£18-05
-2

THE REFORM OF FAMILY LAW IN EUROPE

THE REFORM OF FAMILY LAW IN EUROPE

(The Equality of the Spouses—Divorce—Illegitimate children)

A SEMINAR OF THE UNIVERSITY INSTITUTE OF LUXEMBOURG

Editor: A. G. CHLOROS
Professor of Comparative Law, University of London
Director, Centre of European Law, King's College

KLUWER—DEVENTER—HOLLAND
BOSTON—LONDON—FRANKFURT 1978

ISBN 90 268 0899 2

© 1978, Kluwer BV, Deventer, The Netherlands

Typeset, printed and bound
in Great Britain

CONTRIBUTORS

Preface   By the Editor   vii

Chapter I: General Introduction   1
              by K. H. Neumayer, Professor of Comparative, Civil,
              Commercial and Private International Law,
              University of Würzburg

Chapter II: Dutch Law   19
              by J. de Ruiter, Professor in the Faculty of Law,
              Free University of Amsterdam

Chapter III: English Law   43
              by Joseph M. Thomson, Lecturer in Laws,
              University of London, King's College

Chapter IV: French Law   75
              by Jacques Foyer, Professor in the Faculty of Law and
              Political Science,
              University of Paris XII, Saint-Maur

Chapter V: German Law   111
              by Dieter Giesen, Professor of Private and Comparative Law,
              Co. Director, Institute for International, Foreign and
              Comparative Law,
              Free University of Berlin

Chapter VI: Greek Law   139
              by Alkis Argyriadis, Professor in the Faculty of Law,
              University of Thessaloniki

Chapter VII: Italian Law   151
              by Dr Vito Librando, Judge at the Court of Cassation, Rome

Chapter VIII: Luxembourg Law   183
              by Gaston Vögel, Attorney at the Luxembourg
              Court of Appeal

Chapter IX: Scandinavian Law   201
              by Ake Lögdberg, Professor in the Faculty of Law,
              University of Lund

Chapter X: Socialist Law   227
by *Tibor Pap*, Professor in the Faculty of Law,
University of Pécs (†)

Chapter XI: Civil Procedure   255
by *Savelly Zilberstein*, Professor and Vice-Dean, Faculty
of Law,
University of Bucharest

Chapter XII: Private International Law   283
by *Alfred E. von Overbeck*, Professor in the Faculty of Law,
University of Fribourg, Switzerland

Chapter XIII: Problems of Migrant Workers in Europe   323
by *Tugrul Ansay*, Dean of the Faculty of Law,
University of Ankara

Index   339

PREFACE

In the last few years European Family Law has undergone considerable changes. Although in the past law reform was slow, since 1969 the impetus for reform has gathered momentum. It is no exaggeration to say that the changes that have occurred in Europe in the last six or seven years have radically altered the very concept of the family in Europe. As a distinguished scholar and former editor of the Family Law volume of the International Encyclopaedia of Comparative Law, Professor Max Rheinstein, has put it: 'These transformations are not fully completed anywhere. They have gone farthest in the countries of highest industrialization and in those of socialist rule. But they have set in wherever industrialization has obtained a foothold. The degree of 'modernization' of family law may indeed be used as an index of a society's degree of Westernization.'[1] Yet, such is the force of traditional patterns of thought that, although we are aware of distinct changes in various legal systems, the underlying and implied assumption is that family law can still move within the traditional framework. This is not surprising for, until comparatively recently at least family law was not thought of as a suitable subject of unification. It was claimed that there is a peculiar and distinct element which derives from the mores and innermost beliefs of each people, from a sort of family *Volksgeist* that renders impossible the approximation or unification of family law.

Nevertheless, the overwhelming evidence now available suggests that these ideas and beliefs must be radically revised. As far back as 1968 I wrote: 'Although it can be argued that the law of persons is intensely individualistic and therefore less amenable to unification, I must confess that I have become increasingly disenchanted with this view. It seems that, whatever the strength of local habits in the past, certain leading ideas are clearly emerging which may be called patterns of a future European law.'[2] For if we leave the rest of 'Western' or 'industrialised' societies apart, it may be argued that a distinct movement of reform has emerged within Europe which is converging toward a uniform model of family life and therefore of family law. This has been caused not only by more rapid and extensive travel and communication, but also by the setting up of inter-European political, economic and cultural links which increasingly appear to develop a pattern of a European family life. It has further been encouraged by a peaceful migration of large numbers of workers from one part of Europe to another in search of an improved standard of living. Such a migration may have sociological consequences which may be difficult to estimate at present. It is by no means free from cultural shocks which are felt not only by the migrant workers and their families, but also by those who are indirectly affected in the home country of each worker.

---

1. *International Encyclopaedia of Comparative Law*, 'Persons and Family', Vol. IV, 1-6, pp. 6-7.
2. 'Principle, Reason and Policy in the Development of European Law', 17 *Int. Comp. Law Quart.* (1968), pp. 849, 853.

In these circumstances it has appeared opportune to take stock of the stage of family law in Europe today: not by looking at the whole field of family law, but by focussing attention upon three aspects of family law which appear to be mostly affected by contemporary movements. These three aspects are: the equality of the spouses, divorce and the legal status of illegitimate children. Around these topics a group of scholars was gathered, on the occasion of a Seminar held at the International University Institute of Luxembourg, which was also attended by over eighty participants not only from Europe but from as far afield as South America. As will be seen from the table of contents, each scholar has dealt with these topics in this book from his national point of view; but the book also includes some general chapters which attempt to cut across national boundaries and raise questions which are important in all legal systems.

The picture that emerges is a composite one, but three different trends are clearly suggested. The first is the strong trend of uniformity of treatment. Thus, there seems to be general agreement on principles, e.g. that in European family law there should be greater equality between the spouses, that divorce should no longer provide for penalties for erring spouses but a remedy for difficult human situations; last, that there should be no discrimination based upon illegitimate status.

The second trend is one of divergence, for it is by no means an easy exercise to put these principles into effect. Opinions (and legal systems) may vary as to how to balance the conflicting interests of children with the respect of the equality and freedom of each spouse to decide upon his future way of life. Standpoints may also differ as to how to remove the stigma of illegitimacy from the statute book without removing the special protection generally extended to the legitimate family. It is not surprising, as these divergences show, that we can obtain no clear and unambiguous answers and that the potions concocted by each legal system contain the same ingredients but in different proportions. What is surprising is that, in the open society in which we live, less advantage has generally been taken, where there is agreement on principles, to regulate individual solutions in a uniform European manner. Thus in divorce, for instance, most systems dissolve marriage when the spouses have lived separately for a number of years. But hardly any effort seems to have been made to agree on a uniform solution on how long the period of separation ought to be. Equally, various legal systems find it difficult to work out a generally acceptable and uniform view of the rights and duties of minors born outside marriage.

The third trend clearly relates to the regulation of the illegitimate family. It poses, perhaps, a fundamental question: if the disadvantages of an illicit relation disappear, or—to put it another way—if the advantages of lawful marriage disappear—is there no danger that marriage, unless prompted by a religious motive, will rapidly, if it has not already, become redundant and obsolete? Should we not, in other words, ask ourselves the question whether marriage is really necessary and, if the answer is a negative one, have we not thrown the proverbial baby away with the bathwater?

It is clearly too early to establish any final conclusions on these matters. Indeed, it can strongly be argued that final conclusions in this field are neither possible nor desirable. For society and the family in society are in a constant state of flux. In the sophisticated European society in which we live, changes occur with astonishing rapidity. This does not help to solve the problems of the legislator who must 'fix' the law for the immediate future at least. If the Luxembourg Seminar has not found any definite answers, it is hoped that this book provides at least a useful collection of information and ideas to permit a rational examination of Family Law in our time.

As Editor I wish to thank the contributors not only for their active participation in the Seminar, but also for their supply of a typescript. I also wish to thank the International University Institute of Luxembourg for its far-sighted initiative in organising a Seminar on Family Law, as well as for its help in making this publication possible. Thanks are also due to the individual participants of the Seminar, whose active interest and lively discussions have shown that the new generation of young lawyers lacks neither courage and ideas nor seriousness of purpose. Last, but not least, I wish to thank the Publishers for their support in the production of this volume.

A. G. CHLOROS

CHAPTER I.   GENERAL INTRODUCTION

by K. H. Neumayer

Report on Comparative Law

A. General

The choice of the equality between man and woman as the subject for a Seminar held in the year devoted to women, appears to be singularly fortunate. It is to be hoped that the study of this subject, in the light of comparative law and of the tendencies in the laws of European states in the direction of the equality of the sexes, may help to lead to the elimination of the injustice of unequal treatment which has deprived the woman of her rightful position in the eyes of the law.

It has often been maintained that family law is a subject in which tradition would place obstacles to an attempt at harmonisation across state frontiers, and that a rapprochement would be difficult to realise. The argument was that family law was particularly determined by cultural factors which differed from country to country and which were influenced by ethics and religion. These in their turn have caused divergent historical evolution, both in the economic and in the social field. There can be little doubt that this point of view reflected reality over twenty years ago. Today on the contrary, faced with certain common general principles which appear to dominate the reforms which are being undertaken almost everywhere, we must consider whether family law could be set apart from the general tendency which prevails and which cuts across all the frontiers of the countries of Europe.

If I speak of a rapprochement I use the term advisedly and with reserve in the sense of a levelling out, of a *Rechtsangleichung*, by internal conviction and by the weight of results obtained from the comparison of the laws rather than by the fact of an intentional international cooperation. For what is, perhaps, new is that, even within the traditional conservative field of family law, the inspiration for the solutions which are discussed and adopted comes from experiments that have been carried out abroad. This more extensive knowledge of foreign law, which includes knowledge in depth, that exists in our time, helps to extend across Europe a family law which is less distant from country to country, less varied but more uniform though not unified. It would appear that we are entering into a period which is marked by a kind of *ius commune*, a common law of which we had known in the past and which we have abandoned[2], a symbol of a uniform society which we lost on the morrow of the Grand Revolution. That revolution had as its consequence the formation of national states all with separate national laws, as well as a divergent social evolution of over a century and a half. The time has come for Europe to remember the basic similarities of its cultures, the unity

---

1. Inaugural lecture given on 21 July 1975. The style of the lecture has been maintained, but the text has been brought up to date. Translated from the original French.
2. Cf. Neumayer 'The Role of a Uniform Legal Science in the Harmonisation of the Continental Legal Systems' in *Essays in Jurisprudence in Honour of Roscoe Pound*, New York (1962).

of its culture during long centuries. Europe should also remember the basic simi-larities of its laws and the unity of its law, which includes the law of the family.

Since the end of the last war Europe has been dominated by a movement of law reform which aims at the transformation of the institutions of family law. Every-where the legislator has shown concern for the status of the married woman, as well as for the status of legitimate and natural children. Everywhere reforms are in progress. The movements of reform converge towards the same ideal of justice and matrimonial dignity which tends to satisfy the sum total of the aspirations which for a long time were considered hardly compatible. These aspirations were the equality of the spouses in respect of the independence, as well as in respect of the union, of their interests, and also of a more equitable distribution of the fruits of their labour. In our Western society the woman has acquired her full intellec-tual and economic capacity. In these circumstances, it is important to replace the present remnants of subordination by a regime of coordination. The common factors which inspire these reforms as they occur here and there are, among others, the adaptation of marital relations to a new welfare society without losing sight of the evolution of moral standards and conditions of life. This involves the recognition of the personality of the woman before the law, the transition from parental power to parental service, and the suppression of a status of a natural child which had no recognised rights. It involves the foundation of the law of divorce upon the idea of the breakdown of the marital link, the independence of the spouses in respect of the management of their property relations, and the sharing of one of the spouses of the benefits realised by the other spouse during marriage. In short, within the framework of the general emancipation of the woman before the law, it is important to realise that in marriage as well as in the family the complete equality of man and woman should be given effect.

Laws such as the Belgian law of 30 April 1958[3] or the Luxembourg law of 12 December 1972[4] or, indeed, the most recent Austrian law which has been unanimously adopted by the *Nationalrat*[5], have reorganised family life upon less narrow foundations; they have suppressed the prejudice of the incapacity of the married woman, which we had inherited from the ancient Romans as well as from the ancient Germans. They have abolished the idea of the obedience of the wife to her husband, as well as the idea of the protection owed to her by the husband. The one as well as the other were replaced, in the light of the equality of the sexes, by the obligations which arise from the mutual duty of fidelity, aid and assistance. These laws have put an end to the old-fashioned idea of the head of the family which France, until recently, had thought fit to maintain. Laws such as the Belgian law of 8 August 1965 dealing with the protection of the young[6], have assured to the children a more extensive protection against disorder arising from disunited or warring families. In some cases they have established rules of public policy which go as far as to grant the Courts the power to replace the parents if

---

3. Law of 30.4.1958 (*Moniteur belge* of 10.5.1958) Art. 1; cf. Dubru, '*L'égalité civile des époux dans le mariage*', Brussels (1959).
4. *Memorial du Grand-Duché de Luxembourg*, 22.12.1972, p. 1909 ff.
5. *Bundesgesetz über die Neuordnung der persönlichen Rechtswirkungen der Ehe, No. 1662 der Beilagen zu den stenographischen Protokollen des Nationalrates*, XIII GP.
6. *Moniteur belge*, 15.4.1965.

the well-understood interest of the child so requires. The new provisions have not always avoided creating confusion in the minds of many a spouse and many a parent confronted with the problems, the complexity of which is beyond their understanding. On the other hand, if in fact the husband and father continues to assume the functions of the head of the family, the Courts have power, when there is a conflict between spouses or parents, to deal with the dispute and pronounce a fair judgment.

In a century in which pre-eminence is given to youth, the ancient legal systems which looked at adoption as a measure mainly intended to perpetuate a name or the ownership of property, were no longer suitable. Indeed, they were incompatible with the new tendency of the law of adoption conceived as a measure to protect the child. Thus a very active legislative movement has developed, and all European States appear to have modified the laws of adoption since 1945.[7] All these revisions are inspired by the same principles of legislative policy. This policy is directed on the one hand towards the alleviation of the formal conditions required for adoption but, on the other hand, it is directed towards a more stringent control of the Courts or other adoption institutions, in order to give effect to the principle that adoption should take place in the interest of the child. A committee of experts of the Council of Europe had discussed in detail all the questions relevant to adoption between 1961 and 1964; it has initiated a European convention dealing with the adoption of children, which was signed on 24th April 1967.[8] This contains a certain number of fundamental principles which the contracting parties undertake to introduce into their domestic law. The latest reforms, for instance, in Swiss law, have already felt the influence of that Convention.[9]

In order to illustrate this tendency towards a rapprochement of legislations, but also in order to avoid too superficial a treatment of the subject, I propose to deal in particular with two phenomena. First, I should like to discuss the law of divorce which is one of the main themes of this Seminar. Secondly, I should like to consider the matrimonial systems which apply by operation of law. It is, of course, true that matrimonial systems are not a subject of this Seminar, because they had already been dealt with in a Seminar held in Luxembourg in 1968; they are nevertheless worthy of a brief mention in an introductory chapter such as this. Conversely, I shall refrain from dealing with illegitimate children. To include them in this chapter would have rendered the treatment of the subject much lengthier than I had intended.[10]

---

7. E.g. the Luxembourg law in the form of the coordinated text of 15.3.1974 (*Memorial du Grand-Duché de Luxembourg* 10.4.1974, p. 453 ff.)

8. Council of Europe, *Treaty series* No. 58.

9. *Bundesblatt* 1972 I 1751.

10. With regard to the recent laws which have introduced equality between legitimate and illegitimate children, cf. the German Statute of August 19, 1969; the French Statutes of June 4, 1970 and January 3, 1972; the Austrian Statute of October 20, 1970; the first Book of the New Dutch Civil Code of 1970; and the Swiss reform in course of preparation. For the position in England, where illegitimate and legitimate children have achieved some kind of equality, see Part II of the Family Law Reform Act 1969 and Schedule 1 of The Children Act 1975.

B. *The Reform of the Law of Divorce*

In the first part I propose to deal with the causes of divorce. In the second part I should like to deal more briefly with the consequences that a divorce may have upon the former spouses.

As far as the causes of divorce are concerned, we may distinguish between divorce by a voluntary act and divorce by a judicial decree. Divorce by a voluntary act was already known at the beginning of the nineteenth century, a solution which was inspired by the theory of the Enlightenment. In its original form the French Civil Code admitted divorce by mutual consent. This was maintained—indeed, recently improved—in Belgium[11] and in the Grand Duchy of Luxembourg.[12] Divorce by mutual consent has been reintroduced in the course of last year in France[13] and in Portugal.[14] However, if in this case it was the agreement of the spouses which was at the root of the divorce, it was nevertheless necessary that a judicial authority should pronounce it.

It is in fact Soviet Law[15] which introduced, on the morrow of the Revolution, the dissolution of marriage without any judicial form. A simple unilateral declaration of such intention by either of the spouses sufficed. The registration of such a declaration with the State Registry of Status merely affected the question of evidence of the divorce. The fact of the registration was notified to the other party. This divorce, named 'divorce by postcard' was entirely voluntary.[16] The procedure, which had already become more cumbersome in 1936[17], involved the entry of the divorce into the identity card. It was also expensive. It was replaced in 1944 by a judicial procedure in two stages. The first stage amounted to an attempt to reconcile the spouses. The local Court alone had jurisdiction, if the attempt failed, to pronounce the divorce. However, in 1968, the "Principles of the Law of Marriage" reintroduced voluntary divorce by an administrative act. In effect, "if the two spouses wish to obtain a divorce by mutual consent and if they have no minor children, the dissolution of the marriage is pronounced by the organ having jurisdiction to register acts of civil status".[18] The granting of the divorce and the delivery to the spouses of the appropriate certificate must occur at the Registry Office at the expiry of a period of three months following the introduction of the divorce petition. It should be noted that, side by side with this administrative procedure, there has always existed a judicial procedure which allows the Court, at the request of one of the spouses or at the request of both, to pronounce the divorce if the continuation of the common life of the spouses has

---

11. *Moniteur belge*, 17.12.1969.
12. Law of 6.2.1975 (*Memorial du Grand-Duché de Luxembourg*, 182. 1975, p. 255 ff.).
13. Articles 230 ff. *Code civil* as in the law N. 75-617 of 11.7.1975 relating to the reform of divorce (*Journal officiel* 12.7.1975, p. 7171).
14. Art. 3 of the *Decreto-lei* No. 261/75 (*Diario do Governo* I, p. 733).
15. For Soviet law cf. Rheinstein, *Marriage Stability, Divorce and the Law*, Chicago-London 1972, p. 222 ff.; Bilinsky, *Das Sowjetische Eherecht*, Münich (1961), pp. 27 and 85 ff.; Sorok-Let, *Sovetskogo Prava*, Leningrad (1957), Vol. II, p. 264 ff.
16. *Sobranie zakonov* (1936) No. 34, art. 309.
17. *Ibid.*
18. *Osnovy zakonodatel'stva Sojuza SSR: Sojuznych Republik o brake i o sem'e* (*Vedomosti Verchovnogo Soveta SSSR* (1968) No. 27, Pos. 241). Art. 14 par. 7.

become impossible. It would appear that the Courts are very generous in admitting the breakdown of the marriage when granting decrees of divorce.

In 1965 which was the last year under the old and more restrictive legislation, the rate of divorce was 1.7 per 1000 households. In 1966, which was the first year under the new law, the number suddenly increased up to 3.1 per 1000. At the time, this was 25% below the number of divorces granted in the United States.[19]

It is interesting to note that none of the other East European States would appear to have provided for an administrative procedure in granting divorce decrees. In these States, as well as in the Western countries, divorce is only obtainable by a judicial decision and mutual consent on its own is not sufficient.

In respect of divorce by judicial decision, two things must be distinguished: on the one hand, divorce for a specific ground or for a non-specific ground; on the other, divorce based upon fault and divorce granted on the breakdown of the marital link. These two distinctions are not complementary. However, as a rule divorce on a specific ground is based upon the idea of fault, whereas divorce for an indeterminate or non-specific reason is often pronounced without the fault of either of the parties having been established.

The traditional solution consists of divorce based upon a specific ground. At the beginning of our century there were no exceptions. It was Prussia which at the end of the eighteenth century, inspired by the theory of the Enlightenment, introduced for the first time the idea of the breakdown of the marriage as a ground for divorce.[20] This innovation, which made no reference to fault, admitted divorce as a remedy. When the Prussian Code was abolished in 1900, it was Switzerland which a few years later took over in article 142 of the Civil Code the concept of divorce as a remedy, side by side with the traditional and specific grounds for divorce.

Following the Swiss example, it was the Scandinavian countries[21] and National Socialist Germany[22] which adopted this dual system between the two wars, combining traditional divorce on a specific ground, generally based upon fault and representing the idea of divorce as penalty, with that of divorce as remedy based upon the simple failure of the conjugal union.

However, the dual method would appear to be inadequate. The modern tendency expresses the conviction that only the notion of divorce as remedy is appropriate for modern society. The struggle against fault, the tendency to eliminate fault as an element at the basis of divorce, originates from the large centres of population, the Courts of which were overburdened and had neither the time nor the inclination to determine the true causes that lay behind the allegations of the parties and the testimony of witnesses. This struggle may be found at the basis of all the post-war reform plans. These are, in fact, the considerations which have led the legislator to slide towards breakdown as the basis of divorce, namely, the inadequacy of fault as a ground for divorce once the

---

19. Cf. Rheinstein, *op. cit.* p. 243.
20. *Allgemeines Landrecht für die preussischen Staaten* of 5.2.1794, par. 716 II 1, par. 718a.
21. Norwegian law of 31.5.1918; Swedish law (*giftermålsbalken*) of 11.6.1920; Icelandic law of 27.6.1921; Danish law of 30.6.1922; Finnish law of 13.6.1929.
22. *Gesetz zur Vereinheitlichung des Rechts der Eheschliessung und der Ehescheidung im Lande Österreich und im übrigen Reichsgebiet* of 6.7.1938 (*Reichsgesetzblatt* I p. 807).

notion of divorce as a remedy is accepted. The judge is not bound to establish the true causes of the disintegration of the marital link which leads progressively to the reduction of the joint responsibility which is the foundation of the conjugal union. Moreover, he does not have at his disposal a sure test which will permit him to pass a judgment of value. The longer a conjugal union has lasted, the more difficult it is to establish the fault which was the cause of the failure. The fault could well be the consequence of the pre-existing failure. The search for the fault permeates the whole procedure. The spouses would feel obliged to make mutual allegations of guilt for the sake of obtaining the advantages of maintenance.

Among the more recent reforms which succeed one another at a rapid pace, it is always possible to distinguish the single idea systems, which tend to abolish completely the notion of fault, and the dual systems.

The majority of the East European countries, in so far as they follow Soviet legislation, only recognise a single ground for divorce; namely, the breakdown of the conjugal link. This is variously formulated: for example, in Czechoslovakia, when the relationship between the spouses is so gravely shaken that the marriage could no longer serve its social purpose[23]. Hungary[24], Bulgaria[25], Romania[26] and Poland[27] follow the single system, whereas Yugoslavia[28] maintains the dual system. Thus, side by side with the general clause establishing the breakdown, there is a large number of specific grounds, the majority of which is based upon fault. England, the Netherlands and Germany, in conjunction with the East European countries, adopt a single clause, that is, the permanent failure of the marriage: breakdown of marriage—*duurzame ontwrichting*—*Scheitern der Ehe*.

Nevertheless, even in the case of breakdown the conceptions differ with regard to the attribution of the failure of the marriage. Some believe that it is undesirable to establish which of the two spouses is at fault and that divorce is a consequence of a situation of fact, namely the breakdown. Conversely, others believe that the breakdown can always be attributed to one of the spouses, that is, the spouse who is responsible for the separation. Thus the English Divorce Reform Act 1969 contains an important restriction to the general clause of the breakdown of marriage because the petitioner, in order to obtain the divorce, must establish one of the five conditions of fact enumerated in the law.[29] Properly speaking the new English law does not really accept a general clause, but five specific grounds, though it is by no means excluded that the judge, when deciding upon the application of one or other of these specific grounds, will be led to the investigation of the question of guilt. Nevertheless, it may be worth observing that 98% of divorces in England are undefended cases, which means that the procedure is a non-contentious one.

Dutch law, which has been extensively reformed, has put an end to the comedy which the High Court had described as "*de grote leugen*"—the big lie. The only

---

23. Law of 4.12.1963, para. 24.
24. Law of 6.6.1952, para. 18, modified in 1974.
25. Law of 15.3.1968, Art. 21.
26. Laws of 29.12.1953 and 4.4.1956, Art. 38.
27. Law of 25.2.1964, Art. 56, para. 1; cf. Szer, *Prawo rodzinnie w zarysie*, Warsaw (1969), p. 115 ff.
28. Law of 28.4.1965, Art. 53 ff.
29. Divorce Reform Act, s. 2:

ground of divorce available at the request of either of the spouses is that the marriage has come apart in a lasting manner.[30] The divorce cannot be pronounced until a year has passed from the date when the petition was made, whether at the joint request of the spouses or at the unilateral request of one spouse, which is unopposed by the other; the lasting breakdown is proved by the persistent attitude of the parties. However, there is an important relic of the idea of divorce as a remedy. Thus, the petition of the person who has been mainly responsible for the breakdown is not admissible if the other spouse is opposed to it. This exception appears incompatible with the principle of divorce as a remedy, for it seems to introduce fault through the back door. In the two countries, in England as in the Netherlands, the legislator has made two steps forward but prudence has led him to follow up this progress by taking one step backwards.

In Germany where the Government draft law[31] would appear to be rigid, while introducing Marriage for a Time (*Ehe auf Zeit*), that is, permitting each of the spouses to opt out of the marriage as soon as there is a failure of the marital link, the Germans are known for going back to fundamentals and the result of the parliamentary battle, which will be particularly fierce, is not at all certain. On the one hand, it will have to be established among other things whether the general clause laying down a presumption for the failure of the marriage, will be a simple presumption or an irrebuttable one. The matter has already been debated. On the other hand, there is a hardship clause—*Härteklausel*—the application of which by the Court could bring about a search for fault which, however, had been radically eliminated from the text of the draft.

Thus nothing is less certain than to assume that the problem of fault has been excised once a general breakdown clause is adopted. It is true that the abandonment of the traditional specific grounds, generally based upon fault, results in the disappearance of fault in the first instance. However, fault is by no means dead, for it returns in the second instance. Once the defendant is opposed to the petition for a divorce, he will try to show that if there is a breakdown it is the petitioner who is to blame. In all cases in which the two spouses are not in agreement, the judge will not be able to avoid looking at the reasons for the failure and this is also the case in the single systems of the Eastern countries. For instance, in Romania[32], Poland and Bulgaria, when the judge must establish whether there is a breakdown or not, he is often led to take into consideration the fault of one or other of the spouses. Moreover, in Poland a party at fault cannot as a rule obtain a divorce as a remedy.[33] In Bulgaria, at the request of one of the spouses the fault of the other must be established in the judgment.[34]

---

30. *Nieuw Burgerlijk Wetboek*, Art. 154, para. 1.
31. *Entwurf eines 1. Gesetzes zur Reform des Ehe- und Familienrechts (Bundestagsdrucksache 7/650)*. In the meantime, the Bill has passed through Parliament and the new statute will come into force on January 1, 1977: 1. *Eherechtsreformgesetz Bundesgesetzblatt* 1976, I, p. 1421 ff. The new para. 1565 *Bürgerliches Gesetzbuch* provides a general clause, according to which divorce may be granted if and when the conjugal link has broken down and its re-establishment cannot be expected. Para. 1566 contains an unrebuttable presumption for the breakdown if the case is undefended and the spouses have lived separately for one year or, in other cases, if the separation extends over a period of three years. Para. 1568 contains the hardship clause.
32. Laws of 29.12.1953 and 4.4.1956, Art. 38.
33. Law of 25.2.1964, Art. 56, para. 3; cf. Szer, *op. cit.*, p. 127.
34. Law of 15.3.1968, Art. 21, para. 2.

It is perhaps these considerations which have led to the prudent attitude of the recent reforms which have been introduced into the countries of Latin tradition. In these countries a dual system persists and, side by side with divorce based on breakdown which has been newly admitted, divorce based upon specific grounds —which is the traditional divorce as penalty—has been maintained. This is the case in Belgium, Luxembourg and France where new reforms have recently come into effect.

First, in Luxembourg a reform relates to divorce by mutual consent.[35] The renewal of the petition, hitherto required three times, has now been reduced to one, and the procedure has been considerably simplified.

In Belgium, a new ground for divorce has been introduced. This is actual physical separation lasting over a period of ten years, provided that the rift between the parties is beyond repair.[36] However, the reformers have set a limit. At the basis of this new clause there is a safeguard, that the divorce cannot be granted if the material condition of the children becomes worse as a result. One wonders, indeed, how the material condition of minor children could worsen by a divorce when already the parents have been living separately for at least ten years.

In France, the result of the recent reform has been to introduce the principle of the breakdown "claimed by the petitioner". It is based upon the disruption of the joint marital life and separation for six consecutive years.[37] However, two limitations or restrictions have been placed on this ground: if a cross petition is accepted which is based on the fault of the petitioner, the original petition must be rejected and the divorce must be pronounced upon the fault of the guilty party.[38] The second limitation consists of a hardship clause, following the German model.[39]

The new Italian law also provides for a mixed system. Thus divorce as a remedy is obtainable in the case of a physical separation lasting for a period of five years. This period extends over seven years when the respondent objects to the petition of the guilty party.[40]

The very recent reform in the Principality of Liechtenstein makes divorce available to all citizens, but it insists in a single-minded way upon the concept of divorce as penalty. This means that a divorce cannot be granted to the petitioner if his behaviour is gravely at fault.[41]

Finally, the latest Portuguese reform retains the old subjective grounds based upon the fault of one of the spouses[42], side by side with divorce following separation during five consecutive years and divorce by mutual consent.

We have seen that in spite of the distinct retreat of fault as a cause of divorce even in those countries which only recognise a general ground based upon objective standards, the notion of fault has not been totally eliminated. If the resort to

35. Cf. *supra*, n. 12.
36. Law of 1.6.1974, reforming Art. 232 of the *Code civil* (*Moniteur belge* 17.8.1974).
37. Law no. 75-617 of 11.7.1975 effecting the reform of divorce (*Journal Officiel* 12.7.1975) Arts. 238 ff.
38. Art. 241 of the previous law.
39. Art. 240 of the previous law.
40. *Gazetta ufficiale* of 3.12.1970, No. 306, p. 1338.
41. *Ehegesetz* of 13.12.1973 (*Liechtensteinisches Landesgesetzblatt* of 26.3.1974), Arts. 73 ff.
42. Art. 1778 *Codigo civil* reformed by the *decreto-lei* No. 261/75, *supra* n. 14.

fault sometimes helps to put the brake upon divorce unjustly obtainable, we also find it as a determining factor in establishing the consequences of divorce particularly in regard to the right of maintenance. It is true that maintenance, which for long bore the character of an indemnity, nowadays merely refers to alimony. It is nevertheless true that it is frequently the guilty party upon whom falls the burden for the needs of his innocent ex-spouse. Thus, the recent reform of Belgian law which introduced an objective ground, that is, the physical separation extended over a period of ten years[43], provides that the spouse who obtains a divorce upon that ground is presumed to be the spouse against whom the divorce has been pronounced. According to this presumption of fault, the right to maintenance becomes automatically available for the benefit of the respondent spouse.[44] Of course, the Court could decide otherwise and reverse the presumption if the petitioner could prove the contrary, that the physical separation is attributable to a fault or a failure of the petitioner spouse. It must here be admitted that the Belgian legislator has mixed the concept of divorce as penalty with that of divorce as remedy.

The Dutch law removes the right of maintenance from the notion of fault. Only the spouse in need is entitled to demand maintenance. The judge may, at the request of one party, grant maintenance to him or her even if he or she is the guilty party, provided that that party does not have sufficient resources. Nevertheless, in such a case the judge is entitled to take into account the behaviour of the parties before and after the separation. This could lead to a declaration of guilt.[45] The position is similar in England. The judge must take into account the behaviour of the parties when maintenance is granted. Lord Denning, MR, however, has tried to render innocuous this clause which threatens to reestablish the idea of culpability.[46]

Last, in many countries of Eastern Europe, all of which adhere to the general clause of divorce based upon the breakdown of the marriage, the right to maintenance is attached to the notion of fault. This is the position in Polish, Hungarian, Romanian and Bulgarian law. Only the spouse who is not entirely at fault in the divorce may petition for maintenance, provided of course in all cases that he is in need of it. This is why even in cases of breakdown, the decree of divorce must establish the cause of the breakdown, that is to say, it must establish the extent to which the breakdown can be attributed to one or other of the spouses. It is true that in this context Hungarian law speaks of "unworthiness", but a directive of the Supreme Court specifies that "unworthiness" corresponds with the notion of fault.[47]

---

43. See *supra* n. 36.
44. Art. 306 *Code civil* reformed by the previously cited law.
45. *Nieuw Burgerlijk Wetboek*, Articles 158 and 159.
46. Matrimonial causes Act 1973, s. 23. In *Wachtel v Wachtel* [1973] 1 All ER 829, Lord Denning MR took the view that no discount will normally be made to take into account a spouse's matrimonial misconduct unless the conduct has been "obvious and gross". For examples of "obvious and gross" conduct see *Hamet v Hamet* [1973] 2 All ER 593 and *Jones v Jones* [1975] 2 All ER 12.
47. Tibor Pap, *Das Eherecht in Ungarn*, in *Die Entwicklung des Familienrechts in Mitteleuropa*, Vienna (1970), p. 102.

In effect, it is difficult to conceive that the law could admit that the spouse who is alone to blame could repudiate his or her innocent partner, leaving that partner without help or resources. Worse, that partner could be a wife who has no other training than that of a housewife. It is not surprising that Madame Krämer-Bach, honorary president of the International Federation of Women in Legal careers, has always been opposed to the removal of sanctions against the guilty party. She claims that our Judeo-Christian civilisation is founded upon the ideas of fault and responsibility. She continues: "It is important to act with humanity and wisdom and not to attempt to renovate at all costs."[48]

C. Matrimonial Regimes[49]

For a long time until the end of the last War, the canvas of matrimonial systems was full of variety and colour. A large number of countries expressly or by implication (because the statutes are silent) adhered to the legal system, of Roman tradition, of separation of property pure and simple. This was the case in Italy, Austria, Greece, Scotland and of some regional Spanish systems, such as the systems of the Balearic Islands and Catalonia. The same system prevailed in Turkey in spite of the reception of the Swiss Civil Code, as well as in England and in the Republic of Ireland. In Italy and Greece the system of separation was combined as a rule with the institution of the dowry, thus also following the Roman law tradition. The community systems of Germanic origin were more widespread than the systems of separation, but the extent of the common property varied considerably. It was a system of universal property in the Netherlands, Denmark and Portugal, but only a community of movables and acquisitions in France, Belgium and Luxembourg, and a community of acquisitions only in Spain. In Germany and Switzerland the system was and, in the latter, it still continues to be, a separation of property in which, however, the husband has the administration and enjoyment of the wife's separate property. This was combined in Switzerland with a certain distribution of benefits between the spouses at the time of the dissolution of the community.

Today this picture is in the process of losing its variety and colour. We may distinguish three essential factors which have influenced legislators in different countries in respect of the organisation of matrimonial property in ordinary law. In the first place, economic and social changes in the modern world which have resulted in the diminution of the importance of the distinction between movables and immovables, as well as a change in the role of the woman: formerly a housewife confined to her home, she has come to exercise a profession outside her home. Secondly, the change in the basis of matrimonial systems is due to the emerging idea of the equality of the spouses. Lastly, the change has been due to the reciprocal influence of traditional matrimonial systems. Indeed, contemporary legislative policy appears to be moving towards a combination of separation and community systems. Such a merger appears to lead to a new system which combines the advantages of the two diametrically opposed systems. The new system

---

48. With regard to the law of divorce, *Gazette du Palais*, 1974, 2. 716.
49. Cf. on this matter Kiralfy, *Comparative Law of Matrimonial Property*, Leiden (1972).

attempts to reunite the independence of administration and disposal which are the hallmark of the systems of separation, with the existence of a joint or common fund of the two spouses—a kind of family fund—which, when the marriage comes to an end, is distributed between the spouses and the heirs. Thus, ideas of the separation of property have in part penetrated into the community systems. Conversely, systems of separation are inspired by the ideas of community systems. But beware! The terminology used to describe the legal systems, that is, the systems which arise by operation of law, does not always reveal the essential features of the system. Moreover, even in translation, it is impossible to obtain matching terminologies. "Separation of property" in Finnish law is, in fact, a participation in acquisitions which differs from the *"separation des biens"* of French law, which is pure and simple. The universal community of Portuguese law is similar to that of Dutch law insofar as the composition of the community is concerned, but totally different with regard to the administration of the property during the subsistence of the system.

Such a combination is by no means a novelty.[50] For a long time such a system existed in the Electorate of Hesse, in Hungary for families of the nobility and in old Austria, but as a conventional system preferred in agricultural areas in particular in lower Styria and in Carniole, which are regions inhabited by Slovenes today making up the Federal Republic of Slovenia. Its traces are lost in history. After the Great War the idea of such a mixed system was taken up by the Scandinavians, who have often been progressive in the regulation of human relations. From the great North the light came to Germany where the separation of property, coupled with an equalisation of gains—*Gütertrennung mit Ausgleich des Zugewinns*—became the legal regime as from 1957. However, even prior to that reform the Commission for the reform of the French *Code civil* had already proposed the same system for the new French Civil Code.

Looked at more closely the system could take two forms. One system in which the element of separation prevails and which consists of a separation of property pure and simple while the marriage subsists but which, when the marriage comes to an end, implies the mutual right of each spouse to a share of the value of the clear gains made by him or her spouse during the subsistence of the marriage. This system which has been called a system of participation of acquisitions (*participation aux acquêts*) pure and simple, is based upon the value of the settlement. This is, in fact, the system in force in the German Federal Republic[51], and a conventional system in France[52] and the Grand Duchy of Luxembourg.[53] There are draft projects for introducing this system into Austria and Switzerland. This system also applies by operation of law in Sweden[54] and Finland.[55] But in these two countries the equalisation is not payable in cash, but in kind.

---

50. Cf. Neumayer, *Die Kombination von Vermögenstrennung und Vermögensteilhabe im ehelichen Güterrecht*, Rabels Z 18 (1953), p. 380 ff; Zajtay-Vaz Ferreira, *Regimenes matrimoniales de participacion*, in *Revista de la Facultad de Derecho y Ciencias sociales I* (1950), p. 815 ff.
51. *Bürgerliches Gesetzbuch*, Articles 1363 ff.; for German law cf. 'Les régimes matrimoniaux' in *Travaux de la 2ème journée d'études juridiques Jean Dabin*, Brussels (1966), p. 277 ff.
52. Article 1569 ff. *Code civil.*
53. Law of 4.2.1974 (*Memorial du Grand-Duché du Luxembourg* 22.2.1974), p. 143 ff.
54. Law of 1.6.1920 modified on 4.7.1973, Chap. 6, para. 2, Chap. 11, para. 7.
55. Law of 13.6.1929, para. 34 ff.

The other form emphasises the community aspect of the system. During the subsistence of the marriage a common fund of community property is constituted which differs from the separate property of each spouse. In reality, however, the community is a pure fiction during the subsistence of the marriage, for it only arises at the dissolution of the marriage when the spouses or their heirs divide and share in kind the so-called community property. This is a system which the old Austrian law, which knew no divorce, described very accurately as *Gemeinschaft auf den Todesfall*, that is, community deferred to the moment of death.[56]

In France the reform of 1965 has replaced the system of the community of movables and acquisitions by a system of community of acquisitions which is very different from the old conventional system of community of acquisitions provided for by the *Code Napoléon*.[57] While the Senate wished, as was also clear the wish of the 1959 project, to allow the husband to administer the separate property of his wife, the National Assembly was determined to grant the power of the administration to the wife. The Government, which did not wish to give way to the Assembly, withdrew the bill immediately. In 1965 it introduced a new bill which went a great deal further than the Assembly itself had wished when it granted to the wife not only the administration but also the enjoyment of her separate property. In any event, as far as the joint property is concerned, it is the husband who continues to administer it, but he is no longer the "Lord and Master". He must first obtain the consent of his wife when dealing with the alienation of immovables or the disposal of movables which are subject to publicity, the reception of the proceeds from the alienation of such property, the lease of agricultural land or commercial property or other industrial or handicraft property.[58]

The community only includes the "acquisitions". This term includes property acquired for value during the subsistence of the marriage other than earnings, salary and income. Each of the spouses retains full powers over the proceeds of his work or his capital. As long as these proceeds have not been used to acquire property they remain separate from the common fund, which is contrary to the idea of the community. In reality the new legal regime is inclined more towards separation than towards a community.

To the extent that French law continues to confer upon the husband a power of decision with regard to property described as community, it appears to infringe the principle of the equality between man and woman. It is for that reason that the new Luxembourg law which, in many other respects, follows closely the French model, has not taken up the same provision.[59]

If French law has remained faithful to the idea of the administration by one spouse only, community systems in force in the East European countries have set up an egalitarian administration between the two spouses. They require in a general way, though in different forms, the joint consent of the two spouses for any important act of disposal and, in particular, for any disposition relating to immovables. Conversely, they provide in a general way that each of the spouses

---

56. *Allgemeines Bürgerliches Gesetzbuch* of 24.6.1811, art. 123 ff.
57. Art. 1399 ff, *Code civil* (old text).
58. Art. 1424 *Code civil*.
59. Art. 1421 of the law of 4.2.1974; cf. *supra* n. 53.

can freely administer, as well as dispose of, any property jointly owned. It is this concurrent coadministration which the much-lamented Professor Meijers described as a regime with *twee kapiteins op één schip*—that is, a regime of two captains in the same boat[60]—a system which could conceivably result in trouble if the spouses did not agree upon their actions. It is for this reason that the new Dutch, Italian and Luxembourg laws prefer to follow the example of the Scandinavian countries and leave to each spouse the administration and disposal of the property which entered into the joint property at the instance of each.[61] The right of the spouses to the administration and disposal of the property described as community poses a problem, mainly how to prevent each spouse disposing in excess of goods which, though described as community, are under his sole administration. The majority of recent laws require the consent of the other spouse for certain dispositions which are particularly likely to diminish the family fund and thus put in danger the realisation of benefits and the process of sharing between the spouses. Thus, the Luxembourg and Scandinavian law the consent of the other spouse is required for any act the object of which is to alienate or create a charge upon immovables. The same rule applies to the disposal of commercial property and of any gains entered into the community thereunder. In Luxembourg and Dutch law the same rule applies with regard to dispositions into vivos which are made gratuitously and, in Dutch and Scandinavian law, for dispositions the object of which is to alienate or create a charge or to put an end to the joint enjoyment of the matrimonial home and the furniture therein. The most recent Italian reform adopted the same system.[62] Separation of property, hitherto the legal regime, was replaced by a community of acquisitions of which the ordinary administration is confided to the two spouses, even separately, whereas for acts which go beyond mere administration, the simultaneous concurrence of both spouses is required.

The "participation in acquisitions" is the new conventional regime in France and Luxembourg. It is presented in its purest form, however, in Germany where it is the system that applies by operation of the law. In 1900 the *Bürgerliches Gesetzbuch* introduced, as a legal regime, the administration and the enjoyment of the property of the wife by the husband. This system was openly contrary to the principle of the equality between man and woman. By virtue of the Constitution of Bonn, it has been repealed as from 31 March 1953.[63] In the years that followed and while the preparatory legislative work intended to lead to the substitution of the old matrimonial system by a new legal system appeared to lose its impetus, it was case-law that brought about a temporary change by the substitution of the regime that was abolished by a system of separation of property pure and simple. However, in 1957 legislative activity became aware of a new urgency which eventually led to the promulgation of a law setting up a system of participation in acquisitions. According to this regime of separation of property with an adjustment for the equalisation of gains—*Gütertrennung mit Ausgleich des Zugewinns*—the property of the husband and the property of the

---

60. *Weekblad voor Privaatrecht, Notaris-ambt en Registratie* 84 (1953), p. 344.
61. *Nieuw Burgerlijk Wetboek*, Art. 97; Luxembourg law of 4.2.1974 (cf. *supra* n. 53) Art. 1421.
62. Law of 19.5.1975 (*Gazetta Ufficiale* 23.5.1975), Art. 180.
63. *Gesetz über die Gleichberechtigung von Mann und Frau auf dem Gebiete des bürgerlichen Rechts* of 18.6.1957 (*Bundesgesetzblatt* I, p. 609).

wife, including the acquisitions, at no stage constitute a common fund. However, in respect of dispositions relating to the totality of the separate property of the spouses or relating to any items of the household, the consent of both spouses is required. The essential difference, in comparison with the regime of the deferred community lies in the fact that property which does belong to each spouse separately, that is to say, generally the acquisitions, do not constitute a fund subject to a division, at the moment of dissolution. The main characteristic of this regime is that it does give rise to a settlement in value and not a settlement in kind. In effect, at the dissolution of the regime an account is opened with the view to establishing the gains obtained by each of the spouses during the subsistence of the marriage. The spouse who made the greater gains must share the surplus with the other spouse. It is in this way that it can be said that there is compensation in respect of the benefit of each spouse, for the excess is in principle divided in half and shared between them.

The participation consists, therefore, in the grant of a claim for compensation for the benefit of the spouse whose increase in the value of his property was smaller. That spouse only enjoys the benefit of a simple legal claim which is evidently more fragile than a real right in undivided ownership which each spouse enjoys under a system of community property, differed or not.

Simple though this system appears to be in its principles, it nevertheless imposes calculations which are often complicated. It presupposes that the spouses are inspired by the mentality of an accountant, and that they have consequently established at the moment of their marriage and continue to observe thereafter, a detailed balance sheet in respect of their private fortunes. On the other hand, it further requires an estimate of values at periods which may be substantially distant from one another. This is the reason why this system could hardly be recommended as the system to apply by operation of the law. The legislator in Germany has, indeed, recognised the weaknesses and defects of that system by changing almost entirely the nature of its principles. In effect, when there is dissolution of the marriage on the death of one of the spouses, there is no participation in acquisitions. In its place, the surviving spouse is entitled by right of succession to a share of the estate. However, the trouble is that it is not at all certain that it is the predeceased spouse who made the greater gain of the two. On the contrary, it is often the case that when the wife dies first, it is the surviving husband who has, on the one hand, made the greater gain and, on the other hand, is enjoying a privileged position with regard to the excess, for he obtains an increase of his share, acquired by succession, of the estate left by his wife. This is at least paradoxical. In other cases therefore the laws of other States have refrained from taking up this unique rule of German law. In the case of divorce, the debtor of the claim could often refuse payment by invoking a *Härteklausel*— a hardship clause—on the ground that the break in the conjugal link was caused by the fault of the creditor spouse. This hybrid regime is contradictory and gives rise to considerable inconvenience. It ought to be replaced. In this context, it would be interesting to know how many spouses choose the system of participation in acquisitions in France and in Luxembourg, as a regime of choice. In the variants which are in force in Sweden and Finland, the calculation is always in value, but the payment is in kind. The spouse whose capital exceeds that of the other is entitled to choose the items which the creditor spouse is bound to assign.

14

At present reforms are in progress in Switzerland, Italy, Austria, England and Belgium.

In Switzerland, the system that applies at present, which is the union of property (*unions des biens*)[64] is the residue of the old law of the guardianship of the husband, which had taken over from the guardianship of the father over his daughter. With the exception of the property which was reserved for her own use, the wife's property is subject to a legal charge which is comparable to a usufruct and which deprives the woman of the administration and the enjoyment of her own property. She loses control, in fact, though she retains the right to consent to any dispositions of her husband. But in reality in a large number of households which are in theory subject to this regime, the union of property is no longer observed. Frequently the husband leaves the administration of her own property to his wife, or he allows her to enjoy the income therefrom. The results of a poll which was conducted by the Institute of Sociology of Zürich, have demonstrated that the separate property of the wife is administered in 16% of cases by the husband, in 43% by the wife and in 41% by both spouses jointly and this without regard to the matrimonial system under which the spouses are presumed to live.

The reform appears to be directed towards the adoption of a system which can be described as separate administration, which combines the separatist elements together with the community elements, following the example of the legal regime in Germany. The first project has not attempted to restrain the liberty of administration and disposal of the spouses upon their own private property and gains. At the time of the dissolution of the marriage, the gain which a spouse has made will be divided between the spouses or between the surviving spouse and the heirs of the deceased spouse. In the case of divorce each spouse will receive half the gains made by the other. As to losses, each spouse will bear his own. But there will be a *Härteklausel*—a hardship clause—according to which the judges would be entitled to make adjustments if the division appears to be manifestly unfair.

In England the reform of the matrimonial property law has been on the programme of the Law Commission almost since that Commission was set up in 1966.[65] One of the proposals submitted to the Commission is to replace the present system of separation of property by a regime of limited community, that is, "a community of surplus", or a "deferred community". This regime has been copied from the Scandinavian systems or the system applicable to the German Federal Republic. According to this, each spouse will in effect continue to administer his own private property during the subsistence of the marriage but, at the end of it whether by death or divorce, nullity of judicial separation, the clear gains made during the subsistence of the marriage will be divided equally between the spouses. In case of death they will be divided between the surviving spouse and the successors of the deceased spouse. However, this proposal does not seem to have commended itself to the Law Commission. Consequently, it is not likely that English law will adopt a community system, even if it be of limited effect. Another

---

64. In German, "*Güterverbindung*", Art. 194 ff., *Code civil suisse*.
65. The "First Report on Family Property: A New Approach" was published by the Law Commission on 22 May 1973; cf. *The Law Commission, 8th Annual Report, 1972/3* at p. 9. Cf. also Freeman, "Towards a Rational Reconstruction of Family Property Law', in *Current Legal Problems* (1972), p. 84 ff.

15

proposal was to maintain the separation of property even in respect of acquisitions, but to combine with it the co-ownership of the spouses in connexion with the matrimonial home and the furniture therein.

In Belgium, many plans have been submitted.[66] The latest information was not available during the Seminar. The first project, called the Ciselet project, appears to adopt the Swedish system of matrimonial property. According to this system, all the items making up the property of the family will be subject to a *giftorätt* (marital right). This is a kind of limited and deferred real right consisting of the division of the property between the spouses, this being effected at the moment of the dissolution of the marriage. A second project submitted by M. Vermeylen is similar to the legal regime in Germany, that is, the system of participation in acquisitions. A third project has been submitted recently by M. Wigny which still appears to be the subject of a debate. Its particular feature is a very detailed settlement of the problem of the administration of the property belonging to the community. The principle would appear to be that of the concurrent administration, such as we have seen in the regime of Eastern European countries. Each of the spouses could dispose separately of the joint property, and such acts of disposition could not be attacked by the other spouse. However, what seems to be intended as the rule would more likely become the exception, because the items of property which each spouse would administer to the exclusion of the other freely and in the capacity of owner, would be in the majority. Finally, all important acts of disposal, such as the alienation of mortgage of an immovable would be subject to the joint administration of both spouses. This complex system would entail the division of the property into four parts; the property of which the husband is the owner and which he can dispose of freely; the property of which the wife has ownership and which she can dispose of freely; the matrimonial property in respect of which each spouse can act separately (concurrent administration); and last, the elements of the property the disposal of which is subject to joint administration. It appears that, in Belgium, the adoption of a system of separation of property coupled with a participation in acquisitions, would be contrary to the tradition of the country and would therefore be unlikely to meet with general approval.

In Italy, the discussions in respect of the reforms are now being directed towards the abolition of the legal regime of separation of property by a community of acquisitions. The ordinary administration of these would be entrusted to both spouses, whether acting jointly or separately, whereas for any dispositions of importance, simultaneous performance by both parties would be required.

The Austrian reform[67] tends to introduce a system of participation of acquisitions, but with appreciable improvement in comparison with the more rigid German model. In effect, the claim to participation in respect of any increase of capital obtained by the other spouse will be reduced according to whether the latter can establish that the creditor has contributed to the conservation or the increase of the property of the debtor. A contribution, to be taken into account in this sense, would be the assistance of one spouse in the professional activity of the

---

66. Cf. Baeteman, 'The Modern Belgian Law' in Kiralfy, *op. cit.* (*supra*, n. 49) p. 33 ff.
67. Cf. No. 7 *der Beilagen zu den stenographischen Protokollen des Nationalrates*, XII G P of 13.5.1970.

other, or in the management of the household, or in the care and education of the children, as well as any other acts of assistance. Therefore, the Austrian project provides for a relative participation, depending on the conditions in which the spouses have lived. In this flexible way the new Austrian law will resolve a problem which is generally created by the division into half of the common fund. In effect, this egalitarian rule can give rise to injustice when one of the spouses has contributed to a greater extent than the other to the increase of the family fund in circumstances in which the other spouse has gravely neglected his or her matrimonial duties, such as the obligation to contribute to the charges of the household.

The common element in all these reforms of matrimonial property law—whether the reform has been adopted or is still in process of reform—lies in the principle of the division of acquisitions between the spouses at the termination of the marriage. This principle of separation in half, whether it occurs on the dissolution of the community consisting of acquisitions only or within the framework of simple participation in acquisitions, results not only from modern egalitarian ideas but also from the obligation of cooperation between the spouses. This principle has already been called in question in countries such as Sweden, where this method of division has recently given rise to sharp criticism. In effect, it is claimed that it is the special welfare legislation which, in Swedish society, guarantees to the married woman a substantial part of that economic security that was formerly one of the most important functions of marriage.

At a time of rapid social changes such as our own, one reform leads to another. The next reform in the relations between spouses could be dictated by the problem of the evolution of social security. In effect, discussions in this field are already taking place beyond the Moselle. According to the German project of reform, the husband must assign to his divorced wife one half of the social security claims to which he may be entitled.[68] This problem of the *Rentensplitting*, that is, the splitting up of pension rights, has already produced an effect of shock for German lawyers.

The old family unit, especially among farmers and craftsmen who were in the majority in the middle-class society, often costituted a micro-organism, of which the husband was the master and thus alone responsible.

Today, marriage has ceased to serve as an institution which takes care of the woman for life. Whether it is wise, at a time of growing unemployment, to replace the so-called housewife marriage by the marriage for the professional woman with the consequent changes in the regulation of the family and divorce legislation, only the future will show. In any event, one question must be asked: if the law liberates the woman from her secular chains, it could be asked whether this does not also imply certain risks for her, especially for a woman who is left alone with the income from her work, as if often the case, following a divorce which has been granted too easily to a husband who wants to regain his freedom for the sole purpose of marrying another woman.

For it should not be that *"fiat aequalitas et pereat mulier"*.

---

68. Indeed, the new German Statute (cf. *supra* n. 31) provides that, after divorce, the spouse whose pension or social security rights are higher than those of his ex-partner, must share the surplus with the latter; para. 1587(a) *BGB*.

CHAPTER II. THE REFORM OF FAMILY LAW IN THE NETHERLANDS

(with some comparative remarks)

by Jan de Ruiter

1. General Remarks

Several parts of the Dutch Civil Code have been revised since it came into operation in 1838.

A general revision of Family Law took place by the Act of 3 April 1969[1] by which Book 1 of the new Civil Code, established in 1958 and thoroughly recast by that Act, was put into force.

The law of divorce, however, was not yet revised. This was not done until the Act of 6 May 1971[2], which became effective on 1 October 1971.

Juvenile law, which had been extensively amended in the course of the twentieth century, was altered only very little by the introduction of the above mentioned laws, because the Government wanted to wait for the report of the committee for the revision of the law of child protection, instituted in 1965. The committee was called the Committee-Wiarda after its chairman. The report of the committee, which appeared in 1971, proposed several alterations, none of which has yet been put into effect.

2. Equality of the spouses

(a) History

The Civil Code of 1838 enacted that the husband had the dominant position in the marriage. He was "the head of the marriage", or "the head of the family" and the wife was bound to obey him. This dominant position also had important legal effects in several fields. The husband administered the property of the wife and that of the community if the spouses were married subject to a complete community of property. Furthermore, the husband had the "paternal authority" over the children born of the marriage. The wife had no legal capacity and could not appear in court unassisted by her husband. She was not *persona standi in iudicio*. By law (*ipso iure*) she had the domicile of the husband and was obliged to follow him wherever he was resident. Similarly, the wife had the same nationality as the husband. The husband was legally bound to protect the wife, to receive her in his house and to provide maintenance for her.

After the position of the married woman had gradually become more independent in all these fields both by statutory changes and in practice, the Act of 14 June 1956[3] effected a fundamental change. The equality of the spouses and the

---

1. See *Staatsblad* 187, the official collection of Dutch laws (Gazette) [hereinafter referred to as S].
2. See S. 290.
3. See S. 343.

legal capacity of the married woman became the leading principles. It is true that the adage, "the husband is the head of the marriage" was retained in the law, but this phrase, too, was finally rejected when the new Book 1 came into operation in 1970.

On the face of it, the equal treatment of husband and wife in marriage is now the starting point and the leading principle, though this has not been expressly laid down in a statutory provision as it was in the West German Constitution.[4] Nevertheless, there are still some statutory provisions that point to a certain degree of inequality or at least to a different treatment between the spouses. The following will be mainly concerned with these exceptions.

(b) Maintenance and domestic expenses

Nearly all matrimonial obligations have been laid down in the law as reciprocal obligations. Thus, spouses owe each other fidelity, succour and assistance. They are under a legal obligation to provide for and to maintain each other and to maintain and educate their minor children.[5] The housekeeping expenses are borne by both spouses jointly according to a standard more or less defined[6] and one spouse is liable, together with the other, for the obligations contracted for the purpose of the normal running of the household.[7] Disputes between the spouses about these matters are settled in court.[8]

However, there is one exception to the principle of equality in this connection, at least as far as its legal formulation is concerned. According to the text of article 85-2, the husband is obliged to provide his wife with enough money to do the housekeeping. But a similar obligation for the wife is not laid down in the law. In order to interpret this statutory provision correctly, it should be observed firstly, that we are not concerned here with the formal obligation of the husband to maintain his wife, but only with its practical consequences. He must observe his duty to maintain in such a way that the wife gets an adequate allowance for domestic purchases and does not have to buy on credit from the baker, the butcher, etc. The scope of this provision, in fact, is not very wide. Its only purpose is to enable the wife, who usually does the housekeeping in our present social system, to do so. This implies that, if there is another division of roles between the spouses and the husband does the housekeeping while the wife is the bread-winner, there is no reason why the wife should not have the same responsibility as regards the supply of household money.

During the discussion of the Bill in Parliament, it was argued by the government that such an obligation in fact exists and can, if necessary, be based on the general principle of the law, that the spouses are under a legal obligation to provide each other with the necessaries of life.[9] In another connection the Hoge

---

4. See S. 3, section 2.
5. See art. 82. All articles cited without further indication are from Book 1 of the Dutch Civil Code (*Burgerlijk Wetboek*).
6. See art. 84.
7. Art. 85-1.
8. Art 84-4 and 85-4.
9. Article 81.

Raad[10] has also applied the general principles of article 81 to a case which had not been provided for by law.[11] All things considered, therefore, there is only a apparent difference in treatment between husband and wife.

Considering other legal systems, we notice a general tendency towards equality of the spouses in respect of the duty to provide for each other. However, the specific duties of husband and wife are even more emphasised than in Dutch law. Article 214 of the French Civil Code, for instance, imposes on both spouses the duty to contribute to the day to day expenses of the marriage—which means in practice that the costs are primarily borne by the husband and that the wife contributes, for instance, through her work in the household and by helping her husband with his work. German law similarly emphasises the domestic duties of the wife in several provisions[12], behind the last of which lies the same idea as that behind article 85-2 of the Dutch Civil Code.

English law seems to be more restricted. The principle of the Common law is the obligation of the husband to contribute to the maintenance of the wife. The Matrimonial Proceedings (Magistrates' Court) Act[13] does indeed recognise cases in which the wife is obliged to contribute to the maintenance of the husband, but this is restricted to cases in which the earning capacity of the husband is impaired through age, illness, etc., while the wife has sufficient means to contribute. But there is no restriction now under the Matrimonial Causes Act 1973. Also, for the application of the Ministry of Social Security Act of 1966, the spouses have the reciprocal duty to maintain each other, which is of importance for the recovery of the cost of assistance from the other spouse.[14]

(c) Location of the Matrimonial Home

Of greater importance is the difference between husband and wife as regards the matrimonial home. As stated above, the spouses have the mutual duty to cohabit. The matrimonial home should be determined by agreement.[15] Where spouses find it impossible to come to an agreement, the husband decides. There are a few exceptions to this rule.[16] When the husband is under guardianship, or when he is unable or unwilling to express his choice as to the matrimonial home or when the wife supplies the needs of the family because she is the main breadwinner, then it is the wife who determines the location of the matrimonial home. From this it clearly appears that the husband's power to make decisions is a result of the present social situation as it is usually the husband who is the breadwinner. The spouses are, however, entirely equal in their right to apply for an order of the court. When one of the spouses—and in most cases this is likely to be the husband—has taken a decision which involves serious dangers for the moral or mental interests of one of the members of the family or their welfare,

---

10. The Dutch Supreme Court.
11. HR 25 June 1971, NJ 1972, 58, nt. D.J.V. NJ= (*Nederlandse Jurisprudentie*).
12. §§ 1356, 1357, 1360, 1360a. *Bürgerliches Gesetzbuch* (W. German) [hereinafter referred to as BGB].
13. S.I(1)(i).
14. See Bromley's Family Law, fourth edition, 1971. pp. 402, 413 and 417/8, and 427/8.
15. Art. 83-1.
16. Art. 83-2.

then the other party has the right to apply to the court to annul the decision.[17] This provision closely resembles that of article 215 of the French Civil Code. In England, too, it is accepted without statutory regulation that the husband has the first choice in determining the location of the matrimonial home. Again, the law recognises all kinds of exceptions of the same nature as those laid down in article 83-2 and 3.[18]

This question should be distinguished from that of the domicile of the spouses. Before 1956 the wife had a dependent domicile (she followed that of her husband) but, since this problem of domicile of the married wife is solved according to general rules, she has her own, independent, domicile.

(d) The wife's name

Unlike German law[19] in Dutch law the wife keeps her own name on marriage. It is, however, common practice that in social intercourse the wife uses the name of her husband or, in any case, puts his name before hers. Article 9-1 Book 1 of the Dutch Code expressly entitles her to do so. This applies with equal force to a woman who has been married and has not married again. Where the marriage has been dissolved by divorce and there are no descendants, the husband may apply for an order of the court to deprive the wife of this right, at least if there exist weighty reasons for so doing. The French and German regulations are completely different. According to the former[20], either of the spouses resumes the use of his own name; according to the latter[21], the divorced wife retains the name of her husband. The English system does not deviate very much from the Dutch: the wife is entitled to assume the name of the husband and to keep his name after the marriage has been dissolved, provided she does not abuse this right.[22]

(e) Administration of property

As far as the administration of property is concerned, there is no longer any difference between the spouses in Dutch law. As explained above it was here in particular that great differences existed between the spouses prior to the Act of 1956. Then the husband had—with some exceptions—the administration of both the property of the wife and that of the community of goods, or of property. Today the wife, having acquired legal capacity, administers her own property and the goods of the community which came into the community through her.[22] This concerns not only the goods owned by the spouse at the time of the celebration of the marriage, but also goods acquired by a spouse during the marriage (e.g. succession, delivery). Decisive is the *formal* delivery of a good to a spouse, not the origin of the money used to buy it. Since, in this connection, the terms "husband" and "wife" respectively are substituted for the neutral term "spouse",

---

17. Art. 83-3.
18. See Bromley, pp. 95/6.
19. § 1355 BGB.
20. Art 264-1 *Cc* (French *Code civil*).
21. § 54 Ehegesetz.
22. Bromley, p. 95.
23. Art. 97.

we cannot say much more on this rather extensive and difficult subject, at least if we restrict ourselves to the question of equality of the spouses. In this respect they are completely equal, at least before the law, for everybody agrees that, in this matter especially, the actual relationship presents a much more varied picture.[24]

Of course it is impossible within the compass of this contribution to give a full description of how foreign systems deal with this matter. The author can only observe briefly that in French law either spouse administers his own property, but the husband administers the goods of the community although for certain transactions he requires the consent of the wife.[25] The German system closely resembles the Dutch system, at least as far as the equal treatment of husband and wife is concerned.[26] It is very difficult to compare the Dutch and English systems, because the latter does not recognise the existence of the complete community of goods of the spouses at all. It is considered, however, that there too the principle of equality is incompatible with any legal incapacity of the wife or with any restrictions imposed on her capacity to administer her own property.[27]

(f) Parental authority over the minor child

As mentioned above, when the Dutch Civil Code came into force in 1838, the husband had the paternal authority over the children born of the marriage. By the Act of 6 February 1901, S.62, this was altered to parental authority. However, the father had the sole right to exercise this authority. Not until the revision of the Act of 10 July 1947[28] was the joint exercise of the authority by both spouses recognised.[29] This authority extends only to the maintenance and education of the minor, not to the administration of his property, nor to legal representation (see under (g)). This revision has not yet resulted in equality for the wife.

In case of a dispute, the father's will is decisive. The mother may apply for an order of the court to annul the decision of the father if this decision is obviously in direct conflict with, or involves serious dangers for, the moral or mental interests or welfare of the child.[30] In harmonious marriages, this provision is, of course, hardly ever applied. It has practical significance in a situation where the spouses are living separately and the child lives with the mother. In that case, too, the will of the father remains decisive in matters of education. This is equally true when divorce proceedings are pending before the court and the court has ordered that the child shall remain with the mother pending the proceedings.[31]

This provision has come in for some criticism. In the first place it is rather vague because, while the court is authorised to annul the decision of the father, it does not have a similar power to sanction that of the mother. Thus the situation may arise that no decision can be taken at all. Furthermore, criticism is levelled

---

24. For a description of Dutch law see *Comparative Law of Matrimonial Property*, edited by Albert Kiralfy, ch. I and III by G. Bateman—A. W. Sijthoff, Leiden, 1972.
25. Art. 1421, ss *Cc*.
26. §§ 1408 ss BGB.
27. Bromley, pp. 93 §§ and 355.
28. S. H232.
29. Now article 246-2.
30. Art. 246-3.
31. HR 16 Dec. 1966, NJ 1967, 82.

at the dominating position of the husband, which still exists. The Committee-Wiarda[32] proposes to give both parents the same powers and to render it possible for either of them to apply for an order of the court in case of dispute. The latter should not be bound to the criterion of article 246-3 set out above, but should have the discretion either to subscribe to the opinion of one of the parents or to give any order in the interest of the child.

As appears from § 1627 BGB, German/law takes the view of the joint exercise of parental authority, just as French law[33] does. In cases of dispute the parents must adhere to the course of conduct they followed until the dispute arose.[34] If this proves to be impossible, they may apply for a decision of the "juge des tutelles", who should first of all try to effect a reconciliation between the parents. As far as England is concerned, again the totally different system makes comparison difficult. Since the Guardianship of Infants Act 1925[35], the principle obtains that the claims of husband and wife in matters of education are, in principle, equal and that the interest of the child is paramount.[36]

(g) Parental administration of the property of the minor child. Legal representation

In Dutch law the father administers the property of the minor child and represents him in civil actions.[37] These powers are accorded to the mother when she has the sole exercise of the parental authority, which is possible when the parental authority has been committed to her after judicial separation, or when the father has been deprived of this authority. In this respect, too, the Committee-Wiarda proposes an amendment by instituting the joint authority of the spouses and joint legal representation. In case of dispute, either parent may refer the matter to the decision of the court.[38]

This proposition follows the example of current German law[39] which does not give preference to either of the parents. In French law the father has priority over the mother, if the spouses exercise the authority jointly.[40] In all other cases, the parent who has the sole parental authority administers the affairs of the child. In the English system there is no relation between parental authority and administration of the property of the child, so that this system is unsuitable for the purpose of comparison.[41]

(h) Domicile of the minor child

The minor has a dependent domicile. He follows the domicile of the person who exercises authority over him. If both parents have joint authority, the minor

---

32. Report, p. 92.
33. Art. 372 Cc.
34. Art. 372-1.
35. Incorporated in the Guardianship of Minors Act 1971.
36. See Bromley pp. 267 ff and 300 ff, supplement p. A39.
37. Art. 247-1.
38. Report, p. 90.
39. § 1626 BGB.
40. Art. 389 Cc.
41. Bromley, pp. 458/9.

24

follows the domicile of the father. German and French law refer to the domicile of the parents for that of the minor child, without making a distinction between the father and the mother.[42] According to English law, a person of 16 years is capable of having an independent domicile. Under that age, if his parents are living apart from each other, he takes the domicile of his mother if he has a home with her and has no home with his father.[43]

(i) Name of the children

Also, in respect of the name of the children of the spouses, the Dutch, French, German and English systems give preference to the name of the father.[44] Attempts to make the spouses equal in this respect as well have failed due to complexity.[45]

(j) Nationality

A child receives his father's nationality.[46] This point will be dealt with briefly as, strictly speaking, it does not belong to family law. According to the French *Code de la Nationalité*, a child receives French nationality not only if the father has that nationality, but if *one* of the parents has it. In England, on the other hand, the nationality of the father is given prominence.[47]

(k) International private law

Pursuant to section 2 of the Hague Convention on Matrimonial Property, of 17 July 1905, the national law of the husband governs the consequences of the marriage as regards the property of the spouses in case of the absence of a marriage settlement. Article 4 of the Uniform Law concerning the international private law (Benelux), which has not become operative, is to the same effect. The question whether we should continue to observe this regulation, now that our law has recognised the principle of the equality of husband and wife in the law on matrimonial property, is still a moot point.[48]

The relation between parents and their legitimate children is governed by the national law of their father, which is at the same time the national law of the child—see above.[49]

---

42. § 11 *BGB* and Art. 108-2 *Cc*.
43. Domicile and Matrimonial Proceedings Act 1973, S. 304.
44. See Art. 5-1.
45. See Voigt in *Zeitschrift für das gesamte Familienrecht*, 1972, p. 187 and Destopopoulos in the *Revue trimestrielle de droit civil*, 1969, p. 716 ss.
46. Art. 1, 6, 7. Wet op het Nederlanderschap en het ingezetenschap (the Dutch Act on Nationality).
47. Bromley, pp. 317/8.
48. Meanwhile for that reason the Convention has been denounced with effect from Aug. 23rd 1977 (Act of 10 Febr. 1977, S. 64).
49. HR 12 Feb. 1965, NJ 1965, 199.

(l) Conclusion

The foregoing argument on the equality of the spouses has, in fact, amounted to a description of the points of inequality. To go deeper into the question of equality, one would have to give a detailed treatment of almost the entire family law, which is certainly not the present intention.

To summarise, it is felt that the principle of equality of the spouses in Dutch Family Law has nearly achieved full effectiveness. Although the fact that some questions are still solved by reference to the husband may be explained by the mere wish to make a choice if this is inevitable. For practical purposes and to avoid a deadlock, it would seem better to follow the principle to the end. However, real equality of husband and wife is something that no law can dictate but which should be embedded in society itself.

3. Illegitimate children

(a) History and definition of the term

During the course of this century fundamental amendments have been made in the Dutch legislation in respect of illegitimate children. Until 1947 no legal relations had existed between a mother and her illegitimate child, unless she had acknowledged it in the manner directed by law. Since then, such an acknowledgement is no longer required and legal relations between mother and illegitimate child exist by law (*ipso iure*). However, the possibility remained that no relations whatsoever existed between mother and child in respect of adulterine and incestuous children. The importance of this provision was reduced by the fact that it was often not established judicially whether a child was adulterine or incestuous. Only, if the husband of the wife succeeded in denying the legitimacy of the child, it had to be accepted, as a consequence of the decision of the court, that the child was adulterine. But the Convention of Brussels, which has been in force since 23 April 1964[50], abolished this situation, creating legal relations between every child and his mother. This provision was also laid down in the new Book 1 of the Dutch Civil Code.[51]

In order to create legal relations between "begetter" (the father in the biological sense of the word), acknowledgement is necessary. This has always been required, though the legal character of the acknowledgement has undergone some changes (see below). Originally, there did not exist any legal relationship at all between the begetter and the child which had not been acknowledged by him. But by the amendment of the law of 1909, a duty was imposed upon the former to contribute to the costs of maintenance and education of the child.

Despite extensive improvements in the legal status of the illegitimate child, there are still important differences between them and legitimate children. Those differences will be dealt with below under the several heads. Suggestions for

---

50. Convention of 12 September 1962.
51. Art. 221—an illegitimate child has the status of natural child of his mother.

further amendments have been made by the Committee-Wiarda.[52] These suggestions will also be considered briefly.

(b) Terminology

The following terminology is used in Dutch law. Illegitimate children are all the children who are not legitimate. An illegitimate child is by law (*ipso iure*) a natural child of his mother. He is a natural child of his father after he has been acknowledged by him. Thus the word 'natural' implies the existence of legal relations.

(c) The acknowledgment (general)

Acknowledgment by the father can take place in various ways: in the birth certificate of the child, in a separate act of acknowledgment drawn up by an official of the Registry of Births Deaths and Marriages, or in any notarial act.[53]

Formerly there was much divergence of opinion as to the legal character of the acknowledgment. Did it simply serve as evidence of the biological paternity or was it a legal act which judicially established paternity irrespective of the biological parenthood? The validity of the acknowledgment could depend on the answer to this question. For instance, according to the first view a false acknowledgment would be void. However, the second view has prevailed and has been given legal effect.[54] Consequently, acknowledgment means assumption of paternity in the legal sense. Not the begetting, but the acknowledgment is the source of the legal relations. The biological paternity remains significant here in so far as there is greater scope for the annulment of the acknowledgment if the man who acknowledges is not the biological father (see below). The acknowledgment has no retrospective force. Not until the moment of acknowledgment does the child stand in any legal relation to his father. Legal relations with the mother are, of course, established at the moment of birth.[55] However, acknowledgment of an unborn child is possible because such a child is regarded as already born whenever his interests require this.[56]

Whether it is possible to acknowledge a predeceased child is a controversial issue. As the law stands at present such an acknowledgment would only have emotional significance. In the future, however, posthumous acknowledgment may be important for the child's descendants, in view of the Bill for a new law of succession.[57]

---

52. Committee-Wiarda Report, p. 75.
53. Art. 223.
54. Art. 221-2: "The father of a natural child is he who has acknowledged the child."
55. Art. 222.
56. Art. 2.
57. Art. 4, 2, 3a and 6.

(d) Void acknowledgments

An acknowledgment is void if it has been made:

(1) By a man whose marriage to the mother of the child would be prohibited by Article 41.[58] The category of incestuous children falls under this provision. These children, born as a result of sexual intercourse between a woman and a man who are unable to marry on account of consanguinity or affinity, cannot be acknowledged by that man. Consequently, legitimation is also precluded. Thus these children are in a more unfortunate position than other illegitimate children.

This ground of nullity also covers acknowledgment by a man whose marriage to the mother would be prohibited, even where he is not the begetter of the child, that is, where the child is not born of an incestuous union. In both cases it is argued that such an acknowledgment, since it would openly show or at least suggest that the father, father-in-law, grandfather or brother of the mother is the begetter of the child, would not only be a serious offence against public morals, but would also do irretrievable harm to the child by branding him with the stigma of being the issue of such incestuous intercourse.[59] It is further contended that such an acknowledgment would prevent acknowledgment and legitimation of the child by the husband of the mother when he is willing to accept the child as a member of the family.

Where dispensation is possible, for example in respect of an adopted brother and sister, acknowledgment is equally possible.[60]

The death of the mother does not affect the acknowledgment being annulled.

(2) By a married man whose marriage has been contracted more than 306 days before the birth of the child.[61] Thus the former rule that adulterine children could not be acknowledged continues by virtue of this provision, but there is one restriction. This ground of nullity is only applicable for as long as the marriage of the man continues. The legislator has here tried to find a balance between the moral duty of the biological father to acknowledge the child, the child's interests and the fact that the begetter is married. Just as in (1) above, it is not in the child's interests to be acknowledged by a married man because the latter cannot marry the mother and therefore cannot legitimate the child and such an acknowledgment would prevent acknowledgment and subsequent legitimation by another man. Nor would such an acknowledgment be in the interests of the man's marriage. For it is likely that the acknowledgment of the child, by which it receives the name of the husband, would put too great a stress on a marriage which had already suffered the blow of the birth of the child fathered by the husband. For these cases, too, the rule holds good that acknowledgment is precluded even though the man is not the begetter. This is because there is a presumption of

---

58. Art. 224-1. sub a.
59. PG, p. 524. (*Parlementaire Geschiedenis van het ontwerp-Burgerlijk Wetboek*, by C. J. van Zeben, a collection concerning the discussion of Book 1 of the New Dutch civil code in parliament).
60. PG pp. 514, 571.
61. Art. 224-1 sub b.

adultery even though the child has not, in fact, been born from an adulterous relationship. Here also the interests of the child form a bar to acknowledgment and legitimation by a married man, as long as the possibility remains of acknowledgement and legitimation by another man. If a married man wishes to become the father of a child whom he has not begotten, then it would be more natural for him and his wife to adopt the child.[62]

(3) By a minor who has not yet reached the age of 18, unless the acknowledgment takes place on the day of the solemnisation of the marriage.[63] When a man is 18 years old he may enter into a marriage.[64] It follows that at that age he may also acknowledge a child. After having been granted a dispensation, the man may also marry at an earlier age and, on the day of the solemnisation of the marriage, he may acknowledge a child. This should be understood to mean on the day, but before the solemnisation, for after that he attains majority.[65]

(4) During the lifetime of the mother, without her previous consent.[66] The reason why this provision was incorporated into the Dutch Civil Code in 1838 was explained by the government as follows: "The reason is very simple and has a moral basis. If a man could, without the consent of the woman who has given birth to a natural child, acknowledge that child, every woman who has at one time had a moral lapse would be exposed to the danger that out of hatred, envy or for some other design a person from a lower class, even a person branded in the eyes of society, could declare himself to be the father of the child during her lifetime; which might injure both the honour of the mother and the interests of the child and might equally prevent the marriage of the former with the real father."

(5) During the child's majority, without his previous written consent.[67] However, a minor child can be acknowledged without his will. The question has been asked whether, on analogy with the rules of adoption[68], it is not desirable that he should be heard in this matter if he has reached the age of 14. A provision to this effect has not been incorporated in the law, in the first place because acknowledgment is deemed to be less significant than adoption and, secondly, because consultation with the child would necessitate some juridical procedure and this would undoubtedly complicate the acknowledgment. Moreover, there are some guarantees for the child in the provision that the consent of the mother is required[69] and in the possibility of annulment.[70]

---

62. PG p. 514.
63. Art. 224-1 sub c.
64. Art. 31-1.
65. Art. 233.
66. Art. 224-1 sub d.
67. Art. 224-1 sub e.
68. Art. 227-4.
69. See sub-section 4.
70. See below.

In all these cases the acknowledgment is void by law (*ipso iure*). It is deemed never to have taken place and, consequently, never to have had any legal effect.

(e) Voidable acknowledgments

Besides void acknowledgments the law recognises voidable acknowledgments. First of all, the law deals with the annulment of an acknowledgment a man may have been induced to make by threat, error, fraud or, during his minority by abuse of circumstance (undue influence).[71] This is the only case in which the man who is the biological father of the child has the right to petition for annulment, since it is thought that it is his moral duty to assume paternity. However, under some circumstances this is not in the interests of the child. If, after the acknowledgment, the begetter does not marry the mother, it is impossible for the child to become his or another's legitimate child. One might therefore consider it desirable to make it possible to annul an acknowledgment when the mother marries a man who is willing to acknowledge and legitimate the child.[72]

With regard to the annulment of an acknowledgment *by a man who is not the begetter of the child*, one should draw a distinction between cases in which legitimation has taken place and cases in which legitimation has not taken place. In the former case, only a limited group of persons can seek annulment.

Annulment of such an acknowledgment can be sued for *before legitimation:*

(1) By the child if the acknowledgment has been made during his minority.[73] The child may have a great interest in the annulment if this renders it possible for him to be acknowledged and legitimated by another man. It may also be the child's purpose to evade the duty to maintain his 'father'.[74] Whether this should be complied with will have to depend on what happened previously. If the 'father' has acquitted himself correctly of his duty to maintain the child, one would be more inclined to refuse the annulment than if he had never cared for the child at all.

(2) By any person who is a legal issue of the marriage, if the man was married during the period between the 360th and the 180th day inclusive before the birth of the child.[75]

A man cannot acknowledge a child that has been begotten by another woman during his marriage, as long as that marriage continues.[76] After dissolution of the marriage he is allowed to do so, but that acknowledgment can be annulled on a petition by a legal descendent of that marriage. The interest of the latter will be even greater when the Bill of book 4 of a new Civil Code[77] is enacted, whereby

---

71. Art. 225-1.
72. See Report of the Committee-Wiarda, p. 85.
73. Art. 225-2. sub a.
74. Art. 393.
75. Art. 225-2. sub b.
76. Art. 224-1. sub b. see p. 27.
77. See art. 4.2.3(a).

the illegitimate (natural) child will acquire the same legal status as the legitimate child as far as hereditary rights are concerned. In the Report of the Committee-Wiarda[78] it is suggested that this provision be cancelled as being contrary to "the principle of equal rights for children of the same father." Although this agreement appears rather weak—for the point at issue is that the children do not have the same father—the author is strongly in favour of the cancellation of this unfavourable provision.

(3) By the former husband of the child's mother, if the acknowledgment has been made by virtue of Article 198.[79] The interest of the husband is obvious. He can thus prevent his legitimate child being taken away from him as a result of the statement of the mother. Judging his interest *in concreto*, the court will take particular account of the question whether her former husband, unlike the acknowledger, is indeed the begetter of the child.

(4) By the public prosecutor.[80] An acknowledgment may be against public policy. This will be presumed where it has been made merely in order to obtain Dutch nationality *in fraudem legis* and, also, if the actual relationship between 'father' and child is precluded because, for instance, there is only a very small or, as the case may be, a very large disparity in age between the acknowledger and the child. In this connection the question has been asked whether a minimum disparity in age should be laid down in the law.[81] The legislator, however, has preferred this repressive provision, which seems to be a just one as it makes a flexible policy possible.

Annulment of an acknowledgment (still: by a man who is not the begetter of the child) can be sued for *after legitimation*:

(1) By the former husband, in the case of acknowledgment by virtue of Article 198.[82] The rationale of this provision is to cover the situation where the mother marries the acknowledger shortly after the acknowledgment and, consequently, the child is legitimated. The provision gives the former husband a period after the legitimation to petition for annulment.

(2) By the child, if the acknowledgment has been made during his minority.[83] In this way the child is able to undo the acknowledgment by a man who is not his begetter and to whose acknowledgment he had not given his consent. However he has to wait two years before he can bring a petition and must then do so within one year of that date. If he only learns that the acknowledger is not his begetter after the beginning of that year, then he has a period of one year in which to bring the petition, reckoned from the date of learning of that fact. The

---

78. See p. 84.
79. Art. 225-2. sub e. See also below p. 32.
80. Art. 225-2. sub d.
81. Report of Committee-Wiarda, p. 85.
82. Art. 225-3. See below, p. 32, further about Art. 198.
83. Art. 225-4.

annulment has retrospective effect.[84] After the decree has become final, the acknowledgment is deemed never to have had effect. However, rights acquired in good faith by third parties are protected.

(f) Illegitimate child becomes legitimate

Lack of space forces brevity on this, and the following, subject.

An illegitimate child can become legitimate by (1) legitimation and (2) adoption.

(1) *Legitimation.* When the illegitimate child was acknowledged by the father it acquires the status of his legitimate child. Legitimation takes place (a) by the marriage of the mother and the father of the child, (b) by the acknowledgment by the mother's husband during their marriage, (c) by the acknowledgment by the mother's husband after dissolution of the marriage as a result of her death.[85] Further, legitimation can take place by "letters of legitimation". A request for such letters may be made to the Crown, which makes a decision after obtaining the advice of the Hoge Raad (Supreme Court).[86] However, this possibility is restricted to the following cases:

(i) If, after acknowledgment, the projected marriage is prevented from being contracted owing to the death of one of them.[87] This is an exception to Article 214, acknowledgment but no marriage.

(ii) If the man who, having knowledge of the pregnancy of the woman and intending to marry her dies before the birth of the child without having acknowledged it.[88] Here is neither acknowledgment nor marriage. The aim of this provision is to offer a solution for cases in which the sudden death of the man prevents him from carrying out his intention to marry the mother and thereby make the child, with which she is pregnant, a legitimate child at his birth.

(2) *Adoption.* An illegitimate child can also become legitimate by adoption. In this connection there is a peculiarity in Dutch law, that a child can only be adopted by a married couple.[89] However, a couple cannot adopt a legitimate or natural child, or grandchild, of either party.[90] Consequently, a natural child cannot be adopted by his mother nor by her and her husband together.

(g) Legitimate child becomes illegitimate

Pursuant to Article 197 a child born in wedlock has the husband of the mother as his father. A child born before the 307th day after the dissolution of a marriage has the former husband as his father unless the mother has remarried. In the latter case the general rule again applies that the husband is the father. In all

---

84. Art. 225-5.
85. Art. 214.
86. Art. 215 and 216.
87. Art. 215-1.
88. Art. 215-2.
89. Art. 227.
90. Art. 228, sub b.

these cases the child is the legitimate child of the spouses. This is based on the legal presumption that a child is the issue of the sexual intercourse of the spouses and is begotten by the husband. However, this presumption may be rebutted, with certain restrictions. The man, that is the husband or former husband of Article 197, may petition to disclaim his paternity and rebut the above mentioned presumption. Outside the very restricted regulation of Article 198, this is not open to the mother nor to the child.[91]

There are various safeguards for the benefit of the child. The petition has to be directed against both the mother and the child who, being a minor, is represented by a guardian who has to look after his interests.[92] The ground for the petition is that the husband is not the begetter of the child. Rules of evidence are given in Article 200. The husband has to prove that he cannot be the father of the child.[93] The use of the word 'cannot' indicates that the standard of proof is beyond reasonable doubt. The author does not agree with that rule. There is no reason for this deviation from the general standard of proof in civil cases.[94] There are no restrictions with regard to the method of proof. Evidence of hereditary features or proof of sterility, for example, may suffice and recourse can be made to evidential presumptions. Article 200-2, for example, contains such a presumption. If the man argues that he had no sexual intercourse with his wife because they lived separately during the period of conception, the presumption of Article 197 is rebutted, unless there are certain facts which suggest that the man may still be the father of the child. For it is possible that sexual intercourse has taken place although the spouses live apart, or the child could have been conceived by artificial insemination with the sperm of the husband.

Even though it is proved that the husband is not the father (begetter) of the child, the petition to disclaim the paternity cannot succeed in the cases referred to in Article 201-1. These are the cases where the husband has given his consent to the act which might have resulted in the birth of the child or if he had knowledge, before the marriage, of his wife's pregnancy. This will not be so where she has deceived him as to the begetter. The consent referred to here is permission for her to have sexual intercourse with another man or to undergo artificial donor-insemination. The rationale of these exceptions is that, in such circumstances, the husband must be deemed to have accepted the paternity of the child.

The period within which the petition must be laid before the court is short, namely six months or, in the case where the woman has made the declaration of Article 198, eighteen months after the birth of the child.[95] The legal consequences of an affirmative decree of the court are that the child is illegitimate from its birth. This opens up the possibility of acknowledgment and legitimation by another man so that the new situation need not be detrimental to the child. On the contrary, it paves the way for the acquisition of the status of a legitimate child in the new family to be set up by his mother.

---

91. Otherwise § 1596 BGB.
92. See Art. 199.
93. Art. 200-1.
94. Cf. Bromley, p. 231.
95. Art. 203

We must deal shortly with Article 198, which entitles the mother of a child born within 306 days of the dissolution of her marriage, to make under certain restrictions a declaration that her former husband is not the father (begetter) of the child, provided that at the same time another man acknowledges the child. As this has the consequence that the child becomes a legitimate child of the mother and her new husband, this provision falls outside the scope of this paper. It need only be remarked that if the acknowledgment is annulled in accordance with Article 225[96], legitimation cannot take place, with the result that the child will only be the (illegitimate) natural child of the mother. However, there is an exception where the annulment of the acknowledgment is sought by the man who is the child's father by virtue of Article 197. After such an annulment, the child remains what he originally was, the petitioner's and the mother's legitimate child.[97]

(h) Legal relations between parent (father, mother) and illegitimate child

(1) *General remarks*

In many countries there is a marked tendency to assimilate the legal position of the illegitimate child with that of the legitimate child. Almost simultaneously France (1972), West Germany (1970), England (1969) and the Netherlands made considerable progress towards this end. Nevertheless, these/systems have retained differences between legitimate and illegitimate children which, however, seem to be caused primarily by the inescapable fact that an illegitimate and unacknowledged child does not have a father in the legal sense of the word.

(2) *Name*

The natural child of the father has the latter's name. If he has not been acknowledged and is consequently only a natural child of the mother, then he bears her name.[98] There are some social disadvantages attached to this provision as, in this way, the illegitimate birth of the child is at once revealed. German, French and English law generally contain the same provision.[99]

(3) *Consent to marry*

A minor child may not enter into a marriage without the consent of the parents with whom he has legal relations. Likewise, the father and the mother of a natural child have to give their consent. However, their position is less strong than that of the parents of a legitimate child, because their consent can be substituted by consent of the court which is not possible if the parent having authority over his legitimate child withholds his consent. This totally arbitrary distinction is not found in French, German or English law.

---

96. Art. 203.
97. Art. 198-4.
98. Art. 5-2.
99. §§ 1617/8 BGB, Art. 334-1 *Cc*, Birth and Death Registration Act 1953, s. 10 and Family Law Reform Act, s. 27.

(4) *Authority*

In the Dutch law system parental authority only exists during the marriage of the parents. Consequently, an illegitimate child is under "voogdij" (guardianship). The details cannot be explained here. The substance of it is that the mother of the illegitimate child *ipso iure* becomes the guardian, unless she is *incapax*. The father, that is he who has acknowledged the child, can become the guardian if he is appointed by the court. As there can only be one guardian, the court may have to choose between father and mother. In that case the interest of the child is decisive.[100] Notwithstanding certain differences, other legal systems also give priority to the mother in respect of the authority or custody.[101]

(5) *Duty of maintenance*

The mother and father (he who has acknowledged the child) are legally bound to contribute to the costs of maintenance and education of their illegitimate children.[102] This duty is reciprocal provided that, in respect of the father, he has acknowledged the child during its minority.[103] The biological father (begetter) of a child also has a duty to maintain his unacknowledged child. This duty is not reciprocal and is restricted to the minor child unless, after the age of majority, the child is not able to provide for himself owing to mental or physical infirmity.

In Article 394-3 the presumption has been laid down that the man who has had sexual intercourse with the mother between the 307th and the 179th day before the birth of the child is the begetter. However, the claim of the mother is dismissed if (a) the man can prove that the mother had sexual intercourse with another man in the relevant period (*exceptio plurium concubentium*), unless it is shown that the child could not be the issue of it; and (b) if the court conscientiously believes that the respondent is not the father of the child. This latter situation may be due to various circumstances, for instance when the child is a seven-month baby and it is established that the intercourse did not take place at a time when the child could have been the issue of it. Evidence that the man is not the father can also be proved by blood tests, etc. If another man acknowledges the child he will in future be regarded as the father and the duty of maintenance by the former ceases.[104] As the acknowledgment has no retrospective effect, the biological father remains liable for the maintenance for the period between birth and acknowledgment. On this point also German, English and French legal systems amount to roughly the same thing.[105]

(6) *Law of succession*

According to Dutch law the natural child has a very weak position with regard to the law of succession. He cedes priority to the legitimate children.[106] However,

---

100. See Art. 287 ss.
101. §§ 1705, ss BGB, Art. 374 *Cc* and Bromley, p. 271.
102. Art. 392.
103. Art. 393.
104. HR 21 May 1965, NJ 1965 340, nt. DJV.
105. See §§ 1601 ss and 1615(a) ss BGB, Art. 203 ss, 334 ss and 340 ss *Cc* and Bromley, p. 479 ss.
106. Art. 909 ss.

Articles 4.2.3(a) and 4.3.3.2 of book 4 of the Bill of the new Civil Code assimilates the legal positions of natural and legitimate children.[107]

4. Divorce

Introduction

In the law of divorce, also, Dutch law has recently changed radically. It proved to be impossible to effect any significant changes after 1838 until the Act of 6 May 1971[108] brought a fundamental revision of the law of divorce. The Civil Code of 1838 enumerated a number of grounds for divorce (adultery, etc.). If one of the spouses had been guilty of such conduct the other was entitled to a divorce, unless reconciliation had taken place. The 'guilty' party lost all rights to maintenance. Divorce by mutual consent was expressly prohibited. In the course of time this rigid system became somewhat relaxed. The most important mitigating factor was that the Hoge Raad (Supreme Court) decided in 1883 that, in divorce cases, a recognised uncontested fact pleaded by a petitioner had to be accepted as true (in the procedure) without the need of further evidence. Thus it became possible to obtain a divorce in all cases, provided the spouses agreed to it. The prohibition of divorce by mutual consent thus became a dead letter and numerous divorces were obtained on the ground of adultery alleged by one of the spouses and not contested by the other. Although this method, known as "the big lie", was often criticised, its application was general.

Another mitigation concerned the right to maintenance. If the divorce was granted on the petition of either of the spouses the court had the power to award an allowance for maintenance to a spouse in a case in which he was the petitioner and in which he was not declared 'guilty'.

Notwithstanding frequent requests to amend the law of divorce, all past attempts failed. The Dutch people had such divergent religious and ideological views that no single proposition for a fundamental revision was able to receive enough support. After 1957 when the Minister of Justice instituted a discussion group composed of people representing different groups from Dutch society with the aim of studying the law of divorce, a change set in. The report of this committee was followed by numerous reports from churches, ideological groups and political parties, all of which endeavoured to offer solutions which might be widely approved of. All this led to the Bill of Minister of Justice Polak, introduced in 1969, which became law in 1971.

Restricting the small compass of this paper to the four main points of this law, consideration will be given to the grounds for divorce, maintenance, the relation between divorce and judicial separation and the position of the children.

(a) The ground for divorce

In principle—i.e. unless there are very special circumstances convincing the court that there is no chance of a reconciliation—a decree of divorce cannot be

---

107. See also Art. 757 *Cc* (since the Act of 3 Jan. 1972) and § 1934 a BGB.
108. S. 290, enforced on 1 Oct. 1971.

pronounced within one year from the date of the marriage.[109] This provision is designed to prevent undue haste in obtaining a divorce.

Secondly, if they are judicially separated, the spouses cannot obtain a divorce but only "dissolution of the marriage".[110]

The law contains two procedures for obtaining a divorce: (i) on the petition of one of the spouses and (ii) on the joint petition of the spouses.[111]

(i) *on the petition of one of the spouses* a divorce is granted if the marriage is 'durably disturbed'; these words are the literal translation of 'duurzaam ontwricht".[112] It is considered that these words have the same meaning as the phrase "irretrievably broken down" and this term will be used for the sake of simplicity. By recognising this ground the legislator disregards the principle of guilt in favour of an objective approach. The element of "breakdown" means that continuation of the cohabitation has become unendurable; the expression "irretrievable" means that there is no prospect of the recovery of more or less reasonable conjugal relations. Of course, the subjective element in this argument cannot be denied. If one party persists in his allegation that the marriage has irretrievably broken down, the truth of this allegation may readily be presumed. If the respondent does not contest the divorce, the court will not investigate the matter any further. If he does contest it, evidence of all kinds may be adduced to prove the irretrievable breakdown. For this purpose, any fact, cause or symptom of that breakdown, can serve (e.g. living apart for a considerable time). During the discussion of the Bill in parliament, the retention of one element of the old law was urged, namely that the spouse whose partner is guilty of adultery is entitled to a divorce. Without making a provision in the law, the Minister of Justice declared several times that the court should accept the allegation of the innocent party, in cases of adultery, that the marriage has irretrievably broken down, without any further investigation.

It is certainly not a small merit of the new law that, thanks to this objective criterion, a solution has also been found to the problem of divorce in cases of the mental illness of one of the spouses. Under the old law it was impossible to obtain a divorce in most cases, as the ill party had not been guilty of a ground for divorce nor could he be expected to sue the other party. In the case where he had been put under guardianship, neither did his guardian have this capacity. Under the current law, the court can judge objectively whether the marriage has broken down due to the mental illness and, in case of an affirmative answer, can grant the petition.

It is not difficult for a malicious spouse to disturb the marriage by his own behaviour, thus creating the ground for divorce. In order to avoid this risk, the law has taken account of the guilt of the spouse.

If the spouse who petitions for divorce is chiefly to blame for the breakdown, the court will dismiss the petition and thus protect the respondent.[113] The guilty spouse can only petition for a dissolution of the marriage after three years judicial separation.[114]

---

109. Art. 156.
110. Art. 150 and below sub-para. (c).
111. Art. 150.
112. See Art. 151.
113. Art. 152.
114. See *post* p. 39.

Another defence to a petition for divorce relates to its financial aspect. If a spouse has the prospect of certain payments, such as pension, life-insurance, etc., should the other spouse predecease him or her and if, as a result of the divorce, this prospect is lost or to a large extent reduced, the court will not grant the petition until a fair provision has been made for both spouses in the light of all the circumstances of the case.[115] The wife in particular needs this protection. She risks being left badly provided for after the divorce, in the event of her husband's death, because the alimony payments from the man will then cease and often the payment of pension or life-insurance goes to the woman who is the spouse of the man at the time of his death.

Meanwhile, in relation to pensions, legal provisions have been made according to which the widow's pension is divided between both "widows" in ratio to the duration of their respective marriages. But these rules do not apply to all pensions.

Article 153 is far from providing a satisfactory arrangement of the pension rights of the divorced wife. In the first place, it is only a defence and has to be raised by the respondent and is consequently worthless to a petitioning party. Moreover, the defence can only be raised in the case of an existing prospect so that, if the husband has not made any provisions, the defence is not possible. Therefore a regulation has been laid down in Article 157-2 which makes it possible to grant a spouse alimony payments to such a level that she herself is able to make provision in case the other spouse predeceases her.

Article 153-1 does not apply in the following two cases.[116]

(a) if it can be reasonably expected that the respondent spouse can make sufficient provision for her/himself; (b) if it is the respondent spouse who is chiefly to blame for the irretrievable breakdown of the marriage. The exception referred to under (a) does not require further comment. That mentioned under (b) is a reflection of Article 152. Since it ought not to be possible for the spouse who is chiefly to blame for the irretrievable breakdown to obtain a divorce against the will of the other spouse, he should not be able to prevent a divorce sought for by the other spouse on the financial ground of Article 153-1.

(ii) A divorce is granted *on the joint petition of the spouses* if the petition is based on their joint opinion that the marriage has broken down irretrievably.[117] If the parties persist in their request, the court does not examine the breakdown. Either party, however, may withdrawn the request pending the proceedings.[118] The spouses are obliged to come to an understanding with each other about some main consequences of the divorce, such as children and maintenance, and make known to the court what they have agreed.[119]

(b) Maintenance

In the divorce decree or later the court may award a periodical alimony payment (not a lump sum), payable by the other spouse to a spouse who

---

115. Art. 153-1.
116. Art. 153-2.
117. Art. 154-1.
118. Art. 154-2.
119. Art. 155.

38

has not sufficient means for his maintenance and is not able to acquire them.[120] It is an important principle of the divorce law that a spouse's fundamental right to maintenance is not connected in any way with his or her guilt of a matrimonial offence. A spouse can be granted alimony irrespective of whether he is the petitioner or the respondent.

This situation can be contrasted with that under the old law according to which a spouse was never entitled to alimony if the divorce has been decreed against him alone. On the other hand the Hoge Raad[121] had already decided that, under certain circumstances, the man might be under a moral obligation to contribute to the maintenance of his guilty ex-wife. The moral obligation was of such an urgent nature that it was to be regarded as identical to the natural obligation of Article 1395.

The party entitled to an allowance may be either the husband or the wife but obviously, in practice, it will be the wife. An essential characteristic of the Dutch law is that alimony after divorce is at the discretion of the court. The latter can grant an allowance—which means that it has the power, but is not legally bound, to do so. This had already been decided by the Hoge Raad.[122] As far as the duration and amount of the allowance are concerned the court has complete discretion in applying the legal standards for determining the amount. These include the financial capacity of the spouses and their needs and also other criteria such as the material circumstances, the duration of the marriage and the behaviour of the spouse claiming the allowance. This behaviour could be such that it would be reasonable not to grant an allowance or to change or revoke an allowance already granted.

Article 158 expressly enacts that spouses may agree that, after the divorce, one shall be under no obligation to maintain the other. The consequence of this agreement is that, if an ex-spouse receives support from the State, the payments cannot be recovered from the former partner even if he or she has the financial means to make a contribution.[123] A bill to put an end to this unsatisfactory situation is in preparation.

Parties can stipulate that an agreed allowance cannot be varied by the court because of their changed circumstances. In spite of such a stipulation variation remains possible if the change in the circumstances is so drastic that it would not be reasonable for the petitioner to be held to it.[124]

The obligation to pay maintenance terminates the moment the spouse entitled to it either remarries or cohabits with another person as if they were married (concubinage), but owing to the uncertainty attached to the concept of concubinage, this provision has come in for a great deal of criticism.

(c) The relation between divorce and judicial separation

Notwithstanding severe criticism, judicial separation has been retained in the law. The object is twofold. In the first place, judicial separation is a less drastic

---

120. Art. 157-1.
121. 4 June 1965, NJ 1965, 277 nt. GJS.
122. 21 Nov. 1913, NJ 1913, p. 1320.
123. HR 12 Oct. 1973, NJ 1974, 271 nt ARB.
124. Art. 159-3.

form of divorce for the benefit of those who have religious scruples and also for those who, for reasons given above, are unable to obtain a divorce. Secondly judicial separation serves as a technical juridical means of achieving the aim of the legislator to make it possible to dissolve any irretrievably broken down marriage after a certain time.

It was decreed that after three years from the date of the judicial separation, dissolution of the marriage could be requested without the possibility of the defence of Article 152.[125] However, the defence on financial grounds dealt with above[126] remains available.[127] Since the only defence that can be set up against a petition for judicial separation is that the marriage is not irretrievably broken down and since such a breakdown may easily be brought about by one of the parties, it is obvious that after some time every marriage can be dissolved on the petition of one of the spouses, even against the will of the other. Thus it appears that the question as to who is chiefly to blame for the breakdown[128] should not be regarded as an absolute bar to the dissolution of the marriage, but rather as a delaying factor.

(d) The children

After the dissolution of the marriage Dutch law no longer recognises parental authority but only guardianship. The court appoints one of the parents as guardian[129] and the other parent can be ordered to contribute toward the child's maintenance by periodical payments. Other persons are not allowed to be appointed as guardians. Furthermore, the court appoints a supervising guardian. The court has complete discretion to choose either the father or the mother, the paramount consideration being the interest of the child. The usual practice is for guardianship over very young children to be given to the mother and for the other parent to be appointed as supervising guardian, which is not a very important function.

The guardian has all the rights of custody, care and control. He is responsible for the child's education and for the administration of the child's property. Following the example of several other legal systems, the law controls the right of access to the child by the parent who is not the guardian. The court may make an arrangement[130], the paramount consideration again being the welfare of the child.

(e) Some comparative remarks

For reasons of lack of space, only one aspect can be considered—that of the grounds for divorce.

Western Germany has an elaborate system centering round "tiefe Zerrütung der Ehe" which is, however, related either to the guilty actions of one of the

---

125. I.e. the guilt of the petitioner.
126. See p. 39.
127. Art. 180.
128. See Art. 152.
129. Art. 161-1.
130. Art. 161-5.

spouses or to objective circumstances such as mental illness.[131] A law bearing greater resemblance to the Dutch system is in course of preparation. In England, the irretrievable breakdown of the marriage is the only ground for divorce since the Divorce Reform Act of 1969.[132] This breakdown, however, must be established by proof of certain facts such as the adultery of the respondent, such behaviour by the respondent that the petitioner cannot reasonably be expected to live with him, desertion, etc. The French law of divorce, renewed by the Act of 11 July 1975, does not recognise the concept of the breakdown of a marriage. The possibility of obtaining a divorce is increased by the regulation of divorce by mutual consent.[133] Other grounds are separation for six years[134] and wrongful behaviour on the part of a spouse.[135]

---

131. See §§ 42 ss. Ehegesetz.
132. Incorporated in the Matrimonial Causes Act, 1973.
133. Art. 230 ss. *Cc.*
134. Art. 237 ss. *Cc.*
135. Art. 242 ss. *Cc.*

CHAPTER III. THE REFORM OF FAMILY LAW IN ENGLAND

by Joseph M. Thomson

A. The Equality of the Spouses

At the height of the Age of Enlightenment, Diderot could write these words[1]:

"Dans presque toutes les contrées, la cruauté des lois civiles s'est réunie contre les femmes à la cruauté de la nature."

Nor did women fare much better under the Common law[2]: in particular, a married woman was regarded as little more than her husband's chattel.[3] The purpose of this paper is to examine those areas of family law where formerly there was gross inequality between spouses, in an attempt to assess to what extent spouses now have equal status under English law.

A principal reason why a wife enjoyed so few rights at Common law was the doctrine of the unity of spouses[4], that is, that in the eyes of the law a man and his wife were one.[5] But this did not mean that the spouses participated equally in the personality created out of them: rather, the effect of the law could be summed up by the cynical proposition that, while man and wife were one, the man was the one. Although with the increasing independence of twentieth century women, the concept of the doctrine has become outmoded, nevertheless its influence on the structure of the law was profound and legislation has often been necessary to erase its effects.

On marriage a couple have a mutual duty to cohabit: conversely, they have a right to enjoy each other's consortium. This right formerly belonged to the husband alone, i.e. he had a right to his wife's consortium but she had no right to his and was simply under a duty to give him her society and services. To enforce his right, the husband could chastise his wife and imprison her. In time, the right to physical chastisement was lost.[6] In 1852[7], a husband was refused a writ of habeas corpus to retrieve the custody of his wife: in 1891, the House of Lords held in *R v Jackson*[8] that a husband did not have the right to restrain his wife by putting her under house arrest.[9] In *R v Reid*[10] the Court of Appeal maintained

---

1. *Sur les Femmes*, Oeuvres Diderot, ed. Billy Pleiade (1951) p. 985.
2. This is not surprising since the Common law was equated with natural law as 'the perfection of reason'. Coke Institutes Part I, § 138.
3. For an historical survey see generally *A Century of Family Law* (ed. Graveson and Crane).
4. See generally Williams, *Legal Unity of Husband and Wife*, 10 MLR 6.
5. Even in the days of the unreformed Common law, there never was complete unity. Thus, for example, a wife continued to hold her own freehold property.
6. Today the husband would be guilty of assault.
7. *R v Leggatt* [1852] 18 QB 781.
8. [1891] 1 QB 671.
9. The subjection of a wife to the tyranny of her husband is a recurrent theme in the literature of the nineteenth century. See e.g. the plight of Lady Laura Kennedy in Trollope's *Phineas Finn*.
10. [1972] 3 WLR 395.

that *R v Jackson*[11] swept away any conception that a husband could keep his wife against her will or compel her to return to him by use of force: consequently, a husband can now be guilty of kidnapping his wife.

As emphasised above, today it is thought that both a husband and wife have the right to the consortium of the other. Consortium raises important issues. Since the essence of consortium is sharing marriage life together, a dispute about the place of the matrimonial home can be serious. It was once thought that a husband could determine this question and his wife would have to follow unless he had exercised his prerogative unreasonably, e.g. if the new environment would cause injury to her health.[12] Today it is generally thought that this is a matter of common concern and neither spouse has the casting vote. But if a spouse unreasonably refuses to follow the other to the new home, that spouse will still be deemed to be in desertion.

An important incident of consortium is that each spouse owes the other a duty to consummate the marriage and *after* the marriage is consummated, a mutual right to intercourse continues provided it is reasonably exercised. A spouse can refuse intercourse if the other's demands are inordinate or are unreasonable or are likely to result in a breakdown in health. Since consent to intercourse arises at the time of marriage as opposed to the time of the particular act of intercourse[13], a husband cannot be guilty of raping his wife.[14] He can, however, be guilty of aiding and abetting his wife's rape.[15] The implied consent will be revoked on divorce.[16]

By custom, in England a wife takes her husband's name but there is no legal obligation on her to do so.[17] The law also recognises that the relationship of husband and wife is one of confidentiality: consequently, neither spouse can divulge confidences given by the other during the marriage.[18] For similar reasons, special rules of evidence apply to spouses.[19]

As a result of the unity doctrine a wife suffered several disabilities at Common law. She lacked the capacity to contract until this was remedied by the Law Reform (Married Woman and Tortfeasors) Act 1935. If the wife was the victim of a tort, her husband had to join the action as co-plaintiff: this was abolished by the Married Women's Property Act 1882. Again, if the wife committed a tort,

---

11. *Supra* note 3. Petitions for the restitution of conjugal rights were abolished by section 20 of the Matrimonial Proceedings & Property Act 1970.

12. *Millichamp v Millichamp* (1931) 146 LT 96.

13. *R v Clarke* [1949] 2 All ER 448.

14. Though if he used force or violence, he could be guilty of assault.

15. See now the controversial House of Lords decision in *DPP v Morgan* [1975] 2 WLR 913. However, the rule that a husband cannot rape his wife has been much criticised. See e.g. its purported reform in the Sexual Offences Bill 1976.

16. And also if there is a decree of judicial separation or a separation agreement. But *de facto* separation will not suffice. *R v Miller supra* note 2, but this case was doubted in *R v Reid supra* note 10.

17. In Scotland the law recognises that this is purely a social custom and that the wife retains her maiden name. Consequently, cases are cited by reference to a wife's maiden and married name, e.g. *McAlister or Donoghue v Stevenson* [1932] AC 82.

18. *Argyll v Argyll* [1967] Ch. 302.

19. See generally *Cross on Evidence* (1974) 4th ed. 147-149; 154-162.

the husband had to be joined as co-defendant: the need for this continued until 1935.[20] Neither husband nor wife could sue the other in tort until 1962.[21] There is, however, a discretion to stay an action brought during the subsistence of the marriage if the court takes the view that no substantial benefit would accrue to *either* party were the proceedings to continue or if, in a dispute concerning property, it thinks that the matter could be dealt with under section 17 of the Married Women's Property Act 1882.[22]

Certain anomalies still survive as a result of the unity doctrine. Thus spouses cannot conspire together[23] nor is a communication between spouses publication for the purposes of libel and slander.[24] A wife has a defence[25] to a crime, other than murder or treason, if she can prove that the crime was done in the presence and under the coercion of her husband.[26] Under the Theft Act[27], husband and wife are separate persons and each can be convicted of the theft of the other's property.[28]

Until recently, on marriage a wife automatically acquired the domicile of her husband: and her domicile remained dependent on his for as long as the marriage lasted. Now, by section 1(1) of the Domicile and Matrimonial Proceedings Act 1973, a married woman is empowered to acquire a domicile independent of that of her husband. Any woman who had her husband's domicile by dependence when the Act came into effect is to be treated as retaining that domicile as a domicile of choice if it is not her domicile of origin, unless and until it is changed by acquisition or revival of another domicile on or after the coming into operation of the Act.[29] Married women, however, are still discriminated against under the British Nationality Act 1948. If a woman marries a citizen of the United Kingdom and Colonies, she is entitled as of right to be registered, should she desire, as a citizen of the United Kingdom and Colonies. But the converse does not follow, i.e. a man who marries a citizen of the United Kingdom and Colonies is not entitled to register and must be naturalised.[30] This is an example of the doctrine that nationality passes only through males.

However, the most important issues which must be discussed concern the equality of spouses in relation to their children and matrimonial property. The law relating to parental rights[31] is complex and uncertain because English law has

---

20. Law Reform (Married Women & Tortfeasors) Act 1935.
21. Section 1(1) of the Law Reform (Husband & Wife) Act 1962.
22. Section 1(2) of the Law Reform (Husband & Wife) Act 1962.
23. *Mawji v R* [1957] AC 126.
24. *Wennhak v Morgan* (1888) 20 QBD 635.
25. Stemming originally from the Common law.
26. See section 47 of the Criminal Justice Act 1925. The wife did not have to prove coercion at Common law; that was presumed.
27. See section 30.
28. But the consent of the DPP is needed before proceedings are instigated unless the spouses are separated by a judicial order or where the accused is charged with committing the offence jointly with the other spouse. e.g. if a wife pawns property owned by her husband and herself and *both* then steal it from the pawnbroker.
29. Section 1(2) of the Domicile and Matrimonial Proceedings Act 1973.
30. Section 6 of the British Nationality Act 1948. This is unaffected by the Sex Discrimination Act 1975.
31. The paper is only concerned with legitimate children of the marriage.

never analysed precisely what is meant by that concept and the terminology in the cases has not been used consistently. It is the present writer's view that certain parental rights are fundamental in the sense that they are personal to the spouses and are not dependent on the parents having the custody of the child. These are:

(i) The right to share in the estate of their child should he die intestate.[32]

(ii) The right to appoint testamentary guardians.[33]

(iii) The right to refuse to consent to their child being freed for adoption or to the adoption order itself.[34] But if a parent abandons, neglects or persistently or seriously ill treats the child or cannot be found, or is incapable of giving his consent or is withholding his consent unreasonably[35], the court may dispense with the consent.[36]

(iv) A child will have his father's domicile unless the child is living with its mother and has no home with its father, in which case it will have the domicile of the mother.[37] Accordingly, to the extent that a child will *prima facie* have the domicile of its father, the spouses still do not enjoy equal rights in this area of the law.

(v) A child who is not born in the United Kingdom and Colonies, may have British nationality by descent if his father, but not his mother, is a citizen of the United Kingdom and Colonies.[38] Once again, there is a discrimination against women.

(vi) The parents have a right that the child's surname should not be changed.[39] However, the child's surname can be changed if it is in the best interests of the child to do so.[40] This is not to deny the existence of the right but is an illustration of a principle which is now of the greatest importance in English Family Law, viz. that parental rights must be *exercised* in accordance with what is in the best interest of the child (the welfare principle).

(vii) It is the present writer's contention that the parents' rights to access to their child is one of these fundamental rights. A parent's right to visit his child will be upheld unless it is clearly prejudicial to the child to do so[41]: this will normally[42] only apply when the parent is so unfit to be brought into contact with the child that his mere presence would cause the child

---

32. Section 46 of the Administration of Estates Act 1925.
33. Section 3 of the Guardianship of Minors Act 1971.
34. Section 16(1) and Section 18 of The Adoption Act 1976.
35. On the meaning of 'unreasonably' see now *In re P (an infant)*, [1977] 1 All ER 182, to the effect that Section 3 of The Children Act 1975—now repealed and re-enacted as Section 6 of The Adoption Act 1976—has *not* altered the law on this point. The leading cases therefore remain *In re W* [1971] 2 All ER 49 and *In re D* [1977] 1 All ER 145. Cf. *Re B (an infant)* [1976] 3 All ER 134.
36. Section 16(2) of The Adoption Act 1976.
37. Section 4(2)(a) of the Domicile and Matrimonial Proceedings Act 1973.
38. Section 5 of the British Nationality Act 1948.
39. *In Re T* [1963] Ch. 238.
40. *Y v Y* [1973] Fam. 147.
41. See e.g. *M v M* [1973] 2 All ER 81. There the courts argued that access to his parents was a right of the child and therefore should only be taken away in extreme circumstances.
42. But see *B v B* [1971] 3 All ER 682.

harm[43]. Thus the *exercise* of the right will be regulated by the courts in accordance with the welfare principle.[44]

Except where indicated, these fundamental rights belong to both spouses equally. There are, however, another group of parental rights which have been grouped under the concept of 'the custody of the child' and which will be lost by a parent if he loses the child's custody. These are:

(i) The parent's right to determine the child's education.[45] This right must, however, be exercised in accordance with the welfare principle.[46]
(ii) The parent's right to determine the child's religion.[47] This right, too, must be exercised in accordance with the welfare principle.[48]
(iii) The parent's right to refuse to give consent to the marriage of a minor is dependent on having the custody of the child.[49]
(iv) If a parent has custody then *prima facie* he has the right to the physical care and control of the child. However, the courts may order that one spouse is to have the custody of the child so that he may have a 'say in' the matters already discussed—education, religion, marriage—but give the care and control to the other.[50] Determining which parent is to have the care and control of the child is done in accordance with the welfare principle.[51]

The parent with care and control has the following rights:

(i) The right to consent to medical treatment in respect of minors under the age of sixteen.[52] Consent ought to be given for generally accepted medical treatment unless it is clearly against the child's interests to do so.[53]
(ii) The right to discipline the child, the exercise of which is subject to the welfare principle.[54]
(iii) The right to the child's services would seem to be dependent on his being 'part of a household', i.e. physically present in the home.

---

43. The fact that the parents have committed adultery or failed to maintain the child will not usually be serious enough.
44. This thesis was of immense importance if a local authority had assumed parental rights in respect of the child. See Thomson, *Local Authorities and Parental Rights* (1974) 90 LQR 310; Thomson, *Adoption, Local Authorities and Parental Rights* (1975) 91 LQR 14. But now a local authority can assume all the parental rights and duties in respect of the child. See Section 57 of The Children Act 1975 and Thomson, *A Parent's Right to see his Child* 1976, Local Govt. Chronicle p. 683 ff.
45. *Hall v Hall* (1749) 3 Att. 721.
46. *J v C* [1970] AC 668.
47. *Stourton v Stourton* (1857) 8 De GM&G 760.
48. *In Re W* [1907] 2 Ch 557. *In Re Collins* [1950] 1 Ch 498. *J v C supra* note 46.
49. Schedule 2 of The Marriage Act 1949.
50. See e.g. *Wakham v Wakham* [1954] 1 WLR 366.
51. *J v C supra*, note 46.
52. Sections 8 and 21 of the Family Law Reform Act 1969.
53. See Skegg, *Consent to Medical Procedures on Minors* (1973) 36 MLR 370 and cases cited therein.
54. Section 1(1) of the Children and Young Persons Act 1937. Sections 1(2) and (3) of the Children and Young Persons Act 1969.

It is important to stress again that the exercise of most of these parental rights must be done in accordance with the welfare principle, i.e. to further the child's best interests.[55] Moreover, the welfare principle has also been used to determine who should be given the custody of the child and have the consequent parental rights.[56]

At common law custody is vested in the father and he could exercise the custodial rights to the exclusion of his wife.[57] Moreover, he would only lose custody in the most exceptional circumstances, i.e. when he was so depraved and corrupt as to be unfit to have the custody of the child. During the nineteenth and twentieth centuries, this position has altered radically.[58] Statutory recognition was given to a wife's right to seek custody from her husband, and this process culminated in the Guardianship Act of 1973 whereby[59] the rights and authority of the mother and father are to be equal, and exercisable by either without the other, so that a wife may now, on her own initiative, exercise any custodial right.[60]

Even before the Guardianship Act 1973, it was settled that any superior right which a father might have in respect of the custody of his children, had to be ignored in custody disputes.[61] But, in deciding who should have custody of a child, the court must regard 'the welfare of the minor as the first and paramount consideration'[62] and all other factors such as the wishes of the parents—even when innocent—are subject to the welfare principle.[63] Thus, although the spouses are now on an equal footing in relation to parental rights, this area of the law is dominated by the principle that the welfare of the child must generally prevail.

By Section 17 of the Supplementary Benefits Act 1976 there is a duty on both the father and mother to support their children under the age of sixteen. If the parents fail in this obligation, the children will be maintained by the State and the Supplementary Benefits Commission can recover the sums paid out from the defaulting parent.[64]

---

55. See Hall, *The Decline of Parental Rights* [1972 B] CLJ 248. Eekelaar, *What are Parental Rights?* (1973) 89 LQR 210. For a devastating critique of the welfare principle see Goldstein, Freud and Solnit, *Beyond the Best Interests of the Child* (New York 1973).
56. *J v C supra*, note 46.
57. See *In Re Agar-Ellis* (1883) 24 Ch. D 317.
58. For the history see Bevan, *The Law of Children*, pp. 256-259.
59. Section 1(1).
60. If the parents disagree on any question affecting the child's welfare, either of them may apply to the courts for directions.
61. See now Section 1 of the Guardianship of Minors Act 1971, re-enacting Section 1 of the Guardianship of Infants Act 1925.
62. Section 1 of the Guardianship of Minors Act 1971.
63. Compare *In Re L* [1962] 1 WLR 886, with *In Re F* [1969] 2 All ER 766. In *J v C supra* note 46, Ld. McDermott said at p. 710/11 that the courts had to consider all the circumstances and by analysing them take the course which would be in the best interest of the child's welfare. But in *B v B* (1975) *The Times* (May 15th) doubt was cast by Ormrod LJ on the soundness of Ld. McDermott's dictum and the court gave considerably more weight to the wishes of the unimpeachable parent than is usual.
64. Maintenance for children can be obtained from the husband during the marriage under Section 27 of the Matrimonial Causes Act 1973 or Section 1(1)(h) of the Matrimonial Proceedings (Magistrates Courts) Act 1960 on proof by the wife of wilful neglect to maintain them. A husband can get maintenance for the children from the wife under the Matrimonial Causes Act 1973 but may only do so under the Matrimonial Proceedings (Magistrates Courts) Act 1960

One of the most important incidents of consortium is that on marriage a husband becomes bound to maintain his wife[65]: at Common law, however, this duty was not reciprocal, i.e. a wife was not under any duty to maintain her husband. This duty ends on the termination of the marriage or by agreement or by the wife's misconduct, e.g. her adultery[66] or desertion.[67] However, the only way[68] that a wife could enforce her right to be maintained was by virtue of her agency of necessity, i.e. her right to pledge her husband's credit for the purchase of necessities. The Law Commission took the view that this right was anachronistic[69] and the agency of necessity was abolished in 1971.[70]

Statute, however, has intervened to reinforce the Common law and incidentally to expand the scope of the obligation. A wife can seek maintenance from her husband under the Matrimonial Proceedings (Magistrates Courts) Act 1960[71] on proof of his wilful neglect[72] to maintain her; a husband, on the other hand, can only seek maintenance from his wife under that Act if his earning capacity has been impaired.[73] Alternatively the spouses may use the parallel procedure under the Matrimonial Causes Act 1973 on proof of wilful neglect to maintain.[74] After divorce, nullity or separation proceedings, a whole range of orders are available under the Matrimonial Causes Act 1973 for the financial provision of the spouses.[75] Furthermore, both spouses are under a duty to maintain each other by virtue of

---

if he is handicapped so that his earning capacity has been impaired. Maintenance for the child will, of course, be available after divorce, nullity or judicial separation proceedings under the Matrimonial Causes Act 1973. See Sections 23-25 of the 1973 Act. For an interesting discussion of the problems which can ensue see N. V. Lowe & C. Smith, *Supplementary Benefits and Magistrates*, (1976) Fam. Law. pp. 101 ff. and 132 ff.

65. This obligation remains a striking source for new developments in Family Law. See e.g. *Gurasz v Gurasz* [1969] 3 All ER 822 where Lord Denning MR relied on this concept as a justification for excluding the husband from the matrimonial home, cf. *Brent v Brent* [1974] 2 All ER 1211. In *Richards v Dove* [1974] 1 All ER 888 the concept (*inter alia*) was used to justify the refusal of the court to give a man's mistress an equitable interest in the house they shared.

66. *Wright & Webb v Annandale* [1930] 2 KB 8; *Chilton v Chilton* [1952] 1 All ER 1322.

67. *Price v Price* [1951] P. 413.

68. But see *Gurasz v Gurasz* (*supra*) note 65 where Lord Denning MR thought that a husband could be expelled from the matrimonial home if his conduct prevented the wife from enjoying this right to the extent that it involves the husband supplying her with a roof over her head.

69. Law Commission No. 25, para. 108.

70. Section 41 of the Matrimonial Proceedings and Property Act 1970.

71. See Section 1(1)(h) of the Matrimonial Proceedings (Magistrates Courts) Act 1960.

72. She must not have lost her right to be maintained. Then she must prove that she has not got sufficient means, that her husband knew this, *Stringer v Stringer* [1952] 1 All ER 373, that he did not provide reasonable maintenance and had no valid excuse for failing to do so. *Earnshaw v Earnshaw* [1896] P. 160. Finally, the failure to maintain must be 'wilful'. *Baynham v Baynham* [1968] 1 WLR 1890. It has recently been held that the one-third rule should now be the starting point for assessing the amount of maintenance. See *Gengler v Gengler* [1976] 2 All ER 81, criticised by Ellis in (1976) 92 LQR 482.

73. See Section 1(1)(i) of the Matrimonial Proceedings (Magistrates Courts) Act 1966.

74. See Section 27 of the Matrimonial Causes Act 1973. Secured as well as unsecured periodical payments and lump sum payments are available. See Section 27(6)(a), (b) and (c). Once again, the spouse must not have lost the right to be maintained. See *Gray v Gray* [1976] 2 All ER 225.

75. See Sections 23-26 of the Matrimonial Causes Act 1973. As well as those mentioned in footnote 74 (*supra*) property adjustment orders are available. Sections 23(d), (e) and (f) discussed *infra*.

Section 17 of the Supplementary Benefits Act 1976, and the Supplementary Benefits Commission can recover any sums paid out in relief from the defaulting spouse.

The effect of marriage on the property owned by each spouse has, of course, varied over the centuries.[76] Broadly speaking the effect of legislation[77] during the nineteenth and the first half of the present century was to alter the law from the principle of unity in favour of the principle of separation of property. But as Stein and Shand comment[78]

> "This idea [separate property] may be appropriate to the rare situation where both parties have substantial assets of their own. It has never fitted the usual situation where neither has much capital and the main income is that of the husband. The principle of separate property has meant in practice that the husband keeps his income and his wife is in a state of economic subjection to him. Equality in theory has resulted in injustice in practice."

Attempts have been made to remedy this situation. During the fifties and sixties, the Court of Appeal[79] led by Lord Denning MR developed the doctrine of family assets, i.e. that all property bought for the family ought, in the absence of evidence to the contrary, to be presumed to belong to both spouses equally, regardless of the actual size of the contribution to the purchase made by each spouse. This doctrine was, however, discredited as a result of the decisions of the House of Lords in *Pettit v Pettit*[80] and *Gissing v Gissing*.[81]

These decisions held that, when determining their title to matrimonial property, no special property[82] rules apply between husband and wife. Thus the equitable title to the property will *prima facie* follow the legal title but if there is an express agreement stating the beneficial interests, that settles the issue.[83] However, where there is evidence that the spouse who does not have the legal title to the property has nevertheless made, directly or indirectly[84], a substantial[85] contribution to the purchase of the property in money or money's worth[86], then the courts will infer that there is an "implied, constructive or resulting trust" of the property in his/her favour[87]: the size of the beneficial interest will correspond

---

76. For the history of the subject, see Bromley *Family Law* (1971) 4th ed, p. 347 ff.

77. See e.g. the Matrimonial Causes Act 1857; the Married Women's Property Act 1882; the property legislation of 1925; the Married Women (Restraint on Anticipation) Act 1949.

78. *Legal Values in Western Society* (1974) (Edinburgh University Press) 87.

79. See e.g. *Fribrance v Fribrance No. 2* [1957] 1 WLR 384; *Hine v Hine* [1962] 1 WLR 1124; *Ulrich v Ulrich* [1968] 1 WLR 180.

80. [1970] AC 777.

81. [1971] AC 886.

82. Apart from the operation of the presumption of advancement when a husband conveys property to his wife. In spite of criticism, the presumption of advancement still operates. Compare e.g. *Tinker v Tinker* [1970] 1 All ER 540 with *Heseltine v Heseltine* [1971] 1 All ER 952.

83. *Leake v Bruzzi* [1974] 2 All ER 1196.

84. *Gissing v Gissing* (*supra*) note 81.

85. *Gissing v Gissing* (*supra*) note 81.

86. *Smith v Baker* [1970] 2 All ER 826.

87. See e.g. *Falconer v Falconer* [1970] 3 All ER 449; *Hargrave v Newton* [1971] 3 All ER 866; *Davis v Vale* [1971] 1 WLR 1022; *Hazell v Hazell* [1972] 1 All ER 923; *Cooke v Head* [1972] 2 All ER 38; *Eves v Eves* [1975] 3 All ER 768.

to the size of the spouse's contribution.[88] In spite of some difficulty in reconciling all the decisions with the orthodox rules of equity[89], the courts have been able to redress some of the injustices resulting from a strict application of the separate property principle; but there must be some evidence from which a trust can be imputed[90] and the size of the beneficial interest will remain uncertain until the case is decided.

The legislature, too, has at times intervened in an attempt to achieve greater equality between the spouses in relation to their property. By Section 37 of the Matrimonial Property and Proceedings Act 1970, either spouse who makes a substantial contribution in money or money's worth to the improvement of the other's[91] property will thereby acquire a beneficial interest.[92] Moreover any savings[93] made by the wife from the housekeeping allowance given to her by her husband is now to be shared between the spouses equally.[94]

One of the most serious defects of the separate property principle was that the spouse who owned the matrimonial home could sell it to a third party without the knowledge of the other spouse, with the result that the latter could be rendered homeless. In the *National Provincial Bank v Ainsworth*[95] the House of Lords held that while a wife had a personal right against her husband to provide her with a roof over her head[96], this 'mere equity' could not affect *bona fide* purchasers for value without notice.[97] This situation was remedied by the Matrimonial Homes Act 1967[98] under which[99] either spouse, whether or not he or she had a beneficial interest in the property, is given a statutory right of occupation[100] of the matrimonial home, which on registration will be binding on third parties. Moreover, by Section 1(2) of the Act the court has power, *inter alia* to regulate the exercise by either spouse of the right to occupy the dwelling house, but this does not extend to excluding the owner-spouse from the home.[101] However, the owner-

---

88. *Pettit v Pettit* (*supra*) note 80 and *Gissing v Gissing* (*supra*) note 81. There must not be too free a use of the maxim 'Equality is Equity'.
89. See e.g. *Cowcher v Cowcher* [1972] 1 All ER 943 where Bagnall J discusses some of the difficulties overlooked in the Court of Appeal. See now F. Webb *Trusts of Matrimonial Property* (1976) 92 LQR 489.
90. See *Davis v Vale* (*supra*) note 87.
91. Or property already jointly owned in which case he will acquire an increased share.
92. See *Davis v Vale* (*supra*) note 87; *Kowalczuk v Kowalczuk* [1973] 2 All ER 1042; *Griffiths v Griffiths* [1974] 1 All ER 932.
93. Or property acquired out of such money.
94. Married Women's Property Act 1964. On the difficulties caused by the statute, see now E Ellis *Married Women's Property* (1973) 3 Fam. Law 116, where it is suggested that the 1964 Act is of much wider application than is generally thought.
95. [1965] AC 1175.
96. Another aspect of the right to be maintained discussed above p. 49 and footnotes.
97. In practice this could often be a mortgagee. The courts are reluctant to extend the doctrine of constructive notice in husband and wife situations. See *Caunce v Caunce* [1969] 1 WLR 286, cf. *Hodgson v Marks* [1971] Ch. 892.
98. As amended by the Matrimonial Proceedings and Property Act 1970.
99. Section 1 as amended by Section 38 of the Matrimonial Proceedings and Property Act 1970.
100. For a discussion of the theoretical nature of this right see *Wroth v Tyler* [1973] 1 All ER 897.
101. *Tarr v Tarr* [1973] AC 254. This rule has been reversed by Section 3 of the Domestic Violence and Matrimonial Proceedings Act 1976.

spouse can be excluded in certain circumstances[102], viz. his/her conduct is so intolerable[103] that the accommodation can no longer be shared by the family.[104]

Often these property issues will only arise when the marriage has broken down. Under the Matrimonial Causes Act 1973[105] there are a series of property adjustment orders available after a decree of divorce, nullity or judicial separation. These include an out and out transfer of property from one spouse to another[106] of the settlement of a spouse's property for the benefit of the other and of any children of the marriage.[107] These property adjustment orders are made in the context of the spouse's overall maintenance requirements.[108] The aim of these provisions is "to place the parties, so far as is practicable and, having regard to their conduct, just to do so, in the financial position in which they would have been if the marriage had not broken down."[109] In doing so the courts must have regard to all[110] the circumstances of the case.

It has been stressed[111] that these powers are discretionary and must retain their flexibility so that each case must turn on its own particular facts. Nevertheless, certain trends in the way the courts exercise their discretion is clear. In *Wachtel v Wachtel*[112] it was laid down that when there were children and the marriage had lasted for some time, it was a convenient starting point if the courts used their powers so that a wife would obtain a third of the family's combined income and capital assets. If the children are young, the house can be transferred to the wife to be held on trust for sale for her and her husband in such shares as seem appropriate, the sale being delayed until the children are educated[113]: but then there will usually be a reduction in the periodical payments which the husband has to pay to take into account the loss of his capital assets.

---

102. E.g. if the other spouse *has* an equitable interest, or litigation is pending or, more controversially, by virtue of the wife's personal right to have a roof over her head. See *Gurasz v Gurasz supra* n. 65. Cf. *Brent v Brent* [1974] 2 All ER 1211 and E. Ellis *The right of Occupation of the Matrimonial Home and its enforcement by the Courts* (1975) 4 Anglo-American Law Review 59; Thomson, *The Occupation of the Matrimonial Home and Local Authority Housing* (1975) Local Govt. Chronicle.
103. *Hall v Hall* [1971] 1 WLR 404; *Phillips v Phillips* [1973] 2 All ER 423; *Bassett v Bassett* [1975] 1 All ER 513. Cf. *Parris v Parris* [1976] 6 Fam. Law 10; *Singh v Singh* (1976) 6 Fam. Law 45.
104. The welfare of the children is a very important factor. *Stewart v Stewart* [1973] 1 All ER 31; *Marston v Marston* [1976] 6 Fam. Law 13.
105. Section 24.
106. Section 24(a).
107. Section 24(b). Any existing settlements can be varied or extinguished. See Section 24(c) and (d).
108. Thus a property transfer will be reflected in the amount of periodical payments to be made. See e.g. *Griffiths v Griffiths (supra)* note 92.
109. Section 25(1).
110. Certain matters are expressly mentioned in Section 25(1). See e.g. *Daubney v Daubney* [1976] 2 All ER 453 for a survey of the most recent case law.
111. *Chamberlain v Chamberlain* [1974] 1 All ER 33.
112. [1973] 1 All ER 829.
113. For a survey of the case law on this point see *Smith v Smith* [1975] 2 All ER 19. Sometimes the trust for sale will be in favour of the children rather than the spouses. *Wachtel v Wachtel* (*supra*) note 112. In *Browne v Pritchard* [1975] 3 All ER 721, the Court of Appeal emphasised the importance of keeping the former matrimonial residence as a home for any children of the marriage.

In deciding these questions, no discount will normally be made to take into account a spouse's matrimonial misconduct unless the conduct has been "obvious and gross"[114] "calculated to destroy the marriage in circumstances in which the other party is substantially blameless".[115] Usually adultery *per se* will not be obvious and gross, but it depends on the circumstances of the case. Thus, in *Cuzner v Underdown*[116] a wife was refused half the beneficial interest in the house because she was committing adultery at the time the husband bought the matrimonial home and was solely to blame for the breakdown of the marriage. In *H v H*[117] a wife who walked out on her husband and four children in order to live with her lover was only given one-twelfth of the beneficial interest in the matrimonial home, because the only ground for her claim was the fact that she had looked after the family and that job she had left unfinished. Not surprisingly, violence which resulted in the diminution of the spouse's earning power was held to be obvious and gross, even if it took place after the marriage had ended.[118] The conduct was such that it would be offensive to justice not to take it into account in deciding the appropriate shares of the spouses in the family assets. Finally, although a wife's prospects of remarriage should not be taken into account when this involves pure speculation on the court's part, if in fact a wife has remarried or is about to remarry, then that is a relevant factor.[119] If a husband remarried, that too is taken into account, usually to alleviate his maintenance obligations; for the courts realise that, while the Act attempts to put the parties in the same position as though they were never divorced, this is in effect impossible.[120]

In exercising this discretion the courts have a very difficult task: it is the present writer's view that there is little evidence that the exercise of this discretion is unduly biased according to the sex of the spouses.[121] As Scarman LJ said in *Calderbank v Calderbank*[122], "I rejoice that it should be made abundantly plain that husbands and wives come to the judgment seat in matters of money and property upon a basis of complete equality."

This survey of the law demonstrates, it is thought, that a great degree of equality between the spouses has already been achieved in England. Much still has to be done, in particular in the field of family property.[123] Inevitably the position of married women is dependent on the position of women generally in society. Steps are now being taken to remove some of the more blatant forms of

---

114. *Wachtel v Wachtel (supra)* note 112; *West v West* [1977] 2 All ER 705.
115. Per Bagnall J in *Harnett v Harnett* [1973] 2 All ER 593. The case provides an interesting survey of the early decisions on the issue.
116. [1974] 2 All ER 351.
117. [1975] 1 All ER 367.
118. *Jones v Jones* [1975] 2 All ER 12.
119. *Mesher v Mesher* [1973] *The Times* Feb. 13; *Smith v Smith (supra)* note 113; *H v H (supra)* note 117.
120. See e.g. *Trippas v Trippas* [1973] Fam 134; *Dopson v Cherry* (1975) 5 Fam. Law 57.
121. Compare e.g. *Cumbers v Cumbers* [1975] 1 All ER 1 and *Bryant v Bryant* (1976) 6 Fam. Law 108 with *Dennis v Dennis* (1976) 6 Fam. Law 54.
122. [1975] 3 All ER 333 at p. 340.
123. See O Kahn-Freund *Matrimonial Property: where do we go from here?* (J Unger Memorial Lecture 1971); Law Commission Working Paper, No: 42.

sex discrimination[124] and this will improve further the married woman's lot.[125] Moreover, the law is beginning to recognise the position of the woman who lives with a man outside the institution of marriage[126]; but the rules here are still in an embryonic state[127] and no doubt it will take some time before the law imposes the same obligations on a person in relation to his natural family as it at present demands in the case of his legal family.

B. The Reform of the Divorce Law

Like so many institutions of English life, the system of divorce introduced into England in 1969[128] is the result of a compromise. It is a compromise between two conflicting views on the nature of a sound divorce law. For many years English law had more or less[129] adhered to the principle that divorce should only be granted to an innocent petitioner who could prove that the respondent had been guilty of a matrimonial offence, i.e. had been at fault. In time, however, in response to changes in society's attitude to marriage, the need for moral blame-worthiness in the respondent's conduct amounting to the matrimonial offence was whittled away as a result of judicial lawmaking[130]: moreover, in spite of rules against connivance and collusion, in practice divorces were often obtained by the respondent supplying grounds at the petitioner's request.[131]

In these circumstances it was felt that the retention of the system of matrimonial offences was little more than a hypocritical sham. It was advocated[132] that the purpose of a modern divorce law should be "(i) to buttress rather than to undermine the stability of marriage; and (ii) when, regrettably, a marriage has irretrievably broken down, to enable the empty legal shell to be destroyed with maximum fairness, and the minimum bitterness, distress and humiliation".[133] In other words, a divorce should be available to either party regardless of fault, whenever their marriage has completely broken down. Any fault on the part of a spouse which contributed to the breakdown of the marriage ought to be irrelevant[134]; on the other hand, a spouse who was completely innocent and was not

---

124. The Sex Discrimination Act 1975. A detailed survey is outside the scope of this present paper.
125. In particular in relation to employment prospects. See Thomson, *The Employment Problems of One-parent Families—Can Labour Law Help?* (1976) 6 Fam. Law 250.
126. See e.g. *Dyson Holdings Ltd. v Fox* [1975] 3 All ER 1030.
127. Compare the approach in *Cooke v Head* (*supra*) note 87 with that in *Richards v Dove* (*supra*) note 65 and the approach in *Tanner v Tanner* [1975] 3 All ER 776 and *Eves v Eves* (*supra*) note 87 with that in *Horrocks v Forray* [1976] 1 All ER 737.
128. The Divorce Reform Act 1969, consolidated along with other relevant matrimonial legislation in the Matrimonial Causes Act 1973.
129. The Matrimonial Causes Act 1937 introduced divorce on the ground of the respondent's incurable insanity.
130. See especially *Gollins v Gollins* [1964] AC 644 and *Williams v Williams* [1964] AC 698.
131. For a savage attack on the previous system see Evelyn Waugh's novel *A Handful of Dust*.
132. See e.g. *Putting Asunder—A Divorce Law for Contemporary Society*; Law Commission, *Reform of the Grounds of Divorce—The Field of Choice*.
133. *The Field of Choice*, para. 15.
134. It was believed that a matrimonial offence was a symptom rather than a cause of marriage breakdown.

guilty of any breach of matrimonial obligations, could be divorced against his will.[135]

There were considerable difficulties in this latter approach. How was break-down to be established without some form of inquisitorial procedure alien to the Common law? Would not such an approach entail a completely new system of courts of tribunals manned by social workers rather than lawyers?[136] Was not there some truth in the view that the equation of matrimony with a commercial partnership was too revolutionary for mid-twentieth century English society, some members of which still regarded marriage as sacrosanct and many members of which still felt that divorce should be the exception rather than the rule?[137] The Divorce Reform Act 1969 consequently sought a middle course in an attempt to facilitate divorce without making too great an inroad into the traditional concept of marriage. It is the purpose of this paper to examine the nature of this legislative compromise in the light of the difficulties which have arisen in the interpretation of its provisions, with the intention of assessing how the opposing views on the nature of divorce have affected the development of the new law.

By Section 1(1) of the Matrimonial Causes Act 1973 a petition for divorce may be presented to the court by either party to a marriage on the ground that the marriage has broken down irretrievably. This is the one and only ground for divorce under English law. But it is not a simple question of assessing from all the available evidence whether or not a marriage has completely broken down. by Section 1(2) a court cannot hold that a marriage has broken down irretrievably unless the petitioner proves one or more of the facts laid down in that section, viz:

(a) that the respondent has committed adultery and the petitioner finds it intolerable to live with the respondent;

(b) that the respondent has behaved in such a way that the petitioner cannot reasonably be expected to live with the respondent;

(c) that the respondent has deserted the petitioner for a continuous period of at least two years immediately preceding the presentation of the petition;

(d) that the parties to the marriage have lived apart for a continuous period of at least two years immediately preceding the presentation of the petition and the respondent consents to a decree being granted;

(e) that the parties to the marriage have lived apart for a continuous period of at least five years immediately preceding the presentation of the petition.

But while a court cannot grant a divorce unless a Section 1(2) guideline is established—even if satisfied that the marriage has broken down irretrievably—proof of a Section 1(2) guideline will not automatically satisfy the court that the marriage has irretrievably broken down. If a court is satisfied that a marriage has not broken down irretrievably, then under Section 1(4) it will not grant a decree

---

135. This was only true for the incurably insane respondent under the pre-1969 law. However, the extent of the inroads into this principle made by such decisions as *Gollins* (*supra*) note 130 and *Williams* (*supra*) note 130 remains controversial.

136. But these problems would not necessarily have been insurmountable. See for a fuller discussion, H. A. Finlay, *Reluctant, but Inevitable: the Retreat of Matrimonial Fault* (1975) 38 MLR at p. 157.

137. This raises the fundamental jurisprudential issue of how far it is the role of law to lead rather than be led by social mores. See Devlin *Morals and the Law of Marriage*, Essay IV in *The Enforcement of Morals* (Oxford), 1965.

of divorce even though a Section 1(2) fact has been established. In other words, Section 1(2) guidelines are necessary but not always sufficient proof of irretrievable breakdown.[138] Consequently the courts are constrained (theoretically at least) from allowing divorce to degenerate into a matter of rubber-stamping.[139] In *Ash v Ash*[140] for example, Bagnall J emphasised[141] that even after a guideline fact has been proved, a simple assertion by one of the parties that the marriage has come to an end would not be sufficient to satisfy the court that that was necessarily so: the court was obliged before granting decree to examine the whole of the evidence, including the spouses' assertions, lest after all the marriage had not broken down irretrievably.[142] Conversely, in *Richards v Richards*[143], Rees J refused to grant a divorce because the petitioner failed to establish a Section 1(2)(b) guideline fact[144], notwithstanding that he was satisfied that the marriage had broken down irretrievably.

It is not surprising therefore to discover that in their interpretation of the guideline facts themselves, the courts have often taken a strict approach.[145] It is proposed to consider each guideline fact in turn.

Section 1(2)(a)—that the respondent has committed adultery *and* the petitioner finds it intolerable to live with the respondent.

It is settled that the test whether or not the petitioner finds it intolerable to live with the respondent is subjective and not objective.[146] But there has been much controversy[147] on the question whether or not the petitioner must have found it intolerable to live with the respondent *as a result* of the adultery or whether, once adultery was proved, the guideline was satisfied if the petitioner found it intolerable to live with the respondent for some reason quite unconnected with the

---

138. *Pheasant v Pheasant* [1972] 1 All ER 587. In the course of his judgment Ormrod J (as he then was) said at p. 589, "The Divorce Reform Act 1969 itself in Section 2(1) imposes on the court a species of restriction almost, if not absolutely, unique . . . Having established by S.1 that the only ground on which a marriage may be dissolved is 'that the marriage has broken down irretrievably' the Act goes on to provide in S. 2(1) that the court shall not hold the marriage to have broken down irretrievably unless the petitioner satisfies the court of one or more of the following facts"—thereafter the well-known five 'facts' are defined—"The question of irretrievable breakdown has not, therefore, been left at large for the court to determine, no doubt because it was realised that, except in the clearest cases, this is not a justiciable issue . . . (but) proof of these 'facts' must inevitably raise a very strong inference of irretrievable breakdown."
139. In *Santos v Santos* [1972] 2 All ER 246, Sachs LJ said at p. 256, "Whilst sympathising from experience with these judges who have to take the undefended list, it is still the case that the legislature in our judgment intended the procedure before them to involve judicial care as opposed to rubber stamping."
140. [1972] 1 All ER 582.
141. At p. 586.
142. This approach was approved by Sir George Baker P in *Katz v Katz* [1972] 3 All ER 219. In *Pheasant v Pheasant (supra)* note 138, Ormrod J held at p. 592 that even if a guideline fact had been proved, the marriage in that case had not broken down.
143. [1972] 3 All ER 695.
144. See on this point generally Finlay, *op. cit. supra* note 136, especially at p. 158 ff. and cases cited therein.
145. For a general criticism see Finlay *op. cit., supra* note 136.
146. *Goodrich v Goodrich* [1971] 1 WLR 1142; *Pheasant v Pheasant (supra)* note 138.
147. See generally Barton, *Questions on the Divorce Reform Act 1969* (1970) 86 LQR 348.

adultery, e.g. because the respondent snored. The courts at first instance were divided.[148] But in *Cleary v Cleary*[149], the Court of Appeal purported to resolve the issue by holding that there was no need for a causative connection between the adultery and the petitioner finding it intolerable to live with the respondent. Intolerability could result from the *subsequent*[150] conduct of the respondent, separate and unrelated to the respondent's adultery. However, the Court did insist that a petitioner could not assert his/her own adultery to show that it was intolerable to live with the respondent. This decision was reluctantly followed in *Carr v Carr*[151] when Davis LJ suggested that he thought there was weight in the restrictive view favoured in *Roper v Roper*[152] and that the question should finally be settled by the House of Lords.

Section 1(2)(b)—that the respondent has behaved in such a way that the petitioner cannot reasonably be expected to live with the respondent.

The courts have refused to give a broad interpretation to this guideline but have favoured a narrower, more legalistic approach. Firstly, the respondent must have "behaved" in such a way that the petitioner cannot reasonably be expected to live with him. In *Katz v Katz*[153], Sir George Baker P held[154] that "behaviour is something more than a mere state of affairs or a state of mind . . . (it) is action or conduct by the one which affects the other." He also thought that the respondent's acts or omissions ought to have some reference to the marriage—thus, for example, if the respondent was convicted of a non-sexual[155] criminal offence, that would not be behaviour for the purposes of the Act. And so it was thought that the illness of a spouse *simpliciter* would not suffice although most commentators would have accepted that if, as a result of the illness, the respondent's behaviour towards the spouse altered and became unreasonable, the fact that the change was due to illness would not necessarily provide a defence.[156] However, in the controversial case of *Thurlow v Thurlow*[157] Rees J held that a respondent's negative behaviour, i.e., his inability to fulfil his matrimonial obligations generally, was behaviour for the purpose of Section 1(2)(b) even when this failure was a direct result of illness. This decision also throws into question the view which has hitherto been articulated[158] that a spouse could not be treated as

---

148. *Roper v Roper* [1972] 1 WLR 1314—need for causative connection. *Goodrich v Goodrich* (*supra*) note 146—no need for causative connection.
149. [1974] 1 All ER 498.
150 Ironically, in a decision which was endorsing a broad interpretation of the Act, this insistence on the *subsequent* conduct of the respondent is itself a narrow interpretation of the words of the subsection.
151. [1974] 1 All ER 1193.
152. *Supra* note 148.
153. *Supra* note 142.
154. At p. 960.
155. It is submitted that if convicted of a sexual offence, that would clearly be conduct done with reference to the marriage. See *White v White* 1966 SC 187.
156. *Williams v Williams supra* note 130; *Gollins v Gollins supra* note 130. See Thomson, *Look Before You Reform*, 1976 SLT (News) 25.
157 [1975] 2 All ER 979.
158. See for example, *Smith v Smith* (1974) 124 New Law J, 57.

having in any sense "behaved" when the "acts" complained of were symptoms of mental illness. It remains to be seen whether the very wide interpretation of "behaviour" favoured by Rees J will be followed with approval in higher courts.

What sort of behaviour can a petitioner be reasonably expected to withstand? In an early case[159] Ormrod J thought that the test should be similar to that formerly used in relation to constructive desertion, i.e. that the guideline was satisfied when the respondent had committed a serious breach of his matrimonial obligations. Later cases[160] have rejected this approach. The proper approach is to determine as a question of fact whether the respondent has behaved in such a way that the particular petitioner before the court cannot reasonably be expected to continue living with him, taking into account the whole of the circumstances including the characters and personalities of the parties. The test is objective in order to give force to the '*reasonably* be expected' formula in the guideline, but it must be related to the particular spouse in question, that is, it is not simply a consideration of what the reasonable spouse could withstand. Thus in *Ash v Ash*, Bagnall J held[161] "that a violent petitioner can reasonably be expected to live with a violent respondent; a petitioner who is addicted to drink can reasonably be expected to live with a respondent similarly addicted; a taciturn and morose spouse can reasonably be expected to live with a taciturn and morose partner; a flirtatious husband can reasonably be expected to live with a wife who is equally susceptible to the attraction of the other sex; and if each is equally bad, at any rate in similar respects, each can reasonably be expected to live with the other."

This approach has been criticised[162] as frustrating the object of the Act, that is, easier divorce. But as Bagnall J pointed out in the *Ash* case[163] the purpose of the Act was not to make divorce easier. And anyway, the test can work the other way. Thus, in *Livingstone-Stallard v Livingstone-Stallard*[164] it was held that a young, inexperienced wife could not be reasonably expected to put up with a constant atmosphere of criticism, disapproval and boorish behaviour on the part of her elderly husband. *Livingstone-Stallard* was a borderline case and it turned on the fact that the wife was young and inexperienced while the husband was much older. If the test was not related to the special characteristics of the spouses, it would be difficult to hold that the husband's behaviour, objectively assessed, was sufficiently bad.[165] The simple fact that the petitioner has continued to live with the respondent does not conclusively show that the petitioner can reasonably

---

159. *Pheasant v Pheasant, supra* note 138.
160. See e.g. *Livingstone-Stallard v Livingstone-Stallard* [1974] 2 All ER 766; *O'Neil v O'Neil* [1975] 3 All ER 289.
161. [1972] Fam. 135 at p. 140.
162. Finlay *op. cit. supra* note 136 at p. 162.
163. *Supra* note 140 at p. 140.
164. *Supra* note 160. See also *O'Neil v O'Neil supra* note 160.
165. It will be seen that a respondent's insanity will simply be another factor to be taken into account in deciding whether a particular petitioner can reasonably be expected to put up with his behaviour. The courts seem to be taking the pre-1969 approach, viz. when the respondent's acts are *prima facie* serious and harmful, the petitioner cannot reasonably be expected to put up with them even if the respondent is insane; but where they are merely silly, irrational acts then, unless perpetrated with the intention to hurt the petitioner—which will be unlikely if the respondent is insane—the petitioner can reasonably be expected to live with him. See *Katz v Katz supra* note 142.

be expected to continue living with the respondent because, in the circumstances, the petitioner may have had no alternative but to stay in the matrimonial home.[166]

Section 1(2)(c)—that the respondent has deserted the petitioner for a continuous period of two years.

There has been no doubt that all the highly complex pre-1969 law relating to desertion has been incorporated into this guideline.[167]

In *Stringfellow v Stringfellow*[168] the Court of Appeal held that simple desertion was not *per se* 'behaviour' for the purposes of Section 1(2)(b) and, accordingly, a petitioner in those circumstances would have to wait for two years and then rely on Section 1(2)(c).

Section 1(2)(d)—that the spouses have lived apart for a continuous period of two years and the respondent consents to a decree being granted.

Once again, there has been a tendency for the courts to take a strict, legalistic approach when interpreting this section. The interpretation of 'lived apart' has caused some difficulty. By Section 2(6) of the Matrimonial Causes Act 1973, a husband and wife are to be treated as living apart "unless they are living with each other in the same household". But in *Santos v Santos*[169] the Court of Appeal held that the physical separation of the spouses for one reason or another was not necessarily "living apart" for the purposes of the Act. Although living in separate places, a couple was not "living apart" for the purposes of the Act as long as *both* recognised their marriage as a valid subsisting relationship. However, the extra element necessary to turn physical separation into "living apart" was simply the recognition by one of the parties that their marriage was in truth at an end and had become an empty shell; this change of mind could be a spouse's unilateral decision and did not have to be communicated to the other spouse. The two year period ran from the date when the spouse recognised that the marriage had broken down. It follows, therefore, that when their consortium has been destroyed, the parties will be taken as living apart even though they are not physically separated. Thus, in *Fuller v Fuller*[170] the spouses were held to have 'lived apart' when the wife had been cohabiting with a third party in a house where her husband also lived, but as a lodger. The Court of Appeal held that 'living with each other' in Section 2(6) must be read as 'living with each other in the capacity of husband and wife'. Thus, while *Santos v Santos*[171] had been criticised[172] as an unnecessarily restrictive gloss on the literal interpretation of the Act yet it is consistent with the very broad application of the guideline in *Fuller v Fuller*.[173]

---

166. *Bradley v Bradley* [1973] 1 WLR 1291.
167. See *Pheasant v Pheasant supra* note 138.
168. [1976] 2 All ER 539.
169. *Supra*, note 139.
170. [1973] 2 All ER 650.
171. *Supra*, note 139.
172. Finlay, *op. cit.* (*supra*) note 136 at p. 165. Cretney, "*When does living apart start?*" 115 Sol. J. 295.
173. *Supra* note 170. But compare the different approach in the earlier case of *Mouncer v Mouncer* [1972] 1 All ER 289. There the couple were living in the matrimonial home with their children but had no sexual relationship. Presumably consortium was not at an end; but my own view is that the fact that the wife in *Fuller v Fuller* was living with a third party is the vital distinction between the two cases.

A party must have the same capacity when consenting to the divorce as is necessary to consent to marriage[174], that is, to be capable of understanding the nature of his consent and the effect and result of giving it.[175] The two years are strictly calculated[176] and do not include the first day of living apart.

Section 1(2)(e)—that the parties to the marriage have lived apart for a continuous period of at least five years.[177]

This was the most controversial guideline because it enabled a spouse to seek a divorce from his/her entirely innocent spouse without seeking the latter's consent. In order to protect the spouse, a petition solely[178] relying on the Section 1(2)(e) guideline can be opposed by the respondent on the ground that the dissolution of the marriage will result in grave financial or other hardship to him *and* that it would in all the circumstances be wrong to dissolve the marriage. The courts have tended to construe this defence narrowly, with the result that it has not proved too great a stumbling block to divorces relying on the Section 1(2)(e) guideline.

Considering the elements of this defence:

(i) Grave financial hardships

The courts were quick to point out that most divorces will inevitably result in some kind of financial hardship for the respondent. Accordingly, full effect must be given to the requirement that the financial hardship be grave. Thus in *Mathias v Mathias*[179] Stephenson LJ suggested[180] that the defence would usually only be appropriate in the case of a middle-aged wife whose husband was likely to predecease her and who would lose pension rights etc., as a result of the divorce. It would not normally avail a young woman who could always work for herself and would be likely to re-marry. In *Reiterbund v Reiterbund*[181] the Court of Appeal held that even when a spouse was old and would be likely to lose pension rights, if in the circumstances she was so poor that the value of her pension would be more or less the same as social security benefits she would receive were she divorced, there would be no grave financial hardship involved. Unlike the case of maintenance, the courts had to look at the social security position in order to assess whether there would be grave financial hardship as a result of the divorce.[182] The decision in *Reiterbund*[183] thus further limits the scope of the defence.

---

174. *Mason v Mason* [1972] 3 All ER 315. If the petitioner misled the respondent into giving his consent, the court may rescind the decree nisi before it is made absolute. See Section 10(1) of the Matrimonial Causes Act 1973.
175. In *Re estate of Park* [1954] P 112
176. On the grounds that divorce still carries a stigma. See *Warr v Warr* [1975] 1 All ER 85.
177. The problems with respect to 'living apart' are also relevant here.
178. Section 5(2) of the Matrimonial Causes Act 1973.
179. [1972] 3 All ER 1.
180. At p. 8. See now *Le Marchant v Le Marchant* [1977] 3 All ER 610.
181. [1975] 1 All ER 280.
182. In doing so they upheld the views of Finer J at first instance [1974] 2 All ER 455, who had refused to follow a decision of Sir George Baker P in *Dorrell v Dorrell* [1972] 3 All ER 343 to the contrary. The decision in *Dorrell* was subsequently disapproved by the Court of Appeal in *Reiterbund*. Tragically, *Reiterbund* was one of Finer J's last cases: his contribution to the development of Family Law in England was immense.
183. *Supra*, note 181.

(ii) Other hardship

This part of the defence has again been given a limited scope. In *Rukat v Rukat*[184] the Court of Appeal held[185] that 'grave' qualifies 'other hardship' as well as 'financial'. Lawton LJ, while realising the possibility that the defence might be whittled away by the courts demanding too high a standard of proof, nevertheless held that a case of grave hardship had not been made out in spite of evidence that divorce still carried a social stigma in Sicily, the respondent's home.[186] In *Banik v Banik*[187] the Court of Appeal had earlier held that if a divorced spouse would be a social outcast in his or her community, suffering shame and disgrace, that might well amount to grave other hardship and satisfy the defence. However, in the light of *Rukat*[188] a defence on this ground is unlikely to succeed.[189]

(iii) In all the circumstances it is wrong to dissolve the marriage

Even if (i) or (ii) is made out, the defence will only succeed if the court is satisfied that it would in all the circumstances be wrong to dissolve the marriage. But this will be very difficult to establish because the courts have emphasised[190] that it is contrary to the public interest to preserve marriages which have hopelessly broken down. It will be particularly difficult if the spouses are young and there is a prospect of their finding happiness with another person in the future. Thus, one can agree with Cretney when he concludes[191] that "the section seems thus likely to be used primarily to protect middle-aged and elderly wives against the loss of pension rights and then only very sparingly".[192]

While these cases illustrate the reluctance of the courts to allow this defence unduly to restrict Section 1(2)(e) divorces and, accordingly represents the strongest indication yet of judicial acceptance of the breakdown principle as the basis of divorce, nevertheless they are not the striking contrast to the cases on the earlier guidelines that they might at first seem. It must be observed that, although the courts have here facilitated Section 1(2)(e) divorces, this has been done as a result of the same strict, legalistic approach to the interpretation of the statute which is evident in the cases on the other guidelines. In these latter cases, however, it has tended to have the opposite effect, namely, to make divorce less easy by making it more difficult for a petitioner to prove a guideline fact. The explanation for this dichotomy, it is submitted, does not lie in the predilection of the judges towards the breakdown or the fault principle: it is the inevitable result of

---

184. [1975] 1 All ER 343.
185. Approving the decision in *Parker v Parker* [1972] 1 All ER 410.
186. The couple had been separated for over twenty years and, unless extremely naive, the Sicilians must have known that the marriage was unsuccessful. There was no evidence that knowledge of the divorce would spread to Sicily and, according to most people, the wife's marital position would seem to remain unchanged.
187. [1973] 3 All ER 45.
188. *Supra*, note 184.
189. But the defence did succeed in *Lee v Lee* (1973) 117 Sol. J 616 where the wife would have been unable to look after a disabled son had she been divorced.
190. See e.g. *Mathias v Mathias, supra* note 179; *Brickell v Brickell* [1973] 3 All ER 508; *Rukat v Rukat, supra* note 184.
191. *Principles of Family Law*, 2nd ed (1976) p. 151.
192. As in the case of *Julian v Julian* (1972) 106 Sol. J 763, when spouses were middle-aged and the petitioner was ill.

the compromise nature of the legislation when it is consistently interpreted in a literal manner.

This conclusion can be further illustrated by considering the cases on Sections 10(3) and (4) of the Matrimonial Causes Act 1973. In a divorce where the sole[193] guideline has been a Section 1(2)(d) or Section 1(2)(e) fact, then under Section 10(3) the respondent may petition the court to delay making the decree absolute until it is satisfied either that the petitioner should not have to make financial provision for the respondent or that the provision made is reasonable and fair or the best that can be made in the circumstances. But the decree can be made absolute immediately, in spite of the respondent's application, if there are circumstances making it desirable that it should be made absolute without delay *and* the court receives a satisfactory undertaking from the petitioner that he will make such financial provision for the respondent as the court may approve.

Once again the courts have taken a strict approach. Thus, for example, in *Wilson v Wilson*[194] the Court of Appeal held that before the petitioner could have the decree made absolute on the grounds that he had made reasonable and fair financial provision for the respondent, the financial provision must actually have been put into effect: it was not enough that the petitioner had made proposals for the respondent's financial welfare. And so the decree absolute was delayed until the matrimonial home was sold and the proceeds distributed to the respondent in accordance with the petitioner's proposals. This strict interpretation of "made" considerably widened the scope of the section. Similarly, in *Grigson v Grigson*[195] it was held that even when it was desirable to make the decree absolute without delay, nevertheless the petitioner's undertaking to make such financial provision for the respondent which the courts would approve, must not simply be an undertaking that he will do his best, but must be sufficiently detailed and clear in outline so that the court can decide whether it is reasonable, fair and the best that can be done in the circumstances of the case.

On the other hand, in *Krystman v Krystman*[196] the Court of Appeal made it clear that a respondent would not always succeed in delaying the decree. Davies LJ held that a petitioner was under no duty to make financial provision for a respondent from whom he had lived apart for twenty-six years, having married her simply because she was bearing his child, which was subsequently born dead. This was, admittedly, a strong case but the approach is consistent with the cases on the Section 1(2)(e) guideline.[197] The courts are therefore prepared to make Section 10 an effective protection for the respondent, but only to the extent that this is consistent with the fundamental principle of the legislation, namely, that marriages which are utterly dead should be brought to an end.

The present system of divorce also contains rules which attempt to encourage reconciliation. No divorce can be brought within the first three years of marriage, unless the case is one of exceptional hardship suffered by the petitioner or of exceptional depravity on the part of the respondent.[198] This limitation remains

---

193. See Section 10(2) of the Matrimonial Causes Act 1973.
194. [1973] 2 All ER 17.
195. [1974] 1 All ER 478.
196. [1973] 3 All ER 247.
197. *Supra*, p. 61.
198. Section 3 of the Matromonial Causes Act 1973.

important and the courts are slow to find that there is exceptional hardship or depravity.[199] Resumption of cohabitation for a period or periods not exceeding six months will not break[200] a period of desertion or living apart; nor will it prevent a petitioner from relying on previous adultery or unreasonable behaviour and will not be taken into account in determining whether the petitioner found it intolerable to live with the respondent or whether the petitioner can reasonably be expected to live with him. Most important of all, under Section 6 the solicitor for the petitioner must certify that he has discussed with him or her the possibility of a reconsilation and given him or her the names and addresses of persons qualified to help: the court may also adjourn the proceedings if there is a reasonable possibility of a reconciliation between the parties. Evidence suggests, however, that these provisions are of little effect[201] because reconciliation is unlikely once the parties have gone as far as initiating divorce proceedings.

This survey of divorce law in England has shown the difficulties which arise when legislation is based on two mutually conflicting principles. Because the concept of matrimonial fault was not eliminated from the Matrimonial Causes Act 1973 in favour of a system based solely on irretrievable breakdown of marriage, it is hardly surprising that anomalies have arisen. But in so far as criticism for this has been aimed at the judiciary[202], it is unfair. As I have tried to show, the judges have by and large acted consistently in taking a strict legalistic approach when interpreting the statute[203]: if this has led to the result that it may still be difficult to obtain a divorce if reliance is made on those guidelines which were formerly matrimonial offences[204] while it is relatively easy to succeed on the new separation guidelines[205], this is an inherent defect in the compromise nature of the legislation. The judiciary ought not to be criticised for Parliament's failure to support more than a half hearted attempt at reform.

Many of these difficulties are of theoretical rather than practical importance. In theory we still do not have divorce by consent; in practice we are approximating towards it.[206] Few divorces are defended[207] and in spite of Sachs LJ's[208] strictures that even in undefended cases, divorce is not simply a rubber stamping exercise, it is difficult not to believe that this must often be the case. The statistics speak for themselves.[209]

---

199. See e.g. *Blackwell v Blackwell* 1973, "*Times*" November 12.
200. *Lamb v Lamb* (1976) 6 Fam. L. 83. Though it will not count towards such a period.
201. *Marital Conciliation in England and Wales*, A H Manchester & J M Whetton (1974) 23 ICLQ 339 ff. But they may be useful in helping the parties to settle property and custody disputes in a civilised way.
202. For example, Finlay, *op. cit.*, *supra* note 136.
203. As, under English Constitutional law, they are bound to do in the absence of ambiguity in the wording of the legislation.
204. Sections 1(2)(a)(b) and (c).
205. Sections 1(2)(d) and (e).
206. A parallel situation can be found by considering how the Abortion Act 1967 has worked in practice.
207. For example, of the 111,741 divorces dealt with in 1973, 106,215 were undefended, i.e. approx: 95%.
208. *Supra*, note 139.
209.

	1969	1970	1971	1972	1973
Decree nisi granted	54,151	61,090	88,460	109,944	106,522
Petitions filed	60,134	70,575	110,017	109,822	115,048

In these circumstances reform is unlikely in the near future. However, when the question does arise again, it is to be hoped that it will not simply be the occasion for piecemeal reform of the present divorce legislation, but rather a time for a fundamental re-assessment of the role, if any, of marriage in an increasingly secular society.[210]

C. The legal position of the Illegitimate Child

Discrimination against a person born out of wedlock has been for centuries a fundamental tenet of the Common law.[211] The illegitimate child was looked upon as *filius nullius*, a stranger in law to both his father and his mother: consequently, he enjoyed none of the legal rights deriving from the status of parent and child. While in a feudal, agrarian society this harsh rule was perhaps necessary to achieve certainty in questions of title to land, in later times, however, the legal disabilities of bastardy came to be regarded rather as a just punishment for extra-marital sex. But the twentieth century has seen a revolution in the sexual mores of English society and, as a result, the legal position of the illegitimate child has radically altered. Not only has there been an increase in the circumstances in which children will be recognised as legitimate but, more importantly, the process has begun of assimilating the status of the illegitimate with that of the legitimate child. This process is not yet complete and is inextricably connected with the increasing recognition by English law of the rights and obligations deriving from a person's natural as opposed to legal family. It is the purpose of this paper to examine these developments.

At Common law a child was legitimate if its parents were married when the child was born[212] or conceived. But if a child was born out of wedlock, the child was not legitimated by the subsequent marriage of its parents.[213] However, in 1926[214] the doctrine of legitimation *per subsequens matrimonium* at last became part of English law[215] with the result that, where the parents of an illegitimate person have married one another, whether before or after 1926, the marriage has the effect of making the child legitimate from the time the Act came into force

---

210. For a discussion of this problem see Eekelaar, *The Place of Divorce in Family Law's New Role* (1975) 38 MLR 241 and literature cited therein.
211. For a general survey of the problem, see the *Report of the Sub Commission of Human Rights*, "Study of Discrimination against persons born out of Wedlock", UN Doc. E/CN4/Sub 2/265. Saario, Special Rapporteur.
212. It was irrelevant that conception took place prior to the marriage. Blackstone's *Commentaries* Bk. 1, p. 455. If the child was conceived before marriage, if its parents then married but the husband died before the child was born, it was probably legitimate.
213. The Statue of Merton 1236, when the barons rejected the introduction of legitimation *per subsequens matrimonium* into the law with the words—*nolumus leges Angliae mutare*. Nevertheless the title to freehold could be effected by the doctrine of "*bastard eigné et mulier puisné*" which was abolished in 1833. See generally T E James, "The Illegitimate and Deprived Child: Legitimation and Adoption" in *A Century of Family Law* (London) Sweet & Maxwell 1957.
214. The Legitimacy Act 1926.
215. The enactments relating to legitimacy have recently been consolidated in the Legitimacy Act 1976.

(1st Jan. 1927) or the date of the marriage, whichever came later. The child's father has to be domiciled in England at the date of the marriage. Adulterine bastards were excluded[216], i.e. children one of whose parents was married to a third person at the time of their birth.[217] However, this exclusion was removed in 1959.[218] Thus a bastard, alive[219] at the date of his parents' marriage, is legitimated at the date of his parents' subsequent marriage, unless he was:

  (i) an adulterine bastard whose parents were married before 1959 when he would have been legitimated from October 29th 1959 when the Legitimacy Act 1959 came into force,

  (ii) a non-adulterine bastard whose parents were married before 1926 when he would have been legitimated from 1st Jan 1927 when the Legitimacy Act 1926 came into force.

An interesting problem arises if the parents' subsequent marriage is itself void or voidable. If void, it is submitted that this must depend on the construction of Section 1(1) of the Legitimacy Act 1976[220] (discussed *infra*. If voidable, the difficulties have been removed because decrees annulling voidable marriages no longer have retroactive effect if granted after 31st July 1971.[221]

Children of voidable marriages are legitimate because, by Section 16 of the Matrimonial Causes Act 1973, a voidable marriage is to be treated as a valid subsisting marriage if the decree is granted after 31st July 1971. Children of void marriages may be legitimate, "if at the time of the act of intercourse resulting in the birth (or at the time of the celebration of the marriage, if later) *both* or *either* of the parties *reasonably* believed that the marriage was valid."[222] It is submitted that this could cover children who would have been legitimated *per subsequens matrimonium* if the marriage had not been void: the phrase "at the time of the celebration of marriage if later" is in broad general terms and should not be restricted to ceremonies after the date of conception but before the date of birth. Certain conditions must be fulfilled before the Section can operate. The father must be domiciled in England at the time of the child's birth or, if he has died

---

216. Section 1(2) of the Legitimacy Act 1926.
217. In Scotland at common law a child could not be legitimated if there was a legal impediment to his parents' marriage to each other at the date of his conception or birth. This limitation has now been removed by the Legitimation (Sc) Act 1968. See Walker, *Principles of Scots Law* 1975, 2nd ed, p. 327 ff.
218. Legitimacy Act 1959, Section 1(1). See now Section 2 of the Legitimacy Act 1976.
219. Section 1(1) of the Legitimacy Act 1926; Section 1(2) of the Legitimacy Act 1959. See now Section 2 of the Legitimacy Act 1976.
220. Formerly Section 2(1) of the Legitimacy Act 1959.
221. Section 16 of the Matrimonial Causes Act 1973. The position before 1959 is very complex. Prior to 1937 the decree had retroactive effect, i.e. the voidable marriage was retroactively void. Section 7(2) of the Matrimonial Causes Act 1937 limited the effect of the decree when the marriage was annulled on the grounds of insanity, epilepsy or VD so that children of such marriages should not be bastardised. This was extended to children of voidable marriages generally by S 4(1) Law Reform (Misc. Provs.) Act 1949. As the wording of the section is that "any child who would have been the illegitimate child of the parties to the marriages if at the date of decree it had been dissolved instead of being annulled, shall be deemed to be their legitimate child", it is thought that this was wide enough to cover a child who would have been legitimate through the operation of the doctrine of legitimation *per subsequens matrimonium*.
222. Section 1(1) of the Legitimacy Act 1976. Formerly Section 2(1) of the Legitimacy Act 1959. Italics added.

before the birth, have been domiciled in England at the time of his death.[223] It is enough if one of the parties to the marriage reasonably believed the marriage was valid. But the test whether or not a party has reasonable grounds for this belief is objective[224] and the onus rests on the party upholding the marriage to prove that such grounds existed.

The strict Common law position was alleviated by an unduly generous presumption in favour of legitimacy, i.e. that a child born of a married woman during the subsistence of her marriage was to be presumed to be the child of her husband. The presumption still exists. It arises even though the child must have been conceived before the marriage because, by marrying the mother, the husband is *prima facie* to be taken as acknowledging the child as his own.[225] The presumption does not operate if the spouses are living apart under a decree of judicial separation or a matrimonial order containing a non-cohabitation clause[226]: but, if the couple are *de facto* living apart, the presumption will be more easily rebuttable.

It was with the question of what evidence could rebut the presumption that the Common law operated to preserve the status of legitimacy. It was held[227] that the presumption could only be rebutted if evidence was brought that during the possible period within which the child could have been conceived, no sexual intercourse had taken place between the spouses. The burden of proof could be discharged by showing that sexual intercourse was impossible because one of the spouses was impotent or physically absent—beyond the seven seas: it could also be discharged by showing that all the circumstances were such that sexual intercourse between the spouses, while not impossible, was highly improbable.[228] But if the evidence showed that the spouses did have, or were likely to have had, sexual intercourse at the relevant time, then the presumption was almost impossible[229] to rebut: proof of the wife's adultery at the time was certainly not sufficient.[230] Thus, often a child was held to be the legitimate offspring of the husband as a result of the operation of these presumptions, when in fact he was another man's child.

---

223. Section 1(2) of the Legitimacy Act 1976. Formerly Section 2(2) of the Legitimacy Act 1959.
224. *Hawkins v Att-Gen* [1966] 1 WLR 978.
225. The strength of the presumption in this case will depend, of course, on whether the husband knew of the pregnancy at the date of the marriage. The presumption equally operates where the child is born within the possible period of gestation after the marriage has terminated on the husband's death or divorce. If after the termination but before the birth the mother has remarried, the better opinion is that the child should be presumed to be the legitimate child of the first, and not of the second, marriage on the ground that the mother should not be presumed to have committed adultery. *Re Overbury* [1955] Ch. 122.
226. But the presumption does continue in spite of the couple living apart (i) under a separation agreement (ii) in a state of desertion (iii) under an order not containing a non-cohabitation clause (iv) when a petition for divorce or nullity is filed or (v) decree nisi granted but not yet made absolute. See e.g. *Knowles v Knowles* [1962] P 161 per Wrangham J at p. 166/167.
227. *The Banbury Peerage Case* (1811) 1 Sim and St. 153.
228. *The Aylesford Peerage Case* (1886) 11 Appl. Cas. 1. Factors to be considered might include the opportunities available to the spouses for sexual intercourse, their disposition to having sexual intercourse with each other, their conduct during the pregnancy and after the child's birth and their attitude towards the child.
229. E.g. it was probably sufficient if the child's colour indicated that its father had a different racial or ethnic origin from the husband. *Cotton v Cotton* [1954] P 305. But cf. *Ali Chuck v Needham* [1931] NZLR 559; *Watson v Watson* [1954] P 48.
230. See e.g. *Francis v Francis* [1960] P 17—when, in addition, the husband had always used contraceptives. This factor was still not sufficiently conclusive to rebut the presumption.

Twentieth century advances in the field of haematology now enable scientists to prove with a very high degree of accuracy when a child is not[231] the child of a particular person. Moreover, as a result of the changes in our society's sexual mores, there is less stigma attached to illegitimacy than was once the case.[232] Consequently the view has been taken that it is better that the truth be known so that a child's natural parents should have the rights and obligations of parenthood, rather than have the question of legitimacy settled by the application of an out-of-date presumption.[233]

Consequently, by Section 26 of the Family Law Reform Act 1969, the presumption of legitimacy may now be rebutted by evidence which shows that it is more probable than not that the child is illegitimate and it is no longer necessary to prove that fact beyond reasonable doubt in order to rebut the presumption.[234] In *S v S*[235] Lord Reid took the view that the presumption of legitimacy after the 1969 Act was merely evidentiary, i.e. it simply determined the onus of proof. The onus is therefore *prima facie* on the husband to show that his wife's child is illegitimate and he will succeed if he can adduce evidence which proves that it was more probable than not that he was not the father. Thus the presumption of legitimacy will only be conclusive if no evidence is led by the husband or the evidence led by the wife in return results in the issue being so evenly balanced that the court is unable to reach a decision: even weak evidence on the part of the husband will prevail over the presumption provided that there is no evidence to counter-balance it.[236]

In these disputes evidence from blood tests will play a vital role. Accordingly, Part III of the Family Law Reform Act 1969 confers[237] a general discretionary power on all civil courts to direct adults and children to be blood-tested. These tests are not compulsory: adults[238] can refuse on their own behalf and on behalf of children in their care and control. But the court may draw such inferences from the refusal as appear proper in the circumstances[239], and a person refusing cannot rely on the presumption if he or she is seeking relief.[240] Moreover, it has been held by the House of Lords[241] that, while a court cannot go further than a reasonable parent when ordering a blood test, yet since a reasonable parent

---

231. But the tests cannot show that he is, but merely that he could be, the father. The test may, however, indirectly establish that a man is the father of the child, e.g. if the woman is only having intercourse with a man who could not be the father and a man who could be the father, it must follow that the latter is the father.
232. But it does not follow that the illegitimate child will not suffer certain social disadvantages. See e.g. Crellin, Kellmer, Pringle & West, *Born Illegitimate, Social and Educational Implications*.
233. See e.g. Blood Tests and the Proof of Parentage in Civil Proceedings (Law Comm. No. 16).
234. Cf. the changed attitude to the standard of proof of adultery. *Blyth v Blyth* [1966] AC. 643.
235. [1972] AC 24.
236. For an illustration of how the presumption operates in practice, see e.g. *T(H) v T(E)* [1971] 1 All ER 590.
237. Section 20.
238. I.e. persons over the age of 16. See Section 8, Family Law Reform Act 1969. It would seem that the adult must realise that his blood is being taken for the purposes of litigation: otherwise the evidence may not be admissible. See the *Ampthill Peerage Case* [1976] 2 All ER 411.
239. Section 23(1).
240. Section 23(2).
241. *S v S*, (*supra*) note 235.

would have some regard to the general public interest that the truth be known, the court should order a blood test to be carried out on a child, unless it was clearly against the child's interests to do so. In determining this issue, the likelihood of the child's being proved to be illegitimate will not usually be sufficient to convince the court that an order should not be made: illegitimacy *per se* is generally not against the child's interests when these are weighed—as they must be—in the context of general public policy with its emphasis on the importance for justice that the truth ought to be known.[242]

Thus while the trend of the law in the earlier part of the century was to increase the number of children who were to be treated as legitimate, by the sixties the pendulum had swung the other way, to the extent that the old Common law presumption of legitimacy would not be allowed to mock the truth even if this resulted in the child becoming illegitimate. Of course, many of these children would be legitimated by their natural parents' marriage in due course but, nevertheless, the position might seem strange unless steps were taken to eliminate the legal disabilities of illegitimate children themselves. It is not surprising, therefore, that the Family Law Reform Act 1969 contained important provisions[243] to this effect. But as we shall see this process is not yet completed and anomalies subsist and will continue to do so until the law imposes the same obligations on a person in relation to his natural family as it at present demands in the case of his legal family.

As already emphasised[244], the Common law regarded a bastard as *filius nullius*, having no legal rights whatever. Consequently, the use of the terms "a child" or "children" in a statute or legal document referred to legitimate children only, unless there were express words to the contrary.[245] Thus, even in 1975, Ld. Simon of Glaisdale could say[246], "many members of Parliament do not know the legal rule that when the word 'child' is used in a legal instrument, it is presumptively taken to mean a legitimate child; but the draftsman of the statute does know this; and a court of construction will conclude that his usage was to carry into legal effect what Parliament desired." However, illegitimate offspring could not be ignored completely. Thus, the prohibited degrees of marriage have always included illegitimate as well as legitimate relationships[247] and, from the seventeenth century onwards, legislation was passed "to protect the community against the financial consequences of bastards becoming a charge on the poor relief."[248]

Twentieth century legislation has, however, done much to assimilate the positions of illegitimate and legitimate children. The distinction is not made for entitlement to benefits under the various National Insurance schemes[249], as

---

242. See Hayes, *The Use of Blood Tests in the Pursuit of Truth*, (1971) 87 LQR 86.
243. See Part II of the Act, ss. 14-19. Discussed *infra*.
244. *Supra*, p. 64.
245. Similarly, references to father or parent were *prima facie* concerned with legitimate relationships alone. See e.g. *Re M* [1955] 2 QB 479.
246. *Black-Clawson v Papierwerke* [1975] 1 All ER p. 810 at p. 845.
247. *Haines v Jeffell* (1696) 1 Ld. Rayen 68. *R v Brighton* (1861) 1 B & S 447.
248. Cretney, *Principles of Family Law*, 1st ed. p. 320.
249. See now the Social Security Act 1975 which has consolidated the earlier legislation relating to benefits under the National Insurance Acts and National Insurance (Industrial Injuries) Acts. This trend began with the Workman's Compensation Act 1906.

'dependants' there include illegitimate as well as legitimate children: similarly, it is the natural family as opposed to the legal family which is recognised for Family Allowances.[250]

Since 1934 an illegitimate child has been able to sue under the Fatal Accidents Act 1846 and, since 1959[251] has to be treated as the legitimate child of his mother and reputed father in order to discover whether he falls into the enlarged class of a deceased's dependants who now can sue.

For a long time, however, an illegitimate child had no rights on the intestacy of his parents or more remote members of his family.[252] In 1926[253] an illegitimate child[254] was allowed a share[255] of the intestate estate of his mother *provided* that she did not leave any surviving legitimate children and, similarly, the mother could share in the intestate estate of the illegitimate child. The Family Law Reform Act 1969[256] went further: an illegitimate child[257] now[258] has a right to share on the intestacy of *both* his father and his mother on the same basis as if he had been born legitimate and both his parents have the right to succeed on the illegitimate child's intestacy as if he had been born legitimate. But even this legislation is still restrictive: unlike his legitimate brother, an illegitimate child cannot share in the estate of an ancestor more remote than his parents, e.g. his grandparents, nor can he share in the intestate estate of his collaterals.

The Family Law Reform Act 1969 also contained important reforms intended to benefit illegitimate children in those cases where the deceased left a will. Section 15 reversed the presumption[259] that the words 'a child' or 'children' in a will referred to legitimate children only. Accordingly, in any disposition[260] made after the Act has come into operation[261] any reference to a child or children of a person will be construed as a reference to his illegitimate as well as legitimate children, unless the testator's intention appears to the contrary. Thus a reference to X's children *prima facie* includes his illegitimate children, but a reference to X's 'lawful children' only includes X's legitimate offspring, i.e. the new presumption has been rebutted.[262] Similarly, any reference to persons related in any way to any person, e.g. grandchildren of X, shall *prima facie* include persons who

---

250. Family Allowances Act 1965 consolidating the Family Allowances Act 1948. See also, e.g., the definition of 'family' in the Family Income Supplement Act 1970.
251. Sections 1(1) and (2) of the Fatal Accidents Act 1959. But the surviving parent still cannot sue unless married to the deceased. See *K v JMP Co* [1975] 1 All ER 1030.
252. Similarly, neither parent could succeed on the intestacy of their illegitimate child.
523. Section 9 of the Legitimacy Act 1926.
254. Or his issue if he has died. Issue, of course, was limited to legitimate children.
255. I.e. have such a share as he would have been entitled to had he been born legitimate.
256. Section 14.
257. Or, if dead, his issue, i.e. legitimate children.
258. Since 1970 when the Act came into force. It is not retroactive.
259. Discussed *supra* p. 68.
260. The earlier rule of construction still applies to statutes and other legal documents and, of course, dispositions made before January 1st 1970.
261. January 1st 1970.
262. The term 'heir' or 'heirs' only refers to legitimate children.

would be so related if he, or some person through whom the relationship is deduced, had been legitimate.[263], [264]

Finally, by Section 18 of the Act, illegitimate children were allowed to apply to the court for an order of reasonable financial provision to be made for their maintenance out of their deceased parent's estate under the Inheritance (Family Provision) Act 1938.[265] Thus, while the Family Law Reform Act 1969 removed some of the most glaring inequalities between the succession rights of legitimate and illegitimate children, there are still important limitations on an illegitimate person's rights and the distinction between legitimate and illegitimate persons remains a fundamental feature of the law.

The opportunity was not taken in the Domicile and Matrimonial Proceedings Act 1973 to assimilate the position of legitimate and illegitimate children for the purposes of the law of domicile. A legitimate child still has *prima facie* the domicile of his father. However, if he lives with his mother and has no home with his father, then he will acquire his mother's domicile.[266] An illegitimate child, on the other hand, still has *prima facie* the domicile of his mother.[267] The distinction could have been removed if the rules had been changed so that both legitimate and illegitimate children had *prima facie* their mother's domicile unless they lived with their father and had no home with their mother.[268] Moreover, while almost[269] all children born within the United Kingdom and Colonies are citizens thereof regardless of whether they are legitimate or illegitimate, an illegitimate child cannot claim citizenship by descent because English law holds that nationality may descend only through males and this remains restricted to legitimate relationships.[270]

By Section 17 of the Supplementary Benefits Act 1976 both a man and a woman are obliged to maintain their illegitimate, as well as legitimate, children. But it by no means follows that this obligation can be enforced in the same way in both cases. It is a remarkable feature of English family law that a child cannot

263. Cf. the intestacy provisions which are restricted to parents and their children. On the difficult questions which can arise if the illegitimate child is subsequently legitimated, see Sections 5 and 6 of the Legitimacy Act 1976.
264. Section 15(7) expressly abolishes the rule that dispositions in favour of illegitimate children not in being when the disposition took effect were void. The rule continues for dispositions prior to 1st January 1970.
265. For a full discussion of the problems raised by this aspect of the Family Law Reform Act 1969 see, above all, *Theobald on Wills* (13th ed) Ch. 29; Ryder "Property Law Aspects of the Family Law Reform Act 1969" [1971] *Current Legal Problems*, 158. The current provisions are to be found in the Inheritance (Provision for Family and Dependants) Act 1975. See, in particular, Sections 1(1) and 25(1).
266. See Section 4(2)(a) and (b).
267. Section 4(4) of the Domicile and Matrimonial Proceedings Act 1973. The Common law position therefore remains. See *Udny v Udny* (1869) LR 150 & Div. 941.
268. See on this point E M Clive, *Changes in the Law of Domicile*, 1973 SLT (News) p. 241 ff.
269. For exceptions see Section 4(a) & (b) of the British Nationality Act 1948.
270. See Sections 5 and 32(2) of the British Nationality Act 1948. Parry, *Nationality and Citizenship Laws*, p. 238 ff. On the question of legitimated children, see Section 23 of the 1948 Act.

directly[271] enforce his right to be maintained by his parents: it must be done on his behalf by a third party. If the child is legitimate, the parental obligation to maintain him can be enforced by one of the parties to the marriage bringing proceedings against the other on the ground of wilful neglect to maintain the child.[272] Maintenance for a child can also be obtained by a party to a marriage in the magistrates' courts on proof of a Section 1 complaint[273], and there is an array[274] of orders available in the High Court after divorce, separation of nullity proceedings. Maintenance for an illegitimate child can only be obtained in this way if he has become a "child of the family"[275], by virtue, usually[276] of his mother's marriage.

But what is the position if the illegitimate child is not a "child of the family" for the purpose of the Matrimonial Proceedings (Magistrates Courts) Act 1960 or the Matrimonial Causes Act 1973? Although an illegitimate child can be the subject of a custody order under the Guardianship of Minors Act 1971, maintenance cannot be ordered for him under that Act[277]: similarly, although he can be made a ward of court, unlike the position of the legitimate child, the courts cannot make any provision for an illegitimate child's maintenance.[278] Thus, unless his father has entered into a voluntary maintenance agreement for his benefit[279], the only way in which a mother of an illegitimate child can compel his father to contribute to his maintenance is by way of affiliation proceedings.

These proceedings are now brought under the Affiliation Proceedings Act 1957 as amended by the Affiliation Proceedings (Amendment) Act 1972. A

---

271. There are two limited exceptions to this general principle. Under Section 12(3) of the Guardianship of Minors Act 1971 if a legitimate child has been the subject of a custody order—even if it did not contain provisions in respect of his maintenance—and he is between the ages of 18 and 21, he can go to court to get an order requiring either parent to maintain him until he is 21, provided his parents are not residing together. A similar provision applies in respect of legitimate children who have been subject to a court order making them a ward of court. Sections 6(4),(5) and (6) of the Family Law Reform Act 1969. But see now the very generous approach taken by Payne J in *Downing v Downing* [1976] 3 All ER 474. Cf. the position in Scotland. See Levin, "*Aliment and Financial Provision*", 1976, Fam. Law 164.
272. See Sections 1(1)(h) and (i); 2(1)(h) of the Matrimonial Proceedings (Magistrates Courts) Act 1960 and Section 27 of the Matrimonial Causes Act 1973.
273. See generally Sections 1 and 2 of the Matrimonial Proceedings (Magistrates Courts) Act 1960.
274. See Sections 23, 24, and 25 of the Matrimonial Causes Act 1973. These include *inter alia* periodical payments, secured periodical payments, lump sum payments, property adjustment orders.
275. The definition is different in the Matrimonial Proceedings (Magistrates Courts) Act 1960 and the Matrimonial Causes Act 1973. In the 1960 Act a child of the family is defined in Section 16 as a child of both parties or any child of either party who has been *accepted* as one of the family by the other. In the 1973 Act he is defined in Section 52(1) as a child of both parties or any other child (apart from one boarded out by a local authority or other organisation) who has been *treated* by both parties as a child of their family. On the problems raised by the definition, see e.g. *Kirkwood v Kirkwood* [1970] 1 WLR 1042; *Snow v Snow* [1971] 3 All ER 833 (1960 Act). *W(RJ v W(SJ)* (1971) 3 All ER 303; *A v A* [1974] 1 All ER 755 (1973 Act).
276. But not necessarily always. See especially the definition in the Matrimonial Causes Act 1973, *supra* note 275.
277. See Section 14(2) and (4) of the Guardianship of Minors Act 1971.
278. See Section 6(6) of the Family Law Reform Act 1969.
279. Which are not too uncommon.

single[280] woman with child or who has been delivered of an illegitimate child can apply by complaint to a Justice of the Peace for a summons to be served on the man whom she alleges to be the father of her child.[281] Normally[282] the complaint must be brought within three years of the child's birth.

Although affiliation proceedings are domestic proceedings and not a penalty or punishment for extra marital sexual relations, yet the proceedings are, in some respects, reminiscent of criminal cases. Although since 1973 the woman is no longer obliged to give evidence[283], if she does it must be corroborated in some material particular by evidence which will satisfy the courts that the defendant was the father of the child.[284] Evidence that the complainant associated with the defendant during the relevant period but with no other men could amount to corroboration. As these are civil proceedings, the onus on inference of paternity drawn from blood tests will be discharged if the evidence establishes that it was more probable than not that the man was the child's father.[285]

If the defendant is adjudged to be the father, an affiliation order can be made under which he will be obliged to pay any expenses incidental to the birth[286] and to pay a weekly sum for the maintenance and education of the child. These weekly payments are unsecured, there is no possibility of a lump sum, capital payment, and they only continue until the child is sixteen.[287] If the father dies the payments cease[288] and they cease if the child is subsequently adopted.[289] They do not cease, however, if the woman marries, provided the couple do not adopt the child.[290]

When we compare the affiliation payments, i.e. unsecured weekly payments, with the range of possible orders available for the maintenance of a child under the Matrimonial Causes Act 1973[291]—secured weekly payments, lump sum payments, property adjustment orders, etc.—it is clear that the legitimate child is

---

280. By Section 4 of the Legitimacy Act 1959 an action can be brought by a woman who was a single woman at the date of the birth even though she was not a single woman at the date of the proceedings. Moreover 'single' has been given a very liberal interpretation and will cover not only a spinster but also a widow, divorcee or a married woman separated from her husband either by a decree of separation or a matrimonial order containing a non-cohabitation clause. It also covers a married woman living apart from her husband who has lost the right to be maintained as a result of her misconduct. See e.g. *Jones v Evans* [1944] 1 KB 582.
281. It is enough that the mother, father and child are resident in the UK. This is important in respect to immigrants. See *Reg v Bow Road Justices ex parte Adedigba* [1968] 2 QB 572.
282. The complaint can also be brought at any time subsequent to the birth of the child provided the man has maintained the child within the three years next after the birth or at any time within three years after the man's return to England, provided he left England within the first 12 months after the child's birth.
283. Section 1 of the Affiliation Proceedings (Amendment) Act 1972.
284. Section 4(2) of the Affiliation Proceedings Act 1957.
285. *Simpson v Collinson* [1964] 2 QB 80.
286. Including funeral expenses if the child died before the order was made.
287. And then only if the order expressly directs that they are to continue beyond the age of thirteen. If the child becomes engaged in full-time education, they can continue beyond that age, but not beyond twenty-one.
288. Because unsecured.
289. The former rule that the payments continued where the mother adopts the child herself while remaining single, has now been abolished. Adoption by the natural parent alone is not encouraged. See S.15(3) of the Adoption Act 1976.
290. But the order may be varied at the father's request.
291. See *supra* note 275.

much more favoured because he will always be a 'child of the family' in relation to his parents' marriage.[292] But even here the position is unsatisfactory because orders for maintenance are only available when a party to the marriage has wilfully neglected to maintain the child or when the marriage itself has broken down: and, as has been stressed[293], proceedings cannot be brought by the child himself and have to be brought by a party to the marriage on his behalf.

Often, however, the mother of an illegitimate child will turn to the State for maintenance of her child and herself. The Supplementary Benefits Commission can recover the benefits paid from the putative father either by having an existing affiliation order varied so that payments are made to the Secretary of State instead of the mother, or, if there is no affiliation order in existence, the Commission itself can apply for an affiliation order to achieve the same object.[294] The Commission's right to recover from the father is an independent right and will not be affected even if the mother has failed to obtain an affiliation order against the same defendant in earlier proceedings.[295] A similar procedure exists for local authorities to recover from the putative father a contribution for the cost of maintaining his illegitimate child, if the child has been taken into care.[296] But as Cretney has stressed[297] "only a small proportion of mothers obtain orders, the defendants are poor (so that only small amounts are ordered) and payments are only made irregularly". This problem therefore raises the same social issues as the plight of one-parent families in general and awaits a solution along the lines recommended by the Finer Committee on One Parent Families.[298]

A final issue must be discussed. For centuries the law has assumed that an illegitimate child is *prima facie* a fatherless child, i.e. a child whose father is either unknown or is unwilling or unable to assume parental duties in respect of him. Accordingly, the mother of an illegitimate child was given parental rights to the exclusion of the putative father. It was established by the House of Lords in *Barnado v McHugh*[299] that the mother of an illegitimate child had the legal right to its custody. The father, on the other hand, had no substantive right to custody of the child nor has this been affected by the Guardianship Act of 1973 which expressly states that the powers conferring equal rights on a child's mother and father do not apply in the case of an illegitimate child.[300] However, this total exclusion of the putative father from the enjoyment of parental rights has been alleviated in recent years. As we have seen, he now can share on his child's

---

292. If his parents' marriage has terminated and the parent with custody has remarried, then it will have to be established that he is a 'child of the family' in relation to the second marriage.
293. *Supra* p. 70. But see now *Downing v Downing supra* note 271.
294. Supplementary Benefits Act 1976.
295. *Clapham v National Assistance Board* [1961] 2 QB 77.
296. Children Act 1948, S.26 as amended. Children and Young Persons Act 1933, S.88, as amended; S.5(2) Affiliation Proceedings Act 1957.
297 *Op. cit., supra* note 248.
298. I.e. that a one-parent family should receive a State allowance for each child as of right. See *The Finer Report on One-Parent Families* 1974 Cmnd. 5629. There is little likelihood of the major recommendations of the Report being implemented in the foreseeable future.
299. [1891] AC 388.
300. Section 1(7).

intestacy[301]: by section 14 of the Guardianship of Minors Act 1971, he may apply[302] for custody under Section 9 of that Act and, if custody is granted, he can *then* appoint a testamentary guardian.[303] But although the welfare principle ultimately[304] prevails in custody proceedings, much less weight is given to the father's wishes in the case of an illegitimate child[305] as opposed to a legitimate child.[306]

Nevertheless, the parental rights of the putative father are still limited. His consent to the marriage of his child if under the age of majority is not required unless he has obtained a custody order and the mother has been deprived of custody.[307] More importantly, his consent is not required if the child is to be adopted.[308] But a court must now be satisfied that the putative father has no intention of applying for a custody order or that such an order would be refused if he did apply, before it can free his child for adoption.[309] And if the putative father is successful in obtaining custody of the child, then his consent *is* necessary in any further adoption proceedings.[310]

The denial of parental rights to the putative father can only have a rationale in relation to the situation where the illegitimate child is in fact a fatherless child: to apply this approach when the child is the offspring of an unmarried couple who enjoy a long-standing stable relationship is absurd. The recent strengthening of the putative father's rights is therefore to be welcomed: but until the process is completed, the concept of illegitimacy will still remain a fundamental—if regrettable—feature of English law.

---

301. Section 14 of the Family Law Reform Act 1969.
302. Prior to 1959 he could only apply for custody by instituting wardship proceedings. The right to apply directly for custody and access was given in Section 3 of the Legitimacy Act 1959.
303. Section 14(3) of the Guardianship of Minors Act 1971.
304. *Re Aster* [1955] 1 WLR 465.
305. *Re C(A)* [1970] 1 All ER 309.
306. Where they are at present having a considerable renaissance. *B v B supra* note 42.
307. Sch. 2 of The Marriage Act 1949.
308. *Re M* [1955] 2 QB 479.
309. Section 18(7) of the Adoption Act 1976.
310. He is the guardian of the child within the definition of guardian in Section 72 of the Adoption Act 1976 and his consent is necessary by virtue of Sections 16 and 18 of that Act.

CHAPTER IV. THE REFORM OF FAMILY LAW IN FRANCE

by Jacques Foyer

Introduction

Family law is one of the select areas of comparative studies. As Dean Carbonnier wrote in *Flexible Law*, "all the societies of today, the third world apart,
whether of industrial or consumer character, can appear to be extremely uniform
though their laws are not unified—above all, not their family laws. It is a classical
aphorism of comparative law, that while the law of property and obligations
tends towards homogeneity, family law remains the seat of national idiosyn-
crasies."[1] In truth, this peculiarity, which has been beyond dispute for some ten
years, tended to diminish in western societies at the beginning of the last quarter
of the twentieth century. The laws of the majority of the countries of Western
Europe tended to converge towards a uniform model, and this evolution has
been very rapid.

French law has in no way escaped this movement. Over little more than ten
years it has known, according to the statement of Dean Cornu, a "peaceful
revolution".[2] For more than a century and a half the Civil Code had remained
practically intact. Some laws of varying degrees of importance[3] had hardly
tampered with the conception which the legislature of 1804 had created for the
family. That was based upon powerful ideas, in particular, the principle that only
the legitimate family was recognised by the law. That principle had a whole series
of direct and indirect consequences one of which was the difficulty of obtaining a
divorce, for divorce would disrupt the legitimate family. Another consequence
was the non-recognition of the natural family and the deliberate neglect of free
unions; still another was the inferior condition imposed upon children born out
of wedlock and the possibility of legitimation, which permitted an illegitimate
child to accede to the privileged status of a legitimate child. This principle of the
superiority of the legitimate family was completed by a corollary, no less fundamental, which was that of the legal superiority of the married man. It is true that
this supremacy was not formulated in any precise text of the Civil Code, but it
inspired an entire series of particular provisions, such as those relating to marital
power, according to which the husband was the administrator of the common
matrimonial fund and of the wife's reserved property. He also had the enjoyment
of such fund and property. On the other hand, the married woman was, until the
reforms of 1938 and 1942, legally incapable of performing judicial acts. The effect
of parental power was that only the father had authority over the children of the
marriage and he was the administrator of their assets.

---

1. Jean Carbonnier, *Flexible Law*, 2nd edition 1969, p. 127.
2. Gérard Cornu, *The Impact of the Recent Reforms of the Civil Code on the Theory of Civil
Law*, Course for the DES of Civil Law 1970-71, *Les Cours du Droit*, mult.
3. In the first rank must be placed the Law Naquet of 18 April 1884 on divorce, the Law of
16 November 1912 on natural paternity, and the reforms of 1938 and 1942 on the legal position
of the married woman. See *infra*.

The passage of time and the evolution of morals and ideas have gradually called in question these two fundamental principles of French society. Criticisms multiplied on all sides and these were political, philosophical, sociological or psychological. The main criticisms related to the inegalitarian character of this legislation, which was charged with institutionalising the "law of the males", a masculine privilege which no longer corresponded to the growing part which women were playing in all areas of social and professional life.[4] Over and above these criticisms, the model imposed by the Civil Code was no longer respected by a growing number of individuals who were thus living on the margin of the law.

Those individuals who did not wish to marry, or could not marry, lived in a more or less stable concubinage. This posed the question, among others, of the legal position of children born from such unions, of the recognition of the natural family, and of concubinage. The objects of legislative policy had to be defined— whether the legislator should follow morals or procede them.

These criticisms could hardly have been effective without the joint action of two distinguished jurists, M Jean Foyer who led the work on the recent renovation of French legislation, successively as Minister of Justice and as President of the Law Commission[5], and M Jean Carbonnier who lent his elegant and precise style to the greater part of the texts adopted by Parliament.[6]

It is possible, in 1977, to stand back a little in order to appreciate the extent and the interest of this reform. The method followed by the French legislator is of some interest. His intention was to transform the Civil Code in depth without changing its overall architecture, while modifying as little as possible the numbering of the essential articles.[7] This policy has been followed with remarkable constancy. For twelve years past, almost every year has been marked by reform which has been more or less important:

14 December 1964: Guardianship and Legal Administration.

13 July 1965: Matrimonial Regimes.

11 July 1966: Adoption.

3 July 1968: Protection of Incapacitated Adults.

4 June 1970: Parental Authority.

3 July 1971: Liquidation of Succession.

3 January 1972: Affiliation, Legitimate and Natural.

9 January 1973: French Nationality.

5 July 1974: Lowering of the Age of Majority to 18 Years.

11 July 1975: Divorce.

---

4. See, for example, for the nineteenth century, Charles Morizot-Thibault on the marital authority (Critical Study of the Civil Code), Paris, Chevalier-Maresq et Cie, 1899.

5. In a communication read out before the Academy of Moral and Political Sciences in October 1967, Dean Carbonnier could clearly affirm that "Since 1963 we have seen a legislative thrust in private law which is quite simply historic and which connects it with the person of the *Garde des Sceaux* of the era, M Jean Foyer."

6. All except the last text on divorce, which has been re-written in the vernacular, on the initiative of the President of the Republic.

7. On the technique followed by the legislator, see G Cornu, "The Letter of the Code and the Test of Time", *Mélanges Savatier*, 157 ff.

Setting aside the law of succession and privileges which has, however, been modified in part[8], it is the whole of the personal status in its patrimonial and extrapatrimonial aspects which has been remodelled. Several hundreds of the articles of the Civil Code have been replaced by new provisions. The reforms, which are numerous and varied, can all be explained by a different reasoning; but they fall within an overall policy.

The legislature has pursued various aims. In the first place, the modernisation of legislation. Parliament, and those who have inspired it, wished to decree laws reflecting the state of French society in the last part of the twentieth century. This concern clearly confirmed in the various Parliamentary activities[9], was shown especially in the growing importance assumed by comparative law[10], and, above all, by the sociology of law.[11] The majority of the recent laws have been preceded by research into public opinion, and statistical and sociological studies[12], which well demonstrate the concern to adapt the institutions to French moral standards.

In the second place, the legislator wished to make a liberalisation effective[13] by promulgating laws adapted to a pluralist society. Ways of life tend to diversify. Alongside the traditional legitimate family—fortunately, always in existence— one cannot disregard the existence of deviant conducts: unions, in fact more or less durable[14], experimental marriages, group communities etc. Despite the principle of secularisation, the legislation inherited from the Civil Code remained profoundly marked by the canonical conception of marriage and of the family.[15] Today the legislator is changing his outlook with regard to the different ways of

---

8. The Law of 3 July 1971, in fact, profoundly modified the rules relating to succession and the reduction of privileges affecting the reserve; the Law of 3 January 1972 increased the rights of succession of natural children. But the matter has not been thought out afresh in its entirety. In particular, there is still the question of a reform of the rights of the surviving spouse.

9. See especially the Report of M Jean Foyer, "Report on the Law of 3 January 1972 on Affiliation", *Documents Parlementaires, Assemblée Nationale*, Second ordinary session 1970-71, No. 1926, 13 ff.

10. For example, the Report previously cited of M Foyer includes a translation of the recent laws on descent: English law of 1969, German law of 19 August 1969, Netherlands law of 3 April 1969.

11. The influence of Dean Carbonnier, who is one of the great specialists in the sociology of law, carried considerable authority in this respect. See also F Terre, "The Sociological Significance of the Reform of the Matrimonial Regimes", *L'année Sociologique* 1965.

12. For example, the review *Sondages* published the preliminary studies made before the law on the Matrimonial Regimes and those made in anticipation of a possible reform of the law of Succession.

13. This concern is particularly clear in the Law of Affiliation of 3 January 1972. See especially the studies of Mme. Gobert, "Marriage since the recent reforms of Family Law", JCP 1967, I. 2122; and "Reflections on an Indispensable Reform of the Law of Affiliation", JCP 1966, I I 2207; and Claube Colombet, Jacques Foyer, Danièle Huet-Weiller and Catherine Labrusse-Riou, *Affiliation, Legitimate and Natural*, Paris 1973, p. 9 ff. On the law of Divorce, see J Carbonnier, *The Question of Divorce*. See D 1085 I, p. 117, "if it was necessary to characterise briefly the dominant direction of the reforms most currently demanded, the word which would be most apposite would apparently be liberalisation."

14. R. Rodière, "The *ménage* in fact according to French law", *Travaux de l'Association Capitant* 1960, Dalloz, p. 55 ff.; Ph. Saint-Cyr "Of the free marriage union and article 301", art. 1 of the Civil Code, D. 1975, I, p. 123.

15. J. Carbonnier, "Heaven and Earth in the French Law of Marriage", *Etudes Ripert*, T I, Paris 1950, p. 329.

life and has abandoned the imperious imposition of a uniform collective moral-ity[16]; more than this, he has become inclined to respect such morality.[17]

This liberalisation ought necessarily to lead to a democratisation of the family. Modern French legislation seeks above all to be egalitarian and has tended to put an end to all the unjustified discriminations between individuals. If, in political and professional life, individuals were recognising equal rights in principle, it was not so within the family. As has been seen, until 1965 French law left a whole series of inequalities in existence:

—inequality between the husband and wife;
—inequality between the father and the mother;
—inequality between the legitimate and the illegitimate child.

Without using a constitutional norm of legal equality[18], as does the German legislator, the French legislator, in all his new provisions, has obviously been fired by the desire for egalitarianism and has rediscovered the fundamental principle laid down by the Declaration of the Rights of Man of 1789 and sub-sequent constitutional texts: "Men are born equal and remain free and equal before the law".[19]

However, this new principle offends a part of public opinion that is little dis-posed to admit such novelties. It is for this reason that a certain influence of public opinion and of the State can be seen in the law of the family. More and more frequently judicial authorities have been called upon to intervene[20] either to control the exercise of their powers by the spouses[21], or to re-establish the equality of their rights and duties.[22] The phenomenon is not new, and the Law of 1884 on Divorce showed that the law insisted on judicial control of important acts concerning the family. This has been accentuated in the present time and certain ill-disposed minds felt able to speak of the arrival of a "household of three", the husband, the wife and the judge, which is a gross exaggeration.

These various ideas are included in the three headings chosen for a Seminar of the University Institute of Luxembourg. One might say, by way of witticism, that the legislator wished to sanctify the device of the French Republic, which appears on the facades of public buildings:

Equality between the spouses (I).
Fraternity between legitimate children and natural children (II).
Liberty to divorce (III).

---

16. E.g. while placing on the level of equality legitimate and natural affiliation, the legislator of 1972 showed his preference for legitimacy by developing legitimation. Similarly, in liberalising divorce, the legislator of 1975 has retained Separation, the "divorce of the Catholics" which has less serious effects.
17. See notably the severe criticisms of M H Mazeaud on the Law of Affiliation "a family in the wind", the family outside marriage, D 1971, I, p. 100.
18. See Catherine Labrusse-Riou, "Equality between the spouses in French and German law", *Bib. droit privé*, LGDJ 1965.
19. See notably, J Foyer, *Rapp. préc*, p. 24 *et seq.*
20. See André Rouast, "The judge and family life in French law", *Mélanges Dabin*, T II, p. 865.
21. This is notably the case for the failure of parental authority and measures of assistance in education.
22. This is particularly clear in the relations between the spouses. See *infra* p. 79.

I. *Equality of the spouses*

"Is woman the queen of society, or a slave in submission to man? A treasure of virtue and devotion, or the source of weakness and even of many ills?" Glasson asked himself[23] at the beginning of the twentieth century. To this question the legislator has given very different answers in the course of time.

"The husband owes protection to his wife, the wife owes obedience to her husband", proclaimed Article 213 of the Civil Code in the 1804 edition. "The spouses together ensure the moral and material direction of the family. They provide for the education of the children and prepare for their future." This is what the same Article 213 affirms today, in the edition of the Law of 4 June 1970. Let us evaluate the pathway between these two texts.

In 1804, according to Colin and Capitant[24] a married woman was equated "to a minor or a lunatic". This rule of Article 213, which came in essence from the habits of the country[25], was of an ambiguous nature. It was explained, at one and the same time, by the authority of the husband and the necessity for the protection of the wife, by reason of her weakness (*imbecilitas sexus*). Moreover, it seems that this had been adopted from Bonaparte, who had compared the married woman, whose vocation was to procreate, to "the fruit tree which, producing its fruits, is the property of the gardener."

One could say[26] that the incapacity of the married woman appeared in the legislation as an equivocal institution, descended from two very different tendencies. On to the old basic foundation of marital power was grafted a new idea, that of protection. Mongrel as it was, this institution resulted in important consequences; the married woman could not carry out any judicial act on her own without authorisation by her husband. He exercised considerable powers over his wife, whose personal activity he could control. Without his authorisation the married woman could not move her residence, go on a journey, obtain a passport for herself, undertake studies, choose her doctor, accept the office or guardian by will[27], be appointed as subrogated guardian.[28] Above all, a husband had control over his wife's contacts[29] and could oversee her correspondence.[30]

---

23. L. Glasson, Preface to the work, cited above, of Charles Morizot-Thibault.

24. Colin and Capitant, *Treatise on the Civil Law*, Dalloz, T I 1957, p. 608, No. 1025.

25. "By custom", wrote one author, "the wife is in the power of the husband. It is otherwise in the written law." In particular, the right of correction was recognised. The husband could chastise his wife reasonably and without maiming her.

26. Colin and Capitant, *op. cit.* No. 1029, p. 612.

27. As in the former Art. 405 of the Civil Code, para. 2, edition of 20 March 1917. The law feared that the husband would not take part in fact in the administration of the guardianship and decided that he should be an obligatory co-tutor.

28. Former art. 420 of the Civil Code, repealed by the law of 18 February 1938.

29. The case law admitted, however, that the husband abused his right if he forbade his wife, without plausible reason, to visit her father and mother.

30. This was one of the extreme consequences which resulted from the wife's duty of obedience to her husband. He could have returned correspondence addressed to his wife, and could read her letters, but the unjustified abuse of this right could be considered as a serious injury, and so could be a ground for divorce.

With the development of society the husband's privileges were retained, and the practice of them was tolerated, only with difficulty.[31] Two important laws of 18 February 1938 and 22 September 1942 brought in notable modifications. The Law of 1938 suppressed the duty of obedience and the incapacity of the married woman, and permitted the wife to have a separate profession, other than commercial. The Law of 1942 authorised the wife "to carry on a profession separate from that of her husband, so long as he did not oppose it"[32], without distinguishing between civil and commercial professions. In addition, this Law, by a reform of Articles 212 et seq. of the Civil Code, made fundamental alterations to the whole of the "rights and duties between spouses".

After the Second World War this movement towards the equality of the rights of man and wife was accelerated. In 1946 women found themselves with the vote and were eligible to stand for Parliament, they were given free access to public service, and then awarded equal pay. Equality of the sexes had been gradually recognised, if not in fact, at least in law. But this equality was only evident in the social relations between men and women, whether married, single, widowed or divorced. On the other hand profound inequality remained in marriage itself. The Laws of 1938 and 1942 had preserved the husband's status as head of the family. This was looked on as neither a right nor a more or less discretionary prerogative, but as a function. The law of 22 September 1942, in the first paragraph of Article 213, in fact declared: "The husband is head of the family. He exercises this function in the common interest of the household and the children." The same Article adds in paragraph 2 that "the wife concurs in ensuring the moral and material guidance of the family and its maintenance, in bringing up the children and preparing their settlement in life." Lastly, paragraph 3 permitted the wife to represent her husband should he be unable to express his wishes. The husband was no longer an absolute sovereign, but a constitutional monarch. Nonetheless he kept some important rights. He remained the head of the family, he chose the matrimonial home, he alone could exercise paternal control over the children[33], he could give his French nationality to a foreign wife[34], he could give his name to his wife, and had a privileged status in the case of adultery.[35] These various powers were without doubt more shocking in their principle than in their daily use, when they were largely tempered by the collaboration of the spouses.

However, it is only recently that the legislator has seriously tried to promote a theoretical and practical equality between the spouses. In truth, this reform has not been acquired as easily as might have been thought. The legislator has made three attempts to establish it definitively. The law of 13 July 1965 which reformed matrimonial regimes, was egalitarian in spirit, yet retained a certain number of

---

31. A series of laws had produced partial solutions, especially the law of 13 July 1907, which permitted the married woman to dispose of the income from her own work, but which did not remove the necessity for the wife to obtain her husband's authority for carrying on a separate profession.
32. Art. 216, para. 2, CC. See Colin Capitant, *op. cit.*, No. 1062 ff., p. 633 ff.
33. Art. 373, para. 1. See *infra*, p. 85.
34. Art. 37, Code of Nationality (Ord. 19 October 1945).
35. In the Penal Law the adultery of the wife incurred more severe penalties (Art. 339c) than that of the husband and was more easily incriminated (Art. 337c. pén.).

inequalities.[36] Notably Article 213 continued to affirm that the husband was the head of the family and Article 215 preserved his final say in the choice of the family residence. It was the law of 4 June 1970 that caused the disappearance of the almost wholly unequal provisions[37], proclaiming that the spouses had an equal duty to ensure the material and moral guidance of the family and to choose the matrimonial home. Henceforth, equality of the spouses has been one of the fundamental principles of French law.[38] Lastly, the law of 11 July 1975 on Divorce authorised the wife to have a separate domicile. The proclamation of such a principle was bound to provoke a whole series of chain reactions, the full extent of which has not yet been gauged. The whole economy of the relations between spouses, now established on totally different bases, has been dealt with in great detail.[39] To best appreciate these, consideration must be given to the equality in their relations between themselves (A), and in their relations with their children (B).

A. Conjugal Equality

It is fairly difficult to give an exact picture of French law in this respect. In fact, it seems to be a mosaic of legal provisions from different sources, adapted as has been seen from very different epochs like a patchwork of rules with diverse spheres of operation. In addition, the equality is not always to the same extent. It could be described by distinguishing between relations which are patrimonial and those which are extra-patrimonial, though the dividing line between the two is far from precise. It may be simpler to take up the division inaugurated by Law of 1942, developed by the law of 13 July 1965, between the fundamental status of married persons (1) and their matrimonial status (2).

(1) *Equality in the fundamental status of spouses*

Articles 212 et seq. of the Civil Code, the Law of 13 July 1965 sought to lay down a certain number of common rules for all spouses, whatever their matrimonial regime.

In truth, examination of the legislation gives only a very imperfect idea of the equality which should be effective in conjugal relations. Above all, this equality is a matter of mental approach and involves more sociology than law. According to a saying of Dean Carbonnier[40], in the family there are "long days of non-law

---

36. See, for example, the analysis by Dean Carbonnier in 1969 *Droit civil*, Vol. 2, p. 69 et seq. no. 22 et seq. Add Anne-Marie Bourgeois, "The law of 13 July 1965 and the sequels in the status of legal inferiority of the married woman", *Rev. trim. droit civil* 1968, 68.
37. It was this law that suppressed the principle according to which the husband is head of the family. See Cl. Colombet, *Parental Authority* D. 1971, I, p. 1 ff.
38. This can be verified in private international law. In a judgment of 27 June 1974 (Rev. crit. dr. int. privé 1974, 505) the Court of Paris set aside, in the name of French public international order, the law of the Cameroons which did not ensure real equality between the spouses and only recognised divorce on account of the wife's adultery, and not for the adultery of the husband.
39. For example, Art. 37 of the Code of Nationality (Law of 9 January 1973) affirms that "marriage will not, as of right, affect nationality" but, according to Art. 371, "the foreigner or expatriate who contracts marriage with a spouse of French nationality can acquire this nationality by declaration". The new law no longer distinguishes between husband and wife.
40. Cited by Mirelle Delmas-Marty in *Family Law*, "*Que sais-je?*" PUF 1972, p. 9.

for a few moments of law; for the non-law is of the essence, and the law is incidental."[41] However, the law is not deprived of effect on behaviour and the recent reforms can be presumed to have encouraged democracy in the lives of the spouses, though not being the sole causes of this development.

In order better to understand the complete reversal that has been carried out, it should be remembered that in other times the husband had the benefit of a double superiority: he was at the same time the superior of his wife and the head of the household. If it had been possible to suppress the first privilege in 1965, this would have been a direct clash with the assumption of equality between individuals. On the other hand, the second privilege was less unequal and fitted in with the conception of the management of the conjugal enterprise.[42] It has taken longer to disappear and some consequences remain.

(a) The wife is henceforth her husband's equal at least in law, if not in fact. The legislature wished to conciliate two contradictory rules, in order to leave to the wife liberty of action without going so far as to sever the conjugal link. To quote a well-known expression, it was sought to realise an "independence with the interdependence".[43] In principle the independence is recognised by Article 216 of the Civil Code, according to which "each spouse has full capacity in law". This principle takes the exact opposite view from that established before 1938 and 1942, which made the married woman an incapacitated person. The general rule did not appear sufficiently precise to the legislator of 1965, who provided for a whole series of specified consequences in Articles 221-225 of the Civil Code.

This is how Article 221 recognises the independence of the spouses in banking and investment: "Each of the spouses can open a deposit account and a share account in his or her individual name, without the consent of the other." Although stated in general terms, this right is chiefly useful to married women who can thereby open a banking account for themselves without marital authority. The sphere of application of this text is widely understood. It applies in the relations of each of the spouses with the financial institution, who cannot request proof of the right to dispose of funds and certificates deposited. Moreover, it is effective not only in opening an account, but also for the maintenance of it, including the withdrawal and disposal of funds and certificates deposited. On the other hand Article 221 does not operate in the relations between the spouses and third parties. Nor does it apply to the operation of a bank account abroad and especially to other banking and Stock Exchange operations, such as the opening of a Bank Deposit box, or transactions in bearer or registered shares.[44] For this type of operation it is necessary to apply Article 222, which has an even wider

41. See G Cornu, "Report on the Notions of Equality and of Discrimination in French Civil Law" *Travaux de l'Association H Capitant*, T.XIV 1961-62, Dalloz 1965, p. 102.
42. "In a group of some sort a certain unity of impulse, of direction, responds to a vital necessity. And if the group comprises only two persons unity can only be assured by the leading role of one of them. In the household, following a custom which French habits seemed not to be able to entirely overcome, this favoured role was given to the husband." Jean Carbonnier, *op. cit.* 1969, p. 73.
43. This is the idea which inspired the developments of MM Patarin and Morin, p. 8 no. 2 and p. 34 ff. no. 29 ff.
44. On all these points see Patarin and Morin, *op. cit.*, no. 53 ff., p. 53 ff.; Ponsard, *op. cit.* No. 43 ff., p. 80 ff.

area of application. There it is stated that "if one of the spouses presents himself or herself alone to perform an act of administration, enjoyment or disposition of a movable asset which he or she has in his or her individual possession, then that spouse, as regards third persons of good faith, has the power to perform that act alone." This provision, which is the "key to the vault for the security of third persons and therefore for the independence of the spouses in their relations with third persons"[45] has great practical importance. It applies to all tangible movables, with the exception of the movable furniture in the family home and movables naturally belonging to the other spouse.[46] According to some, it also applies to intangible movables[47], but this opinion is debated[48], at least where the spouse has possession of the movable.[49] This Article applies to all the acts to which the management of an asset can give rise and, notably, to the payment of debts by means of funds in the individual possession of one of the spouses. Lastly, this text protects in a very effective way third parties in good faith, that is, those who are unaware of the lack of capacity of the spouse; in particular, the recipient of a bank cheque or postal cheque who is unaware that the funds deposited were not at the disposal of the drawer, is protected against all objection on the part of the other spouse.

This independence of the spouses in the management of their movable assets must necessarily lead to professional independence. This has never been in quetion for the husband. Henceforth, Article 223 of the Civil Code lays down that "the wife has the right to carry on a profession without the consent of her husband, and she can always dispose of or pledge her personal assets in her own right as sole owner for the needs of that profession". It is on this point that evolution has been most spectacular. Under the aegis of the Civil Code of 1804 case law deduced the principles of the supremacy of the husband and the incapacity of the married woman, who could not validly carry on a profession with the consent of her husband. The Law of 22 September 1942 substituted for this consent *a priori*, a right of opposition by the husband *a posteriori*. Progress was achieved in that the law proclaimed that the wife could carry on a separate profession, but that the husband retained the right of veto. Today it is simply acknowledged that each of the spouses can carry on the profession of his or her own choice[50], either civil or commercial, without the opposition of the other spouse. Such liberty is not without risk for the family. Also, some authors maintain that, if the carrying on of a separate profession by the wife presents dangers for the household, the husband can appeal to the President of the Court of Appeal on the basis of Article 220-1 of the Civil Code, to make an urgent order to prohibit the wife from pursuing the disputed profession.[51] This measure will necessarily be of an exceptional character, such a conflict leading more naturally to a divorce or a judicial separation.

---

45. Patarin and Morin, *op. cit.* no. 30, p. 34.
46. Clothes, linen, chattels and, more generally, all chattels having a personal character.
47. R. Savatier, *The New Conjugal Community*, no. 45.
48. Patarin and Morin, no. 32, p. 36.
49. This idea of possession must be made precise by reference to that of possession in Art. 2279 Civil Code (see Patarin and Morin, no. 34, p. 40).
50. Patarin & Morin, no. 68 et seq, p. 67 ff.; Cornu, p. 87 ff.
51. Patarin & Morin, no. 69, p. 67; Ponsard, no. 55, p. 110.

Lastly, from this professional independence Article 224 has very naturally deduced that "each of the spouses shall receive profits and remuneration and can dispose of them freely after discharging the expenses of the household." The same Article adds in paragraph 2 that the assets acquired by the wife in the exercise of a separate profession become "reserved assets"[52] under her administration and for her own enjoyment and free disposition. Here again the solution is important. The wife has been accorded a real financial independence. The remuneration remains always disposable at the hands of the wife who carries on a profession and no clause of the contract can obstruct this free disposition.[53]

Such an array of provisions should cause a wife to lose all the inferiority complexes she might have had with regard to her husband. But there was also the opposite danger, that the marriage could become a juxtaposition of two opposing wills.

Interdependence is of the very essence of marriage. This has been defined as "the society of man and woman united in order to perpetuate their species, to help each other by mutual assistance in carrying the burden of life, and to protect their joint future".[54] This society aspect operates in the first place between the spouses. Article 212, the wording of which has not changed since its origin, recalls that "the spouses owe each other mutual fidelity, help and assistance. Recently, Dean Cornu[55] could write, "It is possible that fidelity readily passes as the more feminine commitment, while the help and assistance remain chiefly the concern of the husband." In future the equality of rights should include that of the obligations.

Again, Article 213 affirms the common vocation of the spouses to assure "together the moral and material guidance of the family". Article 214, in default of matrimonial agreements, rules that the contribution of the spouses to the matrimonial expenses should be in proportion to their respective abilities." However in the 1965 edition of the same Article 214, paragraphs 2 and 3 laid down that this contribution fell in the main upon the husband and that the wife acquitted herself of it by using her income and remuneration, and by her activity in the home and her collaboration in the profession of her husband. These paragraphs, which seemed to give the wife a subordinate role, have been rescinded by the Law of 11 July 1975 (Article 6).

According to Article 215 the spouses mutually agree to a joint way of life and the family home is chosen by common agreement.

But interdependence also operates with regard to third parties. The law has provided here a series of normal situations, either that when one of the spouses, acting alone, binds the other spouse jointly[56], or when the two spouses are bound to act together, or when one of the spouses must be authorised by the other.[57]

---

52. The reserved assets are those reserved to the administration of the wife, see G Cornu, p.111 ff.
53. Patarin & Morin, no. 73, p. 72.
54. Portalis, cited and discussed by Alex Weill in *Droit Civil Les personnes*, 3rd ed. (Précis Dalloz) p. 145, no. 185.
55. Report on the inequalities, *op. cit. supra*, p. 100.
56. According to art. 220 each spouse has the power to enter into contracts alone which have as their object the maintenance of the household or the education of the children. But the solidarity does not operate for expenditures which are manifestly excessive.
57. Thus one spouse is prohibited from alone disposing of the family dwelling and the furniture therein (art. 215, para. 3). Also purchases under hire-purchase do not make the two spouses jointly liable except when they have jointly concluded the contract.

However, the principles laid down are not rigid. The legislature has provided a whole series of flexible rules. Thus Article 218 permits one of the spouses to give a mandate to the other spouse to represent him or her in the exercise of the powers which the matrimonial regime attributes to him or her; also Article 219, paragraph 2, provides that in default of legal right, mandate or authorisation by the Court, acts performed by one spouse as representative of the other are effective in relation to the other in accordance with the rules of implied contract.[58] Last and most important, the Law of 1965 augmented the cases of intervention by the Judge in the relations between the spouses. Such intervention is provided for in two cases. First, if one of the spouses is not in a condition to express his or her wishes, the other spouse can be authorised by the Court to carry out an act alone[59], for which the consent or the agreement of the other spouse would have been necessary (Article 217), or he could be authorised to represent the other for general or specific arts (Article 219). Secondly, the intervention of the Judge is equally possible if one of the spouses is seriously lacking in the performance of his duties and so puts in peril the interests of the family (Article 220-1). The President of the Court of Appeal can lay down the measures that may be urgent and necessary and can forbid the spouse to dispose of his own or the family assets, or can forbid him to remove a movable.[60] Acts in violation of the order of the President can be annulled at the request of the other spouse (Article 220-3).

The preceding articles, with one exception[61], names the spouses without distinguishing between man and woman, which is an example of the legislator's desire to achieve equality. The husband is no longer the master of his wife.

(b) In principle the husband is no longer the head of the household, the spouses having an equal duty to look after the family. This idea has taken too long to become law. Although in theory it was desired to recognise the woman as equal with the man, the idea of the family as a unit with the husband at the head was firmly established. The reforms in 1938 and 1942 were very characteristic in this respect—that the husband remained the head of the family, the wife only collaborating and occasionally acting as his deputy.

It is remarkable how this concept left such profound traces in French law. The Law of 13 July 1965, although egalitarian, continued to affirm in Article 2213 that the husband was the head of the family. Only in the Law of 4 June 1970 was it affirmed that the spouses should be the family together. Henceforth the major decisions of the household had to be taken in common, and in relations with the outside world each of the spouses, without distinction, represented the family in the eyes of third parties. In practice, however, it is apparent that it will be the wife who continues to carry out the day to day housekeeping.

Nonetheless, some traces of the older concept have remained, and still do so. Thus, a woman takes the name of her husband when she marries and this has

---

58. See Patarin & Morin, no. 81 ff.; p. 80 ff.
59. Patarin & Morin, no. 83 ff and 81 ff.; Ponsard no. 51, p. 96.
60. This provision has already given rise to an abundant case law. See Claude-Isabelle Foulon-Pigniol, the first case law tendencies of art. 220-1 D 1967, Chr. 207; Patarin & Morin, no. 84 ff., p. 84 ff.; Ponsard, no. 53, p. 107.
61. Art. 223 on the separate profession of the wife.

become the social habit in marriage.[62] It is true that the patronimic is as much a matter of custom as of law. All the same, until the Law of 11 July 1975, Article 215 paragraph 3 laid down that, in the case of disagreement between the spouses on the choice of the family home, this should be in a place chosen by the husband, unless the wife appeals to the Court on the ground of serious inconvenience. The authors of the recent Law on Divorce erased this precept as giving to the husband unfair privileges.[63] In the same spirit, it was agreed that the spouses could have a separate domicile.[64] This is an important reform. It is no longer compulsory for the wife to share the husband's domicile. Should she also have a different name?[65] As Dean Cornu wrote on the eve of the 1965 reform, "If the husband, without being master, remains eponymous (i.e. continues to give his name to the family) and continues to choose the home, there will be no equality; if equality is established, this will be to the detriment of the real and symbolic unity of the family."[66] It is perhaps this last idea that explains the retention of a relative inequality in the financial relations between the spouses.

(2) *Equality of spouses in matrimonial regimes*

The equality of the spouses' functions is more or less assured, according to the type of regime adopted. The separation of their assets and the equal participation in new assets make for equality in the division of the spouses' powers. On the other hand, the community regime amounts to an unequal association which, in the traditional view of the community regime of movables and acquisitions, existed as a balanced economy.[67] Corresponding to the important powers of the husband were a whole series of guarantees for the wife against the abuse of these powers, against fraud, negligence, and the incapacity of the husband.[68]

Here only the legal regime will be considered. There is some surprise that, in the atmosphere of equality surrounding the Law of 13 July 1965, the legislator chose to restrict the legal regime to a community of acquisitions (Article 1400-1491 of the French Civil Code). This choice is explained, however, by a sociological law[69], moreover this regime is not only based on the idea of equality.[70] The legislator endeavoured to construct the legal regime on the basis of equality—without completely achieving it—as much in regard to the rights of the spouses during the marriage as to the guarantees extended to them on the dissolution of the marital link.[71]

---

62. See Weill, *Droit civil, supra* no. 45 p. 44.
63. According to art. 3L, 11 July 1975, paras 2 & 3 of Art. 215 were replaced by the following new para: "the family residence is in the place which they choose by common agreement."
64. The new art. 108 of the Civil Code is worded thus: "The husband and the wife can have a distinct domicile without to that extent infringing the rules of community of life."
65. A name which she can resume after divorce (new art. 264 Civil Code).
66. The report cited above, p. 80.
67. Cornu, *op. cit.,* p. 102.
68. Especially, the right for the wife to renounce the community (former art. Civil Code) and the benefit of emolument.
69. Researches into public opinion carried out before the law was drafted revealed that the French had a profound attachment to the idea of community: Cornu, *Treatise,* p. 60.
70. Notably, at the moment of the partitioning of the community which existed between the spouses.
71. See Colombet, "The legal community" in *Rép. Dalloz Droit Civil,* 2nd ed; P Hebraud, "The married woman and the French law of matrimonial regimes", *Annales de la Faculté de Droit de Toulouse,* 1966, T XI Fascicule, 2. 197 ff.

(a) There is equality of rights on many levels, but there remain some traces of the original inequality. The legislator first wished to rebalance the three categories of the spouses' assets, by augmenting the personal assets to the detriment of the common fund. In the regime prior to 1965 this comprised all acquisitions and all the movables of each spouse, whatever their origin. In the current system, the common fund contains only assets acquired by the spouses jointly or separately during the marriage, that is to say, according to Article 1901, the assets "derived as much from their individual work as from economies effected in respect of the fruits and incomes from their personal assets", and the reserved assets of the wife.[72]

In respect of individual belongings, that is, assets owned on the day of the marriage and assets or gifts acquired during the union, personal assets and any subsequently acquired or otherwise obtained, each of the spouses is recognised by Article 1428 as having "the administration and enjoyment of his or her individual assets" and the power "to dispose of them freely". By this rule the regime of legal community approaches the regime of separation of assets and this becomes closer as the legislator favours the control of interference by one of the spouses in the management of the funds of the other. This is considerable progress for the woman in comparison with the previous regime, in which the husband had the administration of all the assets of the community, including the personal assets of his wife. Finally, the legislator tried as much as possible to assimilate the positions of husband and wife by ensuring a correlation between debts and assets, both in respect of individual possessions and the common fund. Thus, debts for which each spouse was liable on the day of the marriage or which are charged on their successions and fall due in the course of the marriage only affect the full ownership of these several assets.[73] Conversely, debts contracted by the husband or the wife for the maintenance of the household and the education of the children, affect the common fund.[74]

However, on different occasions the law has disrupted the principle of equality between the spouses. It did so in the first place by recognising the husband's right to manage the common fund (Article 1421 Civil Code). It is true that, for the sake of symmetry, the wife had the right to manage her personal assets (Article 1425 Civil Code). In the second place, the law allowed the husband to dispose of the common fund under certain conditions and exceptions.[75] From this it follows that all debts incurred by the husband in the course of the marriage become debts on the common fund, at least provisionally.[76] Here we find again, expressed more forcibly, the idea previously examined, that the husband remains the head of the household.[77] The law has also affected the idea of equality in a manner favourable to the wife, in that certain of the wife's debts affect the common fund and the personal estate of the husband, while similar debts of the husband only

---

72. On the composition of the legal community, see Patarin & Morin, no. 98 et seq, p. 100 ff.
73. Patarin & Morin, no. 225 ff.
74. Arts 1413 and 1414 Civil Code.
75. Art. 1424 CC.
76. Art. 1413 CC.
77. See *supra* p. 88.

affect the common fund and not the separate assets of the wife. This applies to debts contracted with the consent of the husband[78], to the obligations of the wife from her professional occupation, to the case of maladministration or to a registered declaration of approval for the wife to carry on an outside occupation.[79]

With these reservations the legal equality of the spouses has been broadly assured. But the legislator did not stop there.

(b) Equality in the guarantees for the spouses has also been sought. In the Civil Code system the wife had effective protection from the husband's mastery in her right to earn and possibly to waive her right to the common fund. As this had diminished appreciably, it seemed appropriate either to extend the same guarantees to the husband, or to lessen those of the wife. Thus it was henceforth recognised that the husband had the same right to earn as the wife (Article 1483 Civil Code). Conversely the wife lost her right to waive participation in the common fund, provided by the former Article 1453 of the Civil Code. Legal equality has its obligations but, here again, the law has been unable to carry the logic of its system as far as it could go. The wife who does not manage the common fund, must be protected from the husband's mismanagement. Also Article 1421, having declared that the husband alone administers the common fund, lays down that he "must answer for any faults committed during his management". On the same lines, Article 1426 provides for the possibility for the wife to ask the Courts to substitute her husband and put her in his place in the exercise of his powers, if he is permanently unable to make his wishes known, or if his management of the common fund reveals ineptitude or fraud.[80] It will be noted that this Article is worded in a bilateral manner and that it can equally serve for the husband to be substituted for the wife in the management of her personal assets, but it is clear that this is a defensive weapon for the benefit of the wife.[81] The last of the wife's prerogatives is that, at the time of the division of the common fund, she may choose her share before her husband chooses his (Article 1471, para. 2, Civil Code).

In terms of this examination of the legal relations between husband and wife, the position of French law appears to be ambiguous. Although equality was desired, and largely realised in the personal relations, there remains a certain inequality in favour of the husband in the financial regulations. The same conclusion will be reached regarding the legal relations between the spouses in their capacities as father and mother.

B. Parental equality

After establishing conjugal equality, it was logical, and necessary, to proceed to parental equality. Moreover, on the very day after 13 July 1965, adverse comments were already made concerning the equality already attained and the inequality that still remained in respect of the position of the husband as head of the family. For he alone is entitled to parental rights.[81] This paternal right had

78. Art. 1419, para. 2, CC. See also Patarin & Morin, no. 236, p. 206.
79. Art. 1420 CC. Patarin & Morin, no. 236, p. 207.
80. See Ponsard, *op. cit.* no. 2220 ff, p. 392.
81. See A. M. Bourgeoix, art. cited above.

88

been much discussed. The point was raised that the specific term had not been used in the Civil Code of 1804. Above all, the discretionary and absolute character of the notion of paternal power itself was queried. It was regretted that this power had been recognised for the father alone and not for the mother.

All changes in the law since the Civil Code, legislative as well as case-law, had greatly attenuated its original character. A Law of 24 July 1889 had provided for the loss of paternal rights by a father who failed to fulfil his duties. An Ordinance of 23 December 1958 had replaced the father's right of chastisement by judicial measures for the protection of infants and adolescents in danger.[82] Last but not least, Article 373 of the Civil Code, in the draft of the Law of 13 July 1942, had stated what authority over the infant belonged to the father and to the mother but that, during the marriage, such authority was to be exercised by the father alone in his position as head of the family.[83] The principle of the father's authority had thus been modified in depth: the individual and discretionary right had gradually been transformed into a function exercised in the interest of the child and of the family, under the control of the judicial authority, but the supremacy of the father was retained. This was virtually abolished in the new Article 371-2 of the Civil Code. "Authority belongs to both father and mother for ensuring the children's safety, health and morals".[84] In the first instance, the change is one of terminology: 'power' has been replaced by 'authority' and the adjective 'paternal' has been changed to 'parental', which was invented for the purpose. But in law vocabulary is not neutral. The new terms indicate basic changes. According to the definition given by M Ponsard, "Parental authority is the amalgamation of the rights and powers which the law accords to the father and mother over the persons and assets of their children while the latter are minors and not emancipated, in order to permit the father and mother to carry out the duties of maintenance and education which fall upon them."[85] Such a definition gives force to the main characteristic of this idea: it is a function recognised by law, having the character of social order and being exercised in common by the father and the mother. Henceforth, the principle of equality of rights and duties permeates, with some exceptions, all the regime of parental authority concerning both of those entitled to it and concerning its content.

(1) *Those entitled to parental authority* says the law, are the father together with the mother. This principle of equality is realised through two complementary ideas: the spouses must exercise their functions in common but, as they have an equal function, they are interchangeable and each of them can deputise for the other. These two principles cover both the normal situation and the exceptional situation that can occur.

(a) For the legislator, the normal situation is when the father and mother are both living and able to exercise parental authority and agree between themselves.

---

82. CC Art. 375 ff.
83. See Colin and Capitant, *op. cit.*, no. 1518, p. 891 ff.
84. On the spirit of the new law, see Cl. Colombet D 1971, I, 1; M Gobert, "The child and the adults", *JCP* 1971 1, 2421; R. Legais *Répertoire Defrenoix;* Y Buffelan Lanore Juris classeur Droit civil art. 371 387 Fasc. I & II A Weill Droit civil above, No. 704 ff. p. 627.
85. A Ponsard, "Parental Authority" in *Rep. Droit civil*, 2nd ed. no. 1.

Article 372, being an application of the principle of Article 3712, affirms that "during the marriage the father and mother exercise their authority in common".[86] Thus, normally all decisions concerning the children should be debated between the spouses and decided by common agreement. But this joint exercise of parental authority might become a strain on the relations between the spouses and become dangerous with regard to third parties requiring proof of the parents' agreement. Article 367-2 introduced a practical flexibility by declaring that, "in regard to third parties of good faith, each of the spouses is considered to have acted with the consent of the other when he or she carries out alone a normal act of parental authority relating to the child's person." Thus the wife is able to decide alone with regard to a whole series of day-to-day acts, such as applying for a passport, registering in a school, or organising a holiday.[87] But, in general, jurists are less interested in the normal than in the pathological.

(b) Exceptional situations provided for are numerous and of varying gravity. In the first place there can be a disagreement between the spouses on a decision concerning a child. By a curious decision, Article 3721 provided that, "if they cannot agree on what is the best interest for the child, the practice followed on similar occasions will serve for lack of a rule." Here the law refers to family custom, making contact between law and non-law. But this remedy is in no way a panacea. Moreover, failing such a practice or in the case of a dispute as to whether it exists or is valid, the guardianship authority can be appealed to by the more responsible parent (Article 372-1, para. 2).

A deeper crisis can arise if either or both of the spouses lose their control of parental authority, or are deprived of it. According to Article 373, this will occur in the case of incapacity, absence or distance, in the case of delegation of authority to another person, of abandonment of the family, of failure of, or withdrawal from, parental authority. If only one of the spouses finds himself in one of the above mentioned cases, the exercise of the parental authority passes, in its entirety, to the other spouse (Article 373-1). The exercise of parental authority is necessarily affected by the dissolution of the marriage, or by the relaxation of its disciplines. In the case of the death of the father or the mother, the surviving spouse will exercise the parental authority alone (Article 373-2), showing that the father and the mother are placed on a level of strict equality. If the spouses are divorced or physically separated, parental authority is exercised by the spouse to whom the Court has granted custody of the child (Article 373-2) which, in the majority of cases, is the mother. But it is recognised that the other parent has a right to visit and to supervise.[88]

Finally, if neither father nor mother remains in a position of authority, either by reason of death, or of failure or withdrawal of authority, this becomes the occasion for creating a guardianship (Article 373-4).[89]

---

86. These articles are themselves applications of the principle of article 212 Civil Code; see *supra* p. 84.
87. On the other hand, the use of surgery would require the consent of both parents. See Colombet, *op. cit.* p. 13.
88. These solutions have not been modified by the Law of 11 July 1975.
89. On guardianship, see A Weill *op. cit.* no. 890, p. 797 ff. and the authors cited.

In all these cases the legislator's desire is clear. It seemed desirable that, for his physical and moral equilibrium the child should be raised by both parents, each of whom, as the saying goes, had a voice in the matter. But these functions, though intended to be joint, could be exercised by either one or the other without distinction.

(2) *The content of the parental authority* is, by nature, very varied. Rights and duties over the person are by tradition distinguished from rights and duties over the child's property.

(a) Rights and duties over the person. According to Article 371-2, the child must be protected "in his safety, his health and his morality". Both father and mother are recognised in this respect as having "right and duty of custody of supervision and of education" (Article 371-2, para. 2), to which must be added the duty of maintenance provided for by Article 203 of the Civil Code.

Here it is impossible to analyse exhaustively all those prerogatives. Custody implies that the child lives in the family home. Article 371-3 lays down that the child may not leave the family home without the authorisation of his parents and that he may not be removed from it except under conditions stated in the law. In practice this usually means where the judge takes measures to facilitate his education.[90] Supervision includes the control by the parents of a child's correspondence and their approval of his friends, but this is not an absolute right. Article 371-4 prohibits the parents from opposing a child's associations unless there are serious reasons, especially the relationships with his grandparents. Paragraph 2 of the same article provides that the Court can, in exceptional circumstances, grant a right to visit or to correspond with other persons whether they are relations or not. Education must be agreed upon in a wide sense, that is, not only with regard to instruction itself but also regarding professional, civic and religious education.[91]

The parents' obligations to the child include the duty of maintenance, which aims at preparing the child to earn his own living later on. Maintenance comprises in particular not only the obligation to care for the child, but to provide him with everything necessary for his existence, such as a home, clothing, medical expenses, and so on. The law has endeavoured to condense a complex reality which is subject to rapid change. Nowadays children acquire their independence much sooner than did their elders.[92] Also, parental authority now carries greater burdens than gains. This is evidenced by the existence of penal or civil sanctions[93], and by placing that authority under the control of judicial authorities. But here again there is an equal balance between the spouses. In particular, Article 1384, paragraph 4 of the Civil Code emphasises the joint responsibility of both father and mother for damage caused by minor children in their care.

---

90. That is to say by placing a child in a special school, or to live with a third party according to the conditions in Article 375-3.
91. See A Weill, no. 714, p. 637.
92. For instance, the fact that minors over 13 years can buy the Pill legally without their parents' permission, is a debatable example.
93. Failure of parental authority (Art. 378 ff. CC).

(b) *Rights and duties over the child's assets.* The Civil Code provided two prerogatives, the legal administration and the enjoyment of the child's assets.

(i) The legal administration was reshaped in depth by the Law of 14 December 1964 and consists in representing the minor in his civil acts. As in the case of the parents' control of the person of the child, the law distinguished between a normal situation, to which the legal administration pure and simple applies, and the abnormal situation involving legal administration under the control of the Court.

Article 389-1 calls the legal administration pure and simple when the minor is a legitimate child whose parents are living, not divorced or physically separated, and who have not been deprived of, nor have they forfeited, the exercise of their parental authority. Here again the two Laws of 14 December 1964 and 4 June 1970 made a subtle distinction between equality and inequality. According to Article 382 both parents are associated jointly in the management of the minor's property. Yet Article 389, paragraph 1, as in the case of the common fund[94], entrusts the exercise of the legal administration "to the father, with the concurrence of the mother." This provision has been criticised. It is explained, however, for practical reasons by the necessity for the child to have one definite agent, particularly in disputed matters. The wife has important powers of control and her consent is required for acts of disposal.[95] But the father can carry out acts of administration alone.[96]

The legal administration is under the control of the Court when one of the parents is deceased, or when the parents are divorced or physically separated, or have forfeited their parental authority. In these situations one parent alone is concerned with the care of the child. This will either be the surviving parent or the one who has been given custody of the infant. The principle of equality, here again, decides their rights, since it is the father or the mother, without distinction, who will be granted legal administration. In the case of divorce it will be the mother. The legal administrator can perform alone acts of administration but, for acts of disposal, he must obtain the permission of the guardianship authority.[97]

(ii) The legal administration described above suffices for the correct management of the minor's assets. However, Article 383 of the Civil Code has retained the parallel right of legal enjoyment. This right is a legal usufruct permitting the father or the mother who is in charge of the legal administration to receive and use the income of minor children who are not emancipated.[98] The retention of this right in the law of 1964 has been much discussed. Some have seen in it an anachronism surviving from the previous law[99] which confers on the legal administrator greater advantages than those of the guardian.[100] However,

---

94. See *supra* p. 87.
95. Art. 389.
96. Art. 389-4 CC.
97. Art. 389-6 CC.
98. Since the Law of 5 July 1974 lowering the age of majority to 18 years, legal enjoyment ceases as soon as the child attains the age of 16 years. Art. 384-1 CC.
99. On this controversy see Y. Bufflan-Lanore, the Art. cited above and A. Weill no. 720, p. 640.
100. Guardianship is in effect gratuitous, while legal enjoyment can be considered as remuneration for the legal administration.

according to Dean Carbonnier, it is an institution in favour of the woman which, in the case of the predecease of the father, precludes a radical change in the mother's habitual mode of life.

It is evident that the lawmakers have wished to work along the lines of modern thought. However, this has its limits. The legislator has not, and has not wished to, pursue the principle of equality to its ultimate conclusion. Although the modern French marriage laws contain the principle of equality, they also include pockets of inequality in the form of masculine supremacy in regard to the management of the assets of both spouses and children. On the other hand the joint authority of the spouses comes up, more and more often, against the mistakes of the young in their newly found independence. Perhaps two parents are needed to oppose young adolescents intent on taking power into their own hands.

II. Illegitimate children

In the law of marriage, the Civil Code treated relationships with a basic inequality. It was considered necessary to distinguish between the legitimate child, the simple natural child, and the child born in adultery, according to a pre-established hierarchy. The first could have his descent established with difficulty and could take advantage of his full rights; the simple natural child, both of whose parents were unmarried, could have his affiliation established, though his rights were reduced in comparison with those of the legitimate child; while the adulterous child, at least one of whose parents was married at the time of conception, was prohibited from establishing his relationship[101] and thus, in principle, had no rights.[102] It is true that subsequent legislation and case-law had weakened the original rigour of the law. This amelioration had chiefly benefitted the simple natural child, who found himself better able to establish his descent[103] and obtained increased rights of succession.[104] On the other hand, adulterous children were regarded as pariahs[105] and outside the law. Certainly, over the years it has become easier to acquire legitimacy, but the chief benefits have accrued more to children born from the adultery of the father than from that of the mother. It has also become possible, by a Law of 15 July 1955, for these children to obtain support from their adulterous father[106] by Court action, but on the whole their fate was at a great disadvantage.

One of the authors of the 1972 legislation has said it was desired to make a "law of justice and equity". Drawing inspiration from the lessons of the past and the teachings of Comparative law, he wished to place children of whatever origin

---

101. To these three must be added the incestuous child whose father and mother were related by blood or marriage within a prohibited degree.
102. In the rare cases where its affiliation could be established (e.g. disavowal of paternity, nullity of marriage for bigamy) he could only claim for necessaries and even this provision disappeared if the adulterous father had taught his child a trade.
103. Law of 16 November 1912, modifying art. 340 CC.
104. Law of 25 March 1896, modifying art. 756 ff. CC.
105. Jean Foyer, Report on the draft law on affiliation, *Assemblée Nationale*, 2nd ord. session 1970-71.
106. Art. 342 bis CC.

on a level of equality. The new Article 334, which is the relevant fundamental provision, claims in fact that "the natural child has in general the same rights and duties as the legitimate child in his relations with his father and mother."[107] The innovation appears in the first instance in the vocabulary. The Civil Code henceforth describes the adulterous child with a paraphrase, as "the child of whom one of the parents was, at the time of conception, linked to another person by the ties of marriage".[108] This formula is not an easy one to use. Some authors have proposed substituting for it the expression, "a natural child conceived during the marriage". It may be supposed that, for greater convenience, people will continue to speak of an adulterous child, but the term has become far less derogatory than it was.

The innovation is primarily in the principle. Equality is the rule and inequality must be the exception. But if all discrimination between children is done away with, it does not follow that certain differences cannot remain. As Madam Riou-Labrusse has written[109], "The legislator and the jurist have a dual concern for justice and for realism in distinguishing that which, amongst the rights and duties of the parents, is common to all affiliations and must consequently be the object of identical rules, and that which is different and so justifies special rules." These two complementary ideas appear throughout the whole length of the study of the legal position of natural children. Though in principle the effects of the affiliation of natural children are the same as for legitimate children, on the other hand, there are great differences in establishing the affiliation on account of the absence of legal links between the parents.

A. Establishing the affiliation of illegitimate children

In practice the affiliation of legitimate and of illegitimate children is established in different ways. In general, proof of the affiliation of legitimate children is an easy matter. Legitimate birth is proved by the production of a Birth Certificate or by the fact that the child was born of a married woman[110] and that the conception and/or birth took place during the marriage. Such proofs are strengthened by the known facts of the length of the pregnancy and by the child's status.[111] For the legitimate paternity it suffices to apply the traditional presumption, *pater is est quem nuptiae demonstrant*.[112] The father and, since the Law of 3 January 1972, the mother can dispute this presumption or bring an action of disavowal.[113] Proof of affiliation of a natural child is concerned only with paternity and is thus

---

107. On the new law, see Colombet, Jacques Foyer, C Labrusse-Riou and D Huet-Weiller, *Legitimate and natural affiliation*, Paris, Dalloz 1973. J Massip, G Morin and J L Aubert, *The Reform of Affiliation Répertoire Defrénois*.
108. See especially arts. 759 and 760 CC.
109. Report to the Franco-Polish Colloquium of October 1974 at Poznan.
110. On the establishment of legitimate affiliation, see Colombet and Others, No. 88 ff., p. 74 ff. A Weill, no. 465 ff., p. 398 ff.
111. Art. 311-1 CC.
112. Formulated by art. 312 CC.
113. This action, provided for by arts. 318 to 318-2 CC, can only be brought at the end of the legitimation of the child, "when the mother, after the dissolution of her marriage, remarries to the real father of the child."

more difficult to achieve. To quote a distinction made by M. Lambert, among illegitimate children there are some "desired children" and some "children who happen"—some wanted children/and some who are not foreseen, accidental children born of a casual union. There are, or used to be, mothers who are ashamed of their maternity and who seek to hide it. There are, and apparently always will be, fathers who refuse to assume their responsibilities towards the children they have sired.

The Civil Code of 1804 provided for two methods of establishing affiliation, common to both fatherhood and motherhood: voluntary establishment—recognition—and judicial establishment—an action claiming natural paternity[114] or natural maternity.[115]

The Law of 3 January 1972 has not modified appreciably the methods of direct proof of the affiliation of illegitimate children. It has only created a new method of proof of maternity[116], but it has extended its application by excluding all discrimination against adulterous children. On the other hand, the new law has brought in noticeable changes in the methods of indirect proof of affiliation of illegitimate children, which establish it after having denied him legitimate affiliation.

(1) Direct methods of establishing the affiliation of illegitimate children tend to have a certain diversity.

(a) Proof of maternity is the more simple of the two. According to a classical adage, *mater semper certa est*. The Civil Code of 1804 estimated that the biological fact of birth did not suffice to prove the maternal affiliation. It was necessary for the mother to volunteer a formal recognition of her child.[117] If the mother refused, or neglected, to make this recognition, the child could bring an action claiming natural maternity[118] founded on status.

This system was fairly rigid and differed greatly from that provided for by many European laws, which contended themselves with the proof of the Birth Certificate.[119] On the introduction of the new law some voices were raised demanding the alignment of French law with these other legal systems. The National Assembly tried to comply but, following a difference with the Senate, a compromise solution was found for the new law.[120] It preserved the traditional methods of proof, recognition and enquiry regarding maternity, but the new Article 337 of the Civil Code added that "the Birth Certificate bearing the name of the mother should be recognised when it is associated with status", that is, when it is reinforced by the traditional elent of the *Nomen*, the *tractatus* and the *Fame*. It is apparent that, in future, this method of proof will become general.

---

114. According to art. 340, this action is only in the case of the abduction of the mother by the defendant.
115. Art. 341 CC.
116. See *infra* p. 94.
117. See C Colombet and Others, No. 173 ff., p. 134 ff.
118. Colombet and Others, No. 191, p. 144.
119. E.g. German law and Swiss law.
120. On this controversy, see Colombet & Others, p. 136 ff., no. 178 ff.

(b) The new Law contains fewer innovations regarding proof of paternity. The Civil Code of 1804 had authorised fathers to recognise their illegitimate children by a signed deed or by will.[121] The rule is the same today, except that Article 335, which formerly prohibited the recognition of adulterous children, has been repealed. This recognition of paternity, as also that of maternity, is not subject to any special basic condition, such as the semblance of affiliation. In particular, the natural mother is not able to oppose this recognition, as may be done in certain foreign laws.[122] If the father refuses or neglects to recognise his paternity the child can bring an action claiming natural paternity, under the new Articles 340 to 340-7, but this action is subject to stringent conditions[123] with short limitation periods.[124] In addition, the defendant can oppose the action by claiming that there is no case to answer in particular, on account of the mother's known misconduct.[125] In this instance French law is more restrictive than some foreign laws which attach greater importance, for example, to status and blood tests between the defendant child and the supposed father. These cannot be regarded as positive proof in substantive law[126] but they can be considered negative proof sufficient to defeat the claim.

(2) Indirect methods of establishing affiliation are quite different from the direct methods. To begin with, indirect methods aim at upsetting the apparent legitimacy of a child and thus demonstrate an illegitimate affiliation, frequently adulterous. They can either be used to enable legitimation by the true father, or merely to demonstrate the biological fact. The latter will now be examined. There will be no discussion regarding the mother's action to dispute paternity, which is one of the innovations of the new law, because such an action can only be brought at the end of legitimation by the mother's second husband.[127] Prior to 1972 the methods of proof were well known. Thus there was the action in disavowal of paternity[128], the action to dispute status and the action for nullity of marriage. One of the chief objects of the new legislation was to enable more thorough research into the biological facts. It was therefore usual to call in question the apparent legitimacy founded on the over frequent use of the presumption 'pater is est quem nuptiae demonstrant'. In this sense although the Law of 3 January 1972 maintained the presumption of legal paternity[129], this was reduced in scope. It even became possible to speak of the 'death' of this presumption.

---

121. Former art. 334 CC.
122. E.g. in Polish law.
123. Abduction or rape, wrongful seduction, written documents for the unequivocal establishment of paternity, notorious concubinage and participation of the putative father in the maintenance of the child. Art. 340.
124. Two years following the birth, and two years following majority. Art. 340-4.
125. Notorious misconduct or relations with another individual, the physical impossibility of being the father, negative proof by blood tests or other certain medical method. See Bl Heno, The diminishing importance of the plea of no case to answer, JCP (1975) 2706 and references cited there.
126. As in German law.
127. On this action see Colombet and Others, no. 123 et seq., p. 97 et seq.
128. G. Champenois, "Has the Law of 3 January 1972 suppressed the presumption 'pater is est quem nuptiae demonstrant' ", JCP 1975 I 2686.
129. Art. 312, para. 1 CC.

(a) First, it has become easier for the father to bring an action in disavowal of paternity.[130] This action is no longer limited by case-law. The second paragraph of Article 312 states that the mother's husband "can disavow the child by legal proceedings if he can justify the action by facts showing that he could not be the father of the child", which is very wide in scope. In addition, the limitation periods have been lengthened.[131]

(b) A newer change was made in Article 313-1, which set aside the presumption of *pater is est* on occasions when the child is registered for civil status without stating the name of the husband, and only has status with regard to his mother.[132] In such a case it is assumed that the mother has not given the name of her husband because he is not the father of the child. There have been severe criticisms of this provision[133], emphasising that a married woman with malicious intentions could thus deny a child to her husband when he is the rightful father. This does not appear to be a serious risk and Article 313-2, in paragraph 2, permits either spouse to claim that the presumption of paternity should be re-established on the grounds that, during the legal period of conception, relationships took place between the spouses confirming the paternity of the husband.[134] However, discussion continues regarding the exact sphere of application of Article 313-1 and the question arises as to whether it should be extended to include other theories such as when the mother, indicated in the Birth Certificate by her maiden name, has not given any status to the child, and the maternity has been declared by a Court.[135]

(c) The new Article 334-9 of the Civil Code[136] has been the most hotly debated. This provides that "every recognition is null and void and all legal claims are inadmissible when the child already has an established legitimate affiliation." On the face of it, this text does not raise difficulties. The legislator intended that legitimate affiliation established jointly by the two normal methods of proof should not be subject to suspicion and could not be put at issue by a third party.[137] This is the price of family peace. However, this Article has been interpreted in the opposite sense, that is, that legitimate affiliation can be attacked when it only rests on the Birth Certificate without status also. There are two variations of this interpretation: either that legitimate affiliation fails automatically[138] as the result of a recognition by a third party or by a Court action against the real father; or

---

130. Art. 312, para. 2; art. 314, paras. 2 & 3 and art. 325. See Colombet and Others, no. 105 ff., p. 84.
131. Art. 316 and 316-1 CC.
132. See G Champenois, art. cited above no. 53 ff., and the references there cited.
133. See M L Rassat, "Critical comments on the law of 3 January 1972" *Revue trimestrielle de droit civil*, 1973, no. 54, p. 245.
134. For one of the first applications of this article see *Tr Gr inst Angers*, 21 May 1974, D 1975-323, note by H Souleau.
135. On this controversy, see G. Champenois, no. 60 ff.
136. For a very complete bibliography of the doctrinal controversy, see Champenois, no. 14, note 18.
137. This article should be compared with art. 322.
138. In this sense, see J Foyer, report cited above, p. 76. Dagot and Spiteri, JCP 1972 I. 2464, no. 67.

that a Court had not been required to mediate in the disagreement over the affiliation.[139] This dispute has not yet been settled but, if this interpretation is accepted in one of its two forms, the true father will be able fairly easily to rebut the presumption of legitimacy and have a natural affiliation declared. Thus, broadly speaking, it will be possible to establish an illegitimate affiliation, even if adulterous. This would be of little interest in the abstract. It would hardly be worth pursuing unless it were to have the expected concrete effects.

B. The effects of illegitimate affiliation

The desire to assimilate illegitimate children to legitimate children, as proclaimed by Article 334, is easier said than done. Various practical and theoretical obstacles get in the way—the absence of a stable family unit, affiliation established in regard to only one parent, usually the mother, rivalry between legitimate and illegitimate children of the same parent, and so on. Thus, the legislator has had to adopt this principle to the specific position of the illegitimate child. If on the whole he has only been able to provide for objective differences, in certain cases he has had to retain some discriminations.

(1) The differences between the legal position of the legitimate child and the illegitimate child are of a technical kind. In principle there cannot be legal equality between the mother and the father because the identity of the latter is not always known. Neither is it possible to attempt to emulate the legitimate family, because the illegitimate family does not exist, apart from the relatively rare cases of stable concubinage. The Law of 1972 thus wished above all to be realistic and this led to the granting of priority to the natural mother, who is usually the only one to concern herself with the child, except eventually to grant rights to the father. In principal the illegitimate child is entitled to the same rights and obligations as the legitimate child: name, parental authority, legal administration and guardianship, maintenance and rights of succession, but the organisation of these rights is appreciably different.

(a) Instead of automatically taking the name of the father, like a legitimate child, the illegitimate child takes the name of the parent to whom he has been affiliated.[140] In practice, this will most often be the mother, chiefly because the Birth Certificate is her proof of maternity.[141] All the same, the child can take the name of his natural father, either when affiliation is established simultaneously[142], or when it has been established later with regard to the father. In the latter case, the father's name will be substituted.[143] The child can have the issue decided when the Court considers the affiliation on a claim presented during the minority of the child, or during the two years following his majority.[144] The name being a matter of usage rather than of right, the rules have been made as flexible as possible.

---

139. In this sense, Massip, Morin and Aubert, no. 74, 52 bis and 98.
140. Art. 334-1 C Civ.
141. Art. 337. See *supra* p. 95.
142. Art. 334-1 CC.
143. Art. 334-2 CC.
144. Art. 333-3 CC. On all these theories, see Colombet & Others, No. 489 ff, p. 263.

(b) It was also so in respect of parental authority.[145] In this case the principles were not stated in the Law of 3 January 1972, but in the Law of 4 June 1972. The new Article 374 of the Civil Code lays down that "the parental authority is exercised by either the father or mother who has voluntarily recognised the child, if it has been recognised by only one of them." In practice, this will be the mother. However, in the case of double recognition, article 374 in paragraph 2 provides a newer solution, stating that "the parental authority is exercised entirely by the mother". The priority of the mother is thus enshrined in the law. Yet, at the request of one or other of the two parents, or of the public authority, the Court may decide that the parental authority shall be exercised by the father alone or by the father and the mother jointly. On this last principle alone is there similarity between the legitimate family and the natural family.

(c) With regard to the legal administration and guardianship, a certain resemblance exists between the two kinds of family. In effect, the law has unified the regime of the split family, for whatever reason that may be so. In effect, the laws of 4 June 1964 and 4 June 1970 distinguish between two principles: first legal administration under judicial control. This applies to every illegitimate child whether simple or adulterous[146], whose affiliation has been established with regard to one or both of his parents. In that case the legal administrator will normally be the mother[147]: secondly, guardianship, which applies to the illegitimate child "if he has neither a father or a mother who has voluntarily recognised him".[148] Before 1972 this regime necessarily applied to adulterous children who were prohibited from having their affiliation established. This prohibition having been lifted by the law of 1972, it seemed that the scope of guardianship would have to be exceptional. This regime only applies to those children born of unknown parents, or whose parents are both dead, or for whom the guardianship judge considers this regime to be the most advantageous.

(d) Maintenance obligations do not require, in principle, any special measures for adaptation. Once affiliation is established, a reciprocal duty of maintenance exists between parents and children. Moreover, Article 203 of the Civil Code, governing maintenance obligations for children born of the marriage extend equally to illegitimate children. In this way illegitimate children are enabled to obtain necessaries from their mother or their natural father, whether the latter is married or unmarried. These necessaries will be calculated with regard to the needs of the creditor and the resources of the debtor[147]; allowance for board may be indexed as a matter of course by the judge.[148] The creditor can be deprived of his allowance, wholly or in part, if he has failed seriously in his obligations towards the debtor.[149] This liability is borne by the heirs of the debtor after his

---

145. See Colombet & Others, no 476 ff., p. 258; R Legeais, *op. cit.*, no. 133.
146. Art. 389-2. 3 CC, *rpr* with an orphan child or issue of divorce parents, *supra*, p. 94.
147. At least when the parental authority is not conferred on the father, *supra*, p. 88.
148. Art. 390, para. 2 CC.
147. Art. 208, para. 1 CC.
148. Art. 208. para. 2, CC.
149. Art. 207 CC.

death.[150] On all these points the judicial regime is exactly the same for both legitimate and illegitimate children.[151]

However, a particular difficulty remains in the fact that illegitimate children cannot always establish proof of the paternity of their father, either because of the latter's refusal to recognise them, or because the child cannot establish one of the five cases for bringing an action claiming paternity, under Article 340. These children therefore find themselves deprived of an appreciable safeguard. Before 1972 this situation was especially serious for adulterous children. A law of 15 July 1955, inspired by the German model in force in Alsace-Lorraine, had enabled them to claim in the Court for necessaries from the man who had had relations with their mother during the time of conception, "without this action having the effect of claiming the link of affiliation, the establishment of which remains prohibited". This "little action" had as its only objective to reveal a *Zahlvaterschaft*, a paternity reduced to maintenance only. To begin with, this limited paternity had been reserved for adulterous or incestuous children but, on the eve of the law of 1972, the Court of Appeal extended it legally to simple illegitimate children.[152] Contrary to the German law[153], the law of 3 January 1972 preserved this action, but renamed it an action for subsidies to show the change in its basis. When speaking of a demand for necessaries a paternity is implied, apparent if not definite, in the debtor. The action for subsidies is no longer based on proof of paternity but on a risk or possibility of paternity.[154] It is in this manner that a claim can be brought against the person "who has had relations with the mother during the legal period of conception" and the judge can give judgment against him without being certain that the defendant is the true father of the child. This action has been much discussed, all the more because in a first draft of the law provision was made for the possibility of condemning jointly all those who had cohabited with the mother during the pregnancy of the child. This "pluri-paternity" involved infringement of privacy and, in its definitive version Article 342-3 only admits such an order for joint liability if there are faults on the part of the defendants or previous undertakings made by them.

The survival of this action marks the limits of the idea of legal equality for, in stating the principle, the legislator has had to admit that it does not always exist in fact.

(e) There is another obstacle to equality, of a different kind, in regard to succession. In principle the illegitimate child has the same rights of succession and can receive equal generosity as the legitimate child. The reform is important and has not been won without conflict. The passing of the inheritance on death is doubtless the touchstone of equality. Conservation of the assets in legitimate families is deeply rooted in people's minds yet, in spite of all, Article 757 provides that in future—"the natural child has, in general, in the succession from his parents and other ascendants, as well as from his brothers and sisters and other

---

150. Art. 207-1 CC.
151. See Colombet and Others, no. 510 ff, p. 269.
152. Civ 20 May 1969, D 1969, 429, Concl. Lindon, note Colombet.
153. See Pedamon, "The German law of 19 August 1969 on the legal condition of the illegitimate child: model for a reform of French law?", D 1971, I, 153.
154. See Colombet and Others, no. 518 ff., p. 273.

relations, the same rights as a legitimate child." There are some provisions influenced by the same principle, that accord to the illegitimate child the same privileges[155] and the same reserve as that of legitimate children.[156] The importance of these new rules is all the greater since the 1972 law recognised the existence of the natural family alongside the legitimate family.[157] The illegitimate child can thus claim the inheritance of the succession from his grandparents, uncles and natural cousins, whereas under the old law he could only inherit from his natural parents and, eventually, from his natural brothers and sisters. In French society of today this rule has greater theoretical importance than practical.

(2) Equality pushed to extremes risk provoking positive wars of succession. The law of 1972 maintained discriminations. However, these were not so much between legitimate and illegitimate children as between simple natural children and adulterous children. In fact the new Articles 759 and 760 revived the idea of adulterous children in cases where the child is in competition with legitimate children or with the father's surviving spouse. These articles provide that, in such a case, the child "one of whose parents was at the time of conception linked by ties of marriage to another person" will receive one half of that which he would have received had he been legitimate.[158] The adulterous child on the father's, or on the mother's side, is thus not deprived of all rights of succession as formerly, but merely has them diminished. These articles have caused real headaches in cases where the adulterous child is in competition with the legitimate children of two different spouses. It should be noted that this discrimination is relative since it only protects the direct victims of adultery, that is, the deceived spouse and abandoned legitimate children. But against other successors, the adulterous child recovers his full rights of succession and will have the same rights as a legitimate child with regard to grandparents, uncles and aunts, or children of a previous marriage.[159]

III. Divorce

"During more than two centuries of France's concern with the problems of divorce, the same ideologies confronted each other, the same arguments were put forward and the same sensibilities were affected", declared M Jean Foyer during debates on the law of divorce.[160]

It is true that divorce has always been discussed in France and has had a fairly active history.[161] Divorce was prohibited by law before the Revolution for the

---

155. Art. 908 CC.
156. Art. 913 CC.
157. Art. 334, para. 2. On the incidence on succession of this article see Colombet & Others, no. 235 ff., p. 167.
158. This was the solution adopted before 1972 for simple illegitimate children in competition with the legitimate children.
159. On the controversy, see Massip, Morin and Aubert, no. 125, p. 107 and, in the contrary sense, Colombet and Others, no. 317, p. 197.
160. Session of 28 May 1975, J O 1975, Debates, p. 3309.
161. A Weill, *op. cit.*, no. 346, p. 277; J Carbonnier, *op. cit.*, no. 39 p. 113.

Roman Catholic religion, which was the religion of the State, condemned divorce as being contrary to the concept of the indissolubility of marriage. On the other hand the law of 20 September 1792 laid down that divorce could be obtained without difficulty by mutual consent, even for simple incompatibility, resulting in fact in unilateral repudiation. The Civil Code of 1804 retained divorce but complicated the procedure, suppressing divorce for incompatibility but bringing in divorce by mutual consent with restrictive conditions and again judicial separation, which had been abolished by the Revolution. The Restoration, by a law of 8 May 1816, re-established the Catholic religion as the official religion of the country and divorce was again abolished.

Divorce was finally reintroduced by the famous law of 18 April 1884, called the Law Naquet after the name of its promoter. It is this law which, with some amendments, became the common law until the most recent law of 11 July 1975.

The new law now being fully operative, it may therefore be useful to explain the two regimes in order to understand better the scope of the reform.

A. Divorce prior to the law of 11 July 1975

Divorce could be obtained, but with difficulty, under the law of 1884. It was considered as a last resort for the difficulties of the spouses. At the outset it was logical for the law to forbid divorce by mutual consent. Despite a certain number of reforms of more or less importance, this concept continued to predominate in the legislation. It ran through all the foundations of divorce, its grounds, its procedure and its effects.

(1) *Grounds for divorce*

Divorce cannot be pronounced by a judge except on grounds provided for by law, but the proceedings can be disrupted by defence pleas. Grounds for divorce are divided by tradition into obligatory grounds and optional grounds.

(a) Obligatory grounds require the Court to grant the divorce when the grounds have been proved by the Petitioner. These are two in number: (i) adultery, when the husband can claim a divorce on account of the adultery of the wife, under Article 229; and when (ii) the wife can claim for divorce on account of the adultery of the husband, under Article 230. The duality of these equal texts results from historical reasons. In the Civil Code system the husband's adultery could not be penalised unless accompanied by a second contributory circumstance, for instance, keeping a mistress in the matrimonial home. On the other hand, the wife's adultery was a ground for divorce in all cases when she had had sexual relations with a third party. The law of 1884 removed this inequality, at least on the civil level[162], but for reasons of convenience allowed the redundancy to remain. A spouse's simple flirtation or imprudence did not constitute adultery but could be regarded as an offence.

---

162. On the other hand differences had remained with regard to the penal law, which have been suppressed by the law of 11 July 1975.

According to Article 231, punishment for bodily harm and defamation comes under the penal law and involves criminal penalties such as imprisonment, the death penalty, solitary confinement with hard labour, imprisonment for life or for a period. Here is involved a serious stain on the family honour. On the other hand, minor convictions of public order are not compulsory grounds for divorce, but may become optional. The strict causes were seldom invoked in practice.

(b) Optional grounds are much more frequent. According to Article 232, bodily harm, cruelty or injuries against one another, when such acts constitute a grave or renewed violation of the duties and obligations of the marriage which render intolerable the maintenance of the conjugal link. This ground has undergone a remarkable evolution. The law of 1884 only provided for very serious bodily harm, cruelty or injuries which conformed with the idea of divorce as a penalty. A law of 20 April 1941, regulated by an Ordinance of 12 April 1945, introduced the idea of divorce as a remedy by considering circumstances which rendered the maintenance of the marriage impossible. In practice, the Courts gave a wide interpretation to these facts. Bodily harm and cruelty, which are often confused, include all material illtreatment, violence or assault and battery. Injuries refer to all faults committed by one of the spouses, all failure to perform the duties and obligations arising from the marriage—attacks on the obligation of fidelity, such as flirtations; to the obligation of help, such as vexatious behaviour, refusal to cook meals, domestic scenes; and to that of cohabitation, such as refusal to consummate the marriage. The catalogue is lengthy.[163] Again, it is necessary that the faults should be such as to cause a shock to the innocent spouse who would feel them as a serious attack on the marriage. Thus, little by little divorce had been made easier to obtain. A certain number of defence pleas remain. These have often been used, with more or less success, to curb the increase of divorces. Thus, the law of 2 April 1941 prohibited spouses from suing for divorce during the three years immediately following the date of marriage. This demurrer, which had little effect, was abolished in 1945. At present there remain demurrers in common law[164], such as prescription, *res judicata* and, above all, the striking out of a suit if the proceedings had been held up for three years, also those fundamental to divorce, such as the death of a spouse, reconciliation and reciprocity of wrongs.

(2) *Procedure for divorce*

It is impossible to study the grounds for divorce without also studying the procedure. Moreover, the forms of procedure have been laid down in the Civil Code and not in the Code of Civil Procedure. The lawgiver of 1884 retained the principle of judicial divorce, underlining the importance of the question, but the procedure remained based on accusation. The competent court is the Court of First Instance, whose jurisdiction is of a public policy. Any clause that delegates competence to another Court or to an arbitrator, is void. In the same way, any

---

163. See A Weill, no. 359 p. 288. For a good synthesis see Mireille Delmas-Marty, "Marriage and Divorce, What do I know?"
164. A Weill, no. 364, p. 297.

compromise is prohibited. This Court is *ratione loci* the domicile of the defendant, in practice, that of the husband.[165] A petition for divorce can only be brought by the spouse who is the victim of a failure to carry out the duties of the marriage, thus allowing the innocent spouse to combat the possible rupture of the conjugal tie. A very detailed procedure has been envisaged, divided into two phases.

(a) The first phase takes place before the President of the Court of Appeal. The procedure opens with a petition, which the spouse had formerly to be present in person; he can nowadays be presented by Counsel.[166] The President then attempts to effect a reconciliation between the spouses. The legislator had hopes that this conciliation would be a means of slowing up divorces, hopes which were not borne out in the event. The spouses must appear in each other's presence, but, before the conciliating magistrate without their Counsel. After this consultation the President may either prepare conciliation proceedings which defeat the action, or may make an order for adjournment to give the spouses a period of reflection, or he may prepare a non-conciliation proceeding and make an order granting the right to file a petition to the Court. In the last two cases, the President can order temporary measures for the separate residence of the spouses, the custody of the children, and for an allowance *ad litem*.

(b) The second phase takes place in the Court. The proceedings follow the usual rules of civil procedure, but there are some particular features, namely, proceedings are debates held in camera. there is an opportunity for the defendant to file a counter-claim[167], judgment may be stayed[168], and some forms of proof are not permitted, such as confessions, sworn statements and children's evidence. Judgment is pronounced either on the exclusive wrongs of the defendant or on the reciprocal wrongs of the spouses. It is subject to appeal or to a petition to quash the judgment and, contrary to common law, this petition suspends the execution; further, acquiescence in the judgment and withdrawal of the petition are prohibited. The definitive judgment has absolute authority over the matter before the Court with regard to third persons, and is given publicity.

As can be seen, the above procedure is intended to be dissuasive on account of its formalities and its effects.

(3) *The effects of divorce*

The effects of divorce also contain the idea of a penalty. Current parlance continues to speak of the innocent spouse and the guilty spouse, of divorce for the

---

165. According to art. 108 CC in the edition of the law of 11 July 1975, "the married woman has in no case another domicile other than that of her husband."

166. Before a law of 3 December 1970 this petition had to be brought personally. This was supposed to have a dissuasive effect which was not achieved. However the new art. 234 lays down that this personal appearance before the Court is obligatory when the petitioner asks for provisional measures. See Michelle Gobert on the new art. 234 of the CC, JCP 1972, 2, 2476.

167. The number of counter-claims has been growing steadily since the beginning of the century and thus, in the words of Carbonnier, marks "the cross-thrust of a legal penalty as in a duel", *Droit civil*, 8th ed. 1969, p. 143, no. 47.

168. This stay is possible in all cases except those where the petition for divorce is based on a criminal charge. It is clear evidence of the anxiety of the legislator to curb the incidence of divorce.

benefit of the one and on account of the misdeeds of the other. The first effect of divorce is to dissolve the marriage for the future while keeping alive the consequences of the past. Thus, each spouse recovers his liberty and is no longer held to the duties of fidelity, help and assistance and are able to remarry, except that the wife must respect the period of widowhood.[169] The wife recovers the usage of her own name, with one exception.[170]

Equally, divorce results in changes in the financial relations of the spouses, such as the dissolution of the common fund and changes in the distribution of the succession.[171] It also has effects with regard to the children, for example, the granting of parental authority to the parent who is granted custody, and the award of the right of access and supervision to the other spouse.[172]

However, the most characteristic effect of divorce used as a penalty is the granting of alimony under Article 301. According to that article, if the spouses gain no financial advantage from the divorce petition, or if those stipulated are not sufficient for the spouse who has obtained the divorce, the Court can grant an allowance for maintenance from the assets of the other spouse not exceeding a third of that spouse's income. The legal basis of this allowance has been much discussed. It is generally recognised as being of a mixed nature, being both for maintenance and as compensation.[173] In addition, the innocent spouse can be awarded supplementary damages[174] independently of all other reparation due from the spouse against whom the divorce has been granted. If the divorce has been awarded on the basis of reciprocal wrongs neither of the spouses are entitled to the allowance or the above mentioned damages. It is against this conception of divorce as exclusively a penalty that the new law has been framed.

B. Divorce according to the concept in the law of 11 July 1975

Before considering the contents of the new law, it may be useful to look into the reasons for it. The more or less distant origins of divorce reform must be sought in a basic criticism of the old system. Grounds for complaint come to light, on the one hand against the foundation itself of the legislation and, on the other, against its practical application. For a long time past men of very different outlook—politicians, jurists, journalists, novelists and kindred spirits—have risen up against the principle of divorce as a penalty. This was criticised as making marriage a cause of guilt and of causing loss of individual liberty. Marriage had been described by Montaigne as "a market to which only the entrance is free". It was also felt that it was absurd to expect people to remain married when they no longer loved, or, worse, hated each other. On the contrary, others proposed substituting divorce as a penalty by divorce for objective

---

169. According to art. 296 CC, the wife must respect a delay of 300 days after the decision granting her a separate domicile.
170. Art. 299 CC. The Court of Appeal recognises that the husband may authorise his wife to retain the use of his surname.
171. Arts. 765, 766 and 767 CC.
172. Art. 373-3. See *supra* p. 90.
173. See Weill no. 416, p. 330 and references cited in the footnotes.
174. These damages, added by the law of 2 April 1941, are an application of art. 1382 CC and have a compensatory character.

reasons: for breakdown of marriage which could be used as a remedy.[175] This last concept is open to various shades of reasoning, the most absolute being the objective reason.[176] In particular, many criticised the prohibition of divorce for unsoundness of mind, which obliged the sane spouse to remain chained to an insane person. It was also felt that restrictions on divorce frequently led to immoral behaviour as one, or even both, spouses could be led to live in extra-marital relationships and possibly bring adulterous children into the world.

Apart from the principles, even the methods of divorce were contested. The basic idea of judicial divorce was queried as resulting in the dramatisation, and poisoning of, the relations between the spouses.[177] Spouses who had agreed initially on divorce were apt to be carried away by the atmosphere of the proceedings and exaggerated minor grievances, even invent them from nothing, so that a separation which could have been peaceable, could lead to implacable hatreds. In addition, divorce by mutual consent, prohibited by the law of 1884, began to appear little by little in judicial practice. Spouses agreed on divorce, they then invented fictitious grievances, wrote letters about false injuries, sometimes dictated by their respective lawyers, and the judges closed their eyes to the comedy[178], whose nature discredited the institution of justice itself.

A number of minds in the legal and para-legal world regretted that the judge's only mission was to apportion the wrongs between the spouses. It would have been preferable if magistrates and judges could have sought amicable solutions in agreement with the spouses in the interests of the family and, especially, of the children. These various criticisms led to the Government proposing a reform of the divorce law.

There have been different versions of this reform, which has not been easy to achieve. In 1973 M. Taittinger, then Minister of Justice, asked Dean Carbonnier to draw up a draft law.[179] The text was considerably modified in form as in content in a draft law presented to Parliament in April 1975.[180] This draft was itself the subject of discussion, often passionate, in the National Assembly[181] and in the Senate, between those supporting the emancipation of divorce and defenders of the sanctity of marriage.[182] After opposition from the two Assemblies, the texts had to be edited by a Commission composed of a balanced mixture of opinions.

In its general outlook the text adopted accords with the intentions expressed by the Government, which had the dual burden of being realistic and of safeguarding

---

175. Divorce as a penalty and divorce on account of marriage breakdown in French and German comparative law. *Annales de la Faculté de Droit de Strasbourg*, T XXII, Dalloz 1969.
176. Intolerable life in common, art. 142 Swiss CC. Irremediable failure of marriage. On divorce, the English Reform Act of 1969.
177. See Jean Carbonnier, *Droit civil*, no. 47, p. 143.
178. In the draft law placed before the National Assembly, the Keeper of the Seals assessed the number of divorces by mutual consent at one-fourth of the total number. On this practice, see C Chesne, H Mazeaud, *Divorce by Forced Consent*, D 1963, 1 141.
179. See Jean Carbonnier, *The question of divorce*, *Mémoire à consulter* D 1975, 1, 115.
180. Recorded on 17 April 1975 in the President's Office of the National Assembly, 2nd ordinary session 1974-1975, no. 1560.
181. See account rendered of the session of 29 May 1975, *Le Monde*, 31 May 1975, p. 13.
182. See especially the declaration of M Jean Foyer, cited above, and that of M Schumann in the Senate.

the essential principles of the family, as well as the anxiety of harmonising the law with the habits and ideals of the time.[183]

Technically, the law of 11 July 1975 wished to make divorce "less dramatic" and "not a matter of fault". These ends are again shown in the triple scheme of divorce, that is, the grounds, the procedure and the effects.

Grounds for divorce[184]

The legislator wished to act in an empirical manner and to be able to find answers for the varied behaviour patterns of the spouses. Divorce as a penalty is not wholly abandoned, but is allied to the application of divorce as a remedy. There are three grounds for divorce[185]:

Mutual consent
Breakdown of marriage
Fault

In divorce by mutual consent[186] the spouses can petition for divorce jointly, without revealing the reasons for the petition. This is provided for in the hope of ending the former judicial comedy. This form of divorce can take two forms. According to Article 230 the spouses can present their petition jointly; or the claim can be presented by one of the spouses and accepted by the other, in accordance with Article 233. In this procedure the spouses must present to the judge a plan concerning the future consequences of the divorce. The new law has aimed at certain safeguards to ensure that the divorce is approached seriously. Thus, the petition cannot be presented within the first six months of marriage. Even so, the judge must be convinced that the spouses' agreement is real and made with freewill. It must also be verified that the safeguards meet the interests of the case.

Divorce on the basis of the breakdown of the marriage was the subject of the most animated debates. This ground also can take two forms: one is that the spouses have in fact lived apart for more than six years[187]; the other is when the mental faculties of one of the spouses have been, for more than six years, so gravely impaired that communal life has ceased to exist and there is no reasonable hope of it being resumed in the future.[188] These provisions are the most substantial innovations in the project. According to the draft[189] they are justified by the necessity of finding solutions for situations which have no obvious outcome. Many members of Parliament have seen in it the risk of repudiation of a spouse. To avoid this serious possibility a hardship clause was introduced by Article 240. The judge can reject such a petition if the other spouse can prove that a divorce would cause exceptional material or moral hardship either for himself on account of age and duration of the marriage, or for the children.[190]

---

183. Draft law cited above, no. 1560, pp. 3 and 9.
184. Note the change in terminology. Instead of "cause" one speaks of "cases".
185. Art. 229 CC.
186. Art. 230-236 CC.
187. Art. 237 CC.
188. Art. 238, para. 1 CC.
189. Draft no. 1560, p. 4.
190. Op. cit., p. 5. This clause will result in different solutions according to the individual considerations of the judge.

Divorce on the ground of fault[191], a more traditional provision, has been retained for the sake of realism. Neither public opinion nor the victim himself would understand if, according to the draft law[192] he were prevented from proving his innocence and obtaining the redress to which he or she felt entitled. However, the law has modernised the definition of 'fault', on the lines of the law of 1941, interpreting it as the grave or renewed violation of the duties and obligations of marriage rendering cohabitation intolerable[193]. According to the new article 243, the conviction of a spouse for a criminal offence is still a ground for divorce. On the other hand, the ground of adultery has disappeared.[194] The rest of the draft is on much the same lines as the earlier law.

There has been less modification of the procedure. The authors of the new law have hesitated between a purely accusatory procedure and a more inquisitorial one. Paradoxically, there are tendencies in both directions. On the one hand, the introduction of divorce by mutual consent places an important limitation on the judge's powers of intervention but, on the other hand, certain provisions greatly increase his ability to act.[195]

For the rest, the Court of First Instance Appeal remains the sole authority for dealing with divorce[196], but a judge of that Court will be delegated to deal with matrimonial affairs.

However, contrary to the preceding law, all methods of proof are admitted, including confession, with the exception of letters or statements obtained by fraud or by unlawful entry into the home or by the invasion of privacy. Also, it is possible to oppose the procedure in divorce by mutual consent, where the judge acts as a conciliator.[197] The same applies to cases where the judge's powers are reduced, and to the two other procedures where divorce is contested and conciliation is exercised, as well as in provisional measures.[198]

In article 260 of the Civil Code the consequences of divorce were noted by a return to the idea of divorce as a penalty. The new law aimed at avoiding maintenance being awarded on the conviction for a wrong. On the contrary it wished to see the financial rights of divorced spouses relying on compensation for the imbalance created for the spouses on the breakdown of the marriage.[199] As already stated[200], this radical change is accompanied by a change in terminology: for the idea of "allowance for necessaries" is now substituted "compensatory provision"[201] which is assessed on the needs of the creditor and the resources of

191. Arts. 242-246 CC.
192. *Op. cit.* p. 5.
193. Art. 242 CC.
194. It has disappeared from among the automatic grounds for divorce, and also as a criminal offence. Art. 17, law of 22 July 1975.
195. Notably art. 238 which permits the judge to reject as a matter of course a petition for divorce on account of unsoundness of mind if the divorce risks consequences that would be too serious for the illness of the spouse.
196. Art. 247 CC.
197. According to art. 232, para. 2, he can refuse confirmation if it is proved that the agreement insufficiently preserves the interests of the children or of one of the spouses.
198. Art. 251, 254 CC.
199. Art. 270 CC.
200. *Supra*, p. 102.
201. Art. 270 CC.

the debtor.[202] This can consist of a lump sum or of an annuity, for which there are detailed regulations.[203] This provision has not altogether lost its character of compensation. Paragraph 1 of article 280-1 states, in fact, that the spouse at fault who has occasioned the divorce has no right to compensatory provision, but the spirit of the reform reappears in the following paragraph which allows such a spouse an indemnity, as an exception, if, taking account of the duration of the marriage and of the assistance given to the other spouse's profession, it would appear contrary to equity to refuse him all pecuniary compensation on divorce.

As regards other effects of divorce the new law is less original. Divorce dissolves the marriage for the future, each of the spouses resumes his own name, with certain exceptions.[204] The custody of the children of the marriage is decided in the light of the children's interest[205]; the obligations with regard to the children remain in their entirety.[206]

However, it is clear that the consequences of divorce differ according to the type of divorce involved. In this respect divorce for fault is closer to the older law and, to that extent, the role of the judge is more important[207] while, in divorce by mutual consent the will of the spouses is the determining factor.[208]

Such is the broad outline of family law in France. In considering whether the changes are good, or final, one may wonder whether one should return to the prophesy of Amiel, repeated by Montherlant: "The age of majority will become lower, the barrier of sex will fall, and democracy will arrive at the absurd in submitting decisions on the greatest things to those who are the least capable." Perhaps we should be more optimistic for society. Only time, the sovereign judge, will tell.

---

202. Art. 271 CC.
203. Arts. 272-279 CC.
204. See art. 264, para. 2.
205. Art 287 CC.
206. Art. 288 CC.
207. Arts. 265-267-1.
208. Arts. 268-268-1.

CHAPTER V. THE REFORM OF FAMILY LAW IN GERMANY

by Dieter Giesen

A. The relation between Article 6 and Article 3 of the Basic Law[1]

Many reforms, actual and projected, in the field of Family Law are at present being introduced or discussed in almost every State in Europe. The major areas affected by these reform measures are Marriage Law on the one hand and the Law of Parent and Child on the other.

In the Federal Republic of Germany the field of Family Law, and likewise the reform of this area, is subject to certain basic values and considerations, deriving from the German Constitution, the Basic Law of 23rd May 1949.

In relation to Family Law, two articles of the Basic Law are of special importance: Article 6 governing the protection of marriage and the family, and Article 3 providing for the legal equality of the sexes.

Article 6 reads:

(1) Marriage and the family enjoy the special protection of governmental institutions.
(2) The care and education of the children are the natural right of the parents and the duty to provide for them lies primarily upon them. The community of the State watches over their exercise.
(3) Children may be removed from the family against the wishes of those entitled to bring them up only on the authority of a law if those entitled fail to bring them up or if for other reasons the children are threatened with neglect.
(4) Every mother has a claim to the protection and care of the community.
(5) Extra-marital children are to receive by legislation the same conditions for their physical and mental development and their position in society as legitimate children.

Article 3 reads:

(1) All men are equal before the law.
(2) Men and women have equal legal rights.
(3) No person shall suffer prejudice or gain preferment by reason of sex, descent, race, language, home and social origins, beliefs or religious or political convictions.

The relation between Articles 6 and 3 of the Basic Law will be discussed by way of introduction.

---

1. *Grundgesetz*, abbreviated to GG subsequently in the text.

1. Article 6(1) is primarily concerned with marriage and the family, while Article 3(2)(3) deals with the relationship between men and women generally, irrespective of whether they are married or not. Therefore, as far as marriage and the family are concerned, Article 6(1) is the more specific provision.[2] On the other hand, the rule of legal equality of the sexes (Article 3(2)(3)) is also valid within marriage and the family.

2. Marriage and the family are given special protection by the State under Article 6(1). This provision is in line with Article 119(1) of the old Constitution of Weimar[3] of 11th August 1919. In this provision for the first time a European State protected marriage and the family by a constitutional rule. The origin of Article 6 shows that the constitutional legislator did not set out to establish a contrast between Articles 6 and 3, but saw the legal equality of the sexes as the basis of marriage and the family.

Article 6(1) provides for:

(a) the protection of the specific private sphere of marriage and the family from outside pressure, by the State. This has both negative and positive aspects: the State must (i) refrain from any measures which might damage the institution of marriage and the family, and (ii) take any corresponding action to benefit marriage and the family.[4]

(b) therefore Article 6 is also the expression of a basic value for the whole area of private and public law concerning marriage and the family, and

(c) the "guarantee of an institution", that is, the guarantee of the continuous existence of the legal institutions of marriage and the family under the special protection of State power.

3. Considering these three important aspects of Article 6(1), one notices that the protection of the private sphere is concerned with the relationship between the spouses and the State, while the "guarantee of an institution" protects the basic structure of marriage and the family and thereby constitutionally guarantees a minimum of rules for Marriage Law and Family Law. This minimum of rules determines the relations between husband and wife or between the members of a family. However, this depends on what one calls the "basic structure" of marriage and the family.

Generally speaking, leading lawyers in Germany almost unanimously agree that the legal institution of marriage and the family provides for a minimum of compulsory rules. These rules bind everybody, even in a pluralistic society. And although the German Federal Constitutional Court has emphasized that ideas of natural or religious law on marriage and the family cannot themselves be the only basis for a discussion of constitutional law[5], certain structural elements in the traditional concepts of the institutions of marriage and the family as handed

---

2. Cf. Federal Constitutional Court (*Bundesverfassungsgericht*), BVerfGE 6, 55(71); for further information on the powers of this court see Wiltraut Rupp-v Brünneck, "The Federal Constitutional Court (1972)" 20 *The American Journal of Comparative Law*, 387-403, 389 ff.
3. *Weimarer Reichsverfassung.*
4. Cf. BVerfGE 6, 55 (71 ss,); 24, 119 (135).
5. BVerfGE 10, 59 (81); but cf. also BVerfGE 28, 324 (336) and already BVerfGE 6, 389 (434-435).

down from generation to generation are still regarded to be protected and guaranteed by the German Basic Law of 1949. According to the Federal Constitutional Court and the German legal literature, the essential parts of such basic facts guaranteed by the German constitution are threefold: (i) marriage is concluded by contract between one man and one woman, (ii) the spouses must adjust to the obligations of undivided conjugal society (*coniugium* and *consortium*), and (iii) marriage is—as a rule—intended for life.[6]

4. For the further protection of the basic structure of marriage as a legal institution, Article 6(1) guarantees (as mentioned above) that the State will protect the specific private sphere of marriage and the family from outside pressure. In this private sphere, the spouses' right of self-determination takes precedence. The spouses' autonomy and right of self-determination as required by the Basic Law can only be guaranteed, however, if intended State measures conform to the principle that the spouses—within the limits of the essential facts mentioned above—can live their lives as they wish, that is, that the State neither sets out a specific model of marriage as an "official guideline", nor treats husband and wife unequally by directly or indirectly influencing them towards fixed and expected roles. This is something which could happen all too easily if the State favoured the impression that, generally speaking, "good" husbands were expected to work outside the home and that "good" wives should look after and work in the household; or if, on the contrary, the State favoured a policy that "good" husbands and wives ought generally to earn their livings in some profession or ought to work outside the home. Decisions of this kind, as to whether spouses both want to carry on with their professional work after marriage or whether they prefer one partner to earn the necessary living and the other to keep the house, must be left to the discretion of the spouses. The State is only allowed, and obliged, to improve the social conditions in which such decisions can be made in the complete freedom of an equally possible and an equally attractive alternative.[7]

Therefore, Articles 6 and 3 of the German Basic Law, providing respectively for the protection of the basic structures of marriage and the family and for the equality of sexes, must be seen not as contradicting, but as complementing each other. The equality of sexes, therefore, is, in the legal field as well as in social reality, an indispensable precondition for the autonomy of the spouses, since the

---

6. BVerfGE 10, 59 (66); 24, 119 (149-150); 31, 58 (82). J. *Gernhuber*, Lehrbuch des Familienrechts, 1964, Section 3 subsection 5 (p. 22), Section 24 IV 2 (p. 207); K. *Larenz*, Allgemeiner Teil des Buergerlichen Gesetzbuchs, 1967, Section 9 I (p. 111), and P. *Mikat*, Scheidungsrecht in einer pluralistischen Gesellschaft, in: (1970) 17 *Zeitschrift fuer das gesamte Familienrecht* (FamRZ) 333 (334-337), with further references.

7. This problem is now being more fully discussed by the present author's more recent publications: D. *Giesen*, Gleichberechtingungspostulat und Familienschutz im Erwerbsleben, in: *Festschrift fuer Friedrich Wilhelm Bosch*, ed. by F. *Gaul*, W. *Habscheid* and P. *Mikat*, Bielefeld 1976. Special regard to the social law problems involved is being paid in: D. *Giesen*, Family Law and Social Security, with special regard to one-parent families, in: *Social Security and Family Law, with special reference to the lone parent*, ed. by Alec *Samuels* for the United Kingdom National Committee on Comparative Law, in their series of publications, London 1977.

latter can only be achieved by establishing equal opportunities and conditions for both women and men: in their capacity both as spouses and parents, and in the latter case certainly subject to the paramount consideration in Family Law, namely the welfare of the possible offspring, their rights to and needs for a proper upbringing and education, which—wherever this is possible—, can best be achieved within the family rather than anywhere else.[8]

5. For the purpose of promoting the principle of the equality of men and women both before the law and in society, various bodies have been set up to find solutions for the problems involved. There is the "Kennedy Report" of 1963, a report by the Commission on the Status of Women in the USA appointed by the late President Kennedy. The United Nations followed suit and, in 1964, appointed a Commission on the Status of Women which, again in 1964, submitted a report dealing with the Influence of Mass Communication Media on the Formation of a New Attitude Towards the Role of Women in Present Day Society; again, in 1974, the German Federal Parliament set up an Enquête Commission on the Rights of Women in Society, a commission of five members of Parliament and five Expert Members, of which the author is one, to inquire about the legal and social conditions of women in today's society with a view to proposing measures which could be adopted by the Federal Parliament and lead to an improvement both in the legal and, more especially, in the social situation of women in our own society.[9] In September 1974 the British Home Office published a White Paper on "Equality for Women"[10] which set out "what needs to be done by legislation to promote equal opportunities for men and women". This formed the basis of the Sex Discrimination Act, 1975. Earlier, on 14th September 1960 the German Federal Government had already submitted a report "on the situation of women in employment, family and society"[11] and a further report, the German "Governmental Report on Measures for improving the situation of women",[12] was published some ten years later, in 1972. In this Report the situation of women in the fields of education, employment, marriage and the family, social security and agriculture, as well as measures already provided for to improve the situation are discussed and further measures are announced or proposed which are now embodied partly in the Federal Government's Second Report on the Situation of Families in the Federal Republic of Germany[13] and partly in the very interesting and detailed documentation on Women in Family, Profession and Society, of the Federal Statistics Office in Germany.[14]

---

8. A discussion of these problems may be found in: D. *Giesen*, Schutz von Ehe und Familie und Gleichberechtigungspostulat im Erwerbsleben, Paderborn 1977, pp. 9 ff., 15 ff., 39 ff.

9. *Deutscher Bundestag*, Drucksache 7/1148; a first interim report of the Enquête Commission to the German Federal Parliament on the Rights of Women and their social position in present day society is now in its final stages of preparation and will be available to the public shortly after the publication of this paper (in 1977).

10. HMSO, Cmnd. 5724, p. 1.

11. *Bericht der Bundesregierung über die Situation der Frauen in Beruf, Familie und Gesellschaft, Deutscher Bundestag*, Drucksache V/909.

12. *Bericht der Bundesregierung über die Massnahmen zur Verbesserung der Situation der Frau, Deutscher Bundestag*, Drucksache VI/3689.

13. *Bericht über die Lage der Familie in der Bundesrepublik Deutschland, Deutscher Bundestag*, Drucksache 7/3502.

14. *Die Frau in Familie, Beruf und Gesellschaft, Statistisches Bundesamt*, 1975.

B. Equality of the Spouses

1. As pointed out in these Reports and emphasised in reports prepared for the 50th German Lawyers' Congress[15], the biggest, if not the most representative, organisation of German lawyers, the problem of discrimination against women in Germany does not exist so much in the legal as in the social sphere, where some prejudice still continues. In the legal field, almost all discriminatory laws have been gradually removed since 1953 and some of the few relatively unimportant laws which remain will be reformed as soon as the new German Marriage Law of June 14th, 1976, will come into force on July 1st, 1977.[16]

2. No one, especially lawyers from outside the German legal system, can understand the law as it now stands without knowing something of the history of these reforms and of the developments which took place between the crucial years, from 1949 and 1953 to, say, 1970 or 1976.

(a) The basic rule of the legal equality of the sexes was and still is laid down in Article 3(2) and (3) of the Basic Law of 1949. This provision is not merely a programme for future legislation, as was Article 119(1) of the old Constitution of the Weimar Republic, but is a binding rule of constitutional law for all fields of public and private law.[17]

(b) But when this basic article of the German Constitution was passed in 1949, many legal writers expected great difficulties and problems to arise if the rule of the equality of the sexes came into force immediately. This was especially so in the case of Family Law because great parts of the law of matrimonial property and of the law of parent and child, particularly with regard to legitimate and illegitimate children, were not at that time in accordance with the equality rule. Therefore, it was provided in Article 117(1) of the Basic Law of 1949 that all law not in accordance with the equality rule should remain valid until its reform by legislation which reform was to be carried out by March 31st 1953 at the latest.

(c) However, the legislature was unable to adapt the old law to the modern rules of equality within this relatively short period. This led to a situation in which, from March 31st 1953 onwards, the courts had to take over the work of adapting the old Family Law to the new rules of equality.[18] With hindsight one can say that the courts managed this task extremely well and, although being without firm legislative rules, and anticipated legal uncertainty did not occur.

(d) In the meantime the Government and Parliament worked out a family reform bill and this Bill, known as the "Law on Equal Rights of Men and Women in the Field of Civil Law"[19], now usually referred to as the "Equality Act"[20], was passed as Statute on June 18th 1957 and became the law of West Germany on July 1st 1957.

---

15. 50. *Deutscher Juristentag* 1974.
16. *Erstes Gesetz zur Reform des Ehe- und Familienrechts (1. EheRG)*, Bundesgesetzblatt (Federal Statute Book) 1976 I 1421 ss.
17. Wolfram *Müller-Freienfels*, "Family Law and the Law of Succession in Germany", in: (1967) 16 *The International and Comparative Law Quarterly* 410-445 (424).
18. Cf. J Leyser, "Equality of Spouses under the new German Law" (1958), 7 *The American Journal of Comparative Law*, 276-287, p. 278.
19. *Gesetz über die Gleichberechtigung von Mann und Frau auf dem Gebiete des Bürgerlichen Rechts.*
20. *Gleichberechtigungsgesetz.*

3. Generally speaking, the patriarchal idea of Family Law as laid down in Book IV of the old German Civil Code[21] of 1896, which granted to the husband the right to determine finally almost all questions relating to family life, was abolished by this Equality Act of 1957.

In particular, the fields of the relations between husband and wife and of matrimonial property law, were revised with due regard to the principle that married spouses must be treated as equal in all respects before the law.[22]

(a) Thus, the rules of the Civil Code on matrimonial property law were completely reformed by the Equality Act 1957. Under the earlier Civil Code of 1896, the regular statutory matrimonial regime was that of "the husband's administration and usufruct".[23] This permitted the husband, within certain limits, to administer freely most of the wife's property. Furthermore, he was legally entitled to the interest resulting from the use of the wife's property as a kind of compensation for his obligation to maintain her. This was the normal statutory matrimonial regime, much more important than the other four matrimonial regimes, the legally, but not in terms of frequency, most important of which were the "separation of property"[24] and the "community of property"[25].

(b) The Equality Act 1957 now introduced an entirely new statutory regime for matrimonial property, similar to the system introduced by the Scandinavian countries in the 1920s and which is still in force in Sweden, Norway, Denmark, Finland and Iceland.[26] One could call the new German system the "community of surplus"[27] or, to be more precise, "Separation of property with equalisation of gains"[28]; that is, each spouse retains equal and, within certain restrictions[29], independent power to own and administer property during the marriage. At the end of the marriage, for example in the case of divorce, each spouse is entitled to half the surplus, that is, the amount by which the total of the property owned by both of them at the end of the marriage exceeds the value of the property owned by them before the marriage.[30] This matrimonial regime of "separation of property with equalisation of gains" applies whenever the spouses have not adopted one of the other two permitted types, namely separation of property or community of property. Although it is possible to contract out of the statutory system, only a few do so. The same applies to the Scandinavian countries.[31]

---

21. *Bürgerliches Gesetzbuch*, BGB. For further sources, the historical development of Family Law and the spirit and structure of the Civil Code, see W. Müller-Freienfels, *op. cit.*, pp. 409-420, and, more elaborate, The same, *Ehe und Recht*, Tübingen 1962, *in toto*.
22. For a comparative study on the equality of the spouses and matrimonial property see W. Müller-Freienfels, "Equality of husband and wife in Family Law" (1959) 8 *The International and Comparative Law Quarterly* 249-267, p. 261 ff.
23. *Verwaltung und Nutzniessung des Ehemannes*.
24. *Gütertrennung*.
25. *Gütergemeinschaft*. For further introductory information cf. J Leyser, *op. cit.*, p. 277 f.
26. Cf. Inger M Pedersen, "Matrimonial Property Law in Denmark" (1965), 28 *The Modern Law Review*, 137-153, pp. 137f and 140f.
27. *Zugewinngemeinschaft*.
28. *Gütertrennung mit Zugewinnausgleich*.
29. Cf. W. Müller-Freienfels, "Family Law etc", *loc. cit.* p. 426 f.
30. §§ 1373 ff *BGB*. For a detailed discussion see *supra* fn. 4 and J Leyser, *op. cit.* pp. 279-283.
31. Cf. I. M Pedersen, *loc. cit.* p. 139.

(c) The Equality Act altered the law in many respects in the matter of relations between husband and wife. It repealed §1354 *BGB* according to which the husband had the authority to determine all questions relating to matrimonial life. The Civil Code 1900 originally vested all parental power in the father, that is all care for the person, care for the property and power to act as statutory agent for the child.[32] The Equality Act 1957 gave the parental custody to both parents but gave the father a casting vote in cases of disagreement between the spouses and reserved to him alone the right to act as a statutory agent for the child.[33] The reason for this ruling was "less the belief in the father's superiority than the fear that the State may have to be admitted as matrimonial arbiter in default of any other authority."[34] However, under the present law there is now complete equality between both parents in German Family Law. In 1959 the Federal Constitutional Court, which administers the Basic Law[35], held that the new versions of §§ 1628 and 1629(1) *BGB*, as introduced by the Equality Act 1957, were void.[36] The ground for so doing was that, by giving the father the casting vote and the right to act alone as statutory agent for the child, these paragraphs were incompatible with Articles 3 and 6 of the Basic Law, which provide for the equality of the sexes and hold that the care and education of the children vest in both parents as basic rights. Now both parents act as joint statutory agents for the child. In cases of disagreement between the parents in matters of custody, as current German legal practice has developed, each spouse may apply to the Guardianship Court[37] for a decision. However, in order to prevent State intervention in family affairs as far as possible, the Court must choose the proposal of either the husband or the wife.

(d) The Equality Act of 1957 also provided that each spouse had a duty to maintain the other spouse and their family, and that, as a rule, the wife fulfils her duty to maintain by working in the household rather than outside the home. The wife, however, is entitled to earn her living outside the house as far as her household duties permit so to do. These provisions of the Equality Act as embodied in the present German Civil Code[38] still show some bias towards the role of a woman who wants to pursue a gainful employment outside the house. Some German authors argue that these provisions are inconsistent with the principle of the equality of the sexes, but it can also be argued that, on the contrary, these rules are not compulsory but merely guidelines for the spouses who can decide not to follow them.

(e) However, these recommendations made by the legislation a couple of years ago, will be revised again as soon as the already mentioned German Marriage Law of 1976 will come into force (July 1st, 1977); this law deals with the reform of consortium, divorce, and the consequences of divorce; it was passed, after hot debates and substantial concessions on both sides of the two

---

32. § 1626(2).
33. §§ 1628, 1629(1) *BGB*a.F.
34. Cf. W. Müller-Freienfels, "Equality of Husband and Wife, etc." *op. cit.*, p. 256.
35. Cf. W. Rupp-v. Brünneck, *op. cit.*, p. 389 ff.
36. BVerfGE 10, 59. See also *supra* fn 3.
37. *Vormundschaftsgericht*.
38. Sections 1356, 1360 BGB (present version, 1976).

houses of parliament (Bundestag and Bundesrat) in 1975-76[39], and received the signature of the President of the Federal Republic of Germany on June 14th, 1976. One of the reforms of this law is to do away with the traditional concept of the present Civil Code, described above, of a married woman as a housewife who confines herself to her household duties. The new law does so by stressing the right of *both* spouses to have a profession and to work in it, or to pursue some gainful employment outside the house, as long as this does not seriously jeopardise their family life, and especially that of their children.[40]

The new law purports to abolish all that is incompatible with the rule of equality of the spouses. The present Sections 1353 ff. of the German Civil Code are to be reformed by laying more stress on the equality between the spouses and by emphasising the idea of partnership between them.[41] For example, under Section 1355 BGB as in force until June 30th, 1976, the name of the husband became automatically the common name for wife and children; the wife was entitled only to add her maiden name to her husband's and their family's name. The new law, which for that purpose came into force on July 1st, 1976, provides that the spouses should adopt a common family name: either the husband's or the wife's name; and only if the spouses at the time of their marriage before the registrar do not declare themselves what name they are going to adopt, it will be the husband's name that prevails as the common family name.[42]

Another reform measure is provided for in Section 1357 of the new Marriage Law. The present law (still in force until June 30th, 1977), enables the wife to act as statutory agent for her husband in the domestic field, and if, for instance, she purchases food or clothing for herself and the children, the husband is liable for such transactions. "But it is doubtful if this provision is consistent with the equality of the spouses in this day and age."[43] This provision is obviously unsatisfactory if the man runs the house and the wife earns the income, or, perhaps more common in the future, if both spouses have part-time jobs. As "the difference in agency powers granted to husband and wife cannot be justified by the mere fact that one is male and the other is female"[44], the provision of Section 1357 (as it now stands) will be revised by Section 1357 BGB (as amended and in force from July 1st, 1977): The reform measure provides that each spouse may equally carry out proper transactions for domestic purposes, for which then both will jointly be liable.

---

39. The necessary three readings of the bill by the *Bundestag* were completed in December 1975; in January 1976 the *Bundesrat* refused to consent, and made suggestions for a further improvement of the bill, which, after substantial committee work in and of both houses, eventually were accepted by the *Bundestag* on April 9th, 1976, in order to secure the passing of the bill.

40. Section 1356 BGB (as amended by the new Marriage Law of 1976, and effective from July 1st, 1977).

41. For a more detailed discussion of the principles involved cf. D. *Giesen*, Schutz von Ehe und Familie und Gleichberechtigungspostulat im Erwerbsleben, *op. cit.*, pp. 15 ff.

42. Section 1355 BGB (as amended by the Marriage Law of 1976).

43. W. *Müller-Freienfels*, "Family law . . .", *loc. cit.*, p. 426.

44. *Ibidem*, p. 426.

118

C. Divorce

I. Introduction: The situation under the present law

1. Alterations of the existing law of *consortium* appear insignificant when compared with the complete reorganisation of the law of divorce and the consequences of divorce, as eventually passed by the new Marriage Law of 1976.[45] Before drafting the Reform Bill that finally and after many discussions and protracted deliberations led to the new Marriage Law of 1976, the Federal Government considered carefully the new laws of other countries, especially the provisions of the Matrimonial Causes Act 1959 (Australia), which in the meantime was superseded by a completely new legislation (1976), the Matrimonial Proceedings Act 1963 (New Zealand), the Divorce Act 1968 (Canada) and the Divorce Reform Act 1969 (England), now embodied in the Matrimonial Causes Act 1973, together with the highly impressive Anglican Report, which become well-known under its name *Putting Asunder*.[46]

2. In order to understand the extent of the reform measures coming into force on July 1st, 1977, it is advisable to look first at the present divorce law in Germany.[47] The present law is governed by the so-called *matrimonial offence principle*. Under Section 48 of the Marriage Law Act of 1946, a divorce may still be granted on the application of one spouse, if both have been living apart for at least three years preceding the application, but it may not be granted if the petitioner was the cause of the marriage breakdown and the respondent wishes

---

45. BGBl. I. 1421 ff. Effective from July 1st, 1977. The following discussion of the future German divorce law is based on the drafts which were available at the time during which the lectures printed here were prepared and held, i.e. until August 1975; the most important draft was the one of 1973 (for which cf. D. *Giesen*, Divorce Reform in Germany, in: 7 *Family Law Quarterly* 351 ff. (1973)): Deutscher Bundestag, Drucksache 7/650 (*Entwurf eines Gesetzes zur Reform des Ehe- und Familienrechts*). In the meantime, this draft underwent some changes, especially in the field of an incorporeal and financial hardship clause (which was eventually introduced) and concerning a less rigid maintenance law including some kind of a maintenance hardship clause (which finally, although very restrictedly, found its way into the statute book, too). Where absolutely necessary, the text of the 1975 lectures has been adjusted to the new development and situation created by the Marriage Law of 1976, partly, and mainly, by referring the reader, in the footnotes, to the final law which either adopts or alters the measures discussed in the text, partly by re-writing the text itself, where this seemed unavoidable in order to secure a proper understanding by the reader of the developments before and after 1976. For a detailed discussion of the events after August 1975, which eventually led to the acceptance of the reform by a great majority of the German Federal Parliament in both houses, cf. D. *Giesen*, Schutz von Ehe und Familie und Gleichberechtigungspostulat im Erwerbsleben, *op. cit.*, pp. 15 ff., 39 ff., especially notes 31, 33 and 55 ss., with further references both to the parliamentary sources and debates and up-dated legal literature; also cf. H.-J. *Vogel* (Federal Minister of Justice), Das Erste Gesetz zur Reform des Ehe- und Familienrechts vom 14. Juni 1976, in: 23 *Zeitschrift für das gesamte Familienrecht* 481 ff. (1976); a discussion in English can be found in D. *Giesen*, Family Law and Social Security, with special regard to one-parent families, *loc. cit.*, *in toto*.
46. A discussion of this report can be found in: D. *Giesen*, "Objektive Ehezerrüttung—alleiniger Scheidungstatbestand?" in: 13 *Zeitschrift f. d. ges. Fam. R.* 524 ff. (1966).
47. For further introductory information on this point, cf. D. *Giesen*, Divorce Reform in Germany, loc. cit., 351 ss., and the very important article by W. *Müller-Freienfels*, "Family Law etc.", loc. cit., p. 412, 433-442, both with further references.

119

to continue the marriage.[48] A divorce has rarely been granted under this Section and only 5% of all divorce petitions are based on it, so that it is of little practical use. Sections 42 and 43 of the still existing Marriage Law Act 1946 are of greater practical importance. Under Section 42 a spouse may present a petition for divorce if the other has committed adultery; under Section 43, if the other spouse is guilty of causing the breakdown through a "grave matrimonial offence", or other guilty conduct. About 95% of all divorce judgments delivered in 1971 were based on these two grounds[49], both of which come under the "matrimonial offence principle". But it is considered that this principle has proved a failure in court practice and, in many cases, aggravates rather than solves matrimonial problems. According to its precepts, one spouse must accuse the other of adultery or some other guilty conduct in order to obtain a divorce decree. Contentious litigation often results in which one spouse blames the other in order to convince the judge of his or her own innocence. This is an important point, because crucial decisions such as custody, care and control of the children, or the right to claim maintenance, depend on this "fight for a pronouncement of guilt against the other spouse."

3. This "principle of matrimonial offence", which requires the court to judge a spouse's actual guilt in causing the marriage to break down, is a questionable one on account of the difficulty of ascertaining the facts required in order to pronounce guilt and enter a decree. Particularly when both spouses want a divorce and decide between themselves who will plead guilty; falsifying facts and feigning an offence in order to obtain a satisfactory court judgment. Without proof of collusion a judge cannot prevent such suits. The fact that 80% to 90% of divorce actions brought on the ground of adultery or some other matrimonial offence, result from such collusion emphasises the wide gap between law and reality and has resulted in the drive towards reform of the divorce laws. Legal commentators all agree on one point, that the legislature must act.

II. Some Principles of the reform in general

1. The various proposals for reform differ on a number of issues, mainly on what should replace the "matrimonial offence principle". Some reformers want complete contractual freedom for the dissolution of marriage, a demand familiar to readers of John Milton's "Doctrine and Discipline of Divorce" of 1643. Other reformers advocate divorce by mutual consent subject to certain safeguards. The vast majority of reformers would abolish the "matrimonial offence principle", whether or not there is mutual consent and even if the parties do not agree on the dissolution of the marriage, replacing it by the "principle of marriage breakdown". The latter was introduced into English law on 1st January 1970 by the Divorce Reform Act of 1969. It is expected that the proposed new principle

---

48. For further discussion of Section 48, cf. J. Neville *Turner*, "Divorce: Australian and German "Breakdown" Provisions Compared", in: (1969) 18 *The International and Comparative Law Quarterly* 896-930, and Michael *Bohndorf*, "Recent Developments in German Divorce Law", in: (1970) 19 *The International and Comparative Law Quarterly* 705-710.
49. Cf. *Deutscher Bundestag*. 7/650, Tabellenanhang, Teil 1, Tabelle 3, p. 242.

would set more objective standards and do greater justice to human dignity. Whether this will be justified will depend on how the new principle is introduced into the new German divorce law.

2. Three different reform suggestions have been put forward.

(a) The first suggestion is to introduce the "principle of marriage breakdown" by means of a "general rule".[50] The wording was proposed by the Commission on Marriage Law established by the German Protestant Churches and adopted, almost verbatim, by the Roman Catholic study group for marriage law, and was approved by leading legal writers on Family Law. It reads as follows:

> "If the spouses' marital relationship has been destroyed so severely that no restoration of relations compatible with married life can be expected, the marriage may be dissolved on an application filed by one spouse."

This type of "general rule" would permit the judge to consider each marriage on its own merit and would enable him to apply the most appropriate standards for each individual case.[51] On the other hand, the generality of the rule would not offer clear standards to the court or to the parties. It would open the door to varied judicial interpretations, including considerations outside the law, with a danger that the results might depend on local practices or on the judge's personal attitude to dissolution of marriage. It would not eliminate the current problem of collusion, the only difference being that the parties might agree on facts supporting marriage breakdown instead of on facts supporting marital offences. This might seriously jeopardise the stability of the administration of justice.

(b) To achieve stability, another proposal suggests an irrevocable presumption of "marriage breakdown" when the spouses have lived apart for a fixed period of time. Fixed periods of time are not open to manipulation by the parties, their lapse is foreseeable and this would prevent what has been called, "the judge's delving into the innermost reasons for the marriage breakdown". This rule would prevent the development of different standards for judging a breakdown. Opponents of the proposal argue that stability might be achieved at the expense of individual case diagnosis and therapy.

3. Because of these problems, a large majority of the 1970 Congress of Representatives of the German Legal Profession (*Deutscher Juristentag*) voted against introducing a general rule. They expressed approval of the marriage breakdown principle, but felt that this should depend only on a fixed period of separation. When the spouses agree on divorce, the marriage should be dissolved if the spouses have lived apart for one year; if only one spouse applies for divorce, a separation of two years should be required.

---

50. *Generalklausel*.
51. Cf. Paul Mikat, "Scheidungsrechtsreform in einer pluralistisches Gesellschaft" (1970). 17 *Zeitschrift für das gesamte Familienrecht*, 333-348, pp. 339, 340; see also D. Giesen, *Aktuelle Probleme einer Reform des Scheidungsrechts*, Frankfurt/M, 1971, p. 39 note 14.

Divorce by mutual consent after one year of separation, proposed by the *Deutscher Juristentag*, is objected to on the ground that it apparently only serves the scruples of those who disapprove of "divorce by mutual consent", and seems designed to give the impression that divorce is not being granted merely because the spouses want their marriage dissolved. Once the spouses earnestly wish to end the marriage, it is doubtful if a separation period serves any useful purpose other than to indicate the breakdown of the marriage. A marriage can be wrecked before separation and, if the spouses wish to terminate their marriage because they find its continuation insufferable, one should proceed on that basis.[52]

4. "Divorce by consent" remains highly controversial, even when based on the "marriage breakdown principle". Those against consider that its recognition by the law reduces marriage to the level of an ordinary contractual obligation which can be freely evaded, that it ignores society's interest in stable marriage and can lead to such trends as trial marriages. It also implies abandoning the idea of marriage as a union for life, the concept adopted by the two highest courts in Germany, the Federal Constitutional Court and the Federal Supreme Court.[53]

5. On the other hand, there seems to be little evidence supporting the contention that marriage will be contracted more irresponsibly if the requirements for divorce are relaxed, or that "divorce by mutual consent" will increase the number of trial marriages. Even now, spouses know that they can obtain a quick divorce with the aid of a clever attorney, yet, despite this, the great majority of couples enter marriage for life "for better for worse, for richer for poorer, in sickness and in health, to love and to cherish, till death us do part", to quote the well-known phrase used in the Book of Common Prayer of the Church of England.[54] One cannot ignore the importance to society of the institution of marriage, but a marital union between two people does not exist for the sake of the institution. Legal arguments in favour of the institutional concept cannot support the continuation of marriages devoid of all life. John Milton's thesis still seems tenable:

> "that the law forbidding divorce, never attains to any good end of such prohibition, but rather multiplies evil . . . (and that) the law can to no rational purpose forbid divorce: it can only take care that the conditions of divorce be not injurious."

Article 6 of the German Constitution can be read as declaring that marriage is intended to be a union for life[55], but it is questionable whether such a concept

---

52. Cf. D. Giesen, "Aktuelle Probleme . . .", *op. cit.*, pp. 11-12.
53. *Bundesverfassungsgericht* and *Bundesgerichtshof*, both residing in Karlsruhe.
54. Cf. D. Giesen, "Divorce Reform in Germany" (1973), 7 *Family Law Quarterly*, 351-379, p. 360 note 43. For a detailed history of the Matrimonial Jurisdiction in England from the eve of the reformation to the beginning of the 19th century cf. D. Giesen, *Grundlagen und Entwicklung des englischem Eherechts in der Neuzeit*, Bielefeld 1973, 836, with ample references to the Common Prayer Book practice since 1549, 1552, 1559 and 1662.
55. Cf. D. Henrich, *Familienrecht*, Berlin 1970, p. 21.

can be legally enforced. However, there is no convincing reason for denying the existence of model concepts of marriage based on ethical concepts of very high standards, such as the Christian marriage ethos, though public law should not compare marriages with such sublime standards but only with the spouses' individual abilities. It should be taken for granted that it is they who, after a period of sharing experience, will know best their individual capabilities.[56] A lasting union will only be morally valuable if it is the result of the spouses' own decision. The fact that 80% to 90% of current divorces are really by mutual consent indicates that current divorce law has little actual effect.[57]

In order to secure public support, a divorce reform law must be based on certain widely accepted principles in the German legal system, including:

(a) The fact that Article 6 of the German Constitution requires the State to protect and strengthen marriage and the family; and, that they are solid and lasting, in recognition of the fact that it is in society's interest to ensure that marriages are contracted only by responsible parties.

(b) A recognition that broken marriages avail no one and that their dissolution is necessary for the protection of the concept of marriage.[58]

(c) The need for a divorce law which will ensure dissolution of marriage "with the maximum fairness and the minimum bitterness, distress and humiliation", as the English Law Commission has put it. It follows that divorce by mutual consent, now practised clandestinely, should, subject to the introduction of certain safeguards against its abuse, be accepted openly.[59]

The following definition of *divorce by consent* would, however, have met these essential requirements: A marriage is broken, or is considered broken, if both spouses declare in person before a court of law that they do not wish to continue consortium and, if the court is satisfied that *both* spouses seriously desire a divorce and have agreed upon proper arrangements both with regard to the welfare of their children and maintenance where appropriate.[60]

III. The Problem of a hardship clause

1. Both in Germany (West) and abroad, stiff opposition has been expressed to dissolution of marriage *against* one spouse's will because of the failure of the principle of marriage breakdown to consider the reasons for the marriage breakdown. It is feared that, by accepting the principle without considering the cause, encouragement might be given to divorce by repudiation. Safeguards

---

56. D. Giesen, "Aktuelle Probleme, . . ." *op. cit.*, p. 13 ff.
57. For similar figures in England after the 1969 Reform, and in Switzerland see Ulrich Magnus, "Jüngste Entwicklungen im Scheidungsrecht Englands, der Schweiz und der DDR—noch bedeutsam für die deutsche Reform?" (1975) 8 *Zeitschrift für Rechtspolitik*, 56-62, p. 56 ff.
58. Cf. D. *Giesen*, Aktuelle Probleme etc., *op. cit.*, pp. 14 ff.
59. For details on such safeguards cf. D. *Giesen*, "Divorce Reform etc.", *loc. cit.*, pp. 363 ff.; for support of the concept cf. U. *Magnus*, loc. cit., p. 58.
60. The German legislation has, however, not accepted such a concept of divorce by consent (cf. Sections 1564 ff. BGB, as effective from July 1st, 1977, BGBl. I. 1421 ff.).

should therefore be introduced to avoid inhuman results.[61] Some experts have suggested a hardship clause comparable to Section 4 of the English Divorce Reform Act of 1969, which prohibits divorce if it would mean an excessive and inequitable *human* or *economic* hardship to the opposing partner.[62] It is, however, doubtful whether this would be adequate compensation for the disadvantaged spouse. A general "misuse" clause prohibiting divorce if it ran counter to traditional concepts of natural justice is also undesirable as it might lead to elements in the law that might get out of hand, such as renewed rules on the institution of marriage disregarding the present disastrous state of so many marriages.[63]

2. A very restricted hardship clause in the original government's divorce reform bill of 1973[64]—restricted to cover extreme situations of an *incorporeal* hardship only—read as follows:

"The marriage is not to be dissolved if the spouse who objects pleads extraordinary circumstances according to which the divorce would mean such a severe hardship to him that, despite the breakdown of marriage, its maintenance appears to be necessary, even with regard to the other spouse's pleading. No economic considerations may be taken into account."[65]

(a) However, it should be recognized that *incorporeal* or human hardship is not a direct result of the divorce decree, but of the couple's estrangement and, possibly, because of one spouse's attachment to a third person resulting in the end of consortium and in that spouse living apart. Nevertheless, this hardship clause of the government's 1973 draft has aroused much criticism on rather different grounds. While the Federal Bundestag[66] wanted to proceed on the lines of the government's reform bill, the Federal Bundesrat[67] was of the opinion that such a hardship clause covering incorporeal hardship only would provide too narrow a basis for decision[68], and, from the beginning of the parliamentary deliberations to its end favoured a hardship clause based on the grounds of both incorporeal and financial hardship: very much on the same line as the English example now in force.[69] Other opinions doubted whether a hardship clause would be useful in achieving more justice in individual cases and mitigating a strict application of the separation period. In their view, the judicial dissolution of a marriage should neither depend on uncontrollable, extra-legal[70] nor on

---

61. Cf. D. *Giesen*, Aktuelle Probleme etc., *op. cit.*, pp. 14 ff.; P. *Mkat*, "Scheidungsrechtsreform in einer pluralistischen Gesellschaft", *loc. cit.*, pp. 333 ff. 341.
62. Now Section 5 of the Matrimonial Causes Act, 1973, Cf. D. *Giesen*, "Divorce Reform in Germany", loc. cit., p. 366.
63. Cf. U. *Magnus*, loc. cit., p. 60.
64. *Deutscher Bundestag*, Drucksache 7/650.
65. Section 1568 BGB (as proposed in the 1973 draft, printed in BT-Drucks. 7/650.
66. The first chamber, with a safe government majority of the SPD and FDP coalition parties.
67. The second (Länder) Chamber, with as safe an opposition majority of the CDU/CSU *Länder* governments.
68. Cf. *Deutscher Bundestag*, Drucksache 7/650, p. 261.
69. A more detailed discussion can be found in: D. *Giesen*, "Divorce Reform in Germany", loc. cit., pp. 351 ff.

financial considerations, since marriage ought not to be regarded as a life insurance institution against financial difficulties.[71]

(b) Of particular concern was whether a *financial* hardship clause should be included in the future divorce law. A former Chancellor said in 1969 that divorce law reform "must aim at avoiding a lowered social status for the divorced wife and children upon divorce." This same sentiment was echoed by the then Federal Minister of Justice, who said: "It goes without saying that in our society the socially weaker spouse must by no means suffer any disadvantages." The question was whether these statements meant that the Federal Government would advocate a divorce decree only if, prior to the judgment of divorce, steps had been taken to ensure financial security for the socially weaker spouse. But the government never planned to reach this goal by means of a financial hardship clause in the *divorce* law, even though many (including the CDU/CSU opposition in Parliament) wanted it. The government argued that financial hardship was not a reason for maintaining a broken marriage, and said economic consequences could be dealt with in a simpler, more straightforward way than by altogether prohibiting divorce in such cases. In principle, it is true, of course, that economic hardship is not properly part of the law of *divorce*, but rather of the law concerned with the *consequences* of divorce. However, social reality demands that we find solutions to these problems without regard to the manner of their proper dogmatic classification. A financial hardship clause, therefore, cannot be dispensed with unless it is rendered superfluous and useless by a thorough reformation of the vast field of social law[72] or at least, in the absence of such a reformation, by an acceptable and flexible enough reform of the laws related to the immediate consequences of divorce, especially of the law of maintenance after divorce.[73] To the present writer it therefore seems acceptable that after long and protracted debates and deliberations in the German parliament the view eventually prevailed that a hardship clause which includes *economic* hardships ought to be introduced.[74] The forthcoming new German Marriage Law will thus include a hardship clause which reads as follows:

"I. The marriage is not to be dissolved, although it has broken down, if and as long as the continuation of that marriage on exceptional reasons is necessary in the interest of the offspring of that marriage, or if and as long as the spouse who objects to the divorce pleads extraordinary circumstances according to which the divorce would mean such a severe hardship to him that despite the breakdown of marriage its continuation appears to be necessary, even with due regard to the other spouse's interests and concern.

---

70. Cf. I. A. *Saunders*, "Protection of an Innocent Spouse in Divorce: Myth or Reality?", in: (1975) 24 *The International and Comparative Law Quarterly* 106-115, with a discussion of the hardship clauses in Australia, Canada, and England.
71. Cf. D. *Giesen*, "Divorce Reform in Germany", loc. cit., pp. 351 (365).
72. Cf. D. *Giesen*, Family Law and Social Security etc., loc. cit., *in toto*, with further references.
73. Cf. D. *Giesen*, "Divorce Reform in Germany", loc. cit., pp. 351 ff. (368 ff.) with further references.
74. It should, however, be emphasised that the *incorporeal* elements in the new hardship clause on the reasons given here and elsewhere ([1973] 7 F.L.Q. 351 ff., 365), are not acceptable to the present author.

II. Subsection I is not applicable in cases in which the spouses have lived separate and apart for more than five years."[75]

IV. Principles of a Divorce Law Reform with regard to the Consequences of Divorce

The 1973 draft also contains a completely new concept of the law relating to the consequences of divorce, such as maintenance and custody.[76]

1. Today about two-thirds of all married women can claim protection under the German social law only if they are insured jointly with their husbands. On divorce, they lose almost all claims made through their husband's insurance; generally, they would not be entitled to health insurance, life insurance, old-age pension or disability annuities, after a divorce. It is intolerable that German social law does not recognize the productive services which housewives and mothers render during their married lives. Section 1587 to Section 1587s of the proposed 1973 draft[77] make important changes in this area of the law, recognizing a "claim for equalisation of pensions and benefits" on the theory that "at least in the legal provisions on family maintenance the spouses' achievements during marriage are regarded as equal, although there may be a distribution of tasks as to who will run the household and who will support the family financially".[78] Because of these equal roles, it is justifiable to "regard claims to future pension and benefits acquired during marriage as based on joint achievements in life and, if the marriage is dissolved, to allot an equal share in the security afforded by pensions and other benefits to both spouses."[79] Under Section 1587 of the new law, a wife not gainfully employed during her marriage would have a rightful claim to an equal share in her husband's rights to pensions and other benefits. Thus, if the husband's initial claim index had been zero and, during marriage, he had acquired a public or private law right to benefits with an index of 500 DM, the wife would have a right to an equal share, in the amount of 250 DM. While this is not a large amount—and for most people of the entire population in Germany the amount would be even smaller than that—it is an improvement over the present law (although the whole construction of this equalisation of benefits and pensions works as an incentive for both spouses to pursue and maintain a gainful employment in order to build up a more secure and comprehensive social security scheme for their own personal needs).[80]

---

75. Section 1568 BGB (as passed by the German Parliament and published in the Federal Statutes Book: Bundesgesetzblatt 1976 I 1421 ff.]1423]).
76. And so does the forthcoming new Marriage Law of June 14th, 1976, with regard to the maintenance law, a more detailed discussion of which can be found in D. *Giesen*, Schutz von Ehe und Familie etc., *op. cit.*, pp. 15 ff.
77. The same is true of the final new Marriage Law of June 14th, 1976, as effective from July 1st, 1977: cf. Sections 1587 ff. BGB (as printed in BGBl. I. 1421 ff.).
78. *Deutscher Bundestag*, Drucksache 7/650, p. 155.
79. *Ibidem*, p. 155.
80. For a detailed discussion of this argument, cf. D. *Giesen*, Schutz von Ehe und Familie etc., *op. cit.*, pp. 15 ff., 39 ff.

2. The 1973 draft[81] also provides for more substantial changes: Under the present law the guilty spouse must pay adequate maintenance to the other spouse.[82] Under the 1973 draft, the proposed law relating to the consequences of divorce, as in the proposed law of divorce itself, does away almost completely with the matrimonial offence principle. Thus, after divorce there will be no general duty for one spouse to pay maintenance to the other, the 1973 draft requiring each spouse to maintain himself after the dissolution of marriage.[83] It must therefore be assumed that the new maintenance law should be read as presuming that both spouses will support themselves by pursuing gainful occupations, having both been gainfully employed prior to the divorce and enjoying economic independence. However, this attitude is unrealistic in the light of present social reality, for two-thirds of all married women are not gainfully employed and the traditional view of marriage still predominates among most German women who view their roles as those of housewives and mothers, rather than as those pursuing a profession, and who wish to see their daughters pursue the same roles in life.[84] The role of law should be to attempt to balance social hardship and not to create new hardship for the weaker parties by an unrealistic view of the social order.[85]

3. It should be considered however, whether it is wise to foster the German woman's conservative view of her role in marriage, a mental attitude which denies women the educational opportunities available to men and has its origin in the lopsided views of past generations. Marriage should not be regarded as life insurance. It is important to move away from the view of maintenance and subsistence and to foster an awareness of personal responsibility. For some time now women have been aspiring to economic independence and this should be encouraged in the woman's own interests, as vocational training is a valuable asset which cannot be taken from her in later years. Outward independence provides inward liberty and, in the case of dissolution of marriage, only those enjoying inward liberty can build a new basis for existence without the burden of financial difficulties. The liberating effect of earning one's own wage or salary should not be underestimated.[86]

4. On the other hand one must not disregard the social hardship which can result during a prolonged transition period. Those who hold that individual spouses should be responsible for themselves, should ensure that everyone has the opportunity to live by this principle. This means more than simply equality of educational opportunity, for it is a fact that even those who wish to maintain vocational independence during marriage, often do not have the opportunity of doing so. Professor Mikat recently described the problem in these terms:

---

81. What is being said about the 1973 draft in this paragraph, is equally applicable to the final German Marriage Law of 1976 (BGBl. I. 1421 ff.).
82. Section 56 Ehegesetz.
83. Cf. D. *Giesen*, Schutz von Ehe und Familie etc., *op. cit.*, pp. 15 ff.
84. Some statistical data of present day Germany in this context are given in the present author's recent publication Schutz von Ehe und Familie etc., op. cit., pp. 9 ff., with further references.
85. P. Mikat, *loc. cit.*, pp. 344-345. This point is also stressed and further discussed in D. Giesen, *Schütz von Ehe und Familie und Erwerbstaetigkeit op. cit.*, pp. 24 ff.
86. Cf. D Giesen, "Divorce Reform in Germany", *loc. cit.*, pp. 351 ff.

"Time will tell how long a modern society can afford not to make use of the frequently neglected manpower potential of female skilled labour who so often cannot pursue their occupation due to a shortage of part-time jobs. This is because although the modern society should be concerned, training costs for men and women are equally high and, in addition, there must be a wage incentive to meet the needs of women with families. A policy which stresses labour performance, espouses equal rights for men and women, and purports to strengthen the position of the family will not stop the trend toward professional activity of women without losing substance. Women must be offered job conditions that allow them the opportunity to be active within their families as well as in the public world."[87]

This means the necessity for more full-time kindergartens, more full-time schools and more part-time jobs. Divorce law reform would be an easier task if these problems were solved.[88]

5. Instead, however, we are faced with the problems of vocational training and rehabilitation for divorced women. Prospects are not bad for the fairly young divorced woman whose training is good and whose gainful occupation was only interrupted for a short time by marriage. For a woman of forty-five it is much more difficult to resume work and, for a woman of fifty-five, it is almost impossible even with favourable economic conditions. The problem is how a woman can be compensated for her years of interrupted professional experience and missed promotional opportunities, and for the years of sacrifice during which the spouses relied on joint planning for the future of their married lives. These years cannot be adequately compensated for by an equalisation claim, however good it is in principle. It is debatable how the socially weak party can be protected from suffering the social hardship of divorce.

6. The 1973 government draft provided for a maintenance claim in only six different instances: (1) as long as the divorced person cannot work because he must bring up and care for a child of the former marriage[89]; (2) if the former spouse cannot work because of old age[90]; (3) or because of permanent disability[91]; (4) as long as the divorced spouse cannot find reasonable gainful employment[92]; (5) as long as the divorced spouse requires educational grants for vocational training or re-training in order to finish school or vocational education interrupted by the marriage[93]; or (6) because he does not receive sufficient pension or benefits on account of not being gainfully employed during marriage or during certain periods after the marriage terminated, subject to some qualifications.[94]

---

87. P. Mikat, *op. cit.*, p. 347.
88. That they are really unsolved is demonstrated by many examples given from the wide field of social security laws: cf. D Giesen, "Family Law and Social Security", *loc. cit., in toto*, with many further references.
89. *BGB* § 1571.
90. *BGB* § 1572.
91. *BGB* § 1573.
92. *BGB* § 1574.
93. *BGB* § 1576.
94. *BGB* § 1577.

7. Although these provisions covered the most important and most frequently occurring situations, they did not cover all the situations where a spouse needs maintenance. One may enquire whether they even appropriately covered the most important and frequent ones. What about the maintenance payments for a child brought into the marriage by one spouse, or to assist a spouse who has been caring for a needy relative in the marital home, with the other spouse's consent? Does the expression "not able to work because of old age" mean age forty-five, or fifty-five or sixty-five, or something else altogether? What does the phrase "not able to find reasonable employment" mean? Why is "reasonable employ- ment" only related to the education and abilities of one spouse and not to the social status jointly achieved by the couple?[95] Does this mean that the wife of, say, a successful medical specialist would have to begin anew, after her divorce, from her pre-marriage position of, for example, a hospital laboratory techni- cian?[96] What about the legal right of a married housewife to financial compensa- tion for her services to the family, and to the husband in particular, at least where the wife worked exclusively as a housewife for many years? Why should the wife be regarded as having worked gratuitously when, on the open market, such services could only be obtained at high cost, if at all?

8. Therefore, the government bill of 1973 has not dealt adequately with most of these problems, and neither has the new Marriage Law done so to the extent one would wish. The Federal Minister of Justice (then Gerhard Jahn) once stated that "life is often more complex than we can imagine" and a judge must have opportunity to provide relief "even in extreme situations." If that is so, then maintenance law should be capable of meeting such contingencies. Therefore it would seem advisable that the 1973 draft should be made more flexible and that a broadly worded provision for hardship cases should be incorporated into the future law.[97]

V. The absolute interdependence of the decisions on divorce and the consequences of divorce

1. Everything will depend on whether the legislature can make a firm ruling that a divorce decree may not be pronounced unless provisions are made relating

---

95. This question is now being answered by section 00 of the forthcoming new Marriage Law of 1976, whereby the marital status at the time of the divorce is declared also to be relevant.
96. This question can now sufficiently be answered by applying the new Marriage Law of 1976, according to which, in contrast to the 1973 draft, the marital status of both spouses as achieved by mutual co-operation of the spouses (as the law presumes) has also to be taken into con- sideration when reaching a divorce and maintenance decisions.
97. As has been pointed out above, a much too narrow-worded maintenance hardship clause was eventually incorporated into the new Marriage Law at the insistence mainly of the *Bundesrat* and a joint committee of *Bundestag* and *Bundesrat*, by re-phrasing the law in Section 1568 BGB (BGBl. 1976 I 1421 ff.). This means an improvement against the 1973 draft, but even in its new form Section 1568 will still fall short of what social justice would require, i.e. to sufficiently protect the socially weaker part of a broken marriage; cf. D. *Giesen*, Schutz von Ehe und Familie etc., *op. cit.*, pp. 15 ff., 39 ff.

to the consequences of divorce.[98] In contrast to the present law, the government's 1973 draft provides that the same court has jurisdiction over both the divorce as such and over the consequences of divorce (including maintenance and custody questions). For this purpose, so-called Family Courts are to be set up[99], which will be special divisions of the *Amtsgerichte*, the lowest courts in existence in the hierarchy of courts in Germany.[100]

The 1973 draft also contains new procedural provisions.[101] According to these, at the request of one spouse the court may give simultaneous judgment regarding the dissolution of the marriage and with regard to the consequences of the divorce.[102] In the case of divorce by mutual consent, a proposal with regard to the consequences of divorce must be presented with the divorce petition.

2. However, in *ZPO* § 627a, the 1973 draft provides for separate actions in certain "closely restricted" conditions: (i) if it is "not possible" to decide on the consequences of the divorce before the divorce has been granted or, (ii) if a decision on both the divorce and its consequences (e.g. custody, maintenance, etc.) would protract the decision on the divorce. The bill still holds to the theory that proceedings on the consequences of divorce should only be initiated by a complaint or application filed by one of the spouses.[103] Only proceedings relating to custody and care and control would be allowed with special applications.[104] Questions of access can only be dealt with on the application of one spouse.[105] These are serious problems because the need to protect the socially weaker spouse is thereby frustrated. By making exceptions to the rule that judgments on divorce and its consequences be made simultaneously, the bill opens the door to the possibility of one spouse pressurising the other in order to obtain a divorce in spite of his or her objections.

3. Another important issue is how claims can be secured and enforced more effectively than in the past. The 1973 draft deals too briefly with this matter. Comparative law demonstrates that the enforcement of maintenance claims is the central problem of maintenance law[106] and that it will cause insurmountable difficulties, especially if the liable *omnimod facturus* changes his job frequently. Other difficulties will arise if there is conflict between the claims of an indigent former spouse and those of a new wife or husband.[107] One solution is to give

---

98. What is being said about the 1973 draft in this paragraph, can also be said, *mutatis mutandis*, of the new Marriage Law of 1976. The problems discussed in the text above, all apply to and remain unsolved by the future law as effective from July 1st, 1977.

99. For a full comparative law discussion of the problems involved, cf. D. *Giesen*, Zur Problematik der Einführung einer Familiengerichtsbarkeit in der Bundesrepublik Deutschland, Paderborn 1975, pp. 7 ff.

100. Section 23a *Gerichtsverfassungsgesetz* (as amended by the new Marriage Law of 1976; BGBl. I. 1421 ff.).

101. §§ 623, 630 *ZPO*.

102. For a similar provision in England, see s. 41 Matrimonial Causes Act, 1973.

103. *ZPO* § 623, I, II.

104. *ZPO* § 623 III 1.

105. *ZPO* § 623 III 2.

106. D. Giesen, "*Entwicklungstendenzen . . .*" *loc. cit.*, pp. 20-23.

107. P. Mikat, *op. cit.*, p. 347.

priority to the former spouse's claims. The official Commission on marriage law suggested this procedure and it has been adopted in the 1973 draft[108], which gives priority, in principle, to the divorced spouse's maintenance claims over the claim of the new partner. Thus, a divorced spouse entitled to maintenance need not fear the loss of maintenance if the liable spouse remarries.

4. When one reflects on the social function of the law, it is apparent "that today the gist of divorce law reform is no longer directed to problems concerning whether divorce should be granted on the basis of guilty conduct or on the ground of marriage breakdown, but rather, to whether or not the introduction of the breakdown principle alone, as the sole basis of divorce law, represents a true achievement without real reform simultaneously of the law on the consequences of divorce".[109] The reform of both the law of divorce and the law of the consequences of divorce is necessary if any reform in this sphere is to have a lasting effect.

D. Reform of the Law of Parent and Child with special regard to Illegitimate Children

I. Reform of the law relating to illegitimate children

In Germany the reform of the law relating to children born outside marriage has already been completed and has been in force since 1st July 1970.

1. The necessity for the reform[110] was occasioned by the fact that Article 6(5) of the Basic Law required that illegitimate children should be entitled to the same conditions of physical and spiritual development as legitimate children[111], and that that Article [112] was a direct commission to parliament to initiate new legislation immediately.[113] Should this not be done, parts of the law concerning illegitimate children would have to be declared void as infringing the principle of equality between legitimate and illegitimate children, and would have to be replaced by judge-made law.[114] In the event, the German *Bundestag* effected the required reform in a few months.

2. The new provisions are to be found in §§ 1591-1600o and 1705-1740g of the German Civil Code and, with regard to the law of succession, in §§ 1934a-e.
One of the most striking alterations in the new law is the use of a new appellation for children born outside marriage. They are now called "nichteheliche

---

108. *BGB* § 1583.
109. P. Mikat, *op. cit.*, p. 348.
110. For previous reform proposals see Michael T Bohndorf, "The New Illegitimacy Law in Germany" (1970), 19 *The International and Comparative Law Quarterly*, 199-308, p. 299.
111. Cf. *supra* at p. 111. Also, M Bohndorf *ibid* at p. 300.
112. *BVerfGE* 8, 210 (216) (1958); 25, 167 (1969). Further to this case see M. Bohndorf *ibid*, p. 301 f.
113. Further to this point and to admonitory decisions of the Federal Constitutional Court, see W. Rupp-v. Brünneck, *loc. cit.*, p. 387 f.
114. Cf. M. Bohndorf, *ibid.*, p. 300 f.

Kinder", instead of "uneheliche Kinder", which could be translated as "non-marital children" instead of "contra-marital children".[115] This is, perhaps, comparable to the English Family Law Reform Act 1969 which now speaks of "illegitimate children" instead of "bastards", as was the old Common law usage. It may also be interesting to note that even more neutral names have been suggested. In the House of Lords debate in England, the argument was put forward that it might be better to speak of "children born out of wedlock" because it is not the children who are illegitimate, but their parents. One could also speak of "children of unmarried parents" as in the New Zealand and East German law reforms[116], or of "children born outside marriage" as proposed by J. Neville Turner of Adelaide.[117]

3. The German reform of the law relating to non-marital children did not lead to complete equality between them and legitimate children. Under the German Civil Code the non-marital child never was a *filius nullius* or, as still seems to be the position in France[118], an *enfant naturel*, without any automatic statutory relationship to either mother or father. Under present German law, the non-marital child is entirely equal to a legitimate child only in relation to its mother, as was the case prior to the reform. The child is entitled to claim maintenance from its mother[119], and is also entitled to succeed to her and her relatives, in the same way as a legitimate child.[120] The mother exercises all parental power over the child, especially custody.[121] There is also a special statutory representative for the child, called the *Pfleger*, which may be translated as "curator".[122] The local Youth-Office[123], which is the *Pfleger*, represents the child in litigation and protects its interests, especially in cases regarding the determination of paternity, maintenance and succession.[124]

The new law provides that the non-marital child should take the mother's surname at the time of its birth[125], in contrast to the old law under which the non-marital child took the mother's maiden name even if she was married at the time.

4. However, equality between legitimate and illegitimate children has not so far been reached in relation to the father. The father-child relationship has been

---

115. Cf. J. Neville Turner, *Improving the Lot of Children born outside marriage. A comparison of three recent reforms: England, New Zealand and West Germany*, National Council for One Parent Families, London, 1973.
116. *Ibid.*, pp. 5, 6.
117. *Ibid.*, pp. 6, 45.
118. Cf. Art. 334, 334-8 *Code civil*.
119. Cf. §§ 1601, 1606 *BGB*.
120. For general principles of the German Law of Succession see W. Müller-Freienfels, "Family law . . .", *op. cit.*, pp. 443-445.
121. § 1705 *BGB*.
122. Cf. J. Neville Turner, *op. cit.*, p. 29.
123. *Jugendamt*.
124. § 170 5 *BGB*.
125. § 1617 *BGB*.

a subject of concern and has been improved, particularly by the recognition that father and child are now regarded as related before the law.[126]

(a) In spite of the fact that the father-child relationship is now legally recognised, and unlike the position in some continental countries[127], under German law the non-legitimate father is still excluded from obtaining custody of the child. However, the father has a right to be heard by the guardianship court before important decisions are made, to serve the best interests of the child.[128] The father's right of access to the child depends on whether, and under what circumstances, the mother considers a meeting would be reasonable. If the parents cannot agree on the terms of access, the matter will be decided by the guardianship court and access will only be granted to the father if it is in the best interests of the child[129]

(b) The new law relating to non-legitimate children has introduced the child's claim to intestate succession from the father, and vice versa. However, if there are legitimate issue or a surviving spouse, then § 1934 (a) *BGB* does not provide a genuine right of inheritance, as is provided in Section 14 of the English Family Law Reform Act 1969, for there is no real participation in the estate itself because the claim of the illegitimate child is reduced to a money claim against his father's heirs[130], the amount of which is equal to what the illegitimate child would have inherited had he been legitimate. He is still not a co-heir with the legitimate children and has no right *in rem* to anything of his father's estate. He only has the right to make a *Erbersatzanspruch*, that is a "claim in lieu of a succession right"[131] or "substitute inheritance portion"[132] if he has been recognised by the deceased, or if the deceased has been legally declared to be the father.[133]

(c) This last condition also applies to the child's own claim for maintenance against the father. Unlike other legal systems, for example England, it is not only the mother who can claim for maintenance, but also the child.[134] Separate claims may be made for the mother's expenses in connection with her pregnancy, delivery, maintenance during a certain period of time after the delivery, and funeral expenses should she die in childbirth.[135] The child's maintenance must be awarded according to the *Lebenstellung*, that is, the standard of living, of both parents and not, as formerly, of that of the mother alone.[136] Unlike some Common Market countries, such as England and New Zealand, the father and his relatives

---

126. § 1589 (2).
127. E.g. Switzerland. See Art. 325 *ZGB*.
128. § 1712 *BGB*.
129. § 1711 *BGB*.
130. Cf. M Bohndorf, "The New Illegitimacy . . .", *loc. cit.*, pp. 306-308.
131. Cf. J. Neville Turner, *op. cit.*, p. 43.
132. *Ibid.*, p. 306.
133. § 1600 (a) *BGB*.
134. Cf. J Neville Turner, *op. cit.*, p. 11.
135. § 1615 k-n *BGB*.
136. Cf. M Bohndorf, *loc. cit.*, p. 305.

may have to pay maintenance throughout the child's life[137], not only during his minority, though usually he will only be liable until the child reaches the age of eighteen.[138] "A most significant and attractive innovation"[139] is the fact that the new law provides a standard minimum amount of maintenance to avoid judicial variation, the present rate being 126-140 DM for children up to 6 years; 153-170 DM for children between 7 and 12 years; and 180-200 DM for children from 12 to 18 years. These rates may be changed by the government according to variations in the cost of living.

5. Another important feature of the reform is that the dichotomy of two independent and distinct actions, one for maintenance and one for "general paternity", has not been retained.[140] According to the old law it was possible for a man to be liable for maintaining a child, who was not necessarily held to be its father with the corresponding parental rights and duties. German legal literature referred to such a man by the ugly term *Zahlvater*, that is "pay-father". Now, according to the new § 1600 (o) *BGB*, the only man liable to pay maintenance is either he who has acknowledged paternity[141] or one who has been established by the court to be the father in an action for "declaration of paternity".[142]

6. Thus it can be seen that the reform of the law relating to non-legitimate children has not achieved complete equality between legitimate and illegitimate children before the law although, as has been stated by a learned Australian colleague, "West Germany on balance gives non-marital children advantages over other children".[143] At the moment, other fields of Family Law are being considered, but it can safely be said that the final word in our legislation has not been said by the 1969 reform with regard to illegitimate children. What can be done in this field is shown in the draft of a Uniform Parentage Act passed in August 1973 in the USA which has been recommended to all States for acceptance. This bill, mainly drafted with the assistance of Professor Harry D. Krause, Illinois, provides for most complete equality non-legitimate children before the law.

II. Reform of the Age of Majority, Parental Custody and Adoption

1. Age of Majority

Until 1st January 1975 the age of majority in Germany was 21 years. Since that date it has been reduced to 18 years, as in several other European jurisdictions, for example, in England by the Family Law Reform Act 1969.

---

137. Cf. §§ 1601, 1606 *BGB*.
138. § 1615 f *BGB*.
139. Cf. J. Neville Turner, *op. cit.*, p. 11.
140. The discussion on this point in J Neville Turner, *op. cit.*, p. 10 f, 15, 24, is not entirely correct.
141. For further discussion on this point, see D Henrich, *op. cit.*, 130-133; J Neville Turner, *op. cit.*, p. 15-18; M Bohndorf, *op. cit.*, p. 303-304.
142. *Gerichtliche Feststellung der Vaterschaft*, § 1600 (n).
143. Cf. J Neville Turner, *op. cit.*, p. 44.

(a) The reduction of the age of majority in Germany was a controversial issue among both politicians and lawyers. In its comment on the draft, the *Bundesrat* voted against the reduction of the age of majority. In German law this term implies absolute contractual capacity, applying in particular to contracts concerning bills and immovables. Under §§ 106-113 *BGB*, young people between the ages of 18 and 21 had only a limited contractual capacity and contracts entered into by them were only valid under certain conditions; an infant under seven years of age has no contractual capacity at all. It was argued that, if the age of majority were reduced, the protection provided by §§ 106-113 *BGB* would be removed.

The principle of attaining legal age by stages exists in other areas of German law. For instance, a minor of 14 has complete religious freedom[144], at the age of 16 he is capable of making a will[145]; since 1972 an 18-year old minor has had the right to vote. There are many more examples. Various German jurists[146] recommended the gradual attainment of full age, rather than the reduction of the age of majority to 18 for most legal purposes. This concept of gradual attainment of majority would solve such important problems as the legal labour age (i.e. vocational education, choice of place of work, disposition of the remuneration, and the solution of conflicts between parents and children in relation to the children's life style.

(b) Apart from the reduction of the age of majority, the marriagable age has been changed from 21 for men and 16 for women, to 18 for both parties.[147] However, the guardianship court may exercise its discretion if the applicant has reached the age of 16 and his or her intended spouse has reached the age of majority.

2. Parental Custody

Parental powers and duties decrease proportionally with the increase of powers granted to young people as they grow older.

(a) The reform of the legal and marriagable ages has a close connection with the changes in the rules for parental care.[148] At present, parental powers are governed by §§ 1616 to 1712 *BGB*.

(b) The comprehensive reorganisation of this area of the law lays special emphasis on the rights of children and on what is in their best interests. The aim behind the decisions of parents, courts and welfare departments should be to

---

144. § 5 of the law concerning the religious education of children, *vom 15 Juli 1921, RGBl.* 939, S. 1263.
145. § 2229 II *BGB*.
146. Cf. F W Bosch, "*Volljährigkeit-Ehemündigkeit-Elterliche Sorge*" (1973) 20 *Zeitschrift für das gesamte Familienrecht*, 489-508.
147. § 1 *EheG*.
148. *Entwurf eines Gesetzes zur Neuregelung des Rechts der elterlichen Sorge, Deutscher Bundestag, Drucksache* 7/2060, 2nd May 1943. For further discussion of this draft see Joachim Kuntze, "*Anmerkungen zum neuen Sorgerechtsentwurf,*" (1973), 22 *Juristische Rundschau*, 273-77.

ensure that the child should grow up to be independent and self-sufficient. Therefore, the new § 1626 (2) *BGB* proposes that the child should have the right to discuss the matter in question and that, depending on his development and age, the child's wishes should be taken into consideration. The exercise of such parental power is called "parental care" in the draft. Under § 1626a, for instance, a minor of at least 14 years shall be entitled to consent to therapeutic medical treatment if he or she is capable of appreciating the reason for, and importance of, such treatment and if he or she is able to make a decision. A similar provision for children over 16 years can be found in section 8 of the English Family Law Reform Act 1969.

(c) An important point in the draft is that the right of access may not be exercised against the will of the child if it is at least 14 years old. The guardianship court should hear the child before making decisions, if the child is old enough to make up its own mind and is capable of doing so.[149]

(d) The competence of the guardianship court will be extended to enable adequate consideration to be given to what is in the best interests of the child. The court would have the authority to settle any dispute between the parents on important issues.[150] The court would also be entitled to intervene in cases where children may be imperilled and to make any necessary arrangements which the parents either refuse to do or are incapable of doing, even where there is no fault on the part of the parents.[151]

(e) Paramount consideration should be given to the best interests of the child when decisions are made, after a divorce, with regard to the custody and the care of the child.[152] This should depend on the child's own wishes if he is at least 14 years old, although his best interests should always be the deciding factor. The prerogative of the "innocent" parent to have the custody and care of the child, which is established in the second sentence of Section 1671 (3) BGB, will be abolished in accordance with the change from the doctrine of matrimonial offence to that of the breakdown of the marriage.

3. Law of Adoption

The law of adoption will also be shortly undergoing a comprehensive reform[153], although it was recently amended, on August 14th, 1973. However, that reform was not considered sufficient and is regarded as a first step only toward the complete reorganisation of this part of the law.

---

149. § 50 *FGG*-draft.
150. § 1628 *BGB*-draft.
151. § 1666 (1) *BGB*-draft.
152. Section 1671 BGB.
153. In the meantime, this part of the reform plans was also passed by the German Parliament, with some minor alterations of the measures which are discussed in this following section. For the text of the final Adoption Law of July 2nd, 1976 (BGBl. I. 1749 ff.), which will come into force on January 1st, 1977, cf. the Federal Statute Book quoted here; for a first discussion of its measures cf. A. E. *Griess*, International Society on Family Law Newsletter No. 3 (1977) and A. *Lüderitz*, Das neue Adoptionsrecht, in: 29 *Neue Juristische Wochenschrift* 1865 ff. (1976).

(a) Essentially, the existing law of adoption still consists of the original provisions of Sections 1741 to 1772 of the Civil Code of 1896. Some have since been changed by part-reforms, such as the bill on the Alteration of Family Law and the Law on Non-marital children discussed above.

(b) The 1973 Adoption Law facilitated adoptions by the alteration of two particular provisions. First, the age requirement for the adoptive person was reduced from 35 to 25 because it was usually small children who were being adopted and it was held to be best for their development if the adopting parents were fairly young.[154] Second, it was made easier for consent to adoption to be given by the guardianship court rather than by the parents. Prior to this, the court could only give its consent under three headings: (i) if the parents had neglected their obligations towards the child, (ii) if the parents withheld consent maliciously, (iii) if it would be detrimental to the child for it not to be adopted.[155] The new provision in § 1747a *BGB* allows for the court's consent to adoption in substitution for that of the parents when this had been withheld through indifference to the child's welfare as, for example, when children for adoption were living in a Home.

(c) The German Federal Government has further put forward recently a "Draft of a Statute relating to Adoption."[156] At the beginning of this century the function of adoption was primarily to enable childless couples to have a child in the family. Today, adoption is looked on as a means of serving the best interests of the child. This alteration in the attitude to, and function of, adoption has resulted in reforms of this part of the law in many States in Europe.[157] In order to fulfil the obligations of the Strasbourg European Convention on Adoption of 24th April 1967 and to provide for ratification of this agreement in West Germany[158] and for the adaptation of the law to these new principles, the draft was submitted to the *Bundestag* in January 1975 and will be discussed during the current period of legislation.

(d) The draft[159] provides for a comprehensive reform of the law of adoption. By this draft the German Adoption Law will turn from the "contract-system" to the "decree-system", that is, by a decree of court on the adoptor's application[160], rather than by a contract of adoption between the adoptor and the adoptee requiring confirmation by the local Court, the *Amtsgericht*. By the provisions of §§ 1754, 1755, a system of "full-adoption" (*Volladoption*) for minors

---

154. *Amt 1. Begr. d. Bundesreg., Teil* B, *zu Art.* 1, *BR-Drucks.* 70/73, S.4.
155. § 1747 III *BGB*, repealed.
156. *Entwurf eines Gesetzes über die Annahme als Kind, Deutscher Bundestag, Drucksache* 7/3061, 7th January 1975. For a detailed discussion of *t*his draft, see Helmut Engler, *Der Entwurf eines Gesetzes über die Annahme als Kind* (1975) 22 *Zeitschrift für das gesamte Familienrecht,* 125-138.
157. Austria 1960, Belgium 1969, Denmark 1972, France 1969, Great Britain 1969, Greece 1968, Italy 1967, Netherlands 1972, Switzerland 1972.
158. The convention has already been ratified by Ireland, Malta, Sweden, Great Britain, Norway and Switzerland.
159. § 1752 *BGB*-draft.
160. § 1755 *BGB*-draft.

will be introduced into German law. By this provision, adoption will result in the cessation of the relationship between the adoptee and his ascendants[161], as in the present law, and, instead, the establishment of a relationship between the adoptee and the adoptor's relatives.[162] In contrast to the present German law, other legal systems provide for these consequences.[163]

According to the present law, the adoptee must be a minor as a rule[164] but the *Amtsgericht* may grant exemption for this requirement. The reform provides for the adoption of adults[165] but the consequences would not be as far-reaching as in the case of a minor.[166]

---

161. § 1754 *BGB*-draft.
162. E.g. England, France (art. 358 *Code civil*, Switzerland (art. 267 *ZGB*.
163. § 1744 (3) *BGB*.
164. §§ 1767 ff. *BGB*-draft.
165. Cf. § 1770 *BGB*-draft.
166. Now the Adoption Law of 1976 (*BGBl*. I. 1749 ff.), which, but not in all details, follows the draft discussed here; for a first discussion of the actual law to become effective on January 1st, 1977, cf. A E Griess, *loc. cit.*, and the references mentioned there.

CHAPTER VI. REFORM OF FAMILY LAW IN GREECE

by Alkis Argyriadis

I. Introduction

The Greek Civil Code[1] came into force in Greece on 23 February 1946. This codification of the civil law replaced pre-existing laws which were: (a) Byzantine Law, codified in the year 1345 in the Hexabible of Constantin Harmenopulos, a Byzantine judge of Thessalonica. This prevailed over the greatest part of Greece; (b) the Ionian Civil Code of 1841 which applied to the Ionian Isles; (c) the Civil Code of Samos of 1899, and (d) the Civil Code of Crete of 1903.

All these laws were modified by a number of more recent Greek statutes. These affected different areas of the Civil Law. For instance, prior to the annexation of the Ionian Isles of Samos and of Crete, two laws of 1861 could be noted in the field of Family Law, on mixed marriages, minors, guardianship and emancipation. After the annexation of these territories, there was Law 2228 of 1920 on divorce and the decree of 14/17 July 1926 on the status of natural children. The two last, i.e. the law on divorce and the decree on the status of natural children, were fairly progressive works for their time in the context of the economic and social situation of Greece. In fact, their provisions have been reproduced in substance in the relevant articles of the new Greek Civil Code.

The preparatory work on the Greek Civil Code goes back to 1930. But the dream of a modern codification of Civil Law had inspired several generations of Greek jurists. Ever since 1821, the first year of the Greek War of Independence against the Turkish domination, the desire to work out such a codification was often expressed officially. But earlier Commissions, which had worked from the 19th century onwards, first under the influence of the Code Napoléon and later, i.e. in the first decades of the present century, under the influence of the German Civil Code, did not produce results. At last in 1930 a Committee, charged with the task of drafting a civil code, was set up by the Liberal Government of E. Venizelos by virtue of Law No. 4680. The Committee was composed of Professors K Demertzis, K Triantaphyllopoulos, G Balis, G Maridakis and P Thivaios. The committee elaborated a draft Civil Code which was published in six parts during the years 1933 to 1936. Two revision Committees were set up in 1930 and in 1934, but they did not make much progress. The dictatorship of 4 August 1936 under General Metaxas dismissed the second revision Committee and entrusted the task to a single member, Professor G Balis. He revised the draft and modified it in a conservative spirit. This was true above all in respect of the part concerning Family Law. The Metaxas government then promulgated the text thus revised by Law No. 2250 of 15 March 1940 but, owing to the War and the subsequent occupation of Greece, it did not come into force. The Code was retroactively enacted by the Law of 23 February 1946.

---

1. Law 2250 of 15 March 1940.

The Greek Civil Code consists of five books: (1) The General Principles of Law, Private International Law and the Law relating to Persons (Arts. 1-286); (2) The Law of Obligations (Arts. 287-946); (3) The Law of Things (Arts. 947-1345); (4) Family Law (Arts. 1346-1709); (5) The Law of Succession (Arts. 1710-2035). The first three books of the Code were mainly inspired by the German Civil Code and the Swiss Civil Code, as well as by the Swiss Law of Obligations. The last two books of the Code reflect the Byzantine law, which had evolved through the centuries and had been modified by modern Greek law in the form in which it applied in Greece at the time the Code was drafted. Some foreign influences, not always happy ones, can also be detected in the last two books. In a final article it was anticipated that the Civil Code would come into force on 1 July 1941. But, following the entry of Greece into the Second World War on 28 October 1940, the struggle of several months' duration against Italy, the attack by Germany and the Occupation in April 1941, the coming into force of the Civil Code was suspended by the *de facto* Government appointed by the forces of occupation. It is very probable that the Occupation authorities did not view with favour the unification of the law over the whole of Greece as, at that time, the country became divided into three zones of occupation.

After the liberation there was a movement to replace the Code of 1940 by a new Civil Code, drafted in some haste by Professors K Triantaphyllopoulos and G. Maridakis, but in a more progressive spirit than the Code of 1940. This Code, which became known as the Code of 1945, was put into effect by the Law No. 777 of 29 December 1945, as from 23 February 1946, by the Liberal Government of Th. Sofoulis. But the Government of the Popular Party (Conservative) of K Tsaldaris that won the elections of 31 March 1946, withdrew the Code of 1945 and, by a decree of 7/10 May 1946, enacted that the Civil Code of 1940 was deemed to have come into force on 23 February 1946.

This history of the Greek Civil Code now in force, i.e. the Civil Code of 1940, shows that the current Greek law represents a pre-war tradition. The modern tendencies that have manifested themselves since 1945 in several countries of Europe in Family Law matters, did not touch the "new" Greek Civil Code. The principle of the equality of the spouses, the abolition of a compulsory religious marriage ceremony, a more rapid emancipation of youth, etc, still remain unsatisfied in Greece. But democratic evolution which has resumed its course since 1974, will no doubt lead to the reform of Family Law.

II. The Equality of the Spouses

The equality of the spouses is not recognised currently in Greek law. On the contrary, Greek Family Law is based on the principle that the husband is the head of the family. The predominant role of the husband was a feature of the law prior to the Civil Code. It derived from the ancient traditions of Byzantine Law and from the old Greek Law. It corresponded to social reality. It should be added that the wife was in a position of inferiority and that, even now, she retains that position in a large part of Greek territory, especially in the villages. On the other hand, it runs counter to the development of life in the industrial and modern centres and in the large towns. There, the emancipation of women and their participation in the economic and social life, often independently of their husbands, has led to an equality of fact between the spouses. In this respect, special reference must be made to Law No. 3191 of 1955. It abolished all obstacles to the acquisition by women of posts in the Civil Service and in Local Government administration. Moreover, women now enjoy the right to vote and to be elected without discrimination in this respect. It is true that there is no strong feminist movement in Greece demanding the abolition of the laws that give to the husband the principal role in the family. This is, perhaps, due to the fact that the social unit constituted by the family provides—as it does in all countries—rules for the common life of its members. Families which live in harmony hardly need to refer to the rules laid down by the State.

The inequality of the spouses and the principal role of the man, whether as husband or as the father of legitimate children, manifests itself in a large number of provisions of Greek substantive law, above all in provisions concerning the personal relations between the spouses.

Relying on the well-known definitions of marriage to be found in Roman and Byzantine law, to the effect that marriage is a *"consortium omnis vitae"*[2], Article 1386 of the Greek Civil Code lays down that marriage creates for the spouses, "the mutual obligation to live in common", provided that the observance of this obligation does not lead to an abuse of rights. This seems to imply that the personal relations of the spouses are based on equality. But the following Article 1387, lays down the principle of the legal superiority of the husband, "The husband is the head of the family and decides on everything which concerns the married life, provided that his decision does not lead to an abuse of rights." Article 1388 of the Greek Civil Code further lays down that the wife receives the surname of the husband while, according to Article 55 of the Greek Civil Code, the wife's home is that of her husband. She can only acquire an independent residence when she is not bound to follow the husband to his own home.

We see here all the legal provisions that were common to the European Codifications of the 19th century[3] and which tended to subject the wife to the domination of her master, the husband. But case law and learned writings have reduced the impact of the superiority of the husband by accepting that the husband's right of decision—according to Article 1387 of the Greek Civil Code— is at the same time a duty which must be exercised for the common benefit of the family. A fairly large degree of autonomy has in fact been recognised for the wife in several matters, e.g. in the carrying on of an occupation by the married woman, in her personal affairs, in her private correspondence, etc. Moreover, according to Article 1389 of the Greek Civil Code, the wife is in control of the management of the household and can meet the "day to day needs of the domestic economy" by making the husband liable through her acts.

Under this concept which is more or less patriarchal, the husband must provide his wife with maintenance appropriate to his own social position and to the extent of his fortune or his resources[4], while the wife is not obliged, save in

---

2. Dig 23, 2, 1: Bas. 28, 4, 1; cf. Inst. 1, 9, 1.
3. Cf. e.g. former Arts. 213-214 of the French Civil Code; former Arts. 1354-1355 of the German Civil Code.
4. Art. 1391 Greek Civil Code.

exceptional circumstances, to maintain her husband.[5] The so-called Mucian presumption—that is, that moveable things in the possession or control of either or both of the spouses are presumed to belong to him for the purposes of satisfying the husband's creditors, is another instance of the superiority of the husband.[6] Only moveable things intended for personal use by the wife, in particular, clothes, jewellery, tools of trade, are presumed to belong to the wife.

An instance of the special place of the wife in a marriage is the obligation of her parents and particularly of her father, to give a dowry to his daughter.[7] The dowry is the property that the wife, or another person acting on her behalf, brings to the husband "as a solace for the burdens of the household".[8] This is because it is the husband who is expected to meet the expenses of the household.[9] In respect of the dowry the husband acquires that part of the property that consists of moveable things, subject to any stipulation to the contrary. He also acquires the administration and usufruct of any moveable assets, subject also to a contrary stipulation.[10] Fairly severe rules exist to prevent the alienation of immoveable assets in the dowry. Alienation by the husband is permitted with the consent of the wife and after authorisation by the court, but only in case of necessity or of manifest advantage.[11] The institution of the dowry, which remains well established in the traditions of the Greek people, clearly gives to the wife a fairly strong position in the family in view of the fact that, in the case of the dissolution of the marriage, the dowry is restored to the wife or to her heirs.[12] It sometimes happens that many parents leave their male descendents practically without inheritance in order to be able to give a "suitable" dowry to their daughters, with the result that a large number of assets, especially immovables, belong to women in Greece. But the "hunt for a dowry" constituted, until the very recent past, a demoralising element in the Greek way of life. Fortunately, the younger generation seems to be free from this preoccupation.

A reform of Family Law should abolish the obligation to give a dowry and, indeed, the whole institution of the dowry. Also in need of reform is the principle set out in Article 1397 of the Greek Civil Code, that "the marriage shall involve no change in the patrimonial autonomy of the spouses". In practice, this principle accords to the husband the whole benefit of efforts that are often made by the spouses in common. A sound reform should replace both the dowry and the separation of property by a community of acquisitions (*communauté des acquêts*). Such community should operate during the marriage and not only at its dissolution.

Finally, the superiority of the husband is exemplified in the relations between the parents and legitimate children. Not only does the child receive the surname of the father[13], but the "paternal power" over the child belongs to the father as of

---

5. Art. 1392 Greek Civil Code.
6. Art. 1396 Greek Civil Code.
7. Arts. 1495-1498.
8. Art. 1406, para. 1.
9. Art. 1398.
10. Art. 1412.
11. Cf. Arts. 1417-1420.
12. Art. 1426.
13. Art. 1493.

right. In this function the father is replaced by the mother only in the case of the father's incapacity to exercise it.[14] The paternal power is accompanied by the father's "right and duty" to the personal protection of the child and to his legal representation.[15] The protection of the child includes his education, supervision and his instruction, the choice of his residence and, should the need arise, "the employment of appropriate means of correction".[16] Only in the case of divorce or of the annulment of the marriage are the father and mother regarded as equal by the law, as far as the protection of the child is concerned.[17]

It has now become necessary to reform Family Law with regard to the equality of the spouses, as a result of the coming into effect, on 11 June 1975, of the new Constitution of the Greek Republic. This Constitution[18] provides for "the equal rights and equal obligations for men and women". It is therefore necessary to change almost all the provisions cited above. The task has fallen upon a Committee of experts appointed by the Ministry of Justice under the chairmanship of Professor A Gazis. He has expressed the opinion, so far a personal one only[19], that it is necessary to introduce a right of joint decision for the two spouses in respect of questions affecting the family. He also advocates equality in connection with the expenses of the marriage and the obligation of support. Moreover, he takes the view that the father and the mother must have equal rights with regard to the children, even after the dissolution of the marriage. It would also be necessary to permit a free choice in respect of the surname of the married woman and the children of the marriage.

III. Illegitimate Children

Greek legislation is more progressive with regard to illegitimate children. This has been so from 1926 onwards. Indeed, the decree of 15/17 July 1926 which governed the matter, was very tolerant for its time. The provisions of that decree[20] provide the basis for the provisions of the Code on natural children. Article 1530 of the Greek Civil Code enunciates the principle that the natural child has the same position as a legitimate child, not only with regard to the mother but also vis-à-vis relatives on the maternal side, and receives the family surname of the mother. If the mother marries, her husband may give his surname to the child, if both mother and child agree to this.[21] It is thus possible to integrate a mother's illegitimate child into the legitimate family created by the mother at a later stage.

Recognition of the natural child by the father is always permitted, even after his death, his absence or his mental illness. This recognition may be effected by

---

14. Art. 1500.
15. Art. 1501.
16. Art. 1502.
17. Arts. 1503-1506.
18. In Art. 4 para. 2.
19. Cf. *Nomikon Vima* 1975, p. 576.
20. Abrogated by Art. 87 of the introductory law of the Greek Civil Code.
21. Art. 1531.

the paternal grandfather.[22] The procedure is either by a unilateral declaration by the father, or the grandfather, whether before a notary or by will (voluntary recognition), or by a court action (judicial recognition). Voluntary recognition[23] is unconditional and irrevocable. However, it can be opposed within certain time limits by the mother, the child or its heirs, as well as by anyone who has a legitimate interest. The only ground for such an attack is that the author of the voluntary recognition is neither the father nor the grandfather of the child.

By a voluntary recognition, the natural child receives the father's surname and, save in two cases, the rights and obligations of a legitimate child. The two cases are: (a) if, at the moment of the voluntary recognition the father is married, the recognised infant can only cohabit in the matrimonial home if the spouse of the father consents to it; (b) the right of succession, on intestacy, of the child who is voluntarily recognised is reduced by one half in respect of the succession of his father, if he competes with legitimate descendants, the father, mother, or the spouse of the father. This last provision, which discriminates against the recognised child, is inserted in the Code in order to favour the legitimate family. But nothing prevents the father from distributing his estate by will. Subject to the legal reserve, he is entitled, for example, to leave equal shares to his children whether legitimate or recognised. The recognised child is indeed a reserved heir vis-à-vis his father, except that he is only entitled to one half of the reserve when he competes with a legitimate child.

Judicial recognition is obtained[24] by the mother or by the illegitimate child through an action in court brought against the father or against his heirs. Paternity is presumed if it is established that the person against whom the action is brought has maintained sexual relations with the mother during the "critical period" of conception, that is, between the 103rd and 124th day before the birth of the child. An action to establish paternity cannot be brought if it can be proved that the mother had sexual relations with others at the time of conception. In other words, Greek law admits the famous *exceptio plurium* of Roman law. But such an exception is no longer justified in our time if the link can be established by medical or physiological means. Furthermore, the action to establish paternity cannot be brought if the mother was married at the time of conception, unless her husband has repudiated the infant. In any case, an action to establish paternity is subject to prescription after five years as from the birth or from the repudiation of the child. The effects of judicial recognition are limited. The father is only under an obligation to support his child "to the extent of the social position of the mother and the patrimonial circumstances of the father". Account is specially taken of the maintenance obligations towards a spouse or the legitimate descendants of the father.[25] The father must pay to the mother the costs of the delivery, as well as the costs of her proper maintenance during the two months prior to, and four months after, the delivery, even if the child should happen to be stillborn.[26] A class sentiment can be seen here. It appears even more strongly in

---

22. Art. 1532.
23. Arts. 1533-1539.
24. Arts. 1540-1555.
25. Art. 1545.
26. Art. 1551.

the rule of Article 1546, to the effect that the alimentary obligation of the father arises only if the child is not in a position to provide for its maintenance by its own means. This includes the minor child's work.

An agreement which settles the obligation to support is admissible and valid, even if a lump sum is fixed which is to be paid in full discharge of the alimentary debt, provided that this agreement is ratified by the Court.

There is a provision[27] in favour of the child and its mother, according to which the obligations of the father concerning the maintenance and costs of delivery are not extinguished by the death of the father, whether the death occurs before or after the birth.

It should be mentioned that, under certain conditions, judicial recognition has all the effects of voluntary recognition.[28] These conditions are that the action has been brought during the lifetime of the father, that the child was conceived while the father was engaged to the mother, or as a result of rape, abduction or seduction of the mother. The same rule applies if the conception occurred when the father was the guardian of the mother, owed her 'protection, or was holding her in a state of subjection, for example as a servant, or if he was simply cohabiting with her.

Greek Law also provides for the legitimation of the natural child, either by the subsequent marriage of its parents, or by a judicial decision.[29]

A child legitimated by the subsequent marriage of his natural parents occupies, in all respects, the position of a legitimate child in respect of its parents. The parents are required, after the marriage, to declare to an official of the Registry of Civil Status that the child is their own. But an omission to make this declaration does not place a child born to them at a disadvantage.

Judicial legitimation is carried out by decision of the Court at the request of the father. The Court admits it if the father has not any legitimate descendants, if the child or his legal representative consents to it and if the legitimation by the subsequent marriage of the mother is impossible, for example, by reason of the death of the mother. Judicial legitimation is excluded if the father and mother of the child were blood relatives in the direct line or collaterals in the second degree. The effects of judicial legitimation are that the legitimated infant occupies, in all respects, vis-à-vis the father, the position of a legitimate child.

There are no plans to reform the Greek Law on Natural Children, on legitimation and recognition. On the one hand this can be accounted for by the relative efficacy of the existing law and, on the other hand, by the fact that the number of illegitimate children in Greece is not very high.

IV. Divorce

At the beginning of the Christian era when the Emperor Constantine the Great, by the Edict of Milan (313 AD) proclaimed religious tolerance and constructed the new capital of the Roman Empire at Byzantium (325 AD)[30] divorce

---

27. Art. 1553.
28. Perfect judicial recognition, Art. 1555.
29. Arts. 1556-1567.
30. The capital that subsequently took his name—Constantinople.

was a private affair of the spouses, especially of the husband who could, by simple repudiation, divorce his wife. This privilege of divorce survived in practice for a long time in the Byzantine Empire, despite the opposition of the Christian Church and even despite Novels 117 and 134 of Justinian. Much later, in the tenth and eleventh centuries, Emperor Leo VI the Philosopher imposed, by his famous Novel 89, the religious celebration of marriage. It was at that stage that the ecclesiastical jurisdiction was extended to divorce. Henceforth, this had to be pronounced by a judicial decision and on the grounds provided for in Novel 117. This regime of divorce remained more or less intact in Greece until the first decade of our century. In 1920 Law No. 2228 introduced a regime of divorce which was more modern and systematic. It provided a general clause on divorce based upon the fault of a spouse, causing the breakdown of the conjugal link. This law was repealed by the Greek Civil Code which, however, did not change the principle of the earlier law. As to jurisdiction, the State Courts had already replaced the ecclesiastical jurisdiction, ever since the time when the modern Greek State was established.

Under present law divorce is pronounced by virtue of Article 1438 of the Greek Civil Code. This requires judicial decision, which is not subject to appeal and on the grounds set out in Articles 1439-1446 only. These are: (a) adultery or bigamy, (b) an attempt on the life of the other spouse, (c) malicious desertion, (d) the breakdown of the conjugal link, (e) unsoundness of mind, (f) leprosy, (g) absence declared by judicial decision, and (h) impotence, of which the plaintiff was ignorant, which existed at the time of the marriage.

Among the reasons for divorce the most frequently applied is the breakdown of the conjugal link.[31] It has been calculated[32] that eighty percent of divorces are pronounced on this ground in Greece. The text of Article 1442 of the Greek Civil Code reads as follows:

"Each of the spouses may petition for a divorce if, through the fault of the other spouse, the conjugal link has been seriously broken to such an extent that the maintenance of the joint married life has become truly intolerable to the petitioner. The latter is not entitled to petition if, while the fault is imputable to both spouses at the same time, the breakdown of the conjugal link is mainly attributable to the petitioner."

There is a very extensive case law based on this Article, a case law that reflects the exigencies of life, the moral ideas of the judge and the social change of our times. Fault relating to the observance of a great variety of family duties, friction regarding the moral standards of the person of the spouse and opposition to social duties and interests, all fall under this general provision. But something which is also hidden under this provision is divorce by mutual consent. This is prohibited by law but, nevertheless, it is fairly commonly practised, indeed tolerated and even favoured by the judge since it gives him the opportunity to make a quick decision in a difficult situation on the basis of a suitable formula which appears as an instance of the application of Article 1442 of the Greek Civil Code.

---

31. Provided for by Art. 1442.
32. See Skorini-Paparigopoulou, *op. cit.* pp. 183-190.

In the case of Articles 1439-1442 of the Greek Civil Code (grounds imputable to one of the spouses), the right to divorce, in Greek law, is cancelled by a pardon. There is a period of limitation that extends to one year from the time when the ground for divorce came to the notice of the innocent party, with the exception of malicious desertion.[33] But the facts, which can no longer serve in themselves as the foundation for a petition for divorce, may be invoked in support of an action for divorce based on other grounds.[34]

The effects of divorce are set out in Articles 1452-1466 and 1503-1504 of the Greek Civil Code. The wife resumes her maiden surname. She has a right to appropriate maintenance, provided the husband is solely responsible for the divorce and the wife cannot provide for her own maintenance from private income or from her employment which she should have been able to pursue taking into account the conditions of her married life. Conversely, when the wife is the guilty party, the divorced husband may only claim maintenance if he is not in a condition to provide for himself.

The obligation of the guilty spouse to furnish maintenance is cancelled in the case of a subsequent marriage of the recipient, but it does not cease on the death of the debtor. If there are serious grounds, maintenance may be paid in one lump sum at the request of the person entitled to it. If there is a serious attempt on the person of the innocent party, the guilty party may be required to pay a sum of money to the injured party as compensation for non-material damage. It is also provided that gifts made during the engagement or during the course of the marriage are revoked.

The most important question, that of the children of the divorced couple, is governed by Articles 1503 and 1504 of the Greek Civil Code. The Court may make an order regarding the protection of the child in accordance with his best interest. It can also entrust his care to a third person, but the law regards this as an exception. The rule is that the care of the child belongs to the spouse who is declared not responsible for the divorce. If both of them are declared responsible, then the custody of a daughter and of a son below ten years of age belongs to the mother; while the custody of a son older than ten years belongs to the father. In any event, the parent who is not given custody always has the right to maintain personal relations with the child. Details of access are subject to the authority of the Court.

No one can ignore the value of marriage, especially in contemporary life, or the value of the family created by the marriage, not only for the spouses but also for the children born of the marriage. Thus, the dissolution of a marriage and the dissolution of the family which ensues, is always and in every case a very serious matter to be considered apart from public and social interests. It is hardly necessary to say that the legislator must find the means of protecting the family and of helping it towards its well-being. Unfortunately it is also true that, in each epoch and each place, there are instances of marriages that can no longer fulfil their function either in respect of the spouses, or in respect of the children. It is necessary in such instances to preserve these formal unions and for how long?

---

33. Art. 1448.
34. Art. 1449.

The question has been posed in Greece in the last few years in the form of a full discussion upon whether to permit "automatic divorce", that is to say, divorce pronounced by the Court after a period of separation of the spouses. Two camps have formed, for and against such a reform. The adversaries to the reform are guided by the Orthodox Church which has declared itself strongly against it although the Orthodox Church of Crete has, by a Cretan Law of 1900, consented to the dissolution of a marriage if it has broken down objectively. On 18 March 1956 a proposal was submitted to Parliament by 65 members (out of 300). It provided for the promulgation of a law permitting divorce after seven years of separation of the spouses, even at the request of the party solely responsible for that separation. In 1966, at the invitation of the Minister of Justice, the Faculties of Law considered the problem. The Faculty of Law of the University of Thessalonica, on the proposal of Professors K Simantiras and J Deliyannis, elaborated a draft law permitting petitions for divorce after seven years of separation, provided that the breakdown of the conjugal link is so serious that it could not be expected that joint life could be re-established. Clauses were included in the draft law intended to prevent divorce in certain special circumstances, that is, if divorce would cause exceptional hardship to the innocent party, or if a divorce would be contrary to "the spirit of the law".

Discussion on this reform was discontinued after the *Coup d'Etat* of 21 April 1967 and the establishment of a military dictatorship. However, it was resumed after the political change of 23 July 1974. Argument for reform and reactions against it, familiar from the earlier debate, were repeated. Nevertheless, the Ministry of Justice has prepared a new draft law permitting divorce after five years of separation and suggested a reform of a number of other aspects of the law of divorce, which had been the object of major criticisms.

This draft, which dates back to 1975, is based on a project of Professor A Gazis. It consists of eleven articles which modify Articles 1442, 1447-1451 and 1453-1454 of the Greek Civil Code and repeal Article 1455. A new Article has been added which permits the contractual regulation of the effects of the divorce on condition that the settlement is approved by the Court.

The most important proposal is contained in the text of Article 1442 of the Greek Civil Code. It is proposed that it should read:

> "Each of the spouses may petition for divorce if conjugal life has been disrupted to such an extent that the maintenance of married life in common has become truly intolerable for the petitioner. In the case of a separation for five years, each of the spouses may petition for divorce, unless a hope exists for the restitution of the conjugal link."

By this modification Greek Law abandons the principle of fault and adopts the objective breakdown as a ground for divorce. Breakdown is presumed in the case of separation for five years. The provisions of Articles 1447 and 1448 of the Greek Civil Code on pardon and on prescription are also likely to be modified in order to take into account the above mentioned changes. Another provision, that of the new Article 1450, will permit the Courts to declare the petitioner to be the person solely responsible for the divorce.

As far as the effects of the divorce are concerned, the project of 1975 provides for the abolition of the obligation of support by the husband if he is declared solely responsible for the divorce. In the spirit of the equality of the spouses, the obligation of support will henceforth burden[35] the spouse declared solely responsible, when the other spouse cannot ensure his or her own maintenance out of his or her estate, or from income from work which may have been carried on during marriage. Other effects of the divorce are not affected by the draft law, with the exception of the obligation to make reparation for non-material damage. By virtue of the new Article 1453, it will be replaced by a wider obligation to make reparation to the innocent spouse for injury caused by the divorce.

The project of 1975 clearly does not introduce the basic reforms needed in Greek Family Law. Its restricted aim is to "liberate" a number of unhappy spouses from a marriage which has failed and give the possibility of a lawful union to illegitimate couples and families. Nevertheless, without doubt, this project constitutes a first step towards the modernisation of Family Law in Greece and a step towards the introduction of a law appropriate to the exigencies of life and of the family in our time.

Appendix

1. The aforementioned Committee which is working on legislation for the new Constitution under the Chairmanship of Professor Gazis to achieve equality between the sexes, has fixed as its target the replacement of the paternal right by the equal right of both parents of a family in respect of support and alimony payments, as well as marriage rights and the use of the family surname. Reform must also be carried out with regard to the financial and property relationship of the spouses. However, the existing Greek system of separation creates in fact fewer problems.

The work of the Committee is somewhat delayed in all these cases and should be accelerated, especially as Article 116, paragraph 1 of the Greek Constitution foresees that the full effect of equal rights must take place prior to 31 December 1982. Should such amendments not be introduced by Statute by that date, equal rights will automatically become law and the courts in the country will have to decide which of the existing laws are applicable and which are not.

2. There is also some delay in the case of divorce reform. Although practically all the Greek Bar Associations and Courts, as well as the Law Faculties of the Universities of Athens and Salonika, have been strongly in favour of such reforms, the opposition of the Church is of such magnitude that it is doubtful when and to what extent such a reform will take place.

---

35. New Art. 1454 of the Greek Civil Code.

CHAPTER VII. THE REFORM OF FAMILY LAW IN ITALY

by Vito Librando

I. Equality of the Spouses

A new legal regime was brought in for the Italian family by a law that was passed in 1975. This chiefly concerned the conditions necessary to contract a marriage, nullity, the rights and obligations in marriage, the family property and affiliation. In defining the relations between the spouses within the family, the legislator was guided by the principle of the State Charter which acknowledged the moral and legal equality of the spouses within the legal limits necessary to guarantee the unity of the family. The achievement of this equality between the spouses has evolved very slowly, as a result of the changing ways of society which has involved the wife more and more in economic and public affairs, and is in sharp contrast to the previous dominance of the husband in all family matters.

Previously, family relations had been based on the principle of the pater-familias, who had control of all the family arrangements.

The Civil Code of 1865, the first code promulgated in Italy after the unification, declared that marriage imposed on the two spouses the reciprocal obligation of cohabitation, fidelity and assistance and also, in harmony with the Code Napoléon, that "the husband is the head of the family". It also stated the principle of the husband's authority. But, taking into account the position which family society occupied at that time and the small appreciation of the wife's contribution to the family economy, this principle was strictly interpreted. Article 134 of the same Code laid down another condition which was clearly disadvantageous to the wife. She was not allowed to give away, dispose of, or charge her movable assets, nor to contract loans, surrender or use her capital or take legal proceedings, following these acts, without the authorisation of her husband. Thus, it was for the husband to implement the will of the wife who consequently had, by virtue of the above mentioned legal provision, only a limited capacity to act concerning the legal acts mentioned, no more than the capacity of a person subjected to the regime of a guardianship. An act carried out by the wife without the authorisation of the husband was null and void, but this nullity could be opposed by either of the spouses, by their heirs or by other interested parties.

This rule regarding authorisation by the husband was abolished by law No. 1176 in 1919, which gave to the wife the full capacity to act regarding her own belongings, but the principle of the husband's power remained and was retained in the Civil Code of 1942, in article 144. That article stipulated that the husband was the head of the family, that the wife shared his civil status, that she must take his name and must accompany him wherever he thinks fit to plan his own residence.

Concerning the husband's power and the resultant consequences relative to the substantial inequality between the spouses, the doctrine agreed, in affirming that the position of privilege attributed to the husband, did not constitute a feudal prerogative of sex. But it was recognised that this position was the result of the requirement, common to every society and of which the legislator was aware, of assuring to the family unit a leader who, at least in certain situations, can assume an exclusive responsibility for the direction of the family in order to safeguard the family as a unit.[1] This can be agreed because the principle of a single direction of the family, traditional in the legal system, necessarily imposed sacrifice on one of the spouses with regard to the other. And this, taking into account the legal tradition and the customs of the country, could only occur by attributing the dominant position to the husband. On this subject it has been remarked that in principle the husband, because of his activity in employment, enjoyed a pre-eminent role in the family concerning the acquisition of the necessary finances and that relations with third parties were generally handled by the husband, the wife most often being relegated to the sphere of the household. The legislator's choice of entrusting the direction of the family to the husband was thus a natural one and conformed with the organisation of the family in practice.

Turning to an examination of the way in which the Civil Code of 1942 arranged the organisation of the family and the position it gave to each of the spouses within the family itself, it is possible to evaluate the diversities in their treatment and to take account some judgments on the subject by the Constitutional Court. It must be said that, in the cases where the said Code spoke purely and simply of the status of spouse and of parents without having regard to the internal organisation of the family and to the necessity of safeguarding its unitary character, the legislator could not have treated the related situations differently and therefore did not make any distinction in the position of each of the spouses. This also applied, for example, concerning the right of opposition by one of the spouses to the marriage of the other, to the grounds for attacking his own marriage, to the reciprocity of the obligations of cohabitation, fidelity and help, to the extent of fundamental duties imposed by the marriage and, in principle, to the right of claiming a separation in cases of violation of these obligations.

When, on the contrary, the quality of being a spouse or a parent was important not for those aspects but for its repercussions in the organisation of the family, the legislator, intent on giving to the latter a unitary orientation, laid down provisions which would ensure the pre-eminence of the husband with regard to the wife. As has been seen, article 144 of the Civil Code laid down the principle of the husband's authority and article 316, after having declared that a child is subjected to the authority of its parents until its majority, attributed to the father the exercise of this authority. In any case it is as well to remember that the inequality between the spouses derived not only from the two provisions cited above, but also from other provisions whose basis was not altogether concerned with the need to assure the unity of the family. It was mainly a question of article 45 of the Civil Code which stipulated that the wife who was not physically separated had the domicile of the husband, of article 151 which did not permit the wife, in the case of adultery committed by the husband, to act separately when

---

1. See Barassi, *The Legitimate Family*, Milan 1947, p. 181; Degni, *The Law of the Family*, Padua 1943, p. 227; De Ruggero-Maroi, *Institutions of Private Law*, Milan 1950, vol. 1, p. 291; Gangi, *Marriage*, Milan 1953, p. 258; Jemolo, *Marriage*, Turin 1961, p. 419.

the fact constituted a 'grave injury', of article 338 which gave the right to the father of fixing for the surviving mother, either by will, by public document or by authenticated private document, conditions on the subject of the education of the children and the administration of their estate.

The disparity of treatment also resulted from other provisions for which no justification could have been furnished other than that of lack of confidence with regard to the wife. In this connection, articles 331 and 340 of the Civil Code will be examined later.

Article 144 of the Civil Code set the principle of the husband's authority and imposed on the wife three particular obligations with regard to the husband:

(a) To share his civil status
(b) To take his name
(c) To accompany him wherever he decides to fix his residence.

Regarding the wife's obligation to share the civil status of the husband, it was emphasised that this provision, because of its indeterminate character, had no very clear meaning. In looking for the reason for this provision, some were of the opinion that it must have derived from the provisions on nationality.[2] It was thought that the legislator wished to insist on the rule that the wife took the nationality of the husband on marriage. But this opinion had been criticised by the fact that the wife's acquisition in her own right of the civil status of the husband had already been provided for by the legislation in article 10 of the 1912 law, No. 555. On this subject one is entitled to maintain that it did not appear logical for the same legislator, in treating the personal relations between the spouses, to repeat in article 144 that which he had already established with clarity in the said law of 1912.[3]

Other authors have maintained that the statement that the wife follows the civil status of the husband only serves to fix the limits and the content of the husband's obligation to provide for the maintenance of the wife.[4] According to these authors the obligation in question falls on the husband not only in proportion to his resources but also in taking into account his standing in society. This theory had been criticised by observing that the provision had been included amongst the obligations of the wife and not amongst the duties of the husband. The law took no account that the content of the obligation of support falls on the husband, and this was defined by a specially inserted provision, that is, in article 145 of the Civil Code. According to another doctrinal opinion[5], the provision in question signified that the wife had to respect the course of life of the family group, which however had been set by the husband. That is, the wife had to adapt her expenditure to this way of life, for herself as well as for the family. This provision, which had already existed in the Civil Code of 1965 and was also necessary to the system of 1942, became all the more essential after the abolition

---

2. Jemolo, *Marriage, op. cit.*, p. 423; Lojacono, *The Power of the Husband in the Personal Relations between Spouses*, Milan 1963, p. 140.
3. Stella Richter G, *Current Profiles of the Power of the Husband*, Milan 1970, p. 85 ff.
4. Spinelli, "Relationship between the parity of the spouses and the unity of the family", in *Iustitia* 1962, p. 168; La Torre, "The maintenance of the wife and the power of the husband", in *Foro it.*, I, c. 996.
5. Stella Richter G, *op. cit.*, p. 91 ff.

of the husband's authority because the wife had acquired the right of disposal of her own property.

The adoption of the husband's name involved as a consequence that the wife, while retaining her own name, had to place before it the name of her husband. The reason for this provision was to affirm the concept of the family unity while retaining the onomastic position of the wife. In this connection it seems opportune to recall that certain authors objected that, in this way, the needs of the married woman could be prejudiced, especially when the wife was carrying on a commercial occupation or liberal profession which was known by the family name. To obviate this inconvenience, the same authors proposed that the obligation of the wife to use the name of the husband remained only in those connections where her belonging to the family group had some significance.[6] The Court of Appeal pronounced on this problem in a judgment of 1970. It recognised that in the sphere of her professional activities and in her business relations, the use by the wife of the only family name could be forbidden to her only in the case where such exclusive use constituted gravely injurious behaviour with regard to the husband. This is authorised when justified by the requirement of a better identification of the wife with regard to persons who, in the past, had occasion to have recourse to her above mentioned activities. Thus the Court of Appeal sanctioned a situation already widespread in practice. According to article 149 of the Civil Code the wife kept the name of her husband during widowhood but was not obliged to keep it on remarriage. This was not only for practical reasons but chiefly because, with a new marriage a new family is established.

Some were of the opinion that during physical separation the obligation of the wife to use the name of the husband ceased. In fact, the unity of the family being profoundly compromised by the fact of separation, the reason for the obligation in question, which was to affirm the principle of the unity of the family, had ceased to exist.[7] On this subject others rightly objected that in reality the unity of the family was not lacking during separation and that only the reciprocal obligations proper to the marriage were suspended, especially those of cohabitation and of assistance, consequently physical separation could not have any effect on the situation regarding the wife's name.[8]

This opinion, doubtless based on correct facts, was corroborated by a provision in article 156 of the Civil Code according to which, in certain circumstances, the Court could prohibit a wife from using the name of the husband in cases where that could be shown to be damaging to him. While a judicial decision is required to relieve the wife of the right to use her husband's name, there was no rule obliging her to continue to make use of it, which was why this obligation remained unchanged in the case of physical separation.

---

6. Briguglio, "On the name of the married woman", in *Riv. trim. dir. proc. civ.* 1957, p. 1625; Delitala, "The assumption of the name of the husband", in *Riv. trim. dir. proc. civ.*, 1963, p. 304.

7. Delitala, *op. cit.*, p. 306.

8. Stella Richter F., *op. cit.*, p. 119. She cites Modugno, "Equality in the unity of the family", in *Iustitia* 1967, p. 177; Mirabelli, "Maintenance of the wife and art. 29 of the Constitution", in *Giur. Costit.* 1967, p. 1700; Perlingieri, "Reflections on the unity of the family", in *Dir. Giur.* 1970, pp. 10-12.

The prohibition of the use of the husband's name had been conceived by the legislator as a means of safeguarding his person. Its obvious aim was to avoid, as far as possible, bringing to the notice of third parties the fact of the marriage. Such a protection was accorded in particularly serious cases where the wife persists in conduct injurious to her spouse. On the other hand, there was the problem of the necessity for a similar protection for the separated wife to have her right recognised not to use the name of the husband in the case where such use would involve damage to her by reason of the misconduct of the husband. The question was submitted to the Constitutional Court in 1970, which declared that article 156 of the Civil Code was unconstitutional so far as it excluded such a right for the wife. The Court held that that article imposed an inadmissible inequality between spouses resulting in a position of unjustifiable superiority of the husband or inferiority of the wife, in contradiction to article 29 of the Constitution. In addition, article 144 of the Civil Code stated that the choice of the matrimonial home was a prerogative of the husband and the wife was obliged to accompany her husband wherever he thought fit to reside. In any case the doctrine and the case law had emphasised the fact that the provision immediately recalled the concept of opportunity, which is synonymous with discretion and which is clearly opposed to the concept of arbitration.[9] Consequently the husband had to exercise the authority in question in the best interests of the family so that the residence chosen may be expedient for the family itself in material aspects as well as in the moral and spiritual aspect. These principles were reaffirmed by article 153 of the Civil Code. This provision enabled the wife to obtain a declaration of physical separation in the case where the husband, without a legitimate reason, had not established a home, or refused to plan it in a way suitable to the conditions of the family.[10]

Article 316 of the Civil Code of 1942 declared that the paternal power rested in both parents but was exercisable by the father, and this had the clear object of ensuring the unity of the family. The exercise of the paternal power passed to the

---

9. Jemolo, *Marriage*, p. 423, 424; Stella Richter G, *op. cit.*, p. 127 ff. The case law has held especially that the discretionary power of the husband concerning the place of residence was not accorded by the law in the personal interest of the husband, but in the greater interest of the family. Consequently the power could not be exercised if inconsistent with this aim and it was excessive if the husband, without taking account of the needs of the family and the requirements of married life, decided to remove the residence elsewhere by imposing his own wishes despotically on his wife [Court of Appeal of Florence, 1953, *Giurisprud. Toscana* 1953, 363; Court of Appeal of Florence *ibid* 1956, 702]. The Court of Appeal (Cass. 29.1.1943, *Foro It. Reper.* 1943-45, See Marriage, n. 87) held that the residence the husband should plan, in conformity with art. 144 Cc. in order that the wife should be obliged to follow him, must be suitable not only to the resources of the husband, but also in the moral sense, which is why the wife could refuse to follow the husband to the house of parents-in-law if such a refusal was justified by grave and serious reasons rendering life with the parents-in-law intolerable.
10. Art. 153 Cc was repealed by art. 34 of the Law of 19 July 1975, n. 151. In fact art. 33 of this Law enunciated a new text of art. 151 Cc in sanctioning the principle according to which physical separation can be judicially claimed when 'facts are produced . . . such as to render intolerable the continuation of the joint life . . .' On the other hand, the fixing of the home is currently deferred to the two spouses, according to the requirements of both and the pre-eminent requirements of the family. It follows from this that even today, when the husband does not wish to settle the matrimonial home, the wife has the power to act separately. This power belongs equally to the husband in the contrary case.

mother in the case of the permanent disability of the father, such as death, or temporary prevention, such as a prolonged absence or a serious illness rendering it impossible for him to exercise his powers. The exercise of the paternal power by the mother occurred again in the case of legal impossibility for the father, such as that stemming from a judicial prohibition or other specific situations provided for by provisions of the law. Certain criminal convictions involved the loss or suspension of the paternal power, while the Court can pronounce the loss of the paternal power by the parent who infringes or neglects his duties to the grave prejudice of the child.

It should be emphasised here that regarding the exercise of the paternal authority, which was entrusted in various cases to the mother, limitations were admitted which created a remarkable inequality of treatment of the parents. Notably, the father could exercise his power by personal decision, except for the duty of respecting moral principles in the education and training of his children and except for the necessity of preliminary judicial authorisation for the most important patrimonial acts concerning the property of his children. Yet limits and conditions were imposed on the mother acting in the same capacity. In effect, the father could fix conditions for the surviving mother regarding the education of the children and the administration of their property. The doctrine emphasised that this limitation could not be explained by the situation of pre-eminence which the Code had established for the father in the sphere of the family, because this superiority of the father was only intended for the purpose of unity of orientation in the direction of the family interests, and to avoid disagreements between the parents remaining unresolved to the prejudice of the children, always providing that the father was actually exercising his paternal authority.[11]

Apart from the above, when the exercise of the paternal power passed to the mother, following a decision of forfeiture by the father, the Juvenile Court could in particular circumstances, such as are provided for in article 331 of the Civil Code, adopt requirements which the mother would be bound to observe. Even for this limitation the doctrine has manifested its opposition by stressing that, beyond the fact that it involves an unjustified inequality of treatment of the spouses, it represents a real and specific lack of confidence with regard to the wife.[12]

A similar objection was expressed on the subject of article 340 of the Civil Code. This article laid down that a mother desiring to contract a new marriage should announce it beforehand to the Court, which could set conditions for her concerning the administration of the children's estate and their education. An obvious diversity existed between the spouses even with regard to separation in the case of adultery. Article 151 of the Civil Code, in including adultery as one of the grounds for separation, admitted the petition by the wife for the adultery of the husband only in the case where particular circumstances rendered the fact gravely injurious to the wife. This distinction between the adultery of the wife and that of the husband, already existing in a more explicit way in the Civil Code of 1865, has been incorporated in the Code of 1942 in consideration of the different

---

11. Degni, *The Law of the Family*, p. 414; Stella Richter G, *op. cit.*, pp. 78, 79.
12. Stella Richter G., *op. cit.*, p. 72.

outlook by society in each situation. In fact, the wife's adultery was held to be more injurious for its effect on the family and even because of the danger of *commixtio sanguinis* which it involved.

The adultery of the husband as a ground for physical separation, constituted a grave injury to the wife, without need of other investigation into the gravity of the matter, in a case where a husband had brought a mistress into the matrimonial home, or elsewhere in a notorious way. The occasional adultery of the husband could only constitute grave injury to the wife in particular cases entailing obvious prejudice to the wife with regard to her social or moral circumstances.

The differentiation between the adultery of the husband and that of the wife in the effects of physical separation were criticised by the doctrine which emphasised that, from the moral point of view, the adultery of the husband is just as reprehensible as that of the wife and that, from the legal point of view the inequality of treatment is unjustified when the obligation of fidelity of both spouses is taken into account.[13] When considering this question the Constitutional Court declared in 1968 that the second paragraph of article 151 of the Civil Code was constitutionally illegal, putting an end to the distinction between the adultery of the husband and that of the wife as far as it concerns the physical separation of the spouses. In the reasons for its decision, the Court stressed that the diversity in the treatment of conjugal infidelity is explained neither in terms of the duty of fidelity to which the two spouses are bound, not by having regard to the guardianship of the family unit, in view of which the legislator can according article 29 of the Constitution, introduce limitations of the principle of moral and legal equality of the spouses. Another difference in the treatment of the spouses stemmed from article 145 of the Civil Code concerning the duty of maintenance. According to that article the husband had a duty to provide for his wife whatever was necessary for the needs of life in proportion to his resources, but the wife was not obliged to contribute to the maintenance of the husband unless the latter had insufficient means of his own. In 1970 the Constitutional Court to whom the question had been submitted declared that the first paragraph of article 145 was unconstitutional in so far as it does not subordinate the duty of the husband to the condition that the wife had not sufficient means. Even on this point the Court recognised the inconsistency in the reasons for the different treatment of the spouses from that dealing with the unity of the family.

It may be recalled that, according to article 10 of the law of 1912, a wife being an Italian national married to a foreigner lost her Italian nationality on marriage irrespective of her own wish, provided that the husband had a nationality which was extended to the wife by reason of the marriage. This rule, provided exclusively for the wife in the case of the loss of her Italian nationality, created an unjustified and irrational inequality of treatment between the two spouses, an inequality which was abolished by a judgment in 1975 of the Constitutional Court when considering the question.

Already under the regime of the 1942 Code and mainly through the intervention of the Constitutional Court taking into account the tenets and public opinion in general, a move was made towards the most rigorous application of

---

13. Degni, *op. cit.*, p. 236 ff; Jemolo, *Marriage*, p. 452.

the principle of equality of the spouses sanctioned by the Constitution. The legislator, involved since 1967 with the reform of the family law, had the task *inter alia* of realising in a concrete manner the above mentioned principle and of establishing its limits.[14] Throughout long and laborious discussions in Parliament, resumed in the course of three legislative sessions, the result was to accept on the broadest lines the principle of the equality of the spouses and consequently to reduce to the minimum the limitations of this principle. In fact, the only limits provided for by the reformed law of 1975 were in practice the use by the son of the father's name—while for the wife it was only provided that she add her husband's name to her own—and the atrribution to the father of the power to take urgent measures if these cannot be deferred, if there is a danger threatening serious prejudice to the child. To summarise, the equality of the spouses is now complete.

Article 24 of the law of 19 May 1975 in fact replaced article 143 of the Civil Code of 1942 by stating that through the marriage, the husband and the wife acquire the same rights and assume the same duties. Reciprocal obligations of fidelity, of moral and material support, derive from the marriage, as well as collaboration in the interest of the family, and cohabitation. The two spouses are bound to contribute to the needs of the family, each in proportion to his own resources and to his capacity for work, either professionally or in the household.

Article 26 of the same law replaced article 144 of the Civil Code of 1942, stating that the spouses should decide between themselves on the direction of the family life and on the situation of the matrimonial home, taking into account the prime requirements of the family and of themselves. Each of the spouses has the authority to realise the agreed orientation.

Article 138 of the new law replaced article 316 of the 1942 Code, stating that the child is subject to the authority of his parents until his majority or his emancipation, this authority to be exercised by the parents in mutual agreement.

Article 25 of the 1975 law introduced a declaration that a wife retains her Italian nationality, unless she expressly renounces it, even if, as a result of the marriage or of a change of nationality by the husband, she takes a foreign nationality.

It could be queried whether the articles providing for this confirmed equality of the spouses are constitutional, in view of the fact that article 29 of the Constitution makes allusion to limitations of this equality with a view to guaranteeing the unity of the family. However, article 29 of the Constitution does not in fact exclude the governing of the family being shared by both spouses; it leaves to the legislator the power to decide whether the question of the family unity is compatible with the equality of the spouses, or whether the latter should be limited in the interest of unity. The legislator has replied in the first sense for reasons which can be summarised as being the necessity of adapting the legal system to the new conditions of Italian life and to the undoubtedly new position of the wife in the family and in present-day social life. It might be maintained that in this way the unity of the family has been sacrified to the equality of the spouses. The

---

14. The first draft law for a major reform of the family law was presented to the Chamber of Deputies by the Minister of Justice, O Reale, in 1967: Doc. no. 3705/C, 4th legislative sessions.

contrary is the case. Having deliberately avoided friction between unity and equality, the legislator has affirmed the principle that equality, which is at the basis of family harmony, constitutes the foundation of unity. It may be significant to recall here that A. C. Jemolo had already denied, in 1961, in his treatise on *Marriage* that the unity of the family is incompatible, or less compatible, with the equality of the spouses.[15]

Undoubtedly the equality of the spouses in the administration of the family and in the exercise of the paternal authority, poses delicate problems in cases where the spouses do not have identical points of view. These cause the most debated problems in the discussion of schemes for reform, for which a great variety of solutions was put forward by academics and in Parliament. In the draft law of 1967 it was provided that in the case of disagreement, the wishes of the husband or father should prevail, subject to the wife's or mother's right of recourse to the Court in cases where the father's decisions were prejudicial to the life of the family. It was then for the judge to resolve the differences between the spouses. The text approved in 1971 by the Chamber of Deputies excluded the dominance of the father's wishes and referred the decision directly to the judge, who could be approached by either of the spouses. It was emphasised that the first solution did not respect the principle of equality in those circumstances which were the most important in family life; also, both solutions were a decisive reverse to the autonomy of the family, on account of the intervention of the judge's decision.

In fact, the reformed law took account of the autonomy of the family by rewording article 145 of the Civil Code and thus providing that, in cases of disagreement between the spouses, each of them could apply to the judge to work out a solution by consent. Where conciliation is not possible and the disagreement related to the situation of the conjugal home, or to other essential questions, the judge, if expressly and jointly required by the two spouses by irrevocable decision, can make an order which he considers the most appropriate to the requirements of the unity of the family. By the two means of attempting conciliation and judicial intervention, the judge practically acting as arbitrator, the legislator has sought to foster family unity while excluding outside interference in the direction of the family life, unless this was not desired by common agreement. If the spouses cannot arrive at an agreement, it is apparent that the family unity is seriously compromised and it may be necessary for the spouses to resort to physical separation.

Article 138 of the new law provides that, even in the ordinary exercise of the paternal authority, either of the two parents can ask for the intervention of the judge in the case of disagreement on particularly important matters, in the hope of a possible conciliation, unless it is a case of a danger for the welfare of the child, in which case the father can take measures which are urgent and ought not to be deferred. If the disagreement persists after attempts at conciliation, the judge will grant the power of decision to that parent whom he considers to be most capable of looking after the interests of the child, on the evidence put forward. It was not possible for the legislator to state that the spouses should

---

15. Jemolo, *op. cit.*, pp. 419, 420 and n. 3 (p. 419).

appear before the judge by common consent, in this case, for they would probably not agree to do so, and he therefore gave the initiative to both of them. This solution, of giving the authority to the parent most suitable to care for the child, is the one which most respects the autonomy of the family.

One of the questions which has been resolved by the new provisions, if only implicitly, inspired by the equality of the spouses is that concerning the work of the wife outside the household. Under the Code of 1942, still in force, the learned opinion[16] had maintained authoritatively that the wife could, even without the consent of the husband, engage herself in employment or could hire out her work. It was confirmed that the contract which the wife made, in this connection, was valid and that she could not use as an excuse for not carrying it out the fact that she had not previously consulted her husband, who would then have refused his assent. The same opinion recognised that in certain circumstances the husband's opposition to the outside work by his wife could be considered as reasonable, so that the wife's refusal to take account of it constituted a grave injury and was thus liable to give rise to separation. Even the case-law was expressed in the same sense, that the husband could not refuse to tolerate the extra-domestic work of the wife so long as it was not irreconcilable with the requirements of a valid family life. This was particularly true when the wife had first started work before marriage, and when the nature of the work was known to the husband.[17] As already mentioned, the new discipline of personal relations between the spouses provides a solution to this question. This results from the moral and legal equality of the spouses concerning their rights and duties, especially with regard to the obligation to contribute to the needs of the family as laid down in the last paragraph of article 24. The principle of the freedom of the married woman to engage in extra-domestic work was recognised in the law of 1975 in connection with the domicile. In comparison with the previous discipline, it permitted in a different way each of the spouses to have the domicile at the place where he or she has fixed the principal seat of his or her affairs or interests. Moreover, of the wife's right to engage in extra-domestic activity must not be stamped out, so it cannot be contested that the wife has a right to her personal domicile, although this right must be adapted to the obligation of cohabitation in order to safeguard the predominant needs of the family.

A more recent rule on this subject has stressed that, following the reform, the question arises in different terms. It is no longer the husband who fixes the residence, both spouses have the right to determine their place of residence by agreement and, if it should become necessary to sacrifice the requirements of one of the spouses, it is not necessarily the wife who must renounce her activities. This doctrine emphasises a particular problem which does not arise in the present state of Italian society and which will not do so until custom and habits are greatly modified—the problem that the natural vocation of woman is to dedicate herself to her children and household, the fact that often the extra-domestic

16. Jemolo, *op. cit.*, p. 422.
17. See in Court of Appeal of Milan, 17 Dec. 1968 in *Giustizia Civile, Rep.* 1969 'Separation, no. 62.' It concerned the particular case of a married woman who, before marriage, had been an actress in radio, television and the cinematograph.

work of the woman is less well rewarded than that of the man, the limited pension facilities for married women, and the fact that all these factors lead the spouses to sacrifice the wife's requirements, as opposed to the man's, for the sake of the family unity.[18]

The development of equality between the spouses takes account of the family fortune to verify the respective positions of the husband and the wife. However, it is not possible to examine this question here as it would involve the study of many delicate institutions and their evolution in the customs and traditions of Italian family society. It may be sufficient to emphasise that the reform law contains considerable innovations in comparison with the preceding systems by laying down the principle that, failing a contrary agreement, a regime of community property is set up between the spouses. The legislator has also introduced the institution of the "family business' according to which a member of the family, and thus the wife also, who engages in specific work within the family and the family business, has the right to maintenance in conformity with the financial situation of the family. That member participates in the profits of the family enterprise and in the assets which were subsequently acquired, as well as in its growth and the enlargement of its custom, in proportion to the quantity and quality of the work done. This is a development of the "family community" foreseen by article 2140 of the 1942 Civil Code, which related only to agricultural enterprises. It recalls the *Communio incidens familiaris* which was elaborated in the Roman law and largely followed during the Middle Ages.

II. Illegitimate Children

In order better to appreciate the problems of the extent of the questions relating to the affiliation of illegitimate children, it is best to consider only two aspects of the relevant provisions, namely:
—the recognition of illegitimate children, and
—the judicial determination of maternity and paternity.

The reform of Italian family law by the law of 1975 introduced important modifications even concerning these two points. Before analysing these new provisions, it seems opportune to explain the rules of the Civil Code of 1942 and of the legislation immediately previous to that.

The Civil Code of 1865 treated illegitimate affiliation with great strictness, not only when the relationship was adulterous or incestuous, but also when the relationship derived in general from all sexual relations outside marriage. Even concerning this category of children the Code of 1865, although admitting enquiry into illegitimate maternity, forbade enquiry into illegitimate paternity except in the case of rape or abduction, provided the occurrence of such rape or abduction corresponded with the time of conception. Enquiry into maternity or paternity was not admitted when recognition was forbidden. Recognition could

---

18. Finocchiaro A and Finocchiaro M, *Reform of the Family Law*, vol. I Milan 1975, pp. 278, 279.

not take place in the case of children born of two persons of whom only one was bound by marriage to a third person at the time of conception. Neither could recognition take place in favour of children born of an incestuous relationship. These are children born of two persons between whom marriage is prohibited on the ground of consanguinity or affinity in all degrees of direct line, and up to the second degree in a collateral line.

The prohibition of voluntary recognition in the cases considered resulted from an anxiety to defend the cohesion of the legitimate family, this being the origin and foundation of an ordered society. The doctrine recognised the pre-eminence of the legitimate family which is united by blood and sealed by marriage. On the other hand it affirmed the need for an appropriate guardianship of the rights of children born of relations which, although reprehensible, could not and should not deprive the innocent victims of a family status and perpetuate for them conditions of complete inferiority, both civil and social.

In order to reconcile the two diametrically opposed requirements, that of defending the legitimate family on the one hand and of protecting the illegitimate child on the other, the legislator of 1942 recognised in certain cases both adulterous and incestuous children. He also allowed enquiry into the paternity in more than the above mentioned two cases which had been provided for in 1865. In fact, the Code of 1942 introduced presumption of paternity in cases where the probability was equal to that in the cases of rape and abduction.

The Code of 1942, while stating the general principle of non-recognition of children born of parents between whom there was a link of consanguinity in all degrees in the direct line or to the second degree in the collateral line or, again, a link of affinity in the direct line, made an exception in the case of children born of incest when the parents were unaware of the link between them at the time of conception. If only one of the parents was in good faith, only that parent could effect recognition.

Concerning children conceived in adultery, the 1942 Code laid down that they could be recognised by the parent who, at the time of conception was not married to another. This was reasonable because only the parent who was married was regarded as being in adultery, and not the parent who was free of marriage ties. The Code went further by stating that recognition could also take place on the part of the spouse who was married at the time of conception if the matrimonial tie had been dissolved by the death of the other spouse.

Although the Code said nothing about it, recognition could also take place when the child was the issue of a marriage afterwards declared null and void: the declaration of nullity of the marriage, by its retroactive effect, terminated the adulterous character of the child.

The law of 1 December 1970, no. 898 which introduced divorce, laid down in article 7 that adulterous children can be recognised by the parent who, at the time of the conception, was married, provided that dissolution or cessation of civil consequences had been pronounced in respect of that marriage.

In addition, it is necessary to recall at once that the third paragraph of article 252 established that, when a marriage was dissolved and legitimate children were born of this marriage or when there were already legitimate children, the recognition had no effects except at the time when the Head of the State, after having heard the opinion of the Council of State, authorised it by presidential decree. There had thus been laid down the norms necessary to verify the opportunity and convenience of admitting or not the recognition of the child born in adultery and this was in order the better to safeguard the interests of the legitimate family, which were considered to be pre-eminent.

To sum up, it can be said that the prescription of the Civil Code of 1942 concerning recognition distinguished illegitimate children in three categories:

Simple natural children for whom recognition was always admitted;

Children conceived in adultery or incest for whom recognition was agreed in the cases indicated above;

Children conceived in adultery or incest for whom, save in cases provided for by the law, recognition was not available.

Resting firmly on the voluntary investigation of natural maternity, the legislator of 1942, with regard to the investigation of natural paternity and taking into account also the widespread opinion which insisted on a better understanding of the problems related to natural affiliation, multiplied the cases where the investigation should be permitted. According to article 259 of the Civil Code, natural paternity could be declared judicially in the following cases:

(i) When the mother and the putative father had publicly cohabited as spouses during the period of the conception.

(ii) When the paternity resulted indirectly in a civil or penal sentence, or in an unequivocal declaration signed by the person to whom the paternity is attributed.

(iii) When at the time of conception there was abduction of a minor or rape.

(iv) When the child possessed the status of natural child.

Article 270 laid down that possession of the status of a natural child could result from several facts giving, when taken together, a serious indication of the parent and child relationship between the child and the person to whom paternity was attributed. In any case there should have been the coincidence of the following circumstances: that the child had been treated as a son by the person from whom he was claiming natural paternity and that this person had provided for his maintenance and education; and furthermore that the child had always been considered, in the social aspects, as the son of the person from whom he was claiming paternity.

While the action for judicial declaration of natural affiliation was not subjected to prescription (Article 272, last paragraph), Article 272 of the Civil Code of 1942 laid down that the action or declaration of natural paternity could be brought by the child, under pain of forfeiture, within two years following the attainment of majority or, in the case of a child conceived in adultery, in the two years following a dissolution of the marriage, if the dissolution of marriage was verified after the attainment of majority on the part of the child.

The action for a judicial declaration of paternity and of natural maternity was not admitted in cases where recognition was forbidden (Article 278). In these cases the natural child could obtain necessaries, which he could also claim in the following cases:

(i) if the paternity or the maternity resulted indirectly from a civil or penal sentence,

(ii) if the paternity or the maternity depended upon a marriage which was declared null and void,

(iii) if the paternity or the maternity resulted from an unequivocal declaration signed by the parents.

The parliamentary work for the reform of the Family Law having started in 1967, the problem of natural affiliation and especially of the recognition of children conceived in adultery, were subjected to examination in Parliament also from the point of view of the need to apply certain constitutional principles. In fact, Article 30 of the Constitution laid down the following principles in the first and third paragraphs respectively:

"The parents have the duty and the right to maintain, instruct and educate the children, even when the latter are born outside marriage."

"The law assures to children born outside marriage the judicial and social guardianship compatible with the rights of the members of the legitimate family."

The account which accompanied the first scheme for the reform of the Family Law[19] affirmed that the Constitutional norms cited above only regroup and, so to speak, "enshrine" the ethical and social conditions which are most widespread among the Italian people concerning children born out of wedlock, in order to avoid the consequences falling upon them of a social and moral irregularity of their parents. It is also in order to assure the enforcement of the Constitutional principles cited above that the draft law conscious of the tenacious aversion of the Catholic world, could not permit more radical solutions, proposed an "attenuated form" of recognition of children conceived in adultery. This form consisted in the possibility, agreed with the natural parent even if married at the moment of conception, provided that he is separated from his own spouse, to make an appropriate declaration before the judge of guardianship, according to which he assumes, in respect of his natural child, the obligations inherent in the *patria potestas*.

In the course of the discussions which took place before the two Chambers and which were prolonged during three successive legislatures, out of consideration for a certain public opinion always more favourable with regard to illegitimate children, an opinion which demanded the full affirmation of the principle that the children should not suffer for the fault of their parents, a different solution from that already mentioned was adopted. Article 102/250 of the law of 19 May 1975, no. 151, establishes that "the natural infant can be recognised by the father or by the mother even if they were married to other persons at the moment of the conception".

Thus the distinction no longer exists in Italian legislation concerning recognition between illegitimate children in the simple sense and children conceived in adultery. There is also the fact that the recognition of children conceived in adultery is effective, according to the new law, even where there are legitimate children. There is no longer the need to follow a particular procedure, that is, to issue a decree by the Head of the State, as was provided for by article 252 of the Civil Code of 1942.

---

19. The draft which carries the number 3705 was presented to the Chamber of Deputies on 9 January 1967.

ILLEGITIMATE CHILDREN

It must be said that the legislator was preoccupied with safeguarding the rights of the legitimate family, to which article 30 of the Constitution makes explicit reference. It has in effect adequately regulated, in consequence of the options chosen, the aspect which is certainly the most delicate relating to recognition, namely the integration of the natural child into the legitimate family of the parent who has brought about the recognition.

Law no. 151 establishes that the integration of the natural child into the legitimate family by one of the spouses can take place following an authorisation by the Judge, who must evaluate the interests of the minor and assure himself that the other spouse and the legitimate children of 16 years and more, who live together, have expressed their consent. The legislator wished to safeguard in this way the harmony and decorum of the family. In effect, the latter may well be perturbed by setting in its midst a person who is not one of its members and who can represent for the other spouse the memory of a conjugal infidelity.

On the other hand, for the recognition of children conceived in incest, the new law has preserved the cases already established by the Civil Code of 1942 and prescribes in addition that recognition must be authorised by the Judge, taking into account the interests of the child and the necessity of avoiding his suffering any prejudice.

The law no. 151 radically reformed another essential point: the quest for natural paternity. By virtue of article 113 of that law the claim of natural paternity, as well as the claim of natural maternity, is now admitted in all cases in which recognition is available. Furthermore, the claim for natural paternity can take place by having recourse to all the means of proof admitted by the law. As a result of article 114 of the same law the action to obtain a judicial declaration of natural paternity is without limitation of time in respect of the child.

A short synthesis of the principle rule which currently regulates the recognition of natural children, also under law no. 151 of 1975, is:
—the parents cannot proceed to recognition until they have attained the age of 16 years;
—recognition of the natural child is effected at the moment of the child's birth, or by a declaration ad hoc made later than the birth or the conception, before an officer of the Civil Status, or before the guardianship judge or, again, by public act or by will;
—the recognition itself is irrevocable and has legal effect only with regard to the parent who has made the recognition, always with the exception of the cases provided for by the law;
—for the parent who has effected it, recognition comprises the assumption, with regard to the illegitimate child, of the same duties and of the same rights as for the legitimate child;
—the natural child takes the name of the parent who first recognises it. In cases where the recognition has been effected simultaneously by the two parents, the illegitimate child takes the name of the father. If the paternal affiliation was verified or recognised after the maternal affiliation, the natural child can take the name of the father by adding it, or by substituting it for that of the mother;
—illegitimate children, in all cases where they cannot bring an action for the judicial declaration of paternity or of maternity, can obtain maintenance and

all that is necessary for their instruction and education until majority. Illegitimate sons who have attained their majority, can obtain necessaries if they are in need.

—natural children who are recognised have the same rights as legitimate children in the succession of their father and mother.

In considering law no. 151, it can be affirmed that the intention of the legislator was to enlarge the possibility of recognition of illegitimate children and also to make the legal treatment of them in almost all respects equal to that of legitimate children. From another point of view it should be noted that article 90 of the statute reforming the Family Law replaced article 232 of the Civil Code by another which, in its second paragraph, limits the presumption of conception during the marriage to the fact that 300 days have not passed from the announcement of the separation by agreement or, indeed, from the date of the appearance of the spouses before the Judge. This applies to the case where the same spouses have been authorised to live separately in the course of the judgment on separation, or of the judgment of annulment, or of dissolution or of cessation of the civil effects of the marriage. In addition, article 93 of the same law modified article 235 of the Civil Code to establish that the judicial claim for disavowal of the child conceived during the marriage—that is, the judicial claim which tends to suppress the status of legitimate child—can also be presented by the mother in all cases where this claim can be presented by the father.

However, having regard to all these norms, it does not seem that one can speak of a "*favor legitimitatis*", or indeed of "*favor illegitimitatis*" as the spirit which animated the reforming statute, but of a "*favor veritatis*". Thus, in the course of the reform of the institution of the family, the legislator clearly wished to make it always possible for the child to be given the status which corresponds to the real situation regarding his parents. In order to realise this objective, the legislator himself limited the scope of certain presumptions of legitimacy of the child which had previously been almost absolute. Furthermore, he has also practically admitted in the article cited above, the recognition of the child who already possesses the status of legitimate son thus introducing an exception to the principle established by article 253 of the Civil Code, confirmed by article 105 of the reforming law, according to which: "In each case, recognition is permitted in contradiction to the status of legitimate child in which the person finds himself". The latitude of the ideas by which the Italian legislator was inspired when implementing the reform of the subject under investigation is thus clear.

III. Divorce

Divorce was introduced into the Italian legal system in 1970 following the law of December 1970, no. 898, published in the Official Gazette of 3 December 1970. This same law came into effect after the normal period of "*vacatio*", that is to say, on 18 December 1970.

It is necessary to make clear immediately that the term "divorce" does not appear anywhere in the twelve Articles of this law. The omission of this term certainly responds to a requirement of the legal situations which the law in question was called upon to govern. In fact, the legislator has correctly distinguished the hypothesis where the marriage was contracted before the Officer of the Civil Status, from that where it was celebrated according to a religious rite with civil effects. In the first case he provided for the possibility of achieving the dissolution of the matrimonial bond. In the second, on the contrary, he provided for the possibility of declaring the cessation of the civil effects of the bond in question resulting from the registration of the marriage in the registers of the Civil State. Taking into account the differences which separate these two situations, it is clear that the term "divorce" cannot represent with adequate exactness the result at which one arrives when there is a claim after a civil marriage or after a religious marriage with civil effects.[20] Thus, if the term "divorce" is sometimes employed, it is only for practical reasons and in order to facilitate the statement, given that it synthesises the principal effects which follow with regard to the legal situations envisaged here. The term "divorce" is not only met with in ordinary social relations, but also in legal reviews and in publications which are generally concerned with the matter. Law no. 898 of 1970 itself, in order to take into account the requirement of resorting to a unique expression, uses in its title the synthetic phrase "regulation of the cases of dissolution of the marriage" which, for the reasons just indicated, does not even answer precisely the two different cases in law dealt with by the legislator.

Regarding the historical precedents of the law it seems opportune to recall that divorce had been introduced under the Napoleonic domination of Italy, between 1800 and 1815, and that it remained effective for several years in the various Italian states to which French law was gradually extended. When Napoleon fell in 1815, divorce was abolished in all the Italian states. The Civil Code of 1865, the first Civil Code of the united Italian State, confirmed the principle of the indissolubility of marriage; but only a short time after the proclamation of Italian unity, the theme of the dissolution of marriage by means of divorce was brought under investigation by Parliament. The first proposal on the subject was presented by Deputy Morelli on 13 May 1878. This proposal, as well as other different proposals which followed in the course of the following decades, were abandoned or ruled out for various reasons without even reaching examination by the parliamentary assemblies. None were able to survive the preliminary phase of the consideration by the Parliamentary Commissions. From 1954 onwards several proposals to introduce divorce were presented to Parliament[21] and, as already indicated, the corresponding law was promulgated on 1 December 1970.

---

20. In another aspect the term "divorce" does not appear in the law no. 898 of 1970 by reason of the preoccupation of Parliament with avoiding the sharper polemics with regard to an institution which is not approved by a great part of Italian society. The Christian Democrat, Senator Leone, moderator and mediator of the modifications of the approved text in its first reading in the Chamber of Deputies—in his intervention in the course of the morning session of the Senate of 8 October 1970, declared "we are all agreed always to adopt in the law the term 'dissolution' and not the term 'divorce' ". Certain words are shocking and thus it is preferable not to use them. (Cf. Acts of the Senate of the Republic, see Legislatura 341 public session, typewritten edition, p. 17403). It should also be remembered that the first proposition of law on this matter (presented to the Chamber of Deputies on 26 October 1954 through the initiative of Deputy Luigi Renato Sansone) spoke of "little divorce" (*piccolo divorzio*) as if it was desired to exclude the intention to introduce a real divorce in the Italian legal system.
21. The proposals which underlay and gave impetus to the law on divorce were presented to the Chamber of Deputies in 1968 by the socialist Deputy, L Fortuna and the liberal Deputy, A Baslini (Docs. nos. 1 & 467, Chamber of Deputies, see *Legislatura*).

It is known that the Holy See, after parliamentary discussions of proposals for a law on divorce, contracted the Italian Government to make known, through the exchange of diplomatic documents which were afterwards published[22] and on the occasion of meetings of its representatives with Italian politicians, its point of view, which was decidedly against divorce on moral and religious grounds. Furthermore, the Holy See explained especially that a law consenting to the dissolution of a marriage celebrated before a Minister of the Catholic faith and having civil effect would constitute a violation of the Concordat with Italy, under article 34. The first paragraph of this document said, "The Italian State, in order to restore to the institution of marriage, which is the basis of the family, a dignity in conformity with the Catholic traditions of its people, recognises that the sacrament of marriage which is governed by the Canon law, has civil effects." As provided by the third paragraph of Article 34 cited above and by Article 9 of the law of 27 May 1929, no. 847 applying the Concordat, the civil effects result from the canonical marriage by virtue of the relevant act in the registers of the Civil Status. The Holy See explained that, under Article 34 of the Concordat, the Italian State, as can be deduced from the literal interpretation of the provision, does not limit itself to recognising the form of celebration of the religious marriage as being as valid regarding the effects of the celebration of marriage governed by the civil law, but indeed, as is established in the Concordats providing for the civil recognition of the canonical marriage, it undertook to recognise the civil effects of a marriage which is governed by the Canon law with its original characteristics, amongst which, in the first place, was indissolubility. The Holy See maintained that this thesis responded to the ratio of Article 34 taken as a whole. This ratio clearly indicates that, by comparison with the canonical marriage under the Concordat, which represents a matrimonial bond for the Church, a civil marriage equally constitutes a bond of marriage for the State.

The Holy See emphasised that, in truth, it would be a contradiction for the State, which had reserved to itself the exclusive competence of the Courts and of the ecclesiastical tribunals, as set out in Article 34, over the causes concerning nullity and dissolution of marriage, it had wished to reserve to itself the regulation of this matter by its own legislation alone. In addition, it is unlikely that in these conditions the Italian State had accepted the formula of the seventh paragraph of that article ("concerning grounds for physical separation, the Holy See agrees to their being judged by the civil judicial authorities"). It is quite clear from this formula that the Holy See did not admit that the civil Courts were judging other matrimonial causes, with the exception of proceedings for physical separation.

On this subject the Italian authorities have argued that the Holy See had based its thesis on the affirmation that, by Article 34 of the Concordat, the canonical discipline of the matrimonial bond had been received by the Italian legal system. On the contrary, this did not happen because the Italian State had bound itself only to prescribe, in its internal legislation, that the celebration of marriage before a minister of the Catholic faith would be equally valid as a celebration of marriage in respect of bringing about civil effects. It is precisely with this aim that it was provided for by Article 34 that the officiating priest should expressly

---

22. Cf. Barbiera, *The regulation of the breakup of the marriage*, Bologna 1971, p. 374 ff.

mention the civil effects resulting from the act celebrated before him and that he should read the legal texts of the Civil Code regarding the said effects. Still with this end in view, the second paragraph of Article 34 provides for pulling up the banns of marriage, apart from the Parish Church, in the Town Hall and for the purpose of recording them in the registers of the Civil Status. Concerning the other provisions of Article 34, providing for recognition of the jurisdiction of the Church, these must also be considered as provisions co-ordinating the two systems of law, that of the State and that of the Church. In fact it was taken into account, on the Italian side, after the conclusion of the Concordat, that the ground for nullity and for ending the marriage were not the same according to the two systems and that these grounds were more numerous according to the Canon law than those admitted by the corresponding provisions of the Italian State law. Without modifying or enlarging the cases provided for by Italian law, the State accepted that these same grounds, once proved by the competent Courts of the Church, would, for a marriage celebrated according to the forms under the Concordat, be equally capable of involving the nullity of the bond of the corresponding marriage celebrated under the Italian legal system. This would be through a procedure which must be followed before the competent Court of Appeal and which recalls in substance the procedure of recognition of foreign judgments. If the legal marriage relationship, governed by Canon law, had really been received into the Italian legal system, the Italian authorities maintained that all the coordination measures mentioned above would not have been necessary because, for the Italian law, the consequences resulting from the creation, or from the cessation, of the Canon law relationship had come into being as a result of the law. Article 34 of the Concordat thus applies to the "act" of the celebration of marriage before a Minister of the Catholic faith, and it is only to this act to which it was desired to attribute civil effects according to the Italian legal system. The effects are the same as a proper marriage contracted before an Officer of the Civil Status, insofar as the possibilities of dissolution are concerned.

To the arguments of the Italian State the Holy See replied by explaining its arguments again and, in order to maintain them, it also invoked the case law of the Italian Court of Cassation. In fact, the Court of Cassation in several judgments, and also in the decision in plenary session of 13 March 1970, which was therefore very close to the time when the law of divorce was being discussed, had confirmed the principle that "the Italian authorities cannot recognise, for marriage under the Concordat, the foreign judgments on divorce because that would be contrary to Article 34 of the Concordat".[23]

---

23. It is pertinent and interesting to recall here the modifications introduced on the subject of marriage in the Concordat between the Holy See and Portugal, stipulated on 7 March 1940 in the *Acta Apostolicae Sedis 1940*, vol. VII, series II, p. 217 ff. Art. XXIV of the said Convention declared: "In harmony with the essential characteristics of the Catholic sacrament it is agreed— *que, pelo proprio facto da celebração do casamento canónico, os côniuges renunciãrao à faculdade civil de requererem o divórcio, que por isso não poderá ser aplicado pelos tribunais civis aos casamentos cátolicos*". The new political situation having intervened, the Portugese authorities have in any case solicited and obtained from the Holy See the modification which was introduced with the additional Protocol of 15 Feb. 1975, *Acta Apostolicae Sedis 1975*, vol. XXIV, series II, pp. 435-436. With this Protocol the text of art. XXIV of the Concordat between the Holy See and the Portugese State was replaced by the following: "*Clebrando o casamento*

After the promulgation of law no. 898 some Courts, and later the united divisions of the Court of Cassation, at different times referred to the Constitutional Court the question of the constitutionality of article 2 of the said law in relation to article 34 of the Concordat, and to articles 7 and 134 of the Constitution. However, the Court by its judgments no. 169 of 1971 and 176 of 1973 rejected the claims of unconstitutionality which had been raised.

In relation to article 2 of law no. 898, there was room to make clear that the formula, "in those cases where the marriage was celebrated according to religious rites and was regularly entered into the register" concerns not only the case of a canonical marriage, but also that of marriage celebrated before the Minister of another faith. In fact, this formula is aimed at respecting, in a regime of equal dignity for all religious persuasions, the eventual religious validity of the marriage and from thenceforth the existence of the bond in the realm of a different system. Consequently, even in relation to the religious marriage which is not canonical but which has civil effects, the judgment must be limited to declaring the cessation of the civil effects. This subject has become more significant because of the repercussions which the promulgation of law no. 898 has had, especially in relation to the canonical marriage under the Concordat and with regard to the existence in Italy of a strong tradition against divorce. The initiative of the referendum for the abrogation of law no. 898 of 1970 is really due to the existence of such a tradition. As everyone knows, the people were consulted on 12 May 1974 and the majority declared themselves against the abrogation.[24]

On examining the contents of the law it will be noticed that, in the case of article 1, as also in that of article 2, corresponding to each of the two hypotheses mentioned above, of dissolution of the marriage and of cessation of the civil effects following the recognition of the marriage according to a religious rite, the relevant decision can only be based on the established impossibility for the judge to maintain or revive the spiritual and material community between the

---

cátolico, os côniuges assumem por esso mesmo facto perante a Igreja, a obrigaçao de se aterem as normas canónicas que o regulam e, em particular de reispeitarem as suas propriedades essenciais". With the second paragraph of the new art. XXIV the Holy See, referring to the doctrine of the Catholic Church concerning the indissolubility of the marriage bond, reminded spouses about to contract canonical marriage that it is their solemn duty not to make use of the civil right to claim a divorce ("*faculdade civil de requerer o divorcio*"). The authorities of the new Portugese State, sooner than make a unilateral declaration of invalidity or of the failure of art. XXIV of the Concordat of 1940, a declaration which perhaps would have been justified in the light of the uncertain efficacy of a renunciation accomplished by the State for its nationals with regard to divorce, or again in the light of the different treatment of these nationals concerning the possibility of claiming a divorce, decided to resort to negotiation and agreement, thus showing their sense of responsibility with regard to international treaties and their respect towards the Church.

24. The referendum was authorised by decision of the Constitutional Court of 25 Jan. 1972, after the Central Bureau of the Court of Cassation had declared that the demand for popular consultation, advanced on 19 June 1971 was lawful. It had for its object the abrogation of all the norms of the law of 1 Dec. 1970, no. 898 and related either to the dissolution of civil marriage or to the cessation of the civil effects of the marriage. The votes registered in the lists were 37,497,091, of which 33,050,679 voted, that is, 88.1%. 13,156,868, corresponding to 40.7% voted in favour of abrogation. 19,162,045, corresponding to 59.3%, voted against abrogation. 768,566 votes were invalid, of which 426,349 voting papers were left blank. (Official data published by the Central Institute of Statistics).

spouses, which is the very core of the marriage. This impossibility must be recognised by the judge by means of an attempted reconciliation. But, according to the principle established by law no. 898 of 1970, except for the particular causes below, on the failure of this attempt and when a ground for divorce is established, the judge must automatically pronounce the divorce.

The spouses can only demand the dissolution or the cessation of civil effects of their marriage in the cases enumerated in article 3 of law no. 898. These cases may be summarised as follows:

(i) Conviction of one of the spouses for certain offences.
(ii) In respect of certain offences, the acquittal of one of the spouses for total unsoundness of mind, or some other reason.
(iii) Judicial separation between the spouses; separation by consent confirmed by the Court; separation in fact.
(iv) Annulment or dissolution obtained abroad by the other spouse of foreign nationality, as well as a new marriage contracted by the latter abroad.
(v) Non-consummation of the marriage.

Convictions which can lead to a petition for divorce must have been pronounced at a time later than the celebration of the marriage, by a definitive judgment, but the object of the conviction can be acts committed before the marriage. The sentences thus taken into consideration are:

(a) Solitary confinement with hard labour in perpetuity, or such imprisonment as extends over a period of more than fifteen years, inflicted by virtue of more than one judgment under the head of one or more offences other than unintentional offences and excluding political offences and those committed for reasons having a particular moral and social content (Art. 3, point (I)(a)).

(b) Sentences of imprisonment for incest, or sexual offences committed on the person of descendants, for the offence of incitement or compelling one's wife or children into prostitution, as well as when there is exploitation of prostitution of the children, or encouragement to prostitution. (Art. 2, Point (I)(b)).

(c) Sentences of the maximum punishment for voluntary homicide on the persons of a descendant or of an adopted child, or for attempted homicide on the person of the spouse or of a descendant or adopted child. (Art. 3, Point (I)(c)).

(d) Sentences on the repetition of an offence, to the full term of imprisonment for intentional personal injury (bodily or mental), called "most grave". By such injuries are meant those which involve an illness which is certainly or probably incurable, the loss of a sense, the loss of a limb or a multilation rendering a limb unusable, or the loss of the use of an organ or of the capacity to procreate, or a serious and permanent difficulty in speaking, the permanent deformation or disfiguration of the face, the miscarriage of the person injured. Also sentences under the head of offences of violation of the obligation to assist the family or of bad behaviour towards the family and towards the children, or of an offence having as its object the defrauding of incapacitated persons, committed with regard to the spouse or a child even if adopted. (Art. 3, point (I)(d)).

In the cases provided for at (d) the judge, in order to announce the dissolution or the cessation of the civil effects of marriage must first verify, taking into account the subsequent behaviour of the defendant, whether the latter is or is not able to maintain or to resume family life in common. (Article 3, point (I), (d) 2nd paragraph). In all cases mentioned of conviction of one of the spouses, the other spouse cannot claim the divorce if he or she has been convicted for participation in the offence, or if the family life in common has been resumed (Article 3, point (I) 3rd paragraph).

The cases of acquittal which can nevertheless give rise to a petition for divorce are as follows:

    (i) when the other spouse has been acquitted on the ground of total unsoundness of mind under the head of one of the offences in art. 3 (I)(b) and (c) mentioned above in the case where the competent judge, in order to pronounce the dissolution or the cessation of the civil effects of the marriage, confirms the incapacity of the defendant to maintain or resume family life in common (art. 3(2)(a)).

   (ii) When the penal procedure involved under the head of the offence mentioned under art. 3(I)(b) and (c) has resulted in a decision that there is no case to answer in respect of proceedings for the offences; in cases where the competent judge who may pronounce the divorce considers that the facts alleged constitute the constituent elements of an offence coupled with the existence of the conditions for its punishment (art. 3, 2(c)).

  (iii) When the penal proceedings for incest result in acquittal or release on the basis that the facts are not punishable for want of a public scandal (art. 3, 2(d)).

Under Article 3, 2(b), divorce can also be claimed in the case of judicial separation, and the latter is without doubt the situation which is most frequently invoked to justify the claim for divorce under Article 158 of the Civil Code. The spouses can obtain physical separation by common consent (*"separazione consensuale"*), but this agreement does not produce effects unless confirmed by the Court. The Civil Code of 1942 provided in Articles 150-153 for separation for fault (*separazione per colpa*) which was only allowed in cases established by the law, that is, under Article 151 (for adultery, wilful abandonment, duress, menaces or grave injuries): under Article 152 (for certain convictions) and under Article 153 (for leaving the residence fixed by the husband). The decision on separation resulting from the observance of the rule of *res judicata*, since Article 3 of law no. 898 of 1970 does not make any distinctions; the claim for divorce could and can be introduced by either of the spouses, and consequently also by the spouse who had been declared responsible for the separation. This has been criticised and stress has been laid on the alleged immorality of a system which permits the dissolution of marriage even in the case where the defendant is innocent and opposes the petition for divorce. In fact, as explained later, the opposition of the defendant in such circumstances only involved the prolongation of the necessary period of separation. Law no. 151 establishing with Article 33 a new text for Article 151 of the Civil Code, by which separation for fault was replaced by separation for acts which are not culpable ("separation for acts which may be independent of the wishes of the spouses which render intolerable the pursuit of life in common . . ."). By the repealing of Articles 152 and 153 above, this situation was made clearer. Now, in fact, even the spouse who was solely responsible for the married life having become intolerable, that is, the spouse who according to the old law would have been declared guilty, could claim separation. This applies also in respect of the spouse whose married life has been unobjectionable and who is opposed to the separation. *This* same guilty spouse can, after the period of separation established by the law, also petition for and obtain a divorce.

In cases of judicial separation, in order to be able to introduce the petition for dissolution or cessation of civil effects of the marriage, the separation must have lasted without interruption for at least five years from the date when the spouses appeared before the President of the Court in separation proceedings. When the defendant spouse objects, the period of separation must be longer—seven years in the case of separation declared to be on the ground of the exclusive fault of the petitioner for divorce, and six years in the case of separation by agreement.[25]

Article 3 2(b) also takes into consideration the case of separation in fact. But such a separation must have commenced at least two years before the law came into operation and the divorce petition can only be made if the separation in fact has lasted at least five years from the date of effective cessation of life together. With reference to the first condition, it seems clear that the norm which provides for the separation in fact as a ground for divorce must be considered as a transitional rule which can only be applied in the case of marriages celebrated at least two years before the law of 1 December 1970, no. 898, came into force.

As stated above, divorce can also be obtained in the case where the other spouse, being a foreign national, has obtained abroad an annulment or dissolution of the marriage, or has contracted a new marriage abroad (Article 3, 2(e)), and also when the marriage has not been consummated (Article 3, 2(f)).

In principle, the case of the foreign spouse who has obtained annulment or dissolution abroad, gives a chance to the other spouse who is an Italian national, to obtain divorce either by means of a judgment introduced to this end, or by means of the enforcement in Italy of the foreign judgment. Doubts have been expressed about the usefulness of this type of divorce, because the Italian spouse has the possibility of having the foreign judgment recognised in Italy. However, there are always particular features in this connection, which justify the rule introduced by the legislator.

Regarding divorce for non-consummation of the marriage, the appropriate rule eliminates the differentiation which previously existed on this point between the regulation of the effects of the canonical marriage under the Concordat and the regulation of the effects of a civil marriage. This is a differentiation which has made people look into the constitutional validity of the rules of the Concordat in the part allowing such a possibility of dissolution of marriage on the ground that it infringes the principle of equality of citizens sanctioned by the Constitution.

---

25. Art. 33 of the law no. 151 of 1975, cited in the text, provides in its 2nd para. that, "the judge pronouncing the separation shall declare, where the circumstances require it and if he is so requested, which is the guilty spouse in view of his or her behaviour contrary to the duties which derive from the marriage." This is the case when the period of seven years separation applies, that is, if the defendant is opposed to the divorce petition.

There is no definition of the *copula coniugalis* in the Italian legal system, although it has been worked out by canonical doctrine and indicated in the Code of Canon Law as "*actus per se apti ad prolem generationem*" (Can. 1081, para. 2). However, such a definition cannot be accepted by the Italian legal system. In fact, the Code of Canon Law declares that the procreation of children (*bonum prolis*) is one of the principal aims of marriage and this requires that the spouses should be capable of accomplishing the *actus per se apti ad prolem generationem* and that, in order that there may be consummation of the marriage, it is necessary that *copula perfecta* should take place. On the other hand, for the Italian Civil Code, the *bonum prolis* is not one of the essential aims of marriage. There is consummation of marriage even by the *copula imperfecta*, that is, intercourse which is incapable of leading to procreation (for lack of the *verum semen* on the part of the man, or for some other reason).

The case under examination presents unique difficulties regarding the method of proof, as it clearly lends itself to fraud. As for the canonical proceedings, it should be said that uncertainty in the opionion of the judge can only be overcome by means of the proof of facts, such as remoteness or impotence, which prevent consummation in the natural way. If, on the contrary, consummation had been possible, the certainty could only derive from the establishment of the virginity of the wife, but it is known that there have been proceedings in the course of which, both the pregnancy of the wife was established and her virginity was also verified.

Article 4 of the law no. 898 proposes an appeal, containing a statement of the facts upon which the petition is based, which must be presented to the Court of the place of residence of the defendant or, again, if the defendant is not to be found or if he resides abroad, before the Court of the place of residence of the petitioner. The spouses are bound to appear together before the President of the Court in person on the date fixed by a decree of the latter, unless prevented by serious reasons, duly proved. The President has a duty to hear the spouses, separately at first and then together, and to try and reconcile them. In the case of reconciliation of the spouses or of a declaration of withdrawal of the petition, the President will arrange the proceedings for the reconciliation or for the declaration of withdrawal of the action. In default of the appearance of the defendant spouse or the prevention of the attempt at reconciliation, the President will entrust to an examining Magistrate the conduct of the affair. He can also order such temporary and urgent measures as he thinks fit in the interests of the children. Paragraph 5 of Article 4 of the law permits the examining Magistrate to revoke or modify these measures.

The intervention of the representative of the Public Prosecutor is obligatory in the course of the proceedings before the Court. Article 5 also gives to the Public Prosecutor power to oppose the decision, but only within the limits of the property interests of the minor children or those who are legally incapacitated.

The decree of dissolution or of the cessation of the civil effects of the marriage contains the order given to the Officer of the Civil Status to proceed to the entering of that decree in the margin of the Marriage Certificate. According to the general principles on the matter, this will take place after registration of the decree in question in the registers of the Civil Status. The dissolution or the cessation of civil effects of the marriage take effect in the terms of Articles 5 and

10, on the date when the decree is entered in the margin of the Marriage Certificate.

Concerning the effects of the judgment granting the divorce and the obligations resulting from it, or which can result from it, the main points to note are:

(1) that the wife, in the terms of paragraph 2 of Article 5 of the law, recovers the name she bore before marriage;

(2) that it is for the tribunal itself, taking into account the pecuniary conditions of the spouses and the reasons for the decree, to provide for the obligation of one of the spouses to make periodic payments to the other in proportion to his own assets and income. In fixing the amount of this annuity, the judge will take account of the personal and financial contribution made jointly for the upkeep of the family and to the origin of the property of each spouse. If the parties are in agreement on the point, the order can be for a single lump sum payment. Paragraphs 4 and 5 of Article 5 lay down that the obligation to pay the annuity shall terminate upon the remarriage of the spouse who benefits;

(3) that the obligation mentioned in the Civil Code to maintain, educate and instruct the children born or adopted during the marriage will continue even in the case of the remarriage of one of the parents. The Court designates the spouse to whose custody the children must be entrusted or decides how, for serious reasons, it will be necessary to provide in some other way for their custody. Article 6 of the law lays down that custody takes place under the surveillance of the guardianship judge;

(4) that Article 7 of the law allows the divorced spouse to recognise his or her children conceived in adultery, under Article 252 of the Civil Code of 1942. This is also the right of the surviving spouse where the dissolution of marriage results from the death of the other spouse. In any case, law no. 151 of 1975 now permits, under Article 102 the text of which replaces Articles 250 and 252 of the Civil Code of 1942, the recognition of the illegitimate child by the father and by the mother "although they may be already married to another person at the time of the conception". The existence of a conjugal link at the time of conception thus no longer prevents the recognition of the illegitimate child in any situation;

(5) that after the dissolution or the cessation of the civil effects of the marriage each of the parents can exercise the paternal power over the children in his or her custody unless the Court has ruled otherwise. The parent awarded custody will administer the assets of the children with the obligation to render an account to the guardianship judge. If the other parent considers that the measures taken by the parent exercising the paternal power are prejudicial to the child, that other parent can present an appeal to the guardianship judge setting out the measures which the applicant considers appropriate (Article 11).

Regarding the various grounds which justify a claim for the dissolution of the marriage or for cessation of the civil effects of the marriage, the judges have no particular question of interpretation to resolve.

Concerning proof of the uninterrupted period of separation required by the law (5, 6 or 7 years), the Italian Courts have been of the opinion that the separation declared by a judgment which has the effect of *res judicata* in addition to separation by mutual consent confirmed judicially, gives rise to a presumption at least *juris tantum* that the separation has lasted without interruption since the presidential decisions under Articles 708 and 711 of the Code of Civil Procedure were pronounced. It falls to the defendant who intends to oppose the petition to rebut this presumption by proving that the separation has ceased. But a reunion of the spouses which is only temporary and occasional would not be enough to establish the said cessation. In fact, to interrupt this *spatium temporis* necessary for the dissolution of the marriage, the spouses must have resumed their life together with *animus conciliandi*. In other words, there is interruption of the state of separation such as is liable to make the *spatium temporis* provided by the law as a necessary condition for the dissolution of marriage pass uselessly. But this only occurs in the case of a total resumption of the married life through the resumption of all the material and spiritual relationships which characterise the bond.[26]

On the other hand, concerning the dissolution of the conjugal link on the basis of a separation in fact, in the absence of the above presumption the petitioner must prove that the interruption of the life together has lasted for the required period of time.

Concerning the nature of the allowance following the divorce, which is governed by the last two paragraphs of Article 5, and the determination of its total amount, the case law has expressed a multiplicity of opinions. In effect, it was affirmed that this allowance has the function of compensating for the loss caused by the divorce of the hopes which the spouse had of marriage and of the subsequent married life.[27] It has been maintained that the allowance in divorce has the same nature as for the maintenance annuity, that is, it almost constitutes the prolongation of the right of maintenance of the spouse during the marriage.[28] Other judges have maintained that the allowance in question has the character of indemnifying the spouse who has the lesser responsibility for the ending of the married life.[29]

However, the fourth paragraph of Article 5 lays down three criteria—appreciation of the financial conditions of the spouses, reasons for the divorce, evaluation of the personal and financial contribution of each of the spouses to the management of the household and to the origin of the property of both spouses. These must be taken into account for the allocation of the allowance and the determination of its amount.

The Court of Cassation has rightly laid down the principle that the allowance has a mixed character: to help, indemnify and compensate. Consequently, after having established which of the two spouses merits a guardianship, having regard to the fact that his or her financial situation has deteriorated following the divorce, the judge will also have to take into account—only in connection with the property—the fault in the failure of the marriage and, lastly, the contribution to the well being of the family. The Court stated that the above criteria are coexistent and bilateral in the sense that the judge is bound to consider them and is bound to keep to them as much in respect of the spouse required to pay

26. Cf. *Trib. Arezzo* 20 Apl. 1971; *Temi* 1971, 307; and *Trib. Roma* 3 Jan. 1972, *Giur. It.* 1973, I, 2, 827.
27. Cf. Court of Appeal of Bari, 24 Feb. 1973, in *Giur It.* 1973 I, 2, 727.
28. Court of Livorno, 13 May 1972, in *Dir. famiglia* 1973, 725.
29. Court of Bari, 12 May 1971.

the annuity as in respect of the spouse who claims it.[30] On this subject the doctrine has highlighted the fact that, since the Italian legal system separates the divorce decree from fault, the allowance for necessaries contributed as occasion demands to one of the spouses has the character of an indemnity.

It is interesting to note the statistical data relating to the judgment of dissolution and of cessation of civil rights of the marriage given in the first years of the application of the law and also the data relative to the separation order, and to confirmations of separation by agreement.[31] In the first semester of 1975 there were 569 orders for dissolution, 4280 orders for cessation of civil effects, 1136 orders for judicial separation and 7796 confirmations of separation by agreement. As can be seen, the number of judgments in divorce has substantially diminished over the years, but this is easily explained as the majority of the judgments are based upon the personal separation of the spouses, that is, on a fact which must have proved itself at least five years before a petition for divorce. Or, if we consider the data relative to confirmations of separation by agreement cited above, it can be foreseen as possible that in the future there will be a certain increase in judgments for divorce.

Having explained the contents of law no. 898, it may be useful also to give a summary of several problems of private international law connected with divorce, namely:

    I. The divorce of foreigners in Italy.
    II. The recognition in Italy of foreign judgments against a spouse not having Italian nationality.
    III. The recognition in Italy of foreign judgments of divorce given against Italian nationals.

I. The divorce of foreigners in Italy

For the Italian legal system, the rules of private international law to which it is necessary to turn in the matter of divorce are Articles 17 and 18 of the provisions on the law in general. Article 17 lays down the fundamental principle by virtue of which the status and capacity of persons and family relationships are governed by the law of the State of which these persons are nationals. Article 18 provides that, if the spouses are of different nationalities, their personal relations are governed by the last national law which was common to them during the marriage, or, in default of such a law, by the national law of the husband at the time of the celebration of the marriage.

Notwithstanding the existence of these rules, the doctrine and the dominant case law have affirmed, prior to the promulgation of the law no. 898, the thesis according to which the Italian judicial authority cannot declare a divorce in respect of foreigners, even if they belong to States whose laws allow divorce. To give reasons for this affirmation it was stressed that the principle of indissolubility of marriage in the Italian legal system ought to be strictly regarded as linked to

---

30. Court of Cassation, United Chambers, 26 Apl. 1974, no. 1124, in *Foro It.* 1974, I, 1335.
31. All these data are shown in the publications of the Central Institute of Statistics. See tables 6 x 4 with headings from p. 29 of the original.

public policy and consequently to be of a nature to constitute, by reason of Article 31 of the provisions on the law in general, a limitation to the application of foreign rules, precisely such rules as the laws to which Articles 17 and 18 refer, which could be contrary to that principle. For the rest, this orientation is consistent with the rule of Article 1 of the Hague Convention of 12 June 1902 for the regulation of conflicts of laws and of jurisdictions in divorce and separation, a rule which declares that the spouses can bring a petition for divorce only when the divorce is allowed, not only by their own national law, but also by the law of the place where the said petition is brought.

Since divorce has nevertheless been introduced in Italy by law no. 898 and which disregards an express statement in the relevant text of the law, it must be affirmed that it is the opposite principle which is operative today, that is, that the Italian judge must be able to pronounce the dissolution of the marriage even against spouses of foreign nationality by application of their national law providing for divorce. On the other hand it must also be stated that an analogous power is vested in the Italian judge in the case where a marriage has been contracted by two persons of whom one has Italian nationality and the other is of foreign nationality. Moreover, when it is a question of a religious marriage having civil effects, it seems that the judge must, according to the principle laid down in Article 2 of the law no. 898, limit himself to declaring the cessation of the civil effects of such a marriage. In any case it is necessary that the Italian judge should have jurisdiction and to this end it is necessary that the defendant spouse should reside in Italy, since the Court which has exclusive territorial jurisdiction in the dissolution and the cessation of the civil effects of marriage by virtue of Article 4 of that law, is the Court of the place where the defendant spouse has his residence. If the defendant spouse resides abroad, or has no known residence, it is necessary for the Italian judge to have jurisdiction that, under Article 4, the spouse who claims the divorce should be resident in Italy.

In the case of foreigners who are nationals of States which have ratified the said Hague Convention of 1902 or have adhered to it, the criteria of much wider connecting links established by Article 5 of the Convention for deciding the competence of the national judge would ultimately be valid, that is, the concurrent jurisdiction of the judge of the place where the spouses have their domicile or where they have had their last domicile in the case of abandonment or a change of domicile brought about after the occurrence of facts which served as grounds for divorce.[32] For the Italian judge to know thoroughly the divorce proceedings introduced into Italy by foreigners under Article 17 above involves

---

32. It is useful to remember that the Hague Convention of 12 June 1902 for the regulation of conflict of laws and of jurisdiction in divorce and separation was ratified by the following States: Germany (1.6.1904); Belgium (1.6.1904); France (1.6.1904); Luxembourg (1.6.1904); Netherlands (1.6.1904); Italy (17.7.1905); Portugal (2.3.1907); Romania (1.6.1904); Sweden (1.6.1904); Hungary (22.9.1911). The following adhered later: Poland (25.6.1929) and Danzig (25.6.1929). On the other hand this same Convention was denounced by: Germany (27.11.-1933); Belgium (30.10.1918); France (12.11.1913); Netherlands (11.6.1968); Switzerland (28.11.1928); Sweden (3.11.1933); Poland (11.6.1969); Hungary (12.2.1974); Luxembourg (14.8.1974, but effective from 1.6.1979). The sphere of application of this Convention is thus currently restricted to a few States only, viz: Italy, Luxembourg, Portugal and Romania.

the application of the relevant rules of law of the State of which the parties in the proceedings are nationals. If the foreign spouses are of different nationalities, or if one of them is of Italian nationality, as in the case of an Italian woman marrying a foreigner without acquiring his nationality[33], the principles laid down in Article 18 above will apply. Consequently, the divorce will be decided on the basis of rules of substantive law of the last national law common to the interested spouses or, failing such a law, by the national law of the husband at the time of the celebration of the marriage. It should be added that the application of the foreign law is not allowed in all cases. In fact in the field under discussion, as for those cases where it is necessary to apply foreign law, the principle stated in Article 31 of the provisions of the general law applies, according to which such laws can have effect in Italy only so far as they are not contrary to public policy and morality. Subject to that, in principle the rule is applied according to which, in the circumstances, the grounds for divorce in the State of which the foreign spouses are nationals can be invoked and applied even if the said grounds are different from those laid down by the law of 1 December 1970, no. 898. It is for the case law to work out the limits of application of foreign grounds for divorce.

II. The recognition in Italy of foreign divorce decrees against a spouse not having Italian nationality

If a divorce has been decreed abroad against nationals of other States than Italy, the relevant judgment can be declared enforceable in Italy by resorting to the special procedure under Article 796 to 799 of the Code of Civil Procedure. This possibility already existed before the legal institution of divorce had been received into the Italian legal system. In fact by ratifying the Hague Convention of 1902 Italy had been obliged, under Article 7 of the Convention, to recognise a divorce decreed by a competent Court in respect of a spouse whose national legislation permitted the ground for dissolution on which the decree had been based.

In this connection it must be added that after the ratification of the Convention the doctrine and the case law, while not without some contrasts, affirmed the legal possibility of enforcing in Italy the divorce judgments given by the courts of States which had not adhered to the Convention on condition, under Article 17 above, that the national law of the interested parties permitted divorce.[34] In fact it was maintained that these decisions could not be considered as contrary to public policy since Italy had received into its own legal system, through the ratification of the Convention, the above mentioned obligation under Article 7 thereof. The orientation just indicated had, however, thrown into relief the necessity at the time of the order for enforcement, of reserving a different treatment for the judgments rendered in states adhering to the Hague Convention in

---

33. Art 10 para. 3 of the law of 12 June 1912, no. 555 on Italian nationality, which is now covered by art. 143 introduced by art. 25 of the Statute of 19 May 1975, no. 151, reforming the family law.
34. Cf. Court of Appeal of Trieste, 15 Dec. 1958, in *Riv. Dir. Matr.* 1959, p. 432; Court of Appeal of Trente, 26 Feb. 1959 in *Dir. Eccl.* 1961, II, p. 136; Court of Appeal of Palermo, 22 May 1959, in *Giur. Sic.* 1960, p. 449.

contrast to those in States which had not adhered. Thus, it was not thought to be necessary with regard to the former States to investigate the grounds for the divorce. This distinction was inferred from a remark while ratifying the Convention, that the Italian State had carried out a preliminary evaluation of the legal systems of the other States that had ratified and, on the other hand, from the fact that by virtue of Article 7 of the Convention itself, the obligation to recognise such judgments was only subjected to the one condition that the judgments should come "from a court which is competent in the terms of Article 5".[35]

Since the coming into effect of law no. 898, it is more necessary than before to affirm henceforth the possibility in general of declaring enforceable in Italy foreign divorce decrees pronounced in proceedings by parties who are not Italian nationals, provided that the relevant ground is not contrary to Italian public policy. The determination of the limits within which public policy must be protected is naturally a matter for case law. In this respect, a recent decision of the Court of Appeal of Rome[36] held that "a unilateral act of repudiation by the husband cannot be recognised in Italy". "In fact", the Court reasoned, "such an act cannot be assimilated to divorce, given the fact that Italian legislation permits divorce only for certain reasons". Referring to these reasons, the Court of Appeal of Rome rejected the claim that the foreign judgment of the Sciaratic Court in Egypt of 3 November 1960 should be declared effective in Italy. The Egyptian Court had declared the dissolution, on the grounds of repudiation of a marriage contracted in Cairo and registered in the registers of the civil State of the commune of Rome, by an Italian woman and an Egyptian national. On the other hand, the Court of Appeal of Milan by its decision of 14 December 1973[37] declared the principle by which the wife who is an Italian citizen but married to a foreigner can obtain in Italy a declaration of effectiveness of the foreign judgment for divorce by mutual consent, provided the foreign law does not allow the wish to dissolve the bond depend simply upon a momentary disagreement between the spouses, even if it is mutual, and insists upon a minimum period to verify that all material and spiritual communion has really evaporated. In the particular case, it was a question of a decision by a Belgian judge declaring the dissolution by mutual consent of a marriage contracted by a Belgian citizen with an Italian woman. The Court of Appeal emphasised[38] that the decision in question was not contrary to Italian public policy, given that the Belgian law which applied did not make the dissolution depend immediately and simply upon the mutual agreement of the spouses. In fact, in Belgian law such an agreement can be admitted as a ground for divorce only after two years of marriage and, in addition, there is a declaration of the spouses that they wanted a divorce. The agreement must be renewed in the course of the fourth, seventh and tenth months, with the same formality as the first declaration and with an

---

35. Court of Appeal of Rome, 1 Apl. 1952, in *Temi. Rom.* 1952, p. 91.
36. 9 July 1973 in *Il diritto di famiglia e delle persone* 1974, p. 653.
37. In *Il diritto di famiglia e delle persone* 1975, p. 828.
38. In addressing itself to the Convention between Italy and Belgium concerning the recognition and enforcement of judgments in civil and commercial marriages, signed in Rome on 6 Apl. 1962 and made operative in Italy by the law of 2 Mar. 1963, no. 596.

appearance before the President of the Court. Only after one year and after a new attempt at reconciliation can the divorce be granted.

In the two cases described, as the Italian woman had acquired the nationality of the husband as a result of the marriage, it had become a question of a judgment pronounced abroad against foreign nationals.

Regarding a foreign divorce of a spouse who has not Italian nationality but whose marriage has been contracted according to a religious rite with civil effects, (that is, a canonical marriage under the Concordat celebrated in Italy according to the forms authorised), it is necessary to consider whether the decision relative to such a divorce can be made effective in Italy concerning only the cessation of the civil effects of the marriage, without prejudice to the maintenance of the religious bond, which would be in conformity with the principle established in Article 2 of the law of 1 December 1970, no. 898. Analogous principles apply equally in the case of a divorce declared abroad when one spouse is an Italian national.

III. Recognition in Italy of foreign divorce decrees against Italian nationals

Concerning the recognition in Italy of divorce decrees relating to marriages of Italian nationals, the case law had in the past constantly excluded the admissibility of these.[39] In fact it had been held that these decisions infringe Italian public policy because of the principle of the indissolubility of marriage sanctioned by Article 149 of the Civil Code, a norm of substantive law from which Italian nationals cannot deviate. On the other hand, this recognition has been admitted by the Italian courts and tribunals with regard to divorce decrees referring to a marriage contracted by foreigners with Italian nationals. This when the latter, under Article 10 paragraph 3 of the law of 12 June 1912, no. 555 on Italian Nationality, had lost their Italian nationality by acquiring that of the foreign husband, as a result of the marriage.[40] In such a case it is thought that the problem of the protection of public policy does not arise because in the final analysis it is a question of a divorce pronounced in proceedings by spouses who will both be henceforth foreign nationals. But since divorce has been incorporated in the Italian legal system, as a result of the coming into effect of law no. 898, it must be said that even in the absence of all explicit affirmation on the subject in the law itself[41], the principle is established for the future that foreign divorce judgments given in proceedings involving Italian nationals can be recognised in Italy. It is for the case law to define when in particular cases of this kind recognition should not be admitted insofar as it would be incompatible with Italian public policy.

---

39. Court of Appeal of Rome, 30 Apl. 1959, in *Dir. Eccl.* 1960, II, p. 238; *Cass*, 16 Mar. 1960, no. 1171 in *Giur. It.* 1961, I 1 181.
40. Court of Appeal of Trieste, 14 Jan. 1957 in *Riv. dir. matr.* 1958, p. 111; Court of Appeal of Milan 6 Dec. 1957 in *Rép. Giur. It.* 1958, see *Delibazione*, n. 27.
41. It is known that the legislation of other States provides that their nationals can obtain divorce abroad. Cf. art. 7 of the Swiss federal law of 25 June 1891 on the civil law relations of established citizens or Swiss citizens visiting a foreign country (LRDC).

Apart from non-recognition of foreign divorce decrees based on grounds contrary to Italian public policy, it is again necessary to emphasise that, concerning judgments given with regard to marriages celebrated by Italian nationals according to the religious rite and having civil effects as a result of their registration, the above limitation for judgments relating to foreigners contracting such marriages is equally applicable, it being understood that the judgment in question can be made effective in Italy only in relation to the cessation of the civil rights of the marriage.

To conclude, the provision of the law to abrogate or modify the regulations governing divorce should be recalled. Considering the result of the referendum, it seems that the proposed law of Christian Democrat Deputy Cavaliere[42] and that of Deputy De Marzio and others of the Italian Socialist Movement[43], have been completely overridden. These two proposals were aimed at the repeal of the law no. 898 concerning the dissolution of civil marriage and the cessation of the civil effects of religious marriage.

Equally, the proposal of a draft law made by M Fortuna, a member of Parliament, was never considered by Parliament. This proposal demanded the repeal of articles 17 and 22 of the law of 27 May 1929 (no. 847). This law laid down provisions for the application of the Concordat between the Holy See and Italy, in respect of marriage and concerning the execution in Italy of annulments of marriages which are not consummated. In this connection it would be appropriate to recall the interesting disputes relating to the recognition in Italy of such judgments and the relevant procedure. These disputes concern the renunciation by the Italian State within its own jurisdiction *in subiecta materia*. These disputes have led to an examination by the Constitutional Court which up to the present has rejected the argument that the above legal standards are unconstitutional. It should be emphasised that the proposed law, presented in the political climate of the referendum on divorce, appeared to be a form of defence to the provisions of the law by which the repeal of law no. 898 of 1970 was demanded.

Finally, the proposals for laws no. 1642, 1644 and 1677, presented to the Senate in 1974, and also those for laws no. 3410 and 3471, presented to the Chamber of Deputies in 1975, aimed at the introduction of rules integrating the social legislation for the protection of the weaker spouse and the children in the case of dissolution or cessation of the civil effects of marriage. Proposal no. 1677 also aimed at "safeguarding for the surviving spouse who has not been responsible for the divorce . . . the rights of succession provided by the legislation in force."

---

42. 19 May 1972, *Doc. Camera dei Deputati* no. 20.
43. 26 July 1972, *Doc. Camera dei Deputati* no. 556.

CHAPTER VIII. THE REFORM OF FAMILY LAW IN LUXEMBOURG

by Gaston Vögel

I. Equality of the Spouses

Until recently the Grand Duchy of Luxembourg recognised the regime of the incapacity of the married woman just as it had been conceived and worked out by the authors of the French Civil Code. Legislation took a very long time to move from this position so that the Grand Duchy was one of the last countries in Europe to have one half of its adult population with legal capacity and one half without it. Article 212 of the Code, governing the respective rights and duties of the spouses, remained without any modification for more than a century and a half, being Napoleonic both in the letter and in the spirit. Advocates were still confronted in 1972 with such out of date ideas as that the husband must protect his wife and that the wife must obey her husband. The practitioner had the unenviable task of explaining to the ladies that they continued to rank with spendthrifts, the feeble-minded and minors in the privileged capacity of those without legal capacity, that they ought on this account to provide themselves with all kinds of authorisations by the husband, and could not become party to any valid document associated with civil life, that they must cohabit with their husband and follow him wherever he happened to decide to live, and in other absurdities of this kind. "All results of this same happy thought that the spouses, united in a life of procreation are one, in the image of the union of the Church with its founder. It is to this image, in fact, that the attitude of the wife must be linked, in submission to her husband."[1] The same principles of inequality were found in those provisions of the Code which were enshrined in the marriage contract and in the economic powers of the spouses. The basis of the Napoleonic wisdom in this area is found in Article 1421 of the Code which stated that the husband alone administers the community assets. He can sell them, alienate them and mortgage them without the agreement of his wife. Today that would be overstating the position. The Luxembourg legislator has at last turned to different concepts just as neighbouring countries have done. The Civil Code inflicted a double incapacity upon the married woman in contrast to the single woman, the widow or the divorced woman. She was placed entirely under the control of her husband and, regarding the exercise of her civil rights, she was prohibited from carrying out a legal act of any sort without the authorisation of her husband. The two guiding principles of the Code concerning the relationship of the spouses were authoritarianism and paternalism. The incapacity of the married woman under the common law was a general incapacity, with the exception of the special provisions for the wife carrying on a profession and for the wife with separate assets. Incapacity was the rule, capacity the exception. The legal equality of the spouses resulted from a reform which was realised by stages. The government took an interest in the problem for the first time in 1963.

---

1. Essay on *The Structural Analysis of the French Civil Code*, by A J Arnaud, p. 72.

The Minister of Justice of the period put forward a scheme for reform which, however, did not touch upon the essentials: the husband would remain the incontestable head of the family. It was not until 1971 that a first pruning of the legislation appeared, though it was altogether too modest and barely perceptible. The law for the protection of the young was published on 12 November 1971. Article 52 of this law repealed Articles 215, 216 and 218 of the Civil Code. Article 215 provided that the wife could not bring legal proceedings without the authority of the husband even when she carried on a trade in public or on her own, or had private assets. Article 216 laid down that the authorisation of the husband is not necessary when the wife is prosecuted on a criminal matter or by the police. Article 218 provided that if the husband refused to authorise the wife to be a party to legal proceedings, the judge could give such authorisation. Of the whole legal complex affecting the equality of the spouses, these were the only provisions to be repealed and even these were in the framework of a text to organise the protection of youth. This mini-reform brought nothing substantial, but only insignificant simplifications of procedure. The real point of departue was the law of 12 December 1972 concerning the rights and duties of the spouses. But this text did not apply to the matrimonial regimes which were the object of the reform of 4 February 1974 so, for nearly two years the legislation remained in mid-air between the former and the new regimes and, on that account, was disfigured by numerous ambiguities and contradictions. The two reforms of rights and duties and matrimonial regimes could not be realised at one and the same time so that, at the end of 1972, the legal commission of the Chamber of Deputies still found itself faced with three different plans concerning matrimonial regimes, without any agreement in sight. These were:

(1) The Government plan, establishing a regime of community limited to property acquired during the marriage, in which each of the spouses administers alone the assets derived from himself or herself.

(2) A draft law establishing a regime of common individual assets, functioning during the marriage as separate assets but which, on the dissolution of the marriage, would be reduced to a common fund, consisting of assets acquired after the marriage.

(3) The plan of the Council of State which also established a common fund limited to property aquired after marriage, but in which the husband retained certain powers of administration and disposition, to the exclusion of the wife.

Despite the inconveniences presented by the separation of the reform of legislation concerning the spouses from that concerning their assets, the Legal Commission of the Chamber of Deputies resigned itself to follow this course on account of the difficulties that remained to be smoothed out regarding the matrimonial regimes, and to record its willingness to ensure the equality of the spouses without further delay. In its notice of 3 December 1972 the Council of State recorded its disapproval of the method of procedure which the Chamber of Deputies had finally chosen.

The first stage in establishing the equality of the spouses was reached in the adoption of the law of 12 December 1972 on the rights and duties of the spouses.

A. Introduction of Law of 12. 12. 1972

This law was unanimously adopted at the first reading on 1 June 1972 and was finally adopted unanimously on 31 October 1972. It abolished the civil incapacity of the married woman and removed most of the discriminations between husband and wife that figured in the Civil Code under the title of rights and duties of the spouses. The 1972 law also organised a primary regime concerning the pecuniary relations of the spouses with regard to the assets. This regime modified some aspects of the former matrimonial regime. The preparatory texts suggested that, without expressly modifying the provisions of the Civil Code, the imperative rules of the new primary regime shall prevail over the relevant provisions of the Civil Code insofar as they conflict. Thus, despite the rules laid down by the Civil Code the wife, whether with common or separate assets, can remove her own immovables without the agreement of her husband and can open a bank account in her own name and freely dispose of the contents without the consent of her spouse.[2]

B. Analysis of the essential provisions

(1) The legislator announces a series of elementary principles which at first sight appear to allow a minimum of progress as they contain so many banalities or mere matters of fact.

The following articles confirm the independence of the spouses in business life:
Article 221: Each of the spouses may open a deposit account and invest in securities in their own name, without the consent of the other . . .
Article 223: Each spouse has the right to carry on a profession or an industrial or commercial activity without the consent of the other spouse.
Article 224: Each of the spouses is entitled to his or her gains and remuneration and the fruits of his or her assets and can freely dispose of them, after having discharged the expenses of the household.
Article 216: The marriage does not modify the legal capacity of the spouses.

(2) Alongside these provisions which establish the equality of the spouses by simple and elementary principles, there is a series of articles governing the life of the couple in truly modern terms.

(a) For the abolition of the idea of the head of the family, the Commission was guided by the principle of complete equality between the spouses. If it was desired in principle to set aside the complete supremacy of one spouse in the framework of the matrimonial regime, it was illogical to retain the idea of a head of the family. Thus the new article 213 of the Civil Code proclaims that henceforth the spouses should agree in the interests of the family, upon the moral and material direction of it, the provision for its maintenance, the bringing up of the children and their preparation for a career. Thus the two spouses are placed on an equal footing. Their agreement is required for everything that relates to the material and moral organisation of the household. In principle, a spouse can act alone only if it is impossible for the other to exercise his or her powers.

(b) Regarding the duty to cohabit, article 215 stipulates that the spouses are bound to live together. In default of agreement between them concerning the

---

2. See Tr. parl. session ord, 1972-73, *Report of the Legal Commission* of 25.6.1972.

matrimonial home, the decision shall belong to the judge who shall fix the place of residence, after having heard the reasons invoked by each of the spouses. Nevertheless, the Court can, for legitimate reasons, authorise the spouses to live separately. In this case, the Court will also decide on where the children should live.

The Luxembourg legislator, anxious not to run the risk of a reproach on the question of discrimination, has abolished all the prerogatives of the husband in the choice of the matrimonial home. With regard to the occasion and circumstance necessitating resort to the Court for a decision, it should be noted that article 215 was interpreted as bearing in mind that the authors of that article emphasised that the reasons invoked by one spouse for a separate residence could (i) result from a disagreement between the spouses as to the choice of the matrimonial home, (ii) be against the good of the family, or (iii) be the result of injurious behaviour of one spouse with regard to the other. This thesis would seem to indicate the possibility that the legislator would have agreed to the installation, alongside divorce and separation, of a new legal regime of the suspension of the obligation of cohabitation.

In Luxembourg case law, a claim for separate residence cannot be introduced in the absence of proceedings for divorce or separation if it is based exclusively on the excesses, cruelties or grave injuries by the husband.

(c) Article 214 governs the contribution of the spouses to the costs of maintenance of the family household, as well as to necessary costs for the education of the children. It stipulated that, if the marriage contract did not specify the contribution of the spouses to the expenses of the marriage, they should contribute in proportion to their respective capacities. This could be acquitted through their professional or domestic work, through the assets brought to the marriage and to their personal contributions to the common fund. Provided one of the spouses does not fail to contribute to the home, the other spouse is obliged to provide for all necessities of life according to his ability and circumstances. If a spouse does not fulfil his obligations he can be constrained to do so by the forms provided in article 864 of the Code of Civil Procedure.

The Luxembourg legislator did not retain the provision in the French Civil Code which preserved the dominance of the husband by stating that the expenses of the marriage fall mainly on the husband.

The remedy provided by article 864 of the Code of Civil Procedure merits careful examination. The Luxembourg legislator based his thesis on the principle that if one spouse fails to fulfil the obligation to contribute to the expenses of the marriage in the circumstances provided for by the Civil Code, the other spouse can, without prejudice to the rights of third parties, be authorised by the Justice of the Peace to receive, to the exclusion of the other spouse, the income of the latter or those which he administers by virtue of the matrimonial regime, the produce of his labour and all other sums due to him from third parties. The judge should fix the conditions of authorisation as well as the maximum amount granted. The law provides that the judge can order the spouses, and even third parties, to give information or to produce account books or vouchers that would establish the exact amount of income. A third party who fails or refuses to furnish the information demanded will be declared debtor pure and simple for the undeclared amounts and will be made liable for the expenses occasioned by him.

Judgment will be effective notwithstanding the subsequent bringing of a petition for divorce or separation, until the decision of the Court or of a judge in chambers.

The question whether the action is admissible arises in the case of a factual separation between the spouses. The question was decided affirmatively in a judgment made on 28 January 1975 by the Justice of the Peace of Esch/Alzette. This decision remains consistent with the case law, according to which the obligation to contribute to the expenses of the marriage is the liability of each of the spouses as long as the marriage lasts. It persists even in the case of physical separation and, as it can no longer apply naturally, the equivalent applies in the form of the payment of an annuity.

Lastly, the law establishes a series of rules to ensure the protection of the original community.

The autonomous power of each spouse to enter into contracts in the interests of the family is affirmed by article 220 of the Statute.

Every debt contracted by one of the spouses for the maintenance of the household or the education of the children places a joint obligation on the other spouse. The joint liability is excluded for expenditures which are manifestly excessive, regard being had to the way of life of the family, to the usefulness or lack of usefulness of the operation, and to the good faith or bad faith of the contracting spouse. Nor does the joint liability apply to obligations resulting from hire-purchases if they were not entered into with the consent of both spouses.

The same article prohibits each spouse from disposing alone of the rights concerning the family home. The last paragraph of article 215 says that neither spouse, without the other, can dispose of the rights by which the family dwelling is assured nor of the furniture therein. The spouse who has not consented to the transaction can demand its annulment within one year from the day when he or she first knew of it without ever being able to bring such proceedings more than one year after the matrimonial regime has been dissolved. In this case it is a question of relative nullity, which can be invoked only by the spouse whose consent was not obtained. The Court would refuse the demand of the plaintiff spouse that he or she has tacitly consented to the act of disposal carried out by the other spouse.

In the same context it is necessary to underline the other provisions of article 864-1 of the new Code of Civil Procedure in the terms of which the Presiding Judge can, if one of the spouses is gravely in breach of his or her duties, or is putting the interests of the family at risk, order urgent and provisional measures required in the interests of the other spouse and the children. The President of the Court can by way of injunction and with the agreement of the Attorney-General, forbid one of the spouses, for such period as he shall determine, to alienate or charge the movable or immovable assets, common or not, without the concurrence of the other and to prohibit the removal of the movables. When the prohibition asked for concerns both movable assets or credits, the President of the Court of the District, in cases of absolute necessity on the request of the plaintiff and before setting down the case for hearing, can by interlocutory order immediately and before the registration, permit the plaintiff spouse to enter a caveat against the other spouse or a third party.

The new article 864-5 provides for the possibility of annulment at the request of the plaintiff spouse of all acts carried through in violation of a judicial decision prohibiting such transactions, from the time of the pronouncement when it is defended and from the time of the notification when it is given by default.

If the law gives to each spouse the power to represent the other when it is a question of assuring the essential needs of the family, it must be permitted *a fortiori* in less essential matters that each may entrust the other with the power to act as his or her agent. The power of contractual representation is laid down in the new article 218 of the Civil Code.

The principle of the fixity of matrimonial agreements had been abolished. The new article 1397 of the Civil Code organises the change of the matrimonial regime. After two years of application the spouses can bring to their matrimonial regime, whether by agreement or by law, all the modifications which they deem to be appropriate and even to change it in its entirety, by a notraial act which will be subject to confirmation by the Court of their domicile.

The procedure of confirmation was severely criticised from the beginning. It was useless, cumbersome and onerous. The power of control by the Court was restricted to a formal verification of the conditions provided for by the law. Extracts of the claim for confirmation and the decision had to be published in the principal national newspapers, which considerably increased the proportional cost of the procedure. As there was a veritable plethora of claims for confirmation, the first section of the civil Court, before which the confirmation proceedings were held, were overburdened and arrived only with difficulty at clearing the ordinary disputes submitted to it. With some rare exceptions, it was generally agreed that it was necessary to change the system as quickly as possible. A recent statute has abolished the procedure of confirmation and the publication of extracts in the newspapers.

The law of 12 December 1972 anticipated in some of its provisions the legislation which had to be adopted two years later regarding matrimonial regimes. The Council of State bitterly criticised the Chamber of Deputies for this, saying that in adopting then and there the rule that each of the spouses obtains the freedom to dispose of the fruits of his own assets and that the wife in community of assets has the administration of her own assets and can dispose of them freely, the Chamber of Deputies had anticipated the option which it intended to reserve until a deeper study was made of the different schemes before it. While provisionally retaining the present regime of the Code, the Parliament had established certain new principles which overthrew the economy of the legislative system and risked being irreconcilable with the provisions retained. Such a hybrid regime would give rise to numerous problems and would foster difficulties which could prove to be insoluble.

The hybrid system was of short duration. A law reforming the matrimonial regimes was promulgated in February 1974. Before this the Legal Commission of the Chamber of Deputies, having regard to the complexity of the matter and being desirous of making a pronouncement only with full knowledge of the matter, took the advice of foreign experts, and two University professors were retained to give information. These were Professor Colomer of the Faculty of Law of Montpellier and Professor Claude Renard, Vice-Rector of the University of Liège. The two experts had been expressly advised that in every aspect of the matter the Legal Commission of the Chamber intended to go as far as possible along the way to equality of the spouses.[3] The expert advice was made available at the end of December 1972. As a result, the law of 4 February 1974 made additions to the rights of the married woman, thereby increasing equality between the spouses.

The legal regime is broadly that of the common fund limited to property acquired after the marriage. In this connection, the law recognised various categories of assets, for example: assets brought into the community by each of the spouses, such as the product of their labour, the fruits and income of their own assets—acquired during the marriage—; assets brought into the community by one of the spouses; individual assets; assets which are personal by their nature, for example clothes, correspondence, family souvenirs, various rights of property, rights of action for damages; trade tools necessary for the profession of one of the spouses; assets of which the spouses were in possession at the date of the marriage, or which they acquired during the marriage by succession, gift or legacy; assets acquired in connection with a personal belonging, as well as new assets and other additions attaching to movable property which is individual.

The Luxembourg legislator abolished the main idea of the husband as the sole administrator of the common fund. Management of the patrimony is now organised as follows:—

One spouse cannot dispose, without the consent of the other, of assets brought into the common fund by both spouses. If one spouse alone performs an act of administration or enjoyment, he or she must have received a tacit mandate from the other spouse. Each spouse is answerable to the other spouse for his or her management, as an agent. He or she is, however, accountable only for the existing profits, and for those which he or she has neglected to receive or has fraudulently consumed, and can be proceeded against only in respect of the last five years. If one of the spouses has interfered in the management of the assets in question in defiance of an expressed opposition, he or she is responsible for all the results of his interference and is accountable without limit for all the profits he has received, or neglected to collect, or fraudulently consumed.

Provided that it be without fraud, each of the spouses administers by himself the assets brought into the community in his or her own right and can dispose of them freely. The preliminary draft stated that the solution which appeared to be the most satisfactory and most logical consisted in leaving to the spouse who had procured the asset the power of managing it for the benefit of the community. In this way perfect legal equality of the spouses is assured, each one having real powers over a part of the common assets, namely that coming from his or her own economic activity and the income from his or her own property.[4]

Article 1421 provides that the spouse is liable for faults committed during his management. The law prohibits the gratuitous disposal of assets brought into the common fund by one of the spouses, even if it be for the benefit of their common children, unless with the consent of the other spouse. Nor can one

3. Report of the Legal Commission of 25.6.1972.
4. Preliminary draft of the law, *Commission d'Etudes Legislatives*, p. 10.

without the consent of the other dispose of immovables, commercial funds or enterprises brought into the common fund in his own right, nor charge them with real rights.

A spouse can demand the annulment of an act performed by the other spouse affecting a common asset when the latter has exceeded his powers or acted fraudulently. The action in nullity is open to the spouse within two years from the date when he first learned of the act, though he may not bring an action more than two years after the dissolution of the common fund.

If one of the spouses finds himself permanently incapable of manifesting his wishes or if in his management of the assets brought into the community in his own right he shows incapacity or fraud, the other spouse can bring an action for his own substitution in the exercise of these powers. In this way the spouse authorised by the Court has the same powers as the replaced spouse would have had. With the authorisation by the Court the spouse can carry out acts for which his or her own consent would have been required if there had not been a substitution.

The right of disposition of the dispossessed spouse is reduced to the bare ownership of his assets, retrospective to the date of the petition.

The principle of individual property is that each spouse has the administration and enjoyment of his individual assets and can dispose of them freely.

In the realisation of the equality of the spouses a third stage was reached by the passing of the law of 6 February 1975 relating to majority, parental authority, legal administration, guardianship and emancipation. The law is the necessary corollary of the laws already mentioned. It conforms to the principles laid down by the laws on the rights and duties of the spouses and, in reforming the matrimonial regimes, grants to the wife and mother the same rights of paternal power, legal administration and guardianship as to the husband and father. Here again, the Luxembourg legislator went further, abolishing all predominance of the father.

The principal stated is that the authority belongs to the father and mother to protect the child in his safety, his health and his morals. In this respect they have a right of custody, supervision and education. During the marriage the father and mother exercise their authority in common. The child remains under their joint authority until its majority or emancipation. The 1975 law also lowered the age of civil majority to 18 years.

The father and mother jointly have the administration and enjoyment of the assets of their minor child, but the latter does not extend to assets which the child can acquire by his own labour.

If the parents cannot arrive at an agreement between themselves as to the requirements for the welfare of the child, the more diligent spouse can call upon the guardianship judge, who will make a decision after having tried to conciliate the parties. If one of the parents dies or loses the exercise of his parental authority, the exercise of that authority devolves in its entirety on the other parent. Upon the death of the father and mother a guardianship will be established.

If the father and mother are divorced or separated, the parental authority is exercised by the one to whom the Court has entrusted the custody of the child, subject to the right of the other spouse to visit and to supervise. In exceptional circumstances the Court which decides on the custody of the child after divorce or separation can decide during the lifetime of the spouses that the authority shall not pass to the survivor in the case of the death of the spouse who is the guardian. In this case he can designate the person upon whom the custody will provisionally devolve.

With regard to parental authority upon the assets of the child, and in the case of disagreement between the father and mother in the joint exercise of the legal administration, the decision is taken by the guardianship judge upon the petition of one of them, subject to the agreement of the other. At least the latter must have been duly summoned to appear. In divorce or separation, the legal administration belongs to the spouse to whom the custody of the child has been entrusted. A distinction is made between the legal administration pure and simple, and the administration under the control of the guardianship judge.

The legal administration is pure and simple when the minor is a legitimate child both of whose parents are living, not divorced or separated and not affected by incapacity. In this regime, both the father and the mother can carry out acts of pure administration alone. For all other acts they must operate together and, in the case of disagreement, it is for the guardianship judge to give the casting vote.

Authorisation by the guardianship judge is compulsorily required for all the following acts—exchange the transfer into a company of an immovable or the assets of a trading business belonging to the minor, the assumption and renunciation of a right. The administration reverts to the guardianship judge on the death or incapacity of one of the parents, on the divorce or separation of the parents, or if the minor is an illegitimate child.

The administrator must obtain the authorisation of the guardianship judge to carry through acts which a guardian can do only with the authorisation of the family council, such as borrowing, alienating or mortgaging the immovables, trading assets, accepting a succession purely and simply, or the repudiation of it, and so on.

The Luxembourg Code still contained non-essentials which it was necessary to get rid of as quickly as possible in the great impetus towards tidying up the law. This had been taking place since 1970. For example, article 229 of the Civil Code stipulated that the husband could claim a divorce on the ground of the adultery of the wife, yet article 230 stated that the wife could claim divorce on the ground of the adultery of the husband when he had kept his mistress in the matrimonial home. An obvious inconsistency in these articles is accentuated by provisions in two articles of the Penal Code: one provided that a wife, convicted of adultery, should be sentenced to imprisonment of from 3 months to 2 years, but another article held that a husband convicted of having kept his mistress in the conjugal home should be sentenced to imprisonment of from one month to one year.

Further, it was necessary to eliminate the curious discrimination made by the law between the wife's co-respondent and that of the husband. Only the co-respondent to the wife was punishable.

There were two possibilities of assuring the equality of the spouses in this area, either by making the Civil law and the Penal law uniform in order to put the spouses on a footing of strict equality, or simply to abolish the provision of a different era. The legislator opted for the second solution, and in 1974 the Minister of Justice presented a draft law which simply removed the penalty for

191

adultery. Just one phrase was required, that of stating that articles 387 to 390 of the Penal Code are repealed.

It seems strange that adultery, although freed from penalty, remains written into articles 229 and 230 of the Civil Code, with all its discriminations between men and women. A plan for recasting divorce as a penalty foreshadows the disappearance of these texts. However, this has not yet been arrived at and, in the interim, the relevant articles of the Civil Code retain their original wording. Adultery remains an obligatory ground for divorce but, while for the wife a single occasion suffices, in the case of the husband it is necessary that the marriage vow should be violated and result from a state of affairs both persistent and particularly injurious for the wife, that of the maintenance of a mistress in the conjugal home.

II. Illegitimate Children

In considering the standing of the illegitimate child, nothing has been done. Society has forgotten it. Illegitimate children thwart the established order and the morality on which it is based. It was consequently thought correct to discard them and thus preserve the acceptable society. There is evidence here of the treatment of some persons as things. Illegitimate children were considered by the law as pariahs, but some pariahs are in greater disfavour than others.

The simple natural child, which is one born neither from an adulterous nor from an incestuous association, has certain rights, limited it is true, but rights nevertheless. He can claim for necessaries against the parent with regard to whom his affiliation is established and he can claim a minimal part in the succession on the intestacy of that parent without becoming a reserve heir. The parents can consequently disinherit him completely. Article 756 affirmed the principle that illegitimate children are not heirs; the law does not grant them rights over the property of their deceased father and deceased mother except when they have been legally recognised. The law accords them no right over the property of the parents of their father or mother. Articles 757 and 758 defined that this right is to one third of the hereditary portion which the illegitimate child would have had if he had been legitimate. It would be one-half when the parents do not leave descendants or brothers or sisters. It is a right to three-fourths when the parents leave neither descendants or ascendants, brothers nor sisters. The illegitimate child has the right to the whole of the property when his parents do not leave relatives in any degree which can succeed to their estates. Nor can his parents grant him a larger share than that which would normally have come to him under intestate succession.

To establish affiliation the child must first cut his way through the judicial undergrowth. If the establishment of maternity is easy, paternity is, by contrast, decidedly not.

A child conceived in adultery or incest has no rights. The law even prohibits him from establishing his affiliation. Legitimation by subsequent marriage is always impossible. This child has then in principle neither the right to maintenance nor to a share in the succession of its parents. Here the singularity of being treated as a thing reaches its cynical height. Article 762 affirms that the provisions which affect the rights of succession of illegitimate children are not applicable to children conceived in adultery or incest. When the father or mother of such a child have had him learn a trade the child cannot claim against the succession. The people who invented such a rule must have been without shame, like animals. One may wonder how it is that a society which has preserved such scandalous laws for more than a century and a half can claim that it is democratic and liberal and can claim to compare themselves with countries considered as dictatorial.

Luxembourg law in this respect is in contradiction to the directive and recommendation made within the framework of the United Nations, under the aegis of the Commission of Human Rights and of the Economic and Social Council. It is in opposition to article 11 of the Constitution, which states that the people of Luxembourg are equal before the law. The discriminations made by the Civil Code between legitimate and illegitimate children, whether simple or complex, can be considered as revolting as those which relate to race or religion. In recent times this subject has been attacked by the contemporary world.

Reforms adopted in the recent past may be summarised as follows.

A law was published in 1974 modifying the regime of adoption. By this law children conceived in adultery have been able to obtain a satisfactory status.

In 1975 a law was passed relating to parental authority, guardianship and legal administration with regard to the illegitimate child. This provided that the parental authority over the illegitimate child is exercised by whichever of its parents has voluntarily recognised the child, if it has been recognised by only one of them. If both have recognised the child the parental authority is exercised wholly by the mother. Nevertheless, the guardianship judge, at the request of one or the other, or of the Attorney-General, may decide that the authority shall be exercised either by the father alone or by the father and mother jointly and, in that case, articles 375 and 375-2 will be applicable as if the infant were legitimate. The legal administration is placed under the control of the guardianship judge, as occurs in the case of a legitimate child on the death or divorce of one of his parents.

The Government has since drafted a law reforming the right of affiliation, which serves the purpose of making the biological truth prevail over legal fictions as far as possible. It affirms the elementary principle that every child has the right to establish its affiliation and, consequently, the establishment of the bond of affiliation is allowed in all cases. The action to establish affiliation is always admissible and is not prevented by a difficult or tricky system of proofs. Thus the draft abandons the archaic conditions to which the disavowal of paternity was subjected. In the description of the grounds it is stated that the comparison of the blood groups constitutes a certain means for establishing the negative proof that a particular man could not be the father of a given child. However, the proposed text does not mean to limit the methods of proof, if only in order not to prejudice future developments which genetics and biology may be able to achieve in this area.

The principle of the assimilation of legitimate and illegitimate children is laid down in paragraph 1 of article 334. This provision puts an end to all discrimination. Each time an article of the Code or of a special law speaks of a child, the term must henceforward be understood as referring to all children, whether issue of a marriage or not. Again it is laid down that the illegitimate child becomes a member of the family of its parent. This had been denied previously by case-law.

However, the rights of succession are not affected by the draft law. This will be dealt with by a special draft which will provide at the same time for the complete recasting of the rights of the surviving spouse. It is to be regretted that the whole problem could not be resolved in one step.

III. Divorce

Luxembourg law recognises divorce on specified grounds and divorce by mutual consent.

The first system, which rests on the principle of fault, obliges the spouses to make a public issue of their real or imaginary wrongs. The second system permits the spouses, thanks to a discreet procedure, to separate with dignity. The two procedures were introduced by the Napoleonic law of 1803, the Luxembourg legislater later retaining them in their original form and tenor and refusing to introduce any modification whatever. The legal complex of divorce has since undergone substantial changes.

A law of 1975 relating to divorce by mutual consent has introduced important modifications simplifying the procedure and facilitating access to this form of separation by the abolition of conditions which were as extravagant as they were painful. The system of divorce on specified grounds is also being completely refashioned.

A. Divorce by mutual consent

In 1975 the matter was governed by articles 275 to 294 of the Civil Code. The conditions set by the law for divorce by mutual consent were heavy, weighty, rigorous and thereby often made illusory the desire of the spouses to separate under this system.

In their book *Divorce: Liberalism or Liberty*, Monique and Roland Weyl emphasise that for the peasant to whom the earth is given, as for the bourgeois who freely conducts family affairs founded upon personal ownership, often based on land, the family remained what it had been—a means of conservation, of extension and of transmission of a patrimony which is still almost exclusively based on land. This peasant, like the burgeois, had absolutely no desire to see his assets at the mercy of the individualistic aspirations of children wishing to marry freely and to be able to divorce freely ... The principle of the immutability of the contract of marriage, the family pact which the spouses cannot modify, is indeed the corollary of the indissoluble marriage. For those families with possessions this contract is more important than the marriage itself and it would not be acceptable to permit its modification. These ideological aspects must be re-membered when trying to understand what seems at first sight to be imbecile or absurd in the ancient law.

Divorce by mutual consent is only possible under the following conditions— The husband must be at least 25 years of age and the wife at least 21 years of age;

194

the consent could only be admitted after two years of marriage; the consent is no longer admitted after twenty years of marriage; it was no longer admitted if the wife had attained the age of 45 years. In any case, mutual consent was not enough if it was not authorised by their parents or by their other living ascendants. Here is strong evidence of the character of marriage as a family arrangement, essentially implementing the union of the two patrimonies and which necessitated the concurrence of the parents, the heads of the family fortune, to prevent the methods of dissolution. Article 305 provided a condition which made it impossible for wealthy folk, the economically strong, to divorce by mutual consent for, in that case, the ownership of one half of the assets of each of the spouses would be acquired absolutely by the children of the marriage, from the date of their first declaration. The spouses could not contract a new marriage until three years after the pronouncement of the divorce. The presence of two notaries was obligatory. The spouses had to appear together before the President of the Court on five different occasions, accompanied by their respective notaries. For the final appearance they had to be further assisted by two friends each who were notables in the district and at least 50 years of age.

The law of 1975 repealed the whole of articles 275 to 294 and proceeded to a complete recasting of the matter. Conditions for divorce by mutual consent were reduced to two: (a) Mutual consent will be admitted only after two years of marriage, (b) It will not be admitted at all if one of the spouses is less than 23 years old.

As a preliminary the spouses are obliged to make, through a lawyer, an inventory and estimate of all their movable and immovable assets and to sort out their respective rights regarding which possessions they will be free to deal with. They will be similarly bound to affirm in writing their agreement concerning the residence of each of the spouses while the proofs are being examined, the administration of the person and property of the minor children, the contribution of each of the spouses to the maintenance and education of the children and the amount of any annuity to be paid by one of the spouses to the other. The spouses must then present themselves together and in person before the President of the Civil Court of their district and must make their declaration to him of their wish to separate, while producing the agreement, the inventory and extracts from the certificates of their civil status. The declaration must be renewed within the six months following. In the month from the day on which the anniversary of the first declaration occurs, the spouses will present themselves together and in person before the President of the Court and will petition the magistrate, but in each other's presence, for the pronouncement of the divorce. The Court, at the instance of the Attorney General who will have the burden of verifying if the conditions provided by the law have been fulfilled, will pronounce the divorce.

Appeal from a judgment refusing a divorce must be made by both parties within one month from the day on which the judgment was notified to them by the clerk by registered post. The proceedings will be instituted and judged by the Court of Appeal as an urgent matter. The appeal will only be admissible against an order refusing the divorce and only when it is brought by the spouses acting jointly.

In the case of divorce by mutual consent, the divorced wife can remarry immediately after the pronouncement of the divorce.

B. Divorce on specified grounds

Divorce rests on the principle of fault. The objective fact of the impossibility of a life together was only taken into consideration if it resulted from fault. The 'innocent' spouse could oppose the divorce even when life together seemed manifestly impossible and intolerable, and the judge must not pronounce the divorce if faults are not established, which amounts to decreeing that spouses who cannot, or no longer wish to, live together shall remain married as if the marriage were indissoluble. The institution is not only of an exclusive character, but an essentially repressive character for it preserves a system of personal vengeance in which the spouse who is 'innocent' or apparently innocent can, at his discretion, keep the other spouse in bonds which are impossible to break, or can make the other spouse pay the price of liberty.[5]

Fault involves economic consequences which are not usually in proportion to the responsibility incurred in the disunion. A responsibility shared during the breakdown, however small the share, suffices to deprive the spouse at fault of all chance of help.

Before going into the numerous and justified criticisms which have been directed at the system in force, it is useful to remember the essential points, while describing the modifications which have been introduced in the recent past.

1. The grounds for divorce: The spouses can reciprocally claim divorce on the ground of adultery. Paradoxically, adultery has been abolished as an offence but is retained as a special ground for divorce. This situation will shortly be brought to an end. The spouses can claim divorce from each other for excess, cruelties or grave injuries by one of them against the other. A further ground for divorce is when one spouse receives a conviction involving dishonour for the family.

2. The following procedure must be followed. A petition setting out the facts must be presented to the President of the Court by the plaintiff spouse in person. This petition can be brought only at the Court of the district in which the spouses have their common residence or, failing that, in the Court of the defendant party at his or her residence. Having heard the petitioner, the judge will order a day and hour for an attempt at conciliation, when he will make such representations as he thinks proper to effect a reconciliation. If this fails he will arrange for a hearing of the disagreement and will grant or suspend permission to sue, for a maximum of twenty days.

3. The debate and discussion comes after the divorce summons, which must be issued within three months following the Presidential order granting permission to bring the case. The ground is judged and stated in the ordinary form. However, apart from children and descendants, other relatives of the parties, or their servants, cannot be approached because of either their relationship or their status.

4. Before modification to the law in 1975, the Court only dealt with divorce. The spouses had to have the divorce pronounced by the Officer of the Civil Status, under pain of nullify. Henceforth, it is the Court that pronounces divorce.

---

5. Monique and Roland Weyl, *ibid*, p. 29.

The judgment or decree is effective with regard to its effects on the property of the spouses on the day of the petition. It will only be effective with regard to third parties from the day of the notice or of the transcription. The judgment or decree pronouncing the divorce must be signed by the Commissioners of the Court.

The period for appeal against, or for quashing, the petition is three months from the date of notification. If notification of the judgment or decree has not been duly made, the President of the Court will make a decision in default by publishing the judgment in a newspaper of his choice.

The period for entering a defence will be fifteen days from the notification to a person, or from the act of publication.

Unfortunately, there are still some anomalies in the law regarding procedure with regard to divorce.

C. Provisional measures resulting from a divorce petition

During any stage of divorce proceedings provisional measures can be made concerning the person of the parties or the children, their maintenance and their property. The Divorce Chamber of the Luxembourg Court gives exclusive competence to the judge in chambers for these measures, yet the Court declares itself incompetent to fix provisional measures if approached by way of interlocutory judgment. This view must be erroneous, as it is not supported by any legal text.[6]

The spouses may apply for separate residence during the divorce proceedings. If one spouse has not sufficient income for his needs he can claim a proportionate maintenance annuity within the capacity of the other spouse. This will be refused if he is in good health, does not have the care of the children, is able to carry on an occupation and can meet his needs through his own efforts.[7]

D. Effects of divorce

(a) Remarriage: Since 1963 divorced persons have been able to remarry provided they celebrate the remarriage afresh. In the case of divorce on the ground of adultery, the guilty spouse was not allowed to marry the co-respondent until after the death of the first spouse, but this provision has since been abolished.

(b) Financial penalties: Apart from the case of divorce by mutual consent, the spouse against whom the petition has been granted loses all the benefits given by the other spouse, whether through the marriage contract or during the marriage. The spouse who is in the wrong also loses all rights to an annuity on the death of the spouse, within the social security system.

There is a serious anomaly in this connection, in that the spouse who petitions for divorce, generally the wife, loses her husband's sickness insurance. This is particularly unfortunate as it occurs before the judge has been able to examine the responsibilities in the marriage failure. However, it does not affect the

---

6. *Kaboth v Gorges*, 22.5.1975; *Back v Thifold*, 7.7.1975.
7. *Carreira v Pütz*, 1975.

children and the Minister of Labour and Social Security can grant a dispensation when there is a common household.

The Court can grant a maintenance annuity to the spouse who has been awarded the divorce, out of the assets of the other spouse, but this may not exceed one-third of the income of the other spouse. This annuity has the character of providing and indemnifying at one and the same time. It is based on the damage caused to the 'innocent' spouse which has enabled him to obtain the divorce. This annuity cannot be made the object of a transaction or of a renunciation and any arrangement between the spouses in this respect is null and void.[8] In fixing the amount the Court takes account of the rank and position the innocent spouse would have enjoyed if the marriage had not been dissolved.[8]

(c) Custody: The law provides that the children shall be entrusted to the spouse who has obtained the divorce unless the Court, at the request of the family or of the Procurator-General, orders that all or some of them shall be entrusted to the care of the other spouse or of a third person, if that is for the greater advantage of the children. In general, the Court entrusts the custody to the spouse whom it considers to be the best able to assure the education and maintenance of the children. The parental authority is exercised by the spouse entrusted with custody, subject to the right to visit and supervise by the other spouse.

The Court making the latest order for custody can always be approached by the family or the Attorney-General in order to nominate a third person as guardian of the child, with or without the setting up of a guardianship. In exceptional circumstances the Court making the order for custody can decide, even during the lifetime of the spouses, that the custody shall not pass to the survivor on the death of the guardian spouse. In such a case the Court can nominate provisionally the person who will be given the custody.

The system in force cannot be said to be satisfactory.

Deficiencies of the present system

It is unacceptable that the judge should have to make painful investigations into the private lives of people for the purpose of establishing the existence or otherwise of problematical wrongs. Respect for human rights should ensure the privacy of intimate relationships. There are no criteria which enable the Court to prove the occurrence or scope of pretended wrongs leading to the break-up of the marriage. The actions of one spouse relate to those of the other and it is mostly impossible to interpret culpability among the nuances which should be taken into consideration. The investigation procedure is apt to lead to bitter rivalry between the spouses, especially when the result will affect the economic position of them both, and thus jeopardise hopes of eventual reconciliation. Furthermore, witnesses cannot be relied upon for factual observation, being actuated by preferences or reluctance to become involved, and these biased statements can influence a judge who has no greater access to any facts. The result

---

8. CSJ Luxembourg—Pasicrisie 17, p. 327.
9. CSJ Luxembourg *Muller v Bydsovska;* CSJ Luxembourg 17.3.1975 *Thiel v Becker.*

-may be a judgment given on a very precarious basis yet carrying severe economic penalties. Only three solutions are possible: to pronounce the divorce for the benefit of one party on account of the wrongs of the other; to pronounce the divorce for equal wrongs on both sides, on a fifty-fifty basis; or to dismiss the petition for lack of evidence. When the divorce is based on shared wrongs the maintenance allowance is forfeited, without account being taken of the individual contributions made to the upkeep of the household and the common fund.

In principle, maintenance should not be dependent on fault, but should be provided by the spouse in the stronger economic position for the benefit of the spouse who is unable to provide for himself or herself by their own means.

As divorce is only granted for grave default regarding conjugal obligations, those whose only fault lies in finding themselves unable to live together are unable to free themselves of a hated link unless they can sue by mutual consent. This they may not be able to do because of failure to agree on preliminary measures, or on account of nationality.

E. Suggested reforms

1. New grounds

It is proposed that specified grounds for divorce should be admissible in both divorce as a penalty and in divorce as a remedy. The former grounds would be retained, which really amount to one ground, that of grave injury, but adultery and a penal sentence involving dishonour should no longer count as grounds for divorce. The tendency is towards the elimination of the idea of fault and the establishment of divorce as a remedy for a broken marriage when the parties have been unable to live together for at least three years and when there is no hope of a reconciliation. There still remains the difficulty of proving an irrevocable breakdown of a marriage; unsoundness of mind and unpleasant physical disease have not been retained as grounds for divorce. However, there is a proposal to reinstate unsoundness of mind for at least five years as a ground for the breakdown of a marriage. Such petitions could be refused if the parties have already separated or if the economic results of a divorce would be unnecessarily harsh for the petitioning spouse or for the children.

2. Maintenance

Maintenance should be separated from the idea of fault and paid to satisfy the needs of the other party, not as compensation for fault. Each spouse, regardless of fault, should pay for his own maintenance, and allowances should only be granted when one or other of them is unable to do so from his own means.

Various detailed rules are suggested with regard to the award of maintenance. Thus the Court giving judgment can take into account the age, health and education of the divorced spouse and consider whether he is likely to successfully rebuild his life and obtain employment quickly. Amounts can be adjusted according to needs and the behaviour of the spouses and in consideration of the contribution of each spouse to the common fund. The amount of maintenance should not exceed one-third of the income of the spouse who must pay it. Maintenance can always be reviewed and altered according to circumstances. On the death of the debtor spouse the debts due shall pass to his heirs.

CHAPTER IX. THE REFORM OF FAMILY LAW IN THE SCANDINAVIAN COUNTRIES

by Ake Lögdberg

I. Sweden

1. Divorce

During this century there has been very comprehensive collaboration in legislative work between the Nordic (Scandinavian) countries. Marriage law is one of the fields where such collaboration has occurred between Sweden, Denmark and Norway, with the result that as lately as a few years ago, the legislation in these three countries was rather similar. As matters stand now, however, there is a wind of change blowing and probably in the near future there will be greater differences than before. As a matter of fact, there are at present great differences between the Swedish legislation on the one hand and the Danish and Norwegian legislations on the other. This is because Sweden has already accomplished some new reforms in this field while, for instance, Denmark is still at the planning stage. But in relation to the field of matrimonial property, Sweden too is at the planning stage.

In the long term, the main causes of these changes in divorce law are undoubtedly the growing secularisation of society and the considerable increase in the number of women working outside their homes. The greater haste displayed by the Swedes is a result of their more radical government with a greater interest in experiments.

During the sixteenth century Sweden officially went over from the Roman Catholic Church to the Lutheran (Protestant) Church. For several centuries since then the thoughts of the reformer, Martin Luther, had a great influence on Swedish marriage legislation. According to Lutheran opinion, the two grounds for divorce were adultery or desertion by the other spouse. In 1863 civil marriage was allowed when the parties were a Christian and a Jew and, in 1908, civil marriage was allowed for other persons also.[1] But the great bulk of marriages are still religious (church) marriages.[2] Thus the Swedish tradition is that marriages should normally last until one of the spouses dies. Even though the number of divorces has risen swiftly in later years, most marriages still last until the death of one of the spouses.

In connexion with the new Swedish legislation of 1973 and the other changes now being planned, the legislator has tried to describe the different functions of marriage. The most important are considered to be the reproductive, the sexual, the fostering and the economic functions. In particular, the supervision of the children is still very important today as is, of course, the reproductive function. More debatable is the role of the family as an economic unit. Among other

---

1. See Schmidt, Folke, *Aktenskapsrätt*, 5 ed. Lund 1974, pp. 14-16.
2. See *Statens offentliga utredningar* (SOU) 1972; 41, p. 335.

functions named in this connexion are the care of sick and old persons, the organisation of leisure time, etc.[3]

The writer considers that the emotional role of the family should be emphasised, not least between parents and children. The importance of the children's sense of security and confidence ought to be highly valued.

Against this background it may be interesting to study what has happened recently to divorce in Swedish legislation. It should first be mentioned that annulment (*återgång*) was abolished. Annulment arose when a marriage was considered to have been affected with a serious fault from the beginning. Other very great changes also occurred in the divorce law of Sweden in 1973 by means of legislation. The most immediate cause was probably the fact that, during the last few years before this reform, it had become more and more common for men and women to live together, and even raise children, without building a family through marriage. Between 1960 and 1971 the number of children born to unmarried mothers during a year had almost doubled to 21.6%. According to an investigation conducted in 1971 about two-thirds of the new unmarried mothers were living together with the father of their child.[4]

However, in the opinion of the legislator there is no doubt that, even in the future, the family will continue to have a central position in the life of society. Therefore he intended to keep marriage as the normal and natural form for the family for the overwhelming majority of people. Perhaps reformed divorce rules may make marriage more attractive. It may be mentioned that even before the reform of 1973 unmarried couples living together in forms similar to marriage had been treated, in other fields of law apart from family law, in much the same way as married couples, for instance, in social law and tax law. This legislation of 1973 was a rupture with the former cooperation with other Scandinavian countries in this field, because it was not possible to obtain unity of opinion.

The Swedish legislator has pointed out that in Sweden between 1920 and 1971 the number of divorces rose tenfold but, at the end of this time, of all marriages which had commenced in a certain year, still only about 14% were dissolved after 20-25 years. However, the legislator did not wish to make restrictive divorce rules.[5] Such rules would also, of course, make marriage less attractive. Instead, it has become rather easier to obtain a divorce.

It was decided that, if the spouses were unanimous about dissolving their marriage, they had a right to immediate divorce and the former necessity for judicial separation (*hemskillnad*), that is, living apart for one year before a divorce, was accordingly abolished. In 1968 a change was made in the law so that, once both the spouses had agreed to a divorce, there was no longer a need for there to have been a deep and long-lasting discord between the parties before a divorce could be granted. The legislator considered that there was not a great risk of there being many ill-considered divorces as a result of the new rule of 1973. However, this opinion is not unanimously held by Swedish experts in family law and different views have been expressed. It is easier to obtain the present type of

---

3. *Ibid*, pp. 63-75.
4. See *Nytt Juridiskt Arkiv* II 1973, p. 114.
5. See *Nytt Juridiskt Arkiv* II, 1973, p. 118.

divorce than it was before, because it is no longer necessary that there should be compulsory mediation between the spouses before a divorce takes place. It is now sufficient that the possibility of obtaining voluntary mediation is available to the spouses. In this connexion it may be mentioned that, also in 1973, the former legal rules attaching to betrothal disappeared.

Before 1973 it was possible for one of the spouses, in certain cases, to obtain judicial separation unilaterally and, in some special cases, divorce. Mostly guilt (*culpa*) had to be displayed by the other spouse, but in some cases discord between the spouses was enough.

In 1973 further changes in these rules were made. It was laid down that when only one spouse wanted a divorce, there had to be a time for reflection and reconsideration. This was also to apply when the spouses were unanimous about a divorce but when either or both had the custody of one or more children under the age of 16. This time for reflection is to begin on the day when the spouses make a common application, or when the application of one of the spouses is communicated to the other. When there are young children, a divorce is considered to have such far reaching consequences for the children that it cannot be regarded solely as the married couple's own business. A couple's adopted children are, in this respect, treated in the same way as their natural children. The time for reflection must be at least six months and at most one year. During this time, in contrast to the former judicial separation period, there is no need for the spouses to live part. After one year, unless there is a demand to pursue the request, the application for divorce is considered void.[6]

Even a stepchild is considered to have the same interests as a child common to the spouses, thus a marriage must only be dissolved after careful reflection.

Some lawyers, for instance the Swedish Bar Society, have expressed the opinion that it is unnecessary for the spouses to have a period for reflection on account of their young children when they both want a divorce. They thought it a completely unnecessary interference by society in the right of two human beings to decide the course of their lives together.

However, emphasis has been laid on the fact that there are often great difficulties for the children in connexion with a divorce. Children will lose close contact with one of their parents, whom they will only meet sporadically after the divorce. Often they will live in a family with only one grown-up person yet it is important for the development of children that there should be in the family persons who can fill both the father's role and the mother's role. But it is also realised that to grow up in an environment marred by discord between the parents can have a prejudicial influence on the children.[7] This point of view has resulted in a Danish committee coming to a different conclusion from the Swedish legislator concerning the need for a period of reflection in this instance.[8]

The most important innovation introduced in 1973 was the disappearance of fault (*culpa*) as an important factor in divorce cases. One consequence is that an innocent spouse no longer has the possibility of obtaining damages. These

---

6. See Marriage Code 11: 1-3.
7. See *Nytt Juridiskt Arkiv* II 1973, p. 142.
8. See *Aegteskab 2, aegteskabs opløsning, betaenkning nr. 697 orgivet af ægteskabsutvalget af 1969*, København 1973, p. 12.

damages could refer to both mental and economic injury—especially the loss caused by "divorce to money", that is, the division of the so-called *giftorättsgods* (marital property) into two halves after a short marriage when the case law in this connexion was very complicated.[9]

Thus, a time for reflection is sometimes necessary and sometimes not. The legislator considered the previous period in the case of judicial separation unnecessarily long. Six months should be long enough to counteract premature decisions. Here it may be observed that it was possible for judicial separation to continue for an unlimited time, but that only one year was necessary for obtaining a divorce. It was thought that a final decision ought not to be deferred for an indefinite period, especially if one of the spouses really desired to continue with the marriage, in which case it was reasonable that the other spouse should make a definite decision without undue delay.

The question whether spouses ought to live apart during the period of reflection has been more controversial. The Swedish Bar Society expressed the opinion that, when spouses disagree, it is hardly possible for them to have a constructive discussion about their problems as long as they are living together. Thus, the old judicial separation was better than the proposed time for reflection. Only when living apart can the parties obtain the experience of what a divorce really implies.

However, reasons were put forward for the new system. One was the difficulty the courts had in checking whether the spouses really lived apart. Close investigation of the personal conduct of the spouses might be necessary. The legal effects of judicial separation were much greater than those of the "time for reflection", especially the necessity of living apart and the fact that property acquired by each spouse during the time of judicial separation was the private property of the spouse, even if the judicial separation later became void. These rules just apply to the time for reflection where the main principle was that the property rights, if the divorce case was dismissed, were in every respect to be the same as though the question of divorce had not been brought up. Under the new rules, property division would not take place until after the divorce decree.[10] (The principal rule during marriage is that one spouse has a so-called *"giftorätt"* (right to marital property) in relation to the property of the other spouse, that is, a right to receive half of his/her property after death or after divorce, unless there is a marriage settlement). Therefore, judicial separation was a more definitive step towards divorce than the "time for reflection", as it was usually followed by an immediate division of the property of the spouses.

One of the spouses can obtain a divorce without a time for reflection if the spouses have lived apart for the last two years of the marriage; formerly, divorce was possible after living apart for three years on account of discord. Neither is there a need for a time for reflection when one spouse desires a divorce on the ground that the marriage was contracted with a person within the proscribed limits of relationship. The same holds good in the case of bigamy and here the spouse of the bigamist's former marriage also has the possibility of having that

---

9. See Saldeen, Ake, *Skadestand vid äktenskapsskillnad*.
10. See *Nytt Juridiskt Arkiv* II 1973, p. 148.

marriage ended without time for reflection. The General Prosecutor may plead in these cases. However, the spouse of the bigamist's former marriage does not have the right to get the later marriage ended,[11] a right which he or she had under the former legislation. Before the reform of 1973 it was possible for one of the spouses to obtain immediate divorce on the ground of maltreatment. According to the new rules it is no longer possible to obtain an immediate divorce on this ground but when one spouse has injured the other marital cohabitation can be suspended immediately and a prohibition issued against visits by the guilty spouse.

A great many grounds for obtaining divorce for special reasons have disappeared since 1973. One of the special reasons was when one of the spouses had disappeared and it was not known whether he had been alive during the last three years. Another reason for immediate divorce was in connexion with venereal disease; if a spouse had knowledge or suspicion of his veneral disease and, through sexual intercourse, had infected the other spouse, who had not known of the danger before intercourse, the infected spouse could obtain an immediate divorce. The infected spouse, however, had to sue within six months of obtaining knowledge of the danger of infection. Such a divorce could also be obtained in a case of one spouse plotting against the life of the other spouse. Again, application for divorce had to be made within six months of obtaining knowledge of the plot and within three years at least of the event. The same possibility existed when one spouse committed similar offences against a child, in relation to whom the other spouse had custody. A spouse's misuse of intoxicants could also lead to immediate divorce if the other party sued. However, the court had to be convinced that there were particular reasons for it. Other grounds for obtaining an immediate divorce arose when one spouse was sentenced to prison for at least three years, or when he had committed adultery. In the latter case, judicial separation could also be obtained in certain cases. There was also the possibility of obtaining judicial separation if the other spouse had flagrantly neglected his duty to provide for the other spouse or the children or neglected his duties towards them to a notable degree, or if he was misusing intoxicants, or leading a profligate life. However, it was up to the courts to decide whether he ought still to continue the cohabitation. There was another possibility for one spouse unilaterally to obtain judicial separation, that is, if there had arisen deep and lasting disagreement between the spouses as a result of differences in disposition and ways of thinking. Here also it was at the discretion of the court to decide whether he still ought to continue the cohabitation.[12]

As already suggested, the greatest difference between the new rules of 1973 and the old ones concerning divorce lies in the disappearance of guilt (*culpa*) as a ground for divorce and also as the foundation of an action on the part of the innocent spouse to obtain damages for economic loss, as well as for pain and suffering. There seem to be important advantages connected with this disappearance. It is often difficult to decide who is responsible for certain circumstances constituting guilt and, above all, investigations and accusations in this

---

11. See Marriage Code 11: 5 and *Nytt Juridiskt Arkiv* II 1973, p. 153.
12. See Marriage Code, chapter 11 in its wording before the new legislation of 1973.

respect can injure or ruin the future life, not only of the spouses but also of their children. Many encroachments on the privacy of one or both the spouses or of the children were unavoidable under the old "guilt" system.

More debatable is the new right of the spouses to obtain an immediate divorce without either judicial separation or time for reflection, provided they desire it unanimously. The idea that unanimous spouses must be supposed to have come to their decision after mature consideration seems not to be well founded. The 1973 legislator criticised judicial separation because the community of property was dissolved and therefore the spouses had taken a greater step towards divorce than is now the case with the new period for reflection. But the new swift divorce after unanimous application really seems to be unnecessarily definite without any certain time for reflection. The rationale that adult independent spouses do not need any time for reflection, because they can always be assumed to act rationally, does not seem to conform with other Swedish legislation in recent decades, as a result of which liberty of contract has been much more limited than before, for instance, in order to protect consumers against premature purchases.

A more important reason why immediate divorce is possible in the case of unanimous decision has, perhaps, been the competition between the institution of marriage and the system in which two people live together without marriage, and the ease with which people in the latter category can separate.[13] In the introductory remarks in this chapter it was said that the legislator ought to be neutral, as far as possible, with regard to different forms of living together. Individual persons should have the freedom to decide what rules they should have for living together in a family. Similar social situations should be treated equally, irrespective of their legal form. At the same time, it was said that marriage has, and ought to have, a central position within family law. It seems that the method used by the legislator to support this central position consisted of detailed regulations for marriage law, as compared with the system of living together without marriage, while making divorce easier than before.[14]

Attention has also been paid to the diminishing role of the family in producing goods and services during the last decades. More and more married women now obtain employment outside the family. Former legislation set out from the assumption that, as a rule, marriage lasted until the death of one of the spouses, but nowadays divorce is much more common than before in Sweden. The stability of marriage can no longer be said to be as important as it was formerly considered. The independence and equality of the spouses are more strongly emphasised. More can be said about the disappearance of guilt as an important factor in divorce cases. It is normally very difficult to decide if one of the spouses and, in that case, which one, is guilty of causing the failure of the marriage. This is easier for the court to handle if the question of guilt is legally connected with a

---

13. Re the system of two people living together without marriage according to Swedish law, see Bengtsson, "*Om Sktenskapsliknande samliv*", in *Festskrift for Carl Jacob Arnholm*, Oslo 1969, pp. 645-667. Cf. also Sundberg, "Recent changes in Swedish family law: experiment repeated" in *American Journal of Comparative Law*, Vol. XXIII, Winter 1975, No. 1, pp. 38-39. As to the state of things in Denmark, see Borum, O. A, "*Kønsrolledebatten og aegteskabslov-givningen*" in *Festskrift for Carl Jacob Arnholm*, Oslo 1969, pp. 671-592.
14. See SOU 1972: 41, p. 91, and *Nytt Juridiskt Arkiv* II, 1973, p. 115.

special occurrence or circumstance, such as adultery. But it has been argued that there may be another, more profound cause of the failure than the adultery—that is, the adultery is a symptom, not the cause, of the matrimonial failure. To point to a certain occurrence can also result in a dangerous dramatisation of the relationship between the spouses. It could also lead to "arranging" such an occurrence to avoid the need for a judicial separation year when the old rules were applied.

As a comment on these arguments, it may be said that they could be made in relation to several branches of the law; that there are often deeper causes to explain human conduct than those usually taken into account by the law. That is one of the reasons for strict liability (without demand for *culpa*) as far as damages for certain actions are concerned. But, as far as marriage and the relationship between the spouses are concerned, it often seems especially difficult to point out one conclusive cause of the crisis in the marriage.

If the stability of the family was of special importance in 1920, the legislator in 1973 emphasised the importance of following the free will of the parties. However, it was considered that this freewill should be based on deliberation and that premature divorces should be avoided. Yet, when the spouses unanimously desire to obtain a divorce it has been shown that it was presumed there would be little risk of a premature decision. This point of view is the very opposite of the thinking behind the former legislation. It is the author's opinion that it must be very uncertain whether these divorces will have been thoroughly considered, as a rule, at least when the old customs in this area of life are beginning to lose their influence. It seems more probable that in previous decades when lifelong marriages were considered to be the normal case, the spouses were much more careful before agreeing to divorce than they are nowadays. In the old days, marriage usually held a more important place in the hearts of the people.

The following situation may be considered under the present legislation. If one of the spouses, who is a dominant person, has a sexual relationship with a third party and wishes for a divorce, both parties to the marriage will perhaps agree to an immediate divorce. But when after a while the sexual interest in the third party has dwindled, because of the divorce prestige feelings may prevent a second marriage between the two former spouses, although they would otherwise have been prepared to draw a line through their discord and continue with their marriage.

It may be queried whether a time for reflection in the new rules is better than judicial separation in the old ones. The thought behind the old rules was that judicial separation should be a time for quiet reflection about the continuation of the marriage, without undue influence from the other spouse. It was considered important that the opportunities for one spouse to exercise pressure on the other should be as few as possible. When they did not live together, they could look at their marriage from outside.

The legislation of 1973 is based on the view that the time of judicial separation was too long, especially because most spouses had probably discussed the possibilities of continuing the marriage, and the practical consequences of an end to their living together, for some time before the application for "*hemskillnad*". If there had been no such discussion, it must be assumed that communication between the spouses was so difficult that there was little prospect of obtaining a better relationship between them and, in that case, the length of time for reflection was not very important. Another point of importance to the legislation of 1973 was the case of the spouses beginning to live together again during the time of judicial separation, in which case the judicial separation became void. This would counteract attempts at reconciliation.[15]

It is interesting to observe the difference in outlook between the legislators of 1920 and 1973, a difference arising from two different conceptions of the factual consequences of living apart for the purpose of a thorough reconsideration of the viability of the marriage in question. However, it may be difficult to gauge the importance of living apart during reconsideration, because of differing circumstances and individual characters of the spouses. In most cases living apart probably gives the best opportunity for mature consideration of the marriage.

The legislator of 1973 considered that the fact that the property system between the spouses was changed as a result of judicial separation—and which remained changed even if the separation became void—made judicial separation appear to be a more or less definite step towards the dissolution of the marriage. However, it is doubtful whether this property change was much of an obstacle to a reconciliation. In many marriages it is arranged by marriage settlement that both spouses own their private property, without the other spouse having a marital right to a share of the combined property. If the spouses break off the judicial separation and begin to live together again, they can revert to the previous system of property by means of a new marriage settlement. Thus, it is difficult to see how these economic consequences really favour the belief that a system of judicial separation leads more easily to divorce than the new "time for reflection". According to the new system, if the divorce case is dismissed, the property rights shall in every respect remain the same as though the question of divorce had never arisen. Property division shall not take place until after the decree of divorce.[16]

It may be mentioned that according to the new rules, property acquired during the "time for reflection" is considered to be the private property of the acquiring spouse if this period is followed by a decree of divorce, or if the spouse dies while the divorce case is pending, but otherwise as "giftorättsgods" (marital property), if not treated as private under a marriage settlement. This seems unnecessarily complicated.

Before the recent change in the divorce rules, at least an attempt had to be made to obtain mediation before the granting of a judicial separation, but now mediation is only voluntary. General rules about its organisation have been inserted in a new statute concerning mediation. The existing organs for mediation are to be retained until the question of the organisation of the Family Counselling Bureaux has been decided. Previous rules on mediation in the Marriage Code have been rescinded. The new rules about voluntary mediation are also applicable to men and women living together without marriage. It is considered essential that the law should contain information as to the possibilities offered by society to couples who have marital difficulties.

15. See SOU 1972: 41, pp. 186-187.
16. *Boskillnad*—settlement of property.

For quite a long time there existed in the Swedish legal system, besides marriage, the so-called "*trolovning*" (betrothal), which was an agreement to marry but which was not always followed by marriage. This betrothal had certain legal consequences. *Trolovning* disappeared through legislation in 1973, but the "*fri samlevnad*" (cohabitation without marriage) plays a role reminiscent of the old betrothal. Some legal consequences of *fri samlevnad* are similar to those of marriage both in civil law and in some other departments of law. In this connexion, the new rules in civil law are based on the general survey of the functions of a family, as mentioned before.

The special functions of marriage are said to be (a) regulation of the mutual relations between the spouses and (b) regulation of the relations of the spouses to the surrounding world. In principle, the legislation expresses equality between marriage and *fri samlevnad*. In reality, marriage still has a better position as far as family law is concerned. The two forms of living together are treated more similarly by the social legislation.

The immediate reason for introducing new rules in connexion with living together without marriage is the great increase in Sweden during the last few years, especially during the last decade, in the number of men and women so living. According to an investigation made some years ago, most of these "paperless families" were childless and few had more than one child. As might be expected, a greater number of unmarried couples than of married couples were young people. This trend is comparatively new.[17] It has also been observed that many couples live together without marriage to begin with and then marry when there is a child, or when a child is expected.

The following are the new rules about *frivillig samlevnad*, which were introduced into Family Law in 1973:

(a) Rules about the right to rent, *bostadsrätt* (right to residence), on dissolution of the living together. It is intended to be equivalent to the statute on the common residence of spouses in a marriage. The right to residence (*bostad*) on the dissolution of the living together is allotted to the party who has the greatest need of it, irrespective of whether he or she was held to be the tenant or holder of the right to rent before the dissolution. These rules are only applicable if the parties had been living together permanently and had communal children, or in other special circumstances. This requirement of permanence can raise evidential problems when the parties separate, especially if great enmity has arisen between them. For instance, if one of the parties is looked upon as the tenant or holder of the *bostadsrätt* and believes that his former companion will be considered by a court to have a greater need for the residence in question, it would be in his interest to deny the durability and length of time of their relationship. In such a case, the assistance of public authorities which is a valuable source of evidence at the start and end of ordinary marriages, is not of course available. If children are the important elements in giving the residence to the father, paternity must have been established. One of the parties is given the lease on the dissolution of the living together. After the death of one of the parties, the surviving party is given

---

17. See SOU 1972: 41, pp. 358-359, 365 and 370.

the lease; in this case, the other party, or the estate of the deceased, must be compensated.[18]

It may be mentioned that there is no corresponding rule as far as "extended families" (*storfamiljer*) are concerned. In this connexion, "*storfamiljer*" means a group of unmarried persons belonging to both sexes who are living together without being relatives.

(b) Rules have also been introduced concerning the custody of the children when an unmarried couple cease living together. This custody implies a duty for the custodian to attend to the child's personal needs and to give it a careful upbringing, but it does not include maintenance for the child. According to the old rules, it was always the mother who was the custodian of a child born outside marriage unless it had been adopted by someone else. According to the new rules introduced in 1973[19], an unmarried father has in principle the same possibility of obtaining custody of the child as a married father in the corresponding situation of the dissolution of a marriage. He has lived with the mother and they have together cared for the child. In both these cases custody of the child is allotted to whichever parent the court decides, according to the best interests of the child. The unanimous opinion of the parents is often important. It is often difficult to decide what is best for the child. Earlier experiences of the manner of deciding the question of custody in divorce cases is not especially encouraging. Investigations made in connexion with such cases are often very unpleasant and the introduction of a better right to privacy in this area seems very important. Despite these investigations, in most cases the child seems to be allotted routinely to the mother. The legislation of 1973 has not fully penetrated this problem and, still less, the concomitant problem as to the father's or mother's right to care for the child for certain periods during the year, when he or she is not the custodian. According to a proposition made in May 1975, the parties can agree that, after divorce, they will continue to have common custody of their children. This would be applicable for married spouses as well as for parties living together without marriage.

There are often great problems when parties living together without marriage separate, in particular with regard to the division of property. It is often difficult to know which party has provided certain goods. The usual Swedish system of dividing the property into two equal parts is here not applicable. For instance, if one of the parties has provided the food and the other party has provided more durable goods, such as furniture, at the time of separation the former will often obtain almost nothing and the latter a considerable amount. This seems unfair. It sometimes happens that the party who is awarded the residence has refused to part with any of the goods from the house to the other party.

In 1973 some changes were also made in the alimony rules. The main rules are that, during the marriage, the spouses are obliged to support one another according to their ability, by means of money, activities in the home or otherwise. After divorce, alimony depends on the need of one spouse and the other spouse's financial situation in the light of all the circumstances. A sum may be

---

18. See *Nytt Juridiskt Arkiv* II 1973, pp. 197-206.
19. See *Nytt Juridiskt Arkiv* II 1973, pp. 187-190.

paid once and for all, or there may be several amounts to be paid at separate times. In the latter case, if the party entitled to the alimony remarries, the alimony must cease. It has already been stated that an important change in the divorce law in 1973 was the disappearance of the role of guilt. In the old law, guilt prevented alimony from being paid to the guilty spouse after divorce. When alimony has been fixed by means of a contract confirmed by the court, or directly by the court itself, it is now possible, as was the position before the legislation of 1973, to change what was decided on in certain circumstances. One reason is fundamentally changed circumstances. It is easier to get alimony lowered than raised and it is not possible to change it when it was awarded as a lump sum payment, once and for all. However, special reasons may enable one spouse to obtain alimony even when none at all was fixed at the time of the divorce.[20]

Even if there are no fundamentally changed circumstances after the decision on the question of alimony at the time of the divorce, the amount can later be changed on account of the original unreasonableness of the amount (*obillighet*). This is only possible if the alimony was awarded by means of a contract between the spouses, not when it is decided directly by the court, because the court is not expected to make unreasonable decisions. Claims must be made within a time limit of one year from the divorce.[21] These rules in the statute on alimony are based on the principle of equality between the spouses. In reality however, when a court decides that alimony shall be paid, it is almost always for the benefit of the wife.

In connexion with judicial separation or direct divorce, the property of the spouses is divided. The principal rule is that each spouse receives the valuable parts of the property in equal shares. But there are exceptions. In the case of a marriage settlement, either before or during marriage, the spouses may have arranged for all their goods, or parts thereof, to be private, with the result that the other spouse has no claim to part of them in connexion with a divorce or after death. Such a marriage settlement must be written and the document requires two signatures of witnesses.[22] If there is no marriage settlement and if the division of the property into two equal parts is considered unreasonable with regard to the economic circumstances of the spouses and the length of the marriage, then division of the property can be made in accordance with the principle of what is considered reasonable. However, it is not possible for one of the spouses to obtain more than the amount corresponding to his own "*giftorätts-gods*" (marital property) under this rule.[23] The *giftorättsgods* is one spouse's marital property in which the other spouse has rights. This new type of division will probably make it easier for disputes to arise. It may be mentioned that there are special rules relating to division of the property of the spouses in divorce.

2. Equality of the spouses

In principle, legal equality between the spouses was introduced in Sweden with the Marriages Act 1920, which came into force in 1921. Before that, the

---

20. See Marriage Code 11: 14-15.
21. See Marriage Code 11: 16.
22. Marriage Code, chapter 8.
23. See Marriage Code 13: 12a.

husband had been the guardian of the wife. However, there is still a privilege for the wife, in that there is a shorter time for prescription for her than for her husband, in relation to certain joint debts. But the great differences are found outside the legal texts, as is instanced in the case of the granting of alimony by the courts which usually award it to the wife plus maintenance for the children. This is partly due to the fact that in many marriages wives still do not have full-time, or even part-time, work outside the home and also to the time when such work was very unusual for women and often ill paid. On the other hand, many divorced husbands obliged to pay alimony to the former wife and maintenance to their children, are almost reduced to poverty on that account.

Another important fact not evident from the legal text, is that custody of the children is usually given to the wife on divorce and, in most cases, the wife usually has more time to care for them than the husband. However, in Sweden as in many other industrialised countries, there is now a tendency for more and more wives to work full-time or part-time outside their homes, a tendency favoured by the general trend to reduce the total number of working hours through shorter weeks, longer holidays, shorter working-hours per day and so on. This will also probably gradually change the division of work between the spouses and thereby bring about a greater similarity between the spouses in relation to court decisions on alimony and the custody of the children after divorce. The mention of "privileges" for the wife are, in fact, established by the courts and are based on the idea that women in fact still have a different status from men.

3. Illegitimate children

In former Swedish law there were several categories of illegitimate children, each giving rise to different legal effects. There were ordinary illegitimate children who were the heirs of their mother and her relatives and whose mother and her relatives were their heirs. Then there were illegitimate children born during betrothal, or in respect of whom their father had issued a declaration of inheritance right ("*arvsrättsförklaring*"), who had an inheritance relationship with their father but not with the father's relatives. Finally there were adopted children, in relation to whom the inheritance rules were complicated and concerned natural relatives as well as relatives created by the adoption. Another category of illegitimate children were those whose parents later married, the children thereby becoming legitimate.

The father had to pay maintenance to his illegitimate child and the mother was usually the custodian.

In 1969 there was a great change in the inheritance rules relating to illegitimate children. The rules are now the same for almost all legitimate and illegitimate children. Illegitimate children, like legitimate children, have the right to a lawful portion ("*laglott*" in Swedish, "*Pflichtteil*" in German). This means a right to half of his share in the estate of his parents, even if it has been disposed of by will.

In special cases there can be another custodian, apart from the mother. This may be, but need not be, the father. If the parents agree unanimously that the father should be a custodian, this will be allowed provided it is not considered obviously unreasonable for the welfare of the child. Otherwise, the father may become custodian if it is considered reasonable with regard to the welfare of the child. These possibilities for the father to become custodian of the child are specially important in cases of the child's parents cohabiting without marriage.

An important problem is the establishment of the paternity of an illegitimate child.[24] In Sweden it can be established either by means of an acknowledgement by the supposed father or, in case of dispute, by the judgment of a court. A certain form is prescribed for acknowledgement. The legal procedure, in the case of a court judgment, has undergone important changes in recent decades. Before the new Parents' Act came into force in 1950, the man indicated by the mother as being the father of her illegitimate child, was considered by the court to be the father if he had had sexual intercourse with the mother at the relevant time and if it was not obvious that he could not be the father, for instance, by means of a blood test. The court generally followed the woman's statement with regard to sexual intercourse. *Exceptio plurium* was not allowed and, in one case, there was an opinion in the Supreme Court considering that kind of evidence as against Swedish public order. The woman was allowed to complete her evidence with an oath before the court.

The Parents' Act replaced this rule by another, by which the man indicated was considered to be the child's father if sexual intercourse was considered to have taken place, but only if it seemed not unlikely that the child had been conceived as a result of the intercourse in question. If there were special reasons, *exceptio plurium* could be allowed.

In 1969 there were important changes in the rules concerning the manner of establishing paternity by court procedure. The most important change was that it must be considered practically certain that the child was conceived during sexual intercourse with the man in question. As far as evidence is concerned, the possibilities have been so widened that *exceptio plurium* is now considered a normal form of evidence. The reason for this improvement in the man's legal position was the introduction of the full right of inheritance for the illegitimate child from his father and his father's relatives. Before the legislation of 1969 the paternity of illegitimate children was only presumed when not admitted by the man. Now it is intended to be a finding of real paternity, even if disputed by the man in question. In this connexion, oaths as evidence have now been replaced by affirmations of truth ("*sanningsförsäkran*"). Blood tests and other anthropological investigations can be of great importance.

Illegitimate children can still become legitimate by means of a later marriage between the parents, or by adoption. On the other hand, it may happen that a child born in wedlock may, by means of legal procedure, no longer be considered the child of the husband and may therefore be made illegitimate. If the child's mother and the real father of the child marry after the mother's divorce, the child is considered legitimate, if paternity has been established by acknowledgement or by court judgment. Children who are made legitimate in this way are considered ordinary legitimate children with the same rights as legitimate children. The same applies to adopted children who generally have the same rights as other legitimate children. There is an exception as far as children adopted some years ago are concerned.

---

24. Not long ago a thorough jurimetric investigation was made by Ake Saldeen, entitled "*Fastställande av faderskapet till barn utom äktenskap*".

As was the position before the changes in his inheritance rights were made in 1969, the illegitimate child has a right to maintenance not only from his mother, but also from his father if the child does not have sufficient resources of his own for his maintenance. When the child reaches the age of 16 years, maintenance is conditional on the capability of each of his parents. The child still has the right to maintenance for his education according to his talents and the position of his parents. An important point is the possibility of the child obtaining State grants, or advances, for his education.

A contract may be drawn up between the parents with regard to the maintenance of a child. If the child is legitimate, he can always claim for a larger sum by way of maintenance despite the contract. If the child is illegitimate, a contract correctly drawn up and signed by two witnesses is binding upon him. Maintenance is usually paid periodically, but may be paid as a once and for all lump sum.

The illegitimate child not only has the right of inheritance from his father, but also his maintenance and the right to his family name.

II. Denmark

1. Divorce

In Denmark great changes are being planned in marriage legislation, including rules on divorce, but until now the divorce legislation since 1969 is similar to the Swedish law before 1973.

As in the former Swedish legislation, there still exists in Denmark what in Sweden was called *"ätergäng"*, that is annulment, and in Denmark is called *"omstødelse"*. This form of dissolution is used when the marriage is considered to have been void from the outset, for example, on account of the bigamy of one of the spouses, or when the spouses were within the unlawful degrees of relationship. Other reasons are mental instability at the time of the marriage, or marriage under duress, or when deluded into marriage in some other way.[25]

In Denmark annulment has the same legal effects as divorce except with regard to the division of the property of the spouses. As in the former Swedish law, division of the property into two equal parts only concerns property acquired during the marriage other than by gift or inheritance. This also applies to the division of the property of the spouses after certain short-lived marriages, which has some resemblance to the rules applicable to short-lived marriages under the Swedish rules of 1973.[26]

In Denmark there is a special court for the division of property after death or divorce, called *"skifteretten"*, but private division is more usual. There is no corresponding authority in Sweden.

To obtain a judicial separation, which is similar to the former *"hemskillnad"* in Swedish law, the usual requirement is that both parties should be unanimous. Yet in some cases a separation can be obtained without the consent of the other

---

25. See Andersen, Ernst, *Familieret*, 3 ed. København 1971.
26. *Se Aegteskab 3, formueordningen, afgivet af aegteskabsudvalget af 1969, betaenkning nr 716*, København 1974, p. 49, and Andersen, *op. cit.*

spouse if he has grossly violated his duties to his spouse and children. A spouse can also unilaterally obtain a separation if the relationship between the spouses is shattered for other reasons, provided this is not principally a result of his own conduct. A spouse can also obtain "separation" if he can obtain an immediate divorce.

The duration of a separation is one year. Some years ago it was one and a half years when the spouses were unanimous, otherwise two and a half years. The Danish rules for separation are very similar to the former Swedish rules of "*hemskillnad*", but there are some important differences. For example, if the separated spouses begin to live together again, the legal effects of separation disappear for the future. This was not the case in former Swedish law. But if the spouses have had one year of separation and have not lived together afterwards, either of them has the right to obtain a divorce, as in the former Swedish law.

In Denmark, as formerly in Sweden, there are many grounds for an immediate divorce, mostly dependent on the guilt of one of the spouses. Such a reason would be the disappearance of a spouse for three years or more, a new marriage, or the adultery of the other spouse, provided the claimant spouse has not some guilt also. A further reason is when a spouse has ceased sexual intercourse for the last two years without adequate grounds. If a spouse has an infectious venereal disease and demonstrates his lack of care (*culpa*) by having sexual intercourse with his spouse, there can also be an immediate divorce. Other grounds are maltreatment, a prison sentence, lunacy, etc. It should be borne in mind that, for better or worse, these special reasons for divorce have now disappeared from Swedish law. According to Danish law mediation is compulsory before separation, as well as before immediate divorce.

If the parents are unanimous about the question of custody of the children after divorce, this is decisive provided it is not considered to be in conflict with the welfare of the children. If this is the case, or if the parents are not unanimous, custody is decided according to what is considered reasonable with special regard to the welfare of the children. In Denmark, as in Sweden, it is usually the wife who is given custody of the children after divorce.

A great difference between Swedish and Danish divorce legislation is that, in Denmark, the decisions regarding separation or divorce are often administrative decisions, not judicial decisions, when the spouses are unanimous. It has been recorded in the legal literature that probably more than ninety per cent of divorce cases are decided by administrative authorities.[27]

As in Swedish law, the chief principle concerning the division of property between the spouses in the case of divorce is that each spouse is entitled to half the marital property. This can be altered by a marriage settlement. The main principles regarding alimony are also similar to those in Sweden.

2. Equality of the spouses

Again, the legal texts are similar in both Denmark and Sweden. *Proposed new rules.*—A committee has presented proposals for new divorce rules in Denmark. These are different in some respects from the current Swedish rules adopted in

---

27. See Andersen, *op. cit.*

1973. Although annulment is to be abolished, the committee wishes to retain both separation and divorce. There will be a right to immediate divorce if the spouses are unanimous that they desire it, even when they have children under age.[28] The committee desire that a spouse should be able to obtain separation without a special ground, even if the other spouse does not wish it, one of the reasons being that it is impossible to force spouses to live together. A unilateral right to immediate divorce is not proposed by the committee, such a right being considered quite another thing than the unilateral right to a separation and would, indeed, imply a rejection of the separation principle which the committee feels to be valuable. Such a separation is looked on as a probationary divorce, allowing time for reflection apart from each other, with their disagreements at a distance. If, after reflection, the spouses no longer want to dissolve their marriage, they can bring the legal effects of marriage into force simply by beginning to live together again, without help from any public authority. This is different from the old Swedish judicial separation.[29] It is also different from the new trend in Swedish divorce law, where there is also a time for reflection when, for example, only one of the spouses wants a divorce.

Special reasons for immediate divorce

Opinions were divided in the Danish marriage committee about adultery as a ground for divorce. In Denmark the trend is not so decidedly against guilt as a ground for divorce as is the case in Sweden. There is a majority in the Danish committee for wishing to keep in some rules about extreme violence as a ground for divorce, but the minority against this feels that occasions of violence against a spouse or the children are very rare, that the violence is evaluated differently by different sections of the population, and that it is debatable whether corporal violence should be given a different meaning from mental violence.

It is desired to keep the rules for bigamy as a ground for divorce. A majority of the committee wishes to abolish insanity as a ground for divorce, since it is considered difficult to distinguish between real mental disease and other phsyical disturbances and also because other disturbances can arise during marriage which are as great a burden for the other spouse as mental disease.

The majority of the committee wants to abolish divorce founded on the annulment of the "*samliv*" on account of discord between the spouses. But some want to keep these rules, only change the time from three to two years. The same viewpoint has been applied in the case of the disappearance of one of the spouses. The committee considers that the fact of one spouse infecting the other with venereal disease should no longer be a ground for immediate divorce. It is felt that this rule is seldom used and has little weight when set beside adultery as a ground for divorce. The rule relating to venereal disease might be useful to keep if the possibility of obtaining divorce on the ground of adultery disappears.

The majority of the committee feels that a prison sentence alone should no longer be a reason for immediate divorce. Spouses have a natural duty to help

---

28. See *Aegteskab* 2, p. 12.
29. *Ibid*, p. 15.

and support each other and this rule could have the effect of destroying an opportunity of fitting the criminal for society once more.[30]

3. Illegitimate children

As early as 1937, according to Danish legislation children born out of wedlock had the same right of inheritance as children born in wedlock, not only as to their mother and her relatives, but also as to their father and his relatives.[31] The child has the family name of the mother, but she can, by announcement, change the child's family name to that of the father. If the mother is, or has been, married and has taken her husband's name as a result of the marriage, the child takes the family name of the mother's husband.

The main principle is that the mother has the custody of an illegitimate child and the father has the right to visit the child. The illegitimate child has the same right to maintenance from the parents as a legitimate child. Illegitimate children born before 1961 could be (i) children whose paternity was established, (ii) children who received contributions from one or several asserted sexual intercourse partners, so-called company children, (iii) children where no such sexual intercourse partner was identified.[32] As in Swedish law, paternity can be established either through acknowledgement or through a judgment.

In Denmark, as formerly in Sweden, it is still provided that if a man has had sexual intercourse with the unmarried mother during the time when the child could have been conceived, he will be considered to be the father, provided that there are no circumstances making it improbable that he is the father. According to the current Swedish legislation, it must be positively probable that he could be the father.

In relation to evidence in establishing paternity, the Danish law is similar to the Swedish law with the difference that, in Denmark, a kind of party oath (*"partsed"*) is still used which has been replaced in Sweden by a hearing under affirmation of truth ((*"sanningsförsäkran"*). In Denmark the party oath is seldom used in this connexion. The use of *exceptio plurium* is older in Denmark and had different consequences from Swedish law. In Denmark, the blood test is usually the most important evidence against the presumed father seeking to avoid the establishment of his paternity, other means of evidence being similar to those in Swedish law.

III. Norway

1. Divorce

Norwegian law in this field has not undergone any significant change in recent years and is very similar to the Swedish regulations before the changes of 1973.

---

30. According to a sociological investigation, a large proportion of the Danish population wants the possibility for a divorced person to obtain alimony from her former spouse to be abolished. A majority does not want the alimony to be paid from public assets. See *Aegteskab 6, aegteskabet i statistisk og sociologisk belysning*, p. 18.
31. See Andersen, *Arveret*, København 1965.
32. See Andersen, *Familieret, op. cit.*

As in Denmark, and formerly in Sweden, there are three ways of dissolving a marriage:
  (i) Annulment (*"Omstøtelse"*), when the marriage is considered to be void from the beginning.
  (ii) Divorce after judicial separation (*"separasjon"*); and
  (iii) Immediate divorce.

Annulment is unusual and the grounds for it are not quite the same as in the corresponding institution in Denmark or, formerly, in Sweden.[33]

The most common form of divorce in Norway is when the spouses apply unanimously, after a period of separation. This *"separasjon"* is granted by the Governor of the Province (*"fylkesmann"*) after mediation has been attempted. In Sweden, the authority for granting time for reflection is the court, as was also its former function in relation to judicial separation. In Denmark the relevant authority is the Minister of Justice or, after his authorisation, the *"overøvrigheden"* where the parties are unanimous. If only one of the spouses wants a divorce, the question must be decided by the court unless both parties want a *fylkesmann* to decide it. The reasons for a separation are similar to those in Swedish law before 1973. The guilt of the other spouse plays an important role. Also, the rules relating to immediate divorce are similar to the pre-1973 Swedish rules, there being only slight differences. Such reasons for immediate divorce include bigamy, venereal disease with the risk of infecting the other spouse, certain crimes and threats of crime against the other spouse, maltreatment of the children, the other spouse being condemned to a long prison sentence, mental disease, adultery, and so on.

Severe criticism had been levelled at the unusual rule about the right to divorce when one spouse—against the wish of the plaintiff and without sufficient reason —has avoided sexual intercourse for two years. This right is said to be very seldom exercised.[34]

The rules about damages in connexion with divorce are similar to those in Sweden before 1973.

The rules relating to alimony are similar in all the Scandinavian countries, except that in Sweden the principle of guilt has been abolished in this connexion. In theory, according to the legal texts, no distinction is made between husband and wife with regard to alimony, but in practice it is almost always the wife who is awarded alimony, if any is granted. Rules about the custody of the children are similar to those of Sweden, as well as those relating to the other spouse's right of access. Custody is usually given to the mother, but there is now a tendency to give custody to the father more often than before, owing to the growing number of women working outside the home.

As in Sweden, there is *"giftorätt"* in Norwegian law, which can be changed by a marriage settlement, in which case the division of goods can be done privately and usually without great cost. If one of the spouses is under 18 years of age, or declared incompetent, a public division must be made by a court (*skifteretten*).

---

33. See Haga, Hilde Wiesener, *Hva man bør vite om separasjon og skilsmisse*, Oslo, 1974, pp. 10-11.
34. *Ibid*, p. 36.

One or both of the spouses can also have the division done by *skifteretten*, if they so wish.[35] This differs from the Swedish procedure.

Committees have been preparing new legislation about marriage and about the legal position of children since 1971.

2. Equality of the spouses

The equality of the spouses in Norway is on a par with the legislation in Denmark and Sweden.

3. Illegitimate children

In relation to illegitimate children, Norwegian law is similar to Swedish law, except that the Swedish rules about maintenance are more detailed. The main rule in Norway is that the mother generally has the custody of the child, though the father may sometimes be entrusted with its care. The parent who is not the custodian is not given as much access to the child as under Swedish law.[36]

Illegitimate children have the same right as legitimate children to inherit, provided they are born after 1 January 1917 and paternity has been established through acknowledgement or judgment. At birth, illegitimate children are given the family name of their mother. The child can later obtain the family name of the father by special decision of an authority.

As to *"odelsrett"*, a special Norwegian form of right to land in the country accompanying some families, the illegitimate child usually has the right to the mother's *odelsrett* only. He may have the right to the father's *odelsrett* also, if there is a registered declaration of paternity from the father. There is another right to land in the country, called *"asetesrett"*, which is the privilege of an heir to acquire such land against comparatively small sums of money as a redemption charge to the other heirs. This only falls to an illegitimate child if the father has decided this in writing.[37]

If the mother is Norwegian, the illegitimate child has Norwegian citizenship, notwithstanding the father's citizenship. If possible, the child must be brought up in accordance with the economic conditions of the parent who is most well off. As in Swedish law, paternity can be established by a man's acknowledgement of the child, or through a judgment of the court, though the procedure is somewhat different.[38] As in pre-1973 Swedish law, paternity will not be established if it appears improbable that the man in question could be the father, though it is not necessary for it to be positively probable that the man in question is the father, as is now the case in Swedish law. This is noteworthy, because in Norway illegitimate children have a similar position in relation to their father as children born in wedlock.

The evidence used to establish paternity by judgment is similar in both countries. It may be mentioned that the *exceptio plurium* has been used in evidence in Norwegian law much longer than in Swedish law. When it is used, one condition

---

35. See Haga, *op. cit.*, pp. 101-102.
36. See *Knophs Oversikt over Norges rett, 6 utgave av Birger*, pp. 174-175 and 178.
37. *Ibid*, pp. 175 and 215-217.
38. See *lov om barn utanom ekteskap* 1956, Ch. II-III.

for establishing paternity is that one of the men in question is more likely to be the father than the others.

New rules on the legal position of children are in preparation by a committee.

IV. Finland

1. Divorce

In Finland there are still rules about annulment (*återgång*) which greatly resemble the Danish rules, although more detailed.

With regard to divorce proper, the law is similar to the law in Norway and Denmark and pre-1973 Sweden. However, in Finland a distinction is made between divorce founded on the principle of guilt and divorce founded on the principle of discord. The principle of guilt can give rise to immediate divorce on account of adultery, venereal disease, plotting against the life of the other spouse, maltreatment, some types of prison sentence, abuse of intoxicants, avoidance of sexual intercourse and living apart for one year. There are some small points in the rules which are peculiar to Finland. Immediate divorce can also be obtained after discord and living apart for two years. The principle of discord gives rise to *hemskillnad* with a subsequent divorce after two years of living apart. Judicial separation is also possible after application by only one of the spouses after living apart for one year. There are two kinds of divorce after judicial separation, one after a joint application and one after application by one of the spouses.

There are also other principles for divorce, besides guilt and discord, namely mental disease and the absence of the other spouse. The latter has been categorised in Finland as a separate principle, but it can often be considered as a case of guilt.

Guilt is an important ground for divorce because, *inter alia*, of the question of damages. The rules about damages are similar to the Swedish rules prior to 1973. The rules about alimony are also reminiscent of the former Swedish law although in Finland guilt is still important. *Giftorätt* also exists in Finland, but there are some differences, in that in Finland a reduction may be made on account of guilt.[39]

What would be in the best interests of the children of the marriage is considered to be of great importance in relation to the question of divorce. In 1969 there was an important change in the marriage legislation, to the effect that the court can decide that there should be a judicial separation instead of a divorce, if that is to the best advantage of the children of the spouses.

Proposed new rules

In 1972 a committee report appeared[40] which suggested changes in the divorce law of Finland. The difference between *återgång* and divorce lies in the legal consequences rather than in the dissolution itself. The report suggested that it

---

39. See *Betänkande av äktenskapskommittén* I, p. 219.
40. Called *Äktenskapskommitténs betänkande* I.

was unnecessary to retain the institution of *återgång* and proposed that it should be abolished. Suggestions were made that changes should be made in the legal consequences of divorce which would lead, in the future, to the same end result as in *återgång*. At the same time it was suggested that a rule should be included regarding immediate dissolution of a marriage on account of bigamy or marriage within certain close relationships.

In suggesting changes, it was considered that, from the point of view of society, the safeguarding of the family and the care of the children are important aspects of marriage. From the point of view of the individual, the important things are emotional satisfaction, consideration of the sexual needs of the spouses, and the creation of harmonious and safe surroundings for the children while growing up. Divorce was assumed to create a conflict between the demands of society and the satisfaction of individual needs. It was considered that feelings of affection between members of the family are likely to play a greater role in the future than they do now. It is also still important that society should protect the weaker spouse and the children in order to obtain real equality between the spouses. It was also considered important to diminish disputes in connexion with divorce cases. The committee considered that the requirement of guilt should be abolished, as a ground for the ending of a marriage. They also wished to abolish the necessity for proof of discord before a court as a ground for divorce, the spouses' own statements to be considered as sufficient.

The cause of the increasing number of divorces was discussed by the committee, which came to the conclusion that the increase was due to the growing importance of the emotional element in family relations, rather than to the effect of discord arising out of the economic independence of the spouses. The latter point is debatable and it might be better to postulate that other types of feelings are more prevalent nowadays than before.

It may be observed that the former Swedish institution of judicial separation was introduced into Finland by legislation in 1948.[41] As mentioned above, the committee has now recommended its abolition. In principle, the committee takes the view that society ought not to prevent a divorce which both spouses desire, or even make difficulties when the spouses' application is unanimous. Immediate divorce should be obtainable by a unanimous application even when there are children of the marriage, though in this case the spouses must also be unanimous in settling the custody and maintenance of the children under sixteen in a satisfactory manner. The committee considered that such an agreement would be hindered by a system which necessitated six months for reflection, such as has been introduced in Sweden when there are children under sixteen years of age. The Finnish committee's proposals differ in this respect from the legal systems of both Sweden and Denmark. The Finnish committee recommended that, in most cases of unanimous application for divorce, the spouses should be heard personally by a court.

When the spouses are not unanimous about the dissolution of the marriage and its accompanying legal consequences, the committee considered that the harm done by the divorce would be much worse than if the application had been

---

41. See Hakulinen, Y J, *Familjerätt*, Tannerfors, 1964, p. 197.

unanimous and therefore recommended the introduction of a special time for reflection as a requirement for divorce when the spouses were not unanimous. When one of the spouses is against a divorce, a time for reflection might prevent a divorce founded on a whim of the other spouse without any serious grounds. This time for reflection would also serve as protection for a spouse who relies on the permanence of the marriage and would give time for solving economic problems. Six months was proposed as the length of the time for reflection, as in Sweden. This period would also give the spouse who does not work outside the home an opportunity to seek work, or to study in anticipation, and to arrange for the care of the children while working and so on.

As already mentioned, the proposed procedure in a divorce case does not require evidence regarding the possibility of preserving the marriage, whether the spouses are unanimous or not. This is based on the fact that only three out of a hundred divorce applications were not allowed in Finland in 1969,[42] and it was therefore considered unnecessary to have an investigation of the relationship between the spouses. Thus it is possible to avoid many conflicts and also to eliminate the regional and local differences caused by the outlook of the individual judge. The principle would also make it easier for the applicant to envisage the outcome of his application and the clarity of the rules would make them more easily understood by the public. Legal proceedings would be shorter and it would be easier for people to plead their own cases in court. Arrangements could be made between the spouses, before the divorce, concerning the custody of the children, alimony and maintenance.

It is important to note that the committee considers that the dissolution of a marriage should take place before a court as this would assist in preventing unpremeditated divorce, owing to the necessary time for reflection. This period should last for two months in cases of unanimous application and from eight to ten months in cases of disagreement. These times do not include delays, or applications for alterations. No evidence is considered necessary for the dissolution itself, but the court must investigate the conditions for the custody and residence of the children and for their maintenance.

To summarise: the committee holds that immediate divorce is possible when the spouses are unanimous and there are no children under 16 years old, or where there are children under 16 provided the spouses have made a satisfactory agreement about their custody and maintenance, or when the spouses have lived apart during the last year on account of their discord. A time for reflection is necessary when the spouses are not unanimous, or when they are unanimous but there are children under 16 years of age and no satisfactory agreement has been arrived at concerning their custody and maintenance. Judicial separation should be abolished, as well as the need for evidence of the condition of the parties in relation to the dissolution. However, evidence is still important regarding the legal consequences of divorce. Alimony after divorce was introduced into Finland in 1929 by legislation, but the situation of women is now quite different. The increasing number of women working outside the home, and the present comprehensive social legislation must be taken into account. Yet, this social

---

42. See *Betänkande av äktenskapskomittén* I, 1972: A21, Helsingfors 1974, p. 185.

protection is not great for women with little or no income and alimony after divorce, though usually granted to the woman, is never large. Alimony for a divorced spouse should be obtained primarily through social protection and the right to claim under private law only allows for alimony during the time of transition. It is felt that this should be possible for a longer length of time, depending on the length of the marriage and the circumstances of the spouses.[43] The committee hopes to abolish the guilt principle as far as alimony is concerned as it has been abolished as a ground for divorce. Alimony claimed under private law should be for a period of three years only.

The committee also wish to change the system of marital property so that each spouse has his or her own property, but the cooperation of both is required for the disposal of the residence and other items particularly important to the economy of the family. However, the basic rule should be that, in divorce, there should be an equal division between the spouses of that which they have acquired during the marriage. Property already belonging to a spouse on marriage and that inherited or acquired by gift or will during the marriage belongs to that spouse alone. These proposals are the same as in previous Swedish law. However, the Finnish committee felt that equal division of communal property should depend on the individual needs of the spouses. Economic position, age, ability to work, income, social protection should determine the alimony for the spouse and the maintenance for the children, also the needs, age and number of the children should be taken into account.

It should be noted that the opinion of the committee was not unanimous, but lack of space prohibits full discussion of the different points of view in this article.[44]

2. Equality of the spouses

The current rules as to equality of the spouses are very similar to those in Sweden, Denmark and Norway.

3. Illegitimate children

In Finland the legislation regarding illegitimate children is similar to that in Sweden, but there is an important difference regarding the rules of inheritance. Only if the child has been conceived during betrothal, or if a man has acknowledged a child as his own, is there an inheritance relationship between the illegitimate child and his father and the father's relatives. However, that is more than allowed for in the Swedish legislation before 1973. The main principle is that an illegitimate child, unless it is ruled otherwise in the relevant statute, has the same legal position in relation to its mother and her relatives as a legitimate child. The child has the mother's family name, even if she is or has been married. There are two exceptions to this; one is that the child takes the father's family name if it later becomes legitimate through marriage.

---

43. See *Betänkande av äktenskapskomittén* I, pp. 211-213.
44. See *Betänkande av äktenskapskomittén* I, pp. 233-277.

The mother is custodian and guardian of the child, but the court can appoint another custodian or guardian if that is considered better for the child. The acknowledged father has the right to see the child. The child has maintenance from the mother and from the man who has had sexual intercourse with the mother and is likely to be the father of the child. This duty to provide maintenance continues until the child attains the age of 17, but can continue longer if the child cannot support himself on account of illness or weakness. The amount is decided principally in accordance with the mother's standard of living but, in some cases, it is the father's conditions of life that can be decisive. Maintenance can also be continued beyond the age of 17 to finance the education of the child.

As has been stated above, a man can acknowledge that he is the father of an illegitimate child. However, paternity cannot be established by judgment in the case of a man who has denied being the father. But a judgment can establish the duty for a man to pay maintenance for an illegitimate child. If there has been sexual intercourse between the mother of the child and a certain man during the time when the child could have been conceived, then that man has a duty to pay maintenance unless it is manifestly unlikely that the child could be his. This rule is similar to the Swedish rule before the last two reforms in this field of law. Maintenance can also be decided by means of a written contract with witnesses and confirmed by a certain authority.

Proposed new rules

According to a proposed Bill in 1974, it is intended to create legal equality between legitimate and illegitimate children and thus obtain similarity in this respect with the other Nordic countries. It is therefore proposed to introduce the possibility of having a man's paternity established by judgment if he does not voluntarily acknowledge his paternity. Before paternity can be established through judgment, an investigation must be made by an administrative authority[45], this being different from the other Nordic laws. This evidence would be similar to that used in Sweden, such as blood tests, anthropoligical facts, *exceptio plurium* and so on, but would be more detailed. In its report No. 5, 1975, the Parliamentary Law Committee has pointed out that the establishment of paternity according to the new proposals would imply more rigorous demands than those at present made for the establishment of a duty to pay maintenance for an illegitimate child. It must be clearly established that a man begat the child. It is also proposed that every child, whether legitimate or illegitimate, shall have full inheritance rights from his parents and their relatives, and that the parents and their relatives shall have the right to be the child's heirs. Both legitimate and illegitimate children would also have the same right to maintenance from their parents.

It is proposed that the basic rule of guardianship for illegitimate children is that the mother should be the guardian, though it is possible for the father to be so if that is considered the best solution.[46]

---

45. *Barntillsyningsmannen.*
46. According to information received, the aforesaid Bill resulted in new legislation in the autumn of 1975.

Some final remarks about divorce, equality of the spouses and illegitimate children in Sweden, Denmark, Norway and Finland

For a long time there has been a trend away from the ideal of the stability of marriage towards a situation in which the emphasis is placed on the importance of the freewill of the spouses. A great deal of concern has been given to the problem of the welfare of the children in connexion with the increasing number of divorces, but no real solution to the problem has been arrived at.

Another trend has been to abolish or diminish the importance of guilt as a ground for divorce, as well as to reduce its importance in relation to alimony in connexion with divorce.

For a long time the formal status of marriage has been the same for husband and wife in the four mentioned States.

In all these countries there has long been a trend towards improving the legal position of the illegitimate child. In Sweden, Denmark and Norway the illegitimate child has about the same legal position as the legitimate child if paternity is established. In Finland, a similar new legislation is planned.[47]

V. Iceland

1. Divorce

The main principles in the Act on Marriage and Dissolution of Marriage of 1972 are the same as in Norway and Denmark, among them the special Nordic system of marital property. It may be noted that in Iceland both separation and divorce are almost always granted by administrative authorities, but it is legally possible to obtain a divorce by going to court. Guilt is still important in some divorce cases. When the spouses are unanimous, they can obtain judicial separation and divorce one year afterwards providing they have lived apart during that year. However, they must also be unanimous about the custody of their children. See the proposed Finnish rules.

One spouse can unilaterally obtain judicial separation and, after separation, divorce, if the other spouse has neglected, to a noteworthy degree, to provide for the first spouse or for the children or has flagrantly neglected other duties towards them. Also, if deep and lasting disagreement has arisen between the spouses which is so serious that continued cohabitation is considered impossible and the applicant is not the guilty party.

If the separated spouses are not divorced, and resume their cohabitation, the legal consequences of the judicial separation disappear.

According to a statement by Professor Tor Vilhjálmasson of Reykjavik, separation is granted in practically all cases, even if only one of the spouses makes the application.

---

47. See previous footnote.

2. Equality of the spouses

In Iceland there is equality between the spouses in much the same degree as in the other Nordic States.

3. Illegitimate children

In Iceland a child born out of wedlock has a comparatively good legal position. If paternity is established, he inherits from his father and his father's relatives in the same way as a legitimate child.

Illegitimate children are very numerous in Iceland. In 1974 illegitimate children accounted for 34% of all children born in Iceland.

CHAPTER X. THE REFORM OF FAMILY LAW IN THE SOCIALIST STATES

by Tibor Pap

Introduction

Before examining the questions of the legal equality of the spouses, the family status of the illegitimate child, and divorce, it may be useful to glance at the family law of the European Socialist States in general. In addition, the legal systems of these countries on these points, prior to the Second World War, should be recalled in brief because it is only by such a comparison that one can perceive the essential changes brought about in the regulation of the legal family relations in those European countries that have since become socialist.

Nevertheless the fundamental principles, typical of family law of the countries under consideration, must be dealt with in a less general way, and this also applies to the system of rules concerning family relations. These often go beyond the family law, in the implementation of which the respective national laws have been concerned when forming their legal institutions. These fundamental principles common to the family laws of all the European Socialist States explain why the family laws of the socialist countries are more or less similar in many respects. At the same time it cannot be denied that, in respect of some rules of the family law, differences which can hardly be called insignificant are evident, especially with regard to the way in which these rules have developed.

In the European Socialist States—except the Soviet Union and, in part in an opposite sense, the German Democratic Republic—the family law in force, prior to the end of the Second World War, was backward in several aspects compared with the bourgeois family law. With a few exceptions, that carried the imprint of ecclesiastic influence and of the feudal institutions. This family law was equally characterised by legal details which were partly the consequence of ecclesiastic influence in matrimonial relations. This can be traced back to historical antecedents. It showed itself in rules regarding material relations within the family, so far as these were matrimonial, as well as in other relations. Different rules helped develop the institutions and helped solve the vexed questions in family law which varied on account of territorial and denominational factors. Also, many traits characteristic of the burgeois law could be seen. There was no equality of the sexes within the family, the supremacy of the husband within the family was assured both in relation to his wife and to the children, as well as regarding the management of the family property. The illegitimate child was discriminated against, adoption was regarded rather as a pecuniary institution than as a concept of family law and, in the sphere of guardianship also, the wife filled a subordinate role. Furthermore, particularly during the expansion of fascism, legislation reflecting concepts based on social discrimination in family relations also made its appearance.

After the War, statutes aimed at the democratisation of family law appeared in the Peoples' Democracies, which created uniform regulation of the family law for all citizens of the countries in question. Between 1946 and 1952, the Peoples'

Democracies created their fundamental laws which laid down at the constitutional level the following principles:

1. the social protection of the marriage and the family
2. the protection of the mother and of childhood
3. the legal equality of men and women, and
4. the legal equality of the illegitimate child.

Later, between 1955 and 1958, after the constitution of the Peoples' Democracies, family codes regulating family relations in the socialist spirit were created, involving the putting into effect of constitutional principles in the area of family relations. Following that, recodification of the family law took place in Czechoslovakia in 1963, in Bulgaria in 1968, in Yugoslavia in 1971-74, and in Hungary in 1974. In the Soviet Union the republican regulations of the 1920s, afterwards modified by partly federal rules of law, were changed in 1968 by "the foundations of the legislation of the Soviet Union and of the Federal Republics on marriage and the family", and the republican family codes depending on them. The family codes in force will now be discussed and earlier rules made after the War will only be mentioned if they explain the development.

Socialist family law, insofar as it is a system of institutions regulating family relations, was developed and consolidated in the Soviet Union after the great October Revolution. The young Soviet State had liquidated rules of a feudal character which were anti-democratic in family relations, in the period immediately after the triumphant revolution. While Lenin established Soviet power in the autumn of 1919, after the issue of the decree on marriage and the creation of the Soviet law on marriage and the family, the power of the workers had already forced a revolutionary transformation of the most radical kind in the law relating to the status of women. The European Peoples' Democracies, developed after the Second World War, found themselves facing a similar task. They were influenced by general socialist ideas, and the rules developed there showed the Soviet methods of working out family legislation in several aspects which indicated the trend of the future. From the time of the creation of their codes, the Peoples' Democracies followed Soviet solutions in their family law.

The legislation regulating the Soviet socialist family, as in the Peoples' Democracies, is concerned that in all aspects of family relations the husband and wife should have equal rights and obligations. These laws also eliminate the traces of ecclesiastical influence in family relations and attribute marriage rights and obligations only to a civil marriage. In Hungary and Germany, however, the obligatory civil marriage was introduced as the result of the so-called "cultural struggles" at the end of the nineteenth century with the Catholic Church and the Holy See in Rome. As a concession to the Church, the law in these two countries still recognises the institution of separation, which is unknown in socialist family law.

From the time of the regulation of the invalidity of marriage, these statutes were concerned with codifying the main sets of facts which were obstacles to marriage in that they excluded or endangered the realisation of firm and durable marriage relationships, having regard to morals and health, the non-observance of which would conflict with existing ways of life in society and would produce consequences capable of damaging future generations. At the same time, they did not make the distinction between void and voidable marriages, eliminating the ideas of degrees of invalidity found in bourgeois law, and also getting away from the further consequence that the declaration of nullity adversely affected the family status of the illegitimate child.

Concerning the dissolution of marriage, the laws considered depart from the principle that only those marriages which are irremediably broken and are denuded of all value from the point of view of the spouses and of society can and ought to be dissolved. They also took greater account of the interests of the minor child. In connection with material relations, the legislation reaffirmed the marriage bonds and the consequent equality in law between the spouses. Regarding the relations between parents and children, moreover, these laws are concerned, not with stressing the rights of the parents, but with the regulation of their equal obligations towards their children giving first consideration to the interests of the latter. The discriminations against illegitimate children were abolished and the institutions of adoption and wardship were also regulated so that they became primarily institutions protecting the interests of the minor child.

The general pattern is equally characteristic of the family law of the Soviet Union and of the Peoples' Democracies, resulting from the manner of regulation of family regulations by the respective family codes. Certainly these matters could not have been dealt with in a uniform way by the Soviet Union and the Peoples' Democracies if they had not been societies of the same type—socialist, or becoming socialist. Nor is it just a matter of chance that family codes figure among the first codes created in the spirit of socialism in the countries of the Peoples' Democracies, as in the Soviet Union. Similar principles also characterised the legislation on family matters of the first Dictatorship of the Hungarian proletariat, in the Hungarian Socialist Republic of 1919, though the number of family law rules of the Republic were relatively few. However, these rules were of great importance because they contained the intention to regulate family relations and marriage according to the socialist ideal. These objectives were realised in significant measure. The legislation of the Hungarian Socialist Republic at the same time regulated questions of no less importance than the family status of the illegitimate child, taking account of the interests of the child; dissolution of marriage and related questions, which are very complex and as highly relevant to society as to the spouses and the children; they attached to family relations and, through them, to broader aspects of family law. This legislation created a system of rules which assured the education and suitable care of the child and the development of the socialist protection of childhood and youth.

The identity of the characteristic principles of the family law of the Soviet Union and the Peoples' Democracies does not necessarily mean the overall identity of the institutions of family law. Different legal regulations evolving from historical divergencies and consequently affecting the views of workers, are equally viable for the implementation of the same principle, the goal being similar to the prescribed scale of social development. Thus, while it is generally established that the socialist family laws agree in their fundamentals, there are some in which differences in certain important questions have not yet been resolved.

In this way the Soviet legislation, as well as the legislation of the Peoples' Democracies, provides that the illegitimate child does not suffer discrimination by comparison with a child born of the marriage, but the legal instruments called up to realise this objective are different. After 1944 and before 1968 Soviet family law did not recognise the possibility of establishing paternity by judicial means, and society took care of the illegitimate child by the protection accorded to the mother or by the placing of the child in an institution. On the other hand, the family law of the Peoples' Democracies made it possible from the beginning for paternity to be confirmed by the judicial method and to oblige the father to furnish the child with necessaries. Hungarian law alone codified the institution of providing necessaries without confirmation of paternity.

In fact, the recognition of the marriage is not met with in the family law of the Peoples' Democracies at any stage of their development. However, in the family code of the Soviet Union, the effective family life in common, when it complied with certain defined criteria, produced in a vague manner obligations and conjugal rights until 1944. From that date only a registered marriage was considered as producing conjugal rights and obligations regarding the spouses and the children. The family law of the Peoples' Democracies controls the material relationship between the spouses more fully than the family codes of the RFSSR, which can be traced back precisely to the fact that the law of the Peoples' Democracies already makes use of scientific experiments and Soviet practice. The socialist family laws of these democracies also contain differences among themselves in the regulation of certain institutions.

For example, in Hungary until the 1974 modification of the family law, the future spouses of both sexes, alone among the European socialist countries, could conclude a marriage with the authorisation of the guardianship authority as soon as they attained the age of 12 years. This regulation did not assure conditions necessary for the establishment of firm and durable family bonds. On the contrary, it contributed to the formation of very early marriages entered into without reflection. Also, only about 10% of marriages were requested by minor spouses. The law of the German Democratic Republic, having regard to the fact that a marriage which results in a family relies from the start on a firm base and that such a marriage would involve the least danger from later complications resulting from the insincerity of the spouses, goes as far as to prohibit a marriage under the age of 18 years. The Czechoslovak code makes it possible "in exceptional cases if this accords with the social aim of the marriage" to authorise marriage for minors older than 16 but, in this connection, the strictness of the legislator is exemplified by the following provision which says, "in the case of minors younger than 16 years, marriage cannot be effected". The Bulgarian legislation provides similarly, but does not contain any rule declaring a marriage entered into under the age of 16 years to be invalid. The Polish family law contains a special solution, guided by the idea of the reaffirmation of the marriage, which establishes the age limit for marriage at 21 years in the case of men but, for certain important reasons, authorises the contraction of marriage by a man aged 18 years and a woman aged 16 years.

The fundamental Soviet law authorises the legislation of the federal Soviet Republics to reduce by up to two years the general age limit of 18 years for contracting a marriage. Only the Uzbekian and Ukrainian legislators have made use of this possibility by establishing the legal age for women at 17 years. A more pronounced difference among the republican laws appeared in the dispensations which can be accorded with regard to the age of consent. In fact, while the code of the Russian Federation makes possible "in certain exceptional cases" the authorisation of the celebration of marriage at 16 for the man as for the woman, the Uzbekian code does not provide at all for the possibility of granting a dispensation. Other republican laws, among which are the Georgian, the Ukrainian and the Lithuanian, permit the authorisation of marriage for either of the future spouses one year before the age limit provided by the law, while the fourth group of codes, especially the Latvian, the Estonian and the Moldavian, assure the possibility of dispensation of age only for the engaged girl, at most for one year before attaining the matrimonial age. Thus, in the last analysis, the laws of the Russian Federation and of the Ukrainian Republic make possible the authorisation of marriage at 16, though for the women only, while the other federated republics allow marriage at an earlier age than 17, some of them for either spouse, and some for the engaged girl only. As in Romanian law, the conclusion of a marriage can be authorised at the age of 15 years for the woman who, under the general rule, can contract a marriage at the age of 16 years. The Hungarian law provides that the man can marry at the age of 18 and the woman at the age of 16, and the guardianship authority can authorise the marriage at the earliest two years before those respective ages. Through this recent provision, the Hungarian law is attached to the rule which exists in the socialist countries of Europe.

The provision of the recent Soviet, Hungarian and Polish legislation, which interposes between the engagement and the celebration of the marriage by an officer of the State a period called a period of waiting, is intended to eliminate marriages conceived on a sudden impulse. The period of waiting is generally one month and, in the codes of the Soviet Federal Republics, is determined by the officer of the State, but cannot exceed three months. The Tadjik law alone allows a waiting period of six months. This is not equivalent to the reintroduction of public banns deriving from Canon law since the reason for the existence of this institution, namely to draw the attention of persons knowing of any impediment to the projected marriage with a view to reporting them, had already been questioned in the bourgeois literature. Several provisions of certain socialist family laws are directed towards a similar end, the assurance of conditions necessary for firm family bonds, conditions designed to record the state of health of the future spouses. These conditions usually lay down that each spouse must be informed of the state of health of the other (e.g. the relevant provision of the Soviet basic principles and the respective codes of the Federated Republics and the Czechoslovak law) while, under the recent Hungarian legislation, future spouses under 35 years of age must take part before the marriage in a consultation for the protection of the family and of the wife. The primary purpose of this consultation is to give information about family planning. The most strict law in this connection is the Bulgarian, according to which a person who is suffering from a complaint which is seriously prejudicial to the life or health of descendants, cannot contract a marriage unless the other future spouse knows of it. Moreover, the future spouses must vouch before a State official, by producing a medical certificate, that they are not currently suffering from such a disease. Omission to present the medical certificate, when there is no disease, can attract the disciplinary responsibility of the State official while, if one of the spouses is actually ill, the marriage can be declared null.

With regard to the celebration of the marriage, while in some socialist laws this can only be done by a State official when the appropriate inscriptions have been entered in the State registers (e.g. in the laws of the Soviet Union, Romania, Bulgaria and the German Democratic Republic), the legislation of other socialist States does not recognise any legal effect to the inscription. Thus, according to the latter laws the agreed declaration by the spouses before the State official itself creates the bond. On this subject, some socialist laws make it possible to contract a marriage through an agent and evaluate in a different manner the legal relations of adoption from the point of view of the grounds for the invalidity of the marriage.

Reference will only be made here to certain differences which occur among the family laws of the socialist States, or which have existed at certain stages of their development. Consideration will now be given to the following points: the admission or rejection of the dissolution of marriage in the case where the petitioner is exclusively at fault, the development of the law of family property on the basis of the separation of assets, the admission of various differences on a contractual basis of the legal system of the law of family property, and the method of regulating the conditions and duration of maintenance between spouses, as well as the name borne by the married woman. However, the most important differences which occur cannot be traced back in this area to the fact that the family laws of the socialist countries have been guided by different aims. The differences result, on the one hand, from the fact that these codes were formed in different times of socialist development and, on the other, from the fact that these national laws originating under the influence of different historical antecedents could not or, more precisely, did not wish to operate completely independently of the earlier rules. Where possible, although not completely achieving the socialist character of the family law, they did not altogether desire a rupture at all costs with all that is old.

It has been indicated above that the relevant differences between the family law of the Soviet Union and that of the Peoples' Democracies does not in the least affect the fact that these legal systems belong to the same type of law—socialist law. On the other hand, the fact is that the resemblance of some institutions of the Soviet family law and the law of the Peoples Democracies does not necessarily derive from the fact that they are examples of the same type of law, especially not of its socialist essence.

Thus, beyond the traits resulting from the socialist character of the family law of the Soviet Union and the Peoples' Democracies, there are to be found similar institutions produced in part by external circumstances influencing the socialist countries at the time of their codifications. Beyond that, even bearing in mind the partial interdependence of the national legal systems, there are similarities which are partly accidental. One of these elements was the prohibition of a marriage between citizens of the Soviet Union and foreign citizens. A similar regulation also existed in several family laws of the Peoples' Democracies. Here we come face to face with a peculiarity which does not result from the socialist essence of the family laws of the Soviet Union and the Peoples' Democracies. This is partly explained by the short time during which the institution has existed and partly by the fact that not all the family laws of the Peoples' Democracies have found it necessary to institutionalise it.

Another resemblance between the family laws of the Soviet Union and those of the Peoples' Democracies which could be called accidental is the institution of the procedure for preparatory conciliation preceding the dissolution of a marriage, separate from the basic procedure and duplicating the latter in a particular way without the characteristic of a decision of principle. This was also introduced at one time in the Hungarian legislation. It follows from the socialist character of the laws mentioned that they contribute to a reasonable framework by their control of the stability of a marriage. But they are also used to achieve the aims of administrative measures which, at least in Hungary before the liquidation of the institution in question, were of very doubtful value and did not derive from the socialist character of these laws.

In order to understand the differences existing between the respective socialist family laws, it must be considered that the relationship of the man to the family and to the marriage is not determined directly by the economic position. In social relations, the development cannot go so fast as, for example, in industrial relations, for socialist society lays down broader possibilities for fostering the organisation of its own economic activity. Furthermore, in the area of family relations, the methods of providing for moral standards have a particular significance and bring into the balance more weight than in any other aspect of social life. That is why there is a particularly close link here between the legal and moral points of view. The human relations controlled by the family law are occasionally much more complex than the most complicated relations in civil matters.

I. Equality of the spouses

Regarding the legal equality of the spouses, it is necessary to take into consideration in the legislation of the European socialist States, and not only in their family law, the physical nature of the woman which makes it imperative to have certain distinctions in the legal systems. The woman is assured the same rights and obligations as men in political and social life, for example in electoral law, assets and debts, the carrying out of functions and the exercise of a profession; but in labour law the physical nature of woman must be generally considered. For certain work it is absolutely forbidden to employ women. On the other hand, a working woman has broad advantages in her role as mother.

In this way the law of the countries under consideration follows the principles fixed by the Constitutions as fundamental laws. On the other hand, the Constitutions declare the full equality of citizens, including the prohibition of discrimination between the sexes. They also contain express provisions with regard to the protection of the family and the wife.

In examining the equality which is at the heart of the family law, the question of the legal equality of the man and the woman must be explained in three aspects: the question of equality in law concerning personal and material relations, parental equality relative to their rights and obligations towards the children, and their duties towards illegitimate children.

In connection with the control of the personal relations of the spouses, the socialist laws of the family aim at realising equality between the spouses in all aspects of family life. This is apparent from the fact that these laws lay down the spouses' rights and obligations regarding essential matters that arise in family life, apart from conjugal fidelity, mutual help and the family name.

These Codes emphasise the importance of the personal relationships between the spouses and thus dispose of these questions first.

Only later do they lay down propositions regulating the material relations between the spouses.

In Czechoslovak law, the Civil Code contains provisions on this point. The family law does not contain positive rules concerning the substantive law of the family. These rules derive from socialist moral principles and are placed ahead of the passages of law concerning the reciprocal relations of the spouses. By means of rules governing the personal relations of the spouses, attention is at the same time attracted to the fact that, in the final analysis, the legal obligations of the spouses are pre-eminently moral obligations of one towards the other. Their reciprocal relations should not be, and cannot in any way become, simply legal obligations and legal powers.

During research into the laws mentioned above, it was found that some socialist laws declare both the principle of the protection of the family and the mother and, at the same time, the equality of the sexes within the family. The family law of the majority of the European socialist States contains provisions concerning the protection of the family and of the mother. The Czechoslovak Code formulates this as follows: "The family based on marriage constitutes the basic link which in all respects protects the family relationships"[1] and goes on, "Society accords to the mother not only a protection, but also multilateral cares".[2] For example, when going into detail, the Soviet bases are concerned with institutions which will protect the interests of the child.

In the Soviet Union and the Federal Republics, the basic principles of the legislation on marriage and the family deal separately with the legal equality of the woman and the man in the family relations and declare among other things that the equal personal rights vest in the woman and the man, adding that "the legal equality of the woman and the man in the family is based on the equality in law established by the Constitution of the Soviet Union, and assured in all areas of life within the State, socio-political, economic, as well as cultural." Among the principles serving as a basis for the control of the family relations, the Bulgarian Code mentions, "the full equality in law of the husband and the wife", and subsequently lays down that the spouses have equal rights and obligations in the marriage. The formulation of the Albanian law hardly differs from this while, according to the family Code of the German Democratic Republic, "legal equality of the man and the woman fixes in a decisive manner the character of the family", and later decrees with remarkable brevity, "the spouses are equal in law". The relevant provisions of the family law in the other countries examined differ only with regard to the wording, but the law of 1973 of the Federal Republic of Montenegro, Macedonia and Serbia, reproducing almost verbatim the wording of the Yugoslav fundamental law on marriage, do not differ from that. The preamble of the family law of the Hungarian People's Republic, as

---

1. Translated from the original French text.
2. Translated from the original French text.

modified in 1974, also declares that the aim of the law is "to ensure the legal equality of the spouses in marriage and in family life", on the basis of the relevant articles of the Constitution.

The legal provisions cited exclude any agreement between the spouses from having any effect upon the equality in law between the husband and the wife. For example, an agreement could not provide that the husband would be considered as the head of the family. Nor would a right vest in him with regard to decision making in questions regarding the family. Any agreement between the spouses by which either would renounce the exercise of these rights for the future would also be contrary to the law.

According to these Codes, the spouses must decide by mutual agreement upon all the essential questions touching upon the married life. This is so in all the European socialist family laws, although they provide for this question in various degrees of scope and intensity. The Yugoslav fundamental law on marriage does not regulate the agreement of the spouses except for the running of the common household, but it lays down that the spouses have identical rights and duties with regard to the children. The Codes of the German Democratic Republic and of Albania and Romania expressly require decisions to be taken by common agreement on every question affecting the marriage and the life in common and the wellbeing of each spouse. The Polish and Czechoslovak laws make a distinction with regard to decisions taken in common on family questions and questions essential to the family, such as those connected with the exercise of parental supervision, decisions about the surname, the education and instruction of the children and decisions on the needs of the family. In general, everything connected with the intellectual and material conditions of the family community. Also, the choice and change of the family home, the place of business, the place of work of the spouses, all come within the sphere of essential questions of married life. All these problems can be directly important from the point of view of the whole family, but can also touch the family to a certain extent when such problems produce a direct change in the circumstances of only one of the spouses.

If the spouses cannot agree over essential problems in the married life, the question arises as to who must decide. The recognition of the husband's right of decision does not constitute a desirable solution for the socialist codifier, because this solution would be contrary to the idea of the equality between the husband and the wife. The above mentioned legal systems adopt various forms. One group of laws, failing agreement of the spouses, submits all the essential questions to organs of the State for decision; another group of Codes provides for the intervention of the organs of the State only in certain prescribed situations. The law of the German Democratic Republic, in its turn, leaves this problem completely open. According to the Polish and Czechoslovak laws, failing agreement the judge is called upon to decide on essential questions in the family. This solution is fully acceptable, since the competent organ of the State bases its solution doubtless upon an examination and careful appreciation of all the circumstances. This serves the interests of the whole of the family and of the wife, it sometimes opposes a possible tendency towards the guardianship of the husband. However, this is only reassuring in appearance. In fact, the Czechoslovak law refers separately to the fact that, concerning the exercise of a profession and the hiring out of the services of the spouses, neither of them is in need of the other spouse's consent.

Other socialist systems contain similar rules which, however, do not generally introduce the possibility of a judicial decision in cases where there is no agreement between the spouses regarding essential questions of married life. Thus, while it is practicaly certain that no consent is necessary, the good sense of the spouses must come into play on the essential questions. It is a different matter when the socialist law can lend its support to neither one nor the other of the spouses in order to prevent them by a judgment from putting obstacles in the way of the other spouse in taking part in productive work according to his or her aptitudes. It is no accident that, in the Polish legal literature a discussion has developed as to whether the choice of a profession and of the place of work must be considered as an essential question. The discussion only took place for the reason that the express provisions of the law could have assured the just result, namely, that the spouses should not be able legally to prevent each other from exercising their fundamental right to work.

Another group of Codes gives to the organs of the State the right to decide questions regarding the supervision by the parents and the question of the child's surname. This right is given to the guardianship authority or to the Courts, for example, in the laws of Bulgaria, Soviet Russia, Hungary and Romania. Regarding both the essential and the less essential questions within the sphere of married life, these Codes do not contain any provision concerning which organ shall make the decision in default of a proper agreement between the spouses. Where an agreement is lacking these laws provide only for questions requiring an immediate solution with regard to the interests of the child. According to the Czechoslovak and Polish literature, these rules achieve the desired effect in this way on the questions of choice of domicile and place of work of the spouses. These decisions are legally dependent neither on the consent of one nor of the other spouse.

Concerning the domicile of the spouses, several laws provide "that they live together", or "are obliged to live together", e.g. Bulgarian, East German, Czechoslovakian and Polish; "they choose their residence by common agreement", according to Yugoslav and Hungarian law. According to the Bulgarian and Hungarian laws the spouses cannot depart from the agreement except for "well-founded reasons". On the other hand, the Soviet legislation grants to each spouse the liberty to choose his own residence.

The Code of the German Democratic Republic, unlike the Codes considered so far, does not name any State organ to be used to decide cases of disagreement between the spouses, or in respect of parental supervision. However, this can also be connected with the fact that, as far as the relations within the marriage and the family are concerned, more particularly in connection with parental supervision, the German codification refers to the intervention by article 44 of the law, "it is the task of the organs of the State, above all the cultural organs, the health and social insurance services, trades unions, parents' groups and tenants' committees, that they protect the parents in the education of the children." However, in the final analysis, this rule of law cannot avoid the possibility of intervention by the State and, in the case of culpable and grave violation by the parents of their obligations, it provides for forefeiture of the right to decide on the child's education.

236

The family law of several socialist countries contains the provision that the spouses owe fidelity to each other and are obliged to help each other. Conjugal fidelity is obligatory not only from the moral, but also from the legal point of view, for both spouses. This fidelity is not limited to sexual fidelity between the spouses, as the Supreme Court of Hungary has held in one of its decisions, although this is without doubt its most significant realm, but 'fidelity' between spouses cannot be interpreted differently from fidelity in other human relations. According to the Supreme Court, a husband who is habitually drunk and shows a brutal and coarse attitude towards his wife and child, does not show fidelity.

The obligation of the spouses with regard to mutual help imposes requirements of character upon them which are partly material and partly non-material. The non-material aspects of this cooperation require that the spouses should do all within their power to help each other and to develop their assistance in all respects, to the full extent of their abilities in the most useful way for the benefit of society and of the family. The personal obligation of reciprocal fidelity and cooperation cannot be achieved by force. Nor is it possible to bring an action for the implementation of this duty. However, there are legal sanctions. In some legal systems the spouse who avoids this obligation can be subjected to various disadvantages, such as the legal consequences of being unworthy of maintenance and of being the guilty party in the dissolution of the marriage.

It is a characteristic of the socialist family legislation that it imposes the task of realising the principale of legal equality of the sexes, as prescribed by the Constitution, also with regard to the family name. This idea is reflected in the most consistent way in the laws of the Soviet Union, Yugoslavia, Bulgaria, Czechoslovakia, Romania and the German Democratic Republic, and Albania. According to these Codes the spouses may choose as the family name the name of either the husband or the wife. Some of these laws permit the retention of the pre-marital name of a spouse, or they may both join together their family names. Yugoslav law also makes it possible that one of them alone takes the family name of the other and attaches his or her own family name to that. All the European socialist laws assure the spouses of complete freedom after betrothal to choose the name by which they will be known during the marriage. However, alongside the agreement on this main question, the Polish and Hungarian laws differ by providing that the family name of the husband alone may be chosen as the common name of the family. This is a major deviation, significantly against the emancipation of women. While in Polish law the omission of the declaration of the wife automatically means that she takes the name of her husband, the Hungarian law lays down that the declaration relative to the name of the future spouse is obligatory. Until the modification of the law in 1974, the Hungarian law, alone in Europe, laid down that the wife could not take the family name of her husband except with a suffix referring to the marriage bond. Today however the law makes it possible for the wife to attach her own first name to the family name of her husband. Moreover, before the modification, the Hungarian and the Polish laws also laid down, in the case of the omission of the declaration by the fiancée, that the future wife should take the name of her husband automatically. The Hungarian codifier modified this provision precisely because it offended against the principle of the emancipation of women. On the other hand the Albanian law, alone among the socialist laws, makes provision that in the case of different family names of the spouses, the children shall carry the name of the father. The special feature of the Bulgarian law in this respect shows that the children, according to tradition, carry only the father's family name, while the requirements of the emancipation of women are satisfied. With regard to the surname of the children, the Soviet law also has the distinction in favour of the father while, according to the usage of Russian names, the children also carry his family name and his first name—"the patronimic name."

The institution of maintenance during marriage is known in the law of all the European socialist States, although not all the Codes provide for it in a formal way. With regard to the joint life of the spouses, the majority of the Codes leave gaps. The literature, as well as traditional practice, have derived the right to maintenance during marriage from the legal obligation laid down with regard to the contributions to the joint family needs and also from the cooperation of the spouses. But the necessity for maintenance during marriage normally arises in cases where the spouses live apart. How far this is typical can also be seen from the relevant text of the Hungarian law, which only mentions the obligation of maintenance for a separated spouse. However, while the Hungarian law clearly ordains that the separated spouse, provided he is deserving, can require conjugal maintenance from the other spouse only if in need, the laws of the other socialist countries give little information on this problem except for the German Democratic Republic, the Soviet Union and the Federated Soviet Republics. This results in different opinions from different standpoints in the judicial practice and the literature of certain socialist countries. Concerning the German and Soviet solutions these laws, and particularly the Codes of certain Soviet Republics, adopt an attitude taken in principle from Hungarian law. In Soviet law the wife has the right to maintenance during pregnancy as well as for a year after the birth of a child. However, these Codes exclude maintenance in the case of a brief marriage, or of the unworthiness of the person claiming the right, or the fault of that person. The law of the German Democratic Republic grants to the unqualified spouse the right to conjugal maintenance for the duration of his or her professional instruction.

Concerning the control under socialist law of the material relations of the spouses, in general few systems of law regulate the material aspect of marriage. Those legal systems which have methods of regulation which are the most appropriate for the realisation of legal equality in such material relations, are seen to be those with a single regulation. Either it is not within the powers of the spouses to deviate from this regulation or, in some legal systems, there is the possibility of agreement between them insofar as it is not contrary to the idea of the legal equality of the sexes.

This legislation exists basically in the field of the community of assets in marriage. It allows for each of the two spouses to participate in the assets acquired during the marriage. Thus it takes into account the work contributed by the spouse concerned with the interior of the home, while assuring to him or her by means of different legal solutions a suitable participation in the assets acquired by the spouse engaged in an activity as the breadwinner. These laws do not only assure a suitable participation on the distortion of a marriage assets but also provide that during the marriage both spouses are required to contribute to a great extent by common agreement, assets which vest in them both. In connection with spouses and third parties, the laws in question recognise the disposal of assets by one of the spouses as valid in certain cases, but only insofar as their economy requires it. In the reciprocal internal arrangements the relevant laws also take care to remedy any interference with the interests of either of the spouses. At the same time, where the laws recognise the idea of the community of acquisitions acquired during the marriage, they recognise the exclusive rights of the spouses to their belongings held before the marriage, and also provide for their exclusive right to certain patrimonial securities acquired during the duration of the marriage. The principles of the Codes under consideration, apart from agreement on fundamentals, contain differences concerning the merits of the questions that arise on the legal basis of the community of assets, the extent of the common assets, the tracing and the demarcation of the common and the individual assets, the possibility of the winding-up of the community of acquisitions during marriage, the method of partitioning the assets for each spouse, as well as the authorisation of the contractual variations of the legal regulation of the property relations between the spouses.

The Codes examined admit, as the legal system of property relations between the spouses, the community of assets during the marriage. In Hungarian law, the institution of the substantive matrimonial law also conditions the existence of the marriage, but here the relation between the two institutions is not necessarily correlative. The fact of the marriage does not mean that a community of assets exists automatically between the spouses. According to Hungarian law, contrary to that of other European socialist States, the community of assets is not the product of marriage but of the communal married life. In that legal regime, separation without the termination of the marriage automatically involves the termination of the communal property. Among the Codes of the Soviet Republics only the Kazakh Code contains a similar ruling, because it authorises the judge to consider as separate assets the patrimonial securities acquired by either of the spouses after the actual termination, though not the legal termination, of the communal life. Here, unlike the Hungarian law, the decision is entrusted to the interpretation of the judge. In default of relevant legal provisions, in Yugoslavia the literature expresses the view that assets acquired by the work of the spouses after the interruption of their communal life constitute the separate property of the spouse who acquired them.

As to the legal basis upon which assets belong to the communal fund, these laws generally consider that all inherited property acquired by either of the spouses and, lacking express provisions to the contrary, not being separate property, belong to the communal fund, including the income from the common assets if they are not separate property. Polish law lays this down in an explicit manner. The laws of Albania, Yugoslavia and the German Democratic Republic make an exception to this rule which, like the regulations previously enforced in certain Republics of the Soviet Union, there relates only to the assets acquired by the spouses in connection with the common fund. The practice of the Supreme Court of the Soviet Union seems at present to rank equally the income from separate assets and the chance increase of the separate assets, in the sphere of separate property.

The Codes determine in a diffrent manner the extent of the assets that belong to the communal fund, because they use different criteria to distinguish those assets that the spouses may dispose of independently, as their personal property.

These Codes refer to the separate assets of the spouses, the assets possessed at the time of the marriage, and the inherited assets later acquired by chance by either of the spouses during the existence of the communal fund, as well as inherited assets replacing separate property and used for the personal needs of either of the spouses. Furthermore, certain Codes eliminate from the communal fund the assets which one of the spouses, although he has acquired them during the marriage, has used them in his profession or occupation. These are sometimes subject to restrictions, for example in Polish law, where such goods are taken out only if they are separate assets. In German law this occurs to the extent that the value of such assets is not disproportionately great in comparison with the income and common assets of the spouses, while the Hungarian law establishes the limit of the relevant measure to the usual quantity of effects for personal use. The assets which contribute to the success of a professional occupation belong to the goods held in common. On the other hand, some Codes of the Yugoslav Republics put this restriction into effect with regard to the inherited assets of separate property in both these categories. Romanian law takes out from the communal fund the broadest area of assets, far surpassing those mentioned above, and classifies them as separate property.

These laws make possible the partition of the communal property during the marriage. In Hungarian law, this occurs during the community of married life, but the methods of partition are not all uniform.

The rules of law entrust the partition of common property primarily to the joint decision of the spouses and only in default of their agreement will the Court carry out the partition. In this connection the Hungarian law bases the participation strictly on a fifty percent basis. The laws of the other socialist countries, on the one hand provide only in principle for partition in equal parts, while on the other hand they primarily take into account the contributions of the spouses to the provision of the common fund. But, despite this difference in point of departure and having regard to the corrections applied, a just result is always arrived at.

In fact, the laws having as their base the principle of equal partition also simplify the application of the unequal participation, by taking into account the contribution of a greater proportion by one of the spouses, the needs of the children living with that spouse, as contrasted with the inaction of the other spouse. The Codes that have the contribution to the building up of the communal fund as their criterion in determining the ratio of participation, take into consideration the cooperation given by the spouse who is not gaining his living, but is occupied in the direction of the household, the education of the children, in contrast to the other spouse who is obtaining the livelihood. This was the position in Albanian, Yugoslav and Romanian law.

Regarding the disposition of the assets belonging to the communal fund, the codifier had to reconcile the interests of the spouses in their character as equal owners in law, with the interests of a third party having business relations with them in connection with the needs of the family. In this area the laws considered whether it is a question of family assets (immovables) or of business assets aimed at satisfying the daily needs. In fact, the Codes generally require that the spouses conclude their business by selling part of the communal fund by mutual consent.

But this rule does not carry much weight except in the case of transactions beyond the needs of daily life, and chiefly concerning immovables in gratuitous transactions. In fact, in this area, the transaction concluded by one of the spouses alone is considered as null and void.

In less important affairs concerning daily needs, the Hungarian law in general recognises as an exception to the principal rule, the validity of the legal act of one of the spouses alone. In fact, it is presumed that they have the consent of the other spouse to a transaction concluded by one of them. The presumption can be contested. This is only done in a case when the third party knew of the lack of consent, or at least ought to have known it. However, while in the case of a transaction to satisfy daily needs, the Hungarian law regards the presumption of consent only counteracted by a statement made in advance before the third party, the Polish law does not recognise this presumption at all and requires the separate consent of the other spouse who has not taken part in the transaction.

Regarding the question of how to modify by contract between the spouses the system of family property law in the legal systems examined, a fairly varied picture is presented. Most of the countries prohibit deviation by contract from the legal order of community property and any agreement contrary to the obligatory provisions of the law. As the Romanian law expresses it—nothing is excluded except the extension of the sphere of community property. The law of the German Democratic Republic establishes the prohibition only with regard to patrimonial assets which are necessary for the common way of life of the family, while according to the Polish law, partly similar to the Czechoslovak law previously in force, the legal community of family property can not only be enlarged by contract, but limited, or even excluded. The commentary on the Polish law refers to the fact that the legislator has chosen this regulation having regard to the interests of the agrarian population.

With regard to the legal equality of the spouses in their capacity as parents, this has been touched upon in discussing the personal relations of the spouses. On the other hand, in explaining the rights and obligations of the parents with regard to the illegitimate child, all questions which are invariably important with regard to him and his parents will be analysed. The chief heads on this point are: it is equally important for the family laws of the socialist States that the parents have the right and the obligation to care for their minor children, to educate and represent them and consequently to supervise the rights and the personal and material interests of their children. These rights fall to both parents together. As Hungarian law also establishes, the parents are bound to exercise these rights in a way best suited to the children's interests. In a case where the parents do not live together, the child must generally be placed according to the agreement of the parents and, failing such agreement, on the basis of the Court's decision in the place where one of them is domiciled. In this case, apart from certain exceptions for various reasons, there is a right of access for the other spouse. However, in case of need, the child may equally well be placed in the home of a third party. In this case, it is necessary to establish which of the parents has the right of supervision. The maintenance of the child is equally the obligation of both parents, bu the Czechoslovakian, Hungarian and Polish laws, in safeguarding the interests of the child also recognise the possibility of a grant for necessaries by the State. This takes the place of the person who finds it impossible to pay for the maintenance or who has not undertaken to provide it. In that event the State finances the necessaries while reserving to itself the right to reimbursement. Some laws, for example Hungarian law, include the naming of the guardian, among the rights of both parents.

II. Divorce

The preoccupation of society with the ideal of durable family communities in which legitimate children can be brought up is evident in the family law of the socialist countries. There are also various socio-economic provisions to the same end and the problem of divorce must be approached from the point of view of this requirement. This is not to say that the law would refuse divorce during the lifetime of the spouses or would seek to maintain a bond desired by neither of the spouses. In fact the law cannot be oblivious of the fact that the harmony and the good sense required in a marriage may decline and it can sympathise with the spouse who anxiously desires to be released from a bond which has become un-endurable. Some European socialist laws show reservations on this point. At the same time it is obvious that these family laws aim at encouraging the development of firm family bonds by the creation of standards for married life that will assist serious and constructive attitudes in the spouses.

However, in the European socialist States a divorce must be granted upon a reasonable petition in cases where there is a lasting, basic breakdown of the marriage. When the marriage has broken down irremediably, some of the socialist laws provide for divorce on the grounds of fault. But socialist family law in general rejects the principle of examining details of family life, and wishes to avoid tying the hands of the judge in divorce proceedings.

With regard to the grounds for divorce, with two exceptions these laws are not concerned with the accusation of the defendant, but rely exclusively on the judge's appraisal of the situation between the spouses at to whether the marriage can still be considered as valid for them and for society. The interests of the minor children are held to be most important and these are taken into consideration first, before deciding whether these interests militate in favour of maintaining or dissolving the marriage. This is especially emphasised in recent Soviet legislation, where the husband can only bring an action for divorce, without the wife's consent, during her pregnancy after a period of at least one year after the birth of the child. The Soviet regulation shows that, on occasion, essential changes can be made in the law as a result of stages in social development. A decree of 1917 placed divorce in the hands of the State, rather than under ecclesiastical control. On a petition by one or both of the spouses, the Court can dissolve the marriage without seeking reasons for the divorce. As a result, it was not possible to reject the divorce petition. A marriage could also be ended by a declaration made by the spouses before an officer of the Civil State. The first Soviet family Code of October 1918 retained these provisions and subsequently the family Code of 1926 of the Russo-Soviet Federation simplified the divorce procedure even more by placing divorce in all cases within the powers of the State organs. This also included the case where the petition was brought by only one of the spouses. In 1944 radical modifications were made to the family law, including divorce. This law departed from the legal recognition of a "marriage in fact" and in future only recognised marriages entailing conjugal rights and obligations which had been celebrated before State officials were held valid. At the same time it was ruled that divorce could only be obtained by the judicial method and then only if the Court was convinced of the hopelessness of maintaining a marriage. Certain restrictions in the 1944 law were done away with in 1965, in particular the provision for an attempt at conciliation before the first hearing on the failure of which a full enquiry was made by a higher Court. After that the spouses had to publish their intention to divorce in the press. Subsequently, in 1968 the basic principles were laid down, on the foundation of which the Codes of the Republics were created.

However, the divorce laws of the European socialist States only present a uniform picture on the principal question, notably on the principle of divorce on the complete breakdown of marriage, with divorce as the remedy. The Codes are uniform in that they all repudiate the principle of fault. They do not attach primary importance to this as a ground for divorce.

In respect of other legal consequences equally bearing on divorce, these laws found it necessary to resort to certain corrections based on contemporary criteria. Thus, they attached more or less great importance to the spouses' attitude of mind to the marriage, an attitude which could be improper from the moral viewpoint and which could lead to the breakdown of the marriage. They consider this attitude as a cause for the breakdown. As a result, they apply indirect sanctions to the spouse at fault, such as the withholding of maintenance, the prohibition of the use of the family name, or the regulation of the participation in the communal fund.

In this connection the Codes are divided into two groups. Most of the laws attach no direct legal consequence to the fault of the spouses for the divorce and thus they do not contain provisions relating to the judge's findings towards the question of the fault of one or both of the spouses, at the divorce hearing. The other group hold that a marriage cannot be dissolved on the petition of the spouse who is solely responsible for the breakdown of the marriage. This is particularly so in the Polish and Yugoslav Codes. The former Bulgarian and Czechoslovakian laws contained similar provisions, while in 1955 the Romanian Supreme Court held that a marriage could not be dissolved on a ground created by the petitioner. In fact, the Romanian codification of 1966 did not mention fault in connection with divorce, but the article providing for the maintenance of divorced spouses contains disadvantageous rules for the spouse on account of whose wrongs the divorce had been granted. These laws provide for a legal appraisal of the conjugal fault directly affecting the possible breakdown. This appraisal, though direct, is only secondary because, whether the innocent spouse consents or not, the possibility of divorce still exists, even if the party solely at fault initiates the proceedings. The relevant rule of the Code of the German Democratic Republic contains a special solution. This Code does not make divorce conditional upon fault but, approaches it from another standpoint. It provides that in divorce proceedings brought by one spouse the Court must carefully examine the history of the marriage and the interests of the children, but also the question as to whether a divorce would produce serious disadvantages for one of the spouses. This clearly refers to the defendant spouse. It is stressed that this examination is specially important in marriages that have lasted for some years, especially when the spouses are of more mature years. The appraisal of fault in these Codes cannot be considered only against the other spouse, for the guilty spouse may also claim the divorce.

With regard to the indirect influence of fault upon divorce, the Socialist laws are much more uniform. Most of the laws do not consider the wrong moral attitude of the spouse responsible for the breakdown of marriage as of no interest from the legal point of view and, consequently, apply sanctions. It is therefore not by chance that the three Codes of Bulgaria, Albania and Czechoslovakia, placed in the first group of Codes above, which attach importance to fault in divorce, lay down that the divorce decree should pronounce, only occasionally and at the request of one of the spouses, on the fault of one of them in establishing the reasons for the breakdown of the marriage. In Polish law, for example, this statement about fault is only ommitted when the spouses jointly claim that the Court should not state its view on the question of fault. The legal consequences are then as if neither of the spouses was guilty.

In this context, the Codes of Hungary and the Federated Soviet Republics do not speak of fault, but of "unworthiness". However, this has the same results as fault if the legal consequences are resolved at the time of the divorce. "Unworthiness" differs from fault leading to breakdown of marriage because the validation of certain claims relating to the unlawful removal of rights occurs considerably later than the event and the conduct of the spouse at fault towards the ex-spouse can also be taken into account.

Another delicate question in divorce in socialist legal systems is that of divorce by mutual consent, that is, when both spouses request the termination of the marriage bond. Here, the family codes of the Socialist countries generally allow, but do not require, that the agreement be taken into consideration. Two Codes clearly make exceptions to this rule, those of the Soviet and Bulgaria. The Soviet law, which is based on the Code of the Russian Federation of 1926, was unable, until, 1944 to consider whether the common consent of the spouses to divorce was sufficient for the ending of the marriage. This is because it recognised that life together in fact creates conjugal rights and obligations. This had the consequence that divorce was not within the judicial power and the petition of one spouse alone sufficed for the ending of a registered marriage celebrated by the officer of the Civil Status. This situation lasted for more than one and a half decades and also made its effect after 1944 in judicial practice, while academic opinions were divided on the matter and disapproved of the admission of mutual agreement by the Courts. However, according to statistics for 1958, in some 60% to 80% of divorce proceedings, both spouses had requested the termination of the marriage and the Courts had admitted these petitions almost without exception. There was frequent subsequent discussion on this point and divorce by mutual consent was finally adopted as a basic principle. In effect this establishes that, where spouses have agreed to the dissolution of their marriage, not only can the marriage be dissolved but it is not necessary to resort to a judicial procedure. The organs of the Civil Status are competent and do not examine the underlying reasons for the breakdown. In this case, however, common consent to divorce is not sufficient in itself, the parties must also come to an agreement with regard to the questions of division of property and maintenance. There is a further legal requirement in these circumstances, which is that the spouses have no minor children. In 1973 the Supreme Court of the Russian Federation laid down that the minor child of one of the spouses should not prevent the divorce where there is common consent.

The other socialist State whose family code recognises divorce by mutual consent is the Peoples' Republic of Bulgaria. Bulgarian law decrees that in the case of sincere and unshakeable mutual agreement, the marriage can be dissolved without the need for the Court to examine the factors influencing the spouses to present their petition. However, such a petition can only be presented after two years of marriage. Consequently, Bulgarian law raises mutual consent to the rank of an absolute ground for divorce and excludes the possibility of an appeal against the decree based on this ground. However, Bulgarian law makes extra conditions to the admission of a petition by mutual consent, in particular it requires that the spouses must agree on the exercise of parental rights, the maintenance of the children, their property interests, the use of the matrimonial home and alimony.

The Hungarian family law solution, after the legal amendments of 1974, is similar to that of Bulgaria. As already mentioned, the Hungarian Code of 1953 rejected mutual consent by the spouses as an absolute ground for divorce, as was formerly the case, and based divorce on the principle of breakdown of the marriage. However, the judicial practice had always been confronted with this question and, after the law had been in force for ten years, the Hungarian Supreme Court laid down a compulsory directive stating that the principle that a declaration of the common desire of the spouses based on a voluntary resolution, uninfluenced and freely entered into, seriously considered and final, is essential to a divorce petition. According to the Supreme Court, the fact of the presentation of such a petition is conclusive evidence that a marriage had irretrievably broken down, taken in conjunction with other circumstances. Consequently an enquiry into further reasons for the breakdown was superfluous. This attitude of the Supreme Court is reflected in the relevant provision of the amended law together with the added conditions that spouses presenting joint petitions for divorce must also mutually consent to provisions regarding the children, maintenance, the matrimonial home or else rely on the judge's decision in the matter. What basically distinguishes the Hungarian system described above from the relevant Bulgarian and Soviet systems is the fact that Hungarian law does not consider mutual agreement of the spouses as an absolute ground for divorce, but only as evidence from which it can be concluded that the marriage has irretrievably broken down. Yugoslav law also recognises that a divorce petition presented by mutual agreement is evidence of a breakdown of conjugal relations, but the partners have to support their mutual agreement by valid reasons and agree to the same provisions as in Hungarian law regarding the children and other similar factors.

The socialist legal systems not mentioned above do not contain provisions regarding the agreement of the spouses on divorce but, in the development of the Polish and Czechoslovak laws there was a period in which legal practice, following the more simple civil procedure, decreed divorce in cases where the spouses had requested it.

It is considered that there can only be a negative answer to the question as to whether the non-observance of the agreement between the spouses calls for a frank examination of their reasons for their petition and also as to whether the divorce procedure can be usefully employed as a stabilising influence on marriage. It is also considered, by the Hungarian Supreme Court, that a failure to observe any agreement to divorce often encourages the spouses to invent reasons to support it.

Before the War, married couples most frequently based their divorce petitions on two absolute grounds which figured in the Marriage Law of 1894, particularly desertion and neglect of the family through an immoral way of life. In 1938 these grounds were put in evidence in 73% and 25.7% of cases respectively, a total of 98.7%. The modification of family law in Hungary took place after the War when, apart from mutual consent, separate residence for five years was also declared to be an absolute ground for divorce. How the grounds for divorce were formed after that is seen in the course of legal proceedings. In 1946 desertion and neglect of the family figured in 23.2% and 6.1% respectively, a total of 29.3% of all grounds for divorce. At the same time, on the basis of common consent and of separate residence for five years, divorce was decreed in 38.4% and 31.4% respectively, a total of 69.9% of all cases. There is a notable connection between the numerical reduction of decrees on the two former grounds for divorce which required fault, from 98.7% to 29.3%, and in the decrees based on the new grounds irrespective of fault, which made it possible to discover the real reasons for the petitions. This leads inevitably to the conclusion that, in a large proportion of divorce proceedings, the spouses have disguised the real reasons for the breakdown of marriage because of necessity, since in the system recognising fault they could not obtain a decree.

At the same time, in the case of mutual consent, a detailed examination of the underlying reasons leading to the breakdown of the marriage can upset the tenuous relations between the parties, already balanced between extremes of feeling, the consequences of which primarily affect the children. Acceptance of mutual consent is not contrary to the public interest and to the interests of the children, as in this case it is one of the conditions of the breakdown. The preservation of an amicable link between separated parents and the avoidance of upsetting this link during divorce proceedings is necessary for the good of the children. There is no contradiction between a divorce decree based on the mutual consent of the spouses and the claim that a decree can be considered as one of the means of social defence against irresponsible petitions. In fact, if the dissolution of a marriage can only take place by a definite intention adequately supported by facts, then the Court cannot refuse to grant a decree of a marriage irretrievably broken down by referring to general prejudice.

Apart from these fundamental questions and when there are many differences, some legal systems held it necessary to enumerate some circumstances as grounds for divorce, such as in the laws of Yugoslavia and Albania. Yugoslav law even requires the assessment of circumstances based on, or independent of, fault as grounds for divorce. It is worth noting that the recent Codes of Montenegro and Serbia follow this basic difference, while Macedonian law not only does not require absolute grounds for divorce, but does not even provide for an assessment.

Two European socialist States, the Soviet Union, and Romania before 1974, decided to establish the legal consequences of a divorce decree according to special provisions. According to these laws a decree only comes into effect from

246

the date of registration with the State authorities and not from the date of the Court judgment. Romanian law requires that this State registration must be delayed for two years, the Soviet law requires three years. Omission of this delay renders the decree null in both countries.

The legal position of the child of divorced parents, the question of the family name and the maintenance of the ex-spouses must now be considered. The laws take into account the moral attitude of the spouses as to whether or not they attach importance to conjugal fault.

Divorced parents can decide by mutual agreement with regard to their parental rights towards their minor children in respect of their maintenance and up-bringing, but the Court has the right to examine and, if necessary, modify this agreement. If required, the Court can also place the child in the care of a third party. In this respect the guilt of the ex-spouse responsible for the breakdown of the marriage is not taken into account, even by those Codes that consider fault as a basis for divorce. Under Yugoslav law the Court can entrust the upbringing of the child to either spouse, irrespective of whose fault caused the breakdown. Before 1974 Hungarian law, failing agreement between the spouses, the Court took into account the age and sex of the child.

With regard to the family name, with the exception of the Polish and Hun-garian laws according to which a single woman retains the family name of her ex-husband, all European socialist countries allow the ex-spouses to use their own family name. Even those laws that recognise fault as a basis for divorce, consider fault to be irrelevant in this respect, and leave to the discretion of the spouse whose name changed on marriage to retain it, or resume the original name used before marriage. The Court can make rulings on the family name in certain instances. For example, in Bulgarian and Albanian law, although it is usual for the wife to revert to her maiden name after divorce, the Court may allow her to retain the name of her ex-husband if good reasons are advanced. Romanian law can implement this even when the ex-husband opposes it. In Hungary an ex-wife can be forbidden to use the name of her ex-husband if she has been imprisoned for some offence. The Yugoslav law of 1965 contained a similar provision.

In the whole of family law the most complex problems are those connected with the maintenance of divorced persons. Hence, this field contains the most varied legal provisions among the laws of European socialist States. In Soviet law the obligation of support and the right to maintenance have undergone important changes. In the majority of the Federated Soviet Republics before the basic laws of 1968, conjugal maintenance was only valid for one year after divorce. In another group of Codes the divorced spouse was entitled to maintenance for three years after divorce, while a third group of Codes imposed no time limit. The Codes granting maintenance for a short time did not date it from the time of the ex-spouse's inability to work; but the Codes giving maintenance for a longer, or unlimited, time considered the beginning of the inability to work as the date of the start of the maintenance.

With regard to the legal basis of maintenance, the Codes of the European socialist States refer to the poverty of the person entitled to it as the indispensable requirement to the right of maintenance. Certain Codes make an exception only in instances in which the fact of marriage has prevented the needy spouse from acquiring some professional skill necessary for his own support, or the further-ance of his scholastic studies. The laws of some countries required additional conditions apart from the poverty of the recipient. In some, maintenance could only be considered when the other spouse's inability to work dated from before the divorce or was acquired only a short time afterwards. In the German Demo-cratic Republic maintenance could only be granted when the spouses had cohabited for at least one year. Others stipulate that a short marriage entitles only to short-term grants.

The laws of all the socialist States attach importance to the moral aspect of the conjugal relations when considering maintenance, and consider the right to it forfeited by the spouse guilty of causing the breakdown of the marriage. How-ever, all Codes do not agree on this point or on the fundamental principles. There are diverse means of implementing this viewpoint. To summarise, however, although some legal systems attach importance to fault as a cause of divorce and reflect it in the conditions of maintenance, this point of view is declining.

III. Illegitimate children

As already mentioned in the introduction, the legal order of the European socialist States is phasing out the existing discriminations against the child born out of wedlock. Certain of the countries mentioned also express this principle in their Constitution and, where the fundamental laws omit a separate reference, family law has created positive rules in this connection. The attitude of the family codes to this question is chiefly characterised by the fact that they do not in fact use the expressions, "child born out of wedlock" and "illegitimate child". By this means these Codes show that they do not make any distinction with regard to the legal status of the child according to whether its parents are married or not. The Albanian law clearly established that "the family status of the child born out of wedlock is identical with that of the child of the marriage". There is the single presumption of paternity. The consanguinity of the child with its mother and the mother's parents is recognised in all cases and the identity of the father is established on the basis of the relevant presumptions relating the child with its father's family. The Hungarian draft law governing all questions of affiliation states the essential fact that the child's status is entirely identical both for the legitimate and the illegitimate child.

Consideration for the child also results in the regulation that the facts of the birth are disguised, even before the confinement, in a society which is still inclined to discriminate.

We will now discuss the single presumption of paternity constituting the affiliation of the marriage, the conditions governing certain variations of this presumption as well as its ending, as also the problems in connection with the family name, the child's maintenance, the exercise of parental rights, and the legal status of the child regarding the law of succession.

With regard to the affiliation of the child, the family law of the European socialist States departs from the thesis known in Roman law as "patrum nuptiae demonstrant."

The husband of the child's mother must be considered as its father if the child is born during the marriage or, in general, during a period of 300 days from the termination of the marriage. The same rule applies equally to the paternity of the child of parents who are, or were, living in a void marriage. It follows that, in the sense of the laws examined, the declaration of nullity of the marriage, for whatever reason, has no influence on the recognition of the child's affiliation. The question arises, however, as to who must be considered as the father of the child if the mother was divorced at the time of the presumed conception, or had become a widow and has subsequently remarried where, in the relevant period, two men in their capacity as husbands of the mother could possibly have been the father. This question is important because these legal systems do not recognise the "period of waiting" (the period of widowhood) established in some systems of law for the woman who is widowed or divorced.

Except for the Soviet basic rules which, without mentioning the question expressly, draw a similar conclusion, the Codes examined lay down that sometimes the previous spouse of the mother must be considered as the child's father. On this point, the Yugoslav basic law and the corresponding Serbian law of 1975, alone contain a different rule. According to these laws, in the case of the mother remarrying, her previous husband also qualifies as the father of a child born during the 270 days after the termination of the previous marriage who recognises the child as his own with the consent of the mother.

Most of the laws examined also contain provisions relating to the establishment of maternity. Thus the Albanian and Romanian laws contain detailed rules for the denial, the recognition, and the legal establishment of maternity, Serbian law applies the same rules as for the resolving or dispute of paternity, Hungarian law only legislates for the judicial confirmation of maternity. At the same time this also means the non-recognition of the maternity of another woman. The Supreme Court of the Soviet Union mentions the dispute of maternity and, concerning the countries examined whose Codes do not provide for this question, the academic view holds this problem to be soluble on the basis of the rules of procedure. As this presumption is that the mother's husband should be considered the man who is the father of her child, it is necessary to establish the identity of the father. The law of the European socialist States recognised many cases of this presumption concerning the paternity of the illegitimate child. In particular, each of the legal systems mentioned permits the voluntary recognition and judicial establishment of paternity. Hungarian, Yugoslav and German laws accept the effect of the presumption of paternity upon the subsequent termination of the marriage.

These laws recognise a voluntary declaration acknowledging paternity, if a man declares the same before the competent authorities. For the declaration to be valid, the mother's acknowledgment is necessary in respect of an irfant of a specific age. The Bulgarian, Yugoslav and Albanian laws make detailed provisions regarding the legal consequences of the acceptance or refusal of the acknowledgment. The last two laws arrive at the same solution as the laws of the other countries mentioned. This is that the mother's contribution—her opposition or her silence during a stated period—prevents the recognition from becoming definitive. Bulgarian law considers the omission of opposition of the recognition during a stated period as the equivalent of the contribution. In general, recognition can also be made with regard to an unborn child already conceived. The Hungarian, Polish and Czechoslovak practice does not examine the question whether the man who has recognised the child is in reality the father. On the other hand, the German, Romanian and Albanian Codes only permit recognition of a child already born. A child can be recognised after its death, according to the laws of Bulgaria, Poland, Romania and Hungary, except that the last named allows such posthumous recognition only in the case where descendants survive the child. The Serbian Code does not allow the declaration of paternity of a deceased child except by the judicial method. The Soviet law is unique in that it allows, in the case of the death of a man who during his lifetime maintained the child but was prevented for certain reasons from acknowledging paternity, that the Court may establish the recognition of paternity. But it is a special provision of Soviet law that the fact that the parents are married to other persons does not constitute any obstacle to the voluntary recognition of the child. Thus, we face here a very simple denial of the presumption of the husband's paternity, because it is only necessary that the mother should make a declaration together with the man in question in relation to the child's paternity. On occasion, however, the Soviet rules make it possible for the real father of the child to oppose the recognition and to demand verification of paternity by the judicial method. The Soviet rules also deal with the case where the mother makes a declaration, together with her husband, regarding the paternity of a child when in reality he is not the real father. In that case the real father can, in his turn, apply for the judicial declaration of his paternity. There is a similar rule, although without the premises existing in Soviet law, in the Albanian Code and the relevant Yugoslav law of 1947. In fact, according to these rules, the person who considers himself to be the father of an illegitimate child can oppose the presumption of paternity of another person who has recognised the child. This is not so, however, in the Serbian law of 1975.

It is characteristic of the uniform style of the family law of European socialist States that, when the identity of the child's father cannot be verified, either by the principal rule of presumption or on the basis of voluntary recognition, it is possible for a judicial declaration of paternity to be made. Some legal systems give judgment in favour of voluntary recognition, others grant recognition of paternity in cases where the father has not recognised his child. Others declare the paternity of a man who wishes to avoid the responsibility of caring for his offspring.

Soviet law permitted the judicial declaration of paternity without restriction until 1944. Until 1926, it even made it possible for several men to be made responsible for the joint obligation of the child's maintenance. The year 1944 brought radical changes. It abolished the mother's right to appeal to the Court for a declaration of the paternity of her illegitimate child, including the provision of necessaries. At the same time the law authorised the mother to receive State benefits of regular assistance for the maintenance of the child or to place him in a children's home, as had been possible previously. However, since the middle of the 1950s in the Supreme Soviet of the Soviet Union and in the Soviet literature on family law, attitudes which became more and more clear were taken with regard to the illegitimate child. These made it possible on the one hand to confirm the voluntary recognition of paternity and, on the other, to declare the identity of the father by the Court. In this context, people looked back to the fact that historically the effects of the War which had justified the provisions introduced in

1944 had come to an end. The regulation of the basic principles mainly satisfied these claims. It is true that they did not entirely return to the provisions of the 1926 legislation. According to that legislation the putative father could protest, during a period of one month, against the civil declaration of paternity. During a period of one year, he could oppose the declaration before a Court. Failing such protest, the man declared by the mother was registered as the father of the child. The 1933 regulations had authorised the State to register the paternity of the man indicated by the mother, regardless of his opposition, but reserving the possibility of rectification of the registration when the man brought an action in nullity. The basic principles facilitate the judicial declaration of paternity only in cases where the man voluntarily proves in some way that the child belongs to him, for example, if the man had lived in a common household with the mother before the birth of the child, or when they had reared and maintained the child together, or when there is proof that makes it probable that the man has recognised his paternity. These principles disclose the existence of such circumstances as relate to the fact that the man and the mother were together involved with the creation of a family.

Albanian law closely resembles these provisions, mentioning among the facts relating to paternity, the rape of the mother, the promise of marriage, or the indirect verification of paternity in the course of penal or civil proceedings. The Albanian Code removes all these restriction in the case where the mother was a minor at the time of conception.

The restrictions in Romanian law are a little different. An action for the declaration of paternity can only be brought within one year from the birth of the child, or of the denial of the previous presumption of paternity, except when the mother has cohabited with the putative father, provided that the limitation period begins from the end of these circumstances. Details vary between the countries. Thus, the Bulgarian, Yugoslav and Romanian laws contain references to paternity being established by the judicial method only when the man has refused to undertake the obligations himself. Other systems are more concrete in that they require as a condition for the judicial declaration of paternity proof that the man and the mother had sexual intercourse during the period of conception. According to Hungarian law, the Court can declare as father of the child the man who (a) cohibited with the mother during a longer time during the time of conception in conditions indicating a communal life, or (b) had intimate relations with the mother during the same period. From a careful scrutiny of all these circumstances, a reasonable conclusion can be arrived at that the child resulted from the relationship. German, Czechoslovak and Hungarian rules refer to the inability of establishing a man's paternity, or to the exclusion of his paternity under certain circumstances.

The lack of a similar legal provision in the laws of other socialist countries does not prevent judicial practice or learned writings from taking a similar view. Where there is a reference in the rules to the possibility of legal action, intercourse during the critical period must have occurred. Paternity cannot be established in the case of others, if there is impotence or a negative result from a blood test. However, *exceptio plurium concubentium* is not brought in and, according to Polish law, the fact that the mother had intercourse with another man during the relevant period cannot serve as a ground for the denial of paternity even when the paternity of the other man is the more likely. Similarly, in German law in the case of equal probability of paternity, it is necessary to establish the paternity of the defendant but, if the paternity of another is more probable, as suggested by the plaintiff, the latter can be brought into the proceedings and declared to be the father. In German law if a blood test is ordered it is obligatory and can be imposed by subpoena but, in the other countries under review, a refusal to undergo the test is a reason for a decision in favour of the other party.

Apart from the above mentioned grounds, Hungarian and German law also attribute paternity to a subsequent agreement to marry. This is not identical with the true *legitimatio per subsequens matrimonium*, which alone gives rise to the integrated family. While the German law attributes the birth to the expectation of a marriage between the child's parents, the Hungarian law regards it as im- material whether the man marrying the child's mother is really the child's father. In any case it is necessary that the husband should recognise the child before a State official, before the celebration of the marriage. Yugoslav law contains a similar provision that, on the marriage of the parents, the child must be con- sidered as born of the marriage, but the husband's paternity must be established either by recognition or by judicial decree. Yugoslav literature calls this 'legitima- tion' and, in this case only, the illegitimate child obtains family status with the legitimate child in all respects, including maintenance and succession rights. German law makes certain restrictions for illegitimate children in the right of succession and makes a condition that the child be an adult. Hungarian law also admits maintenance without proof of paternity. Here it is a case where a decree, while not establishing a relationship in family law, or consanguinity, lays the obligation of maintenance for a child on a man who had intercourse with the mother during the time of conception and whose probable paternity cannot be excluded although the Court may not be convinced of it.

The laws also recognise the practice of the denial of the presumption of paternity, but this can only take place in an action brought within a short period, usually a year or six months. It is intended to protect the status of the child in the family. Some laws also admit the reinstatement of the recognition of paternity, others take into consideration the latest possible date for conception from which it is probable that the child was not conceived during the marriage. It is enough to deny the presumption of paternity; the husband makes a declaration ex- cluding his paternity during the nullity proceedings. However, this does not apply when the mother can prove that, in the presumed period of conception, she had intercourse with her husband after he first knew she was pregnant. The putative father, the child and occasionally the mother have the right to bring an action for nullity, also, in Soviet law, against the man who considers himself to be the father of the child. Some laws permit the latter to oppose the paternity of the man recognising the child. In some laws an action to nullify the presumption of paternity of the supposed father can only be brought in his lifetime.

An action to nullify the presumption of maternity can be brought on the same lines as a similar action with regard to paternity.

The Codes of three European socialist States contain provisions concerning the legal effects of artificial insemination with regard to birth and the presumption of paternity. When this is effected with the consent of the husband an action for denial of paternity cannot take place, as affiliation is the consequence of medical intervention.

With regard to the surname of the illegitimate child, the legal systems, despite their concern with equality before the law, were obliged to differentiate according to whether the identity of the child's father had been established or not. However, this is not to the disadvantage of an illegitimate child because, even as the legitimate child may do, he can adopt his mother's surname when she has kept her maiden name after marriage. If the identity of the child's father was not confirmed, the child takes the mother's surname. In some laws the mother, with the consent of her husband, can choose any family name for her child, even for a legitimate child. In Hungary a mother may indicate a fictitious person as the child's father, which will also affect the surname taken.

When the father's identity is confirmed, in general the illegitimate child takes the family name in the same way as the legitimate child. He may take his father's surname or retain the previous name. In Serbia this only applies to a child who has been recognised, whose parents have married, or who has been declared born of the marriage. When a mother makes a subsequent marriage and takes the name of her husband, the child's name also changes automatically unless, on reaching a stated age, he also gives his consent.

When the presumption of paternity has been overthrown, the child takes the name of his mother, whether or not this includes the addition of the husband's name.

When both parents are unknown the relevant authority is obliged to give him a name and establish his rights.

With regard to parental supervision of the illegitimate child, this reverts to the mother alone, who has exclusive rights and obligations of a parent until the identity of the father is proved on the basis of one of the presumptions.

If affiliation has been established with regard to both parents, the same rules as those for legitimate children must be applied with regard to the rights and obligations of the parents. Romanian law applies the rules in the case of divorced parents with regard to the residence of an illegitimate child. Generally, parental rights are exercised by the parent who has custody of the child, usually the mother unless the parents come to some mutual arrangement. On essential questions of the child's best interests, the father must also be consulted unless he has been given sole parental rights by the Court. When he has not been authorised to exercise parental supervision, he must have the right of access and communication with the child in the custody of his mother. The guardianship authority alone can deprive him of this right if the interests of the child require it.

The situation with regard to child maintenance is the same as in the case of parental supervision and the use of the surname. Until the father's identity is established, the obligation to maintain the child is vested solely in the mother. There is a partial exception in the laws of Poland and Czechoslovakia in which the father, who is not the mother's husband but whose paternity is probable, can be ordered by the Court to maintain the mother and to reimburse her for the pregnancy and delivery costs, over a period ofsix months. For this to take effect it is not necessary that the child be born alive. However, should the Court later establish the paternity of another man, that man can be ordered to reimburse the first man's expenditure.

With regard to succession, the child takes priority over all others having a claim and parents are required to support their minor child by putting his interests before their own. If this does not create enough difficulties for them, they are also required to maintain their older child while he is still a student. Some legal systems also require a brother to support another brother who may be in need, though some laws only require this for a minor brother. This obligation is sometimes extended to parents-in-law in respect of their son- or daughter-in-law who has been brought to live in the family. It is said that the provision of maintenance is in keeping with the concept of communal social life.

There are various methods of establishing the amount of maintenance for a child, some more complicated than others. Some European socialist States set fractions of the income, such as one-fourth for one child, one-third for two children, or one-half for several children; others base their calculations on a percentage, such as 20%, 40%, 50% in similar cases. Variations of income also have to be taken into account and the Court makes rulings with regard to this. Apart from the duty of maintenance, parents may have to contribute more for a child who is seriously ill, infirm, or still at school. The State may be called upon to provide maintenance when the parents' obligation to do so has not been discharged, though failure to observe the obligation also involves penal sanctions.

In general, the legitimate child and the illegitimate child have the same rights of succession, but the German Democratic Republic and Yugoslavia have different rules. German law, seeking to protect the interests of family unity, only allows the illegitimate child to inherit from his father, on his majority, if his paternity has been established either by recognition or by Court decree and if he still lives at home and requires maintenance. Yugoslav law contains a restriction on inheritance with regard to the relatives of the child's father.

A child is, in turn, liable for the maintenance of his parents if they are in need and he is in a position to provide for them.

CHAPTER XI. CIVIL PROCEDURE AND THE REFORM OF FAMILY LAW. THE VIEW OF SOCIALIST LAW

by Savelly Zilberstein

I. Equality between spouses

The Personal Relationships

Although a major part of this book deals with certain essential features of family law, it may be suggested that civil procedure cannot be readily understood without the substantive law which it is intended to bring into operation. In other words substantive law and procedure cannot be dissociated from each other. It is hoped this view will emerge clearly from the account presented below. Moreover, the reference to the rules of substance as they exist in Romanian law will permit the exposition of certain particular features of Socialist law which, perhaps, have not yet been mentioned but which ought to be mentioned if one wishes to give an idea of the totality of the family law of the Socialist countries of Europe. We shall also observe through the rules which will be mentioned, how much concern there is—in the terms of the programme of the Communist Party of Romania, adopted by the Eleventh Congress of the Party, a programme which carries the imprint of the personality of Nicolae Ceausescu, Secretary-General of the Romanian Communist Party and President of the Socialist Republic of Romania—in continually developing and perfecting the judicial activity in conformity with the new realities of Romania, on the basis of the ideology of dialectical and historical materialism, and on the basis of the ideal of Socialism and Communism.

The equality between spouses

This is one of the fundamental principles of Romanian family law, a principle which is no more than a manifestation of another, more general, principle proclaimed in article 17 of the Romanian Constitution of 1965. In its first two paragraphs it provides that, "The citizens of the Socialist Republic of Romania, without distinction of nationality, race, sex or confession, have equal rights in all areas of life, economic, political, legal, social and cultural.

The State guaranteed equality of rights to its citizens. No restriction on these rights and no discrimination in their exercise based upon nationality, race, sex or religion are tolerated."

Already, article 21 of the Constitution of 13th April 1948 had provided that a woman has equal rights with a man in all aspects of the life of the State, economic, social, cultural, political, as well as in private law. This provision was taken up again and strongly stressed in article 83 of the Constitution of 27th September 1952. The status of inferiority of women is now a matter of history in Romania.

Equality between spouses can be envisaged, in the first place, from the point of view of the relations of the spouses between themselves. These relations can either be personal, or relations concerning property. This is the distinction which is normally drawn. In respect of the one type as of the other, it is convenient to mention from the beginning the provision of a principle contained in article 1, paragraph 3, of the Family Code:[1]

"In the relations between the spouses . . . the husband and wife have equal rights";[2] again, article 25 of the Family Code states: "The husband and wife have equal rights and obligations in marriage." This is the reason why—to begin with personal relationships—according to article 2 of the Family Code the spouses (just as other members of the family) are obliged to give each other the moral and material support which each may need.[3] This is also why, according to article 27, the spouses decide by mutual agreement upon all matters that affect the marriage. Moreover, according to the same article 27, at the end of the marriage ceremony the future spouses must declare to an authorised officer of the civil State, by what name they have agreed to be known during the marriage. The article specifies that the spouses may keep the surname they had before marriage, just as they may take the surname of one or other of the spouses, or their joint surnames. Lastly, according to article 29, the spouses are obliged to contribute to the expenses of the household in proportion to their means.

How are all these provisions put into effect? It is in this respect that the rules of procedure become relevant. To be truly effective, substantive law must rely upon the civil procedure. In case of diagreement the spouses have the right to resort to the Courts. It should be made clear here that, when we speak of Courts, we mean the common law Courts. In fact, in the Socialist Republic of Romania there are other institutions which have jurisdiction. In particular, for a whole

---

1. In Romania today Family Law consists of an autonomous branch of law. Detached from the civil law, it was incorporated in a Family Code of 4th January 1954. This became operative on 1st February 1954. The question has sometimes been asked in learned writings in Socialist countries whether this separation between the Civil Code and the Family Code is really justified. In this connexion it is important to bear in mind that the relationships of the Civil Law are relationships, in the first place, of a patrimonial character. This is not the case—or is no longer the case—for family relationships. In reality this is precisely the difference which provides the justification for such a separation. However, it must be made clear that where there are no special rules in the Family Code, or, more generally, in the statutes dealing with family law, the rules of the Civil law must be applied (so far as they are compatible with the nature of the family relationships). I.e. for all branches of the law which have from time to time been separated from the Civil law, the latter represents the common law, and in this respect both the written and the case law are unanimous. It should be added in order to cover all the Socialist countries of Europe, that in all these countries family law consists of an autonomous branch of law, whether the law is contained in a Family Code or in special laws ("fundamental laws") which constitute the family law.

2. The quotations from the Family Code, reproduced above between inverted commas, are reproduced according to the translation given in the official edition in foreign languages (Ed. note: the text above is a translation from the French).

3. The reference to material support clearly also represents an aspect of relations of a patrimonial character. The author considers, however, that a distinction must be drawn between personal relationships and relations concerning property. The obligation to agree among themselves concerning material support arises, in this classification, from personal relationships.

series of disputes between natural persons, there are what are called the Commissions of Judgment.[4]

However, it should be mentioned that disputes between spouses, arising from their position of equality, can never be brought, in whatever form, before the Commissions of Judgment. Jurisdiction for deciding such disputes belongs exclusively to the common law Courts.[5]

Let us now see which are the disputes that occur in respect of the relationship between spouses. It has already been said that it is necessary to distinguish

---

4. The Commissions of Judgment were created by Law No. 59 of 27th December 1968 re-enacted, after some modification, on 9th March 1973. These Commissions were created in response to the constant preoccupation with reinforcing the legal means for the defence of socialist legality. They were also created in order to strengthen the more active participation of the masses in the promotion of a just attitude with regard to work and to socialist property. The object was to ensure correct behaviour in society and to bring about a concentration of the activity of welfare organs into a unique jurisdiction and a unique procedure.

The Commissions of Judgment function alongside the organs of management, enterprises, other economic organisations, the institutions and other socialist organisations of the State and also the co-operative organisations and the other social organisations. They also function alongside the executive committees of the popular councils, the municipalities and the sectors of the municipality of Bucharest or, in respect of town and communes, alongside the executive offices of the popular councils. (For the administrative organisation, see below). It should be stressed that these Commissions of Judgment are elected by general meetings of workers or, when they relate to commissions functioning alongside the committees or executive offices of popular councils, by the meetings of the popular councils. As organs of social welfare, the Commissions of Judgment are also sometimes Courts, especially in the case when rules of social behaviour are lacking (art. 11) and also under certain conditions (art. 27) in circumstances covered by penal law.

At the same time, the Court aspect is more evident in some labour disputes or in disputes between a co-operative and its members, or in other patrimonial litigation. There, decisions have the force of *res judicata*. In other cases, the social welfare aspect is different from the Court aspect, the welfare aspect being realised, above all, by the attempt at conciliation by the parties when it is a question of certain offences or of certain patrimonial disputes.

However, the control exercised by the Law Courts over the Commissions of Judgment confirm the preeminent position of the former.

5. According to Law no. 58 of 27th December 1968 on judicial organisation, the Law Courts of Romania are: (a) the Justices of the Peace; (b) the District courts; (c) the Supreme Court; (d) Courts Martial, which are special courts. The District Courts can have several sections (civil and penal).

All disputes for which the law has not provided other jurisdiction are within the jurisdiction of the Justices of the Peace at first instance; and jurisdiction at the last instance is regulated by law. There are District Courts in each department, while the Municipal Court of Bucharest has a substantive jurisdiction which is of the same order. The District Courts try, at first instance, suits provided for by the law, either by reason of their value (more than 15,000 lei) or by reason of their nature. (Ed. note: On January 1 1977 the commercial rate for £1 =

The main task of District Courts is that of pronouncing upon appeals against sentences pronounced by the Justices of the Peace acting within their territorial limits. A jurisdiction of a special character of the District Courts is to pronounce upon the extraordinary appeals introduced by the Procurator-General against judgments pronounced by the Justices of the Peace at last instance.

The Supreme Court (Civil section) decides appeals against decisions pronounced by the District Courts at first instance. It also decides on the extraordinary appeals introduced by the Procurator-General against all first judgments, with the exception of the extraordinary appeals within the jurisdiction of the District Courts. The Supreme Court, sitting as a full court, issues directive-decisions aimed at the uniform application of the law by all the law Courts.

personal relationships—which are the most important—from relations concerning property. With regard to personal relationships, it will be recalled that article 2 of the Family Code relates to the obligation of the spouses to agree between themselves in respect of the moral support to which each is entitled. For example such support is the attentions of a personal nature which one of the spouses is required to give to the other when occasioned by the age of a spouse, his or her state of health, or an informity of some kind. The law describes such moral support. Is it a question of a moral obligation or, despite the term used by the law, is it a question of a legal obligation, that is to say, one for which there is a sanction? This is a problem that has been widely discussed. Several authors argue that it is a question of a legal obligation. However, it is a legal obligation that shows a peculiarity in that its execution is assured not only by civil procedure but also by the Penal Code. Consequently, from this standpoint, it can be considered in the average case, where the objective is to ensure the execution of an obligation of substantive law, as serving the purpose of the rules of procedure.

In fact, according to the Romanian Penal Code[6], article 305a: "If a person who is bound by the legal obligation to maintain commits, in respect of the person who has the right to maintenance, one of the following acts:

(a) he abandons, or expels, or leaves that person without assistance, thus exposing him or her to physical or mental suffering, . . . he shall be punished (for the act provided at (a) above) by three months to two years imprisonment or a fine . . ."

There is therefore a sanction which the law has introduced to punish the refusal to provide moral support. Since there is a sanction, it cannot be said that this is not a legal obligation. Indeed, this is not the only sanction. In certain circumstances, failure to observe this obligation could provide grounds for the divorce of the spouses. This will be considered separately.

In discussing article 2 of the Family Code we must also consider the obligation of the spouses to agree, as between themselves, on the material support for each other. Here we must mention the provisions of article 86 which provides, in respect of the allowance for necessaries which the spouses (and other members of the family) are obliged to accept as between themselves, that such an allowance is due to a person who finds himself or herself in need because, owing to physical inability to work, he cannot earn his living by his labour.[7]

During the marriage, the right of a spouse to the allowance for necessaries is enforced by an action brought before a magistrate. This is clearly a personal action. The jurisdiction is territorial and depends on the domicile of the defendant, assuming that the spouses do not have—which, as we shall see, is theoretically possible—a common domicile. This is an application of article 5 of the Code of Civil Procedure. The application will be brought before the Court of the domicile of the defendant. If the domicile of the defendant is located in a foreign country, or if there is no known domicile, the application will be brought before the Court of his or her residence in Romania. If that residence is not known, then

---

6. The current Penal Code dates from 21st June 1968. It came into effect on 1st January 1969. It was modified and re-enacted on 23rd April 1973.
7. A minor, however, need not prove the cause of the need in which he may find himself (art. 86, para. 3, of the Family Code).

jurisdiction is exercised by the Court of the domicile or of the residence of the applicant.

The situation is no different in the case of divorce. Article 41 of the Family Code provides, in fact, that in respect of the regulation of divorce, the obligation to maintain continues to subsist between the spouses up to the moment when the divorce becomes final. But what of the period after the divorce? Assuming that a separate action has not been initiated, it is the decree of divorce that regulates the allowance for necessaries. This is so because the spouse has a right to maintenance even though divorced, provided that the incapacity to work existed before the marriage or provided that it arose during the marriage. A divorced spouse also has the right to maintenance if the incapacity to work arose during the year after the dissolution of the marriage. If the incapacity was determined by circumstances connected with the marriage, an action for maintenance could clearly be initiated even after the dissolution of the marriage. Such action will be brought according to the rule of jurisdiction established by article 5 of the Code of Civil Procedure. However, it should be emphasised that, according to article 41 of the Family Code, the spouse whose fault has led to the divorce does not have the right to claim the benefit of the provisions just mentioned—that is, the provisions granting maintenance in spite of the divorce—except for one year after the dissolution of the marriage. In any event, the right to maintenance ceases upon the remarriage of the spouse who enjoys the benefit. Last, it is generally recognised, even before the legislative modification that has been indicated, that in order to meet the need of the spouse who has a right to such maintenance, provisional measures may be taken by means of an application in chambers under art. 581 of the Code of Civil Procedure. According to that article, in cases of urgency the Court can order provisional measures for the preservation of a right that may be impaired by the delay, to prevent imminent damage which could not be compensated, and to set aside the obstacles that might defeat a compulsory execution. The order may be issued *ex parte*. This is so even where there would be proceedings on the substance of the right. The order is provisional and executory. The Court can decide that the execution should be effected without notice and without delay.

Today a solution is expressly provided by article 6132 of the Code of Civil Procedure.[8] It provides that for the whole duration of the proceedings the Court can decide, by way of an order by the presiding judge, upon provisional measures in respect of the person to whom a child is to be entrusted. These measures concern the obligation to maintain, the amount to which the children are entitled, and the use of the family residence. As it realates to everyday life, it is important to give immediately the means of subsistence to the spouse who fulfils the conditions imposed by the law. It is hardly necessary to add that, since the factual circumstances may change, the total sum of the maintenance may be reduced or increased, according to the circumstances. To this end, at the level of Civil Procedure, it is necessary to bring an action—a personal action—before the appropriate magistrate under article 5 of the Code of Civil Procedure. It is of

---

8. This provision was introduced by Decree No. 174 of 1st August 1974, which modified the Code of Civil Procedure.

some interest to recall that, as has been seen above, the Penal Code is used to support the application of the Family Code. Article 3051 of the Penal Code has already been noted. Articles 305b and c add: "If a person who is bound by the legal obligation to maintain commits, in respect of the person who has the right to maintenance, one of the following acts:

. . .

(b) fails to perform, in bad faith, the obligation to maintain provided by the law;

(c) fails to pay, in bad faith, during a period of two months the maintenance which has been judicially ordered, such person shall be punished for such acts as provided by (b) with three months to two years imprisonment or a fine, and for such is as provided by (c) with six months to three years imprisonment."

It is easy to see how these statutory provisions are applied in the different situations which have been envisaged. In addition, refusal to provide maintenance of the spouse who fulfils the conditions prescribed by the law can lead, in certain circumstances, to the dissolution of the marriage by divorce. Moreover, in view of its importance, the right of the spouses to maintenance (like the right to such allowances in general) is strengthened by other guarantees and also by other means of protection, both of which arise from the rules of Civil Procedure.

To take first the means of protection. In Romanian law there are two kinds of attachment. One with a Court validation order and the other without such an order. Thus, when it is a question of maintenance, article 461 of the Code of Civil Procedure provides: "In respect of the sums due by virtue of maintenance when compulsory execution relates to the salary[9] or other income resulting from work, as provided by article 409, the Court which has issued the order for execution shall decide, as a matter of routine, that attachment should be effected. In these cases, the attachment is enforceable without the need for a validating judgment, the third person upon whom it is levied being obliged to pay to the creditor the sum charged on the salary of the debtor or on his other income derived from work, within the period of five days from the date on which the payment was due. Appeals against the writ of attachment can be brought, within a period of fifteen days from the date of the first payment made to the debtor sued by the attached third party, after the order of execution of the writ of attachment."

As regards the guarantees, the beneficiary of the maintenance enjoys a right of priority in relation to other creditors. In fact, according to article 409, paragraph 2, of the Code of Civil Procedure, to cite only the article which is most often applied, if there are several compulsory executions on the same salary, they cannot all be satisfied except to the extent that the total does not exceed one-half of the basic nett monthly pay. Thereafter the following order of priority applies:

(a) maintenance

---

9. Socialist law no longer speaks of a salary. It is a question—a new vision that has emerged from new realities—of the reward for work which is charged on the remuneration fund. This is stated in art. 3(1) of Law No. 57 of 1st November 1974 "on the remuneration according to the quantity and quality of the work". The remuneration fund represents that part of the national revenue allocated to individual consumption, which is distributed directly to those who work.

(b) the payment of damages due as compensation for the damage caused by death or by injury to the person

(c) the payment of sums due to the State as duties and taxes

(d) the payment of damages due for the compensation for damage caused to socialist property

(e) all other debts.

To sum up, it can be seen that care has been taken to ensure the realisation of the right to maintenance. In this respect the role and the importance played by civil procedure can clearly be seen.

There is little to say on the subject of article 29 of the Family Code: "The spouses are bound to contribute, each according to his means, to the expenses of the household." The text is rarely commented upon by the workers. Nor does there seem to be any case law upon it. However, it is necessary to underline the fact that, if the wife must contribute to the expenses of the household in proportion to her means, this does not mean, as will be seen later, that the care which she takes of the household will not be considered as a contribution in the sense of article 29. On the contrary, the unanimous view held is that it should be recognised as such and that this care can be estimated as the equivalent of the earnings of the husband from his work in the process of production.[10]

However, if there is little to say on the subject of article 29 of the Family Code, there is much to say on the subject of the domicile of the spouses. Article 26 of the Family Code expects, as has been seen, that the spouses should decide by agreement between them, upon all matters concerning the marriage. It is not useful to consider here which are these matters concerning the marriage. But there is one question which is particularly important and which should be mentioned; it relates to the domicile of the spouses.

In this respect it is clear that the common domicile of the spouses is of the nature or essence of the relations between the spouses. One could not conceive, in principle, that the spouses should live separately; but there could be situations— those that are really exceptional—in which the spouses would be obliged, even though temporarily, to have distant domiciles. But in that case the separate domiciles would result from an agreement between the spouses, which itself is evidence of the fact of the equality between them. It follows that, if the spouses have decided nothing on the subject of domicile, the latter can only be common. Let us consider what the solution would be if it is supposed that, at a given moment without asking the consent of the other spouse, one of the spouses wished to have a separate domicile, or if it is supposed that the spouses cannot come to an agreement to have separate domiciles. It is clear that, as a result of the equality existing between the spouses, the problem could not be resolved by one of them imposing his or her will upon the other. In the case of the wife, the restoration of the common domicile *manu militari* is a thing of the past. It is doubtful if the spouses can have recourse to a Court to decide between them. There are cases where the Family Code expressly provides for the possibility of

---

10. See Serbanescu, *Codul Familiei Cementat Si Adnotat*, Bucharest, Ed. Stiintifică, 1963, p. 48. The Romanian literature on this and other topics dealt with in this chapter is ample. However, the bibliographical references have been reduced to a minimum. It was not thought useful to refer here to all the learned literature, nor even all the authoritative works.

recourse to law. But, generally speaking, there is no legislative authority for this particular problem. However, it would seem that in the absence of such a statutory provision, it would be contrary to the principles of Romanian Family Law to ask the Court to intervene in a dispute, whether more or less serious, which may arise between spouses. Save for exceptional situations, notably those provided for by the law, the spouses must decide between themselves what suits them best, just as they will have to bear the consequences of the decisions they take. That is to say, in order to resolve the conflicts from time to time between the spouses as regards their domicile, from the procedural point of view the only possibility is that of divorce, a possibility—as will be seen—which should only be used with the greatest circumspection. It is for the judges to try to effect a reconciliation between the spouses regarding rifts which are often the result of a misunderstanding.

As is normally the case in learned literature, it must be added that equality between the spouses means that the husband has no right of control over the correspondence and over the social relationships of the wife, just as the wife does not require the consent of the husband in order to pursue a profession or occupation. The Family Code does not mention these points but the matter is nevertheless clear in law. If the husband is tempted to act differently, that is, to assume the rights which he no longer has, and to make difficulties for his wife, the judges who hear the divorce suit will try to act as conciliators between the opposing views or opinions which, as has been said before, are usually the result of a misunderstanding.

This account of the personal relationships between the spouses cannot be concluded without a reference to the sanction in respect of the obligation of fidelity. However, Family Law does not make express mention of it. As regards the wife, the obligation is the foundation of the presumption established in article 53 of the Family Code, according to which a child born during the marriage of its parents is the child of both spouses. And, as a matter of principle as much for the husband as for the wife, the obligation of fidelity results from the very nature of the socialist family, which is based on affection and is untrammelled by material considerations.

We must consider what the sanction is for this obligation of fidelity and what is the role played by the Civil Procedure in this respect. Of course, if there is a breach of the obligation by the wife or by the husband, the only sanction is divorce. In socialist law, however, divorce appears to have a particular complexion. It has already been mentioned that this will be dealt with separately. In doing so, note will be made of the circumstances in which divorce can be granted and what are the grounds in general that justify the dissolution of a marriage. It should be added that here the Penal Law also has a role to play. According to article 304 the fact that a spouse has had sexual relations outside marriage is punished by imprisonment, from one month to six months, or by a fine.[11]

II. Relations regarding property and divorce

In the socialist family, personal relationships are the most important, but they are not the only kind of relationships. There are also relations concerning

---

11. The penal action can only be initiated at the instance of the innocent spouse.

property and these must be mentioned in turn so that the whole picture may be fully understood. According to the Family Code, the principle is that certain goods that have been bought during the marriage by one or other of the spouses, constitute what is called the common fund. Apart from the common fund, each spouse is also entitled to own exclusively his or her own personal property. It is not useful to enumerate here the assets which, according to articles 30 and 31 of the Family Code, constitute the common fund or the separate property. Suffice it to say that the common fund is reserved, in the first place, to the creditors of both spouses, in other words, for the payment of debts incurred during the marriage and, in principle, in the interests of the marriage. This is the purport of article 32.

There is no need to repeat the legislative texts which have been referred to previously which, recognising the realities of life, establish the equality in the relationships between the spouses. It is how this equality manifests itself in the relations concerning property, and the way in which Civil Procedure intervenes to ensure the realisation of this equality, that is important now.

First, the assets will belong to the common fund, or will be part of the separate property according to the provisions of articles 30 and 31, without reference to the question of whether it is the husband or the wife who is involved. Apart from equality as regards the principle, there is also equality as regards the means of proof. With regard to the common fund, the final paragraph of article 30 of the Family Code is categorical: "The origin of the common fund need not be proved." Whether the goods have been acquired during the marriage by the husband or by the wife, the law applies to both the common fund and to any separate property. No distinction of any sort is recognised.

We must go back to a provision which figures, not in the Family Code, but in Decree No. 32 of 31st January 1954 to discover the position of the regime of separate property with regard to the means of proof. This Decree brought into effect the Family Code. Decree No. 31 of 31st January 1954, which concerned physical persons and legal persons[12], must also be referred to. Moreover, according to the first paragraph of article 5 of Decree No. 32, proof that an asset is part of separate property can be brought, as between the spouses, by any means available.[13] It will be seen that third persons may also be interested, indeed, very closely interested, to know if an asset is part of the common fund or not. When the interests of third parties are concerned, the security of legal transactions requires that the means of proof should be those of the ordinary law. Also paragraph 2 of article 5 of the Decree No. 32 of 1954 lays down that, in

---

12. Decree No. 31 of 1954 embodies the principle of protection of the civil right of natural persons and of legal persons and the principle of the exercise of these rights in conformity with their economic and social aim. The Decree also regulates the civil capacity—capacity to enjoy and capacity to exercise—the name and the domicile of a natural person, the judicial declaration of absence and of death, and also the proof of civil status. In relation to legal persons, this important decree provides the conditions for the existence of a legal person or socialist organisation, for the exercise of its rights and the performance of its obligations. Lastly, Decree No. 31 of 1954 is also concerned with the protection of personal rights of a non-patrimonial character.
13. The provision spoken of in the text is found in the Decree which brings the Code into effect, since the second paragraph of art. 5 contains, in relation to that which is laid down by the first paragraph, a regulation of a transisional nature.

respect of marriages concluded before the coming into effect of the Family Code, proof that an asset is part of separate property can be made, even as regards third parties, by all means of proof.

However, equality between the spouses does not end there. The first paragraph of article 35 of the Family Code is explicit with regard to the administration of the common fund, and lays down that it must be administered by the spouses, acting together. Thus, it is necessary that there should be agreement between the spouses. However, the second paragraph of article 35 adds a further expression of equality by stating that each spouse, when acting alone, is presumed to have the consent of the other. If consent has not been given and the third party, who is a party to the contract, knew it, then the act of administration can be annulled. The action must be brought before a magistrate who has territorial jurisdiction determined by the domicile of the defendant. This is an application of the ordinary law.

The rules providing for acts of administration have their equivalent, in the same legislative texts, in respect of acts of disposition. This is a subtle distinction, but an important one. According to article 35 paragraph 2, one of the spouses cannot alienate an immovable. Equally, he or she cannot burden himself with a real right without the express consent of the other spouse—the 'express consent' should be noted.

If it is supposed that the rules have not been respected there will be an action in nullity, for the purpose of combating the irregular act, brought before the Justice of the Peace whose territorial jurisdiction is that of the court of the place where the immovable is situated.

A problem of procedure, raised more than once, is that of knowing whether the spouses have at their disposal, during the marriage, what is known as an action for verification. This is an action, the sole object of which is to determine what property constitutes the common fund and what represents separate property. The difficulty comes from the fact that, according to the provisions of the Code of Civil Procedure (article 111), the action for verification is only admissible when the plaintiff has no substantive action (action for realisation) available.

Legal authors are divided in their opinion since, it is said, that according to article 36 the "realisation" can be achieved by an action for partition.[14] It is submitted that the better view is that an action for verification is admissible.[15]

Lastly, the common fund also poses the problem of the liquidation of the community. On this subject article 36 of the Family Code lays down, in the first paragraph, that in the case of dissolution of the marriage by divorce, the common fund is to be divided in conformity with the decision of the spouses. If the spouses do not arrive at an agreement, the Court must decide. Paragraph 2 adds a provision, which should be stressed, that for good reason the common fund, either in its entirety or in part, may be divided by judicial decision even during the marriage. The fund thus divided takes on the character of separate property.

---

14. For the text of article 36, see next paragraph.
15. This is also the point of view embodied in the directive-decision of the Supreme Court, sitting in plenary session, No. 3 of 1974, *Revista Romana de Drept* No. 6 of 1974, p. 39.

The assets that have not been the object of this partition, as well as assets subsequently acquired, remain part of the common fund.

In this matter of the liquidation of the community one of the main problems is to know whether, at the time of the dissolution of the marriage, the common fund is terminated as a matter of law or whether it is necessary that a voluntary partition, or the action for partition, so far as assets attributed to each spouse are concerned, should transform the common fund into separate property belonging exclusively to the spouse to whom they have been allocated.[16] There is much Romanian literature on this problem. It seems that, at the time of the dissolution of the marriage, the common fund is transformed as a matter of law into a regime of co-ownership, which is ownership by aliquot shares. Thus it is submitted that the legal relationship concerning the common fund is not an autonomous legal relationship. It necessarily presupposes the existence of another legal relationship on which it rests, which is the marriage. From the moment the marriage ceases to exist, the community also cannot exist.[17] Moreover, there are other reasons, though they need not be stated here. The aim is not to debate the problem but to state the regulation and some solutions which derive from it. For the rest, all the reasons are only consequences of the cessation of the fundamental relationship of the marriage. At that moment we are faced with joint property. As to the partition, either voluntary partition or action for partition, it will be necessary to determine the extent of the aliquot shares reverting to one or other of the spouses or, more precisely, to the former spouses.

In the case of an action for partition, rendered necessary by divorce, it is necessary to decide on which Court should make the declaration. The question has been amply debated. It is generally held that each spouse has the choice of three actions: a main action, after the dissolution of the marriage, for which the Court having jurisdiction is that of the domicile of the defendant;[18] a claim brought before the Court seised of the divorce, that is, a claim that figures in the action for divorce itself; and lastly, an action distinct from the action for divorce, but introduced at the same time. Nevertheless, the last two actions must be treated as being connected.[19] In addition, supposing neither of the parties have claimed partition and, in view of the active role of the judge in Socialist Civil Procedure—an active role which is an essential feature of the civil process of Romanian law—the Courts seised of the action for divorce have a duty to draw the attention of the parties to their right to ask for partition of the fund. The Court will then pronounce upon that claim at the same time as on the action for

---

16. It is supposed that in the case of divorce, the action for divorce has not a distinct head, although it can be seen that this is possible, regarding the partition of the common fund. If such a distinct head does exist or, more broadly, if the action for divorce and the demand concerning partition are judged at the same time, there is no problem. At the moment when the decision pronouncing the divorce becomes definitive then, at the same moment, the common fund will be divided. There will be no interval between the dissolution of the marriage and the partitioning of the common assets.

17. See Dr Mihail Eliescu in his *Casatoria în dreptul R.P.R* (marriage in Romanian law), Ed. of the Academy of the Socialist Republic of Romania, Bucharest, 1964, p. 332.

18. If among the community assets there is also an immovable, the action for partition will be within the jurisdiction of the Court of the place where the movable is situated.

19. Dr Mihail Eliescu, *loc. cit.*

divorce. This duty derives from the concept of the neutrality of the judge. The ignorance of the parties cannot be a reason for causing them to lose their rights. It is also decided that if the claim concerning partition requires numerous types of proof likely to cause delays, the Court can proceed to the separation of the two claims, one for divorce and the other for partition, for the Family Code does not impose on the Court granting the divorce the obligation to proceed at the same time to partition the fund.

We are not concerned here with the manner in which the rights will be determined, that is, with the extent of the rights of each spouse over the assets forming the object of the partition. This would be a matter of substance rather than of procedure. Also there is no need to insist on the fact that the work of the wife in the home and her care of the children create for her rights over the assets to be shared. This has already been dealt with. What may be said, because here it is civil procedure which is in question, is simply to state that the division will be made in conformity with the rules of Law No. 603 of 10th September 1943 for the simplification of judicial partitions.[20]

Division of the community assets can also be made without the intervention of the Courts. It is only in default of a voluntary division that there will be proceedings for a judicial division. But it has sometimes been said that, in the case of a voluntary decision, it is necessary that such a division should be confirmed by the Court. However, it is submitted that the solution to this question cannot depend upon any legislative text. Evidently, faced with a voluntary division, the Court must ascertain that there has been no fraud on the law and that the rights of third parties have not been prejudiced. The Court will, in fact, do this in respect of all legal transactions or, in other words, in accordance with the ordinary law. The agreement to share is not a plan. It is a definitive act.

We have seen, however, following article 36 of the Family Code, that the division of the community assets can be demanded by one or other of the spouses, even during the marriage. The Court that has jurisdiction in this connexion depends upon the value of the assets, whether above or below 150,000 lei, and can be the Court of the Justice of the Peace, or the district Court of the domicile of the defendant. The *situs* of any immovable determines jurisdiction in the case of immovable property being involved. Such claims must be based on a good reason. In general, it is thought that good reasons are the impossibility or

---

20. Law No. 603 of 1943 has simplified the procedure of judicial partition. It is no longer such as had been provided by the Civil Code and the Code of Civil Procedure. In fact, if the partition involves two phases, the admission in principle and then the formation and allocation of the shares, the former is made by an interlocutory judgment which can no longer form separately the object of the proceedings; it cannot be attacked except at the same time as the substantive claim. On the other hand, and this is different from the previous regulation, Law No. 603 of 1943, when it deals with co-partitioners having equal rights, always leaves it to the discretion of the Court to proceed either directly to the allocation, or by drawing lots. The partition takes place, in principle, in specie. But if the assets cannot be conveniently divided in specie, they will be sold by agreement or, when the co-partitioners cannot agree upon it, by way of public auction. The sale by way of public auction is also classified as a sale by agreement, subject to an action for annulment and the price will be included in the fund to be divided. The Court can decide, for good reason, that an asset shall be allocated to one of the co-partitioners, the other co-partitioners having the right to an equivalent award either in assets or in money.

extreme difficulty of administering the community assets together, or of exercising the right of disposal over the community assets. Again, good reason is the impossibility or extreme difficulty for one of the spouses to make use of the community assets. Such situations could be encountered especially where the spouses are in fact separated.[21] There are certainly other reasons equally appropriate to justify a claim for partition during the marriage, but it is not necessary to refer to them here.

As far as procedure is concerned, it is thought very often that the character of the alleged good reasons must, as far as the Court seised of the matter is concerned, provide *prima facie* evidence. Before proceeding to the division the Court must be of the opinion that a *prima facie* claim has been made out.[22] In any event, division claimed by one of the spouses during marriage can only result in a judicial partition. A division by agreement of the parties would amount to a modification by agreement of the legal matrimonial regime. That would be a modification which is absolutely null and void under article 30 paragraph 2 of the Family Code. According to that text every agreement contrary to the regime of matrimonial property established by the law is absolutely null and void.

Division of the community goods could also be claimed by creditors. Here, reference must be made to the basic regulation. This is one of the examples which prove, if this is still necessary, that the rules of civil procedure cannot be understood if, in describing them, one dissociated them from the rules of substance. In this connexion it should be mentioned briefly that there are creditors for whom the real security available, in the first instance, is the community assets. These creditors or, more exactly, these claims, are dealt with by article 32 of the Family Code. The personal creditors of one or other of the spouses can only enforce their rights against the separate property of their debtor. This rule is laid down in the first paragraph of article 33. The common creditors can levy obligatory execution against the separate property of the spouses if the community assets have not been sufficient to permit them to recover the amounts due to them (article 34). Lastly, the personal creditors of one or other of the spouses can themselves be paid out of the community assets. In other words, they can claim during the marriage the division of the community assets, but only so far as it is necessary for the recovery of their debts. The assets reverting to each spouse as a result of the division will become separate property (article 33).

To begin with the last of the hypotheses mentioned, it is certain that the division of the community assets claimed by the personal creditors can only be effected by judicial means. Usually, this involves a main action within the jurisdiction of the Justice of the Peace or the District Court, depending on the value of the action (above or below 150,000 lei). The territorial jurisdiction belongs to the Court of the domicile of the defendant spouses or of the *situs* of an immovable, according to whether the action is a movable action or an immovable action.

The right of the personal creditors to recover their debts against the community assets is subject to the sufficiency of the separate property of the debtor

21. Dr Mihail Eliescu, *op. cit.*, pp. 372-373.
22 *Idem*, p 374.

spouse. This in an aspect with which the Court must concern itself *ex officio*. The safeguarding of the community assets is not an interest which one can ignore.

A main action is not always necessary, however. In fact, within the framework of the procedure of judicial execution, article 42 of Decree No. 221 of 1960 (concerning the claims Socialist organisations have against physical persons, or the confiscation of the assets) gives power to the Court at the instance of any interested party to oppose the execution involving an interested spouse and to decide upon the division of the community assets. Decree No. 52 of 1969 has generalised this solution by introducing in the Code of Civil Procedure, article 400[1]. According to that article, in the framework of every judicial execution, the Court if seised of a counter-claim to stop execution, can proceed to re-partition the community assets.[23] To conclude this account of the relations concerning property, it should be mentioned that the benefit of a composition can be offered, if there are grounds for it, to the common creditors who intend to have the judicial execution levied against the separate property of the spouses. Since the right of the creditors to have the judicial execution levied against the separate property of the spouses is subject to the insufficiency of the community assets, one can clearly take advantage of the fact when this is not the situation.

Here the regulation of the relations concerning property has only been described by sketching the principal features, in the same way as those concerning the personal relationships between the spouses have been described earlier. What has been said is sufficient to show that, if there is true equality between the spouses, the rules of procedure make their contribution, a contribution which is truly of primary importance, to the realisation of one of the fundamental principles of Romanian family law.

III. Illegitimate children

Romanian family law makes no distinction between the infant born of a marriage and the infant born out of wedlock. In their relations with their father and mother, both have the same rights. Equality is established by article 97, paragraph 1, of the Family Code. Conversely, according to the same article 97, paragraph 1, the father and mother have, in regard to the infant whether he be born of the marriage or born out of wedlock, the same rights and the same duties. Here again—equality. Lastly, the parents can only exercise their rights in the interest of the infant. This principle is enunciated in article 97, paragraph 2. Thus, by a short sentence in a single text—article 97—an entire past of suffering, humiliation and injustice has been abolished.

Yet we must consider what are the concrete manifestations of equality between children and what role civil procedure is called upon to play in the realisation of one of the fundamental principles of the family law, such as this.

In the first place, and this is a necessary introduction, in order that the infant born out of wedlock may enjoy the rights which he possesses as the child of his father and of his mother, it is necessary that his descent should have been

---

23. See I Stoenescu and S Zilberstein, *Drept Procesual Civil* (The law of Civil Procedure) supplement, Bucharest, 1975, p. 84.

established, in respect of the father or in respect of the mother. Legal relationships only exist between the child and the father, or between the child and the mother, if his status as the child of one or the other is established. It could not be otherwise.

Descent with regard to the father can be established, following article 56 of the Family Code, by recognition effected by the father. However, we are not concerned with it here because it is a subject of interest to substance, not to procedure. For this reason we are not concerned with recognition. The action for paternity is a personal action within the jurisdiction of the Justice of the Peace of the domicile of the defendant. It is also personal in the sense that, according to article 59, it is an action which belongs only to the infant. It can be brought in the infant's name by the mother, even if she is a minor, or by its legal representative. It cannot be brought by the creditors of the infant.

Opinions vary concerning the right of the Department of the Public Prosecutor to bring the same action by virtue of article 45 of the Code of Civil Procedure. Some authors recognise such a right of the Department.[24] Others do not admit it, invoking the strictly personal character of the action.[25]

The action for paternity does not pass to the heirs of the infant; but they can continue an action already started on condition that they can show a patrimonial interest.[26] The action can also be directed against the heirs of the putative father. Clearly, this is a rule which does not submit the action to a condition of substance. It is not subject to rejection by the Courts on the ground of *exceptio plurium concubentium*. Consequently, the judges will have to decide by relying upon all the proofs available, of whatever kind they may be. Here the law has created for the infant born out of wedlock easy means of proof which will allow him or her, as far as possible and in accordance with the circumstances, the affiliation which he seeks.

It is not without interest to mention that literature and the case law have queried whether the mother, or the legal representative who has brought the action, can withdraw it. It is submitted that they have no right to do so. To initiate the action is in the interest of the infant but to withdraw it, or to make it the object of a compromise, could cause damage to the infant.[27] Such a solution would tend to be contrary to the general sense of the regulation.

The action for paternity must be brought during the period of one year after the birth of the child. But supposing that, as the result of a judicial decision, a child is no longer considered as illegitimate, the period of one year would be calculated from the moment that decision became definitive. If the mother had cohabited with the putative father or if the latter had provided for the mainten-

---

24. They claim it would protect the interests of a general character and ensure the application of the law to social life.
25. See, V. Economu in Rudenia (*Relationship*), Editions of the Academy of the Socialist Republic of Romania, Bucharest 1966, p. 95.
26. *Ibid.*
27. See on this matter, the decision of the Supreme Court, No. 1161 of 8th November 1965; Dr Ioan Mihuta; Dr Alexandru Lesviodax Repertoriu de practica judiciara in materie civila a Tribunalului Suprem si a alter instanta judecatoresti pe anii 1952-1969 (Directory of the judicial practice in civil matters, of the Supreme Tribunal and of other courts of justice, for the years 1952-1969), Scientific Editions, 1970, p. 63.

ance of the child, the period of one year would be calculated from the time when the cohabitation ceased or from the time when the putative father ceased his support. These rules are stated in article 60.

Affiliation with respect to the mother is established by the certificate which certifies the birth of the infant, without distinguishing between an infant born of the marriage and an infant born out of wedlock. This is the proof in ordinary law. In the rare cases where identity is contested, it is necessary to prove identity between the infant who seeks to take advantage of this certificate and the child described by the certificate. As it concerns a matter of substance, all evidence is admissible.

However, there are exceptional cases where the proof allowed by the law is not possible. These cases are provided for by article 48 of the Family Code. In these cases the mother can recognise the child.[28] Lastly, according to article 50, when proof of the affiliation cannot be made by the document of birth or when the facts of the statement in the certificate are contested, proof of the affiliation with regard to the mother can be made in Court by any means of proof. Civil procedure is again called upon here to ensure that the affiliation will be established in conformity with the facts. It should be emphasised that in Romanian law the character of affiliation, whether for a child born of the marriage or a child born out of wedlock, has no influence on the means of proof relating to affiliation by the mother. The Civil Code contained a certain discrimination in the past, in that the status of the "natural child" was considered with disfavour. This is no longer so. It is once more a thing of the past.

The action which seeks to establish affiliation is also clearly a personal one, in the two senses set out in dealing with the action for paternity. As stated in article 52, this action belongs only to the child and can be brought by the legal representative of the child if the latter is a minor or if he is interdicted. However, the legal representative cannot renounce an action after commencing proceedings. The reasons are those invoked on the occasion of an action for paternity. Again, in this case, the action cannot be brought by the creditors of the child.[29] The action, as in the case of an action for affiliation, does not pass to the heirs of the child. The heirs can, however, continue an action already instituted if they can prove a patrimonial interest. The action can also be directed against the heirs of the putative mother. Lastly, during the life of the child the action is not subject to prescription.

In order to discuss the rights of the child born out of wedlock, or the rights and duties of the parents, it must be supposed that affiliation has been established. It can be established with regard to the mother, with regard to the father, or with regard to both. The fundamental principle of equality between legitimate and illegitimate children should also be borne in mind. To take the example of a child born of the marriage, the question of whether the parents still exercise (or

---

28. Recognition by the mother and recognition by the father can both be contested by any interested party if such recognition does not correspond with the truth (arts. 49 & 58 of the Family Code). These would be actions within the jurisdiction of the Justices of the Peace of the domicile of the defendant.

29. Concerning the right of the attorney to introduce a similar action, opinions are divided, just as in the matter of an action for paternity. See *supra*, p. 36.

exercise in the same manner) all the rights and are bound by all the duties provided for by the law in their relations with the child, must be answered in the negative. There are cases which involve a divided protection, in respect of the rights and duties which together form the protection owed by the parents. Such a situation occurs in the case of divorce. Nevertheless, in the case of an illegitimate child, the situation is the same as in that quoted above relating to a legitimate child whose parents are divorced. The rights and duties of the parents with regard to the child are equal, but the methods of application of the rights will not always be the same. In any event it should be noted that there is a difference in the legal regime between the legitimate and the illegitimate child, but certain factual situations lead to the same consequences, as much for the one as for the other.

To understand what happens when the protection is split, one should consider what the rights and duties of parents are, whether in regard to illegitimate children or to those born of the marriage. One should also consider the role of Civil Procedure. As the rights are only means enabling the parents to discharge their duties,[30] it will be necessary to consider the duties. These concern the person, and consequently, the property of the infant.

To begin with the duties concerning the person of the child, after declaring that "the parents have the duty to take care of the person of the infant" in article 101, first paragraph, of the Family Code, paragraph 2 adds that "they are obliged to raise the infant, care for his health and physical development as well as for his education, his learning and his professional training, according to his aptitudes, in conformity with the aims of our Socialist State so as to render him useful to the community." It could be, however, that the parents do not take sufficient account of these requirements of the law. Moreover, article 102 provides that the guardianship authority may authorise the infant, at his request if he has attained the age of 14 years, to change the type of instruction or of professional training that has been established by his parents.

Thus, we may consider the important institution of guardianship authority. It is necessary to recall that the law has provided an entire mechanism of control intended to permit the checking of the manner in which parents exercise their rights or discharge their duties, this control being exercised through the tutelary authority which, according to article 58, is the executive committee of the Popular Council of each sector of the Municipality of Bucharest, or the executive bureau of the Popular Councils in the communes or towns.[31]

---

30. Eugen A Barasch, Ion Nestor, Savelly Zilberstein, *Ocrotirea Parinteasca* (paternal protection), Scientific Editions, Bucharest, 1960, pp. 16-17.
31. The popular councils are the local organs of the authority of the State in the territorial administrative units in which they have been elected. They direct local activity, ensure the economic, socio-cultural and municipal development of the territorial administrative units, safeguard the protection of Socialist property, the protection of the rights of citizens, socialist legality and the maintenance of public order. The popular councils organize the participation of the citizens in the administration, at the local level, of State and civic affairs. They work in sessions convened by the executive committee or the executive bureau, as the case may be, of the relevant popular council and they take decisions. The executive committee and the executive bureau of the popular council are the local organs of the State administration which have general jurisdiction in the territorial administrative unit in the place where the popular councils have

The importance of the role of the guardianship authority will be seen in the course of this account. The first paragraph of article 108 of the Family Code lays down in general terms that "the guardianship authority is obliged to exercise an effective and continuous control of the way in which the parents fulfil their duty with regard to the person and the property of the child." Therefore, if at the request of the child the guardianship authority can decide upon a change of the type of instruction or professional training, it is easy to see how civil procedure or the rules of procedure of the Family Code are invoked to ensure the effective application of the substantive rules.

The change in the type of instruction or professional training can also occur independently of a request by the child. In fact, by the application of Law No. 3 of 26th March 1970, "Relating to the regime of protection of certain categories of minors", the infant whose physical, moral or intellectual development or whose health is threatened if he continues to live with his parents, can be entrusted by the Commission for the Protection of Minors to a family or to a person or even, according to the distinctions of the law, to an institution for protection. In the case where the child has been entrusted to a family or a person, according to Article 3 paragraph 2 of the law, they will have the rights and duties of the parents concerning the person of the infant.

The performance of the duty of bringing up the infant is also assured by the Penal Code. In fact, according to Article 306c.p., if the physical, intellectual or moral development of the minor is put in serious danger by measures, or treatment, of whatever sort on the part of the father or mother or of the person to whom the minor has been entrusted for the purpose of education, the guilty party is punished by imprisonment for from one to five years.[32]

Again, with a more general field of application, there is a specific sanction in family law, applied by decision of the Court at the request of the guardianship authority, through the rules of procedure. In fact, according to Article 109 of the Family Code, if the parents exercise their rights in such a way as to imperil the health or physical development of the child, or if they seriously neglect the performance of the duties incumbent upon them, or if the education, instruction or professional training of the child are not carried out with devotion with regard to the socialist State, the Court of law will pronounce the withdrawal from the father or from the mother of the rights which they have with regard to their infant child, on the application of a guardianship authority. Such an action will come within the jurisdiction of the district Court (Article 2 of the Code of Civil Procedure) of the domicile of the defendant parent.[33]

---

been elected. In the exercise of these powers, the executive committee or the executive bureau of the popular council issues decisions on the basis of the law and with a view to implementing them. The popular councils set up alongside their executive committees or, as the case may be, alongside their executive bureaux, specialised organs of the State administration, subordinate so far as the popular council and the executive committee or executive bureau is concerned, to the local and central organs of the State administration which are superior in the hierarchy.

32. Certain facts relating to the obligation to bring up a child can also amount to offences punishable by a fine: Decree No. 153 of 13 April 1970.

33. It should be added that the Prosecutor also has a right to ask for the withdrawal from the father or from the mother of the rights which they have with regard to the infant child.

Another duty of the parents must now be considered. It must be remembered that duties and rights exist as much for an illegitimate child as for an infant born of the marriage. The rules which have been considered and the following rules are both the same unless differences are indicated.

The new duty in question is to provide for the needs of the child, that is, the obligation to provide for the maintenance of the infant, which amounts to the obligation to supply necessaries. As it is only procedure which is concerned here, it is not necessary to discuss the substance of this obligation. If there is a disagreement as regards the extent of the alimentary obligation and also in some other aspects, such as for example, with regard to the contribution of each of the parents, Article 107 of the Family Code provides that the Courts must pronounce on this after the guardianship authority has also been heard. The action would be a personal one within the jurisdiction of the Justice of the Peace of the domicile of the defendant parent. It should be added that the child can require from each of its parents all the support he needs. In other words, the debtors of the obligation to maintain have a joint and several obligation (*in solidum*) subject to the right of each parent who has had to provide the whole, to ask for a contribution from the other. This is done by an action within the jurisdiction of the Justice of the Peace of the domicile of the latter parent in his capacity as defendant. Having regard to the respective means of the parents, the obligation of one can be different from that of the other.

The action by which the alimentary obligation is put into effect is initiated in the ordinary way by one of the parents against the other. It has to be decided in what capacity the plaintiff acts. In other words, what is the legal entitlement that the action hopes to realise. The plaintiff certainly represents the interests of the infant. At the same time he is a person who is, himself or herself, bound by the obligation to maintain. The plaintiff thus has a double character and, in initiating the action, he acts as much in one of these capacities as in the other. If this is so, it can be seen once again that the basic rules interpenetrate with the rules of procedure, even though in principle the minor, aged between 14 and 18 years, should himself initiate the action. If the right is that of the infant only, a parent would no longer have the right to initiate an action on his own, intended to realise the interests of the infant. It is submitted it can be started by one of the parents acting alone, precisely because in starting the action he is claiming or enforcing interests which are proper to him.

In addition, neglect of the obligation to provide maintenance for the child is met with a penal sanction, provided by Article 305 of the Penal Code, the text of which has already been noted.

Finally, to conclude this description of the alimentary obligation from the standpoint of procedure, it should be emphasised that the obligation can be reduced or increased by the Courts on the basis of a change in the particular factual situations.

One may now pass on to the rights of parents with regard to the person of their minor child.

Their first right is that the infant should live with his parents. This is provided for by the first paragraph of Article 100 of the Family Code. It is this which leads to the rule in article 103, first paragraph, according to which the parents have the right to demand that the child should be returned to them, should he be with a person who has no legal right to look after him. This is a right which enables the parents to perform their duty of bringing up the child. However, with regard to the child's professional training, as in the case of the type of professional training concerned, the guardianship authority may authorise the infant, if he has attained the age of 14 years, to live wherever is considered most suitable to enable him to achieve the instruction or professional training he may require.

If the solution is not contrary to the interests of the infant, the Courts, in principle, should return the infant to his parents. To this effect a civil sanction is available, but in theory it is possible for a penal sanction to apply. In fact, article 307, first paragraph, of the Penal Code provides that where in fact one of the parents is keeping his minor child without the consent of the other parent, or of the person to whom the infant has been entrusted by law, he shall be punished by imprisonment or by a fine if the development and education of the child are endangered.

A second right, intended to permit the performance of the obligation to bring up the child, may be called the "right of orientation". The significance of this right is to "orientate" the acts of the infant, to give them direction and to decide, within the limits of the law, on all matters which concern the health and physical development, the education, instruction and professional training of the infant. One of the manifestations of this right is the capacity of the parents to appreciate the associations, that is the friends, of the child and to examine his or her correspondence certainly not in a discretionary way but under the control of the guardianship authority.

It is hardly necessary to add that the right of orientation does not in any way exclude the infant receiving advice from other persons or youth organisations, according to the rules in force. It is a method of ensuring by joint efforts that a child is brought up in accordance with his capabilities and in conformity with the aims of the socialist State, so that he or she may become a useful member of the community.

Lastly, mention should be made of the right of parents to consent to the adoption of their infant child.[34] This is also a means intended to permit the performance of parental duties. Since by the effect of the adoption the rights and duties of the parents in their relations with their infant child will pass on to other persons, it is important that the parents should agree in their appreciation or verification of such other persons as being able to perform their duties and exercise the correlative rights. However, failure to consent to the adoption does not necessarily imply the nullity of the adoption. Nullity—a special type of

---

34. In Romanian law the adoption can either be full adoption or an adoption having only restricted effects. The first of these adoptions confers on the infant the right of descent which is substituted for his original descent. The adopted child ceases to belong to his family. Marriage between all the ascendants and descendants in the direct line will, however, be prohibited. Marriage between relatives to the fourth degree in the collateral line will equally be prohibited. The second form of adoption does not involve bonds of relationship except between the adoptor, on the one hand, and the adopted child and his descendants on the other. The rights and duties of the parents (i.e. the parental authority) pass to the adoptor. The adopted child and his descendants retain, with respect to the father and the mother by blood and their relatives, all the rights and are bound by all the obligations resulting from the descent.

nullity, since it only operates for the future—must be in the interests of the infant.[35] This is one illustration of the fact that it is the interest of the infant which is paramount in the rules.[36]

It must be considered how the rights and duties will be complied with in the case where the protection of parents is divided. For example, in the case of divorce. When the child is born out of wedlock the position is regulated by the rules governing the divorce.[37] The first paragraph of article 42 of the Family Code requires that, in pronouncing the divorce, the Court must decide to which of the two parents the infant children will be entrusted. Article 42 (1) adds that, for good reasons the children could be entrusted to other members of the family or to other persons, with their consent, or even to welfare institutions. Equally, according to paragraph (3), the Court must determine the contribution of each parent to the expenses required for the upbringing and education of the children to enable the child to be brought up in conformity with the requirements of the Family Code. According to article 43, first paragraph, the parent to whom the infant has been entrusted must exercise the rights of the parents in respect of the child. Lastly, according to paragraph 3 of article 43, the parent to whom the child has not been entrusted retains the right to have personal relationships with the child, as well as the right to supervise the manner in which the infant is brought up, is educated or obtains his instruction or his professional training.

It follows from these requirements that the alimentary obligation also remains a burden on the father and mother. This is also the case with the obligation to bring up the child. It could not be otherwise. Moreover, the solution is expressly established by the first paragraph of article 97 of the Family Code, which provides that the parents have equal rights and duties in regard to their infant children. It is the same for other duties. The parent to whom the child is not entrusted must also have the duty of bringing up the child, with the correlative right of orientation. However, all the rights which the parents enjoyed before the divorce will not necessarily correspond to the duty of the parents to bring up the child. Clearly, there can no longer be a right of the parent to whom the child has not been entrusted, to have the child living with him or her. In the same way, the right of orientation will no longer be exercised by that parent. Having separated, the parents can no longer be asked to take measures concerning the person of the child by agreement between themselves, as required by the first paragraph of article 98. That is, the duty of bringing up the child or the right of orientation will be expressed in a different fashion. This is exactly why article 43 paragraph 3 requires that the parent to whom the child has been entrusted should retain the

---

35. In addition, the infant's consent must be sought if he has attained the age of 10 years.
36. It is necessary to mention that, in the application of law No. 3 of 26th March 1970 relating to the regime of protection of certain categories of minors, one could take, in regard to the minors subjected to this regulation, a whole series of measures the result of which would be that certain rights and certain duties of the parents would go to third persons. Nearly all the measures provided for by law No. 3 are decided by the Commissions for the Protection of Minors. This is a law which will also be mentioned later.
37. This is why the consequences of the divorce as regards the distribution of the duties and rights between the parents, are examined here. Without this examination it would be difficult to understand the rules relative to children born out of wedlock. It will be seen that this is a consequence of the technique adopted by the Family Code.

right to supervise the manner on which the child is brought up, his education, his instruction and his professional training. In practice, this means that the parent to whom the child has not been entrusted is entitled to consider, *post factum*, whether the child is being brought up in conformity with the requirements of article 101, paragraph 2. Such a parent should inform the guardianship authority if he does not approve of the child's upbringing. It is for the guardianship authority to intervene in the application of the legislative provisions of article 99, which are of a general character. These state that whenever there is a disagreement between the parents on the subject of the exercise of the rights, or the performance of the duties, which the law has granted to them as parents, the guardianship authority, after having heard the parents, must decide in conformity with the interests of the child.

Indeed, the parent to whom the child has not been entrusted retains the right to have personal relationships with the child, so that he may take account of the manner in which the child is being brought up and inform, if necessary, the guardianship authority accordingly. An agreement between the parents regarding the care of the children, or regarding the contribution of each of them to the expenses required by the education, instruction and professional training of their children, can have no effect unless it is approved by the law Court. This is an application of the more general principle according to which one cannot derogate from the legal rules by means of a private agreement.

Concerning the right to consent to the adoption of an infant child, this right is equally available to the father and to the mother. Divorce will not influence the manner in which this right may be exercised.

However, the child can also be entrusted to a third party. In this respect, paragraph 2 of article 43 of the Family Code provides that the third party will only have the rights and duties attached to the person of the infant child. Regarding the position of the parents in this situation, the Family Code lays down that the alimentary obligation remains an obligation of the parents. Law No. 3 has, in any case, modified this rule. When the child is entrusted to a person or a family, such person or family must provide for the maintenance of the child. For this purpose they will receive from the State a maintenance allowance.[38] The persons who are obliged according to the law to provide for the maintenance of the child will be compelled, as a result of the decision taken on this matter, to pay to the State a monthly contribution during the whole time that the measure is applied.[39]

But all the evidence shows that the child will not be allowed to live elsewhere except at the home of the third party to whom he had been entrusted.

On the other hand, as far as the duty of the parents to bring up the infant is concerned, and the right of orientation, these may continue to exist but will be expressed in different ways. Such rights will amount to interventions post factum, whereas the obligation on the guardianship authority to settle a dispute provides a

---

38. Article 3 (2).
39. Article 91 (1) of the Law. The other legislative provisions are concerned with the way in which this contribution will be determined. The rule is that the minor who benefits from an income as successor or from other income will defray the disbursements required for the care of his person.

means of enforcement. In order to make these post factum interventions possible, the parents retain the right to have personal relationships with the infant. Lastly, it should be stressed that, in applying article 44 of the Family Code, the Court in the case of a change of circumstances may modify the measures concerning the personal or patrimonial rights and obligations between the divorced parents and the children. This can be done at the request of the father or of the mother, or of the child if he has attained the age of 14 years, of the guardianship authority, or of an institution for protection.

Lastly, the parents retain the right to consent to the adoption of the child.

The legal position of the illegitimate child must now be considered. Article 65 of the Family Code leaves no doubt about this. If the descent of the child born out of wedlock is established either with regard to the father or with regard to the mother, the question of the person to whom the child is entrusted and also the contribution of the parents to the disbursements required by the maintenance, education, instruction and professional training of the infant are decided in conformity with the provisions of articles 42-44. That is to say, in accordance with the rules provided in the case of divorce, which have already been discussed. It follows that the solutions described when discussing the situation in the case of divorce will also be the solutions which have to be applied in the case of illegitimate children. The law is explicit.

Some details may be of help. Such is the rule that the measures envisaged by article 65 will only be taken by a decision of the Judge and, also, the rule that an agreement between the parents cannot be effective except when approved by the Court. If it were supposed that such an agreement, approved by the Court does not exist, it would seem that the effect would be as follows:

(1) The child would be expected to live both at the home of the father and at the home of the mother. Since in fact he cannot do so, the effect would be that the presumption of civil liability would exist as far as the parent is concerned, with whom the child does in fact live, rather than with regard to the other parent;

(2) The duty to bring up the child and the right of orientation could no longer be expressed in different ways. The measures concerning the person of the child would have effect only if the measures were decided by agreement between the parents or, in case of disagreement, by the guardianship authority. In other words, the effects could not be the same. There must be a distinction between the position where the legal rules have been respected and the position where they have not been respected.

This is also the case in divorce. It is unnecessary to add that, if the descent of the child has been established only with regard to the father, or only with regard to the mother, the rights and duties which have been mentioned, as well as those concerning the property of the child, will exist only as an obligation of, or in favour of, the parent with regard to when descent has been established.

As already stated, the duties and rights of the parents also relate to the property of the child. A brief mention of these is given.

First among the duties, there is the duty of administering the property of the child, as indicated in the first paragraph of article 105. It is a duty which comprises the acts of conservation, as well as the acts of administration properly so called and, under the name of acts of administration of the patrimony, certain acts of disposition. These are envisaged by the final paragraph of article 129.[40] This duty will be performed differently according to whether it concerns the assets of an infant of more or less than 14 years. This aspect arises from the civil capacity. The acts which the Family Code designates in article 129 paragraph 2[41], such as acts which go beyond the right to administer, can only be executed with the authorisation of the guardianship authority. Lastly, there are some acts which are forbidden to the parents. These are the acts referred to in article 128[42] and article 129.[43]

There are also other duties, which need only be enumerated here. They are:

The duty to demand that an inventory of the child's assets be drawn up by an agent of the guardianship authority. This must be approved by that authority, but it is not necessary if the infant has no other assets than those intended for his personal use (article 105, paragraph 3, and article 126).

The obligation to declare certain debts (article 126, paragraph 2).

The obligation to demand that the guardianship authority should determine the annual sum required for the maintenance of the minor and the administration of his property (article 127, first paragraph).

The obligation to deposit certain sums of money and securities in a State bank (article 131, first paragraph).

The obligation, in order to obtain a discharge, to render to the guardianship authority, annual accounts which concern the administration of the assets (articles 105, paragraph 3, article 134 and 135).

The obligation to present to the guardianship authority, when "the duty and the right to administer the property" has ceased to exist, a general account intended to permit a general discharge (article 141).

In passing from the duties to the rights, it is necessary to mention the right of the parents—a right which is also an obligation—to represent the child in civil acts, up to the moment when the minor attains the age of 14 years and, from that moment, to give previous approval to his or her acts, assuming that they find them useful to the minor (paragraphs 1 and 2 of article 105).[44] This matter

---

40. Article 129, final paragraph sets out: "Nevertheless, the tutor can alienate, without the previous authority of the guardianship authority, those assets which are subject to waste or deterioration as well as the assets which have become useless for the minor, if the value of such assets does not exceed the sum of 250 lei." This text refers, as do others which will be mentioned, to the powers of the tutor. But, by the effect of an article of principle (article 105), these are the rules which apply equally to the parents.

41. Article 129, para. 2: "The tutor cannot, without previous authorisation of the guardianship authority, validly alienate or bind the property of the minor, nor surrender his patrimonial rights, nor conclude any other act which exceeds the right to administer."

42. Article 128: "It is forbidden to conclude legal transactions between the turor, the spouse, a relative in the direct line or brothers and sisters of the tutor on the one hand and the minor on the other."

43. Article 129, paragraph 1: "The tutor cannot, in the name of the minor, make donations, nor enter into a guarantee of the obligation of another." Acts performed in violation of articles 128 and 129 are voidable, that is to say, are affected with relative nullity.

44. It is important to notice that the right spoken of exists even if the child has no property. That right is also exercised in connexion with the person of the child (as, for example, when the parents approve the contract which the child must enter into to follow courses at certain schools).

arises from civil capacity. It must be underlined that the right will have to be exercised by the father and the mother. The representation of the minor, or the approval of his acts, requires the participation of both parents.

We must go back to the example of divorce to see what is decided when the protection of the child is divided. Article 43 of the Family Code establishes a distinction. According to the first paragraph of that article, the divorced parent to whom the child is entrusted will exercise the rights, or will be under the duty of the parents in their relationships with the minor child. Consequently, the rights and duties concerning the property of the child will also belong to the parent to whom the child has been entrusted. If the child has been entrusted to another person or to an institution of protection, atricle 43, paragraph 2, provides that the Court in pronouncing the divorce will designate the parent who will exercise the right to administer the property of the child and the right to represent him or her, or to approve his or her acts.

In the application of article 65 of the Family Code, the situation will be the same if it relates to an illegitimate child. When the child is entrusted to one of the parents, it is that parent who has the duties and the rights regarding the property of the child. When the child is entrusted to a third person, it is necessary to determine which of the parents will have the duties and the rights concerning the property of the child. But, in either case a decision by the Judge will be necessary, as laid down by article 65, referring expressly to article 42 and article 43, paragraph 2.

Even though a decision of the Court is necessary, it does not follow that this matter will always be regulated. Assuming that a decision of the Court has not designated the parent who is to have the duties and rights concerning the property of the child, it is necessary to consider whether the duties and rights will be the obligation and right of both parents. Of course, it could be that the child is entrusted to one of the parents by agreement between them, without any application to the Court. But an agreement between the parents, if it has not been approved by a decision of the Judge, can have no effect (article 42, paragraph 4, to which article 65 refers). Here again, for the reasons given when dealing with the rights and duties concerning the person of the infant, the rights and duties will revert to both parents. Their joint liability may be invoked under one form or another, e.g. when one or other of the parents happens to apply to a Court which is within the jurisdiction of the Justice of the Peace of the domicile of the defendant. Thus, the law will eventually be enforced.

In order that this account concerning illegitimate children should not be incomplete, reference must be made to the name of the family of the child and of his rights of succession.

As far as the name is concerned, article 64 of the Family Code provides that the child will carry the family name of the parent in respect of whom descent has first been established. If descent has been established with regard to the other parent as well, the Court can authorise the child to carry the family name of the latter parent. Where the infant would have been recognised by both father and mother at the same time, article 62, paragraph 2, concerning infants born of the marriage (the article to which article 64 refers) provides that the parents will decide the family name of the child by agreement. This could be the family name of one of the parents, or their combined family names. In the absence of such an agreement it will be for the guardianship authority to decide.

Lastly, reference must be made to the rights of succession. In Romanian law the illegitimate child and the child born of the marriage have the same legal position. They are called to the succession under the same conditions, whether it be the succession of the father or the succession of the mother. To mention only some of the conscquences capable of having procedural implications, it follows that the illegitimate child also has the equality of beneficiary entitled to a reserve. The sum which constitutes the reserve may be subject to an action for reduction which belongs to the illegitimate child in his own right and which is not transmitted by way of succession.[45] It also follows that the illegitimate child has seisin and that he need not demand to be put into possession, the effect of the seisin—which is its most characteristic effect—being that the heir acquires the right, by operation of law, as plaintiff, to bring actions of a patrimonial character which belonged to the deceased and, as defendant, to oppose actions which third persons had initiated against the deceased and which they now direct against the heir.

The quality of an heir can be proved by a certificate of inheritance delivered by the State Notary, who has jurisdiction according to the place of the opening of the succession.[46] But in order to succeed in an action for the succession, the heir may also prove his status by means other than the certificate of inheritance, which is not obligatory. It will then be a question of proving the descent. It should be mentioned that it is disputed whether the petition of heredity, that is, the action for the succession, is a real action, a personal action, or a mixed action. It is submitted that it is a mixed action.

When there is a petition of heredity, the Court may declare, in appropriate circumstances, the unworthiness of the heir. This is only a declaration, since the sanction for unworthiness is that it produces its effect by operation of law.

As there can be several heirs, there will be an undivided estate between them, so far as certain assets are concerned. This is an estate which is ultimately shared out. When there is no agreement between the heirs the division may be claimed by way of action by each of the heirs. But the partition of the property may be deferred for a period of five years at the most. This is provided by article 728 of the Civil Code.

The action for partition, as provided by article 14 of the Code of Civil Procedure, will always be within the jurisdiction of the Court of the last domicile of the deceased, the Justice of the Peace or the District Court, according to the value of the object of the action, that is, whether it is below or above 150,000 lei.

Nowadays the judicial partition takes place according to a simplified procedure established by Law No. 603 of 10th September 1943, of which mention has already been made.[47]

---

45. According to the facts, the right to a reduction can be exercised equally by means of an exception.

46. For the procedure for the delivery of the certificate of inheritance, see Decree No. 40 of 22nd January 1953, republished in 1960.

47. If one of the owners is the State, the partition will be made according to special rules laid down by Decree No. 841 of 3rd January 1965.

Certainly, the succession is a matter which raises many problems. However, they do not concern us here, first because they very often raise rules of substance and also because it was important to put in evidence the equality of the legal positions of the legitimate and the illegitimate child.

To conclude, if it is true that the equality of the legal situations between the two has only been established by stages, it is apparent from the development of Romanian law that, in all the aspects examined, the equality is institutionalised today. This is a great and moving realisation in the battle for more justice, which is being fought to some extent everywhere in the world.

CHAPTER XII. PRIVATE INTERNATIONAL FAMILY LAW IN EUROPE

by Alfred E. von Overbeck

Introduction

The object of the present chapter is to describe some interesting developments in the private international law in Europe, in respect of descent and divorce and the alimentary obligation. It in no way pretends to give a systematic comparative account.[1]

The three subjects which will be dealt with here, namely equality of the spouses on the one hand and natural children and divorce on the other, do not occur on the same level. The first subject concerns a general principle which has inspired the recent internal legislative reforms and which can have repercussions on the rules of the conflict of laws in a number of spheres. Discussion on this subject is particularly fostered in the Federal Republic of Germany. The other two subjects figure amongst the most important of the private international law of the family.

Equality of the spouses

In respect of the principle of equality of the spouses, the rules of private international law can be criticised from various points of view:

(a) It is possible that a rule of conflict leads to apply a substantive law which does not embody the principle of equality of the spouses. In such a case it is a question of determining, in the specific case, if the discrimination is sufficiently serious for the public policy of the forum to lead to the setting aside of the law in question.

(b) The rule of conflict itself can treat the husband and the wife unequally, for example, by submitting the divorce of the spouses of different nationality to the national law of the husband. Does this fact in itself constitute a discrimination? It is important to underline, in the first place, that it is in no way certain that the wife suffers damage from the fact that the law of the husband is applied. On the contrary in some cases, this law can be more favourable to her than her own national law, for example, because it prevents a divorce to which the wife is opposed, or in the case of divorce, because it gives her more extensive rights.

It is no less true that such conflict rules are nowadays themselves objected to as discriminatory and that the new codifications and draft laws seek to avoid them.

---

1. For the rules of substantive law cited, see especially Bergmann-Ferid, *Quellen des internationalen Privatrechts* 3rd ed.; Makarov, *Internationales Ehe-und Kindschaftsrecht*, 2nd ed.; and T M C Asser Institute, *Statutory of Private International Law*, Oslo, 1971. For the recent Hague Conventions, see *Recueil des Conventions de La Haye*, The Hague 1973, and the principal periodicals.

The question does not, however, arise in the same way in all matters. In the case of divorce, the husband and wife oppose each other on the basis of equality. One cannot see why preference should be given to the nationality of one rather than of the other. On the contrary, in respect of descent, whatever the wish may be to realise the equality of the spouses, the natural difference and the normal course of things cannot be disregarded. Maternity is certainly one of these differences, with exceptions which tend to disappear. Thus, most commonly the natural children live with their mother. Consequently if it is desired to realise the unity of the regime applicable to descent, one can argue that it is as well to have a connecting factor derived from the inherent qualities of the mother, and this even when it is a question of determining the relations between the child and the father.

(c) Lastly, more specifically for example domicile or nationality, can be the cause of a certain discrimination. This is notably the case when the domicile of the wife does not depend on her choice, but upon the domicile of the husband, as is still provided by many laws.[2] The "Convention on the Recognition of Divorces and Legal Separations", signed at The Hague on the 1st June 1970 Article 3 paragraph 2, does not take into account the domicile of the wife when it is bound by law to that of the husband.[3]

All the same, the wife frequently acquires the nationality of her husband from the mere fact of the marriage, without her being consulted or being able to contest it. In such a case, it can be discriminatory to take into account her acquired nationality while neglecting her former nationality which, according to many systems, the wife retains in her own right or by virtue of a declaration. Equally, the recent Convention of the Hague Conference on the law applicable to matrimonial regimes takes into account, in several circumstances, only a national law which has been voluntarily acquired.

Among these three aspects, whether public policy intervenes against a discriminatory law depends essentially upon the individual case. On the other hand, no reform of the private international law could neglect the principle of equality of the man and the woman in respect of its double aspect of the person or persons which the rule cf conflict takes into consideration and in respect of the choice of the connecting factors.

Natural Children

The typical problem in this region is that of the establishment of a legal bond with the father. As has already been said, legal systems tend to abandon the system of the "unknown mother"; the principle *mater semper certa*, already

---

2. The English and Italian laws have recently introduced the independent domicile of the wife; see The Domicile and Matrimonial Proceedings Act 1973, Section 1, and Italian law No. 151 of 19th May 1975, Reform of Family Law article 1, modifying article 45 of the Civil Code.
3. See on this Convention, the Hague Conference on Private International Law, Acts and Documents of the Eleventh Session (1968), tome II, divorce.

established by the laws of Germanic origin, seems to be taking the lead.[4] More-over, even before the recent reforms of the substantive law, disputes over maternity have hardly been frequent.[5]

The evolution of internal law tends to facilitate the establishment of paternal descent by resort to law and, at the same time, to make the bonds of such descent more substantial. Recognition and legitimation are also facilitated. The tendencies of the internal law in this region are reflected in the national rules of conflict and, on the international level, in two conventions drawn up by the International Commission on Civil Status: the Convention on the Extension of the Jurisdiction of the appropriate Authorities to Register the Recognition of natural children, of 14th September 1961, and the Convention on Legitimation by Marriage, of 10th September 1970.

Another problem affecting paternity which is worthy of reflection is that of the disavowal. In many cases, the disavowal relates to children born after the spouses were separated and whose true father is perfectly well known. Often, divorce and remarriage will follow and the objective sought finally consists in having the child enter into the new family.

However, this can pose problems of private international law, which are well illustrated by a case decided by the Cantonal Court of Zürich on 26th January 1973.[6] In the case in question, a Yugoslav woman domiciled in Switzerland had given birth to a child a short time after her divorce from her Yugoslav husband from whom she had already been separated for many years past. She subsequently married an Italian, who was the true father of her child. The lower court had refused to acknowledge its jurisdiction to hear the action in disavowal to which, in fact important exception could be taken. According to Articles 8 and 32 of the Swiss law on Conflicts of 1891 (LRDC), Swiss law gives jurisdiction to the courts of the country of the nationality of the husband of the mother and declares his national law to be applicable. On grounds, founded essentially upon the interest of the child, i.e. to make its legal position agree with biological reality, the Cantonal Court admitted its own jurisdiction. Yet it examined the possibility of the recognition of its judgment in Yugoslavia. It declared that the action could be admitted equally well on the basis of Yugoslav law, as well as on the basis of Swiss law, and that the Yugoslav courts would not thus consider themselves as having exclusive jurisdiction.[7]

In this particular case the Zürich court to some extent had anticipated the situation which would present itself after the action was admitted. This point of view appears even more clearly in an earlier decision of 4th September 1969.[8]

---

4. See also the Convention relating to the Establishment of the Maternal Affiliation of Natural Children, of 12th September 1962, elaborated by the CIEC.
5. See M Simon-Depitre et J Foyer, Le nouveau droit international privé de la filiation (Loi du 3 janvier 1972), Paris, 1973, No 15, p. 23.
6. Revue suisse de jurisprudence (SJZ), 1973, p. 87; Annuaire suisse de droit international (ASDI), 1972, vol. XXVIII, p. 407.
7. See also another judgment of the same court, of 30th May 1972, SJZ, 1973, p. 122 and the other decisions published in ASDI, 1972, vol. XXVIII, pp. 399 et seq., note P Lalive.
8. SJZ, 1969, p. 377; ASDI 1969/70, vol. XXVI, p. 291.

The court had taken into account the fact that the infant in the case of the admission of the action in disavowal, would acquire the right to the Swiss citizenship of its mother.

It is remarkable, in these specific cases, that the main difficulty arises from a singularity of Swiss law: the rule which founds international jurisdiction on nationality. But the problem can arise in any country which applies the national law of the father, if that national law does not know the action in disavowal or if it makes such action subject to very restrictive conditions.

Divorce

In the matter of divorce the solutions of private international law are fairly tightly bound up with the internal law. The States whose internal law does not recognise divorce are clearly restrictive in the recognition of a foreign divorce. The situation in Italy, where divorce has only recently been introduced without any change of the rules of private international law[9], presents a particular interest.

The tendency is towards an enlargement of international jurisdiction which carries the risk, in its turn, of the creation of more "limping" divorces. Such divorces are not recognised in all the interested countries.

Certain difficulties in the matter of divorce result from the principle of nationality. Thus, where the right to divorce is accorded only to the husband who had the nationality of the forum, as is the case in Switzerland, there is a discrimination based on nationality. The problem of remarriage of the divorced foreign spouse under such conditions has only recently been resolved in Switzerland and Germany.

On the other hand, nationality can intervene in a restrictive sense as certain States reserve to themselves the exclusive jurisdiction to pronounce the divorce of their own nationals, or recognise a foreign divorce only if the national law has been applied.

The effects of descent and of the divorce

Once descent has been established or a divorce granted, the problem of their effects comes to the fore.

Amongst these effects we may note the problem of the name of the wife or of the natural infant, the question of the exercise of parental authority, the guardianship of the natural children or the children of divorced spouses, and the rights of succession of the natural child.[10] Of these effects, one related to the descent

---

9. With the exception of "divorce as a ground for divorce". See *infra* p. 319.

10. This problem is in large measure solved by the Convention on Jurisdiction and Applicable Law, relating the protection of minors, signed at the Hague on 5th October 1961, which is in operation in the following States: the Federal Republic of Germany, Austria, France, Luxembourg, the Netherlands, Portugal and Switzerland. (See Acts and Documents of the Ninth Session, 1960, tome IV, Protection of Minors). It is true that Article 15 thereof allows the exclusion by reservation of protective measures after divorce.

as well as divorce is particularly important: it is the maintenance obligation which arises. The maintenance due to a divorced wife and to her children frequently presents problems. On the other hand, if it is true that Germany has recently replaced the *Zahlvaterschaft* by an affiliation with full effect, and that Switzerland has done the same, the cases will be fairly rare where the declared fathers will be truly concerned with the children and will voluntarily supply their needs. Most frequently, the order to pay maintenance and its recovery will remain the most important questions.

It will be difficult to understand that here there is a considerable social problem which goes beyond the purely individual sphere. In fact, where the father is at fault in fulfilling his obligations, it is often the community which has to contribute to the maintenance of the child. This is a burden which the mother often cannot appropriately assume alone. There is also a tendency in internal law to charge public funds in respect of the necessaries and to seek to recover these from the father subsequently.

On the other hand, the law of alimentary obligations is of special interest because in this area the solutions are by agreement much more developed than they are for descent in general and for divorce.

Many European States have ratified the Convention on the Law Applicable to Maintenance Obligations Towards Children, signed at The Hague on 24th October 1956, and the Convention Concerning the Recognition and Enforcement of Decisions relating to maintenance Obligations Towards Children, signed at The Hague on 15th April 1958. This instrument was completed by the Convention on the Recovery Abroad of Maintenance signed in New York on 20th June 1956. The latter, without directly controlling jurisdiction and the law applicable, provides for a system of aid among public authorities. New Hague Conventions signed in 1973 have as their aim to replace the former Conventions by developing this system and by extending it to alimentary obligations between adults.

Lastly, the regime of alimentary obligation has influenced directly the law of descent in at least one country, Germany. Certain solutions in favour of the child, applicable in respect of maintenance, tend to be extended to affiliation proceedings.

In the first place, these declarations lead us to some extent to put the cart before the horse and thus to treat alimentary obligations first as a common result of descent and divorce. The private international law of descent will be discussed below and also certain questions relative to divorce.

A. The Maintenance Obligations

Article 5 of the Bulgarian Family Code of 15th March 1968 states: "The obligation of support is governed by the national law of the person claiming such support". That is a clear rule, unfortunately fairly exceptional in existing private international law. More frequently, it is necessary to deduce the law applicable to obligations of support from rules of conflict which are more general, and which are related, for example, to relations between the parents and the children or between spouses. It is then not always easy to know which, amongst different rules that have to be considered, is effectively applicable to the

287

alimentary obligation. Such uncertainties exist also in the matter of jurisdiction.

Once the national rule of conflict which is applicable has been determined, the question clearly arises of knowing if it is truly appropriate to the matter. Details cannot be entered into here but a survey will be made of the system of the Hague Conventions which, at least in central and western Europe, has broadly replaced the rules of the common law.[11]

Outline of the system of the Hague Conventions

Here we have to distinguish among three things: the substantive law, the two Conventions on private international law drawn up by the Hague Conference in its eighth session of 1956, and the new law of the two Conventions drawn up at the twelfth session of 1972/3. The first Conventions are only applicable to the alimentary obligations towards the children, while the new Conventions apply equally to adults.

The two sets of Conventions have this in common, that they govern the question of the law applicable and of the recognition and execution of the awards. The rules concerning the law applicable on the one hand and concerning recognition and execution on the other are derived from similar principles and constitute a coherent system. But they are formally independent, if only because the States are free to accept some without the others.

As distinct, for example, from the EEC Treaty on Jurisdiction and on the Enforcement of Judgments of 27th September 1968, the Hague Conventions do not govern international jurisdiction directly. They do not affect such jurisdiction except as regards recognition and enforcement of judgments. Regulation of the direct international jurisdiction would certainly be useful. Its absence does not seem, however, to have been felt to be a serious inconvenience.

After having described the origin of the Hague system, we shall examine more closely the problem of the law applicable. We will then examine the influence of the Conventions on the Italian law.

The Status of the Conventions of 1956/58

The "Convention on the Law applicable to Maintenance Obligations towards the Children", of 24th October 1956, is in force in the following States[12]: the Federal Republic of Germany, Austria, Belgium, Spain, France, Italy, Liechtenstein, Luxembourg, the Netherlands, Portugal, Switzerland and Turkey.

The "Convention concerning the Recognition and Enforcement of Judgments in the matter of Alimentary Obligations towards the Children" of 15th April 1958, was in force at the same date between the following States: Germany,

---

11. M M Verwilghen, reporter on the subject at the Twelfth Session of the Hague Conference on Private International Law, is preparing an exhaustive work on the alimentary obligations, which will especially highlight their specific character.
12. 1st March 1977.

Austria, Belgium, Denmark, Spain, Finland, France, Hungary, Italy, Liechtenstein, Norway, the Netherlands, Portugal, Sweden, Switzerland, Czechoslovakia and Turkey.[13]

Given the great difficulty there is to obtain the ratification by States of Conventions on private international law, the number of States who are parties to the Conventions of 1956/58 must be considered impressive. This is all the more so because, at the level of the law applicable, the Convention of 1956 modified the existing law for many countries in a fairly radical way by replacing the connecting factor of nationality by the connecting factor of the habitual residence of the child. How can this success be explained? It is submitted that the principal merit is attributable to the late Professor L I de Winter, of the University of Amsterdam. As a reporter, he could defend in a convincing manner some simple and persuasive principles which are at the basis of the Conventions. Thus he could carry conviction with delegates at the Conference and, consequently, with Governments.

The Principles at the basis of these Conventions

The first idea was a deliberate legislative policy: that of favouring the infant. It is sometimes claimed that private international law can achieve indirect justice only, for its method is to attribute each legal relationship to the legislation with which it has the closest ties. It is not allowed to pursue aims of a substantive nature. But this concept has been sufficiently refuted, so that it need not be elaborated any longer.

In respect of support, it has been thought justified to give a certain number of advantages to the child, who is the weaker party. The person who owes this support, more especially the natural father, has already a number of means, in the internal law, of evading his obligations. The possibilities open to him to do so are amplified if he can add to the internal opportunities those afforded by international law. This policy in favour of the infant is realised first by the choice of the connecting factors in respect of the applicable law, which consists of giving to the infant a second chance by the application of a different law if the first law applicable refuses him the necessary support. It also consists in according to such an infant, on the question of enforcement, facilities which go beyond what is permitted in other areas. The delegates of the States which met at the Hague in 1956 thus adopted, at the international level, a legislative policy which, in many internal laws, only appeared much later.

---

13. For the genesis of these Conventions reference can be made to the two volumes published by the Hague Conference on Private International Law: *Acts of the Eighth Session* (1956) and *Documents relating to the Eighth Session* (1956), notably to the two reports of L I de Winter, p. 124 of the first and p. 310 of the second volume. For the numerous commentaries, etc., see the biliographies published periodically by the Hague Conference on Private International Law, and lastly in the *Acts and Documents of the Twelfth Session* (1972), tome I, Miscellaneous, p. 139, and the book published by the T M C Asser Institute at The Hague: M Sumampouw: Les nouvelles Conventions de La Haye: leur application par les juges nationaux, Leiden, 1970, Supplément 1972 (*Recueil Asser*). This book also relates the case law; on this see also A E von Overbeck, L'application par le juge interne des conventions de droit international privé, Recueil des Cours de l'Académie de droit international (*Recueil des Cours*), tome 123, 1971, I, p. 1.

(a) The connecting factor of the habitual residence of the child

The second paramount idea was to choose the habitual residence of the child as the principal connecting factor. The national rules of private international law most often submit the alimentary obligation to the national law of one of the interested parties or to the law of a domicile fixed by reference to some other person than the person who owes the support. In 1956 it was thought desirable to accord to the infant the regime of the environment in which he effectively lives. On the one hand the needs of the child can best be measured in accordance with the social conditions of his milieu and, on the other, all the children living in the given environment can be placed on the same footing in this way. Lastly, in attaching the alimentary obligation to the person of the child, his claims against several debtors can be submitted to the same law. On the practical side it can be added that it is the judge of the habitual residence who will be best able to appreciate the situation of the child. It is on this ground that a number of statutes provide, in derogation of the general principle *actor sequitur forum rei*, a forum of the domicile or of the habitual residence of the child. The Conference did not think that it could, in the present stage of development of the law, impose such a jurisdiction directly on the States, but it provided for the enforcement of judgments rendered such a forum.[14]

The expression "habitual residence" was chosen as an autonomous term, not tainted by national qualifications. It was intended to express this integration in a specific situation. It can be appreciated that the circumstances in which the child lives will determine his habitual residence. In any case, the latter is not identical with the domicile of dependence, fixed by reference to the domicile of the person entitled to exercise the powers of the father or of the guardian, as is the case in many legal systems. Even less can "habitual residence" be identified with domicile in the English sense.[15]

This said, it is necessary to agree that it is not easy, and probably even impossible, to define habitual residence in a satisfactory manner. It is not exactly true to say that habitual residence is a pure notion of fact. The elements of intention can play a part. Thus, if a small child is placed in the home of foster parents for a long period, it is certain that he will have his habitual residence there as from the beginning of his stay. It is the judge who has to appreciate the existence of a habitual residence, taking account of the policy underlying the Conventions.

It cannot be denied that there could be embarrassing marginal cases. One of these was recently decided by the German Federal Court.[16] A Spanish mother who, temporarily, could not look after her child who had to start school, placed him in a boarding school in Spain. The German judges considered that the child had at all times his habitual residence in Germany. It would seem that this point of view is justified if the placement had been purely provisional but that,

---

14. The possibility of reservation open to the States on this subject (Article 18) in the Convention of 1958 was not repeated in 1972.
15. See on English case law, C Hall, *Cruse v Chittam: Habitual Residence Judicially Explored*, *ICLQ* 1975, p. 1.
16. BGH 5.2.1975, *Zeitschrift für das gesamte Familienrecht (FamRZ)* 1975, p. 272.

if studies of a certain duration had been envisaged, then the habitual residence of the child ought to have been in Spain. The Court considered that the habitual residence must be in the place where the interested person had his main interests.[17] The Court considered that it was a matter of the domicile of fact which was not differentiated from the domicile in the sense of German law except by the lack of will to make the place of habitual residence the centre of the interests. According to this opinion, habitual residence is thus a concept very close to that of domicile in Continental law, but of course without the rules concerning the domicile of dependence.

The reasons which have led to the adoption of the law of habitual residence has as a natural corollary a variable connecting factor. When the habitual residence of a child changes, the law applicable to the alimentary obligation also changes. The consequences of this system will be discussed later.

(b) The separate rules on maintenance

The third fundamental idea of the Conventions of 1956/58 was to establish specific rules concerning choice of law, and recognition and enforcement of foreign judgements, only in the field of maintenance obligations. As the Convention lays down, only that part of the effective terms of a judgment relating to the obligation to support should be recognised and enforced.[18] The Convention on the law applicable also specifies that the judgments handed down as a result of an application of the rules of the Convention, cannot prejudice questions of affiliation and of family relationships.[19]

These provisions were absolutely necessary in order to obtain the agreement of the States who favoured the principle of nationality.

The development of the system by the Conventions of 1972/73

The "Convention on the Law Applicable to Maintenance Obligations" of 2nd October 1973 and the "Convention on the Recognition and Enforcement of Decisions Relating to Alimentary Obligations" of 2nd October 1973, have so far been ratified by three or four states.[20] However, their ratification is in progress in several countries. The delays which, to impatient youth may appear to be long, must be accepted, though with a certain resignation, by those who recognise the slow pace at which government machines operate. The new Conventions remain on the lines of the former ones but they nevertheless contain certain important innovations which are indicated below.

---

17. *Der Schwerpunkt der Bindungen der betreffenden Person, ihr Daseinsmittelpunkt.*
18. Convention on Enforcement, Article 1, para. 2.
19. Article 5, para. 2, second phrase.
20. On these Conventions see *Acts and Documents of the Twelfth Session*, 1972, tome IV, Obligations alimentaires, especially the Report by M Verwilghen, p. 384 (cited *Verwilghen Report*); the Bibliographie ibid., tome I, p. 147, and: H Batiffol, La Douzième session de la Conférence de La Haye de droit international privé, Revue critique de droit international privé (*Revue critique*), 1973, p. 261; P Bellet, Les nouvelles Conventions de La Haye sur les obligations alimentaires, Journal du Droit international (*Clunet*), 1974, p. 5; A E von Overbeck, Les nouvelles Conventions de La Haye sur les obligations alimentaires, *ASDI*, 1973, vol. XXIX, p. 135.

(i) The inclusion of adults

In the first place, as has already been said, the Conventions are now applicable to all persons to whom support is owed, and not only to children. For certain adults specific solutions have been established. It is the same, in this respect, with regard to the alimentary obligations towards the relatives by marriage and the collaterals. In addition the States have certain possibilities, which need not be considered here, for restricting the area of application of the Conventions.[21]

Originally, at its Twelfth Session the Conference had the intention of completing the treaties on the alimentary obligations towards children by adding to them treaties on adults. However, it appeared that it was convenient, at the least, to coordinate the various instruments. Finally, there was a preference for drafting new Conventions intended to replace totally the former ones. This permitted, notably, the extension of benefits to the infants through a number of improvements which, after fifteen years of experience, have shown themselves to be useful. These considerations have outweighed the inconveniences resulting from the fact that, during a certain number of years, it will be necessary according to the facts to apply either the earlier or the more recent Convention.

(ii) The consideration of the common nationality in certain cases

Habitual residence has been maintained as the principal connecting factor.[22] The new Conventions give a wider place to nationality, which is retained in the second line in respect of the law applicable; on the other hand the judgments handed down by the Court of the common nationality of the creditor and the debtor will be equally enforced.

(iii) The "universal" character of the rules on the applicable law

The rules laid down in respect of the law applicable become now the general private international law of the contracting States.[23] The rules of the ordinary law disappear completely. This was not the case under the Convention of 1956, which applied only to children having their habitual residence in the territory of a contracting State.[24] In the same order of ideas, the new Convention on the law applicable is open without restriction to the signature of any State.[25]

(iv) The inclusion of settlements and, optionally, of authentic acts

The recognition and enforcement has been extended to settlements.[26] This permits the avoidance of proceedings, which are altogether formal, against debtors who are ready to fulfil their obligations. Such proceedings were hitherto

---

21. Convention on the Law Applicable, articles 13 and 14; Convention on Enforcement, article 26.
22. Article 15 of the Convention on the Law Applicable, maintains the possibility for the States, already provided for by Article 2 of the 1956 Convention, of applying the *lex fori*, when the habitual residence of the creditor is the only foreign element.
23. The Convention on the Law Applicable, Article 3.
24. Article 6.
25. Article 21.
26. Convention on Enforcement, Article 21.

necessary to obtain a right capable of being enforced in case the debtor should change his attitude. The contracting State can even agree to enforce official deeds (*actes authentiques*).

(v) *The rules relating to public authorities*

Lastly, in proceedings for support, the new Conventions take account of the increasingly more important role of public authorities. Articles 18 to 20 of the Convention on Enforcement fix the conditions in which public institutions can obtain the enforcement of foreign judgments. Article 9 of the Convention on the Law Applicable contains a corresponding rule on choice of law.

The Law Applicable According to the Conventions – solution favouring the person entitled to support

Among the principles which form the foundation of the Conventions on the Law Applicable, which we have examined, that of the connecting point of the habitual residence, which is an expression of the environment where the creditor lives, gives way, at the end of the day, to the principle of favour to the creditor. But such is not the case regarding the obligations between divorced spouses and between collaterals and relatives by marriage.[28] While setting the principle of the application of the law of the place where he lives, it was not intended to deprive the person entitled to support of the possibilities which could result from the application of other laws with which such a person had some connections. Has this not gone too far? It could be answered that, in these international cases—the only ones which are of interest here—the creditor is a prey to additional difficulties which do not exist in purely internal cases. It is justified, then, to come to his aid with remedies which are also specific to international cases.

(a) *The various possibilities of favouring the creditor by means of rules of conflict*

Before describing the solutions of the Conventions, let us see how a person entitled to support can be favoured by extending to him or her several alternatives.

In the first place, one can state that the most favourable among several laws which can be taken into account, will be applied. However, this solution, generous in itself, presents serious difficulties when it is sought to put it into practice. Thus, in respect of affiliation, which law is the most favourable? —that which permits the establishment of paternity fairly easily on the basis of presumptions but which limits the income as regards its duration—or that which lays down more severe requirements but which is consequently more generous? The uniform law of the Benelux on private international law originally

---

27. Article 25.
28. Convention on Alimentary Obligations 1973, Articles 7 and 8.

contained a rule of this type, which has been subsequently abandoned.[29] In any case, the comparison can be meaningful only in the particular case. It is then up to the judge to apply the law which produces the best result for the child.

A fairly similar system consists in providing an alternative choice of several laws, without retaining the criterion of the most favourable law. In this respect it must be asked whether the choice is exercised by the judge, or whether the plaintiff should decide. The choice by the judge is provided for by the French law of 1972 in questions of legitimation and recognition. According to Articles 311-16 first paragraph and 311-17 of the French Civil code, the desired result can be achieved according to one amongst several laws.[30]

The choice between the laws provided for as alternatives can be left to the plaintiff, Article 311-18 of the French Civil code provides for the choice of the plaintiff in the action for a subsidy, but the authors are not altogether in agreement about the conditions of this choice.[31] This places a fairly heavy responsibility on the shoulders of the creditor or, more exactly, since it is a question of a child, on the shoulders of the persons charged with the defence of his interests. Madame Simon Depitre and M Foyer[32] rightly ask whether that is not a poisoned gift.

Lastly, one can make use of the system of subsidiary or successive applicable laws.

It should be remembered that this proceeding is commonly employed where a first connecting factor does not give results. Thus, for example, failing a common nationality of the interested persons, the law of their common domicile will be applied.

If it is desired to make use of such a system in favour of the infant, the process is a little different. To begin with, a first law is chosen, as the main one. If it is then established that that law does not grant support to the child, a second applicable law is provided.

In existing law, Article 9 of Chapter 7 of the Spanish Civil Code, as amended by the law of 17th March 1973, provides for such a system. Between parents the obligation to support is governed by the national law common to the creditor and the debtor. But the law of the habitual residence of the person entitled to support applies if the latter cannot obtain support according to the common national law. Lastly, failing these two applicable legal systems, or when one of them does not permit the Court to grant support, the *lex fori* is applicable.

The Hague Conventions on the law applicable are based on the same technique.

(b) *The technique of the Hague Conventions*

The Convention of 1956 has provided in Article 3 for the case where the law of the habitual residence of the child refuses him or her all rights to support. It

---

29. Article 9, former para. 3 and, on the other hand, Article 5, para. 3 of the new text. See especially I Kisch, La loi la plus favorable (réflexions à propos de l'article 9 al. 3 deuxième phrase de la loi uniforme Benelux), Ius et Lex, Festgabe für Max Gutzwiller, Bâle, 1959, p. 373.
30. M Simon-Depitre and J Foyer, *op. cit.*, No. 58, p. 43.
31. H Batiffol et P Lagarde, L'improvisation de nouvelles règles de conflit en matière de filiation, *Revue critique*, 1972, p. 26; A Ponsard, La loi française du 3 janvier 1972 et les conflits de lois en matière de filiation, *Clunet*, 1972, p. 789; M Simon-Depitre et J Foyer, op. cit., No 57, p. 43.
32. *Op. cit.*, No. 56, p. 42.

makes provision for the application of the law designated by the national rules of conflict of the authority seised of the problem. This subsidiary reference to national law was possible, since that law must, in any case, subsist for cases, not covered by the Convention, of children who do not have their habitual residence in one of the contracting States. Evidently this would provide a second chance only in so far as the national rules of conflict permit the application of a different law.

Given the universal application of the rules of conflict of the Convention of 1973, it was no longer possible as a subsidiary matter to rely cn the national rules of conflict. It was therefore sought to insert a subsidiary connecting factor in the Convention. It is natural to think at first of nationality as a connecting factor, as is the case according to many national rules of conflict. It was thought, however, that only the common nationality of the creditor and the debtor, and not the nationality of one of the two, was a sufficient connection. Lastly, the Convention provided in the last resort for recourse to the *lex fori* of the authority seised with the problem, in default of a common nationality or when the common national law did not lead to the allocation of support.[33]

This system again expresses the legislative policy in favour of the person entitled to support: a court should allocate support by applying the law of the habitual residence, or the common national law, in some cases in which its own law does not provide for it. But the opposite is not true. Never will a judge refuse support if his own *lex fori* does allow him to allocate it. It will be found that, if the person entitled to support has the same nationality as the person owing it—which can result from the slightly arbitrary interplay of the various laws on nationality—he has one more chance. The solution can nevertheless be defended by the consideration that, in the normal course of things, a common nationality expresses a link of a certain intensity with the law of a given country.

The importance of the system of subsidiary connecting factors must not be overestimated. The evolution of the internal law has the consequence that the hypothesis that the law of habitual residence will refuse support in cases where other laws accord them, will be more and more rare. And the subsidiary solutions will only operate in the case of a refusal of all support, not when the second choice of applicable law is simply "more favourable.".

It is fitting to add that the Convention of 1973 permits the applicable law to be corrected in certain cases: for the fixing of the allowance, both the needs of the person entitled to support and the resources of the defendant must be taken into account.[34] It should be recalled that the former German law did not meet this requirement.

The Law Applicable continued – More Restrictive Solutions for Certain Alimentary Obligations

(a) Divorced Spouses

Article 8 of the 1973 Convention on the law applicable, subjects the alimentary obligations between the divorced spouses to the law which had been applied to

---

33. Articles 5 and 6.
34. Article 11, para. 2.

the divorce. The same rule is valid for legal separation, nullity or annulment, or for any modifications of all these judgments.[35] This solution is justified by the firm link which exists between the decree of divorce and its effects. The considerations of *favor obligationis* are not necessarily valid here. The rule supposes that the divorce has been given in the country of the judge who pronounces on the obligation to support, or that it will be least be recognised there. If one of these two conditions is not fulfilled, that means that the spouse is considered as still married in the State in question. He or she may be able to provide for the allocation to himself or herself of the support owed to a spouse who is not divorced, in accordance with the rules of Articles 4-6.

(b) The collaterals and the relatives by marriage

The alimentary obligations between collaterals were excluded from the 1956 Convention. Such obligations are known only in certain countries, while other countries do not favour their recognition. Analogous considerations are valid for the relationships between relatives by marriage. Consequently, the two categories of persons are subjected to a restriction which the Conference had at one time envisaged for all the alimentary obligations between adults. Article 7 of the 1973 Convention on the law applicable permits, as a defence to the action, the pleading of the absence of an obligation to support according to the common national law of the creditor and of the debtor, or, in the absence of such law, according to the law of the habitual residence of the debtor. The States can, moreover, in applying Article 14 of the Convention on the law applicable, exclude this case completely from the field of the Convention.[36]

The determination of the legal link on which the maintenance obligation is founded

(a) The problem

Reference has just been made to the obligation between well-defined persons, the divorced spouses, and between others who form a wider circle, i.e. the collaterals and the relatives by marriage. In addition we have referred to the alimentary obligations for which the Hague Conventions have established a distinct set of conflicts rules, in a completely general way. This has left open an essential question, that of knowing which are the relations on which maintenance is based aimed at by the Convention. In other words, how to establish which person owes support to whom.

It must be admitted that, in this respect, the Conventions of 1956/58 are not very precise, this defect having given rise to many difficulties in practice.

The Conventions of 1973[37] contain the following definition: "Maintenance obligations arising from a family relationship, parentage, marriage or affinity, including a maintenance obligation in respect of a child who is not legitimate".

---

35. See Verwilghen Report, No. 152 *et seq.*, p. 447.
36. Article 26, chapter 2 of the Convention on Enforcement provides for an analogous possibility.
37. Law Applicable, Article 1, Enforcement, Article 1.

296

This definition is also valid in the framework of the Conventions of 1956–58. It is aimed at the legal obligations to support (as distinct from those which are purely the result of agreement), between relatives in the widest possible sense. Moreover, the legal basis of the obligation is unimportant. In mentioning illegitimate children specially, it was particularly desired to express the fact that the alimentary obligations, founded on the natural affiliation, were always intended to be covered even if they were qualified, for example, as purely patrimonial or delictual.[38]

The law of the habitual residence of the person entitled to support (or possibly one of the applicable laws in the subsidiary group) will govern the alimentary obligations between all the relatives in the broad sense. But the support due by the legitimate father, the natural father, or also by an aunt or a relative by affinity, are not the same; according to certain laws, those mentioned last do not owe anything at all. It is thus a question of defining more closely the links which unite the person entitled to support and the person owing support.

At the outset it is necessary to cite Article 10 of the first chapter of the 1973 Convention on the law applicable, which was taken from the 1956 Convention: "The law applicable to a maintenance obligation shall determine *inter alia*: 1. whether, to what extent and from whom a creditor may claim maintenance . . ." This legislative provision expresses the idea that the Convention wished to govern the law applicable, not only as to the quantum of the alimentary obligation, but also as to its principle. But, according to Article 2, paragraph 2, of the 1973 Convention on the law applicable, the decisions taken under the Convention do not prejudice the existence of "family relations . . ." etc provided for in the first Article.[39] According to this provision and according to the corresponding rules of the Convention on Enforcement, only the decision on support involves obligations for the other contracting States.

This extension of the treaty law to the cause of the obligation to support on the one hand and, on the other, the restriction of the effects of the decisions only to the level of support which arises from the cause thus established, has raised several difficulties of interpretation. In fact there is, at least at first sight, a paradox in condemning a man to pay an allowance to a child, while refusing to take up a position concerning him on the question of whether he is that child's father.[40]

The difficulties appear only when the relation "of family" (still in the broad sense) is itself the subject of litigation. If the position of the parties is clear because they are, without contradiction, husband and wife, or the adopting father and the adopted child, etc., it is a different question. Once the link "of family"— e.g. stepmother and stepson—is known, the question of whether support is due

---

38. Such is the case according to a widespread opinion in Italian law; see *infra* Section C. See on this question the Verwilghen Report Nos. 14 *et seq*, p. 390.
39. See also Article 3 of the Convention on Enforcement. These provisions are repeated from the Conventions of 1956/58 (Convention on the Law Applicable, Article 5, para. 2, second phrase; Convention on Enforcement, Article 1, para. 2).
40. See also H Batiffol, *op. cit.*; *Revue Critique* 1973, p. 266; and Verwilghen Report, Nos. 129 *et seq*., p. 437.

devolves upon the question of whether the law of habitual residence has established an alimentary obligation between the persons whom the bond unites.

The main cases can be stated.

(b) Divorced spouses

The particular solution given in Article 8 of the 1973 Convention may be recalled. Here reference is expressly made to the law of the forum to determine if a spouse is divorced. In more technical terms it is said that the preliminary question of divorce is decided, independently, according to the private international law of the forum.

(c) The creditor already having a certain status

This is a second common case—a creditor who already enjoys, in comparison with the debtor, an established status such as that of a recognised infant, or a nephew, or a stepson. In the case of a legitimate child who finds himself constrained to claim support from his father or from his mother because the parents are separated, when the legitimacy of the child is not in doubt, the rules of the law of habitual residence relative to support due to legitimate children will be applied, for example, in respect of the question as to what age the maintenance must be paid to students. In fact, if one wished to push the principle that the law of habitual residence also governs the ground for the alimentary obligation to its ultimate consequences, it would be necessary to verify afresh, according to the substantive law of habitual residence, whether the marriage of the parents was valid, whether the infant was born at a moment which renders him legitimate, etc. This will not occur to any sensible judge.

(d) The child having no status

This is a critical hypothesis, where the tie between creditor and debtor is disputed. This is the case of a child presenting himself before a judge for the first time without having the benefit of some status. He claims maintenance from a person whom he indicates as his father, but who denies paternity. There will be no great difficulty here if both the State of the forum and that of the habitual residence provide—as Swiss law did until 1978 and as former German law did—a purely alimentary action founded on the fact of the biological paternity.[41]

---

41. The entry into force of the Illegitimacy Act in Germany (*Nichtehelichengesetz*) on July 1st 1970 has raised problems relating to the connection between the purely alimentary action and the declaration of affiliation. Article 1600a of the German civil code (*BGB*) lays down in fact that the declaration of paternity is a condition of the obligation to maintain. The German courts have set on one side the separate connecting factor for the declaration of paternity, and have finally adopted a solution which amounts to subjecting the question of status to the law governing the obligation to maintain. The point will be returned to below, p. 308. The modification of the German law could not, however, remain without some effect on the attitude of the courts of other countries. In the *Siesky case*, decided on 30th May 1972, the Paris Court of Appeal had to recognise an action brought before the court at Meaux according to the German law, which was the child's law of habitual residence. The change of law in Germany occurred

But what happens when the laws in point, or one of them, do not provide for the alimentary obligation except insofar as there has been an affiliation established by a judgment or a recognition? Such States regularly have a specific rule of conflict for the establishment of the affiliation founded, for example, on the nationality of the father. Supposing that to be so in "Ruritania" and that, moreover, this fictitious State has a right corresponding to that of the French Civil Code before the reforms, that is to say, that the declaration of paternity is possible only in certain well defined cases and that no support is to be granted beyond these cases. Supposing that a Ruritanian judge had to decide the action of a child, who has his habitual residence in Switzerland, against a Ruritanian defendant. It has to be assumed that no ground of paternity according to Ruritanian law exists. If he applies purely and simply the Swiss code, the judge will order the father to pay an alimentary pension. The limitation of the effects of the Convention to the obligation to support will prevent that Ruritanian from being considered the father from the standpoint of other questions of family law. However, on the assumption that the Ruritanian rule of conflict relative to the affiliation designates the *lex fori*, could the Ruritanian judge, even with this purely alimentary effect, condemn a Ruritanian when, according to Ruritanian law, there is no paternity in that particular case?

The question has been raised—and certain authors have defended the thesis—that affiliation should, at first, be determined according to the rule of conflict of the forum applicable to this question (independent solution of the preliminary question). This opinion results in that a negative reply by the applicable law concerning the affiliation—for example, by the national law of the father—would put an end to all possibility of allocating support. The decision on the principle of maintenance would, in reality, be taken according to the law applicable to the affiliation, and not according to the law of habitual residence, as the Convention wishes it.

In particular, one could not found this opinion on the provisions of the Conventions which limit the effect of the judgments to the alimentary point. On the contrary, the provisions are necessary precisely in order to permit of judgments on the affiliation according to the law of habitual residence, but only as a ground for a maintenance order, and without any other international effect.

---

during the course of the case and the Court of Appeal was of the opinion, according to the transitory provisions of German law combined with certain rules of procedure in French law, that it should allow time to the plaintiff to bring an action for declaration of paternity in the sense of the new provisions of the German law (*Revue critique*, 1972, p. 660, note Lagarde). Which law will be applied, and which judge will be competent? Professor Lagarde in his note defends vigorously the solution that the court already seised should deal with the matter and should do so, according to the principles of the 1956 Convention, by applying internal German law. M Lagarde adds some remarks on the effects of the new French rules of conflict which came into effect in 1972. He advocates giving the Convention priority, but observes that article 311-18 concerning the action for subsidies in the last analysis gives to the creditor more possibilities than the Convention. The creditor has in fact the choice between the law of his and that of the debtors habitual residence. This remark applies to the 1973 Convention on the Applicable Law. In fact the law of the habitual residence of the debtor could at the very most become applicable as the *lex fori*.

Moreover, it would also be completely erroneous to solve the preliminary question of affiliation according to the rules of conflict of the law applicable to the alimentary obligation. Far from that being the case, the substantive provisions of this law must be consulted in order to judge the principle of the obligation to support.[42]

(e) The law applicable to the preliminary question of affiliation

By way of summary, if one wishes to see affiliation as a preliminary question, it should not be judged according to any of the branches of the classical alternatives between allocation to the law of the forum and allocation to the *lex causae*, but according to the substantive law which governs the principal question of the alimentary obligation.

The great majority of authors and decisions have interpreted the Conventions of 1956/58 in this sense. This interpretation has also been shared by the delegates who have worked out the Conventions of 1973.[43] The Conference has even thought of expressly introducing this solution in the text. According to the report, it has not done so, above all for fear of seeing the desirable solution drafted in an ambiguous fashion.[44]

However, as we have seen, the application of the conventional law to the principle of the alimentary obligation has limits at the point where the pre-liminary question has already been resolved in the eyes of the judge. In these cases, the creditor has already a label, for example, of a legitimate, recognised or an adopted child. In our previous example, if the father had already recognised the child in a way valid in the eyes of the Ruritanian judge, the latter would certainly not verify a second time, according to the Swiss law, whether paternity could be established On the contrary, he would allow the support provided by Swiss law for a natural child which has been recognised. It can also be seen that the system just described operates in favour of the person entitled to support. If he appeared "with empty hands", he could be allowed support on the basis of the

---

42. If the question of the affiliation could be solved separately, these provisions would lose all relevance each time the forum and the State of enforcement decide the affiliation according to the same criterion.

43. On the contrary, the draft scheme in Article 13 (*Acts and Documents of the Twelfth Session*, 1972, tome IV, p. 90, III p. 126) left to the authority seised of the matter the trouble of con-necting the preliminary question as the authority intends. But it concerned only the adults for whom the Convention submitted the most important case, that of divorced spouses, to special rules.

44. The Verwilghen Report No. 127 i.f., p. 437. See, on the whole question, this report No. 24 *et. seq*, p. 435; and also, especially, A E von Overbeck, Une règle de conflit uniforme en matière d'obligations alimentaires envers les enfants, Nederlands Tijdschrift voor Internationaal Recht (*NTIR*), 1958, p. 255, especially p. 264; Id. *Recueil des Cours*, tome 132, No 32 et s., p. 62; K Siehr, Auswirkungen des Nichtehelichengesetzes auf das Internationale Privat- und Verfahrensrecht, Bielefeld, 1972, p. 85 (*Auswirkungen*); P Lagarde, note under C A Paris 20 mai 1972, *Revue critique*, 1972, p. 666; P Bellet, Comité français de droit international privé, *Revue critique*, 1975, p. 169; the references given by these works and Sumampouw, op. cit. Contra see J Déprez, Les conflits de loi en matière d'obligations alimentaires, *Revue critique*, 1957, p. 391; Y Loussouarn, Les Conventions de La Haye relatives aux obligations alimentaires envers les mineurs, Liber Amicorum Baron Louis Frédéricq, Gand, 1965, p. 703; F Sturm, De alimen-torum statuti vi attractivo, Juristenzeitung (*JZ*), 1974, p. 206, with many references to various opinions.

law of habitual residence, provided that the latter permitted that the defendant, as father, should be taken into account. If, on the other hand, the person entitled presents himself as a recognised natural infant, or as an adopted child, and the judge seised of the matter recognises such status, the law of habitual residence will not be applied except to decide whether the bearer of such a status has the right to some support, and for the purpose of fixing the methods and the total sum. But it could not be invoked in order to put the disputed status in issue again.[45]

(*f*) *The example of adoption and the limits of the independence of the maintenance obligations*

In order to demonstrate that the question of the independence of the maintenance obligation arises primarily for the natural child we can, as it were, envisage the case of adoption as counter-evidence or as a *reductio ad absurdum*. It is quite clear that a child cannot receive maintenance in the capacity of an adopted child unless the judge seised of the case finds himself faced with an adoption which he can recognise. Suppose that a child has lived with his foster-parents in Luxembourg and that thereafter he had his habitual residence in Switzerland. He clearly could not claim that, according to Swiss law the conditions of adoption are fulfilled and that, consequently, his Luxembourg foster-parents must be liable for maintenance due to an adopted child. Adoption as the legal ground for the alimentary obligation assumes the joining of two elements which are lacking here: the wish of the parents to adopt and a decision on the part of an authority.

This does permit us to observe more closely the limits of the independence of the maintenance obligations in the sense of the Hague Conventions. The obligation must always be founded on a pre-existing cause. In paternity suits, the pre-existing cause is a fact. It is the biological paternity, which is subject to confirmation. On the other hand, in cases where the creditor already has a status (for example, that of a child who has been recognised, or of a legitimate or adopted child), the pre-existing cause is precisely this status. It can be the result of the law (legitimate child), of a legal act (recognised child), or of a decision by an authority (adopted child).

Change of the connecting factor (conflits mobiles)[46]

Article 4, paragraph 2, of the Convention of 1973 on the law applicable, repeating Article 1 paragraph 2 of that of 1956, provides that a change in the habitual residence involves the application of a new law. Although the Convention does not say so expressly, the same thing must be true for those laws which are applicable as if the law of habitual residence does not apply.

This changeability of the connecting factor can also benefit the creditor. If he has obtained nothing according to the law of a first habitual residence he can, in

---

45. An adaptation can be necessary between the pre-existing statute and the categories of the law of habitual residence. If, for example, the latter law does not know adoption, it will be examined whether an adopted child should receive the maintenance due to a legitimate child.
46. See Verwilghen Report, No. 140/141, p. 442.

fact, have another chance after a change of country. It is true that, in principle, if he subsequently establishes himself in a third country, his right lapses and he would have to start entirely afresh. In fact, the judgment has no effect beyond the obligation of support, and the basis of that obligation falls as a result of the change in the habitual residence. That can appear unfavourable for the creditor. In reality, many factors in this field alleviate the apparent rigour of the system:

(a) First, a judgment remains executory until it is replaced by another decision, even if the law according to which it was given has lost its applicability.[47]

(b) Secondly, in fresh proceedings it will generally be possible to produce the first judgment in evidence.

(c) Lastly, nothing prevents the States from recognising a first judgment beyond the purely support aspects. If the judgment contains a true declaration of paternity and if it can be recognised according to the rules of ordinary law, the descent will be considered as having been established.

Although the text of Article 2, paragraph 2 of the Convention of 1973 on the law applicable can dispel doubt, one cannot see how a Convention could prevent a judgment from having the force of *res judicata*, in the country of the forum as much in respect of the establishment of the paternity as of the obligation to maintain. Only the international effects founded on the Convention are limited to maintenance.[43]

The Influence of the Conventions on Italian Law. The Partial Exequatur

The solutions of the two Hague Conventions of 1956/58 have had a particularly interesting influence upon the evolution of the Italian case law on the law outside the Conventions. Here we can only sketch this influence. Further references may be found in two very interesting articles of A Giardina and of Mlle. P De Cesari. The later in time gives a complete picture of the case law and of the doctrine in the matter.[49] These decisions have been taken, not within the framework of the application by the Italian judge of the foreign law of the habitual residence, but in the context of the *delibazione* of foreign decisions which make a person liable to support in cases where the affiliation could not be established according to the Italian law. Several courts of appeal at first refused the enforcement of such decisions, notably on the ground that the limitation on actions for affiliation in the Italian law was part of public policy and that it could not be admitted that the support had been founded on a wider research for paternity.

The *Cour de Cassation*, on the other hand, has recognised in several judgments the possibility of enforcing separately the alimentary part of the decision, even within the framework of national law.[50] The Court has admitted that, once

---

47. *Ibid*, No. 140 p. 442.
48. Cf. Siehr, *Auswirkungen*, p. 92.
49. A Giardina, L'exequatur partiel en Italie des décisions étrangères en matière de filiation, Multitudo Legum Ius Unum, Mélanges Wengler, vol. 2, Berlin, 1973, p. 337, also in italian in Foro italiano, 1971, I, p. 2661; P De Cesari, Diritto agli alimenti del figlio naturale, Convenzioni dell'Aja e Ordine pubblico, Rivista di diritto internazionale privato e processuale (*RDIPP*), 1974, p. 238.
50. The Conventions are often invoked only as a complement, for which the authors reproach the Court.

Article 279, Chapter 1 of the Italian Civil Code provided for support in certain cases where recognition was forbidden, there was no reason not to recognise, even in other cases, decisions imposing a liability to support. The Court expressly admitted that the affiliation proceeding only had the character of a condition of fact, and that its effect was limited to the alimentary obligation. Moreover, the Court considered such obligations as having a purely patrimonial and not a family character. This qualification had the consequence that, according to the private international law of Italy, Article 25 paragraph 2 of the preliminary part of the Civil Code applies. This lays down that "obligations not arising from agreements are governed by the law of the place where the fact from which they flow occurred." The Court thereby came to eliminate all reference to Article 20 of the preliminary part which governs the relations between parents and children.

The above mentioned authors[51] see in these judicial decisions a clear influence of the system of the Hague Conventions. They do not question the possibility of recognising a foreign judgment concerning maintenance deriving from a descent admitted outside the cases provided for by Italian law. Indeed, they even demonstrate that the Italian law knows, for example, in the matter of nationality "special" declarations of paternity, that is, declarations that have no effect except in a very precise area. But they contest the qualification according to the criteria of Italian law, of such decisions, as purely patrimonial and would prefer in any event to speak of family relations of a particular character. This would also have the advantage in their eyes of permitting the intervention of Italian *ordre public*, in certain cases, for example when several men are ordered to pay maintenance for the same child.

This reasoning seems to conform with the Convention, which sees in the alimentary obligation the consequence of a family relationship in the broad sense. It may well be as these authors suggest, that this autonomous qualification of the alimentary relationship is preferable to a qualification established by the law of the forum, drawn from the cases where the internal law of Italy provides for an alimentary obligation held to be purely patrimonial. On the other hand it would be wrong that the appeal to *ordre public* should become too frequent.

B. *Natural Children*

The Establishment of descent from the father

The study of the effect—often the most important—of illegitimate descent, that is to say the establishment of the alimentary obligation, has already permitted certain glances at the question of the establishment of such a descent. In Germany and in Italy, certain modifications of the substantive law have taken place but these have not been accompanied by new rules of conflict. On the other

---

51. See p. 302.

hand, in France such rules have been introduced[52], but they have been sharply criticised by the highest authorities in the land.[53]

The New Swiss Child Law of 25th June 1976 which contains considerable innovations for it abolishes the distinction between legitimate and illegitimate children is accompanied by rules of conflict.[54] These rules will, perhaps, only have a transitory character, given that a complete codification of the Swiss Private International Law is in preparation.

Spain and the greater part of the countries of Eastern Europe have recently codified their rules of conflict in the matter. Alongside this there exists a certain number of drafts.

Our plan is not to describe one or other system, but rather to examine the possible solutions and their advantages or disadvantages. We must restrict ourselves to principles, that is, to possible connecting factors as to the laws applicable and to combinations of them. They will be considered, above all, under the heading of the judicial establishment of paternity. In the majority of systems recognition is subjected to the same law, but the new French law for example contains special rules which favour recognition.[55]

This examination will be limited essentially to the countries of continental Europe who have rules of conflict of laws in the matter of declaration of paternity. In fact in the United Kingdom, although the situation of illegitimate children has been much improved, there still exists no declaration of paternity properly so called. The rights of natural children are always examined in the particular context.[56] The situation in the Nordic States equally merits deeper examination, though it has not been possible to examine it here. It would seem that the courts apply above all the *lex fori*, so that it is in the last analysis the criteria of jurisdiction which determine the law applicable.

The possibilities mentioned below are clearly not the only ones. They remain in the traditional framework of the European rules of conflict which have as a starting point the precise connecting factors. This does not exclude the possibility of bringing into them the necessary flexibility. It is known that, according to other theories, such rules and the foreseeability which they involve have been given up in order to seek uniquely the most just solution at the moment of the judgment.

---

52. Civil Code, Articles 311-14 to 311-18.
53. See especially H Batiffol and P Lagarde, *op. cit., Revue critique*, 1972, p. 1; on the whole of this codification see Simon Depitre and Foyer, *op. cit.* For the French law, German law and Swiss law see Les Conflits de lois en matière de filiation, en droit international privé français, allemand et suisse, Actes du Colloque des 13-14 octobre 1972, Annales de la Faculté de droit et des sciences politiques de l'Institut de recherches juridiques, politiques et sociales de Strasbourg, XXV, Travaux de l'Institut de droit comparé, Paris, 1973 (*Actes du Colloque*).
54. Message of the Federal Council to the Federal Assembly concerning the modification of the Swiss civil code (Affiliation), of 5th June 1974, *Feuille fédérale* 1974, No. 27. The law came into force on 1st January 1978.
55. Article 311-17. The French law submits, at least in principle, to the same rules for legitimate and natural affiliation while, on the other hand, many laws distinguish between these hypotheses.
56. See M Piret, Les principales réformes modifiant les droits patrimoniaux des enfants illégitimes en droit anglais, Revue internationale de droit comparé, 1973, p. 277.

Survey of possible systems

(a) Law of the place of conception or of birth

The moment of conception or of birth can play a role in fixing the connecting factor as far as time is concerned. By contrast, these places, which can be fortuitous, cannot serve to define the laws in terms of space.

(b) A quality of a single person: for example, to the nationality of the father, or to the habitual residence of the child

This solution has the advantage of providing for a single law. In fact, apart from exceptional cases of stateless persons or of refugees subjected to special rules, every person has a nationality, a domicile and a habitual residence. But in relying in this way on the father or the child, one wonders if sufficient account is taken of the fact that the relationship of affiliation is, by definition, of interest to both.

(c) A common element shared by several persons

It seems more convincing to chose the applicable law according to a common circumstance of the three interested persons—mother, father and child, or at least to two of them. Such a solution supposes a second choice, or even several such choices, in cases where the principal common element does not exist. For example, the first choice may be the common nationality, and a secondary choice the common domicile. A more subsidiary choice may be the *lex fori*.

(d) Dependence on the law governing another question

A connecting factor retained in another matter can also be extended to the affiliation, and that connecting factor can be founded in its turn on an individual element or a common element. Thus the French case law before the law of 1972 submitted the legitimate affiliation to the law applicable to the effects of the marriage (national law, common to the parties, in the absence of such law, to the law of the common domicile and, in the absence of the latter, to the *lex fori*).[57] It will be seen that, in Germany, it is the law of habitual residence, applicable in the matter of maintenance, which has been extended to affiliation.

(e) Alternative systems

In the law of alimentary obligations we have noted a tendency to put at the disposal of the person to whom the support is owed several laws, all giving him several opportunities of obtaining something. The evolution of social and moral concepts has led from the protection, more or less unintended, of the father, to a tendency to improve as far as possible the position of the natural child.

---

57. See P Lagarde, *Destinées de l'arrêt Rivière*, Clunet 1971, p. 249.

This suggests the idea, even for the establishment of affiliation, of providing several systems of law in the alternative.[58] This favourable position can operate in space: for example, it makes available at the same time the law of the domicile of the child and that of the domicile of the father. It can also operate in time: if the child has changed nationality between his birth and the moment when he brings the action, he can be permitted to found his action either on the first national law or on the second.

Connecting factor relating to one person only—Nationality

(a) The nationality of the father

This solution is often found in the rather older laws based on nationality.[59] It can also be met in more recent codifications and projects[60]. Before the reform of the law of affiliation, the German case law and doctrine applied the national law of the father to relationships, other than alimentary ones, between the natural child and the father[61].

The application of the national law of the father has the advantage of providing a certain solution, at least when the father has only one nationality. One can criticise the rule, but these criticisms are directed generally against the principle of nationality, and so we shall not go into their details.[62] It will be enough to cite the case where the father is a migrant worker. His nationality—which is perhaps that of a distant country with very different concepts—is the only foreign element, as all the other elements of the matter (domicile of the mother and of the infant and often also their nationality) point to the country to which the father has come to work. As long as the national law is restrictive as to affiliation proceedings—as is notably the case for the laws of the Arab states—the temptation will be strong to ressort to the *lex fori* on the ground of *ordre public*.[63]

---

58. On the interest of the child and, in particular, on the case law of the Swiss Federal Court, see F Knoepfler, L'intérêt de l'enfant et le droit international privé, Recueil offert au Tribunal fédéral à l'occasion de son centenaire par les Facultés de droit suisses, Bâle, 1975, p. 467.
59. Italy, Art. 20 of the Preliminary Provisions of the Civil Code; Greece, Art. 19 of the Civil Code; Switzerland, former Art. 8 LRDC.
60. Portugal, Art. 59 Civil Code; Benelux project, art. 5; Italian draft Prospettive del diritto internazionale privato. Un simposio. (Projet, rapport, et observations de juristes de divers pays), Milan, 1968, report and commentary by jurists of various countries], Milan 1968.
61. This was by virtue of the principle enshrined in Arts. 18, 19 & 20, *EGBGB*. German Federal Court (*EGH*) 28.2.1973 (*Neue Juristische Wochenschrift*) (*NJW*) 1973, p. 948 and *infra* p. 308.
62. Among innumerable contributions on the question, see L I de Winter, *Nationality or Domicile?* (The present state of affairs), *Recueil des Cours* 1969, III, tome 128, p. 349; A Bucher, *Staatsangehörigkeit und Wohnsitzprinzip* (A comparative law summary), *ASDI* 1972, vol. XXVIII, p. 76; B Dutoit, L'avenir possible du rattachement à la loi nationale en droit international privé suisse, ibid., 1969-70, vol. XXVI, p. 41.
63. On the problems of Private International Law of foreign workers, see for Germany—T Ansay and V Gessner (eds.) Gastarbeiter in Gesellschaft und Recht, München, 1974 (Beck'sche Schwarze Reihe, Bd 108), especially p. 144 and 172.

(b) The nationality of the mother

This connecting factor is found in Articles 20 and 21 of the German *EGBGB*, but these articles are concerned with the alimentary obligation. It is established in a more general way in the existing law of Austria[64] and in the draft now before parliament.[65] The French law of 1972 provides in Article 311-14, in general terms and in respect of affiliation, for the national law of the mother at the date of the birth of the child.[66]

At first sight, it might be considered discriminatory with regard to the father if the national law of the mother is applied in the establishment of paternity. However, it is submitted that this solution finds a certain justification in the nature of things. If one wished to speak of the "natural family", one could hardly dispute that the mother is normally the centre of it.

In fact, however, in the current state of the laws on nationality, the natural child will most often have the nationality of the mother, the reference to her nationality thus frequently leads to the same result as the reference to the nationality of the child. It should be noted that French law retains the nationality of the child as a secondary solution in cases where the mother is not known.

(c) The nationality of the child

The desire to favour the condition of the child, which dominates the whole matter under consideration, suggests the choice of a connecting factor depending on the person of the child. It is, in any case, apposite to recall that, in a specific case, the law of the child can very well be less favourable to him than another law.

The application of the national law of the child is fairly general in the States of Eastern Europe. An example is Article 23 of the Czechoslovak law of 4th December 1963:[67]

"(1) The action (for confirmation or disavowal) of the paternity is subject to the law of the State the nationality of which is attributed to the infant by reason of his birth.

(2) When the child lives in the Socialist Republic of Czechoslovakia, he can bring an action for affiliation (or its confirmation or disavowal) in the terms of Czechoslovak law, if that is in the interest of the infant.

(3) It is enough for the validity of the recognition of paternity that it be entered into according to the law of the State where it occurred."

---

64. Decree of 25 October 1941, Art. 12.
65. See also preliminary draft by Schwind. Para. 22, *Zeitschrift für Rechtsvergleichung*, 1971, p. 169.
66. See M Simon-Depitre and J. Foyer, *op. cit.*, No. 15, p. 22, and the critique by MM H. Batiffol and P Lagarde, *Revue critique*, 1972, p. 14 which, however, is directed more towards the fact that the connecting factor should be unique, while the old case law allowed an option to the child.
67. On the law of the Socialist countries, see in general R Bystricky, Les conflits de lois en matière de filiation dans les pays socialistes, *Actes du Colloque*, op. cit., p. 191.

Similar legislative provisions can be found, especially in the German Democratic Republic,[68] in Poland,[69] in Bulgaria[70] and in Albania.[71] These laws provide that the determining factor is the nationality at the moment of birth.

It should be pointed out that the Hungarian legislation, of older origin,[72] subjects the action for affiliation to the national law of the presumed father at the moment of the birth of the child. But a new Hungarian draft of 1974[73] provides for the national law of the child. Article 93 also lays down that Hungarian law will apply if that is more favourable to the child.

Connecting factor relating to one person only—domicile or habitual residence of the child

(a) General observations

Several of the arguments which are used to justify why the alimentary obligation towards the infant is subjected to the law of his habitual residence, can also apply to the declaration of paternity. It will be seen that the last Swiss draft takes this connecting factor into account.

However, the most interesting phenomenon, which will be examined next, is the extension of the law of the alimentary obligation to the law applicable to affiliation proceedings, as the case law has established in the German Federal Republic.

(b) The extension to the affiliation of the law governing the alimentary obligation in the Federal Republic of Germany

Before the law of July 1970, the German Civil Code knew only an alimentary action against the father which was subjected most often to the law determined by the Hague Convention of 1956. When this was not the case, Article 21 of the *EGBGB* declared the national law of the mother at the moment of birth of the child to be applicable. However, the case law had equally established an action of status in confirmation or denial of affiliation (*Abstammungsklage*). Article 644 of the Code of Civil Procedure, introduced in 1961, also provided that in such a case the judgment on status overrides a previous alimentary judgment. Hence the question arose as to what law was applicable to this action for the establishment of affiliation. The case law is orientated towards an application of the national law of the father, by analogy with other provisions of the *EGBGB*.

The law on illegitimate descent, which came into force on 1st July 1970, has very profoundly modified the internal law. The action for paternity or for recognition now lays down that the establishment of a descent is effective

---

68. Art. 18 of the law of 20th December 1965.
69. Art. 19 of the law of 12th November 1965.
70. Art. 96 of the Family Code of 15th March 1968.
71. Art. 9 of the law of 21st November 1964.
72. Law on marriage, family and wardship of 1952, revised 1957, Art. 17 para 1.
73. Art. 87.

for and against all. It is the condition of an action for maintenance.[74] It is the so-called *Sperrwirkung*. Maintenance cannot be provided except when paternity has been formally declared. But how can these provisions be reconciled with the system of the Hague Conventions which have been described here, and according to which the declaration of paternity is only a ground for the alimentary judgment? It will be seen that, at the beginning of 1973, the Federal Supreme Court pronounced on the law applicable to the declaration of paternity. In the two and a half years which preceded this decision, legal writing and some forty judicial decisions proposed a series of solutions. It is correct to mention that, among these decisions, only four applied to the maintenance question, a law other than German law. In the other cases, German law was applicable, either according to Article 21 of the *EGBGB*, or according to the Hague Convention of 1956.[75]

In the majority of cases the courts applied to the establishment of descent, not the judge-made rule referring to the national law of the father, but the German law applicable to maintenance. The explanations have been various. The argument especially favoured is that the introduction of the new law could not adversely affect the situation of the natural child, by requiring him to obtain a declaration of paternity according to a foreign law. M. Siehr remarks, not without reason, that it would have been even more convincing to say that the Hague Convention prohibits the submission of the alimentary obligation, governed by the law of habitual residence, to the consent of another law. The ambit of Article 1600a has been exaggerated by certain courts which have seen in it, for example, a procedural provision requiring a separate declaration of paternity even when the law applicable did not impose such a requirement.[76] It has also been claimed that a child of German nationality could not claim support from a foreigner except when paternity had been declared according to German law.[77] It has also been proposed that judgments be given limited to certain effects only of the declaration of paternity.

The German Federal Supreme Court decided on this question in three judgments of the Fourth Chamber, namely, a judgment and an order (*Beschluss*) of 28th February 1973[78] and a judgment of 30th October 1974.[79] In the first case, it was a question of the action of a German child of a German mother against an Egyptian. The child had his habitual residence in Germany. The Court admitted

---

74. Article 1600a of the German Civil Code actually enacts: "*Bei nichtehelichen Kindern wird die Vaterschaft durch Anerkennung oder gerichtliche Entscheidung mit Wirkung für und gegen alle festgestellt. Die Rechtswirkungen der Vaterschaft können, soweit sich nicht aus dem Gesetz ein anderes ergibt, erst vom Zeitpunkt dieser Feststellung an geltend gemacht werden.*" (For illegitimate children the paternity shall be established with effect for and against all, by recognition or by judicial decision. The legal effects of the paternity can, in so far as no other regulation results from statutory law, first be made effective as from the point in time of such establishment.)
75. For a detailed survey of this case law, see K Siehr, *Die Vaterschaftsfeststellung im deutschen internationalen Privatrecht, Der Amtsvormund (DAVorm)* 1973, p. 126; and the account by M Beitzke in *Actes du Colloque, op. cit.,* p. 131.
76. Swiss law, OLG Karlsruhe, 18.1.1971, *Die deutsche Rechtsordnung auf dem Gebiete des internationalen Privatrechts, IPRspr.* 1971, No. 77; cf. Siehr, *FamRZ,* 1971, p. 402.
77. See the authors cited in Siehr, *op. cit., DAVorm,* 1973, p. 147, note 45.
78. *NJW,* 1973, p. 948; *FamRZ* 1973, p. 257; *NJW* 1973, p. 950.
79. *NJW* 1975, p. 114; *FamRZ* 1975, p. 26.

that, as far as the alimentary obligation was concerned, the declaration of paternity should be subject to German law. The Courts set aside the solution applying to the preliminary question of descent the judge-made rule of conflict, referring the matter to the nationality of the father. This by reason of the prejudice it would bring to a large proportion of illegitimate children. The Court considered that the aim of the Hague Convention would also be compromised. It could be added that this solution would, in every way, be contrary to the Convention but, unhappily, in Germany the Treaty law does not override the internal law.

The Court rejected a solution which consisted in excluding the requirements of Article 1600a, second paragraph, in international cases and in examining the affiliation only as an incidental matter. It is decided, on the other hand, that only a declaration with complete effect is now possible in German law. The Court went on to give the solution of private international law: it is only by submitting the establishment of paternity to the law applicable to maintenance that the first aim of substantive law can be attained: namely, to ensure that there is always an obligation to pay maintenance.

A declaration of paternity with partial effect is rejected. However, the Court does not draw the conclusion that all effects of the declaration of paternity should be submitted to German law. For such questions as the name, etc., the old rule of conflict referring to the national law of the father can remain. But the decision of the German judge confirms once and for all who is the true father of the child. For similar reasons the Court rejects the proposition of restricting the judgment by implying, for example, that the declaration only applies to the effects provided for by German law. It is for the rules of private international law to determine the international effects of a declaration of paternity. In the Order of the same day, the Court also declared that even a foreign father should be mentioned in the margin of the Birth Certificate of the child.

The judgment of 28 February 1973 only envisaged the case where the action for maintenance was subjected to German law. It did not envisage the case where a foreign law was applicable. The judge-made rule was formulated in a unilateral manner.

The case where a foreign law is applicable was considered by the Fourth Chamber of the Federal Supreme Court on 30 October 1974.[80] Here it was a question of an action against a Pakistani father, domiciled in Germany, and of a child whose mother was Finnish when the child was born. Both mother and child subsequently acquired Swedish nationality and had their habitual residence in Sweden. As the Hague Convention did not apply in this case, the action for maintenance was subjected to Finnish law, according to Article 21 *EGBGB* (the national law of the mother at the time of birth). The Court held that the rule of conflict of the judgment in 1973 was not applicable since the maintenance obligation was not subject to German law. The ground for this solution is, in fact, the *Sperrwirkung* provided for by German law.[81] According to the Court, this provision has neither the authority of a rule of procedure, which ought to be

---

80. *NJW* 1975, p. 114; *FamRZ* 1975, p. 26.
81. Article 1600a, second paragraph of the German Civil Code, *BGB*.

applied in all cases judged in Germany, nor effects in private international law. The Court thought that there is no reason to ask for a declaration of paternity when the law applicable to the alimentary obligation does not require it and that, in these conditions, the rule of conflict based on the nationality of the father can continue to be applicable to the declaration of paternity. The Court was not unaware of the inconveniences of this solution, for example, that it leads to the submission of the relationship of the child with his parents to different laws. But only a legislative revision could introduce a remedy here. In the case at hand, the Court found that the national law did not permit a declaration of paternity. However, it was of the opinion that the situation was not contrary to German public policy, nor was it contrary to Constitutional law. Given the tenuous links of the case with Germany and the lack of interest for such a declaration, which was not indispensable in the particular case for obtaining maintenance.

The superior courts had been seised of this case after a suspension the alimentary action until the establishment of affiliation. The Court gave instructions to the Court of First Instance to proceed with the action for maintenance. In these circumstances descent should be examined as a preliminary question, to be solved according to the law applicable to the alimentary obligation, if such law does not provide a different solution.[82]

These judicial decisions inspired numerous commentaries. Without doubt, the last word has not been said since, according to M. Sturm, the constitutionality of the decision in 1974 has been challenged.[83] It is not intended here to pronounce on the difficult questions of constitutional law, nor is it intended to enter upon a detailed discussion of this case law.[84] From the international point of view it should be stated that, when the obligation to maintain is brought before a German judge, there will always be a complete declaration of paternity, even when the Hague Convention of 1956 is applicable. Despite the hesitations of M. Beitzke,[85] the solution seems to be compatible with the restriction of the Hague Conventions to maintenance. It may be recalled that one should not deduce from the Conventions a prohibition to give judgment on the paternity itself, at the same time as the decision is taken on the obligation to maintain. The provisions of the Conventions simply restrict the international recognition of the

---

82. " . . . *wobei die Abstammung als unselbständig anzuknüpfende Vorfrage nach demselben Statut zu prüfen ist, wenn dieses nicht eine andere Regelung vorsieht.*" It is not altogether clear if this means that the Court seeks to apply the internal law governing the alimentary obligation or, on the other hand, the rules of conflict of this law. In the case in question the Court recorded that the Swedish courts subjected the establishment of affiliation to the *lex fori*.

83. *NHW*, 1974, p. 493.

84. See especially G Beitzke, *Vaterschaftsfeststellung bei Ausländerkindern, Zentralblatt für Jugendrecht und Jugendwohlfahrt*, 1973, p. 365; W Kumme, *Die Wirkungen der gerichtlichen Vaterschaftsfeststellung bei Klagen nichtehelicher Kinder gegen einen ausländischen Erzeuger, ibid*, p. 260; H Reichart, *Rechtswirkungen der Vaterschaftstellung mit Ausländsberührung, Das Standesamt (StAZ)* 1973, p. 181; Menikheim, *Das Unterhaltsstatut als Kollisionsnorm für die Feststellung der Vaterschaft und seine personenstandsrechtliche Bedeutung, ibid,* 1974, p. 72; F Sturm *op. cit. JZ* 1974, p. 201; H J Sonnenberger, *Vaterschaftstellung und Unterhaltsanspruch internationalen Privatrecht, FamRZ* 1973, p. 553; M Ferid, review of Siehr, *Auswirkungen, op. cit., RabelsZ* 1974, p. 772.

85. *Actes du Colloque, op. cit.*, p. 133.

decisions to maintenance. The extent to which other States will recognise a declaration of paternity, effective against everybody according to the law of the habitual residence of the child—which will often also be his national law—will depend on the national private law.

The case law described apparently ought not to influence the hypothesis that the court of another country should submit maintenance to German law. It will also apply this law to the establishment of affiliation but that, from the point of view of the Conventions, only as a ground for the decision on maintenance.

Connecting factors relating to several persons

For the establishment of an illegitimate descent, the existing law does not appear to furnish examples of this type of rule. Perhaps the reason for this is that, in trying to elaborate such solutions, one is inclined to end with both principal and subsidiary rules which are too complicated.

Nevertheless there are some drafts which provide for rules which take into account several interested persons. The proposals put forward by the German Council of Private International law could be cited first.[86] Illegitimate descent is subject to the national law of the parents but, if they have no common nationality, then the applicable law is that of the habitual residence of the child. As a subsidiary link, the Council preferred the habitual residence to the personal law of one of the parents as the habitual residence is a connecting factor determined directly according to the factual situation of the child. Its relations with the two parents are thus subject to the same law. The Council also emphasised the coincidence with the law applicable to the alimentary obligations. For similar reasons, the variable connecting factor has been retained.[87]

The new Swiss Child law submits the establishment and the denial of descent to the law of the country where the child and both parents have their domicile. Failing this, the common national law of all three interested persons shall be applied. Lastly, if neither of these two elements apply, Swiss law will be applicable.[88] Finally, an escape clause has been added, as follows: "In any case, when the particular case presents prevailing links with a different country, the law of that country is applicable."

It may be felt surprising that the nationality and the common domicile of the three persons interested has been insisted on. However, the mother and the child will usually have the same nationality and the same domicile. Domicile is here understood in the sense of Swiss law; thus is depends on the domicile of the parent who has the parental authority, or on the seat of the guardian. Recourse in the last resort to the *lex fori* is not too surprising. At least it will always be the

---

86. W Lauterbach, *Vorschläge und Gutachten zur Reform des deutschen internationalen Kindschafts—Vormundschafts—und Pflegschaftsrechts, Materialien cum ausländischen und internationalen Privatrecht,* No. 7, 1966, p. 2; see also K Siehr, *Die Reform des deutschen internationalen Privat—und Zivilverfahrensrechts, ASDI* 1973, vol. XXIX, p. 247.
87. *Ibid,* p. 19 et seq.
88. Art. 8e *LRDC.*

law of the domicile or of the nationality of one of the three parties, failing which the Swiss judge would not have had jurisdiction.

Switzerland has mainly returned to the principle of domicile, which was at the root of the *LRDC* of 1891, but which was depreciated by the modifications to it of 1912. The Commission of Experts, charged with revising the whole private international law of Switzerland, has based its propositions on the principle of domicile. It may be wondered why the common national law still figures amongst the rules of conflict concerning affiliation. The principal aim of these rules is to abolish the exclusive criterion of nationality in respect of international jurisdiction.

A solution of the same kind would be the common national law and, failing that, the law of the common domicile, with the *lex fori* as the third choice. This was retained by the Yugoslav project of 1970. There was no wish to provide for the national law of the infant, not even as a subsidiary choice.[89]

It has already been mentioned that a Commission of Experts is preparing a new codification of the whole of Swiss private international law. As far as descent is concerned, the solutions currently admitted are as yet very provisional. The Commission has orientated itself towards a system of applying the law of habitual residence or of the domicile of the parent by whom the child is brought up. Failing this, the law of the habitual residence of the child would be applicable. It is thought that these provisions will be completed by a rule requiring the authorities to take further into account the rules of the national law of the infant or of one of its parents if, without it, the judgment would not be recognised in the country in question and if that would involve grave inconvenience for the child.[90]

Alternative Systems in Space and Time

The solution of the Czechoslovak and Hungarian laws has already been mentioned, that is, the application of the *lex fori* if it is more favourable to the child. The rule of the Swiss draft of 1974, permitting the setting aside of the normal links in order to apply the law to which the case is most nearly allied, can equally operate in favour of the plaintiff.

The French law of 1972 includes numerous options for the recognition, legitimation and for the action for subsidies. As for affiliation, Article 311-15 derogates from the personal law of the mother, provided by Article 311-14, in favour of the French law relating to the consequences of proof of civil status. Reference here is to the work of Mme. Simon-Depitre and M Foyer for the

---

89. F. Sadar, *Evoluzione del processo di codificazione del diritto internazionale privato di famiglia jugoslavo*, *RDIPP* 1973, p. 758, especially pp. 808, 823.

90. For a comparable system regarding adoption see Art. 8c of the Swiss *LRDC*, 1973, and the critique of M Knoepfler, *op. cit.*, p. 481. It will be noticed that the problem is different for descent and adoption. It is certainly better to establish an affiliation, even a 'limping' one, than to renounce it entirely. On the contrary, it is precisely the practitioners in international adoption who insist that 'limping' adoptions should not be created.

explanation of this rule, of which clarity is not the most conspicuous quality.[91] These authors show that the rule could be understood almost as a complete submission of affiliation to the French law of status, a solution which the Senate would have wished to establish in the text. If this is so, it is a question of a special attachment to the habitual residence in France of the two interested persons, rather than a provision in favour of the child.

MM Batiffol and Lagarde regret that the text of Article 311-14 refers to the personal law of the mother at the date of the infant's birth.[92] This seems to set aside the old case law which left to the child the choice between its national law at birth and its national law at the time of the action. Mme. Simon-Depitre and M Foyer advocate an interpretation which retains this possibility.[93]

It has just been shown that a certain benefit in the establishment of the affiliation can result from the manner in which the connecting points are fixed, or not fixed, as to the relevant time. Thus, the Swiss law of 1976 does not provide for the exact moment when the national law or the law of domicile are taken into account. This could be interpreted as permitting the choice of the moment when the connecting points indicate the most favourable law. It is true that in the matter of natural affiliation it is unlikely that the three interested persons will all change their nationality or domicile. But one could uphold the possibility of choice between the law of the domicile at the time of the child's birth, applicable because at that time all the interested parties would not have the same nationality, and the law of a common nationality which could be acquired subsequently, when one person changed domicile.

Using the approved technique of private international law one could have certain doubts about this use of moveable conflicts for the purpose of promoting the interest of the child. In the first place, the number of cases in which there are such changes of domicile or of nationality and where these really improve the situation of the child, seem necessarily to be rather restricted. Moreover, it should be remembered that, at least in European private international law, the rules of conflict are directed towards submitting a legal relationship to a national law indicated by a precise criterion. This criterion is supposed to make applicable the law of the country with which, according to the normal course of events, the relationship in question has the closest links. It must be recognised that the idea is somewhat theoretical and that the solutions chosen depend in particular on the opinions which are possible concerning the links with the nationality or with the domicile. It always happens that even the closest link can appear or disappear in time. The question of knowing whether a connecting point is adequate should be considered under the heading of the determining moment. Thus the law of a domicile which has been abandoned for several years, or that of a nationality since replaced by another, can no longer claim to be applicable. It is thus unrealistic to maintain that choice, in order to favour a child in whose life such changes have occurred. If it is desired to set up generous solutions which profit all children, it is necessary to provide for alternative application or the subsidiary

---

91. *Op. cit.*, No. 26 *et seq.*, p. 29.
92. *Op. cit.*, *Revue critique*, 1972, p. 16.
93. *Op. cit.*, No. 78, p. 53; No. 94, p. 61.

application of several legal systems and to fix the determining moment for each. What this moment should be will be examined in the next section.

Change of connecting factor. (*Conflit mobile*)

(a) Nationality

The older laws often omit to indicate the moment when the person or persons interested should possess a given nationality. By contrast, the majority of modern texts are precise on this point. Thus, the statutes of Eastern Europe, the new French law and the Italian draft of M Vitta, refer to the moment of the birth of the child. This corresponds to the idea that a link must be fixed at the moment when a decisive event occurs: a succession is subject to the law of the domicile or of the nationality of a testator at his death; a contract is subject to the law of the habitual residence of the seller at the moment when a contract is concluded, etc. Concerning affiliation, the moment of the birth or, again, that of the conception has traditionally been retained. But this may be the reflection of a point of view which considers the natural affiliation as the effect of a tort whose consequences should be controlled according to the law applicable when it was committed and which would subsequently benefit from a sort of prescription.[94] In fact, on the contrary, the establishment of natural affiliation is based on the biological link between two persons, which can be confirmed at any moment in time. The new scientific techniques permit this to be done with more and more certainty. The Swiss Federal Court has clearly highlighted this aspect of affiliation, that is, the lasting factual situation, as a foundation of the declaration of paternity in a matter involving transitory conflict of private international law.[95] An action which is statute-barred according to the Swiss law applicable under the national rules of conflict has become possible on the ground of a foreign law which has become applicable by the coming into effect of the 1956 Convention. There it was a question of paternity purely for the purpose of maintenance, but the reasoning applied also to the declaration of affiliation. It would lead to the application of the national law at the moment of the court action.

(b) Habitual residence or to the domicile

It is easier to change the habitual residence, or the domicile, than it is to change nationality. While supporting these connecting factors, it cannot be denied that this is somewhat inconvenient, especially when it is a question of giving judgment on status. Perhaps one should keep to habitual residence or domicile at the time of birth. The German case law which has been reviewed above has equally accepted the variable connecting factor for the declaration of paternity, when the German law becomes applicable. The project of the German Council on Private International Law provided for this solution by a bilateral rule.

---

94. In internal law this is expressed by brief periods of limitation for the action, such as the period of limitation of one year from the birth in former Swiss law.
95. Pattavina C Novak, 12th March 1970, ATF 96 II 13; cf. A E von Overbeck, *op. cit.*, *Recueil des Cours*, tome 132, No. 110, p. 95.

The reasons advanced concerning the determining moment in time for nationality are equally valid here. It should not be that each time the habitual residence is changed the status of the child is put in question. Certainly, in a country in which the affiliation order has been rendered, descent would be deemed to have been acquired once and for all. It is impossible to forecast with certainty what is likely to happen in other countries. It must be admitted that, to facilitate the establishment of affiliation, in the absence of an international treaty, could involve more frequent refusals of recognition in other countries. Here one again finds the principles of nationality and of domicile in opposition. Countries attached to the first principle will be reluctant to recognise judgments on civil status affecting their nationals, given in accordance with the law of habitual residence.

(c) The effects of the variable connecting factor

If the establishment of illegitimate affiliation is subjected successively to the law of each habitual residence of the child, it is undeniable that the removal of habitual residence would, on occasion, be favourable to the child. This could also be true of successive changes of nationality. To consider a hypothetical case, a child could first have his habitual residence in Italy, where he would obtain nothing at all; he could then move to Switzerland where he would discover that, according to the law of that country, the action is statute-barred; he could subsequently settle in France and there the conditions for an action for subsidies would be fulfilled. He might then establish his habitual residence in Germany where, as has been seen, according to German law he could have his affiliation established and maintenance granted at the same time; on that basis he could profit from that declaration of paternity in all countries where German decisions are recognised.

The significance of such examples should not be exaggerated. To begin with, the evolution of internal laws has the result that at least the child is able to obtain maintenance according to most laws. Also, frequent changes are fairly unlikely. If a child is not brought up by its mother, it will either be adopted or placed under the supervision of a public authority, which will maintain it in the same country. If, on the other hand, it is the mother who brings up the child, it can normally be expected that she will eventually settle, probably by marrying. One can question why the definitive consequences of the biological link existing between the child and his father should not be decided according to the law of the country where the mother and child have become established. That law appears to have more claim to be applicable than a law applicable at the moment of the child's birth, with which the interested parties have, perhaps, no link at all. It is submitted that, in the final analysis, the advantages of the variable connecting factor outweigh those of a link fixed at the time of birth.

In conclusion it should be mentioned that the Yugoslav project spoken of above, provides in its thesis no. 17 for the establishment of the paternity or maternity to be subjected to the law applicable at the time when the Court decides the question.[96]

---

96. *RDIPP* 1973, p. 823.

C. Divorce

It is intended to restrict this section to a very brief general summary. Thus, only the situation in Italy will be examined since it presents a particular interest owing to the fact that that country has recently introduced divorce into its internal legislation.

General Outline[97]

Recent legislative revisions generally tend to increase the possibilities of divorce. Thus, the Belgian law of 27 June 1960 was intended to permit the divorce of Belgians who had married a national of a country in which divorce is not recognised. The Greek and Dutch reforms aimed at creating new grounds of jurisdiction, in particular in favour of a Greek wife and of Dutch persons who do not have a domicile or a residence in the Netherlands.

In Sweden a law of 1964 provided for some supplementary possibilities over and above the cases falling within the law of 1904. In these cases, the *lex fori* is applicable, to the exclusion of the foreign national law.[98]

There is still a strong tendency only to pronounce a divorce when the grounds in the foreign law are equally existant in the *lex fori*.

As it stands at present, the draft of the Swiss Commission for the reform of Private International Law provides for very liberal solutions.[99] The jurisdiction belongs to the judge of the Swiss domicile of one of the spouses, however the judge of the domicile of the plaintiff only has jurisdiction if the domicile has lasted for at least one year. There is also a jurisdiction founded on nationality, but only if it is not possible to bring an action in a foreign country.

As regards the applicable law, the law of the common domicile and secondly the law of the common nationality, prevail. Failing a common domicile or a common nationality, Swiss law is applicable unless the spouses declare that they accept the law of the domicile or of the nationality of one of them. Lastly, if the foreign law applicable does not cater for divorce, or makes it very difficult, Swiss law applies; but always on condition that one of the spouses has been domiciled for three years in Switzerland, or is a Swiss national.

In Great Britain, a law of 1965 provided for English jurisdiction provided the wife had resided in the country for three years. The Domicile and Matrimonial Proceedings Act 1973 introduced a more important reform, which is of interest under the heading of the equality of the spouses. The wife can now have her own domicile independently of that of her husband. The rules of jurisdiction have also

---

97. See Reports by countries published in *NTIR* 1972, p. 217 *et seq:* Canada, Denmark, United Kingdom, France, Greece, Israel, Italy, Switzerland, Sweden; and 1974, p. 51; Belgium, p. 171; Spain. On the Greek and Dutch laws of 1967 and 1969, see P Kokkini-Iatridou, *Deux nouvelles réglementations de compitence internationale en matière de divorce*, *RDIPP*, 1971, p. 5. On the German, English and Swiss law, see Pi-Song Tsai, *Anerkennung ausländischer Ehescheidungen und Wiederverheiratung im internationalen Privatrecht*, in *Etudes suisses de droit international* No. 2, Zürich 1975. On the more recent developments in the United Kingdom see Dicey and Morris, *The Conflict of Laws*, 9th edn., 1973 second cumulative supplement 1974.
98. See T S Schmidt, *Private International Law of Divorce in Sweden*, *NTIR* 1972, p. 352.
99. For the current case law, see the *Ventura* judgment, given on 15 February 1973 by the Federal Court, *ATF* 99 II, p. 1, and the decisions and opinions cited there.

been widened by this law. According to section 5(2), English courts have jurisdiction if, at the time of bringing the action, one of the spouses has had his or her domicile or habitual residence in England or Wales for one year. Section 7 lays down corresponding rules for Scotland, and section 13 for Northern Ireland.

English legislation has also increased the possibility of recognising foreign divorces. It brings into operation the "Convention on the Recognition of Divorces and Legal Separations" which was signed at The Hague on 1st June 1970, and to which the following states are parties (1st June 1975): Denmark, United Kingdom, Sweden, Switzerland and Czechoslovakia. It is to be hoped that other countries will follow suit. The increased possibilities for divorce can lead to "limping" divorces, with all the complications these involve for the interested parties. Only a solution by Treaty can ensure the legal security necessary in this matter.[100]

The Situation in Italy. General Observations

The introduction of divorce into Italian law by Law No. 898 of 1st December 1970,[101] later confirmed by plebiscite, only touches upon the internal law. However, it can be claimed that this is one of the principal factors affecting the Private International Law of divorce in Europe during the last few years.

A large number of Italians had been divorced in other European countries before this legislative change. Many of them remarried and were consequently regarded as bigamists by their national law. Switzerland and Germany have for long divorced Italians at the request of their German or Swiss wives, but those countries later refused the right to remarry to the Italian husbands.[102] Many went to remarry in the United Kingdom or in Denmark, but these marriages were not recognised in the countries which had granted the divorce. This situation came to an end with the decisions of the German Federal Constitutional Court of 4th May 1971,[103] of the German Federal Supreme Court of 19th April 1972,[104] and of the Swiss Federal Court of 3rd June 1971.[105]

Without going into detail, it should be mentioned that the Swiss Federal Court, which recognised a marriage concluded in England which did not fall within the ambit of the 1902 Hague Convention on Marriage, was of the opinion that that Convention continued to prevent divorced Italians from remarrying even in Switzerland. The Convention was consequently denounced by Switzerland. On

---

100. See on this draft the *Acts and Documents of the Eleventh Session* 1968, tome II, Divorce, and the bibliography in the *Acts and Documents of the Twelfth Session*, tome I, p. 145.

101. Text *RDIPP* 1971, p. 193; French translation in *Revue critique* 1971, p. 367.

102. See A E von Overbeck, Le remariage du conjoint divorcé selon le projet de convention de La Haye sur la reconnaissance des divorces et selon les droits allemand et suisse, *Revue critique*, 1970, p. 45.

103. *StAZ* 1971, p. 189; *IPRspr.* 1971, No. 39, p. 101; *RabelsZ* 1972, p. 145, and the commentaries of various authors, *ibid*, pp. 2 *et seq.*

104. *IPRspr* 1972, No. 41, p. 86; *StAZ* 1972, p. 170; *NJW* 1972, p. 619.

105. DalBosco, *ATF* 97 I 389; *ASDI* 1972, vol. XXVIII, p. 357; on all the decisions and their consequences, see especially Pi-Song Tsai, *op. cit.*, B Dutoit and P Mercier, La nouvelle jurisprudence du Tribunal fédéral suisse concernant le remariage de l'Italien divorcé en Suisse, *RDIPP*, 1972, p. 5.

the other hand, the introduction of divorce in Italy has drastically altered the situation since the Swiss divorce of an Italian can now be recognised in Italy, or at least serve there as the foundation for a new action for divorce.

In Italy itself the new law has given rise to a certain number of problems of international law and has already lead to a number of decided cases and to ample and diverse doctrinal opinions. It will only be possible here to cite some of the most important examples.[106] Questions of constitutionality, which have also occupied the Italian courts,[107] will not be considered here. The volumes of the *Revista di diritto internazionale privato e processuale* from 1971 onwards contain numerous decisions and commentaries on the various questions.

Italian divorce law does not include rules of conflict of laws or rules of jurisdiction expressly intended as such. Case law was obliged, therefore, to operate materially with rules of conflict already in existence and notably with Articles 17 and 18 of the Preliminary Title of the Civil Code. These legislative rules provided for the application, in questions of civil status and of personal relationships between spouses, of the common national law and, in the absence of this, of the last common national law. In a more subsidiary capacity, the national law of the husband at the time of the marriage should apply. As far as the jurisdiction of the court is concerned, the general rules are considered to be equally applicable.

However, the divorce law contains two rules aimed especially at international cases. One of these rules is amongst the grounds for divorce. Article 3 specifies, in effect, that the dissolution or the cessation of the civil effects of marriage may be demanded by one of the spouses: " . . . 2. In cases where: . . . (e) the other spouse, being a foreign national, has obtained abroad the annulment or disolution of the marriage, or has contracted a new marriage abroad." On the other hand, Article 4 provides that a petition for divorce must be presented before the court of the place where the defendant spouse resides and, when this place is unknown or the defendant resides abroad, before the court of the petitioner's place of residence.

An attempt will be made to sketch the problems imposed by these rules, without giving definitive answers, as many questions are still controversial even in Italy.

The scope of Article 3 Chapter 2(e)

(a) The first question that arises is why the case of a marriage contracted in a foreign country should be added to the supposition of the annulment or the

---

106. See especially F Pocar, La loi italienne sur le divorce du premier décembre 1970 et le droit international privé, *Revue critique*, 1971, p. 175, completed italian version, in *RDIPP*, 1971, p. 33; E Jayme, Zu den Auswirkungen des italienischen Scheidungsgesetzes auf den deutsch-italienischen Rechtsverkehr, insbesondere Scheidung als Scheidungsgrund, *FamRZ*, 1971, p. 221; P Picone, Divorzio straniero come motivo di divorzio italiano, Multitudo Legum Ius Unum, Mélanges Wengler, vol. 2, Berlin, 1973, p. 655; P Nascimbene, Sentenze straniere di divorzio e legge italiana sul divorzio: primi orientamenti della giurisprudenza, *RDIPP*, 1973, p.337; R P Mazzeschi, Sulla giurisdizione italiana in materia di divorzio, *RDIPP*, 1975, p. 306; L Condorelli, Le sentenze straniere di divorzio e l'ordino pubblico di ieri, *RDIPP*, 1975, p. 301; F Mosconi, La legge del 1970 sul divorzio e la Convenzione del Aia del 1902. Una difficoltà di coordinamento, *RDIPP*, 1975, p. 5; B Dutoit et P Mercier, Les premières décisions suisses rendues en application de la nouvelle loi italienne sur le divorce, *RDIPP*, 1971, p. 826; A Giardina, Nullité du mariage et divorce en droit international privé italien, *NTIR*, 1972, p. 300.
107. See especially the Constitutional Court, 8th July 1971, *RDIPP* 1971, p. 597.

dissolution of the marriage which, in the majority of cases, are to be the condition of the marriage. The extreme case of polygamy could be cited. The rule on marriage appears, above all, to be in need of application in a case where the first marriage was not recognised in the country where the second marriage is contracted. One can think, in particular, of a civil marriage of a Greek national.[108]

(b) One may ask what should be understood by "the other spouse, who is a foreign national". In fact, the most frequent case of a divorce granted abroad is that of a wife who, while having become Italian by marriage, has kept her first nationality, for example, German or Swiss. If, according to a very general principle, the Italian judge in this case does not take account of the Italian nationality, the rule in (e) would be ineffective in far the greatest number of cases.[109]

(c) The question also arises whether the foreign decision, in order to be invoked in a divorce procedure in Italy, would have to have received the *delibazione,* which is generally the condition not only of enforcement but also of the recognition of a foreign judgment in Italy. A similar requirement would paralyse the rule, or make it useless because, if the *delibazione* could be obtained, there would no longer be any need for a new divorce in Italy. The Court of Cassation, acting as a full Court, explained in a recent judgment that this was one of three cases in which a foreign decision produced its effect in Italy without *delibazione.*[110]

(d) One wonders whether the Italian judge can exercise any control if the decision invoked within the framework of Article 3 Chapter 2 (e) is recognised by the country of which the foreign spouse is a national or, by the country of his habitual residence or his domicile. M Picone[111] is opposed to such a condition, but the point does not seem to have yet been settled.

(e) The text of (e), by saying that the foreign spouse "has obtained abroad the annulment or the dissolution . . ." seems to indicate that only a divorce pronounced on the petition of the foreign spouse can be invoked as a ground for a divorce in Italy. It has even been suggested that the spouse who did not oppose to the petition could not invoke the foreign decision. This opinion is opposed by M Picone.[112] In the first place he invokes the spirit of Italian law, which is based essentially on the principle of the breakdown of a marriage (*Zerrüttungsprinzip*) as opposed to the principle of fault (*Verschuldensprinzip*). The reason for which a foreign divorce can be invoked is henceforth essentially that it has become a fact a marriage does not exist any more (*Disfacimento delle società matrimoniale*). In this light, no reference should be made to the question of which of the spouses brought the action abroad, especially if it was founded on the principle

---

108. Picone, *op. cit.,* note 18, p. 664.
109. See especially the Court of Naples, 28th March 1972, *RDIPP* 1974, p. 156.
110. 15th July 1974, *RDIPP* 1975, p. 113, especially p. 118; in this case the Court of Cassation decided, on the contrary, that a foreign divorce, not being the object of a *delibazione,* could not terminate the Italian nationality as the status of citizenship is entirely governed by Italian law. It is unimportant that it was the ground for a divorce being refused by the foreign judge; Court of Appeal of Milan, 20th April 1973, No. 945, *RDIPP* 1973, p. 885.
111. *Op. cit.,* p. 669.
112. *Op. cit.,* p. 657 *et seq.* In this sense, the Court of Naples, 23rd February 1972, *RDIPP* 1974, p. 165.

of fault. M Picone adds another argument, which seems even more decisive. In not permitting an Italian to invoke the foreign judgment except when it was requested by the foreign spouse, some sort of privilege would be conferred on the party at fault or, at least, on the spouse responsible for the divorce. Conversely, the innocent Italian who had himself brought an action for divorce according to the foreign law, would also be prevented from obtaining a divorce in Italy. It should be added that, when the two spouses are in agreement about divorce, in the majority of countries they can arrange to attribute the role of petitioner to the foreign spouse. The opinion of M Picone appears to be the correct view, but this question also remains open.

(f) M Jayme[113] raised the question whether (e) could be applied by a foreign court. The question does not seem to have been investigated. It seems that the answer envisaged by M Jayme is the right one, if it relates to a rule of immediate application such as only Italian courts can put into operation. It seems to correspond to the character that many authors, and the Italian courts, attribute to the law of 1970.[114]

The International Jurisdiction of the Italian Courts

It is not disputed that Article 4 of the Italian Code of Civil Procedure on the jurisdiction of Italian courts towards a foreign party applies to divorce, even a divorce between two foreigners. It also seems to be true that when the two spouses are Italians, Italian tribunals always have jurisdiction. However, Article 4 of the above mentioned law on divorce has also been taken to include an additional rule of jurisdiction, the effect of which could be notably to accept the forum of the petitioner in addition to that of the respondent. The international jurisdiction could thus be based either on the ordinary rules or on Article 4 of the law on divorce. The Court of Cassation has decided that in every case where the petitioner or the respondent is not resident in Italy, in the sense of Article 4 of the Law on Divorce, that non-residence will not deprive the Italian judge of jurisdiction.[115] When jurisdiction is based on a ground such as the reciprocity provided for by Article 4 sub-para. 4 of the Code of Civil Procedure, in the absence of residence of one of the spouses in Italy, there is no rule relating to the internal territorial jurisdiction of the court. In such a case, it is for the petitioner to choose the court.[116]

M Picone[117] recommends as a criterion for the application of Italian law, as well as for the jurisdiction, the single fact that one of the spouses is Italian. In any case this seems preferable to other opinions based on the place of marriage, or on the fact that it is or is not a marriage under the Concordat.[118]

---

113. *Op. cit.*, *FamRZ* 1971, p. 229.
114. See for example Court of Milan, 18th March 1974, No. 2271 *RDIPP* 1975, p. 330.
115. 15th July 1974, *RDIPP* 1975, p. 119.
116. P Mazzeschi, *op. cit.*, *RDIPP* 1975, p. 320; Court of Milan, 18th March 1974, No. 2273, *RDIPP* 1975, p. 332.
117. *Op. cit.*, p. 681.
118. Cf. Giardina, *op. cit.*, p. 307.

The law applicable

The application of Italian law to marriages between Italians and to mixed marriages does not seem to raise many doubts. The authors admit that a foreign law can be applied in respect of divorces between foreigners.[119] What is remarkable is that it does not seem to be necessary that the ground for divorce according to the foreign law should also be recognised by the law of the forum. In that sense, this country, formerly hostile to divorce, seems to be one of the most liberal.[120]

The recognition of foreign judgments

As far as divorces pronounced abroad between Italians are concerned, these can be recognised but, as one might expect, the ground for divorce, or at least an analogous ground, must also be known in Italian law. This principle has been recently laid down in a complicated decision of the Court of Appeal of Milan.[121] The Court underlined the importance of decisions on personal status, for which even the Common Market Convention of 27th September 1968 provides a possibility of control.

It has been seen that decisions dissolving mixed marriages could be invoked as a ground for divorce in Italian law. This method seems to be more certain than that of a *delibazione* of the foreign judgment itself, which remains theoretically possible. But in such a case the judge would, without doubt, investigate whether the ground for divorce is recognised in Italian law. However, M Picone[122], on the basis of the reasoning in Article 3 chapter 2(e), suggests an increase in the cases where the *delibazione* is possible. It should be granted every time that a divorce has been pronounced on a ground founded on the idea of the irremediable breakdown of the conjugal tie, which is also the basis of Italian law.

---

119. Preliminary Rules of the Civil Code, Arts. 17 and 18.
120. Giardina, *op. cit.*, p. 308.
121. 3rd December 1974, *RDIPP* 1975, p. 356.
122. *Op. cit.*, p. 690.

CHAPTER XIII.   PROBLEMS OF MIGRANT WORKERS IN EUROPE

by Tugrul Ansay

I. Introductory Remarks

At the outset the term "migrant" should be distinguished from the term "immigrant". Whereas immigration is the long recognised process of the movement of persons who have no intention of returning to their original country, migration of workers implies that they do not always intend that their stay in a country should be permanent. Migration is the outcome of modern industrialisation and there have been many instances of it during the last two decades. Many European countries have tolerated, indeed encouraged, foreign labour for various reasons. Some considered them as a temporary labour force; others, being more generous, gave immigrant workers the possibility of becoming more fully integrated into society, culminating with their acquisition of a new nationality, and allowed them to use certain rights which are normally reserved to the nationals of that particular country. Bilateral or multilateral treaties have also given additional rights to incoming foreign workers.

Most of the migrant workers in Western Europe come from the Mediterranean areas. The largest group are Italians, followed by the Yugoslavs and the Turks. The highest number of migrant workers are to be found in the Federal Republic of Germany and in France. The following table* shows the origins of the migrant workers and the countries in which they are working.

If we include the members of their families and also workers illegally present in the countries—which are estimated as 10% of the total migrant workforce—the number of foreigners will be much higher than shown in the table.

We shall take the situation in the Federal Republic of Germany as illustration of the family law problems of foreign workers, mainly because there is more reliable information relating to migrant workers living there. However, the problems are basically the same in almost all labour receiving countries. Also we shall concentrate our attention on six labour exporting countries, namely Italy, Yugoslavia, Greece, Turkey, Spain and Portugal, because almost 90% of the foreign workers staying in Germany originate from these countries.

2. What law should be applied?

The laws in Europe dealing with family matters have not yet been harmonised. The recent trend of reform based on the constitutional principle of equality in the family has reached different stages in various countries. What law should be applied to migrant workers is a very important and troubling issue.[1]

---

1. For a recent discussion see Gamillscheg, Vorbemerkung vor Art. 13, N. 69 ff. (in Staudingers *Kommentar zum BGB*, Teil 3, 1973).

*see p. 338.

As a result of its inclusion in the French Civil Code and the support it received from the influential nationality theory of Mancini during the last part of the 19th century,[2] very many countries on the Continent have applied the law of nationality to the family conflicts of foreigners living in their countries.[3] Only after the second World War do we notice a strong tendency towards the "*lex domicilii*". In the United Kingdom, however, the applicable law has always been the law of domicile.[4]

This is not the place to discuss in detail the benefits and shortcomings of the different principles. Mention will only be made of some of the criticism. There are certain difficulties arising out of the nationality principle. It is weak in cases where a person is stateless or has double nationality or belongs to a Federal State where the family laws are not unified. Critics of the nationality law stress that decisions of domestic courts should be harmonious and, by minimising the need for harmony in the extra-domestic sphere, do not accept that there should be different legal solutions for different nationals living in the same country. They also consider the nationality rule to be unsatisfactory in that it applies the national law of the husband as opposed to giving weight to the legal emancipation of a married woman. Furthermore, the difficulty of finding out the foreign law is held to be one of the serious shortcomings of the law of nationality.

Supporters of the nationality principle, on the other hand, argue that nationality can be ascertained with greater certainty than domicile. They also mention that those who have been "born and bred in a Western civilisation cannot accept being subjected to the law of domicile whereby bigamy, child marriages and repudiation of wives are permissible."[5]

On the other hand, the principle of domicile has much to be said in its favour. In addition to the great advantage for the receiving country that the problems of migrant workers will be solved in accordance with its own law, the application of the law of domicile does signify the "connection with the legal atmosphere elected by the person in question himself". "This is especially true of immigrants who are keen to become part of the community of the country where they have settled as soon as they possible can."[5a] The main criticism directed against the principle of domicile is the different meaning attributed to this concept and, as a result, the difficulty of determining what the domicile of a worker is in many cases. Because of this the "habitual residence" criterion has won considerable support during recent years, especially in multilateral conventions.

Whether the law of nationality or domicile is used, the so-called limping relations will arise unless the same principle is applied in both of the countries involved, that is, the country which receives and the country which exports foreign labour.

---

2. Rabel, *The Conflict of Laws*, 112 (Vol. I 1945); Korkisch, *Der Staatsangehörigkeitsgrundsatz im Kollisionsrecht*, 103 (in Festschrift für Hans Dölle [1963]).

3. See in general Nadelmann, *Mancini's Nationality Rule and non-unified Legal Systems. Nationality versus domicile*, 17 A J C L 418 ff. (1969).

4. See in general Braga, *Staatsangehörigkeitsprinzip oder Wohnsitzprinzip?* (Erlangen 1954); De Winter, *Nationality or Domicile?* 128 Receuil des Cours, 378 ff. (1969 III).

5. De Winter, *op. cit.*, 403.

5a. De Winter, *op. cit.*, 407.

Among the different possibilities, which law is the most suitable for the migrant workers? The reason for using the law of nationality in the German Civil Code was to enable German law to be applied to those German emigrants who left their country.[6] In so doing it was perhaps thought that future difficulties would be avoided if and when they came back to Germany. If we look at the issue from the point of view of migrant workers, this ground is perhaps similarly valid for them in our own day. The answer certainly requires further knowledge about migrant workers.

3. Facts about migrant workers[7] (and the possibilities of integration)

(a) Origins of migrant workers

Migrant workers come mainly from the less developed, less industrialised areas of labour exporting countries. This is especially true of Italians, 75% of whom come from Southern Italy, Sicily and Sardinia. Almost 75% of the Greeks come from the Northern part of the country or from Epirus or Attica. The main exception to this situation is Yugoslavia. Most of the Yugoslavs working in Germany have their origins in the more developed Northern areas of the land.[8]

Other statistics show that more than 50% of foreign workers who have moved into Germany come from towns with populations of more than 50,000; an even higher percentage were born in towns with less than 50,000 inhabitants.[9]

(b) Educational background may show to which stratum of society the workers belong. Various enquiries show that between 5% and 10% of the workers might be considered as illiterate. The percentage is even higher among the women. Only a small number of the workers was able to study beyond primary education.[10] Lack of means to communicate with the nationals of the host country seems to be a major problem for foreign workers. The majority has very little, or insufficient, knowledge of the German language.[11] As a result, they have little chance of contacts with Germans outside of their work. In fact,

---

6. Melchior, *Die Grundlagen des deutschen internationalen Privatrechts*, 28 (Berlin 1932); Niemeyer, *Das internationale Privatrecht des Bürgerlichen Gesetzbuches*, 59 (Berlin 1901).

7. On the characteristics of migrant workers compare: Manfrass, *Entstehung, Ursachen* and *Antriebskräfte der internationalen Arbeitskräftewanderung*, 41/42 (in Lohrmann/Manfrass, *Ausländerbeschäftigung und internationale Politik*, München 1974).

8. *Bundesanstalt für Arbeit, ausländische Arbeitnehmer* 1971, 32 ff. (Nürnberg 1972). The figures show the situation in 1971. Furthermore, Kiefer, Belgrade: *Rückführung hat den Vorrang*, 114 (in *Gastarbeiter Problem, Rotation? Integration? Arbeitsplatzverlagerung?* Südosteuropa-Gesellschaft, München 1975).

9. Bingemer/Meistermann-Seeger/Neubert, *Leben als Gastarbeiter—Geglückte und missglückte Integration*, 118 (Köln/Opladen 1972); Braun, *Soziokulturelle Probleme der Eingliederung italienischer Arbeitskräfte in der Schweiz*, 40 (Zürich 1970).

10. Repräsentativuntersuchung '72, *Beschäftigung ausländischer Arbeitnehmer*, 28 (Herausgeber: Bundesanstalt für Arbeit 1973); Mehrländer, *Beschäftigung ausländerischer Arbeitnehmer in der BRD*, 19 ff. (Koln/Opladen 1969); Mehrländer, *Soziale Aspekte der Ausländerbeschäftigung*, 29 (Bonn-Bad Godesberg 1974).

11. Represäntativuntersuchung '72, p. 29; Mehrländer, 37 (1969); Kommunalpolitische Aspekte des wachsenden ausländischen Bevölkerungsanteils in München, 121, table 132 (Herausgeber: Stadtentwicklungsreferat, München 1972).

they live in areas where migrant workers predominate, or with their fellow nationals in dormitories not too far from where they work. This concentration is particularly obvious in the larger cities, where almost 50% of the foreigners live in houses with more than ten other migrant workers and thus create modern ghettos.[12] Migrant workers mostly read their own newspapers or listen to programmes in their own language, they visit amongst themselves and spend their holidays at home. All these factors indicate that these people are basically incapable of integration.[13]

(c) There are other grounds which make the integration process even harder. The length of stay is, of course, one of the main obstacles. Figures show that the percentage of foreign workers who would like to stay in Germany permanently varies from 24% for Italians to 9% for Turks.[14] About 9% of foreign workers have stayed for more than ten years.[15] What the workers think and what happens are not the same. During economic crises very many workers lose their jobs and consequently have to return home, even if they do not desire to do so. This occurred during the 1966/67 recession.[16] The workers have been experiencing similar pressures since the autumn of 1973. The interests of the exporting and the importing countries seem to be against full integration. In fact, both encourage returning home and maintaining connections with the country of origin. For a long time the rotation of workers has found strong support in certain parts of Germany. The continuous presence of migrant workers in the receiving country puts an additional burden on their governments as far as infra structural expenditure is concerned.

For exporting countries such as Yugoslavia, the migration is only a temporary process due to unemployment. The government is taking steps necessary to create new jobs and to attract Yugoslav workers back to their country.[17] In countries such as Turkey, the length of stay in another land is unimportant, but the strength of the ties between the workers and Turkey is regarded as essential, for it is desirable that such workers should send foreign exchange back home and thus help to solve the economic problems of Turkey.

(d) The typical migrant worker who comes, directly or indirectly, from the country districts of the less developed areas around the Mediterranean brings his values to the new land in which he works. The traditional family with which the migrant is familiar at home is a large type of rural family, or an extended family as the sociologists describe it. Even if the individual does not live with relatives, other than parents, brothers and sisters, the family ties are close. The man, usually the oldest man in the household, has parental power. Inequality between husband and wife is obvious. The wife and children have very little say in solving family problems. Marriage is under the supervision of family or kin groups.

12. *Kommunalpolitische Aspekte*, pp. 44, 143; Zieris, *Betriebsunterkünfte für ausländische Mitbürgern Nordrhein-Westfalen*, pp. 147, 154, 210 (1972); *Der Spiegel*, No. 31, pp. 24 (30 July 1973); Borris, *Ausländische Arbeitnehmer in einer Grossstadt*, 131 (Frankf. 1973).
13. Kayser, B. *Manpower Movements and Labour Markets*, 201 (Paris 1971).
14. Repräsentativuntersuchung, 37.
15. *Wirtschaft und Statistik*, p. 199* (1974); compare Kayser, 203.
16. *Bundesanstalt für Arbeit, Ausländische Arbeitnehmer*, 1972/73, p. 5 (1974).
17. Baucic, *Die Auswirkungen der Arbeitskräftewanderung in Jugoslavien*, pp. 195 (in Lohrmann/Manfrass, *Ausländerbeschäftigung und internationale Politik*). (München 1974).

Illegitimacy is regarded as shameful, breakup of the family through divorce is rare.[18] As this description suggests, there is little indication that these people could give up their traditional values on arrival in the labour receiving countries.

(e) To conclude the background information, some figures are given concerning the family life of foreign workers in the Federal Republic of Germany.

In 1973 there were 1,640,209 foreign men and 706,591 foreign women working in Germany.[19] The Greeks had the highest percentage of women with 40% and the Turks the lowest with 22% (1972).[20] In some areas of Germany the percentage is higher than the average. In Berlin, for example, 47% of the Yugoslav, 45% of the Greek and 45% of the Turkish workers were women[21] (1972).

Most of the foreign workers are married. An inquiry giving figures for 1972 showed that 21.6% of male workers coming from the six major exporting countries were not married. This is slightly lower than the figure for 1968. The highest number of unmarried male workers are Italian. The percentage of unmarried female workers is 26.5%, a little higher than the percentage for males.[22]

Not all the married workers are able to bring their wives to join them in Germany. This may be a result of the German law which not only prohibits the worker's family from entering Germany during his first year in the country, but also requires that they have living facilities which meet the standards laid down in certain rules and regulations.[23] For other personal reasons, workers may live separately from their spouses in Germany. In 1972, 61% of the workers had their wives with them (this was lower in 1968). Of the women workers, 93% had their husbands with them in Germany.[24] Moreover, 66% of the women who were living together with their husbands were also working. When this question was asked of the women, 97% of them said that their husbands were also working in Germany.[25]

It is difficult to discover the exact number of migrant workers' children in Germany, mainly because children below 16 need no residence permit. A representative enquiry made by the Federal Labour Bureau showed that about 630,000 children from six labour exporting countries were living with their parents in Germany in 1972.[26] The number has probably risen since the new law on Children's Allowances, which has made a considerable difference in favour of children who live with their parents in Germany. In any case, not all children

---

18. König, pp. 33 (in *Persons and Family*, Chief Ed. Chloros, *International Encyclopaedia of Comparative Law*, Vol. IV, Ch. I, Introduction); U Planck, *Die ländliche Türkei, Soziologie und Entwicklungstendenzen*, pp. 238 (Frankfurt, 1972).

19. *Ausländische Arbeitnehmer*, 1972/73, pp. 70/71. The number of foreigners in the FRG on 30.9.1973 as 3,966,200. *Statistische Umschau*, Wirtschaft und Statistik, 260 (1974).

20. *Ausländische Arbeitnehmer* 1972/73, pp. 70/71, Also *Amtliche Nachrichten der Bundesanstalt für Arbeit*, pp. 572 (1973).

21. Abschlussbericht des Planungsteams "Eingliederung der ausländischen Arbeitnehmer und ihrer Familien", p. 55 (Drucks. 6/739 des Abgeordnetenhauses, 1973).

22. Repräsentativuntersuchung, 19/20.

23. Rittstieg, *Gesellschaftliche und politische Perspektiven des Ausländerrechts*, pp. 73 (in Ansay/Gessner, *Gastarbeiter in Gesellschaft und Recht*, München 1974).

24. Repräsentativuntersuchung, 19/20; Mehrländer, 203 (1974).

25. Repräsentativuntersuchung, 19/20.

26. Repräsentativuntersuchung, 23; Wirtschaft und Statistik, 262 (1974).

live with their parents for the same reasons that spouses may have to live separately.

The birth rate of migrant workers in Germany is considerable. In 1972 the following number of children were born there:[27]

Year	Italy	Yugoslavia	Turkey	Greece	Spain	Portugal
1970	9,764	6,196	12,748	9,362	4,166	1,005
1971	10,833	9,825	20,457	12,062	4,616	1,303
1972	11,077	11,715	26,796	13,207	4,976	1,849

In 1972 the following number of marriages were performed among the migrant workers in Germany:[28]

Italy	Yugoslavia	Turkey	Greece	Spain	Portugal
745	1,454	442	2,688	1,026	123

If the number of Consular and religious marriages are added, the number will be much higher.

The number of mixed marriages, which should only be performed before the German marriage officials, produces the following table:[29]

Men of the following nationalities marrying German women—

Year	Italy	Yugoslavia	Turkey	Greece	Spain	Portugal
1971	2,234	791	422	373	358	46
1972	2,361	902	365	387	454	47

German men marrying women of the following nationalities—

Year	Italy	Yugoslavia	Turkey	Greece	Spain	Portugal
1971	505	2,144	215	314	320	49
1972	453	2,171	221	347	318	82

4. Legal Problems

(a) The German Basic Law on the family and migrant workers

The Basic Law of the Federal Republic of Germany protects the family and requires full equality between the spouses in articles 3 and 6.

The family under the protection of the Basic Law is comprised of a nucleus of husband, wife and children.[30] Other relatives who may belong to the rural concept of a large family are not included in the urban family of the industrialised nations. One of the main outcomes of this difference is the restrictions on

---

27. Wirtschaft und Statistik, 60* (1974).
28. Wirtschaft und Statistik, 60* (1974).
29. Wirtschaft und Statistik, 60* (1974). For the number of mixed marriages in 1973, see NJW, p. IV (1975).
30. Rittsteig, 73.

bringing members of the family other than spouses and children into the Federal Republic of Germany. Owing to the practice of the administrative courts, residence permits may be given exceptionally to parents or brothers or sisters, if they come to Germany to look after the children of their relatives already working there, or if they themselves need the special care of these relatives.[31] As mentioned earlier, not only relatives, but even spouses or children have difficulties in following their husbands, wives or parents into Germany.

The family also have no protection if one of the spouses commits an act which might cause him or her to be expelled from Germany under the provisions of the "Law of Foreigners". The practical result of such a rule is double punishment for the person concerned and the compulsory split up of the family.[32] For a long time the administrative courts in Germany argued that even in cases of mixed marriages the German wife should have realised from the beginning that she should be prepared to follow her husband to a foreign country some day.[33] However, this argument is inconsistent with the rule of modern family law, under which the wife is not necessarily bound to follow her husband. Only recently the courts have begun to adopt a more favourable test and expel a foreigner only when his presence "is seriously endangering important interests of the Federal Republic of Germany."[34]

Equality of the spouses was one of the issues in cases of mixed marriages. Until the new enactment of 1974, the children of such marriages in Germany acquired only the nationality of their father. This was found to be unconstitutional by the Constitutional Court and subsequently the new law gave to children of a mixed marriage the chance to acquire German nationality also.[35]

In the area of the choice of laws, the question of which law should be applicable has been one of the controversial issues of recent years in Germany. The application of the national law of the husband in cases of mixed marriages was, in particular, under severe attack. It is claimed that it is against the equality rule of the Constitution.[36] Those who support the negative view, however, argue that the application of the national law of the husband does not necessarily mean that the husband is privileged, unless this law in the particular case does indeed favour him.[37] Whatever the outcome of this dispute, the courts no longer apply the national law but apply German law instead if there is a strong "inland relation", for example if the wife is German and the family is sojourning in Germany. Article 30 of the BGBGB on public policy also assists the judges.[38]

Equal treatment of the spouses during their communal life within the marriage has little practical value except when the marriage ends by divorce, where the

31. Rittstieg, 74.
32. Franz, *Die aufenthaltsrechtliche Stellung der ausländischen Arbeiter*, p. 43 (in Ansay/Gessner, *Gastarbeiter in Gesellschaft und Recht*, München, 1974).
33. VGH Mannheim, 9.3.1970, NJW 2178 (1970).
34. Endemann, *Tendenzen der Rechtsprechung zum Ausländerrecht*, Baden-Württembergerische Verwaltungsblatt, pp. 180 (1973).
35. Gesetz zur Änderung des Reichs-und Staatsangehörigkeitsgesetzes dated Dec. 20 1974.
36. Sturm, *Durchbruch der Grundrechte in Fällen mit Ausländerberührung* Fam. RZ. 16 (1972). For others see Gamillscheg, Vorbem. vor Art. 13, N. 50.
37. See in general Kegel, *Internationales Privatrecht*, p. 292 (1971).
38. Ansay/Martiny (in Ansay/Gessner, *op. cit.*, München 1974).

wife demands alimony, or in cases of the family name. It is true that in some labour exporting countries the tradition and the legal order are still based on inequality between the husband and the wife. In Greece, for example, the patriarchal authority and the inferior position of woman has not completely disappeared. The laws recognise this unequal situation. According to the Greek Civil Code, the man is the head of the family and it is he who decides on family matters.[39] In Turkey, too, the tradition of the superiority of the husband is predominantly practised, although the Civil Code gives the same rights to each spouse. There also, the wife and children carry the family name of the husband and, in cases of disagreements on such matters as the education and religion of the children, or on the question of where the family should live, the husband has the final word.[40] The Yugoslav law is perhaps the most advanced among the labour exporting countries as far as the equality in the family is concerned.[41]

The German rule on the choice of law in personal relations between the spouses in the family, is stated in Article 14 of the BGBGB. It states that German law is applicable if both the spouses have German nationality. This one-sided rule is also applied to foreign spouses if both have the same nationality. In cases of mixed marriages the prevailing opinion is to apply the national law of the husband.[42] The position of the husband in the family and his right to make decisions are, therefore, subject to the national law of the husband if the spouses have different nationalities. However, German public policy is often taken into consideration if there is a "strong inland relation".[43]

On the problem of family name, the German Federal Court has recently applied the law of habitual residence where the wife has German nationality.[44] As stated in another Court decision, "from a foreign man married to a German girl, with habitual residence in Germany, it is expected that he behaves as would a German man".[45] That the same behaviour should be expected from a foreign husband whose wife has the same nationality can be defended, because this may not cause limping relations. A suit brought by the wife for equal treatment in the family may imply that she has already adapted herself to the values of the new society. Yet this is not always a matter between only the husband and wife. As long as the family lives together with other workers from the same country, the pressure of tradition is unavoidable. The application of the new values to people who are not ready to accept them may result in extreme acts on the part of husbands. In addition to beating incidents, there are instances of murder attempts by Turkish husbands. In some cases husbands have thrown out their

---

39. Stefanopoulos, *Die eheliche Lebensgemeinschaft nach griechischem Recht*, 160 AcP 58, 95 (1961); Boschan, *Europäisches Familienrecht*, 1973 (1972).

40. Arts. 152, 153, 154, 259, 263 of the Turkish Civil Code.

41. Chloros, *Yugoslav Civil Law*, pp. 48 (Oxford, 1970). For other countries see, Alexandre, *The Status of Women in France*, 20 Amer. J Comp. Law 647, 649 (1972); Grunsky/Wuppermann, *Italienisches Familienrecht*, p. 46 (Frankfurt, 1971); Cabanillas, *Die neue Rechtslage der Frau im spanischen Recht*, 158 AcP, p. 352 (1959/60).

42. Gamillscheg, Art. 14, N. 9 ff.

43. Gamillscheg, Art. 14, N. 128. On equality of parental authority compare BGH 20. 12, 1972, BGHZ 79 (1973).

44. 60 BGHZ 12.5.1971, NJW 988 (1972), 1001 (1972). Gamillscheg, Art. 14 N. 208 ff.

45. KG 17.2.1969, Fam RZ 338 (1969).

wives from the home and, furthermore, have requested the cancellation of their wives' residence permits.

The problems of family support are of a rather different nature. The figures given above show that a considerable number of men leave their wives and children at home and are not always willing to send money for their support. It is perhaps easier to bring a suit of alimony in the country of origin and afterwards seek the enforcement of the decree in the country where the husband is working. The enforcement of such decrees will cause hardship if no bilateral or reciprocity agreement exists between Germany and the respective country. For alimony suits brought in Germany, the applicable law is the national law of the husband.[46]

(b) Divorce

The exact number of marriages terminated by divorce is unknown. The German statistics give figures without making a distinction between Germans and foreigners. But very many of the published Court decisions involving foreigners are concerned with divorce.[47] There is also no information on the number of divorce suits brought in the countries of origin. It is more likely that divided families are divorced in the country of origin of the spouse who remained at home.[48]

It may not be incorrect to state that more mixed marriages are terminated than are normal marriages. Difference of mentality is one of the main reasons for divorce in mixed marriages.[49] The difficulties of adapting to the new life constitute a ground for divorce in cases of separated families. There are some Turkish Court decisions in which the husbands went to a foreign country, found jobs and wished to bring their wives to the new country, only that the wives were not willing to leave their country of origin.

There are two main difficulties concerning the divorce of foreigners in Germany: the jurisdiction of the Courts and the question of which law to apply. The German Courts have jurisdiction to hear divorce suits involving foreigners if the divorce decree will be recognised under the national law of the husband.[50] Greek,[51] Yugoslav[52] and recently Italian spouses are therefore applying to German Courts for divorce. Again, in mixed marriages in which one of the spouses is a German national, the parties may obtain a divorce decree in Germany. There are difficulties here for Spanish and Turkish workers. Since Spanish internal law does not recognise divorce as such[53], and since under

---

46. On the application of German public order, see Gamillscheg, Art. 14, No. 236 *op. cit.*, Art. 13, No. 361, 364.
47. Luther, *Gastarbeiter vor deutschen Zivilgerichten*, 164 (in Ansay/Gessner, *op. cit.*).
48. For Turkey, see Ansay, *Isci göcü ve Federal Almanyadaki Türk iscilerinin aile hukuku sorunlar* 1, 593 (Kologlu Armagani, Ankara, 1975).
49. Luther, 164.
50. Art. 606b ZPO. Compare the Dutch practice, Dist. Court of Dordrecht, Feb. 2 1972, Verheul, *Netherlands Judicial Decisions*, 21 Nederlands Tijdschrift voor Internationaal Recht, 84/85 (1974).
51. LG Ulm, 25.9.1970, IPRspr. 1970 Nr. 55; LG Düsseldorf, 13.1.1971, FamRZ 298 (1972).
52. OLG Stuttgart, 11.10.1972, FamRZ 38 (1973).
53. LG München I, 15.11.1973, FamRZ 257 (1974). German courts may have jurisdiction in divorce cases of Portugese nationals, LG Hamburg 12.12.1973, FamRZ 257 (1974).

Turkish law the Turkish courts have exclusive jurisdiction on the family matters of Turkish nationals,[54] divorce decrees of German courts will not be effective in Spain and Turkey. Turkish spouses must obtain a Turkish divorce, even if both have their habitual residence in Germany. This is especially true of a Turkish-German family, where a divorce may put the Turkish party into a complicated situation. Since the Turkish man will be considered as married under Turkish law, he cannot remarry. The divorced German woman will still be considered as his legal wife and, consequently, all her subsequent children will be his legitimate children under Turkish law unless he rejects them within a stated period of time after the knowledge of their birth. The woman and the children will be his legal heirs in Turkey.

When the German Courts have jurisdiction to hear a divorce suit, they apply the national law of the husband (Art. 17 I EGBGB).[55] In cases of mixed marriages, German law will be applied if the German wife brings the suit or counter suit.[56] (Art. 17 III EGBGB). The aim of this provision is not only to protect the German woman against the nationals of those countries where no divorce exists or a divorce is made extremely difficult, but at the same time to protect her against easy divorces. A German woman may, as a result, divorce her Spanish husband, although they will still be considered as married in Spain. The situation of a Spanish national who has divorced his German wife in Germany would not be different, for this divorce will also be ineffective in Spain. Recent Court decisions in Germany make it possible for divorced persons to marry in Germany for the second time.[57]

(c) Illegitimate children

Illegitimate children constitute another significant aspect of the family problems of migrant workers and of the importing countries. Inability to integrate, difficulties in adopting to sexual freedom and the disappearance of environmental pressure are, perhaps, the main reasons for illegitimacy. Not only the women of the importing country, but also those coming from the exporting country have children from relations outside the marriage.

The number of illegitimate children born of a German mother and a foreign father is not known. German figures only give statistics for all illegitimate children born to German mothers. Nonetheless, very many Court decisions and

---

54. Ansay, *American-Turkish Private International Law*, 62 (New York 1966).
55. Dutch court decisions are contradictory. Long presence in the Netherlands is a ground to apply Dutch law. District Court of Amsterdam, Jan. 29, 1970, 21 Nederlands Tijdschr. v. IR 87. Compare with other cases where Yugoslav and Italian law was applied: Court of Appeal of 's-Hertogenbosch, Nov. 3, 1970 (p. 87), Court of Appeal of Arnhem Feb. 1, 1972 (p. 89). However, see Court of Appeal of Amsterdam, Oct. 18, 1972 (p. 89). See further the Note on p. 90.
56. See Jayme, *Zur Gleichberechtigung in der deutsch-italienischen Ehe.* pp. 9 (in Juristische Beiträge der deutsch-italienischen Vereinigung, Bielefeld 1971).
57. B Verf. G, 4.5.1971, NJW 1509 (1971). For an English summary of this decision see Rabels Z, pp. 141 (1972); BGH 19.4.1972, MDR 124 (1973). Juenger, *The German Constitutional Court and the Conflict of Laws* 20 AJCL pp. 290 (1972).

expert reports deal with the illegitimate children of a foreign father and a German mother.[58] In Hamburg there were 252 illegitimate children with foreign fathers born between June 1971 and May 1972.[59] The number of illegitimate children born to foreign mothers is as follows.[60]

Year	Mother: Greek	Italian	Yugoslav	Portugese	Spanish	Turkish
1972	312	334	1,750	57	170	680
1970	369	269	1,316	35	154	488

The number of illegitimate children born in the labour exporting country are not so high as to make it a serious problem. As mentioned above, most of the married women working in Germany also have their husbands with them there. A different problem exists for those separated families where the man works in Germany and the wife stays at home. The children of these women from men who are not their husbands are legitimate, since they are born within the marriage unless the legal father rejects the relationship in due order. Otherwise he must fulfil all the duties of a legal father.

There are still differences between the legitimate and illegitimate children in the legal systems of various countries receiving and exporting labour. The degree of inequality between legitimate and illegitimate children varies from one country to another. In Turkey the illegitimate child does not bear the family name of the natural father; in cases of inheritance, his share is less than that of the legitimate child.[61]

No child is legitimate unless it was either born or conceived in wedlock. However, there are some examples of illegitimacy even though the children were born during the marriage. This occurs when the marriage has not been properly enacted. In particular, Greek religious marriages enacted in Germany were not considered as valid under German law and consequently the children born during such marriages were treated as illegitimate.[62] In one case[63] a Greek man refused to recognise his child when he and his Greek wife were told that the child was illegitimate owing to the lack of a valid marriage under German law. This was true, even though the spouses had declared that they were returning to Greece.

A woman and her child born out of wedlock are considered legally to be of blood relationship in Germany. A few countries, such as Spain and Italy, do not combine the natural and legal motherhood and require the recognition of the

58. The information was obtained privately.
59. Wirtschaft und Statistik, 60* (1974).
60. From June 1 1970 until the end of 1972, there were about 70 published Court decisions dealing with the determination of the father by Court decisions. Suhr, *Die Vaterschaftsfeststellung im deutschen Internationalen Privatrecht*, Der Amtsvormund, p. 125 (1973).
61. Art. 443 of the t C C.
62. On this problem see Dorenberg, *Hinkende Rechtsverhältnisse im internationalen Familienrecht*, p. 73 ff. (Berlin, 1968).
63. A G Hamburg, 15.1.1970; IPRspr 1968-69, Nr. 58; OLG Köln, 14.7.1971; StAZ 140 (1972). See also IPG 1969, Nr. 26 (Heidelberg). If the marriage is valid under German law, but not under the Greek law, then the children will be illegitimate in Greece. AG Hamburg, Wandsbek, 6.1.1969 IPRspr, 1968-69, Nr. 139.

child by the mother.[64] Whether there is a legal relationship between the mother and the child is determined by the national law of the mother under German law.[65]

The legal relationship between the natural father and the child may be established either by recognition or by a Court decision. The subsequent marriage of the mother and the natural father makes the child legitimate and puts him in an equal position with the legitimate child. This is significant in those countries where some differences still prevail between legitimate and illegitimate children. German authorities therefore encourage a subsequent marriage if the natural parents are not already married. This is one of the reasons for mixed marriages in that country. One inquiry on 46 mixed marriages showed that in 21 cases the women were expecting a child before the marriage.[66]

Recognition of the child, or determination of paternity by a Court decision, causes problems if the natural father is already married. Contrary to German law, under the laws of certain countries such as Turkey, Italy and Greece, married men are not allowed to recognise their illegitimate children[67] and accordingly, no affiliation may be established between these men and the children by the decision of a Court. The law applicable in this matter is not directly stated in the EGBGB. The current approach in Germany is based on the Hague Convention of 1956 on Children's Alimony. Although this Convention dealt with the payment of support, the rule of "habitual residence"[68] used for this purpose has also been applied recently by some of the German Courts in relation to the recognition of illegitimate children and all its resultant legal consequences, without considering whether the child carries the nationality of the country which has approved the Convention.[69] The result is a limping relationship between the father and the child. The child will still be considered as illegitimate under the laws of the countries where married men are not allowed to recognise their illegitimate children. This may cause complications when the mother and father are not German and where she some day returns with her child to her native country.

On the determination by Court decision of affiliation between the child and the father, the question of proof becomes a significant problem.[70] In some countries, including Germany, there is a presumption that the man who lived with the mother during the time of conception is the father. However, this is not

---

64. Danzig, *Kindschaftsrecht*, Anhang V (Darmstadt 1974).
65. Art. 20 EGBGB.
66. Schramm/Steuer, *Ehen zwischen deutschen und ausländischen Arbeitnehmern, Öffentliche Gesundheitsdienst*, p. 487 (1965).
67. Boschan, 179, 252, 551.
68. There have also been problems on deciding whether a child has his "habitual residence" in Germany or not, if he is sent home for educational or other purposes. BGH, 5.2.1975; FamRZ 272 (1975); NJW 1068 (1975); OLG Koblenz 17.12.1974; NJW 1085 (1975); FamRZ 230 1975.
69. Ansay/Martiny, pp. 194 (in Ansay/Gessner, *op. cit.*). BGH 19.3.1975, DA Vorm. 178 (1973). Compare OLG Karlsruhe, 19.9.1972, FamRZ 652 1972.
70. There might be different rules as to the person entitled to bring such a suit. According to German law, this is the child. But in Turkish law the mother brings the suit. This is not against German public policy. OLG Düsseldorf, 21.4.1971, StAZ 304 (1972).

accepted in Yugoslavia and therefore causes difficulty in establishing that a Yugoslav man[71] is the father of an illegitimate child. Blood tests are the common method used in Germany for the establishment of affiliation between the father and the child. There are some cases in which Italian courts have refused to take blood tests, arguing that such a method would be against Italian public policy.[72]

Another issue worth mentioning in the context of illegitimate children is that of parental authority. Under Yugoslav law, the mother of an illegitimate child acquires parental authority *ex offlcio* over the child at birth.[73] This is also the case under German law. The Hague Convention on the Protection of Children,[74] which is effective in Germany, requires the application of the law of habitual residence with the exception of *ex lege* parental authority. It therefore seems that a Yugoslav mother of an illegitimate child, living in Germany, automatically acquires parental authority. However, a Turkish mother can only obtain this authority through a Court order.[75]

5. Final Remarks

After this short survey of examples from German practice, we may again ask our basic question, "Which law should be applied to migrant workers?" Is there any strong reason for the labour importing countries to depart from their nationality principle for the principle of the law of domicile, or that of habitual residence? Most of the industrialised countries of Western Europe, such as Germany, France, Holland and Belgium are still solving the problems of the conflict of laws by applying the common natural law of the spouses.[76] Efforts to the contrary have not been successful so far in completely changing the whole system. The basic rule in cases of conflict of laws on family matters in labour exporting countries is also to apply the national law of the spouses. In Italy, Greece, Turkey, Spain, Portugal and Yugoslavia, family problems involving foreigners are still solved according to the natural laws of the parties.[77] As the German example illustrates, the result of a unilateral move away from the nationality principle in family matters may be limping relations.[78] As long as there exist basic differences among internal laws, the application of local law will produce problematic repercussions when the workers someday move back to their country of origin.

---

71. LG Ravensburg, 9.5.1972, DAVorm, 248 (1972).

72. Jayme, *Das nichteheliche Kind im deutsch-italienischen Rechtsverkehr*, 7/8 (Frankfurt a.M. 1972); Beitzke, *Familienrecht*, 1952/153 München 1974).

73. See LG Osnabrück, 17.12.1973, 28 *Niedersächsische Rechtspflege*, 184 (1974).

74. Dated October 5, 1961.

75. AG Fürth, 22.6.1973, VII 240/73 (not published).

76. Gamillscheg, *op. cit.* 13, N. 92, Art. 13, No. 18, ff., Art. 14, N. 80, ff. Compare for divorce, Art. 17, N. 76, ff. Delaume, *American-French Private International Law*, 100, 104 (New York 1961); Kollewijn. *American-Dutch Private International Law*, 100, 104 (New York 1961). For Sweden, Eek, *The Administration of Justice in Conflict Cases Involving Refugees*, 24 (in *Scandinavian Studies in Law*, pp. 23, 1959).

77. Gamillscheg, *op. cit.*, Art. 13, N. 92, Art. 13, N. 18, ff., Art. 14, N. 80, ff., Art. 17, N. 59, ff; Ehrenzweig/Fragistas/Yiannopoulos, *American-Greek Private International Law* 73 (New York 1957); Ansay, *American-Turkish PIL*, pp. 48.

78. The German Constitutional Court does not give much importance to avoiding limping relations. See *supra* N. 57 (C IV 2).

Taking into consideration the role of tradition in family matters, the unpleasant complications of limping legal relations owing to the high probability of returning home and the social, educational and cultural background of the migrant workers, one might be inclined to give more weight to the humanitarian aspect of the problem. The answer must be in conformity with the basic governmental policy on migrant workers; there should be harmony between this policy and the legal rules. If full integration of the migrant workers is desired, the application of the laws of habitual residence or domicile will, to a certain extent, help to promote integration. However, this is only justifiable if the migrant worker is given the opportunity of acquiring the new nationality[79] with all legal rights, so that in both theory and practice migrant workers are treated as the equal of the nationals of the country without any discrimination whatever. Despite the speeches of high government officials, this has not been the case—at least, not in Germany. If integration is not desired, there is no urgent necessity to avoid using the law of nationality[80] for migrant workers, unless the worker himself has personally achieved a certain degree of integration.

This results in a compromise solution between the adherents of the law of domicile and the law of nationality. If the social aspects of domicile are emphasised, the outcome may be the application of the law of domicile to migrant workers. As Braga describes it, domicile is the centre of life of a person, thereby implying his cultural, political, economic and personal relations with a legal community.[81] De Winter terms it his "social domicile"[82] and suggests applying the law of the community to which he "sociologically belongs".[83] As De Winter says, "if an Italian has, e.g., a house in Italy where his wife and children are living whilst he works in Holland, he will probably be deemed to have his social domicile in Italy."[84] However, it may be that, even if a migrant worker has his wife and children with him, his social domicile might not be the country of residence. The background described earlier makes it difficult to consider most migrants as socially domiciled in Germany. There are, however, workers who might be considered to be domiciled in the country of residence. Other factors than the length of stay,[85] such as his knowledge of the language, the degree of his social contacts, and similar factors should be taken into consideration.[86] Marriage to a German woman is certainly one piece of evidence of a high degree

---

79. In 1973 18,900 persons acquired German nationality. Most of these were of German origin, coming from Yugoslavia, Romania and Poland (NJW p. V, 1975). Compare Schiffer, *Sind wir ein Einwanderungsland?* Arbeit und Sozialpolitik, pp. 189 (1973).
80. Compare Jahr, *Die privatrechtliche Stellung der Gastarbeiter*, 99 (in *Arbeitsplatz Europe*, pp. 88, Europa Union Verlag, Köln 1966); Neuhaus, *Die Grundbegriffe des internationalen Privatrechts*, 162/163 (1962).
81. Braga, 66; compare Papenfuss, *Der gewöhnliche Aufenthalt*, 165 (Köln 1963).
82. Compare Neuhaus, Rabels Z 394; Neuhaus, *Bundesverfassungsgericht und internationales Privatrecht*, 138 (1972).
83. De Winter, 431. Compare with "legal atmosphere" criterion of the recent Dutch writers, 21 Ned. Tijdschr. v. IR, 91 (1974).
84. De Winter, 431.
85. Kegel, 172; Gamillscheg, Vorbem. vor Art. 13, N. 111.
86. Gessner, *Das soziale Verhalten der Gastarbeiter*, pp. 36 ff (in Ansay/Gessner, *Gastarbeiter in Gesellschaft und Recht*); *Gastarbeiter, wirtschaftliche und soziale Herausforderung* pp. 95 (Herausgeber: Ökonomische und soziologische Studien Wien, Wien 1973).

of integration and, as a result, is a justification for the application of the laws of the country of residence. This is probably similar to what the German Courts describe as the "strong inland relation".

If it is desired to make a move away from the law of nationality to the law of domicile without any social content, as the recent popular trend suggests, this move must be accompanied by bilateral agreements to avoid limping relations. Better still, it should be supported by multilateral conventions, effective in all the labour importing and exporting countries. Unilateral moves may bring temporary solutions but, in the long run, this may result in more difficulties than might be expected. To avoid such difficulties was the main purpose of the Hague Conventions, which have been applied by the German Courts even to nationals of those countries in which the Convention has not yet become effective. It should be realised that the problems of millions of workers cannot be solved simply by stating that they are not "migratory birds" or "they are in Germany until they die". All these arguments lead to the conclusion that activities to harmonise domestic laws should be encouraged. Here, possibly, migrant workers with their innumerable problems may act as the stimulus to the law makers. This will be their contribution to the unification of law in Europe.[87]

---

87. See Suhr, *Das Recht des Personalstatuts im Zeichen der europäischen Integration* (Hamburg 1967).

MIGRANT WORKERS IN WESTERN EUROPE ACCORDING TO THE COUNTRY OF ORIGIN*

Country of origin	Total	Federal Rep. of Germany	Switzerland	France	Belgium	Netherlands	Luxemburg	Austria	Sweden	U.K.
						Receiving Countries				
Portugal	487,000	85,000	3,000	380,000	3,000	4,000	9,000	—	1,000	2,000
Spain	599,000	190,000	75,000	260,000	25,000	20,000	2,000	—	2,000	25,000
Italy	1,140,000	450,000	306,000	230,000	70,000	10,000	11,000	1,000	4,000	58,000
Yugoslavia	821,000	535,000	23,000	55,000	—	9,000	—	165,000	26,000	8,000
Greece	282,000	250,000	5,000	5,000	6,000	2,000	—	—	9,000	5,000
Turkey	724,000	610,000	14,000	25,000	10,000	33,000	—	27,000	3,000	2,000
Morocco	204,000	20,000	—	130,000	30,000	24,000	—	—	—	—
Algeria	423,000	—	—	420,000	3,000	—	—	—	—	—
Tunisien	91,000	15,000	—	75,000	—	1,000	—	—	—	—
Finland	105,000	—	—	—	—	—	—	—	105,000	—
Others	2,924,000	445,000	159,000	320,000	73,000	111,000	19,000	32,000	65,000	1,700,000
Total	7,800,000	2,600,000	585,000	1,900,000	220,000	214,000	41,000	225,000	215,000	1,800,000

*Source: Kayser, Les Travailleurs immigrés et la 'crise' en Europe, Le Monde Diplomatique, Febr. 1975.

INDEX

A

access 40, 105, 130, 133, 136, 147, 218, 219, 241, 253
account   14, 82, 185, 278, 279
acknowledgement (*see also Posthumous acknowledgement and Void acknowledgement*) 26, 27, 28, 29, 30, 31, 32, 33, 34, 35, 213, 217, 219, 249
acquisition 10, 11, 12, 13, 14, 16, 17, 33, 45, 86, 87, 141, 142, 152, 153, 239, 323
act 4, 12, 13, 16, 17, 19, 21, 22, 23, 27, 33, 36, 41, 44, 45, 48, 49, 50, 51, 52, 53, 55, 57, 58, 59, 62, 63, 64, 65, 67, 68, 69, 70, 71, 72, 73, 74, 75, 78, 79, 83, 85, 90, 92, 103, 114, 115, 116, 117, 119, 120, 124, 132, 133, 134, 136, 141, 151, 156, 165, 168, 169, 171, 172, 180, 183, 187, 188, 189, 190, 191, 197, 211, 213, 225, 241, 258, 260, 264, 266, 274, 277, 278, 279, 292, 301, 317, 329, 330
administration 10, 11, 12, 13, 15, 16, 22, 23, 24, 40, 76, 83, 84, 87, 92, 98, 99, 116, 121, 141, 142, 153, 156, 159, 184, 188, 189, 190, 191, 193, 195, 264, 277, 278
administrator   75, 92, 99, 189, 191
adolescent   89, 93
adopted child 28, 171, 212, 213, 297, 300, 301, 316
adoptee   137, 138
adoption 3, 29, 32, 46, 74, 76, 134, 136, 137, 138, 154, 193, 212, 213, 227, 229, 232, 274, 276, 277, 301
adoptor   137, 138
adulterine child (*see also Bastard*) 26, 28, 65
adulterous child 93, 94, 95, 96, 99, 100, 101, 106, 162
adultery 28, 36, 37, 41, 49, 53, 55, 56, 57, 63, 66, 80, 93, 101, 102, 108, 120, 146, 152, 156, 157, 162, 163, 164, 172, 175, 191, 192, 193, 196, 197, 199, 201, 205, 207, 215, 216, 218, 220
affiliation 71, 72, 73, 76, 93, 94, 95, 96, 97, 98, 99, 100, 151, 161, 163, 164, 165, 192, 248, 249, 253, 269, 270, 287, 291, 293, 297, 299, 300, 302, 303, 305, 306, 307, 308, 310, 311, 312, 313, 314, 315, 316, 334, 335
age 21, 29, 31, 35, 43, 47, 48, 74, 76, 107, 109, 118, 128, 129, 134, 135, 136, 137, 147, 165, 190, 194, 195, 199, 203, 214, 216, 218, 221, 222, 223, 224, 230, 231, 247, 249, 253, 258, 271, 274, 277, 278, 298
agency of necessity   49
agreement 4, 7, 21, 31, 39, 49, 50, 71, 84, 85, 90, 106, 107, 137, 145, 158, 159, 160, 161, 166, 172, 173, 175, 177, 180, 183, 184, 185, 187, 188, 190, 195, 209, 221, 222, 235, 236, 237, 238, 239, 240, 241, 244, 245, 246, 247, 252, 256, 261, 264, 266, 267, 275, 276, 277, 279, 280, 287, 291, 294, 297, 303, 321, 331, 337
alimony 9, 38, 39, 105, 149, 210, 211, 212, 215, 218, 220, 222, 223, 225, 245, 330, 331, 334
allowance 20, 36, 39, 51, 69, 99, 104, 105, 108, 176, 177, 199, 258, 259, 260, 276, 295, 297, 327
annulment 27, 29, 30, 31, 34, 143, 166, 171, 173, 182, 187, 188, 190, 202, 214, 216, 218, 220, 296, 319, 320
artificial insemination   33, 252
asset 50, 52, 53, 75, 83, 84, 85, 86, 87, 88, 89, 92, 93, 100, 105, 127, 142, 151, 161, 175, 183, 184, 185, 186, 187, 188, 189, 190, 191, 194, 195, 198, 232, 233, 238, 239, 240, 241, 263, 264, 265, 266, 267, 268, 278, 280
assistance 2, 16, 17, 20, 21, 84, 105, 109, 134, 151, 154, 209, 237, 250, 258
Austria   10, 11, 15, 288, 289, 307
Austrian law   2, 12, 17
authorisation 79, 85, 91, 142, 151, 156, 165, 183, 184, 186, 190, 191, 218, 230, 231, 239, 278
authority (*see also Parental authority*) 4, 19, 23, 24, 34, 35, 40, 48, 73, 75, 76, 78, 79, 82, 89, 90, 91, 92, 93, 98, 99, 104, 105, 108, 111, 117, 136, 140, 147, 151, 152, 153, 154, 155, 156, 158, 159, 160, 168, 169, 177, 184, 190, 191, 193, 198, 209, 214, 215, 216, 218, 219, 224, 225, 230, 231, 236, 247, 249, 253, 262, 271, 272, 273, 274, 276, 277, 278, 279, 285, 286, 287, 293, 295, 301, 304, 310, 312, 313, 316, 330, 334, 335

B

bank account   82, 185

339

bastard (*see also Adulterine child*) 65, 68, 132
bastardy 64
battery 103
begetter 26, 28, 30, 31, 33, 34, 35
begetting 27
behaviour 57, 58, 59, 63, 82, 103, 106, 107, 154, 171, 172, 186, 199, 330
Belgian law 2, 9, 180, 317
Belgium 4, 8, 10, 15, 16, 288, 289, 335
benefit 2, 9, 10, 13, 14, 33, 45, 48, 50, 52, 60, 68, 70, 71, 73, 82, 88, 93, 105, 126, 128, 141, 142, 189, 197, 199, 211, 237, 250, 259, 268, 292, 298, 314, 324
Benelux 293
betrothal 203, 209, 212, 223, 237
bigamist 318
bigamy 146, 204, 214, 216, 218, 221, 324
birth 27, 28, 29, 30, 32, 33, 34, 35, 65, 66, 72, 94, 95, 132, 133, 144, 145, 165, 219, 238, 242, 248, 251, 252, 269, 270, 285, 305, 306, 307, 308, 310, 314, 315, 316, 328, 332, 335
birth certificate 27, 94, 95, 97, 98, 310
blood group 193
blood relatives 145
blood test 35, 67, 68, 72, 96, 213, 217, 224, 251, 252, 335
breach 55, 58, 187, 262
breakdown (of marriage) 2, 4, 6, 7, 8, 9, 37, 38, 40, 41, 44, 53, 54, 55, 56, 61, 63, 105, 107, 108, 119, 120, 121, 122, 123, 124, 125, 131, 136, 146, 148, 196, 199, 242, 243, 244, 245, 246, 247, 248, 320, 322
brother 28, 69, 100, 101, 192, 254, 326, 329
bulgaria 6, 7, 228, 232, 236, 237, 244, 245, 250, 308
Bulgarian code 234, 287
Bulgarian law 9, 230, 231, 236, 238, 243, 245, 247, 249, 251

C
capacity 2, 19, 20, 21, 22, 23, 37, 39, 44, 49, 59, 60, 82, 83, 88, 114, 135, 151, 156, 158, 171, 177, 183, 185, 186, 197, 241, 249, 273, 274, 278, 279, 301, 319
capital 12, 14, 16, 50, 52, 72, 151
care 16, 40, 47, 67, 73, 91, 92, 111, 117, 120, 122, 130, 135, 136, 147, 197, 198, 202, 215, 219, 221, 222, 229, 234, 247, 261, 266, 271, 276, 329
cause 4, 5, 6, 9, 21, 49, 52, 55, 59, 62, 63, 65, 71, 72, 82, 103, 105, 119, 123, 168, 171, 201, 202, 207, 221, 243, 284, 301
certificate (*see also Birth certificate*) 4, 27, 82, 174, 175, 195, 231, 270, 280
child 2, 3, 4, 8, 19, 20, 23–36, 38, 40, 45–48, 52, 53, 62, 64–76, 78–81, 87, 89–101, 104–107, 109, 111, 115, 117, 118, 120, 123, 125, 128, 129, 131–137, 139, 141–145, 147, 152, 153, 156, 158–166, 171, 174, 175, 182,
185, 186, 187, 189–199, 201, 202, 203, 205, 206, 209, 210, 212–227, 229, 230, 233–238, 240–243, 245–254, 259, 262, 266, 268–280, 284–292, 294, 295, 297–301, 303, 305–316, 324, 326–336
citizen 45, 46, 70, 173, 180, 227, 232, 233, 255
citizenship 70, 219, 286
civil code 75–77, 79–83, 86–89, 91–97, 99, 102, 103, 108, 116–118, 137, 139, 140, 151–159, 161, 163–167, 169, 172, 174, 175, 181, 183–186, 188, 191–194, 234, 270, 280, 294, 303, 319, 330
civil marriage 173, 201, 228, 320
civil status 4, 97, 145, 151, 153, 165, 167, 169, 174, 195, 244, 285, 313, 316, 319
clause 6, 7, 8, 9, 14, 15, 66, 84, 103, 107, 123, 124, 125, 146, 148, 312
Code Napoleon 12, 139, 151
cohabitation 37, 63, 103, 108, 151, 152, 154, 158, 160, 186, 205, 209, 225, 270
co-heir 133
collateral line 162
collaterals 69, 145, 292, 293, 296
collusion 54, 120, 121
commission of human rights 193
common fund 11, 12, 14, 17, 75, 87, 88, 92, 105, 184, 186, 189, 190, 199, 200, 263, 264, 265
common law 21, 43, 44, 48, 49, 55, 64, 66, 68, 103, 104, 132, 183, 256, 257, 288
communal fund 239, 240, 243
community (*see also Universal community*) 10, 11, 12, 13, 14, 15, 16, 17, 19, 22, 23, 61, 68, 77, 86, 87, 111, 116, 142, 161, 170, 183, 184, 187, 188, 189, 190, 206, 235, 238, 239, 240, 241, 242, 264, 265, 266, 267, 268, 271, 274, 287, 324, 336
comparative law 1, 75, 77, 93, 130
compensation 14, 105, 108, 109, 116, 124, 129, 147, 199, 261
conception 33, 65, 93, 94, 97, 100, 101, 144, 145, 161, 162, 163, 164, 165, 166, 175, 208, 249, 251, 252, 305, 315, 334
conciliation 104, 108, 159, 196, 233, 243
concubinage 39, 76, 98
condition 2, 3, 6, 8, 75, 85, 96, 102, 111, 113, 114, 122, 128, 130, 131, 133, 135, 145, 147, 151, 153, 155–158, 162, 164, 168, 172, 173, 175, 176, 179, 180, 186, 188, 193–195, 219, 222, 224, 230–232, 235, 245, 246, 248, 251, 252, 259, 260, 269, 280, 286, 290, 293, 294, 296, 301, 303, 307, 309, 311, 316, 317, 320
conduct (*see also Misconduct*) 24, 36, 52, 53, 54, 57, 77, 120, 131, 155, 204, 207, 215, 244
confession 104, 108, 255
confidence 44, 202
consanguinity 28, 162, 248, 252

consent (*see also Mutual consent*) 4, 5, 8, 12–14, 23, 29, 31, 33, 34, 36, 41, 44, 46, 47, 60, 63, 74, 82, 83, 85, 88, 90, 92, 102, 106–109, 120, 122, 123, 129, 130, 137, 142, 146, 159, 160, 165, 171, 172, 175, 180, 185, 187, 189, 190, 194–197, 199, 214, 230, 236, 240–242, 244–246, 249, 252, 253, 261, 262, 264, 274, 275, 309
consortium 43, 44, 49, 59, 117, 119, 123, 124
consummation of the marriage   103, 174
contract 84, 85, 113, 135, 137, 160, 183, 186, 187, 194, 197, 206, 211, 214, 224, 241, 264, 315
contribution 23, 39, 50, 51, 73, 84, 151, 175, 176, 186, 195, 199, 200, 217, 238, 240, 249, 261, 268, 273, 275, 276, 277, 337
convention 3, 25, 26, 137, 284, 285, 287, 288, 289, 290, 291, 292, 293, 295, 296, 297, 298–303, 310, 311, 312, 315, 318, 322
co-ownership   16, 265
correspondence   79, 91, 141, 189, 262, 274
Council of Europe   3
couple 32, 43, 59, 66, 72, 74, 122, 124, 129, 137, 147, 149, 185, 202, 203, 208–210, 246
court 2–5, 7, 9, 19–24, 26, 31, 33–40, 43, 45–53, 55–63, 67, 68, 70–72, 74, 85, 86, 88, 90–93, 97–100, 102–105, 108, 112, 115, 117, 120–123, 130, 133–137, 142, 144–149, 152, 154–157, 159, 168–176, 178–182, 186, 187, 188, 190, 195–199, 204–206, 209–214, 218–222, 224, 225, 236, 240–247, 250–254, 256–262, 264–270, 272–277, 279, 280, 285, 286, 290–292, 294, 295, 302–304, 309–312, 315, 316, 318–322, 324, 329–332, 334, 335, 337
court of appeal 43, 50, 57, 59–62, 83, 85, 100, 104, 154, 169, 180, 195, 302, 322
court of cassation 169, 170, 176, 302, 320, 321
credit   49, 187
creditor 14, 16, 99, 108, 142, 260, 263, 267, 268, 269, 270, 292–298, 300–302
cruelty   103, 186, 196
culpability   9, 198
custody 35, 40, 43, 46–48, 71, 73, 74, 90–92, 104, 105, 109, 117, 120, 126, 130, 132–136, 147, 175, 190, 191, 198, 203, 205, 210, 212, 215, 217, 218, 219, 221, 222, 225, 253
Czechoslovak code   230
Czechoslovak law 231, 234, 235, 236, 241, 243, 245, 249, 251, 307, 313
Czechoslovakia 228, 237, 244, 253, 289, 307, 318

D

damage 91, 105, 147, 149, 189, 198, 203–205, 207, 218, 220, 259, 261, 269, 283
daughter   15, 127, 142, 147
daughter-in-law   254

death 12, 14, 15, 27, 28, 32, 38, 66, 90, 96, 100, 103, 122, 143, 145, 147, 156, 162, 175, 190, 191, 193, 197, 198, 200, 201, 204, 206, 209, 211, 214, 250, 261, 315
debt 83, 87, 88, 145, 187, 212, 233, 261, 263, 267, 278
debtor 14, 16, 99, 100, 109, 147, 186, 200, 260, 267, 273, 290, 292–296, 298
deceased 15, 69, 70, 92, 133, 192, 210, 250, 280
declaration 4, 9, 33, 34, 88, 134, 144, 145, 155, 158, 162–165, 174, 180, 195, 212, 219, 229, 232, 237, 242, 245, 249–252, 265, 280, 284, 287, 299, 302–304, 308, 309–312, 315, 316
declaration of the rights of man   78
decree 4, 5, 9, 32, 33, 36, 38, 52, 55, 56, 59, 62, 65, 66, 120, 124, 125, 129, 137, 139, 140, 143, 163, 164, 174, 175, 177, 179–182, 197, 204, 208, 228, 242, 244–247, 252, 254, 259, 263, 268, 296, 331, 332
defamation   103
defence 45, 57, 60, 61, 102, 103, 182, 197, 246
defendant 7, 72, 73, 96, 100, 104, 172–174, 176, 178, 196, 242, 243, 252, 258, 264–267, 269, 272, 273, 279, 280, 295, 299, 301, 319
delivery   22, 133, 144, 145, 253
Danish law   215, 217
Denmark 10, 116, 201, 214–221, 223, 225, 289, 318
dependant   69
dependence   45, 305
descendant 22, 27, 30, 142, 144, 145, 171, 192, 196, 231, 250
descent 46, 70, 93, 111, 268, 269, 277, 279, 280, 283–287, 302, 303, 308–313, 316
desertion 41, 44, 49, 58, 59, 63, 146, 147, 201, 246
disability   44, 64, 68, 126, 128, 156
disease (*see Illness*)
dispensation   28, 29, 198, 230, 231
disposal 11, 12, 13, 15, 16, 82, 83, 92, 154, 187, 223, 239, 267
dissolution 4, 10, 12, 14–17, 30, 32, 34, 37, 40, 86, 90, 120, 121, 123, 124, 127, 130, 142, 143, 147, 148, 162, 163, 166, 167–180, 182, 184, 190, 195, 208–210, 214, 220–222, 225, 229, 232, 233, 237, 244, 259, 260, 262, 264, 265, 319, 320
divorce 2–9, 12, 14, 15, 17, 19, 22, 36–41, 44, 49, 52, 54, 55, 56, 58, 60–64, 71, 75, 76, 78, 81, 83, 92, 101–109, 116, 117, 119–127, 129, 130, 136, 139, 143, 145, 147–149, 162, 166–173, 175–182, 186, 187, 190–199, 201–208, 210–218, 220–223, 225, 227, 242–248, 258–260, 262, 264–266, 271, 275–277, 279, 283–287, 296, 298, 317–322, 327, 329, 331, 332

divorce reform act   6, 41, 55, 119, 120, 124
domicile 19, 22, 24, 25, 45, 46, 70, 81, 86,
  104, 152, 160, 178, 188, 196, 236, 258, 259,
  261, 262, 264–267, 269, 272, 273, 279, 280,
  284, 290, 291, 294, 305, 306, 308, 312–318,
  320, 324, 335–337
dowry   10, 142
duress   172, 214
Dutch Civil Code 19, 21, 22, 23, 26, 29, 36
Dutch law 6, 9, 11, 13, 21, 22, 23, 24, 25, 26,
  27, 32, 35, 36, 39, 40, 41
duty 2, 21, 28, 30, 35, 43, 44, 48, 49, 62, 73,
  78, 80, 81, 85, 89, 91, 92, 94, 99, 103–105,
  108, 111, 117, 118, 127, 134, 135, 141, 143,
  146, 152, 153, 156–158, 160, 164, 165,
  183–185, 187, 190, 205, 210, 215, 216, 224,
  225, 233, 235, 237, 254, 261, 265, 266, 268,
  270–279, 333

E
earning   12, 21, 49, 53, 261
East European countries 5, 6, 7, 9, 12, 16,
  304, 307, 315
East German   132, 236
economy   86, 87, 141, 151, 188, 223, 239
education 16, 23, 24, 26, 35, 40, 47, 72, 79,
  87, 89, 91, 111, 114, 117, 128, 129, 135,
  143, 153, 156, 163, 166, 186, 187, 190, 195,
  198, 199, 214, 224, 229, 235, 236, 240, 271,
  272, 274–277, 325, 330
emancipated   89, 92
emancipation 2, 139, 140, 158, 190, 237,
  238, 324
engagement   147, 231
England 6, 7, 9, 10, 15, 22, 24, 25, 34, 41,
  43, 44, 54, 63, 65, 66, 132–134, 318
English law 15, 21–25, 34, 35, 43, 45, 54, 55,
  64, 70, 74, 120
equality (see also Parental equality) 1, 2,
  10, 12, 13, 19–21, 23, 25, 26, 43, 45, 50,
  51, 53, 78–82, 84–90, 92–94, 98, 100, 101,
  111–118, 127, 131, 132, 134, 140, 141, 143,
  149, 151, 157–161, 173, 183–185, 189–191,
  206, 209, 211, 215, 219, 221, 223–229,
  233–235, 237, 238, 241, 253, 255, 257,
  261–264, 268, 270, 280, 281, 283, 284, 317,
  323, 327–330
equity   51, 93, 109
estate 46, 69, 70, 87, 133, 144, 149, 153, 156,
  192, 210, 212, 280
estimate   14, 195
Europe 1, 2, 111, 183, 231, 237, 255, 283,
  288, 304, 318, 323, 335, 337
European 1, 3, 95, 112, 227, 242, 243, 246–
  250, 252, 254, 287, 318, 323
evidence 4, 27, 33, 35–37, 44, 50, 51, 53, 55,
  56, 61, 63, 66, 67, 72, 104, 122, 159, 192,
  195, 199, 209, 213, 217, 219, 222, 224, 245,
  246, 261, 267, 270, 276, 281, 302, 336

ex-spouse   9, 39, 244, 247

F
failure 5, 6, 7, 9, 57, 63, 90, 103, 104, 120,
  123, 171, 176, 197, 199, 206, 207, 243, 246,
  254, 258, 274
family 2, 11, 13, 16, 17, 19, 21, 28, 33, 50,
  52–54, 64, 68–71, 73, 75–81, 83–86, 89–91,
  97–101, 103, 106, 107, 111–118, 123, 126,
  128–130, 137, 140–144, 146, 147, 149,
  151–166, 168, 171, 172, 175–177, 185–189,
  191, 194–196, 198, 201–203, 206, 207, 209,
  210, 214, 217, 219, 221, 223, 227–238,
  240–248, 251–254, 256, 258–264, 266–273,
  275–279, 283, 285, 287, 291, 296, 297, 299,
  303, 307, 323, 324, 326–333, 335, 336
family council   191
family law 1, 2, 19, 25, 26, 43, 46, 67–70, 75,
  109, 111, 112, 114–117, 121, 132–134, 136,
  137, 139, 140, 142, 143, 149, 151, 158, 161,
  164, 166, 183, 201, 202, 206, 209, 227–235,
  237, 242, 245–248, 250, 252, 255, 262, 268,
  272, 323, 324, 329
family law reform act 67–70, 132–134, 136
father 3, 15, 23–25, 27–35, 40, 46, 48, 64, 65,
  67, 69–75, 78, 88–101, 117, 132–134, 141–
  145, 147, 152, 153, 155, 156, 158, 159.
  163–166, 175, 190–193, 202, 203, 209, 210.
  212–214, 217, 219, 220, 223, 224, 226, 230,
  238, 248–253, 268–270, 272, 275–277, 279,
  280, 284–287, 289, 290, 297–301, 303,
  305–311, 316, 329, 332–335
father-in-law (see also Parents-in-law) 28
fault 5–10, 14, 54, 61, 63, 88, 100, 103, 107–
  109, 136, 146, 148, 164, 172, 173, 176, 177,
  189, 194, 196, 199, 202, 203, 232, 238,
  242–244, 246–248, 259, 287, 320, 321
fidelity 2, 20, 84, 103, 105, 151, 152, 157,
  158, 234, 237, 262
finances   152
financial hardship   60, 124, 125
Finland   11, 14, 116, 220–223, 225, 289
Finnish law   11, 310
foreign 80, 173, 179, 180, 181, 188, 232, 258,
  286, 302, 306, 310, 317–327, 329–333
foreign judgment 169, 173, 177, 180, 291,
  293, 303
foreign law 1, 23, 96, 179, 180, 309, 310, 315,
  317, 321, 322, 324
fortune   14, 141, 161, 195
France 2, 4, 8, 10–14, 34, 75, 101, 109, 132,
  288, 289, 304, 314, 316, 323, 335
fraud   30, 86, 88, 108, 174, 189, 190, 266
free union   75
French Civil Code 4, 11, 21, 22, 183, 186,
  294, 299, 324
French law 11, 12, 22–25, 34, 35, 41, 75, 76,
  78, 81, 85, 88, 95, 96, 167, 294, 304, 305,
  307, 313–315

furniture 13, 16, 83, 187, 210

G

gain 11, 13–15, 91, 111, 116, 185
German Civil Code 116, 117, 118, 131, 132, 139, 140, 250, 308, 325
German Constitution 111, 113, 115, 122, 123
German Democratic Republic 227, 230, 232, 234–239, 241, 243, 248, 254, 308
German Federal Republic 15, 111, 114, 118, 283, 288, 308, 323, 327–329
German law 14, 17, 21, 22, 23, 24, 25, 34, 35, 100, 115, 116, 123, 126, 132, 133, 135, 138, 240, 249, 252, 254, 291, 295, 298, 306, 309, 310, 312, 315, 316, 325, 327, 329, 330, 332–335
Germany 5–7, 10, 11, 13–16, 111, 112, 114, 115, 119, 122, 123, 126, 130, 131, 134, 135, 140, 228, 286–288, 290, 303, 305, 309–311, 316, 318, 323, 325–337
gift 87, 147, 189, 214, 223, 294
good faith 32, 83, 90, 162, 187
goods 13, 22, 23, 206, 210, 211, 218, 240, 263, 267
grandchild 32, 69
grandfather 28, 144
grandparents 69, 91, 101
Greece 10, 139–142, 146, 148, 149, 323, 328, 330, 333–335
Greek 317, 320, 325, 327, 331, 333
Greek Civil Code 139–143, 146–148, 330
Greek law 140, 144, 145, 147, 148
ground 5–9, 36, 37, 40, 41, 54, 55, 60–62, 66, 71, 97, 102, 103, 105, 107, 108, 117, 120, 122, 124, 131, 144, 146–148, 152, 156, 157, 162, 168, 169, 171–173, 175, 178–180, 182, 191–194, 196, 197, 199, 201, 204, 205, 215, 216, 218, 220–223, 225, 232, 242, 243, 245, 246, 251, 252, 258, 262, 268, 269, 285, 290, 298, 299, 301, 302, 306, 309, 310, 312, 315, 317, 319–322, 325, 326, 331
guardian (*see also Subrogated guardian*) 33, 35, 37, 40, 46, 74, 79, 92, 145, 190, 191, 198, 212, 224, 242, 290, 312
guardianship 14, 21, 35, 37, 40, 48, 71, 73, 74, 76, 90, 92, 98, 99, 117, 133, 135–137, 139, 151, 157, 162, 164, 165, 175, 176, 190, 191, 193, 198, 224, 227, 230, 231, 235, 236, 253, 271–274, 276–279, 286
Guardianship of Infants Act 24
Guardianship of Minors Act 71, 74
guilt 6, 9, 37, 39, 105, 120, 191, 203, 205, 206, 211, 215, 216, 218, 220, 221, 223, 225, 247
guilty 8–10, 36, 127, 147, 173, 197, 205, 206, 211, 225, 237, 244, 248, 272

H

habeas corpus 43

haematology 67
Hague Convention 25, 178, 179, 284, 287, 288, 294, 296, 301–303, 308–311, 318, 334, 335, 337
hardship 7, 8, 14, 15, 60–63, 107, 123–125, 127–129, 148, 331
harm 28, 46, 103, 221
head of the family 2, 3, 19, 80, 81, 85, 88, 89, 140, 141, 151, 184, 185, 195, 235, 330
head of the household 82, 85, 87
health 44, 89, 91, 122, 126, 190, 197, 199, 228, 231, 236, 258, 271, 272, 274
heir 11, 12, 15, 99, 133, 142, 144, 151, 192, 200, 212, 219, 224, 269, 270, 280, 332
heredity 280
hire-purchase 187
Holland 335, 336
homicide 171
House of Lords 50, 51, 57, 67, 73, 132
housekeeping 20, 51
housewife 10, 17, 118, 126, 127, 129
Hungarian Code 245
Hungarian law 9, 230, 231, 233, 236, 237–242, 245, 247–249, 251, 252, 308, 313
Hungary 6, 11, 228, 230, 233, 234, 236, 237, 244, 246, 247, 250, 253, 289
husband 2, 3, 10, 12–17, 19–26, 28, 31–34, 38, 39, 43–45, 48–53, 58–60, 66, 67, 75, 78–88, 96, 97, 102, 104, 112, 113, 116–118, 126, 129, 130, 140–144, 146, 147, 149, 151–161, 172, 177, 179–181, 183–186, 189–192, 194, 197, 212, 213, 217, 218, 225, 227, 228, 234, 235, 237, 242, 248–250, 252, 253, 256, 261–263, 283–286, 297, 317–319, 324, 326–333

I

Iceland 116, 225, 226
identity card 4
illegitimate child 3, 26–28, 31–35, 64, 67–75, 78, 93–96, 98–101, 115, 131–134, 143–145, 161–166, 175, 191–194, 212–214, 217, 219, 223–230, 233, 241, 248–250, 252–254, 268–271, 273, 277, 279–281, 297, 304, 310, 332–335
illness 21, 37, 57, 156, 171, 224, 231
immovable 10, 12, 13, 16, 135, 142, 185, 187, 189, 191, 195, 240, 241, 264, 266, 267
impotence 146, 174, 251
impotent 66
imprisonment 103, 171, 191, 205, 215, 216, 218, 220, 258, 260, 262, 272, 274
incapacitated 76, 82, 171, 174
incapacity 2, 23, 79, 80, 83, 86, 90, 143, 172, 183, 185, 190, 259
incest 162, 163, 165, 171, 172, 192, 193
incestuous child 26, 28, 100, 162
incestuous intercourse 28
income 12, 15, 17, 50, 52, 84, 87, 92, 105,

income *continued*
118, 147, 149, 175, 186, 189, 197, 198, 200, 223, 239, 240, 254, 260, 293
indemnity 9, 109, 177
independence 2, 11, 43, 82–84, 91, 93, 127, 185, 206, 221, 301
inequality 20, 26, 43, 70, 78, 80, 81, 86–88, 92–94, 102, 141, 151, 152, 155–157, 183, 326, 330, 333
infirmity (*see Physical or Mental infirmity*)
inheritance 70, 100, 101, 133, 142, 212–214, 217, 223, 224, 254, 280, 333
injury 44, 103, 106, 149, 153, 157, 160, 171, 172, 186, 196, 199, 204, 261
injustice 1, 17, 50, 51, 268
insane 106
insanity 216
institution 2, 3, 10, 17, 54, 77, 79, 82, 93, 106, 111–113, 122, 124, 125, 142, 161, 166, 168, 179, 196, 206, 218, 221, 227–234, 238, 239, 256, 271, 272, 275, 277, 279, 293
insurance (*see also Life-insurance*) 68, 126, 197
intention 4, 26, 32, 69, 74, 76, 97, 106, 246, 323
intercourse (*see Sexual intercourse or Incestuous intercourse*)
international private law 25, 283–290, 292, 293, 298, 303, 304, 310–315, 317, 318
intestacy 69, 74, 144, 192
intestate 46, 69, 133, 192
Ireland 10
Italian 13, 157, 173, 177, 180–182, 323, 325–327, 331, 333, 336
Italian law 8, 13, 169, 288, 302, 303, 318–322
Italy 10, 15, 16, 140, 151, 167, 168, 170, 173, 177–182, 286, 288, 289, 303, 316–321, 323, 325, 328, 333–336

J
joint property (*see also Property*) 12, 13, 16, 265
judge 6, 7, 9, 15, 61, 63, 78, 85, 91, 99, 100, 102, 106–109, 120, 121, 129, 131, 139, 146, 159, 160, 164–166, 170–172, 174–176, 178, 180, 184, 186, 187, 190, 191, 193, 196–198, 222, 235, 239, 242, 243, 245, 259, 262, 265, 266, 269, 277, 279, 290, 294, 295, 298–302, 309–311, 313, 317, 320–322, 329
judgment 3, 6, 7, 53, 100, 104, 120, 125, 130, 152, 154, 157, 166, 169–171, 173, 175–177, 179–182, 187, 195, 197, 199, 213, 217, 219, 224, 236, 247, 250, 257, 260, 285, 288, 290–293, 296, 299, 302–304, 308–311, 313, 315, 316, 320–322
judicial decision 5, 145, 146, 154, 188, 215, 236, 264, 269, 303, 309, 311
judicial separation (*see also Separation*) 15, 24, 36, 37, 39, 40, 52, 66, 83, 102, 171–

173, 177, 202–208, 211, 214, 216, 218, 220–222, 225
jurisdiction 4, 103, 130, 134, 146, 169, 178, 182, 256–259, 264–267, 269, 272, 273, 279, 280, 285–288, 290, 304, 313, 317–319, 321, 331, 332
justice 2, 53, 68, 93, 94, 106, 121, 124, 125, 129, 143, 148, 184, 187, 191, 218, 264, 266, 267, 269, 273, 279–281, 289

K
knowledge 32, 33, 51, 188, 205, 325, 332, 336

L
labour 2, 128, 135, 198, 233, 258, 323–325, 327, 330, 333, 335, 337
land 64, 194, 219
law commission 15, 49, 76
law of divorce 19, 36, 39, 54, 63, 78, 86, 101, 106, 119–121, 123, 125, 127, 128, 131, 139, 201, 211, 216, 220, 321
law of succession 27, 35, 77, 131, 140, 248
lease 12, 209, 210
legacy 189
legal representation 23, 24, 143
legal representative 145, 269, 270
legal system 3, 10, 11, 13, 21, 35, 40, 95, 133, 138, 152, 158, 166, 168, 169, 174, 177, 179–181, 209, 221, 227, 232, 233, 235, 237–239, 241, 244–246, 248–250, 253, 254, 284, 290, 294, 315, 333
legislation 3, 5, 17, 26, 43, 50, 62–64, 68, 69, 76, 77, 79, 81, 93, 96, 102, 105, 111, 114, 115, 117, 119, 131, 134, 137, 143, 149, 153, 161, 164, 168, 179, 180, 182–184, 188, 201, 202, 205–211, 213–215, 217, 219–223, 225, 227–230, 232–234, 237, 238, 242, 251, 289, 317, 318
legislative policy 3, 10, 76, 289, 295
legislator 2, 5, 7, 9, 10, 14, 28, 31, 37, 40, 76–80, 82, 85–89, 91, 93, 94, 97, 98, 100, 104, 107, 112, 147, 151–153, 155, 157–159, 161–163, 165–167, 173, 183, 185, 186, 189–191, 194, 201–204, 206–208, 230, 241
legislature 51, 75, 77, 82, 85, 115, 120, 129, 164
legitimacy 26, 65–68, 93, 96, 98, 166, 298
legitimate child 2, 25, 26, 30–36, 64–66, 68–72, 74, 75, 78, 92–94, 98, 100, 101, 111, 115, 131–134, 141–145, 162, 164–166, 191–193, 212–214, 219, 223–226, 242, 248, 252–254, 270, 271, 281, 296, 298, 300, 301, 304, 332–334
legitimation 28–34, 64, 75, 96, 145, 192, 252, 285, 294, 313
leprosy 146
libel 45
liberty 105, 127, 196, 206, 236

Lichtenstein 8, 288, 289
life-insurance (*see also Insurance*) 38, 125–127
lump sum (*see also Sum*) 38, 72, 109, 145, 147, 175, 211, 214
Luxembourg 2–4, 8, 10, 11, 13, 14, 78, 183, 186, 189–193, 197, 288, 301
Luxembourg law 2, 12, 13, 193, 194

M

magistrate 104, 106, 258, 259, 264
maiden name (*see also Name*) 97, 118, 132, 147, 247, 253
maintenance 6, 9, 19–21, 23, 26, 35, 36, 38–40, 49, 52, 53, 60, 70–73, 80, 82, 87, 89, 91, 98–100, 103, 105, 108, 120, 123–134, 141, 144–149, 153, 157, 161, 163, 165, 176, 181, 185–187, 192, 195, 197–199, 200, 210, 212, 214, 217, 219, 221–224, 232, 237, 238, 241–245, 247, 248, 250, 252–254, 258–261, 269, 273, 276–278, 287, 288, 291, 296–299, 301–303, 305, 309–312, 315, 316
majority 29, 35, 74, 76, 98, 109, 134, 135, 152, 158, 163, 166, 190, 254
man (*see also Married man*) 2, 12, 13, 28–35, 38, 39, 43, 45, 54, 66, 70, 72, 78–80, 84, 85, 100, 105, 111–115, 118, 127, 128, 134, 135, 141, 143, 161, 174, 192, 193, 202, 208, 209, 212, 213, 217, 219, 220, 223, 224, 228, 230, 231, 233, 234, 249–253, 255, 284, 297, 303, 326–328, 330–335
management 2, 83, 87, 88, 92, 93, 141, 176, 189, 190, 227
marriage (*see also Mixed marriage*) 2, 4, 6, 7, 11, 12, 14, 15, 17, 19–23, 25, 27–30, 32–35, 37–41, 43–45, 47, 49, 50, 52, 53–57, 59–66, 68, 71, 73–75, 77, 80, 84, 86, 87, 89, 90, 93, 94, 96, 99, 101–109, 111–114, 116–131, 136, 139–143, 145–147, 149, 151–164, 166–187, 189, 190, 192, 194–199, 201–223, 225, 228–232, 234–240, 242–249, 251–253, 256, 258–268, 270, 271, 273, 279, 280, 284, 285, 292, 293, 296, 298, 305, 318–322, 324, 326, 328, 329, 331–334, 336
marriage settlement (*see also Settlement*) 25, 204, 208, 211, 215, 218
married man (*see also Man*) 28, 29, 75, 334
married woman (*see also Woman*) 2, 17, 19, 20, 22, 43–45, 53, 54, 66, 75, 79, 80, 82, 83, 94, 97, 118, 126, 127, 141, 143, 154, 160, 161, 183, 185, 189, 206, 232, 324, 333
maternity 95–98, 161, 163–165, 192, 249, 284, 285, 316
matrimonial 2, 3, 10, 13, 15, 17, 49, 52, 66, 75, 119, 168
matrimonial home 13, 16, 21, 22, 44, 51, 53, 59, 62, 80, 81, 102, 155, 157, 158, 186, 191, 245
matrimonial property (*see also Property*) 15–17, 25, 45, 50, 51, 115, 116, 201, 267
matrimonial regime (*see also Regime*) 10, 76, 80, 81, 85, 86, 116, 184–188, 190, 267, 284
matrimony 55
medical expenses 91
medical treatment 47, 136
mental 21, 23, 107, 111, 214, 258
mental infirmity 35, 37, 41, 58, 143, 216, 218, 220
minor child 4, 8, 20, 23–25, 29, 33–35, 47, 48, 71, 74, 79, 89, 91, 92, 135–139, 145, 163, 165, 174, 183, 190, 191, 195, 229, 230, 241, 242, 245, 247, 254, 270, 272–274, 278, 279
minority 30, 31, 35, 98, 134
misconduct 49, 53, 96, 155
misdeed 105
mistress 102, 157, 191, 192
mixed marriage (*see also Marriage*) 139, 322, 328–332, 334
money 20, 22, 50, 51, 53, 133, 147, 204, 210, 219, 278, 331
moral 2, 21, 23, 28–30, 77, 146
morality 78, 91, 179, 192, 233
morals 76, 89, 190, 228
mortgage 16
mother 23–35, 40, 46, 48, 64, 66, 69–71, 73, 74, 78, 88–101, 111, 126, 127, 132, 133, 143–145, 147, 153, 156, 159, 163–166, 175, 190–193, 202, 203, 210, 212–214, 217–219, 223, 224, 228, 230, 233, 234, 248–253, 268–270, 272, 275–277, 279, 280, 284–287, 290, 298, 305–309, 312–314, 316, 332–334, 335
movable 10, 12, 83, 85–87, 142, 187, 189, 195, 267
mutual consent (*see also Consent*) 4, 5, 8, 36, 41, 102, 106–109, 120, 122, 123, 130, 146, 175, 180, 194–197, 199, 240, 244–246

N

name (*see also Maiden name*) 3, 22, 25, 28, 34, 44, 80, 82, 85, 86, 95, 97, 98, 102, 105, 109, 118, 132, 151, 153–155, 158, 165, 175, 185, 214, 217, 219, 223, 232, 234, 237, 238, 243, 247, 248, 253, 256, 269, 277, 279, 286, 310, 330, 333
nationality 19, 25, 31, 45, 46, 70, 76, 80, 153, 157, 158, 171, 177–179, 181, 199, 255, 283–286, 289, 291, 292, 294, 295, 299, 303, 305–317, 320, 323–325, 328–330, 334–337
natural child 2, 27, 29, 31, 32, 34–36, 78, 93, 94, 100, 101, 139, 143–145, 163–166, 192, 203, 270, 283–286, 300, 301, 303–307, 309
neglect 111, 246, 273
negligence 86
Netherlands 6, 7, 10, 19, 34, 288, 289, 317

New Zealand 132, 133
non-consummation of the marriage 171, 173
non-recognition 75, 162, 182, 249
Norway 116, 201, 217–220, 223, 225, 289
Norwegian law 217, 218, 219
Null 97, 151, 162, 163, 198, 231, 241, 247, 267
nullity 15, 28, 49, 52, 71, 96, 151, 162, 168, 169, 187, 190, 229, 249, 251, 252, 264, 274, 275, 296

O
obedience 2, 79, 80
obligation 2, 17, 20, 21, 39, 44, 48, 49, 53–55, 57, 58, 64, 67, 68, 70, 71, 75, 84, 88, 91, 98, 99, 103, 108, 109, 113, 116, 122, 137, 140–145, 147, 149, 151–154, 157, 158, 160, 164, 171, 175, 179, 180, 186, 187, 199, 228–230, 233, 234, 236–238, 241, 243, 244, 247, 250–254, 256, 258–260, 262, 266, 273–279, 283, 287–303, 305, 307–312
occupation 51, 88, 127, 128, 141, 154, 189, 197, 240, 262
offence 28, 39, 54, 57, 63, 102, 108, 119–121, 127, 136, 171, 172, 196, 205, 247
one-parent family 73
order 21–24, 159, 287, 299, 309, 310, 316, 335
owner 16, 51, 83, 240
ownership 3, 14, 16, 87, 190, 194, 195, 265

P
pardon 147, 148
parent 2, 3, 8, 24, 25, 34, 35, 40, 46–48, 64, 65, 67–71, 73, 90–94, 98–101, 105, 111, 114, 115, 117, 131–133, 135–137, 142, 145, 147, 149, 152, 156, 158–160, 162–166, 175, 190–195, 202, 203, 210, 212–215, 217, 219, 224, 229, 236, 241, 242, 246–250, 252–254, 262, 268, 270–279, 287, 290, 294, 298, 301, 303, 311–313, 326–329, 334
parental authority (see also Authority) 23, 24, 35, 40, 76, 89–92, 98, 99, 105, 190, 191, 193, 198, 286, 312, 335
parental equality (see also Equality) 88, 233
parental rights (see also Right) 45–48, 73, 74, 88, 134, 245, 247, 248, 253
parenthood 27, 67
parents-in-law (see also Father-in-law) 254
participation 11, 13, 14, 16, 17, 86, 88, 133, 141, 238, 240, 243, 279
passport 79, 90
paternity 27, 30, 33, 72, 94–97, 100, 132, 134, 144, 161–165, 192, 193, 209, 213, 217, 219, 220, 224–226, 230, 248–254, 269, 270, 285, 293, 298–304, 307–312, 315, 316, 334
payment 14, 38–40, 52, 72, 73, 83, 129, 149, 175, 187, 211, 260, 261, 263, 334

penalty 5, 8, 9, 72, 103, 104, 105, 107, 108, 191, 192, 197, 199
pension 17, 38, 60, 61, 126, 128, 161, 299
permission 33, 92, 196
personality 2, 43, 58
petition 4, 7, 8, 30, 31, 33, 36–38, 40, 55, 60, 104, 105, 107, 120, 130, 147, 148, 156, 171–174, 176–178, 187, 190, 191, 196, 197, 199, 242–246, 280, 319, 320
petitioner 6–9, 34, 36, 39, 41, 54–59, 61–63, 102, 119, 146, 148, 173, 174, 176, 196, 232, 243, 319, 321
physical infirmity 35, 258
physical separation 8, 9, 59, 154, 155, 157, 159, 168, 187
physically separated 90, 92
Poland 6, 7, 250, 253, 308
Polish code 243
Polish law 9, 230, 231, 235–237, 239–241, 244, 245, 247, 251
Polish practice 249
population 5, 183, 216, 241, 325
Portugal 4, 10, 288, 289, 323, 328, 335
Portuguese law 8, 11
posthumous acknowledgement (see also Acknowledgement) 27
posthumous recognition 250
power 2, 3, 12, 21, 23, 24, 36, 39, 51–53, 67, 73, 75, 78–80, 83, 85–89, 92, 93, 108, 112, 116–118, 132, 135, 136, 142, 143, 151, 155, 156, 158, 159, 174, 175, 178, 183–185, 187–190, 228, 234, 237, 238, 242, 244, 268, 290, 326
predecease 93
predeceased child 27
pregnancy 32, 33, 94, 100, 133, 174, 238, 242, 253
prejudice 2, 111, 115, 155–158, 165, 181, 186, 246, 310
presumption 7, 9, 33, 35, 66–69, 94, 96–98, 121, 142, 162, 166, 175, 176, 241, 248–253, 262, 277, 293, 334
principle 1, 3, 4, 7, 8, 13, 14, 16, 17, 20, 21, 23–26, 31, 36, 37, 39, 46–48, 50, 51, 54, 61–63, 74–78, 80–83, 85, 87, 89, 90, 92–94, 98–101, 103, 105–107, 113, 114, 116, 117, 119–123, 126–128, 131, 135, 137, 140–143, 146, 148, 151–162, 164, 166, 167, 169, 171, 173, 174, 176–181, 183, 185, 186, 188, 190, 192–194, 196, 204, 211, 215–218, 220, 222, 223, 225, 227–229, 231, 233, 234, 237, 239, 240, 242–245, 248, 251, 255, 256, 262, 263, 268, 270, 276, 283, 284, 286, 288, 289–291, 293, 297–300, 304, 306, 313, 316, 320, 322–324, 335
prison (see Imprisonment)
privacy 100, 108, 198, 206, 210
procedure 4, 5, 6, 8, 29, 36, 37, 55, 73, 102–104, 107, 108, 131, 144, 164, 169, 172,

179, 182, 184, 188, 194, 196, 197, 198, 213, 219, 222, 233, 242, 244–246, 249, 255, 256, 258–273, 280, 310, 320
proceeding 23, 38, 45, 49, 51, 63, 70–74, 97, 102–104, 106, 119, 130, 151, 168, 172–174, 178–181, 184, 186–188, 195, 197, 222, 242–244, 246, 251, 252, 259, 266, 270, 287, 292–294, 302, 303, 306, 308, 317
profession 80, 83, 84, 109, 113, 114, 118, 127, 154, 183, 185, 233, 236, 240, 262
prohibition 36, 99, 106, 122, 155, 156, 162, 187, 205, 232, 233, 241, 243
proof 33, 41, 49, 55, 56, 61, 66, 67, 71, 82, 90, 94–98, 100, 104, 108, 120, 165, 174, 175, 193, 195, 221, 251, 252, 263, 264, 266, 269, 270, 313, 334
property (see also Joint property, Matrimonial property, Separate property) 2, 3, 10–16, 19, 22–25, 40, 44, 45, 50–53, 72, 75, 79, 91, 92, 115–117, 142, 149, 151, 154, 156, 161, 174–176, 184, 189, 190, 192, 195, 197, 201, 204, 206, 208, 210, 211, 214, 215, 223, 225, 227, 232, 239–241, 244, 245, 258, 261–268, 271, 277–280
protection 2, 19, 38, 62, 76, 79, 88, 89, 111–113, 123, 126, 135, 143, 145, 147, 155, 181, 182, 184, 187, 222, 223, 228–231, 233, 234, 260, 271, 272, 275, 277, 279, 305, 328, 329, 335
provision 3, 12, 20–23, 26, 28, 29, 31, 32, 34, 37–39, 49, 52, 55, 62, 63, 68, 70, 71, 75, 77, 78, 81, 83, 84, 92, 94, 97, 100, 101, 107–109, 112, 115, 117–119, 126, 129–131, 136–139, 141, 143–146; 148, 151–156, 160, 161, 168, 169, 177–179, 182–188, 191–193, 197, 230, 231, 233–243, 245–247, 249–252, 254–256, 258–260, 262, 263, 264, 276, 277, 291, 295, 297, 299, 300, 308, 309, 311, 313, 314, 329, 332
public interest 61, 68, 246
public order 31, 103, 181, 213, 303, 306
public policy 2, 68, 103, 178–182, 283, 284, 302, 311, 329, 330, 335
public prosecutor 31, 269
publication 45, 197
publicity 104
punishment 64, 72, 103, 171, 172, 329

R
race 111, 193, 255
rape 44, 145, 161–163, 251
rate of divorce 5
recognition 76, 95–97, 99, 122, 123, 133, 143–145, 161–166, 168–170, 175, 177, 179, 181, 182, 230, 235, 243, 249, 250, 252, 254, 269, 284–288, 291, 292, 294, 296, 299, 303, 304, 307, 308, 311, 313, 316, 318, 320, 322, 333, 334
reconciliation 24, 36, 62, 63, 103, 104, 171,

174, 181, 196, 198, 199, 208, 262
reform 1, 2, 3, 5, 6, 8, 9, 11–13, 15–17, 19, 41, 43, 44, 54, 63, 64, 67–70, 75–77, 80, 82, 85, 86, 100, 102, 105, 106, 109, 111, 115, 117, 118–121, 123–126, 128, 131, 132, 134–140, 142, 148, 149, 151, 158–161, 164, 166, 183, 184, 193, 199, 201, 202, 205, 224, 227, 255, 283, 284, 285, 299, 306, 317, 323
regime (see also Matrimonial regime) 2, 10–16, 86, 87, 89, 99, 100, 102, 116, 146, 151, 157, 161, 170, 183–186, 188, 189, 191, 193, 239, 263, 265, 267, 271, 284, 287, 290
registration 4, 51, 167, 174, 182, 187, 247, 251
registry 4, 27, 145
relationship 6, 23, 26, 29, 31, 44, 59, 68, 70, 74, 91, 93, 97, 106, 112, 121, 132, 133, 138, 149, 161–163, 169, 176, 177, 183, 196, 198, 204, 207–209, 212, 214, 215, 221–223, 228, 230, 233, 234, 251, 252, 255–258, 262, 263, 265, 268, 269, 275–277, 279, 289, 291, 296, 303, 305, 306, 311, 314, 319, 333, 334
religion 1, 47, 102, 193, 255, 330
religious 40, 91, 111, 112, 135, 145, 167, 170, 181, 182
religious marriage ceremony 140, 146, 167, 168, 170, 178, 182, 201, 328, 333
remarriage 53, 154, 175, 197, 259, 285, 286
repudiation 102, 107, 123, 144, 146, 180, 191, 324
reserve 144, 280
residence 79, 81, 104, 141, 143, 151, 153, 155, 160, 172, 174, 178, 186, 195, 197, 209, 210, 222, 223, 246, 253, 259, 289–299, 301, 302, 305, 308–310, 312–321, 324, 327, 329–332, 334–337
resources 9, 10, 99, 108, 141, 153, 157, 158, 214, 295
respondent 54–63, 119, 321
responsibility 6, 10, 20, 91, 95, 127, 152, 176, 196, 197, 231, 250, 294
right 2, 11, 14, 15–17, 21–23, 30–32, 36, 38–40, 43–49, 51, 60, 61, 64, 67–71, 73, 74, 78, 80, 82–89, 91–94, 98, 100, 101, 104, 105, 108, 109, 111, 113–118, 120, 126, 128, 129, 133–136, 141, 143, 144, 147, 149, 151–155, 158–162, 164–166, 175–177, 182–187, 189–195, 197, 198, 202, 203, 205, 206, 208–219, 223, 224, 228–230, 233–236, 238, 239, 241–244, 247, 248, 250, 252–256, 258–262, 264–280, 283, 284, 286, 293, 294, 299, 301, 302, 304, 318, 323, 330, 336
roman law 10, 248
Romania 6, 7, 232, 236, 237, 246, 250, 255, 256, 258
Romanian code 243, 250, 258
Romanian law 9, 231, 240, 241, 247, 249, 251, 253, 255, 260, 265, 268, 270, 280, 281

rule 2, 28, 29, 33, 38, 44, 50, 51, 54, 55, 62, 64, 68, 70, 79, 81, 82, 84, 85, 87, 90, 94, 96, 98, 101, 104, 112, 113, 115–118, 121, 124, 130, 135, 138, 141, 142, 145, 147, 151, 153, 154, 157, 160, 161, 172, 173, 177–179, 182, 183, 185, 187, 188, 193, 199, 202–225, 227–232, 234, 236, 239–241, 243, 244, 248–251, 253–256, 258–260, 264, 266–270, 272–277, 281, 283–288, 290–300, 302–306, 309–315, 317–321, 324, 327, 329, 330, 334–336

S

salary   12, 127, 260
sale   52
sanction 10, 254, 258, 262, 272–274, 280
Sardinia   325
savings   51
Scandinavian countries 5, 11, 13, 116, 201, 202, 218
Scandinavian law   13, 15
Scotland   10, 318
security 125, 126, 185, 202, 239, 263, 267, 278, 318
separate property (see also Property) 14, 15, 50, 51, 239, 240, 267, 268
separation (see also Judicial separation) 6, 8–13, 15–17, 24, 36, 37, 39–41, 49, 50, 52, 59, 63, 66, 71, 83, 86, 87, 102, 106, 116, 121, 122, 124, 142, 148, 149, 152, 154–157, 159, 160, 166, 168, 171–173, 175–178, 184, 186, 187, 190, 191, 194, 203–208, 210, 211, 214–216, 218, 220–222, 225, 228, 232, 239, 266, 284, 296, 318
service 2, 43, 47, 126, 129, 206, 236
settlement (see also Marriage settlement) 14, 25, 52, 80, 148, 292
sex 1, 2, 53, 58, 64, 80, 109, 111–115, 117, 149, 151, 210, 227, 230, 233, 234, 237, 238, 247, 255
sexual 64, 67, 72, 102, 144, 161, 171, 207, 221, 237, 262, 332
sexual intercourse 28, 33, 35, 44, 65, 66, 174, 205, 213, 215, 217, 218, 220, 224, 251, 252
Sicily   61, 325
single   80, 183, 247, 248
sister   28, 100, 101, 192, 326, 329
social security 17, 60, 114, 126, 197, 198, 236
socialist countries 227, 230–234, 237–242, 244, 245, 247, 248, 251, 255, 271, 272, 274
socialist law   255, 262
society 1, 2, 5, 17, 26, 29, 36, 43, 53–55, 64, 67, 75–77, 79, 80, 84, 101, 109, 111–114, 122, 123, 125, 128, 151–153, 157, 160–162, 192, 193, 201–203, 208, 217, 228–230, 233, 234, 237, 242, 248, 323, 325, 330
solitary confinement   171
son   147, 158, 163, 166

son-in-law   254
Soviet law 4, 6, 228–231, 236, 238, 242, 244, 247, 250, 252
Soviet Union 227–230, 232–234, 236–239, 244, 246, 247, 249, 250
Spain 10, 228–291, 304, 323, 328, 332, 333, 335
Spanish law   10, 331
spouse (see also Surviving spouse) 2–4, 6–17, 19–26, 33, 36–41, 43–54, 56–61, 66, 78–91, 93, 97, 101–109, 112–127, 129–131, 133, 135, 140–144, 146–149, 151–153, 155–166, 171–191, 194–212, 214–216, 218–223, 225–227, 229–249, 255–268, 283–287, 293, 295, 296, 298, 317–321, 327–333, 335
state 39, 48, 73, 78, 102, 111–113, 117, 123, 134, 137, 141, 146, 151, 162, 164, 167–169, 177–180, 182, 184, 188, 214, 225, 228, 231, 232, 234–236, 241–243, 247, 250–252, 254–256, 261, 276, 278, 280, 286, 288–293, 295–299, 302, 304, 306, 307, 312, 318, 324
status 2, 4, 26, 31–33, 43, 64, 66, 75, 77, 80, 81, 94–97, 114, 125, 129, 139, 152, 162, 163, 166, 177, 193, 196, 212, 225, 227–229, 244, 248, 252, 255, 269, 270, 280, 288, 298, 301, 308, 314–316, 322
statute 10, 49, 61, 63, 68, 115, 137, 139, 166, 187, 188, 208, 209, 211, 223, 227, 228, 290, 315, 316
stepchild   203, 297, 298
stepmother   297
sterility   33
stillborn child   144
subrogated guardian (see also Guardian) 79
succession 14, 22, 27, 35, 70, 76, 77, 87, 93, 98, 100, 101, 105, 131–133, 140, 144, 166, 182, 189, 191–194, 248, 252, 254, 279–281, 286, 315
successors   15, 101
sum (see also Lump sum) 48, 50, 72, 147, 186, 200, 210, 214, 219, 259–261, 278, 280, 301
supervision 105, 190, 201, 235, 236, 241, 253, 316, 326
Supreme Court 9, 32, 36, 39, 122, 213, 237, 239, 243, 245, 246, 249, 309, 310, 318
surname 46, 132, 141–144, 147, 149, 235, 236, 238, 253, 256
surviving spouse (see also Spouse) 14, 15, 90, 101, 133, 175, 182, 194, 209
survivor   190, 198
Sweden 11, 14, 17, 116, 201, 202, 206, 209, 211–225, 289, 310, 317, 318
Swedish law 16, 212, 214, 215, 217–220, 223
Swiss Civil Code   10, 140, 299
Swiss law 3, 285, 286, 298, 300, 301, 304, 312, 314, 315, 317
Switzerland 5, 10, 11, 15, 285–289, 299, 301, 313, 316–318

T

testator   69, 315
testimony   5
third party 32, 51, 59, 71, 82–85, 90, 97,
   102, 152, 155, 186, 187, 197, 207, 239–241,
                   247, 260, 263, 264, 266, 276
third person 65, 83, 104, 124, 147, 162, 198,
                        260, 263, 279, 280
tort   44, 45, 315
tortfeasor   44
transaction 82, 118, 187, 188, 198, 241, 263,
                                              266
transfer   52, 191
treason   45
tribunal   55, 168, 175, 181, 321
trust   50–52
Turkey 10, 288, 289, 323, 326, 328, 330,
                                    332–335
Turkish law   332

U

unacknowledged child   34, 35
unborn child   27, 249
uniform law   25, 293
union 2, 5, 6, 15, 28, 75–77, 87, 95, 122, 123,
                        147, 149, 183, 195
United Kingdom 45, 46, 70, 304, 318, 324
United Nations   193
United States   5
unity 43–45, 50, 151, 152, 154–159, 161, 202,
                                    254, 284
universal community (see also Community)
                                              11
unreasonable   44, 57, 63
unsoundness of mind 106, 146, 171, 172,
                                             199
usufruct   15, 92, 116, 142

V

valid 65, 66, 90, 112, 115, 135, 145, 160,
   168, 178, 183, 239, 242, 243, 245, 247, 249,
                   296–298, 300, 316, 325, 333
validity   27, 170, 173, 241, 307
value 6, 11, 12, 14, 51, 60, 111, 112, 116,
   147, 229, 233, 240, 266, 267, 280, 326, 327,
                                    329, 330
venereal disease   205, 215, 216, 218, 220
violence   53, 103, 216
virginity   174
void 29, 65, 97, 103, 117, 131, 151, 162, 163,
   198, 203, 204, 208, 214, 218, 228, 241, 249,
                                             267
void acknowledgement (see also Acknow-
      ledgement)   28, 30

voidable   30, 65, 228
voluntary   4, 144, 145

W

ward of court   71
wardship   229
wedlock 32, 64, 75, 132, 164, 213, 217, 219,
              226, 248, 268–270, 275, 277, 333
welfare 2, 17, 21, 23, 40, 46–48, 62, 74, 114,
   123, 135, 137, 159, 190, 212, 215, 225, 275
West German constitution   20
West Germany   34, 40, 115, 134, 137
widow   38, 80, 183, 249
widowhood   105, 154, 249
wife 2, 9, 12–17, 19–26, 33, 38, 39, 43–45,
   48–53, 58–61, 66, 67, 75, 78–88, 90, 92,
   102, 105, 112, 113, 116–118, 125, 126, 129,
   130, 140–142, 146, 147, 151–161, 171, 174,
   175, 180, 183–185, 188, 190–194, 194–197,
   211, 212, 215, 218, 225, 227, 228, 231,
   233–235, 237, 238, 242, 247, 256, 261–263,
   266, 283, 286, 287, 297, 317, 318, 320, 324,
                              326–333, 336
wilful abandonment   172
wilful neglect to maintain   49, 71
will 23, 29, 38, 40, 44, 55, 69, 79, 84, 96, 109,
   123, 135, 136, 144, 151, 153, 165, 207, 212,
                                    223, 261
witness   5, 198, 211, 214, 224
woman (see also Married woman) 1, 2, 10,
   12, 13, 15, 17, 22, 28–30, 32, 33, 38, 43,
   45, 46, 53, 54, 60, 70, 72, 76, 79, 84, 85,
   87, 93, 111–115, 117, 127, 128, 135, 140–
   143, 160, 161, 179–181, 183, 192, 201, 202,
   208, 209, 212, 213, 218, 222, 223, 228, 230,
   231, 233, 234, 237, 238, 247, 249, 255, 284,
      285, 325, 327, 328, 330, 332–334, 336
work 12, 17, 21, 76, 87, 113, 115, 128, 135,
   139, 145, 149, 158, 160, 161, 164, 186, 201,
   212, 222, 233, 235, 236, 238, 239, 260, 261,
                                    266, 313, 325
worker 228, 229, 261, 306, 323–328, 330–
                                    332, 335–337

Y

young   2
youth   3, 229, 274
Yugoslav code   243
Yugoslav law 234–237, 240, 245–247, 249–
                   252, 254, 285, 330, 335
Yugoslav project   313, 316
Yugoslavia 6, 228, 237, 239, 246, 254, 285,
                   323, 325, 326, 328, 335